Fifth Edition

Communicating for Results

A Canadian Student's Guide

Carolyn Meyer

OXFORD
UNIVERSITY PRESS

OXFORD
UNIVERSITY PRESS

Oxford University Press is a department of the University of Oxford.
It furthers the University's objective of excellence in research, scholarship,
and education by publishing worldwide. Oxford is a registered trade mark of
Oxford University Press in the UK and in certain other countries.

Published in Canada by
Oxford University Press
8 Sampson Mews, Suite 204,
Don Mills, Ontario M3C 0H5 Canada

www.oupcanada.com

First Edition published in 2007
Second Edition published in 2010
Third Edition published in 2014
Fourth edition published in 2017

Library and Archives Canada Cataloguing in Publication
Title: Communicating for results : a Canadian student's guide / Carolyn Meyer.
Names: Meyer, Carolyn, 1962- author.
Description: Fifth edition. | Includes bibliographical references and index.
Identifiers: Canadiana (print) 20190219688 | Canadiana (ebook) 20190219718 | ISBN 9780199036127
(softcover) | ISBN 9780199036226 (EPUB)
Subjects: LCSH: Business communication—Canada—Textbooks. | LCSH: Business writing—Canada—Textbooks.
| LCGFT: Textbooks.
Classification: LCC HF5718 .M49 2020 | DDC 651.7—dc23

Cover image: cnythzl/DigitalVision Vectors/Getty Images
Cover design: Laurie McGregor
Interior design: Laurie McGregor
Image credits for infographics: Cube29/Shutterstock.com; Telman Bagirov/Shutterstock.com;
kornn/Shutterstock.com; davooda/Shutterstock.com; IhorZigor/Shutterstock.com; BABAgraphicstudio/
Shutterstock.com; Dstarky/Shutterstock.com; kornn/Shutterstock.com; matsabe/Shutterstock.com;
Shpadaruk Aleksei/Shutterstock.com; Nitichai/Shutterstock.com.

1 2 3 4 — 23 22 21 20

Brief Contents

Contents

3 Getting Started: Planning, Writing, and Revising Business Messages   79

4 Business Style: Word Choice, Conciseness, and Tone   117

5 Business Style: Sentences and Paragraphs   151

6 Memorandums, E-mail, and Routine Messages   181

11   Informal Reports   368

From the Publisher

With the expansion of the knowledge-based economy, Canadian employers are—now more than ever—increasingly interested in hiring individuals who are able to communicate clearly and effectively.

Building on the foundation of its predecessors, the fifth edition of *Communicating for Results* continues to address the needs of today's students by providing them with a thorough understanding of how to communicate effectively in multicultural Canadian business environments. A thorough, hands-on approach engages students in the processes of critical thinking, stylistic development, and content evaluation. Extensive models and organizational plans for letters, memos, e-mails, reports, and presentations—as well as extensive exercises based on real-life situations—help to simplify the writing process, banish writer's block, and ease fears about public speaking.

Throughout, this highly effective approach emphasizes practical knowledge that will give students a head start in the business world. They will develop confidence in their skills and will ultimately have everything they need to become competent and successful communicators who get their message across, get noticed, and get results.

Highlights from the Fifth Edition

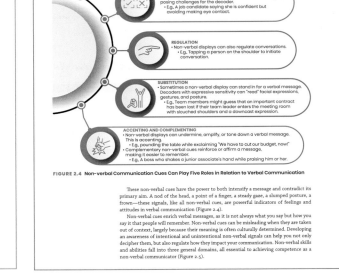

FIGURE 2.4 **Non-verbal Communication Cues Can Play Five Roles in Relation to Verbal Communication**

New coverage on Indigenous Peoples in business and business communication prepares students to be informed and culturally sensitive communicators within the Canadian context.

A dynamic new full-colour design, featuring new infographic presentation of concepts, engages students and helps reinforce key concepts.

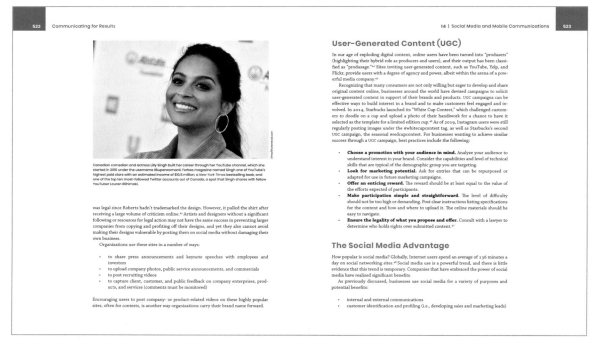

The most up-to-date coverage of business communication available, the fifth edition of *Communicating for Results* provides relevant, engaging, current coverage, including topics such as the Gen Z workforce, managing team conflict, and optimizing your online personal brand.

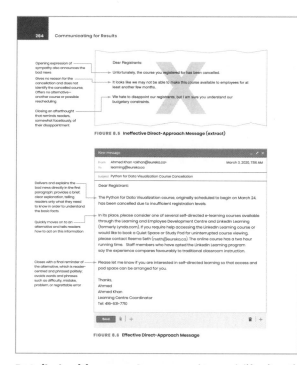

Detailed writing samples respond to real-life situations and show students the level of excellence they should strive to achieve in their own writing. Marginal tips draw students' attention to important features of the samples, and "ineffective" samples show students what to avoid in their own writing.

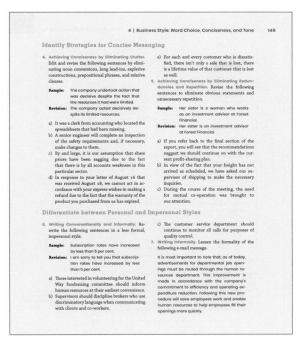

Extensive new and updated end-of-chapter exercises—featuring individual and group activities, writing improvement exercises, case study exercises, and online activities—provide realistic business situations that encourage students to develop their critical-thinking, problem-solving, and collaboration skills.

Learning objectives and chapter previews prepare students for what they will encounter in each chapter.

Chapter-opening vignettes illustrate each chapter's main themes with real-life examples.

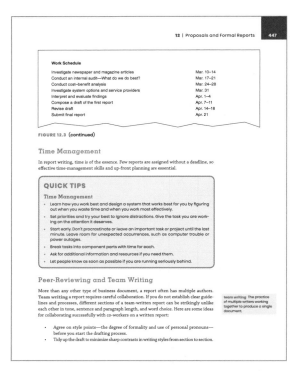

Checklists and quick tips boxes summarize key points for easy reference.

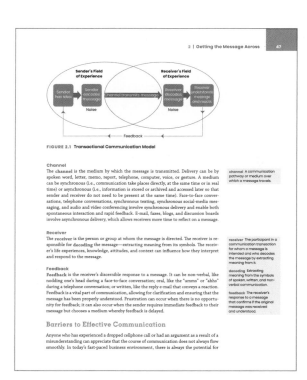

A marginal glossary defines key terms and concepts at their first appearance in the text.

 Ancillary Resource Center

Student and Instructor Resources

Communicating for Results is accompanied by a comprehensive package of online resources for students and instructors alike, all designed to enhance and complete the learning and teaching experiences. These resources are available at www.oup.com/he/Meyer5e.

For Instructors

- A comprehensive **instructor's manual** provides an extensive set of pedagogical tools and suggestions for every chapter, including overviews and summaries, concepts to emphasize in class, suggestions for class discussion, additional exercises, and an answer key for end-of-chapter exercises.
- Newly updated for this edition, classroom-ready **PowerPoint slides** summarize key points from each chapter and incorporate figures and tables drawn straight from the text.
- An extensive **test generator** enables instructors to sort, edit, import, and distribute hundreds of questions in multiple-choice, true–false, and short-answer formats.

For Students

- *Communicating for Results* is available in various formats, including print, loose-leaf, and—new for this edition—**enhanced ebook**, which includes all of the content as well as quizzes and reviews through¬out that further enhance the learning experience.
- The **Student Study Guide** includes chapter summaries, study questions, and self-grading quizzes to help you review the textbook and classroom material.
- Other available resources for students include case studies, additional grammar quizzes, interactive activities, videos, and flashcards to further support your understanding of the material in the textbook.

Dashboard: OUP's Learning Management System platform

Dashboard is an integrated learning system that offers quality content and tools to track student progress in an intuitive, web-based learning environment. It features a streamlined interface that connects students and instructors with the functions used most frequently, simplifying the learning experience to save time and put student progress first.

Dashboard for *Communicating for Results* is available through your OUP sales representative, or visit dashboard.oup.com.

 **www.oup.com/he/Meyer5e**

Acknowledgements

The development of a new edition is a process that involves the expertise, insights, and dedication of many people. I am grateful to have worked alongside and in collaboration with the editorial and production team at Oxford University Press, including developmental editor Peter Chambers. I wish to also offer my sincere thanks to Brenda La Rose, Partner, Leaders International Executive Search, for her advice and generosity in speaking with me.

To my colleagues and associates, internationally, across Canada, and in the School of Professional Communication at Ryerson University, I owe my gratitude for their inspiring engagement with the field of professional and managerial communication.

I also thank the many reviewers from across Canada who originally recommended the project and who have since offered insightful recommendations that helped in the process of shaping and re-shaping *Communicating for Results* over editions to meet the needs of faculty and students. In addition to those who provided anonymous feedback for the fifth edition, I would like to thank the following individuals:

Robert C. Ackroyd, Northern Alberta Institute of Technology
Matt Archibald, University of Ottawa
Heather Burt, Langara College
Leda Culliford, Laurentian University
Sara Earley, Mount Royal University
Karen Grandy, Saint Mary's University
D.A. Hadfield, University of Waterloo
Susan Hesemeier, MacEwan University
Linda Howell, University of the Fraser Valley
Laurie Jackson, Camosun College
Keith Johnson, University of the Fraser Valley
Brenda Lang, Mount Royal University

Heather Madden-Johns, British Columbia Institute of Technology
Patrick Michalak, Centennial College
Karen Riley, Southern Alberta Institute of Technology
Diana Serafini, Dawson College
J.A. Sharpe, University of Manitoba
Oksana Shkurska, Dalhousie University
Gillian Suanders, University of Victoria
Tara Williams, Medicine Hat College
Aidan Wyatt, Southern Alberta Institute of Technology

Finally, on a personal level, I want to thank my family—Margaret Meyer, the late George Homer Meyer, Dr. Bruce Meyer, Kerry Johnston, and Katie Meyer—whose unfailing support, kindness, and patience have made it possible for me to produce the first edition and to do it all again a second, third, fourth, and now fifth time.

Carolyn Meyer

To my mother, Margaret
—and in memory of my father, George Homer

Issues and Trends in Professional Communication

Chapter Preview

This chapter introduces you to the contemporary workplace and what it takes to be a professional, both individually and as part of a team. You'll see why it's important to be honest and principled and to keep private information private.

Learning Objectives

1. Identify the link between effective business communication and personal career success.
2. Understand professionalism and professional boundaries.
3. Identify the importance, types, and characteristics of workplace teams and models for team decision-making.
4. Recognize key changes and trends in the workplace.
5. Identify the goals and standards of ethical business communication.
6. Understand workplace privacy issues and identify strategies to safeguard personal information.

Case Study

By permission of Centre for Aboriginal Human Resource Development Inc.

Brenda LaRose lives her values in her approach to business communication.

Values of honesty and respect for differences, a commitment to trust and relationship building, collaborative and virtual-team practices, and open and transparent communication: these are the cornerstones on which Brenda LaRose has built her outstanding 25-year career as an executive search company head. As the 2019 recipient of the Aboriginal Business Hall of Fame Lifetime Achievement Award from the Canadian Council for Aboriginal Business and as a Métis Anishinaabe citizen, Winnipeg-based LaRose lives the values of her culture while applying a wealth of expertise as a Certified Management Consultant and a Certified Professional in Human Resources. She is the founder of Higgins Executive Search, a national leader in diverse and Indigenous executive recruitment, and is now a partner at Leaders International, as well as the co-founder of SheDay. For LaRose, communicating is about more than just getting the message across. "It's extremely important. You are projecting your values and image every day when you're interacting with people, including clients. It's all about communicating from an ethics-and-values perspective—that's key for communicating. Our job is to make sure that we are communicating well, that we're managing the expectations [of clients and candidates] and that we're making sure they understand how we work and understand the process."

LaRose's ethics-and-values perspective makes good business sense but it comes from a wider world than business. It comes from who she is and who her people are, as embodied in part by Indigenous knowledge, the Anishinaabe Seven Sacred Laws (respect, love, courage, honesty, wisdom, humility, and truth), and millennia-old practices of storytelling and conflict resolution—practices that have been emulated in the mainstream business communication toolkit. LaRose stresses that working in the Indigenous community demands an understanding of its diversity—there are more than 600 First Nations, different from one another in more than just geographical location—and a nuanced appreciation of communicative differences. That respect for differences carries over to LaRose's respect for the communication preferences of her Indigenous and non-Indigenous team. LaRose encourages them to communicate both verbally and in writing and to use Teamer, a tool for interoffice communication, to promote sharing and clear up uncertainties.

With a team of 12 and offices in Winnipeg, Vancouver, and Ottawa, LaRose knows the importance of collaborative software tools and strong relationships between team members based on trust and mutual respect as the keys to productive virtual meetings and on-site project partnerships. When she founded Higgins Executive Search 20 years ago, she realized that many interactions among staff were virtual and that her team needed to be in regular contact to work on a number of different projects at once. She invested heavily in technology for virtual communication, a practice she continues in using GoToMeeting for regular once- to twice-a-week meetings with her dispersed workforce.

For LaRose, GoToMeeting comes with the added advantage of enabling participants to see as well as hear each other. "You've got to be able to work together, trust each other, and like each other to be part of a team. If you're not communicating, not working together, and not spending time together, you can't be a team."[1]

The ability of businesses to manage and adapt to change is a popular topic with communicators. According to Andy Canham, president of SAP Canada, and Tony Olvet, president of research at IDC Canada, the changes facing Canadian business not only involve global competition, but transformations brought by the digital revolution. Machine learning, the Internet of Things, cloud computing, artificial intelligence, big data, and blockchain are all part of what they call "the wave of change [that] is washing over Canadian business."[2] Digital transformation—applying technologies to change the way something is done—is resulting in new ways of creating, selling and delivering products and services.[3]

Communicating for Change— and a Stronger Bottom Line— in the New Economy

Innovation, according to the Conference Board of Canada, is the process of extracting economic and social value from knowledge and transforming ideas into marketable products and services. Whether it involves radical technological breakthroughs such as the adoption of disruptive technologies, like 3D printing, or the use of new, productivity-boosting **information and communication technologies** (ICTs), innovation is important to the success of organizations, communities, and nations. How innovative is Canadian business? In 2018, the Conference Board of Canada, in its How Canada Performs: Innovation report card, awarded Canada a "C" grade and ranked its innovation performance twelfth among 16 major industrialized nations.[4] Although Canada continues to lag behind many other industrialized nations, communication and the ability to work creatively and in teams are seen as increasingly important to attaining productivity and innovation benchmarks.

A 2018 study from Microsoft and Ipsos-Reid showed that driving growth and innovation depends on the ability of business leaders to foster a culture of creativity and collaboration. According to Bruce Mau, co-founder and chief executive officer of Massive Change Network, "Historically, the workplace was designed to prevent communication. What we realize now is that communication flow within an organization is the most powerful creator of wealth, so we as business leaders need to find the synthesis between our physical and digital workspaces to facilitate this communication."[5] Creativity, critical thinking, communication, and collaboration skills are all factors in business success.

information and communication technologies (ICTS) Technologies, such as mobile phone systems and the Internet, used for transmitting, manipulating, and storing data by electronic means.

In today's global business environment, everyone communicates for a living. It is impossible to work in an office without writing reports, dashing off e-mails, composing formal letters, participating in meetings, speaking on the telephone, networking and collaborating with colleagues, giving presentations, or using digital technologies to carry out any of these functions. Spoken and written **communication** that is focused, reliable, and disciplined has the power to influence opinion and shape perceptions on which an organization's competitiveness, productivity, and success depend. Good communication plays a crucial role in building credibility and upholding standards of accountability. In a global business environment where relationships thrive on trust, how you write, speak, and listen reflects who you are professionally.

Done well, your communication can empower you and lead to promotion and success. Language is, after all, a powerful tool worth the effort of learning to use well. Effective communication can cut through the complexities of business, clarifying fuzzy concepts and making masses of data both meaningful and manageable for those who must use it and make decisions based on it.

Successful communication on the job doesn't happen by chance. It is the result of learning how to structure information strategically using text, design, and relevant technologies flexibly to achieve an intended purpose for a clearly defined audience. Delivering information effectively can depend on a fine balance between you and your audience, between a commitment to your business goals and an awareness of your audience's needs. Delivering information at Internet speed, as so many jobs now require, demands more than simply familiarizing yourself with the basic rules of grammar, spelling, and punctuation. It also requires keeping up with changes and developing an accessible, functional style of communication that is flexible enough to be applied to the many forms of communication in your workplace.

Good communication makes good business sense. Even though the ability to communicate effectively is considered a "**soft skill**"—a social and self-management behaviour—as opposed to a "**hard skill**"—technical know-how, tool, and/or technique that equips people to work in a professional capacity—research has shown that communication is important to success at work. Among the 95 Canadian HR specialists surveyed for *Navigating Change: 2018 Business Council Skills Survey*, maintaining a "human touch" and hiring grads with a comprehensive mix of skills were key priorities.[6] Topping the list of skills employers are looking for in entry-level hires are

- collaboration/teamwork/interpersonal/relationship building skills
- communication skills
- problem-solving skills
- analytical capabilities
- resiliency

In a 2016 survey of 90 leading private-sector employers, Canadian hiring managers ranked communication a close second to teamwork skills as the capability most important for entry-level job candidates.[7] Communication capabilities are not just a pathway to career advancement, but also a route to satisfied customers and a healthy bottom line. Terry Matthews, founder and chairman of Wesley Clover, a private equity and investment management firm, sees new graduates with specific skill sets as part of the formula for corporate success in the future economy: "It's not always the ones with

communication A transactional and relational process involving the meaningful exchange of information.

soft skill A social, interpersonal, self-management, or language skill that complements a person's technical skills.

hard skill A technical skill (know-how and abilities) that a person requires for a specific job.

the highest marks. Rather, it's the people with the hard work ethic, creativity and good communication skills."[8]

Businesses across North America collectively spend billions every year training their employees to communicate effectively, in part because business practitioners can spend up to 80 per cent of a work day engaged in oral and written communication[9] and companies with effective communication outperform less communication-savvy competitors.[10] The Conference Board of Canada argues that progress in the work world depends on the ability to do the following:

- read and understand information in many forms;
- speak and write to command attention and promote understanding;
- actively listen and appreciate other points of view;
- use scientific and technological skills to clarify ideas;
- share information via a range of technologies;
- manage information by gathering and organizing it through the use of technologies and information systems; and,
- apply and integrate knowledge and skills from other disciplines.[11]

Developing these skills leads to advantages that have lasting benefits for organizations and stakeholders. Advantages include enhanced problem-solving and decision-making; increased efficiency, workflow, and productivity; and improved professional image, business relationships, and group dynamics.

Communicating in the Current Workplace

Contemporary changes in the Canadian workplace—and beyond—have implications for learning, job requirements, sought-after business talent, hiring, and the quality of work life. Despite these changes, communication is a constant cornerstone for successful professionals.

The Knowledge Economy

Whereas Canada's economy used to be based on the products people made from raw materials through manual labour and industrial production, the information age has made it knowledge-based. Information is a valuable commodity and now, more than ever, it is easily accessed and disseminated through computer technology. The knowledge worker makes and sells some kind of idea-based product, such as software, consulting and financial services, music, design, or pharmaceuticals. The advantage that knowledge products have over products produced through manual labour is that their value can dramatically increase as the global market expands; challenges in a knowledge economy include ensuring continued funding for research and development (R&D), drawing on an educated workforce trained in critical thinking, and fighting the problem of "brain drain," which is the loss of experts to other countries. Richard Florida, an urban studies theorist and director of cities at the Martin Prosperity Institute at the University of Toronto's Rotman School of Management, believes that creativity is the driving force of economic progress and the source of competitive advantage. He claims that "the creative age" has seen the rise of two social classes: the creative class—consisting of workers in science and technology, arts and culture, entertainment, health care, law, and management—and the service class.[12] A 2015 study by the Martin Prosperity Institute shows that Canada's economy is at a crossroads: it is transitioning from a natural resource–based economy to a knowledge-based economy but lags behind its international peers.[13]

Publicly accessible search engines (such as Google) and open-access business engines and databases have spurred the spread of information and made the acquisition of knowledge more democratic. Today, workers are expected to have both the skills necessary to find and evaluate information through these resources and the know-how to process and communicate that information effectively. The information age makes researchers of us all, no matter our occupation or job profile. Common for large businesses and, increasingly, smaller ones is algorithm-based big data analytics, the practice of collecting, analyzing, and comparing large data sets, and identifying patterns in them to better understand consumer preferences, forecast trends, and attune strategies, products, and services. Although many companies do not have fully data-driven cultures, 73 per cent of surveyed businesses reported gaining value from the data and artificial intelligence (AI) projects they launched in marketing, customer-relationship management, data sharing, human resources and hiring, and security enhancement.[14] The Toronto Raptors front office has drawn insights from big data since 2016, when it partnered with IBM to use its AI-based Watson technology to make the strategic draft picks that helped it clinch the 2019 NBA championship.[15] Companies now also rely on competitive intelligence—the practice of deriving data insight from external sources to gain a competitive advantage by utilizing information about a competitor's products, services, and customers to make business decisions.[16] These analytical practices

yelo34/©123RF.com

The Toronto Raptors are just one of the businesses, ranging from large to small, that are using the power of big data and AI to improve their products, market knowledge, and processes.

are part of the Insight Economy, a data-driven approach to business and business processes. Shared workspaces—areas hosted by a web server where colleagues in any location can share information and documents—and company intranets—private communications networks that allow employees to share insider information in a protected web environment—are prime examples of how this era is radically reshaping business environments.

The Risk Society

Unprecedented modernization and globalization have brought not only unprecedented progress but also unprecedented risk. Recognizing this, sociologists Anthony Giddens and Ulrich Beck have called our modern society a "risk society."[17] Risk is the potential for loss. When we act to gain something, we must often assume a certain level of risk. Today's businesses face challenges from a complex threat landscape and carry out extensive assessments to identify potential risks and avoid risk-related losses. Dangers include not only environmental risks, such as natural disasters, but also manufactured risks that have the potential to be catastrophic and affect many people. Examples of manufactured risks in ICTs include **piracy**, **cyberwarfare**, and **identity theft**. According to Statistics Canada, even with cybersecurity spending of $14 billon, more than 20 per cent of Canadian businesses suffered data breaches in 2017. Cybersecurity expert Claudiu Popa, CEO at the Informatica Security Corporation, believes the actual number may be much higher due to lack of detection. Large companies are not immune: in May 2018 the Bank of Montreal (BMO) and the Royal Bank of Canada (RBC) reported that 90,000 of their customers had been affected by data breaches. Air Canada experienced a similar issue in August 2018 when 20,000 of its mobile app users were targeted. Security breaches result in lost or compromised data, as well as a loss of trust; they can harm commerce and a company's credibility, reputation, and bottom line through legal costs, settlements, and PR costs. Institutions such as governments and businesses attempt to control such risks by building trust, establishing cross-border co-operation, and forging networks. Under federal privacy protection law, Breach of Security Safeguard Regulations in effect as of 1 November, 2018, require companies to report breaches to the Privacy Commissioner in writing or face penalties of up to $100,000. The report must specify the nature and cause of the breach, the time/date/period of occurrence, the type of information breached, the number of people affected, an account of how they have been informed of the breach, and actions taken by the company to reduce the risk of harm to those affected.

Managing risk is essential for the active risk-taking that allows a dynamic economy to continue. Preventive measures and regulation are part of this stabilizing effort, as are the specialized protocols of crisis and **risk communication**. Data security, cybersecurity, and defence against a spectrum of threats to communication from computer viruses, hacking, and other forms of cyberattack continue to be top concerns for organizations.

Sustainability and Corporate Social Responsibility

Corporations hold significant power and influence in the world. In fact, 42 of the 100 largest economies in the world are companies.[19] According to Kristen Coco, strategic communications consultant at the UN Global Compact (UNGC), the

piracy The unauthorized reproduction and distribution of copyrighted material, including video games, software, music, and films.

cyberwarfare A form of information warfare, usually the conducting of politically motivated sabotage through hacking.

identity theft The act of acquiring and collecting an individual's personal information for criminal purposes.

risk communication An interactive exchange of information and ideas on risk among risk assessors, risk managers, and other interested parties.[18]

corporate social responsibility (CSR) movement was born in the 1990s amid growing stakeholder concerns over environmental catastrophes (such as the sinking of the *Exxon Valdez* oil tanker), the first sustainability reports from forward-looking companies such as Ben & Jerry's, and the emergence of the anti-globalization movement.[20] Today, important initiatives such as the UNGC drive transparency on how corporations earn their money, treat their employees, and protect the planet's finite resources. The UNGC asks companies to embrace, support, and enact core values related to particular areas:

- human rights
- labour standards (such as bans on forced and child labour, recognition of collective bargaining rights, and elimination of employment discrimination)
- the environment (adoption of environmental protection initiatives and environmentally friendly technologies, and use of precautionary approaches to environmental challenges)
- anti-corruption (zero tolerance for all forms of corruption, including bribery and extortion)[21]

Communicating these values to stakeholders has become more important as interest in **sustainable development** and other CSR-related topics like corporate ethics, citizenship, accountability, and the triple bottom line of environment, economy, and society continues to grow.[22] In 2015/2016, 79 per cent of publicly listed Canadian companies published a sustainability report. Reporting sustainable development is more than a PR exercise.[23] Through a combination of voluntary and mandatory disclosures, sustainability reporting can accomplish many objectives:

- strengthen the link between a company and its stakeholders and increase stakeholder value
- boost financial performance
- showcase efficiency in production and lead to better use of company assets and innovative technology
- increase the company's appeal to socially responsible investors
- build industry credibility, set an example, and enhance company reputation

Business on a Global Scale

The world's economy is becoming increasingly global—to the point where, since 2000, the world seems to have shrunk. This is due, in large part, to several key factors:

- web browsers promoting connectivity and the free flow of information
- software (such as PayPal) and other communication platforms promoting wider co-operation
- open-source software (software that users are permitted to change and improve)
- outsourcing and offshoring (designing at home and redistributing customer service functions and production facilities to distant countries)
- "amplifiers" that are digital, virtual, mobile, and personal (cellphones, smartphones, chips, file-sharing networks, VoIP, WiFi).

This globalized business structure provides new opportunities as well as challenges for Canadian workers and their organizations. Canadian products must compete in international markets, yet the brands we may think of as 100 per cent Canadian may in fact be produced, in whole or in part, in other countries. For example, Canadian aerospace and transportation giant Bombardier has facilities in 28 countries.[24] Furthermore, investment from foreign-based companies and emerging super economies such as China has jumped dramatically, and the trend toward outsourcing and offshoring customer service functions continues. The need to explore new and emerging markets, negotiate, buy and sell overseas, market products, and enter into joint ventures is anchored in effective communication with people from around the world; without this communication, none of these functions could be accomplished. The ability to communicate across cultural differences, time zones, and language barriers—and to exercise intercultural sensitivity by respecting differences in customs, lifestyles, religions, and business etiquette—is crucial to the success of operations in this new global economy.

More Diverse Employee Base

Most Canadian employee constituencies reflect differences in ethnicity, age, race, gender, physical ability, religious belief, and sexual orientation. This diverse, multi-generational workforce is not simply the outcome of Canada's success in attracting talented immigrants or in cultivating social responsibility through fair and equitable employment policies; it is a matter of good economic sense, as companies capitalize on talents, expertise, creativity, and strengths across diverse groups to obtain greater productivity and competitive advantage. A company's human capital, or the individuals that make up an organization, either fuel or curb its success and are arguably its greatest asset. Without a deep talent pool based in diverse organizations, Canada could very well lose out on opportunities for growth. RBC Financial Group refers to this practice as "the diversity advantage" and cites it as a defining business trend in the twenty-first century.[25] The demographic makeup of most workplaces and the interactions brought about by a worldwide economy makes promoting **diversity** an important component of management. Organizational policies and practices will continue to be vital in sustaining an equitable, diverse, and inclusive work environment in which all individuals are valued, respected, and treated with dignity.

diversity Differences among people with respect to gender, race, ethnicity, age, sexual orientation, religious belief, and physical ability, which are to be acknowledged, valued, and celebrated in today's workplaces.

The Growing Millennial and Gen Z Workforce: A "Generation Disrupted"

The term *millennials* refers to individuals born between 1981 and 1996, and Gen Z refers to those born 1997 or after.[26] According to the Conference Board of Canada and researcher Ruth Wright, millennials represent one-third of Canada's population and are the "largest demographic cohort to come after the Baby Boomers."[27] By 2020, they will represent the "largest cohort of working Canadians"—64 per cent—marking a major generational shift.[28] Millennials bring unique talents and competencies to the workforce, but their numbers alone make for a competitive labour market. Their work styles and preferences show desire for

- financial rewards and benefits
- flexible hours

- work-life balance
- ongoing learning, coaching, and real-time feedback
- fulfillment—work that is authentic and allows them to be themselves and develop their strengths
- being kept in the loop—having access to all workplace information that they perceive to be relevant to them and to their jobs.[29]

Millennials are also known for their willingness to work in teams, communicate openly with managers, embrace new communication technologies, and change jobs frequently, in fact twice as often as previous generations, in order to achieve career goals.[30] A full 70 per cent of millennials prefer to work from home,[31] making telecommuting, mobile offices, online collaboration tools, and cloud software more than just passing trends. Eighty per cent of millennials and Gen Zs find the **gig economy**, based in freelance and contract work, appealing, because of the opportunity to work part time and supplement existing employment.[32] If this new generation of employees has a personality, it could be summed up as the Pew Research Center has described it: confident, connected, and open to change.[33]

gig economy a labour market characterized by a high number of freelance and contract jobs.

Team Work Environments

In the twenty-first century, business is conducted by teams. A desire to collaborate and engage in creative problem solving is something business leaders surveyed by Microsoft Canada and Ipsos Canada believe drives growth and innovation. According to Gale Moutrey, vice president of communication at Steelcase, creativity demands different work modes and types of technology: "People need to work alone, in pairs and in different size groups throughout a creative process, and they need a range of devices that are mobile and integrated into the physical workplace."[34] Collaboration in the broadest sense is at work in "open data" and crowdsourcing initiatives, such as apps that allow users to report and share information about heavy traffic or road closures.

Collaboration through cross-functional teams, in which individuals with different areas of expertise come together to share information for a common goal, makes the most of a workforce's creative potential by increasing individual involvement in decision-making and project development. Innovations in information technology and mobile communications have made it possible for employees to be part of globally distributed teams and virtual project teams, which can eliminate time and space barriers—by allowing team members to contribute outside of traditional work hours and from various locations—and still provide quality, low-cost solutions to organizational problems. Working in teams, however, depends on strong communication and interpersonal skills to overcome conflicts that arise when people with differing viewpoints must make joint decisions. Organizations often invest in special training to help teams boost performance, manage conflict, and practice open communication.

Disruptive Technologies

Technology and language-use shaped by technology now filter our perspective of the world. Our communications are mediated through many different technologies and electronic forums. Many of these are what Harvard professor of business administration

Clayton Christensen calls **disruptive technologies**—affordable, accessible products and services that take root at the bottom of the market then move up to displace established competitors and make some existing products and services obsolete.[35] A fourth industrial revolution, commonly referred to as Industry 4.0, is transforming the world of manufacturing through new forms of automation and data exchange as well as machine learning.[36] These breakthroughs have brought us closer to a fully digitized society, complete with smart home security systems, "smart factories", cyber-physical system integration and blockchain record-keeping technology.[37] Many technologies that are now essential communication tools are disruptive technologies: laptops; e-mail; tablets; smartphones; Bluetooth technology; instant messaging (IM); text messaging; voicemail; proprietary Voice over Internet Protocol services (VoIP) such as Skype; podcasts; mobile apps such as WhatsApp; space-defying video conferencing and web conferencing; presentation software such as PowerPoint and Keynote; interactive software that can change the sequence of information; blogs; wikis; augmented and virtual reality; cloud computing; smart and virtual assistants; and wearable computer components. These technologies allow us to communicate farther, faster, and around the clock—to the point where we are always using one technology or another.[38] As political theorist Michael Sandel has noted, "developments in information technology are enabling companies to squeeze out all the inefficiencies and friction from their markets and business operations."[39]

> **disruptive technologies**
> Innovative, transformative products and services that create new opportunities and move up the market to replace established competitors.

Digital Connectivity

Digital technologies have had an extensive impact on communication, relationships, and marketing across Canadian workplaces.

- **Social networking sites: Facebook, YouTube, LinkedIn, Tumblr, Instagram, Pinterest, and Twitter.** Facebook began as a tool to "give people the power to share and make the world more open and connected . . . to stay connected with friends and family, to discover what's going on in the world, and to share and express what matters to them."[40] Facebook lets users control the information they share with others, which is a tool that marketing-savvy corporations have quickly embraced for their self-presentation. Similarly, the popular micro-blogging site Twitter offers corporate representatives the chance to build trust and promote corporate values such as transparency.
- **Web 3.0.** Unlike Web 1.0, the read-only Internet of the 1990s, and Web 2.0, the read-write Internet of blogs, wikis, and peer-to-peer file sharing, Web 3.0 encompasses AI technology, social media, the semantic web (which allows for more sophisticated and personalized searching), and the Internet of Things (dubbed IoT, a network of web-enabled objects and devices).[41] Many business leaders believe that Web 3.0 will transform business; it promises the unprecedented ability to not only connect and communicate with customers but also, through real-time analytics, capture data about their online activities that can then be used for sales and marketing as well as product development. A wide variety of "things"— from cars to health-monitoring devices to personal fitness trackers—are already equipped to automatically collect and exchange data over the Internet. Moreover, technology research group Machina Research predicts that the number of such devices will grow to 27 billion by 2025, and that these devices will generate

several trillion dollars in revenue by that time.[42] Companies that have embraced Web 3.0 include Dell, which has created a community of one million online users to test products and provide feedback on design, and Amazon, which uses AI to provide customer recommendations based on individual browsing histories.[43]

- **Mobile apps for business.** Smartphones, tablets, and other devices with mobile Internet capabilities are used across Canada and, increasingly, across the globe. Many businesses have taken advantage of mobile apps as part of their technology solutions.[44] Business-to-business (B2B) apps are used to support an organization's internal business processes such as customer-relationship management, warehouse management, and salesforce automation. Business-to-consumer (B2C) apps fulfill different needs:

  » Content-oriented apps, such as Twitter and IM+, answer the need for information, communication, entertainment, and socialization.
  » Marketing-oriented apps promote brands and target them to young, digitally native demographics.
  » Service-oriented apps allow users to perform tasks such as banking, shopping, or consulting schedules.

- Various apps also benefit businesses by boosting productivity. Examples include note-taking apps such as Evernote, business-planning apps such as StratPad, file-syncing apps such as Dropbox Business, scheduling apps such as Google Calendar, and virtual personal-assistant apps such as Assistant. Best practices for using mobile apps for business involve selecting secure business app vendors, following secure downloading procedures, evaluating app performance, and preventing inappropriate app use.[45]

New Economies: Attention, Distraction, and Share

The rise of the Internet and social media has made information glut and overload a central fact of daily experience. Surging volumes of content bring endless choices about what to view, read, listen to, and know. Though capital, labour, information, and knowledge are plentiful, attention is scarce, and businesses must compete and manage information strategically to attract it. Media observer Nicholas Carr believes the more the Internet seizes our attention, the more it shortens our attention spans, encourages shallow thinking, and lessens our capacity for critical thinking and ability to absorb and filter information.[46] A state of what tech writer Linda Stone calls "continuous partial attention" is the new reality,[47] especially for knowledge workers whose reliance on digital technologies can result in constant distractions on the job. Attention has become the new currency because it is always at a premium.[48] The term **attention economy** thus refers to a system centred on seeking and receiving attention from other human beings. Having the greatest number of views, tags, followers, or likes is a badge of success, and quantifying and measuring this attention is a big part of what businesses now do.[49] The aim of attracting or interrupting customers' concentration, which is the idea behind the **distraction economy**, has implications for how we present ourselves on online platforms, how businesses market their brands and manage their online images and interactions, and even how we manage our lives. The distraction economy has also brought the need for **mindfulness**, or the ability to "manage [a] wandering mind and external distractions."[50] For businesses and

attention economy An economic system centred on seeking and receiving attention from other people (particularly consumers).

distraction economy An economic system centred on drawing people's (particularly consumers') attention away from one source and to another source.

mindfulness The ability to focus one's thoughts by tuning out external distractions.

their stakeholders, getting attention quickly and memorably and forging connections and affinities online matters more now than it has ever before.

Social media, along with mobile communications, play an equally important role in the **share (or peer) economy**. The share economy is based on the idea of collaborative consumption, or sharing as reinvented through network technologies, with a "shift in consumer values from ownership to access."[51] This new peer-to-peer economic model is based on some old and familiar concepts: sharing, renting, swapping, gifting, lending, bartering.[52] App-based services such as Airbnb (accommodation), Lyft (ride sharing), and TaskRabbit (micro jobs) have disrupted previously regulated taxi, car-rental, and hotel industries. Because share economies place a monetary value on access to assets, they enable people who control that access to become part-time entrepreneurs.[53]

> **share (or peer) economy** An economic system centred on access to rather than ownership of resources.

Indigenous Economic Empowerment

Since the 1990s, there has been extraordinary growth in Indigenous business in Canada; however, there is still far to go in reintegrating Indigenous people into the economy through a process of economic reconciliation and overcoming a history of economic segregation of Indigenous Peoples. In 2016 alone, the annual contribution of the Indigenous economy was estimated at $30 billion, with 45,000 businesses across many sectors.[54] The term *Indigenomics* describes the effort of Indigenous peoples to build their future and improve their communities and quality of life through equity ownership, environmental planning, and procurement.[55] According to the Social Sciences and Humanities Research Council of Canada, Indigenous entrepreneurship can be distinct from mainstream understandings of entrepreneurship because of its emphasis on collectiveness and community development and its foundations in Indigenous knowledge (IK)—understandings and ways of knowing that are cumulative and interconnected and emphasize the relatedness of all living things.[56] For Winnipeg-based Manitobah Mukluks, whose 300-strong workforce creates handmade moccasins and mukluks sold around the world, with sales topping $25 million annually, being an Indigenous business means supporting Indigenous communities, sharing success, keeping traditions alive, and celebrating Indigenous values.[57] Its Storyboot Project embodies these values by creating partnerships with elders and artisans and guaranteeing them 100 per cent of the proceeds for every pair of mukluks or moccasins they craft the traditional way. Behind the steady growth of Indigenous business are organizations such as the Canadian Council for Aboriginal Business (CCAB), which supports the building of relationships between Aboriginal and non-Aboriginal businesses and communities. Business success stories represent a broad range of sectors:

- Spirit Bear Lodge, owned and operated by the Kitasoo/Xai'xais Nation, employs 10 per cent of the local population and practices a community-driven, non-extractive method of eco-tourism.
- The Toquaht First Nation of BC is building a $1.35-million marina.[58]
- The Fisher River Cree Nation north of Winnipeg is behind the first utility-scale solar project in Manitoba, a megawatt facility that will supply revenue to the community and link to the province's power grid.[59]
- Nk'Mip Cellars, the #2 winery in BC according to WineAlign 2018, is one of many ventures from the Osoyoos Indian Band and has the distinction of being the first Indigenous-owned and -operated winery in Canada.[60]

territorial acknowledgement
a statement that recognizes the traditional territory of the Indigenous Peoples who inhabit, or once inhabited, the land on which an event happens or people have gathered.

A fact of living and doing business in Canada is that our lives and work are conducted on the traditional territories of First Peoples.[61] Acknowledging territory shows respect for and recognition of Indigenous Peoples and helps build reciprocal relationships necessary for achieving understanding and reconciliation. **Territorial acknowledgements** are statements read out or displayed at the beginning of meetings, conferences, ceremonies, presentations, courses, and community events. More than mere formalities, they are important cultural protocols (based on formal protocols long used by Indigenous people to acknowledge their surroundings) and are an essential part of doing business.[62] There is no single land acknowledgement statement that can be used Canada-wide—only context-specific statements are true acknowledgements. Each is dependent on geographical location[63] and on the past and continuing presence of specific Indigenous groups or nations, named in the statement, who called and continue to call that place home. Educational tools, such the Whose Land app and website, make it easy for people to identify the Indigenous land they are on.[64]

At its most essential, a land acknowledgment names and recognizes a specific Indigenous group or groups: "We want to acknowledge that we are on the traditional territory of [nation names]." International human rights organization Amnesty International proposes a reflective process for writing a land acknowledgement:

1. Naming the Indigenous territory you are on.
2. Explaining why you are acknowledging that land.
3. Speaking to the relevance of Indigenous rights to the event.
4. Incorporating answers to 1–3 in a meaningful statement.[65]

Some statements go further in "breathing life into" obligations to Indigenous communities and treaties[66] or, in the case of the City of Ottawa Land Acknowledgement, in bearing witness to a colonial past that saw lands taken away from Indigenous peoples:

> We recognize that Ottawa is located on unceded territory of the Algonquin Anishinabe Nation.
>
> We extend our respect to all First Nations, Inuit and Métis peoples for their valuable past and present contributions to this land. We also recognize and respect the cultural diversity that First Nations, Inuit and Métis people bring to the City of Ottawa.[67]

Britco, a British Columbia manufacturer of modular buildings, has made respect for First Nations protocols and recognition of Indigenous rights and title to traditional territories part of its business practice. According to Colin Doylend, the company's director of Aboriginal relations, "Simply, recognizing and supporting Aboriginal culture and traditions within your business encourages more value and principle-based conversations and actions." One of Britco's many initiatives is to feature a land acknowledgement on its business cards.[68]

Checklist

Communication Skills and Trends in the Canadian Workplace

❑ How do hard skills and soft skills contribute to success?

❑ What is the knowledge economy?

❏ How does risk affect business decisions?

❏ Why are sustainable development and corporate social responsibility important in modern business?

❏ What is global business?

❏ Why is it important for organizations to promote diversity in the workplace?

❏ What strengths do millennials bring to the workforce?

❏ How do disruptive technologies affect business practices?

❏ How are attention, distraction, and sharing economies reshaping the ways sellers and service providers connect with customers?

❏ How are Indigenous businesses making their mark, and what are the core values on which many are founded?

Professionalism and Employee Engagement

Why Professionalism Is Important

A professional is a worker or a practitioner (e.g., a doctor, a lawyer, an engineer, a performing artist, or a fundraiser) in whom others put their trust. **Professionalism**, or the act of being professional, requires a worker to demonstrate they are worthy of that trust through their attitudes and actions. Workers can show professionalism through

- putting clients first
- maintaining confidentiality
- using their knowledge for honest, legal, and ethical purposes[69]

professionalism The act of being professional, which requires demonstrating the competence and/or skill expected from a professional.

Professionalism involves aspiring and committing to appropriate work identities, conduct, and practices.[70] A starting point for many new workers is getting to know and understand their shared work identity. This identity links them to others who do the same work and reinforces a sense of belonging based on what they have in common, including their

- educational background
- professional training
- experiences and expertise
- membership in professional associations
- shared work cultures
- shared ways of solving problems and helping clients and customers deal with uncertainty and risk[71]

Becoming professionalized, or achieving status as a professional, isn't about wearing the right suit or looking the part. It's about standing out as someone who can act decisively and knowledgeably, adapt to new situations, and add value to an organization through their high-quality work.[72] As an employee, professionalism is an ongoing process of social learning that involves thinking about and carrying out your duties according to a set of shared values, objectives, norms, and expectations important to you, your organization, and its stakeholders.

The link between organizations and professionalism is strong. In fact, professionalism is embedded in every aspect of the workplace, including its systems, structures, rules, and procedures.[73]

An organization's policies, mission statement, codes of conduct, training manuals, and communication standards make professionalization a priority, in part because professionalism is considered desirable, appealing, and rewarding. Respected organizations often capitalize on professionalism's allure or appeal in the advertising and marketing slogans (e.g., "join our professionals," "trust it to a professional") they create to attract new recruits and customers.[74] For example, in 2014–2015 the Chartered Professional Accountants of Canada raised awareness of its new professional designation by promoting its brand with the tagline "Need a PRO?"[75]

A commitment to professionalism increases the chance that your behaviour, interactions, communications, and achievements will be viewed positively. For individuals, these outcomes can lead to higher status and authority.[76] For organizations, professionalism, by reducing risk of conflict and error, can improve workflow, the quality and conditions of work life, and the customer-client experience. In the end, professionalism is good for business because it enhances a company's efficiency, productivity, competitiveness, and reputation.

Qualities, Characteristics, and Expectations

No matter your profession or occupation, being professional depends on your capacity to act in the best interests of customers and colleagues, never purely out of self-interest.[77] It involves not just a single skill or capacity but a whole range of integrated skills and qualities (highlighted in Figure 1.1). The combined characteristics each organization values are as unique as the organizations themselves. Such characteristics also define organizational culture. Demonstrating these characteristics and being a good "corporate citizen" are what most organizations expect of their employees. Some people interpret this expectation as a way for organizations to exercise domination and control over their members.

This negative interpretation of organizational expectations explains why businesses may opt to become "**authentic organizations**."[78] Authentic organizations aim to foster creative, innovative environments that will attract top talent and thereby bring meaning and engagement back to the workplace. **Employee engagement** has to do with harnessing an employee's "self" to their work role in a way that makes the employee not just attentive to the role but fully immersed in it.[79] Engaged employees boost organizational performance and increase revenues,[80] making engagement a top priority for managers. Canadian employee engagement, at just under 70 per cent, is above the global average but faces challenges from the introduction of new workplace technologies.[81] Many companies in Canada now survey employee engagement and satisfaction frequently (weekly, even daily) and have introduced measures to increase it. IT company Cisco Systems Canada, for example, has set up a reverse-mentoring program that gives new recruits the opportunity

authentic organizations Organizations that encourage employees to be their best selves by valuing and nurturing their perspectives and differences in attitude.

employee engagement Employees' genuine enthusiasm for and commitment to their work and organization.

to share tips with corporate leaders and motivates the new employees by making them feel they can make a difference.[82] The Aboriginal Peoples Television Network Inc. (APTN), one of the *Globe and Mail*'s Top 100 Employers, formed a committee to foster long-term employee engagement through a collaborative approach.[83]

Professional Boundaries and Behaviours

Relationships are defined by the boundaries we set to map out what is acceptable behaviour and what is off-limits in particular contexts. Boundaries create transparency and help build strong, respectful relationships. **Personal boundaries** are the limits (emotional, physical, and mental) we establish to protect ourselves and set our own thoughts and feelings apart from others'. **Professional boundaries**, on the other hand, define the roles and responsibilities of employees in the workplace. Professional boundaries help employees work safely, comfortably, and productively. They help each member of an organization know where they stand, what is expected of them, and what they can rightfully say "yes" and "no" to. Recognizing and respecting boundaries helps people work together more effectively, and it helps build an environment of transparency in which there is less chance of stress, blame, or bullying.

Defining and establishing professional boundaries begins with recognizing the limits of your personal boundaries. It also requires you to understand the guidelines your organization has set to regulate how you will behave toward others and how others will behave toward you. To start, you should be able to answer the following questions:

- What is your role according to your job description?
- What are your duties and responsibilities?
- Who do you support and report to?
- Who assigns your work and sets your priorities?
- Who evaluates your work and provides feedback?

You should also be aware of different types of boundaries and how they relate to communication on the job:

- organizational rules and regulations (positive/negative sanctions)
- norms (obligations that must be met)
- cognition (ways of thinking)
- individualized self-regulation (self-control and personal commitments, such as pride in performance, that guide you where organizational regulations leave off)

Reading your job description, perusing your employment manual, reflecting on your personal values, and having appropriate conversations with superiors or supervisors are all good ways to gain the insight and information you need to set professional boundaries. Observing workplace culture and paying attention to how others interact can also yield valuable information. For example, you may learn that being helpful to a colleague or a customer involves maintaining a proper social distance and striking a balance between being under-involved and being over-involved. Learning about organizational culture and respecting professional boundaries are both essential to professionalism.

personal boundaries
The emotional, physical, and mental limits individuals establish to protect themselves from harm and set their thoughts and feelings apart from others'.

professional boundaries
The emotional, physical, and mental limits that define what employees should and should not do and how they should be treated in the workplace.

Accountability (owning up to and making amends for mistakes)	**Commitment to excellence** (having high expectations for your performance and doing your best)	**Dedication** (being hardworking and finishing what you start)
Action orientation and autonomy (knowing how to self-direct and executing tasks self-reliantly)	**Commitment to service** (understanding and responding to the needs of employers and customers)	**Discretion** (keeping private information private and avoiding causing offence)
Altruism (not letting self-interest prevent you from acting in the best interests of others)	**Competence** (being able to do a job well, usually based on the possession of appropriate practical and theoretical knowledge)	**Ethical awareness** (identifying ethical dilemmas and assessing the impact of values and behaviours on others)
Attention to detail (being thorough and accurate in completing tasks)	**Confidence** (maintaining a calm, well-spoken demeanour and inspiring trust by having confidence in yourself)	**Etiquette awareness** (being familiar with codes for polite behaviour; avoiding making assumptions about people based on appearances)
Audience-focused communications (considering the needs of your readers and listeners)	**Co-operation and mutual support** (committing to and helping to achieve common goals)	**Expert judgement** (making decisions and finding solutions based on specialized knowledge, training, experience, and skill sets)
Collegiality and corporate citizenship (sharing power and authority among colleagues; being pleasant, co-operative, and ready to help)[a]	**Cultural sensitivity and cultural fit** (respecting diversity and adapting to social groups at work)	**Fairness** (making judgements that are free from discrimination and treating people in a reasonable way)

[a] From Shin Freedman. (2009). *Collegiality matters: How do we work with others?* Proceedings of the Charleston Library Conference.

FIGURE 1.1 Skills and Qualities that Indicate Professionalism

Unprofessional behaviour is often the result of loose boundaries or a lack of respect for established boundaries. Crossing these unseen limits, for example, by intruding on someone else's space or sharing too much personal information, can cause confusion, conflict, embarrassment, and loss of respect and reputation. Such behaviour can shift attention off-task and away from a customer's needs or disrupt co-worker relationships. It can also cause irreparable damage to an individual's reputation. Former Toronto mayor Rob Ford learned first-hand the negative repercussions of violating boundaries in the workplace when, in 2013, he knocked over and caused injury to Toronto City Councillor Pam McConnell in the city council's chambers—their shared place of work. Toronto citizens and media criticized Ford's behaviour, and widespread media reports of the incident

Honesty (being forthright and authentic; telling the truth)

Organizational skill (prioritizing important tasks and planning ahead)

Reliability (demonstrating that others can count on you to show up and get the job done well)

Image awareness (meeting basic context-specific standards for grooming)

Poise (maintaining self-control and remaining calm even when others are angry)

Respect and consideration (showing respect and consideration for authority, other people, rules and policies, and differences)

Industry-standards compliance (having appropriate credentials; acting in accord with your organization's goals and objectives)

Politeness and modesty (practising good manners and staying humble about your accomplishments)

Responsibility (taking charge of your own actions and the actions of others)

Integrity (having strong moral principles)

Pride and satisfaction in work (deriving satisfaction from work that is well done and up to standards)

Service orientation (focusing on customers and their needs and concerns)

Knowledge and commitment to professional development (keeping up-to-date on important information and maintaining the right credentials)

Problem-solving skills (finding effective solutions to difficult or complex issues)

Team orientation (actively contributing to the achievement of group and organizational goals)

Objectivity and professional detachment (maintaining proper distance; selectively withholding expression of personal values, emotions, and preferences)[b]

Punctuality (being on time and prompt in your communications)

Trust (placing confidence in things and others and inspiring others' belief in you; not abusing customers' trust)

[b] From Mike W. Martin. (2000). *Meaningful work: Rethinking professional ethics*. New York: Oxford University Press, p. 85.

did little to improve Ford's already sagging reputation.[84] Unprofessional behaviour takes many forms, including the following:

- gossiping about colleagues
- bullying and intimidating colleagues
- using cliques to ostracize certain colleagues
- using profane language
- ignoring messages or responding to colleagues in an inappropriate way
- sabotaging a colleague's efforts
- blaming a colleague unfairly for your mistake
- not acknowledging a colleague's presence or contribution

Professional lapses draw criticism, especially when they happen repeatedly. As a result, they can have costly consequences, lowering morale and hurting employee retention.

How can you tell if you are being professional? Professionalism is subject to self-judgement and the judgement of others.[85] Periodic performance reviews may flag boundary issues. Even before that stage is reached, informal feedback and reactions from colleagues may help you understand how you are measuring up as a professional. This measuring of professionals in fact takes place on several levels:

- self-reflection and self-regulation (measuring yourself based on adherence to your internal standards and those of the organization)
- evaluations, reactions, and feedback from colleagues, managers, and other stakeholders
- awards, merits, and citations
- acceptance into professional associations and accrediting bodies

Although there is no secret formula for professionalism, there are some general rules of thumb: check your emotional baggage at the door; stay principled, committed, and respectful; and be the best employee you can be.

Checklist

Professionalism

- ❑ What is professionalism?
- ❑ What are some factors that help to foster a sense of belonging among professionals?
- ❑ How is professionalism embedded in the workplace?
- ❑ How do workplaces communicate professional standards to their employees?
- ❑ What are the benefits of being professional?
- ❑ What skills (attitudes, beliefs, behaviours) are associated with professionalism?
- ❑ What is employee engagement?
- ❑ How do companies measure employee engagement?
- ❑ What are professional boundaries and why are they important?
- ❑ What constitutes unprofessional behaviour?
- ❑ How can professionalism be measured?

Teamwork

Part of the professional identity practitioners work hard to develop involves supporting teamwork and its knowledge-, attitude-, and skill-based competencies. Teams are now the modern organization's method of choice for responding to change and bettering their chances of survival.[86] A **team** is a specific type of group whose members have complementary skills and work toward a common mission or goal. Teams are different from work groups in that they focus on the collective production of a product rather than individual

team A group whose members have complementary skills and work toward a common mission or goal.

accountabilities and goals. Team orientation is a sought-after skill because teams are the foundation of organizational life.[87] Teams are formed deliberately and carefully to help organizations perform crucial functions, including meeting work needs, realizing specific outcomes, and sustaining a competitive advantage. Teams are an essential feature in organizations because of their capacities in

- accomplishing projects too large or too complex to be completed by individuals
- forming bonds and a sense of community
- proposing and evaluating solutions to organizational problems
- facilitating innovation

Teams can be measured and understood in terms of three dimensions of performance:

- quantity
- quality
- satisfaction[88]

Teams may be of several different *types* according to the context and their purpose (Figure 1.2):

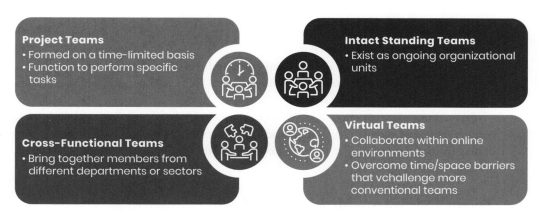

Project Teams
- Formed on a time-limited basis
- Function to perform specific tasks

Intact Standing Teams
- Exist as ongoing organizational units

Cross-Functional Teams
- Bring together members from different departments or sectors

Virtual Teams
- Collaborate within online environments
- Overcome time/space barriers that vchallenge more conventional teams

FIGURE 1.2 Types of Teams

A successful example of cross-functional teams comes from Canadian Tire's R&D division, which has set up labs in Waterloo, Winnipeg, and Calgary that are staffed by teams of behavioural scientists, game and virtual-reality developers, and statisticians. These teams work on a range of projects, including an interactive, 3D-style patio-building app and an app that enables anglers to post photos, share their fishing locations, and mention fishing equipment they may have purchased at the store.[89]

Characteristics of High-Performing Teams

Team performance refers to the degree to which teams meet objectives for time, quality, and cost.[90] High-performance teams establish a record of working well together and succeeding according to these objectives. The experience of working on

High-performing teams encourage open communication of ideas and rely on an established decision-making model that gives all team members a chance to participate.

such a team can be exhilarating and empowering for its members; however, optimal experience and success depends on adhering to specific principles and boundaries (Figure 1.3).

An environment that encourages the open, respectful sharing of ideas and deals with conflict fairly and supportively is essential. It is also essential that all team members recognize the decision-making model and understand who makes decisions and how others are involved.

Team Decision-Making Models

The team leader plays a central role in group performance. The team leader can help build **cognitive trust** among team members and enhance the team's shared sense of **collective efficacy**.[91] Several models, with differing team-leader roles, are open to teams for guiding the decision-making process:

cognitive trust In a team setting, individuals' beliefs in the reliability and dependability of fellow team members.

collective efficacy In a team setting, the group's belief in the ability of the team to organize and execute activities that will enable them to achieve their goal(s).

- unilateral decision-making by the team leader, who then informs other members of the decision (often preferred in time-sensitive situations)
- decision-making by the team leader with input from team members based on their expertise
- decision-making through delegation to team members
- decision-making through a consensus model with input from all members
- decision-making through a majority-rules model

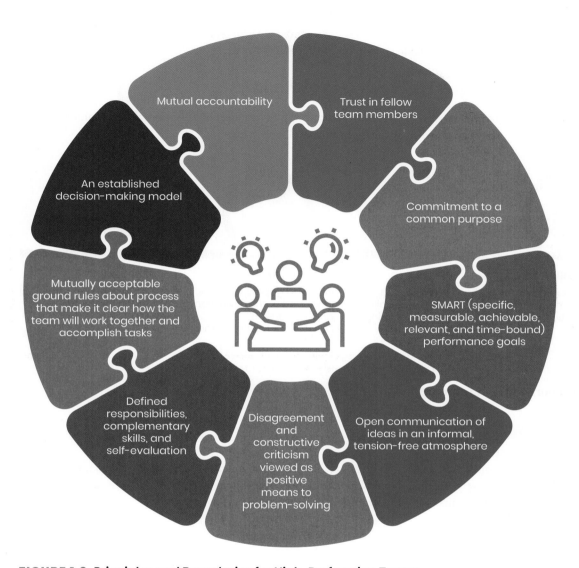

FIGURE 1.3 Principles and Boundaries for High-Performing Teams

Consensus decision-making has specific requirements that must be met in order to be effective: a commitment to hearing and understanding the positions of all members, a willingness to change viewpoints to strengthen the team position, and a general acceptance that the decision reached through the collaboration and co-participation of team members is the best one. It may take time and adjustments before team members reach the level of trust and comfort with one another that is required for interacting co-operatively and making decisions in this way.

Regardless of the model, quality decisions involve a process where group members engage in open communication, respect each other's input, and actively support any decision that is made. There must be a sound and logical rationale for every decision, based on reliable information that has been shared with all team members and, when appropriate, input from outside stakeholders affected by the decision.

Stages in Team Development

Teams need to evolve and pass through four stages of behavioural development before they can perform at the highest level (Figure 1.4).

FORMING

- Phase of initial excitement
- Group members meet and engage in initial goal-setting

STORMING

- Phase of frustration over roles and responsibilities
- Requires a re-focusing of goals to overcome dysfunction

NORMING

- Resolved gaps and issues
- Improved communication and interaction
- Greater confidence in the expression of ideas
- Fresh focus on goals and productivity

PERFORMING

- Realizing progress in attaining satisfaction and achieving goals

FIGURE 1.4 The Four Stages in Team Development

Managing Team Conflict

Conflicts in teams are common. The way team members respond to and manage conflict can affect a team's overall performance.[92] Facing up to conflict and developing effective ways to manage it can therefore improve team performance.

- Rely on co-operative approaches to conflict centred not only on concern for yourself but concern for others on the team[93]
- Think of conflict as a mutual problem that needs to be dealt with in order to complete a critical task rather than as a clash of interests where only one person can win[94]
- Keep in mind that success for one member can promote success for all
- Express ideas, feelings, and positions without animus and look for areas of agreement—goodwill and good feelings can lighten the mood and ease interactions
- Listen carefully to what others are saying and concentrate on asking each other for more information rather than each person stubbornly defending their position
- Combine good ideas to arrive at creative solutions[95]
- Adjust your perspective by recognizing that success for one really means success for all—avoid competing
- Develop a sense of team identity to improve loyalty and trust while refusing to engage in power struggles
- When leading a team, enhance team identification by increasing team member input into decision-making

- Encourage active participation to promote a sense of belonging[96] and co-operation
- Have confidence in overcoming interpersonal difficulties and handling oppositions and disagreements
- Focus on common goals rather than letting individual priorities take you off-task

Virtual Teams

With the growth of offshoring (a company practice of subcontracting of a business unit to a different company in a different country), flexible work arrangements, and rapid advances in technology, virtual communication has become increasingly common for business meetings and critical tasks by dispersed, often global, work teams.[97] Virtual teams use technology to overcome differences in space, time, and sometimes outlook in order to work together to achieve project and enterprise goals. According to a 2017 survey from Regus Canada, Canada's workforce is increasingly mobile, with 47 per cent of Canadian workers spending half of their work week or more working outside of their employer's main office[98] and interacting virtually. Communication in virtual teams is different than face-to-face communication and comes with unique advantages, namely saving time and money, but also challenges.[99] Geographically dispersed team members may be less able to use informal communication approaches and pick up on non-verbal cues. They may not have the benefit of contextual information that is typically shared among team members. Misunderstandings may be more common.[100] Communication tools and techniques can compensate for some of the challenges of leading and being part of a virtual work team:[101]

- **Communication frequency**: expectation of regular communication between the team leader and team members that promotes team cohesion, stronger relationships, and better performance
- **Communication predictability**: a commitment to regular and accurate task feedback that team members can count on to stay informed and apply to procedures and outputs
- **Responsiveness**: asking for and receiving timely answers to questions
- **Clarity**: communicating clear expectations, goals, and directions as well as guidelines for communication and interaction that allow team members to regulate their performance; following agreed-upon protocols for language choice, team member introductions, and turn-taking; speaking in a well-projected voice and adapting word choice for multinational participants, if necessary providing a written transcript as follow-up
- **Mode**: using a synchronous (at the same time) or asynchronous (at different times) communication tool that is the best fit for team members[102] and ensuring all members have installed necessary software, are trained in using that technology, are prepared and ready to use it, and are logged on before the meeting or project consultation begins; being mindful of time zone differences when communicating synchronously (e.g. videoconferencing) in order to schedule meetings at mutually convenient times; taking steps to limit background noise so speech is intelligible

Tools for Online Collaboration

Collaboration apps are productivity tools that enable teamwork. For every task or function, there are categories of collaborative software that help people get work done together and scores of options to fit individual teamwork needs.

a) Communication and videoconferencing tools: Skype, Zoom, Flowdock, Slack, GoToMeeting, Microsoft Teams
b) Documentation tools: Google Docs
c) File-sharing tools: OneDrive, Dropbox, Google Drive
d) Task and project management tools: Asana, Zoho, LiquidPlanner, Teamwork Projects

---

Checklist

Teamwork

❑ What is a team? How is a team different from a work group?

❑ What do teams help organizations achieve?

❑ What are the three dimensions of performance associated with teams?

❑ What types of teams are typically found in organizations?

❑ What are the characteristics of high-performing teams?

❑ What does consensus decision-making require?

❑ What are the five team decision-making models?

❑ What are the stages of team development?

❑ How can teams manage conflict?

❑ What is conflict management and why is it important to teams?

Ethical Communication

Ethics and Legal Responsibilities of Business Communication

When you communicate on the job, you not only represent your organization but also assume responsibility for its actions. Every document (letter, e-mail, or report) you write is in reality a contract acceptable as evidence in a court of law. Signing a letter means you agree to its content. It makes your promises and agreements legally binding and makes retractions next to impossible to carry out without proof of altered circumstances. For the good of your company, its image, and its bottom line, communicating legally and ethically is of the highest importance.

Business ethics stipulate that employees at every organizational level "do the right thing" with regard to both relationships with stakeholders (employees, customers, investors, and the public) and the administration of products and services. In fact, an ethical

business ethics The socially accepted moral principles and rules of business conduct.

imperative is so important that among the Fortune 500 company communications officers surveyed for the 2017 Corporate Communication International Practices & Trends Study Final Report, trust, integrity and candour ranked number one among critical issues in corporate communication.[103] Behaving ethically in business settings involves an awareness of how the choices you make affect and influence others, for better or worse. Corporate codes of ethics—upholding equal commitment to values such as honesty, integrity, fairness, social responsibility, accountability, and respect—sensitize managers and staff alike to how they should behave. The growing emphasis on business ethics is more than just a trend or bandwagon effect. Most public- and private-sector firms across Canada have instituted a code or policies to deal with matters such as conflicts of interest, external and customer relations, the handling of company assets, relationships with competitors, and employee workplace issues. Canadian companies are being recognized for their commitment to values-based leadership and ethical business practices. BMO was one of two Canadian companies honoured by the Ethisphere Institute in 2018 as one of the world's most ethical companies. BMO scored high for its ethics program and culture of ethics, corporate citizenship, governance, and reputation. According to Darryl White, CEO, BMO Financial Group, ethical business practice is a matter of "weighing the impact of every decision start[ing] with a basic question: What do our stakeholders expect?"[104]

Having moral and interpersonal ground rules in place in the form of policies, training programs, and other initiatives helps companies weather crises and controversies by allowing them to distinguish right from wrong in times of fundamental change. A company's ethical practices speak to its social responsibility and integrity—an invaluable asset in an age weary of corporate corruption. Ethical business conduct and communication create a marketplace advantage, enhance employee performance, promote a strong public image, prevent legal challenges, save huge sums in legal fees, and provide incentive for leniency in legal proceedings. The consequences of ethically questionable practices were seen in 2017, when a Competition Bureau of Canada investigation revealed that several major bakery wholesalers and grocery retailers had engaged in bread price-fixing for up to 14 years. Many Canadian consumers took to social media to voice their concerns over long over-paying for a loaf of bread and over the Competition Bureau's immunity program, which enabled some companies to secure immunity from prosecution in exchange for their co-operation in the investigation.

Ethical Lapses and Why They Happen

Ethical lapses occur for a variety of reasons, but mostly they are the result of all-too-convenient excuses, beliefs, and rationalizations. Here are a few of the better-known ethical traps:[105]

- **The safety-in-numbers rationalization:** the belief that such behaviour is excusable or guaranteed immunity.
- **The head-in-the-sand rationalization:** the belief that remaining silent about wrongdoing will make it go away, or fear that taking action to correct it will be seen as "rocking the boat."
- **The between-a-rock-and-a-hard-place rationalization:** the belief that a positive or favourable outcome justifies any means said to be necessary, even if they are unethical.

- **The it's-no-big-deal rationalization:** an attempt to excuse wrongdoing as unimportant and minimize its consequences.
- **The entitlement rationalization:** self-deception based on the argument that one is entitled to break the rules and be free from consequences.
- **The team-player rationalization:** the reluctance to expose or confront colleagues about their wrongdoing out of fear that it will harm professional relationships and career advancement (also known as the yes-man syndrome).

Responsible and accountable workplace communication, especially written communication, plays a big part in ethical business conduct. Here are some tips for becoming a good and ethical corporate citizen:

- **Tell the truth.** Avoid deceptive language, words with double meanings, and extremes of overstatement and understatement. Misrepresentation, especially when in the form of false advertising, is punishable by law. Make sure that your motives are clear, with no indications of a hidden agenda, and that others will perceive them as such.
- **Avoid language that attempts to evade responsibility.** The passive voice, used improperly, can mislead readers through its failure to assign responsibility for certain actions.
- **Don't suppress or de-emphasize important information, including information that the public deserves to know or that people need to do their jobs.** Ensure facts are presented accurately, are relevant, and are used in a reasonable way to reach conclusions and make recommendations. Include any information the reader would want and need to understand your recommendations (as long as the information is within your authority to disclose). Don't hide facts or conflicts of interest, or emphasize or de-emphasize certain facts to give readers a false impression; avoid half-truths and exaggerations. Give clear warnings of risks and dangers when issuing safety information—the liability of your company, not to mention someone's life, could depend on it.
- **Offer good value for money.** Back up and never falsify any claims about the value of a service or performance of a product, including claims made through visual images.
- **Be timely in your communication.** Avoid unjustified delays in replying to or processing information and be sure to direct your message to the right person.
- **Consider your obligations.** Keep in mind to whom you are responsible when you carry out communications on the job—your managers, co-workers, suppliers, customers and clients, the company, regulators, shareholders, other stakeholders, the public and community, and society at large.
- **Show respect and consider ideals and impacts.** Speak, write, and act with the inherent dignity of others in mind. Think about how your communication impacts and helps stakeholders and how it reflects the positive values to which you aspire. Provide the opportunity for stakeholders to give input into decision-making.
- **Avoid libel. Libel** is printed and recorded defamation and is characterized by false, malicious, or derogatory remarks—remarks that arouse hatred, contempt, or ridicule toward the individuals to whom they are applied. Common law protects every person against libel.

libel A false published statement that is damaging to a person's reputation.

- **Distinguish between fact and opinion.** Let readers know the difference between conjecture and a verifiable fact. Passing off an opinion as a fact is misleading and unethical.
- **Use a layout that doesn't hide information.** Style elements such as lists, bullets, and spacing should be used to spotlight important information, not hide it.
- **Know what you can and cannot disclose to certain parties.** Careless publication or misuse of your company's intellectual property and confidential information, even in the form of an offhand remark, can be detrimental to your organization and might result in charges of wrongdoing. Not advising investors of major corporate events that affect such things as share prices can, on the other hand, expose companies to lawsuits under new legislation. Knowing company disclosure practices and terms of confidentiality agreements you sign is essential.
- **Be especially careful communicating online.** Remember that you have virtually no control over where e-mail and text messages are forwarded after you send them. Many companies now have regulations in place regarding the type of information their employees can transmit via e-mail and how long information is archived before being destroyed. A general rule is to not electronically send anything you would not want your employer, colleagues, friends, or the general public to see.
- **Don't claim authorship of documents you have not written.** Disclose how you obtained your information and how you used it in making your arguments. The consequences of plagiarism—not giving due credit for borrowed words or ideas—are serious. Always acknowledge your sources by using quotation marks, notes, and/or citations.

Checklist

Ethical Writing

- ❑ Is the document truthful?
- ❑ Is the action the document endorses legal?
- ❑ In writing the document, do you treat others in a way you would like to be treated, with respect and concern for their inherent dignity? Have you violated anyone's rights?
- ❑ Are you willing to take responsibility for what the document says?
- ❑ Would your perspective on an issue still seem fair if you were viewing it from the opposite side?
- ❑ Is the information in the document based on thorough research from recent, reliable, and unbiased sources?
- ❑ Do you use sound and logical reasoning and avoid exaggeration?
- ❑ Are you acting in the best interest of your employer and your client?
- ❑ Are ethical standards applied consistently to your writing?
- ❑ Have you discussed any ethical dilemmas with someone who will give trusted advice?

Privacy in the Workplace

Privacy, according to legal scholar Alan Westin, is "the claim of individuals, groups, or institutions to determine for themselves when, how and to what extent information about them is communicated to others."[106] Doing business actively involves the collection and retention of personal information from customers, clients, patients, and employees. In Canada, the *Privacy Act* explains how federally regulated public bodies can collect, use, and disclose individuals' personal information. The *Personal Information Protection and Electronic Documents Act* (PIPEDA) applies to commercial transactions in the private sector and organizations that are federally regulated. According to PIPEDA, "personal information" includes a person's:

- name, age, ID numbers such as a Social Insurance Number (SIN), income, ethnic origin
- bank account number, credit records, loan records, transaction histories, tax returns
- medical records, employee personnel files, and even voiceprints and fingerprints.[107]

The central role of technology in business means that concerns about privacy and data security have never been greater. Despite companies' efforts to safeguard personal information, privacy breaches are still common. Here are just a few cases:

- In 2019, the Desjardins Group, the largest association of credit unions in North America, suffered a massive data breach when a disgruntled employee leaked the personal data of 2.9 million members, including their social insurance numbers, their addresses, and details of their banking habits.[108]
- In 2018, Loblaws drew complaints from customers who applied for gift cards in the wake of the bread-price-fixing scandal and felt they were asked for too much personal information.[109]
- In 2017, hackers gained access to Equifax systems through a security vulnerability the credit monitoring company had known about for months. The result was a data breach affecting 143 million people around the world, including 19,000 Canadians whose personal information had been transferred to a third party in the United States without their knowledge. The Privacy Commissioner of Canada criticized Equifax Canada for falling short of its privacy obligations to Canadians on several accounts: retaining information too long and having poor security safeguards and consent procedures.[110]
- The Ontario Court of Appeal case of *Jones v. Tsige* began with a love affair and ended in 2012 with a landmark decision that created a new remedy for privacy invasion. The defendant, Winnie Tsige, was in a common-law relationship with the ex-husband of the plaintiff, Sandra Jones. Both women worked for the Bank of Montreal (BMO), but they had never met. Tsige was involved in a financial dispute with her partner and was determined to find out if he was making support payments to Jones. She used her office computer to access Jones's personal accounts 174 times over a four-year period. She admitted to her actions when confronted by BMO and received a one-week unpaid suspension. Jones made a claim for invasion of privacy and damages, but the motions judge held that no right to privacy

Under PIPEDA, Canadian organizations must provide safeguards to protect the personal information they collect from their employees and their customers.

existed under the Canadian Charter of Rights and Freedoms. This decision was overturned when the courts recognized the tort of "intrusion upon seclusion." This refinement to privacy law involves three elements: intentional or reckless conduct, intrusion on privacy, and the perception by a reasonable person that this action would cause distress or humiliation.[111]

To combat problems of this kind, PIPEDA and the Privacy Act set down rules for the management of personal information. Under the law, personal information should be collected, used, and disclosed only for the legitimate purposes for which it is intended and with an individual's knowledge (and sometimes consent). PIPEDA's privacy principles form the cornerstone of most corporate privacy agreements and state that organizations must meet ten criteria:

- provide accountability
- identify their reason for collecting personal information
- gain valid consent (consent is considered valid only if individuals can reasonably be expected to understand the nature and reason for the collection)[112]
- collect only necessary information
- use the information for the intended purpose only
- maintain the accuracy of the information
- provide safeguards
- inform individuals of what the information will be used for

- give individuals access to their information
- develop straightforward procedures for complaints

Canada's 2015 *Digital Privacy Act* requires organizations to notify affected individuals when a privacy breach has occurred and poses significant harm.[113] Because governments and businesses collect such a wide array of information, compliance with PIPEDA has implications for communications practices at every level. Adopting new protocols is a step in the right direction, and problems can be minimized or avoided altogether with a few simple safeguards. There are several steps you can follow to help ensure your organization meets privacy standards:

- Learn about the federal and provincial privacy legislation that apply to you and your organization.
- Identify what constitutes "personal information" in your workplace—what can be legitimately collected, used, and disclosed by fair and lawful means. Many organizations, such as TD Bank Group, have their own privacy agreements (see www.td.com/privacy/agreement.jsp).
- Obtain written, verbal, electronic, or (in some circumstances) implied consent from customers for the collection, use, and disclosure of any of their personal information.
- Be accountable for the personal information you collect, use, and disclose and be proactive in protecting it to prevent unwarranted intrusion, release, or misuse.
- Understand what you are agreeing to when you accept a service-related privacy agreement—how much privacy are you giving up in exchange for user privileges?
- Adjust privacy settings on all devices you use for business, install anti-virus software and keep it up-to-date, and ensure you have firewall protection.
- When using smart speakers such as Alexa, Amazon Echo, and Google Home and Assistant, be mindful of their full listening capabilities. Some Alexa conversations, for example, may be analyzed by human reviewers.

Giving up some privacy is something you can expect on the job because the premises and the equipment you use belong to your employer, the company's human resources department needs your personal information to manage your pay and benefits, and your employer needs to ensure that work is being done properly. Infringements on employee privacy, however, are becoming much more common. On-the-job drug testing, web-browsing records, and keystroke monitoring are part of an employer's need to know, but this need must be balanced with employees' rights to privacy.[114] Fair employers have clear policies that tell their employees exactly what personal information can be collected and how it will be used. Employees should be well advised of web, e-mail, and social media policies, random surveillance, and any monitoring of their Internet use.

Checklist

Chapter Review

- ❑ What role does communication play in today's business environments?
- ❑ What trends and issues define communication and doing business in the contemporary workplace?

- ❑ What are the differences between soft skills and hard skills?
- ❑ What is professionalism? What are the characteristics and boundaries of workplace professionalism?
- ❑ What does teamwork help organizations achieve?
- ❑ What are the characteristics of high-performing teams?
- ❑ What models for decision-making are available to teams?
- ❑ What does the term *business ethics* refer to?
- ❑ What reasons or lapses account for unethical behaviour?
- ❑ What strategies and practices can you employ to be an ethical communicator?
- ❑ What is privacy? What laws govern privacy protection and regulation in Canada?
- ❑ What steps can you follow to help ensure your organization meets privacy standards?

Exercises, Workshops, and Discussion Forums

1. **Brainstorming Elements of Effective Communication.** As a class or in small groups, discuss the skills and characteristics essential to effective business communication and, from your discussion, devise a list of words that accurately describe it. Rate each skill on a scale of 1 to 10, with 10 being most important, and provide examples to support each characteristic.

2. **Gen Z: Career Priorities and Expectations.** According to the 2019 Deloitte Global Millennial Survey, millennials and Gen Zs have career expectations that are dramatically different from previous generations. They seek a positive work culture, flexibility and work-life balance, financial rewards and benefits, and support for continuous learning. Have employers caught on to what Gen Zs are seeking from their jobs? Using a junior or entry-level job title linked to your future career (e.g., Junior Communications Coordinator, Assistant Social Media Manager), conduct a brief job search on a job site such as Indeed.ca (www.indeed.ca). How, if at all, does the language of the recruitment ad demonstrate that employers are keeping up with the Gen Z needs and priorities listed above?

3. **Taking a Professional "Selfie."** Using a smartphone, take a "selfie" that could be used for professional purposes and posted on a social media site such as LinkedIn. As you take the photo, consider the qualities of professional identity you would like to project. How is this professional "selfie" different from the photos you may post to Facebook, Twitter, or Instagram? What qualities and values do you hope viewers will associate with this image? How could you make this photo look more professional?

4. **Exploring Professional Codes of Conduct.** Almost any profession or industry has at least one professional association that provides its members with guidelines for conduct and practice as well as networking and professional-growth opportunities. For this activity, find at least one professional association connected to your area of study or planned career path. Locate the association's professional code of practice. Identify three core values and responsibilities, and for each list a behaviour or action that could demonstrate it or put it into practice. Share your findings in a small group and discuss the values and prescribed behaviours the codes have in common.

5. **Assessing the Impact of Online Disinhibition.** Professionals who use social media may sometimes face boundary issues when they choose content to post online. These professional lapses happen as a result of online disinhibition, or the tendency to behave differently online than in face-to-face interactions. In a small group, view the photo below and imagine you have come across it through social media. What is your impression of this person? Now imagine that this person is your doctor, your dentist, or your financial advisor. Discuss your changing reaction to the photo.

iStock.com/DragonImages

6. **Establishing Boundaries for Self-Disclosure.** Begin on your own by circling the most appropriate recipient(s) for the following self-disclosures.

a) Your fear about a new job: (i) a long-time personal friend or trusted family member; (ii) Facebook friends; (iii) a co-worker or manager; (iv) almost anyone; (v) no one.

b) Your worst break-up experience: (i) a long-time personal friend or trusted family member; (ii) Facebook friends; (iii) a co-worker or manager; (iv) almost anyone; (v) no one.

c) Your favourite YouTube celebrities: (i) a long-time personal friend or trusted family member; (ii) Facebook friends; (iii) a co-worker or manager; (iv) almost anyone; (v) no one.

d) Your most inspiring mentor: (i) a long-time personal friend or trusted family member; (ii) Facebook friends; (iii) a co-worker or manager; (iv) almost anyone; (v) no one.

e) A conflict you had with past employers: (i) a long-time personal friend or trusted family member; (ii) Facebook friends; (iii) a co-worker or manager; (iv) almost anyone; (v) no one.

f) Inconsiderate co-workers: (i) a long-time personal friend or trusted family member; (ii) Facebook friends; (iii) a co-worker or manager; (iv) almost anyone; (v) no one.

g) Your guiltiest social media pleasures: (i) a long-time personal friend or trusted family member; (ii) Facebook friends; (iii) a co-worker or manager; (iv) almost anyone; (v) no one.

h) Your proudest academic or work experience: (i) a long-time personal friend or trusted family member; (ii) Facebook friends; (iii) a co-worker or manager; (iv) almost anyone; (v) no one.

i) Your grade-point average: (i) a long-time personal friend or trusted family member; (ii) Facebook friends; (iii) a co-worker or manager; (iv) almost anyone; (v) no one.

Go back over the list and draw X's through the least suitable recipients of your disclosures. Form a small group to compare responses. After your discussion, did your thinking on self-disclosure change? Were exceptions ever possible?

7. **Team-Building Activity.** Imagine that you and members of a small group are part of a project team at your college or university tasked with of designing and staging an event to raise awareness of either (a) student hunger and food insecurity on campus, with the ultimate goal of securing donations and volunteers for a campus or community foodbank OR (b) student wellness and resiliency, with the ultimate goal of funding an expanded pet therapy program. (Alternatively, form a Facebook group dedicated to a particular cause or common interest for social justice or social good.) Your team has a modest budget of $250 from your college or university's student administrative council to advertise and stage the event and four to six weeks to plan, organize, and promote it. At this point your focus

will be on assembling your team and planning the event and related advertising and promotion, which involves several tasks and phases of team development:

a) Discuss and decide on the structure of your team, including team leadership and responsibilities. Reach a consensus on how you will communicate with each other and advisors, troubleshoot problems, make decisions, and work together during the project.

b) Formulate an event name and concept (what it involves, where and when it takes place, who and how many it is meant to attract, and how you will measure the success of the event) and decide on the communication channels (e.g., posters, social media posts, student newspaper features) that could be used to promote the event.

c) Discuss the timeline for your project, how you will monitor progress and how you will spend your budget.

During your planning meeting(s), track the progress of your interactions by providing an example of each stage of your team's development. Together, prepare a one-paragraph reflection on your group experience.

8. **Establishing Guidelines for Ethical Workplace Communication.** Working in a small group, assume that you and your fellow group members are the co-CEOs of a new business. You are meeting to establish an ethical framework for your company's internal and external communication. Draw up a concise list of guidelines, or code, for ethical communication in your workplace. If you need help in starting your discussion, refer to "Five Questions that Corporate Directors Should Ask" at *www.ethics.ubc.ca/papers/invited/5questions.html.*

9. **Facing Ethical Challenges.** In a group, discuss the following situations and decide whether they are permissible under any circumstances:

a) using a company phone to make long-distance calls to friends and relatives

b) using a very small, barely readable font to inform consumers about the weaknesses in the side-door impact panels of your company's best-selling SUV

c) exaggerating qualifications and experiences on resumés and in job interviews

d) leaking the employee surveillance practices of a well-known tech company

e) revealing details of a patient's medical history to a prospective employer without the consent of the patient

f) rounding up items on an expense report

g) lying on a performance review to protect a colleague who is also a friend

10. **Discussing the Instagram Phenomenon.** In a small group, discuss your answers to the following questions:

a) How long have you used Instagram?

b) How long do you spend per day on the site, and how many times per day do you log on?

c) What is on your profile?

d) Who has access to your profile?

e) What privacy settings do you use?

f) What are your online interactions?

g) What positive outcomes have resulted from your use of Instagram?

Share your findings with your instructor and compare them with findings and viewpoints from the rest of the class. What conclusions can you draw about Instagram and social networking platforms in general?

11. **Considering Privacy.** In a small group, review each of the following scenarios and discuss whether it constitutes a breach of privacy according to the ten principles set out in PIPEDA (see pp. 30–32).

a) You work at the reception desk in a local bank branch. A customer rushes in and says that her boyfriend has insufficient funds in his account due to a banking error and desperately needs her to look into the matter for him. She explains that he is away on business in

Turkmenistan and is off the grid. You ask her for her boyfriend's name and banking information and review his recent transactions with her.

b) You use your mobile device outside of work, including from home, commuter trains and cafes, to access company e-mail, project files, and human resources-related information. One day, mobile service from your network provider fails so you log on to a public network in a café just for a few minutes. You use your usual password—your birthday—to log in. Your organization is only now introducing two-factor authentication and you aren't using a Virtual Private Network (VPN), so there is nothing else for you to enter to gain access. Because your device is new, you haven't gotten around to installing anti-virus, anti-spyware, and firewall programs yet.

c) Your office computer is malfunctioning and you ask an IT engineer to troubleshoot. He is busy but tells you he will drop by your workstation after 5pm and instructs you to leave your username and password on a post-it. You leave your username (your first name) and your password (123456) fastened to your computer screen in an area frequented by cleaners and couriers.

d) You are the owner of a costume rental business and have found ideal premises to lease for your first retail shop. As you complete the commercial lease agreement with the landlord, he demands your social insurance number and tells you the lease can't be finalized until he has conducted a background check by examining your social media accounts. Hint: Refer to the Office of the Privacy Commissioner of Canada's fact sheet on social insurance numbers at

www.priv.gc.ca/en/privacy-topics/sins-and-drivers-licences/social-insurance-numbers/protecting-your-social-insurance-number/

Writing Improvement Exercises

1. **Establishing Your Goals in Business Communication.** Write an introductory memo to your instructor in which you explain your reasons for taking the course, the outcomes you hope to achieve, your strengths and weaknesses as a writer, the role communication will play in your chosen profession, and the type of writing you currently do or expect to do on the job.

2. **Writing a Personal Statement.** A personal statement (sometimes referred to as a "career summary" or a "career objective") is a short summary or profile (50 words) that defines you and your mission as a professional. It identifies who you are (e.g., degrees/diplomas completed or in-progress, internships, industry experience, core skills), what you can bring to the job, and what your objectives are. Imagine that you are applying for a job in your field or updating your LinkedIn account, and write a personal statement that describes you as a professional. Keep in mind your audience's needs and interests, and try to include your most relevant qualities, skills, and experiences.

3. **Assessing Communication Needs for Employment.** Refer to an employment website and review several advertisements, noting the communication skills required for each position. Write a memo or an e-mail to your instructor summarizing the skills employers want most. Variation: Create a word table (or matrix) in which you provide examples from your own work history and experience that correspond to the skills employers seek.

4. **Communicating with Team Members.** Review the notes you made while you participated in the team-building activity described above. Identify

a development or a decision that you think could lead to another team project, and then write a memo to your fellow team members outlining your new plan and asking for their input.

Case Study Exercises

1. **Land Acknowledgment Rethink.** The following land acknowledgment was posted at Pride Toronto events in 2019 but drew criticism that sparked an apology from organizers.

LAND ACKNOWLEDGMENT

What is that? Let us journey together...

Take a moment to connect with the land that you are currently standing on.

Now introduce yourself spiritually; build a relationship with Mother Earth that provides for all our relations.

No matter what part of Mother Earth our family originates from, we all have a relationship and a responsibility to the land. Let's build a healthy relationship together.

CHI MIIGWECH*

*an Ojibwe expression of gratitude

---

a) What is missing from the acknowledgement?
b) What needs to be revised or added? How would you re-word it to ensure the land acknowledgement fulfills its purpose?
c) Research the land acknowledgment for your community using your town council or municipal website, the interactive map or search box on the Whose Land app or website, or the Native Land website. Identify the Indigenous nations or groups whose lands your community now occupies. Were you aware of the Indigenous groups in your community before you started your research?
d) What is unique to the land acknowledgment for your community? How could it be made more meaningful or relevant?
e) If you were to include a land acknowledgment on a business card, what would it look like?

Remember to be professional and polite, and follow the principles that contribute to high-performing teams.

Whose Land

www.whose.land/en/

Native Land

https://native-land.ca/

2. **The Ethics of Job Blogging.** Workplace-related social media use, an employee's right to freedom of speech, and an employer's right to protect its reputation and earning ability are often at odds. The recent case of *Alberta v. Alberta Union of Provincial Employees* is one instance where social media use crossed the line from unethical to illegal. In 2008, a bereaved Alberta government employee attended therapy provided through her employee assistance program. Her therapist advised her to deal with feelings of anger and hopelessness by writing them down. Over the following months, she vented her emotions through publicly accessible personal blogs, some of which attacked management and ridiculed supervisors and co-workers. It was clear from the postings that the employee lived in Edmonton and worked for a department of the provincial government. Although she used aliases to refer to her co-workers, they could easily identify themselves and were certain they could never work with her again. The employee was terminated with cause. The arbitration panel upheld the termination on the grounds of the blog's destructive impact on work relationships.

a) What issues explored in the chapter does this case raise?
b) Do you agree with the decision in this case? What ethical breaches was the employee guilty of? At what point did she cross the line?

c) Is it ever acceptable to discuss work experiences and colleagues via social media platforms? What are the limits to free speech when expressing personal opinions may damage professional relationships?

d) What could the employer do in terms of best practices, regulations, and policies to prevent similar occurrences? In terms of ethical practice in the workplace, what could be considered reasonable constraints and levels of ethical achievement?

e) What lessons can be learned from this case?

3. **Ethical Dilemmas in Fundraising.** As an assistant advancement officer, your job is to help your university with its capital fundraising campaigns and its legacy, bequest, and planned-giving initiatives. One of your prospects is George Salerno, aged 92. Salerno is an alumnus and pensioner with a modest income and limited savings, yet he is determined to endow a large scholarship in memory of classmates who were killed in the Second World War. This commitment, as he envisions it, would require him to make a monetary gift in excess of $500,000 during his lifetime, which would likely leave him and his 73-year-old wife in financial distress. Since Salerno first met with you a month ago to discuss his options as a major gift donor, he has telephoned you every day to re-affirm his intention to endow the scholarship. Respecting his generosity of spirit, you gently but repeatedly suggest that a planned tribute gift—arranged in his lifetime but not available to the university until after his death—would be a better option, as would giving at a lower level, but he won't hear of it. He wants to see big results right away, to honour and commemorate his friends.

When you e-mail the vacationing chief advancement officer about Salerno's intentions, he is overjoyed. The rate of scholarship endowment and major giving has been decreasing, and your institution has failed to meet targets for five successive years. Your unit has lost two members to downsizing as a result. Still, you're not sure he appreciates the complexities of the situation.

Today, you receive a panicked phone call from Mrs. Salerno, who tells you that her husband has put their house up for sale without her knowledge. Lately, she said, he has been behaving oddly and has been uncharacteristically forgetful. Before today, he had never mentioned the scholarship to her. She thinks that he may be showing signs of dementia. As a fundraiser, you must abide by an established ethical code, but you also face pressures to meet defined fundraising targets.

a) What are your options for acting ethically in this situation?

b) What communication failures contributed to this situation, and how could they be addressed?

4. **Improving Virtual Team Interaction.** As the executive director of an international professional association, Tedi Lundry is responsible for organizing its annual day-long board of directors' meeting. This year, the meeting takes place in Halifax and twenty-five board members are expected to attend. On short notice, Tedi is informed that seven globally dispersed board members will be unable to attend. According to the association's charter, all regions must be represented at the annual AGM, so Tedi informs the seven absentee board members they will have to participate remotely. She quickly looks into options for videoconferencing and decides to use Zephyr, a new system she hasn't used before recommended to her by a colleague. Tedi spends the next day learning about Zephyr and liaising with the on-site technology specialist who will assist with set up. He isn't familiar with Zephyr either. A day before the AGM, Tedi discovers the meeting board room is poorly lit and not well configured for camera setup—only a few people seated at the front of the room will be murkily visible from remote locations and no one off-site will be able to contribute to breakout sessions. Later that day, Tedi e-mails the remote participants and provides them with a Zephyr link and download instructions along with a reminder that the meeting begins "tomorrow at

8 am AST sharp." At the time of transmission, however, participants in the Middle East, Asia, and Australia are already asleep. Tedi wakes up the next day to find her inbox full of questions from them. It is 8:45 a.m. before troubleshooting is completed and the meeting can begin. Still, one participant has no audio connection and will communicate via chat box; two others complain they can't hear anyone and sign off. Board members back early from lunch are upset to see overseas members, caught unawares on camera, eating their dinner, texting, and making personal telephone calls.

a) What best practices for virtual meeting and interaction did Tedi not follow?

b) What suggestions can you offer Tedi for a better virtual meeting outcome?

5. **Privacy Breach and Reporting Ethics.** Imagine that you work for InvestED, a small, app-based investment company that began as a startup and has grown steadily through exceptional word-of-mouth from a growing client base. As part of your work responsibilities, you discover that just before Breach of Security Safeguard regulations were introduced in 2018, a privacy breach occurred at your company that compromised the personal data of 20 new clients. You are not certain what types of data were exposed, but you are working on the answer and immediately report the breach to your manager, Marco Gentile. Marco informs you that the company will most likely upgrade systems to prevent a recurrence; however, he waffles when asked if the 20 affected clients will be informed. He insists that because the breach occurred before the new PIPEDA requirements were introduced the company is, technically, not obligated to inform the clients in question. (You aren't absolutely sure he is right.) Reporting, in his view, is not worth the effort, expense, or risk because so few clients were involved, so much time has passed, and no one has complained. Marco believes that reporting the breach would damage the reputation the company has worked hard to build and quite possibly erode its client base and result in lawsuits.

a) Beyond the steps you have already taken, what are your options for acting ethically in this situation?

b) If clients were to be informed, what details would your company need to share with them?

Online Activities

1. **Best Practices and Winning Strategies of Leading Communicators.** In a small group, go to the International Association of Business Communicators Toronto's Communicator of the Year (COTY) Award website, review the evaluation criteria, and select a name from the list of past winners. Inform your instructor of your choice. Find one or two articles in which the award-winner's approach to communication is reported or discussed. From the article, identify the winner's most important strategies and prepare an informal two- or three-minute presentation in which you share those strategies with the class. At the end of everyone's presentation, draft a list of the top 10 strategies and practices that are shared by all COTY winners.

http://toronto.iabc.com/awards/
communicator-of-the-year/

2. **Innovation and Entrepreneurship.** The Digital Media Zone (DMZ) at Toronto's Ryerson University is a world-leading accelerator for tech startups in Canada. MaRS, also in Toronto, is a community linking talented innovators and cutting-edge startups to capital and customers. From either of the following sites, find a startup of interest to you and write a three-sentence reflection

summarizing how the startup and its concept embody the definition of innovation on page X.

https://dmz.ryerson.ca
www.marsdd.com/

3. **Employability Skills Quiz.** Make an account and take the short quiz offered on the Government of Canada's Service Canada website. Answer each question by rating yourself at one of three levels: (1) I'm not as skilled as I'd like; (2) I'm skilled; (3) I'm very skilled.

www.jobbank.gc.ca/workpreference

4. **Corporate Mission Statements.** Analyze the following corporate mission statements from prominent Canadian companies. In each case, how does the company portray itself? Based on language choices, what is the company's expertise? Does it claim to have more expertise than its competitors? What values are most commonly represented and how do they connect to the company's CSR and commitment to social good? What does the organization in each case promise to do for stakeholders (customers, employees, owners, and society at large) in exchange for their loyalty and commitment?

Canadian Tire

https://corp.canadiantire.ca/English/about-us/default.aspx

Gildan Activewear Inc.

www.genuinegildan.com/en/company/our-approach/

Lush

www.lush.ca/en/story?cid=article_we-believe-statement

McCain Foods

www.mccain.com/about-us/our-purpose-values/

RBC

www.rbc.com/aboutus/visionandvalues.html

Shopify

www.shopify.ca/about

Suncor Energy

www.suncor.com/about-us/our-mission-vision-and-values

Wattpad

https://company.wattpad.com/press

WestJet

www.westjet.com/en-ca/about-us/index

5. **Corporate Mission Statements: Engaging with Indigenous Business.** Most organizations, including businesses, have a mission statement or vision statement that summarizes the values a business aspires to and the goals that underly its operations, outputs, and relationships with stakeholders. In a small group, read the following mission statements representing some of Canada's most successful Indigenous businesses. Identify the values that feature in these statements and describe what is unique to the business models and ways of knowing they embody:

Manitobah Mukluks

www.manitobah.ca/

Leaders International

https://leadersinternational.com/about

Nk'Mip Cellars

www.nkmipcellars.com/About-Us

6. **Facebook as a Business Tool.** Find a company that has a Facebook profile. How does this company use the site to promote its products and services or to put forth its mission statement and increase its market share?

7. **Corporate Social Responsibility.** Watch these corporate CSR videos and make a list of the values each company associates with its practices and the initiatives that demonstrate them. How does each tell its CSR story?

BMO

www.youtube.com/watch?v=MeJzs2RxjvU

Magna

www.youtube.com/watch?v=ArTZ1lPbSgs

Detour Gold

www.youtube.com/watch?v=cyf4OSlXo7s

8. **Sustainability and Corporate Social Responsibility Reporting.** Individually or in a small group, select three companies that have made the most recent list of Canada's Top 100 Employers. Visit each company's corporate website and find information related to the company's sustainability or corporate social responsibility reporting. What measures and practices contribute to sustainable development in each case?

www.canadastop100.com/national/

9. **Accolades for Social and Environmental Accountability.** Mountain Equipment Co-Op (MEC), incorporated in Vancouver in 1971, ranks high on surveys of corporate reputation such as the 2018 CR RepTrak and the Corporate Knights 2019 Best Corporate Citizens list. Review the MEC page below devoted to its efforts in social and environmental accountability. In what ways does MEC seek accountability and how does it use words and images to benchmark its progress and chart its success in reaching targets in these areas?

www.mec.ca/en/explore/sustainability-innovation

10. **Canada's Best Diversity Employers.** Individually or in a small group, choose three companies that have made the most recent list of Canada's Best Diversity Employers and find out why they won by clicking on the corresponding links. Prepare a short presentation in which you summarize the measures employers have begun to adopt in order to address diversity and inclusion.

www.canadastop100.com/diversity/

11. **Identifying Factors in Employee Engagement.** Working in a small group, visit the popular job site Glassdoor.ca. Glassdoor gives annual awards to employees' choices of the best places to work across Europe and North America, including Canada. (A sign-up and sign-in may be required to access reviews.) Select two or three businesses and read three reviews of each. From among the pros and cons, what are the factors that most consistently contribute to employee engagement and job satisfaction?

www.glassdoor.ca/Award/Best-Places-to-Work-Canada-LST_KQ0,26.htm

12. **Company Ethics Codes.** Read the ethics codes for the following companies and look for similarities between them. Summarize your findings on the fundamental standards of most organizational ethics codes.

BMO

www.bmo.com/home/about/banking/corporate-information/codeofconduct

RBC

www.rbc.com/governance/_assets-custom/pdf/RBCCodeOfConduct.pdf

13. **Privacy and Your Workplace.** Individually or as a group, watch the following YouTube video, which summarizes privacy principles as outlined in PIPEDA. Discuss how your knowledge of the 10 principles could affect your own practices on the job.

www.youtube.com/watch?v=kwoN8e9stEI

14. **PIPEDA.** Watch the video or read the print version of an overview of PIPEDA. When you are done, write a two- or three-paragraph summary.

www.priv.gc.ca/en/privacy-topics/privacy-laws-in-canada/the-personal-information-protection-and-electronic-documents-act-pipeda/pipeda-compliance-help/bus_pipeda_intro/bus_101_04/

15. **Privacy Quiz: How Well Do You Know Your Privacy Rights?** Try the Office of the Privacy Commissioner of Canada's interactive Privacy Quiz for Businesses. Click on an answer to receive an explanation of the issue highlighted by the question.

https://services.priv.gc.ca/quiz/index_e.asp

16. **Cybersecurity Knowledge Quiz.** Answer the 10-question cybersecurity quiz from the Pew Research Center and perform an audit of your own cybersecurity practices to reduce potential risks to your data and online interactions.

    www.pewinternet.org/quiz/
    cybersecurity-knowledge/

17. **User Privacy on Social Networking Sites.** Many users rely on default settings when it comes to their social networking practices, and most do not pay close attention to terms of use agreements or privacy policies. How much privacy do these agreements, policies, and settings guarantee you? Review your privacy setting and any agreements you have accepted. Note your concerns. Do the privileges of using the site outweigh those concerns? What aspects of your privacy have you traded in exchange for your right to use social networking sites?

2 Getting the Message Across

Chapter Preview

This chapter presents essential communication principles and explains how communication happens, how it can fail, and how you can apply strategies to ensure it succeeds. You'll learn how business communication involves many modes beyond the written word, and you'll discover how messages flow between individuals within and between organizations. Finally, you'll see why writing for the broadest possible audiences is an important skill in today's global work environment.

fizkes/Shutterstock.com

Learning Objectives

1. Describe the communication process.
2. Identify communication barriers and apply strategies for overcoming them.
3. Identify core competencies for interpersonal communication.
4. Explain the importance of non-verbal communication.
5. Analyze the systems and mechanisms for communicating inside and outside organizations.
6. Examine the organizational flow of communication.
7. Contrast high-context and low-context cultures.
8. Ease the flow of communication between and across cultures.

Case Study

fizkes/Shutterstock.com

Successful businesses recognize what their customers need to know, when they need to know it, and how to get the message to them in a timely, effective way.

Effective communication is essential to success in the business world, as no organization can exist or develop without it.[1] Employees who are able to communicate their ideas and report on their progress with clarity are more likely to gain recognition from their managers and advance in their careers. Likewise, businesses that are able to keep their employees, customers, and other stakeholders well-informed about their business practices and values are more likely to gain positive reputations and advance their organizational goals. Ineffective or incomplete communication, on the other hand, can harm an individual's or a company's reputation and may potentially lead to failure. In 2018, Walmart Canada announced it would no longer participate in a program that provided on-the-job training for people with intellectual disabilities in Québec.[2] Their original message emphasized that ending the program was a "difficult decision," but it did not explain that the people affected by ending the program would not be losing paid positions—instead, they would no longer hold unpaid, vocational training positions in Walmart stores. Members of Québec's provincial government and a provincial health agency voiced their frustration to the media and expressed their distrust of Walmart for cutting jobs held by people with intellectual disabilities. A national outcry followed, especially on social media. Two days after the announcement, Walmart Canada issued an apology for the "confusion and disappointment" caused by their original communication. Yet their apology did little to appease critics, who took to social media saying they did not believe the retailer would provide support for people in the program.[3]

To avoid such public-relations blunders, businesses must recognize the power that communication has to impact their business relationships and image, and they must establish pathways and protocols to ensure effective communication with external stakeholders. Similarly, establishing rules and processes to govern communication within an organization is essential to maintaining employee satisfaction and ensuring that business objectives are met.

Communication Defined

The word "communication" comes from the Latin *commūnicātiō*, meaning "common." Having something in common through sharing knowledge and exchanging information, ideas, and emotions lies at the heart of communication. Communication has been defined as "a transactional process of sharing meaning with others"[4] and as "a human process through which we make sense out of the world and share that sense with others."[5] More simply, communication is the sharing of symbols—words, images, gestures—to co-create meaning. Through communication we assign meanings based on our social and cultural contexts and regulate the world around us by the stories that we make up about it and share. If storytelling, as narrative theorists believe, is one way to view communication, then it is also a means by which we act on the world, whether to persuade or dissuade or simply provoke a response from others.

Communication as a Field of Study

Communication does not simply happen—it is learned and requires practiced skills and competencies. Without such skills and active sensemaking (the process of applying meaning to experience based on past experience), communication can easily break down; when it does, **communication theory**, based on empirical research and observation, can help explain what happens when we communicate and be the lens that brings communication experiences into focus.

communication theory A system of ideas for explaining communication.

Communication theory is part of a global, interdisciplinary, and extraordinarily diverse field of research aimed at seeking answers to these types of "urgent social problems involving communication":[6]

- Impacts of technology
- Communicating and organizing in a global society, including between and among cultures
- Intergroup and interpersonal communication
- Public relations involving communication between and among organizations and target groups
- Visual media and representation

The US-based National Communication Association notes that this growing field "focuses on how people use messages to generate meanings within and across contexts, cultures, channels, and the media" and "promotes the effective and ethical practice of human communications."[7] Communication studies has many branches and shares theories and assumptions multiple disciplines, including sociology, psychology, political science, law, philosophy, and linguistics.

rhetoric The use of language to persuade an audience.

semantics The study of the words and symbols we choose.

semiotics The study of how meaning is assigned and understood.

Similarly, discovering how we can approach learning to communicate effectively through many different theoretical frameworks—from the study of the practical art of discourse (**rhetoric**) and the way our behaviour is influenced by the words and symbols we choose (**semantics**) to how meaning is assigned and understood (**semiotics**) and how information is processed and communication systems function (**cybernetics**). Throughout this book, we will explore what these frameworks have in common, as well as the distinctive branches of communication that are integrated in the workplace.

cybernetics The study of how information is processed and how communication systems function.

The Communication Process

The idea of exchange and interaction—the flow of information from one person to another—is fundamental to modern communication and to the theories that systematically explain how meaning is created, shared, and managed;[8] communication without one or more partners is like a tennis match with just one player. It is important to remember that communication is

- situated (i.e., embedded in a particular environment or socio-cultural context)
- relational (i.e., involves the ability to interact effectively and ethically according to what is needed at a given moment)
- transactional (i.e., exists as a co-operative activity in which people adapt to one another)

Communication isn't something that just happens as a part of work life. It is a process or series of actions aimed at achieving a desired outcome or goal. Senders and receivers of information are involved in this partnership. Communication is therefore the means by which we create our professional world and relationships and conduct business activities.

This partnership involves an exchange that takes place through language or a set of signs and symbols (e.g., words or gestures). In this exchange, a sender transmits a thought that carries an agreed-upon meaning within a particular context with the aim of eliciting a receiver's response. The receiver must be able to understand what is significant about the data and make meaning out of it in order for this exchange to be truly effective. Through communication, we assign meanings to the world around us, though the realities we create are shaped by our cultural experiences and individual knowledge.

Elements of the Communication Process

How does communication "work"? Many conceptual models have been developed to explain it, including the Shannon-Weaver model from Bell Telephone Laboratories, the mother of all conceptual models developed by scientist Warren Weaver and engineer Claude Shannon, the father of the computer age. For communication to occur, Shannon, Weaver, and others claimed, there must be both a source and a destination—someone at one end to formulate and launch the **message** and someone at the other end to receive and respond to it (see Figure 2.1).[9] The goal is for the message to be understood as it was intended. The process, unfortunately, is not always as simple and straightforward as it sounds. Difficulties with transmission, reception, and interference can disrupt the communication process.

Sender

The **sender**, also called the transmitter or the communicator, is the person or group with a particular idea or purpose in mind and an intention to express that purpose in the form of a message. The form that the idea ultimately assumes—its content, tone, emphasis, and organization—is shaped by the sender's context, knowledge, attitudes, background, and other assumptions based on the sender's experience. Taking ideas and putting them into a code is known as **encoding**. The message can be encoded verbally or non-verbally—in writing, speech, or gestures—with the goal that it will eventually be understood. For this to happen, however, the sender must consider the receiver's context, knowledge, attitudes, and communication skills and then choose the right code to convey the intended meaning; otherwise, the communication transaction can fail.

message Any type of oral, written, or non-verbal communication that is transmitted by a sender to a receiver or audience.

sender The participant in a communication transaction who has an idea and communicates it by encoding it in a message.

encoding Converting ideas into code in order to convey a written, an oral, or a non-verbal message.

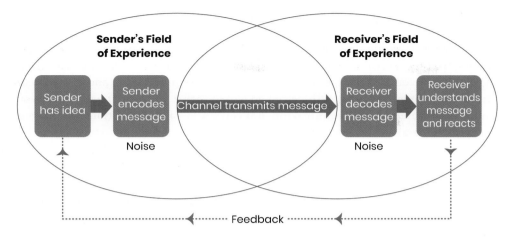

FIGURE 2.1 Transactional Communication Model

Channel

The **channel** is the medium by which the message is transmitted. Delivery can be by spoken word, letter, memo, report, telephone, computer, voice, or gesture. A medium can be synchronous (i.e., communication take places directly, at the same time or in real time) or asynchronous (i.e., information is stored or archived and accessed later so that sender and receiver do not need to be present at the same time). Face-to-face conversations, telephone conversations, synchronous texting, synchronous social-media messaging, and audio and video conferencing involve synchronous delivery and enable both spontaneous interaction and rapid feedback. E-mail, faxes, blogs, and discussion boards involve asynchronous delivery, which allows receivers more time to reflect on a message.

channel A communication pathway or medium over which a message travels.

Receiver

The **receiver** is the person or group at whom the message is directed. The receiver is responsible for **decoding** the message—extracting meaning from its symbols. The receiver's life experiences, knowledge, attitudes, and context can influence how they interpret and respond to the message.

receiver The participant in a communication transaction for whom a message is intended and who decodes the message by extracting meaning from it.

Feedback

Feedback is the receiver's discernible response to a message. It can be non-verbal, like nodding one's head during a face-to-face conversation; oral, like the "umms" or "ahhs" during a telephone conversation; or written, like the reply e-mail that conveys a reaction. Feedback is a vital part of communication, allowing for clarification and ensuring that the message has been properly understood. Frustration can occur when there is no opportunity for feedback; it can also occur when the sender requires immediate feedback to their message but chooses a medium whereby feedback is delayed.

decoding Extracting meaning from the symbols of spoken, written, and non-verbal communication.

feedback The receiver's response to a message that confirms if the original message was received and understood.

Barriers to Effective Communication

Anyone who has experienced a dropped cellphone call or had an argument as a result of a misunderstanding can appreciate that the course of communication does not always flow smoothly. In today's fast-paced business environment, there is always the potential for

noise Any form of physical or psychological interference that distorts the meaning of a message.

communication barriers Problems that can affect the communication transaction, leading to confusion or misunderstanding.

miscommunication. No person or workplace is immune to human error, and the technology on which organizations rely may not always be reliable.

Noise refers to physical and psychological obstacles that can interfere with the communication process and lead to misunderstandings. Noise can be any factor that makes the outcome of the communication process less predictable, and it can occur anywhere, at any time. If something can go wrong with a message, it will, unless you understand potential **communication barriers** and take precautions to prevent them (Figure 2.2).

Channel Overload
This occurs when the number of messages transmitted through a channel exceeds its capacity. You may, for example, try to leave a voicemail only to find that someone's voicemail box is full.

Information Overload
This occurs when a channel carries too much information for the receiver to absorb or when too many messages are transmitted simultaneously, leaving receivers unable to handle them and feeling annoyed and confused.

Emotional Interference
Strong feelings can interfere with an individual's ability to communicate objectively, thereby preventing them from either encoding or decoding a message. Aggressive, impulsive e-mails, for example, demonstrate the damage emotional interference can cause.

Semantic Interference
Words do not have assigned or fixed meanings. In fact, one word may mean different things to different people, and its meaning can also change in various contexts. This creates a wide margin for misinterpretation and thus miscommunication. This is known as **bypassing**. Shifts in meaning, faulty diction, and misplaced emphasis can all lead to miscommunication.

Physical and Technical Interference
Every so often, technical difficulties arise—phone lines jam, computers crash, and mobile connections drop.

Mixed Messages
Some messages give off conflicting signals, resulting in misunderstanding when the receiver can't decide which signal to observe. A speaker might express agreement but raise their eyebrows or roll their eyes, suggesting lingering doubts or reservations.

Channel Barriers
Choosing the wrong communication channel—for example, by e-mailing a contentious message—can lead to a breakdown in communication.

Environmental Interference
People's frames of reference—or ways of seeing the world based on their own experiences, culture, personality, and education—can be miles apart. Age and cultural gaps, for example, can create differences in perception that influence how a message is interpreted.

FIGURE 2.2 Communication Barriers

channel overload The inability of a channel to carry all transmitted messages.

information overload A condition whereby a receiver cannot process all messages because of their vast number.

emotional interference A psychological factor that creates problems with the communication transaction.

Overcoming these barriers involves becoming more reflective about your own communication practices and more responsive to the needs and expectations of receivers. A few guidelines can help you:

- **Be timely and time-sensitive.** In routine situations, respond as soon as you have the information you intend to pass on; in emotionally charged situations, choose the right time, when others will be receptive to your communications. Ease tensions by giving others the opportunity to cool down before responding.
- **Be purposeful.** In all but the very briefest message, state your purpose for meeting, talking, or writing at the beginning.
- **Be a good listener and a careful reader.** Give your full attention to the message and its context.

- **Be context-sensitive.** Consider whether the communication channel is right for the situation and audience. Factors to consider include the physical context (the time and location of the exchange), the history or previous communications between the participants, the type of relationship that exists between the participants, the moods or feelings each participant may be experiencing, and the values, attitudes, and beliefs each participant brings to the interaction.
- **Be proactive.** If you are unsure about what you have heard or read, verify the facts and get more information before proceeding. Reducing uncertainty is vital to effective communication. Being an effective communicator means reducing the margin for uncertainty.

Communication Contexts

Communication can be thought of in terms of several forms or contexts that involve differences in the numbers and proximities of interactants, the relationships between roles of the sender(s) and receiver(s), the nature and amount of feedback, and the degree to which messages are adapted to their audiences. Effective business communication relies on skills related to five forms: interpersonal communication, small-group communication, organizational communication, intercultural communication, and mass communication.

Interpersonal Communication

Interpersonal communication is an interactional process between two people (sender and receiver), either face-to-face or mediated. This form of communication is also called **dyadic** (referring to two people) and is typically informal, spontaneous, and done within a specific context so as to achieve interpersonal goals. Interpersonal communication involves attitudes, behaviours, and cognition (ways of thinking) and the roles they play in creating and managing relationships. In this context, messages serve the following purposes:

- **Sharing meaning.** Shared meaning occurs when there is similarity between the sender's intentions and the receiver's interpretation of a message.
- **Meeting social goals.** Examples include making acquaintance, gaining compliance, and reducing conflict.
- **Managing personal identity.** Personal identity distinguishes you from other people and has three dimensions: (i) who you think you are, as reflected in your values, beliefs, and attitudes; (ii) who other people think you are; and (iii) who you want others to think you are. In interpersonal communication, self is very important to the communication process.
- **Conducting relationships.** Interpersonal communication provides the means for managing our relationships.

Interpersonal communications reflect the emotional temperature of the relationships in a workplace. Those relationships are constructed and sustained through differing levels of

- **trust.** Trust is the faith people have that others will not harm them.
- **control.** Control is the relative power each person has.
- **intimacy and distance.** Intimacy refers to the emotional or intellectual closeness and candour between people. This candour is sometimes referred to as

semantic interference Interference caused by ambiguity, jargon, language or dialect differences, or different ways of assigning meaning.[10]

bypassing Misunderstanding that results from the receiver inferring a different meaning from a message based on the different meanings of the words that are used.

physical and technical interference Interference external to the sender and receiver.[11]

mixed messages Conflicting signals or messages that may result in miscommunication.

channel barriers Inappropriate choices of channel that impede communication.

environmental interference Interference that results from preconceptions and differing frames of reference.

dyadic The form of communication that involves two people.

"self-disclosure," or "the act of revealing personal information to others."[12] There is information, for instance, that people disclose only to their friends. Self-disclosure therefore depends on social distance and the nature of relationships. True self-disclosure must be significant, deliberate, and not previously known by the other person. The tendency to self-disclose is often greater in online interactions.[13]

emotional intelligence
The ability to be in touch with one's emotions, manage one's behaviours, and understand and respond to others' emotions so as to foster strong interpersonal relationships.

Interpersonal communication involves flexible skills that can be improved through practice. When practised and applied effectively, those skills produce appropriate messages that fit the social, relational, and ethical expectations for a given situation. **Emotional intelligence**, which is a quality in each of us that "affects how we manage behavior, navigate social complexities, and make personal decisions that achieve positive results,"[14] is essential to creating competent, appropriate messages. Emotional intelligence is based on personal and social competence. Personal competence involves self-awareness and self-management, and social competence involves social awareness and social management. Four skills based in these two key competencies are associated with emotional intelligence:

- **personal competence**, or the ability to stay in touch with your emotions and use this awareness to manage behavioural tendencies. Personal competence is based on

  » **self-awareness** (the ability to perceive your emotions) and
  » **self-management** (your ability to use your emotional awareness to stay flexible and direct your behaviour positively and productively).

- **social competence**, or the ability to understand other people's moods, motives, and behaviours in order to improve given relationships. Social competence involves a combination of

  » **social awareness** (the ability to read emotions in other people) and

Effective interpersonal communication requires emotional intelligence, active engagement, and a shared understanding of the social, relational, and ethical expectations of a given situation.

iStock.com/MStudioImages

» **relationship management** (the ability to manage relationships through an awareness of your emotions and the emotions of others).[15]

Improving interpersonal communication also requires motivation and a commitment to

- **building communication skills**. Learning and applying message templates to achieve specific purposes and rehearsing mental scripts for interactions can boost competency.
- **building plasticity** (behavioural flexibility, or the ability to change). Building plasticity involves developing capabilities such as forethought, reflective self-regulation (self-control), and self-consciousness.[16] Building plasticity can boil down to analyzing communication situations, assessing the effects of your actions, and adapting your communication skills to fit those situations. A way to begin is training yourself to think about responses before you give them.

Interpersonal and personal-management skills are important because they are linked to performance and align with the employability skills and behaviours identified by the Conference Board of Canada.[17] They are essential to reducing drama in the workplace, dealing with insubordination, giving and receiving criticism, dealing with rudeness, having difficult conversations, counselling employees, avoiding "bad boss" behaviour, and repairing relations with other individuals.[18] There is, however, a dark side to interpersonal communication that can involve lying, conflict, and ethical lapses. Barriers can also prevent us from perceiving others accurately: over-simplifying or ignoring information from our interpersonal interactions, over-generalizing or focusing only on negatives, stereotyping others, avoiding responsibility for deteriorating relationships, relating only to yourself and not to others, and blaming others when they seem to have more power. You can avoid or overcome these barriers by using the tips in Figure 2.3.

Small-Group Communication

Small-group communication is an interactional process that occurs among three or more (up to 20) people and pursues common goals. The size of the group must allow all participants to interact freely, and the links between participants are vital to successful outcomes. Forming and coordinating groups can be complex because it raises psychological and interpersonal issues, which the study of collaborative communication (see Chapter 3) helps us to understand. An example of a situation that uses small-group communication is a project-planning meeting.

Organizational Communication

Organizational communication pursues common goals. However, it takes place within a hierarchical social system composed of interdependent stakeholder groups, such as current and potential employees, clients, customers, suppliers, and regulators). This form of communication takes place in large businesses and industries, as well as government institutions. Individuals within this system assume specialized functional roles that are defined by the formalized behaviours and rules of an "organizational culture"—the dynamic and emotionally charged set of assumptions, values, and objects of human workmanship that arise from interactions between organization members and define outlook

> **Don't get lost in the details.**
> • Commit to seeing a specific interaction more fully from a broader perspective or as part of an ongoing story shaped by your ultimate goals for a relationship.

> **Be empathetic.**
> • Consider a situation or an interaction from the other person's perspective.

> **Avoid stereotypes and maintain cultural sensitivity.**

> **Use active listening skills.**

> **Show self-esteem and respect for others.**

> **Be assertive, but not pushy.**

> **Be likeable, but don't give in too easily.**
> • Getting along doesn't always mean giving in. Being likeable involves being trustworthy, showing empathy, and taking an interest in other people's views while maintaining a clear concept of your own interests and goals.

> **Be patient and don't interrupt.**
> • Take turns and allow others to finish their thoughts before taking your turn to speak.

FIGURE 2.3 Tips for Achieving Interpersonal Success

and what the organizational environment feels like.[19] An organization's culture is created through communication and develops as its members create and market products and services, respond to the concerns and demands of customers and external stakeholders, and coordinate employees and their tasks and initiatives.[20]

Intercultural Communication

Intercultural communication is the management of messages between people and groups of different cultural backgrounds, with necessary adaptation to account for differences between socially constructed forms of communication behaviour. For example, an e-mail sent from an English-speaking organization in Winnipeg to a supplier in Shanghai involves careful consideration of intercultural issues.

Mass Communication

Mass communication is a one-to-many, public interaction in which media professionals send messages to a large anonymous audience. Mass communication is distinct from face-to-face public communication in which a speaker addresses a multi-person audience made up of individuals they do not know. Instead, the transmission is indirect and often mediated through radio or television broadcasts or newspaper or magazine articles. An example of mass communication is a webcast of a CEO's address at an annual general meeting of shareholders.

Checklist

Communication Contexts

❏ What is interpersonal communication? What is its purpose?

❏ What factors set the emotional temperature of workplace relationships?

❏ What is emotional intelligence and what competencies are associated with it?

❏ How can interpersonal communication be improved?

❏ What is behavioural plasticity and why is it important?

❏ Why are interpersonal and personal-management skills important?

❏ What strategies contribute to successful interpersonal communication?

❏ What is small-group communication? What makes for successful small-group communication?

❏ What is organizational communication? What role does organizational culture play in organizational communication?

❏ What is intercultural communication?

❏ What is mass communication?

Non-Verbal Communication

Communication involves more than just spoken and written words. Messages are also actively conveyed through a subtext of non-verbal language, both unwritten and unspoken. As communications researcher and UCLA professor Albert Mehrabian found, the impact of spoken communications containing an emotional or attitudinal element comes largely from non-verbal elements:

- 7 per cent of the meaning is in the words that are spoken
- 38 per cent of the meaning is paralinguistic (voice quality)
- 55 per cent of the meaning is in non-verbal expression[21]

While this finding is intriguing, if somewhat misleading, other research has shown that non-verbal cues have over four times the effect of verbal cues.[22] This alone suggests that **non-verbal communication** is very important to social interaction.

Non-verbal messages communicate emotions, attitudes, greetings, and cues of status.[23] Effective non-verbal skills and abilities can therefore play an important role in building and maintaining interpersonal relationships and managing impressions,[24] which are key components of successful careers. How a message is encoded with any of the following non-verbal cues can influence how it is interpreted:

- tone, inflection, and other acoustic properties of speech
- eye gaze and facial expression
- body movements, posture, gestures, and touch
- appearance (bodily characteristics and clothing)
- personal space and the use of time

non-verbal communication Communication that does not use words but takes place through gestures, eye contact, and facial expressions.

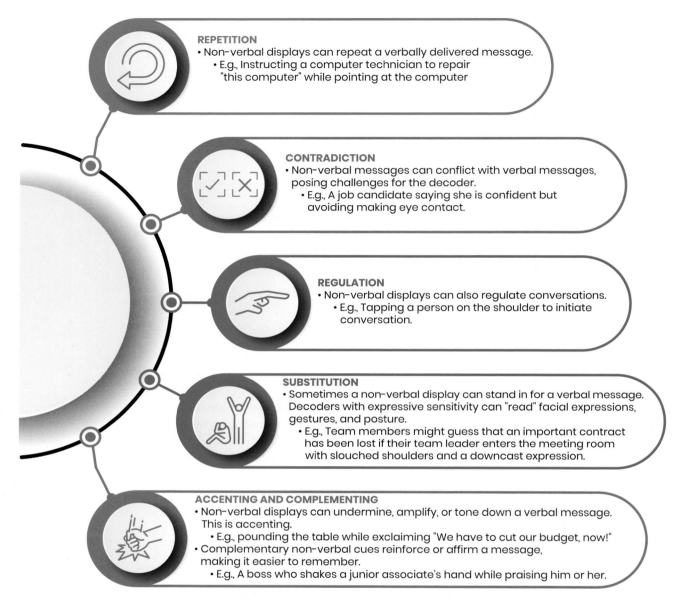

REPETITION
- Non-verbal displays can repeat a verbally delivered message.
  - E.g., Instructing a computer technician to repair "this computer" while pointing at the computer

CONTRADICTION
- Non-verbal messages can conflict with verbal messages, posing challenges for the decoder.
  - E.g., A job candidate saying she is confident but avoiding making eye contact.

REGULATION
- Non-verbal displays can also regulate conversations.
  - E.g., Tapping a person on the shoulder to initiate conversation.

SUBSTITUTION
- Sometimes a non-verbal display can stand in for a verbal message. Decoders with expressive sensitivity can "read" facial expressions, gestures, and posture.
  - E.g., Team members might guess that an important contract has been lost if their team leader enters the meeting room with slouched shoulders and a downcast expression.

ACCENTING AND COMPLEMENTING
- Non-verbal displays can undermine, amplify, or tone down a verbal message. This is accenting.
  - E.g., pounding the table while exclaiming "We have to cut our budget, now!"
- Complementary non-verbal cues reinforce or affirm a message, making it easier to remember.
  - E.g., A boss who shakes a junior associate's hand while praising him or her.

FIGURE 2.4 Non-verbal Communication Cues Can Play Five Roles in Relation to Verbal Communication

These non-verbal cues have the power to both intensify a message and contradict its primary aim. A nod of the head, a point of a finger, a steady gaze, a slumped posture, a frown—these signals, like all non-verbal cues, are powerful indicators of feelings and attitudes in verbal communication (Figure 2.4).

Non-verbal cues enrich verbal messages, as it is not always what you say but how you say it that people will remember. Non-verbal cues can be misleading when they are taken out of context, largely because their meaning is often culturally determined. Developing an awareness of intentional and unintentional non-verbal signals can help you not only decipher them, but also regulate how they impact your communication. Non-verbal skills and abilities fall into three general domains, all essential to achieving competence as a non-verbal communicator (Figure 2.5).

Encoding (emotional expressivity)
The ability to send non-verbal messages accurately to others.

Decoding (emotional sensitivity)
The ability to accurately read another person's non-verbal cues.

Regulation
The ability to control one's non-verbal displays and expressive behaviour to suit social situations. Regulation may require a deeper awareness of the subconscious choices that result in non-verbal displays and the meaning that other people infer from those displays.

FIGURE 2.5 The Three General Domains of Non-Verbal Skills

Tuning in to the signs and signals of human behaviour can help you "read" people and their attitudes, not just the words they speak or write, and make you a more effective and confident communicator. Non-verbal cues are also an important source of feedback that can tell you how successful your communications are—what the mood of a group is, when the group has heard enough, and whether someone in the group would like to speak or raise a question.

Components of Non-Verbal Communication

Non-verbal communication consists of a range of components that are frequently used together to aid expression.

Use of space (proxemics). **Proxemics** refers to the study of the human use and perception of space, specifically the amount of space that individuals maintain between each other during a conversation or interaction according to their cultural backgrounds. How space is used and manipulated, and how the framework for defining and organizing it is internalized, is yet another form of non-verbal communication and one that can lead to serious failures in communication. Proxemics explains why invading someone's personal space—by standing too close or overstepping what is appropriate in a particular social context—can lead to misunderstanding and negative interpersonal perceptions. Cultural anthropologist Edward T. Hall has identified four territorial zones that define spatial requirements (see Table 2.1).[25]

Hall's classification helps explain why a North American might back away when conversing with someone in Europe or South America, where the expected social distance is roughly half of what they are accustomed to. Physical environment, owing to factors such as lighting conditions and interior design, can also affect communicators' behaviours during interactions. The size of an office, its colour, and even its arrangement of furniture conveys information about the occupant(s) that can, in turn, influence how people feel and respond. Productive and efficient business communications depend on maintaining respectful workplace distances and enhancing approachability and interaction.

proxemics The study of the use and perception of space.

TABLE 2.1 Hall's Spatial Zones (North American norms)

Intimate distance	46 centimetres	for interacting with family and close friends
Personal distance	46 centimetres–1.2 metres	for communicating among close business associates
Social distance	1.2 metres–3 metres	for business conversations
Public distance	beyond 3 metres	for formal business exchanges and public speeches

chronemics The study of the use and interpretation of time in non-verbal communication.

paralanguage (vocalics) Non-verbal vocal qualities of communication.

Use of time (chronemics). **Chronemics** refers to the study of how people use and interpret time in non-verbal communication. For professionals, time is a valuable commodity that is uniquely connected to status. The timing and frequency of an action—how punctual a person is, how long someone is willing to listen or wait for a reply, the pace of speech or tempo of a conversation—are factors that influence the interpretation of that interaction.

Paralanguage (vocalics). **Paralanguage** refers to the acoustic or non-verbal vocal qualities of verbal communication, the way a message is spoken in terms of three classes of vocalic cues (Figure 2.6).

Because they can reveal underlying emotions and are used to infer personality traits, these voice patterns sometimes come across more strongly than the actual words that are spoken, at times creating mixed messages when the words and vocal cues clash. Shifts in meaning

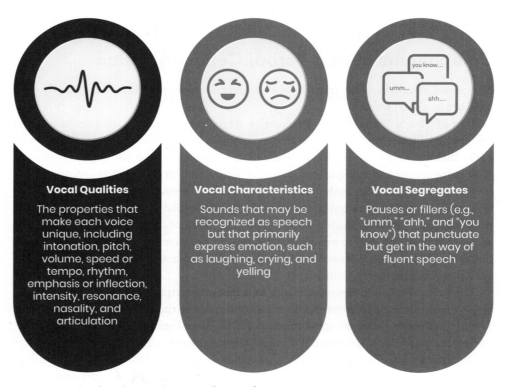

Vocal Qualities

The properties that make each voice unique, including intonation, pitch, volume, speed or tempo, rhythm, emphasis or inflection, intensity, resonance, nasality, and articulation

Vocal Characteristics

Sounds that may be recognized as speech but that primarily express emotion, such as laughing, crying, and yelling

Vocal Segregates

Pauses or fillers (e.g., "umm," "ahh," and "you know") that punctuate but get in the way of fluent speech

FIGURE 2.6   The Three Classes of Vocalic Cues

can occur with the subtlest changes in volume and emphasis. A change in vocal inflection can turn a general observation, such as "Oh, really," into an expression of sarcasm. "We can't fill your order" is a factual statement if said at normal volume but may terminate a customer relationship if it is shouted. "I'm very concerned about this problem," spoken with equal emphasis on each word, delivers a different message than when you say "*I'm* very concerned about this problem" (other people may not be); "I'm *very* concerned about this problem" (my concern is strong); or "I'm very concerned about *this* problem" (there are other problems). Becoming an effective speaker is a matter of learning to capitalize on paralanguage and the specific qualities of your own voice to complement and reinforce the words you use.

Body language (kinesics). Kinesics is a field of research that examines communication through body movements, based on the assumption that all humans—consciously or unconsciously—act and react both verbally and with their bodies. The meaning of these signals and their positive and negative value can shift depending on the receiver's culture, personality, and experience.

body language (kinesics) Non-verbal communication conveyed by gestures, posture, eye contact, and facial expressions.

- **Gestures.** Various hand and arm movements and specific body positions express special meanings—often culturally determined ones—that may both complement and contradict other forms of communication. Psychologists Paul Ekman and Wallace Friesen suggest that gestures can be categorized into five types:

  » Emblems—gestures that can be easily translated into unequivocal verbal statements, for example, waving goodbye or holding a palm outward to signal "stop."
  » Illustrators—non-verbal behaviours that accompany speech and depict what is said verbally, such as wagging a forefinger at another person in a verbal interaction that involves reprimand or disagreement.
  » Affect displays—gestures that convey emotion, primarily through the face, such as a smile.
  » Regulators—gestures that control interaction, such as leaning forward to signal entry into a conversation.
  » Adaptors—body movements that aid in the release of bodily tension due to new or anxious situations, for example, crossing your arms, running your hand through your hair, or tapping a pencil.[26]

  Most gestures convey unconscious messages on the sender's part, so excessive gesturing is a distraction that should be kept in check.

- **Posture.** Open body positions (arms uncrossed and away from the body, legs uncrossed, leaning forward) suggest ease, comfort, and agreement. Closed body positions (arms folded across the torso, legs close together or crossed, hands in pockets) may suggest defensiveness, a lack of receptivity, or discomfort.
- **Eye contact.** Eye contact is a powerful form of communication. What it conveys depends very much on its degree, duration, and context (both interpersonally and culturally). Direct and purposeful eye contact is a sign of honesty, sincerity, respect, and recognition. It is difficult, after all, to fake eye contact or to look someone in the eye and lie. More than a passing glance between strangers, however, can make both parties uncomfortable. Averting one's eyes can communicate

stress or dishonesty; deliberately averting one's eyes can indicate anger or a lack of interest, although in some cultures it is interpreted as a sign of deference. Knowing how to maintain good eye contact is important to the success of public speakers and presenters, who may use it as a means of holding an audience and assessing their receptivity, levels of interest, and attitudes.

- **Facial expressions.** Most expressions are short-lived, but they can nonetheless indicate personality traits, judgements, attitudes, and emotional states. There are, regardless of culture, six universally recognized facial expressions: happy, sad, afraid, surprised, angry, and disgusted. Facial expressions provide a useful, if not always reliable, source of feedback. It is easy to misjudge how people feel by the expressions on their faces, just as it is often common for people to mask their true feelings, especially in a professional environment. Individuals may have their own "display rules," such as "never show your anger in public," which inhibit emotional displays and limit their expression or cause someone to replace a genuine expression with a more socially acceptable one.

- **Image.** Personal choices pertaining to such things as clothing and accessories can be communicators of professional identity and corporate culture; therefore, they require reflective thought about the professional context (based on your role, interactions, and location) and general workplace norms. Many organizations have begun to rethink and relax dress codes that promote their brand and image needs. Business style now ranges from business formal to casual, with many interpretations in between and flexibility in honouring and embracing

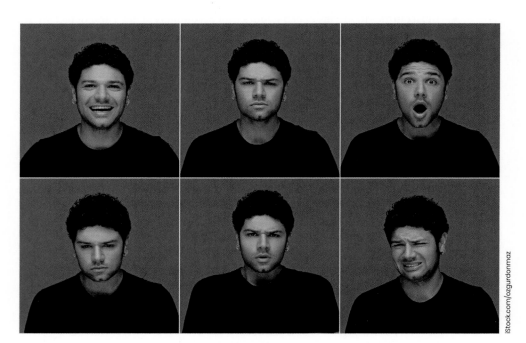

iStock.com/ozgurdonmaz

Facial expressions can communicate information about a person's thoughts, personality, and emotional state.

equity, diversity, and inclusion. Generally, as a rule of thumb, dressing for law, finance, and business settings as well as the boardroom requires more formal attire (e.g., business suits), whereas creative industries favour casual dress (e.g., dark denims, casual collared shirts, and skirts).[27] Yet standards are changing and may continue to change as younger workers join the workforce. A reasonably neat, clean, and appropriate appearance is a basic standard for which to aim. Research has also shown that clothing can affect the wearer's behaviour, with the potential to promote productivity, self-confidence, and more positive experiences for customers.[28] CIBC welcomes its new employees with this advice: "We're all expected to look professional and businesslike, but that differs by role and location. For example, an employee who deals with clients may be expected to dress more formally than someone who never deals with clients. The best way to find out is to ask your manager before you start. It's always safe to dress conservatively on your first day."[29] Ultimately, it is not so much a matter of what you wear as how you stay aware of who you are, where you work, and how others see you.

Communication Competence

Communication is functional—it produces certain outcomes. Communication competence—the ability to demonstrate knowledge of communication—is a measure of how well those outcomes are achieved. Business roles demand communication competence.

Communication competencies (the abilities that enable you to carry out tasks proficiently) fall into several areas of knowledge and literacy:

- Language competence: Knowledge of word choice and language, applicable rules, and what can be achieved through language
- Context-sensing competence: The ability to reflect and know what is right in a given situation
- Procedural knowledge: Practical knowledge for constructing messages and navigating communication systems
- Strategic competence: Knowledge of verbal and non-verbal strategies and how to apply them flexibly for peak performance
- Digital, computer, and media literacy: Knowledge of the use, benefits and limitations of digital communication technologies and how to read and judge digital messages[30]

Being a competent communicator involves knowledge, skill, and motivation[31]—each component can either build or inhibit your performance. Knowing how to write a report may not mean you have the skill or the initiative needed to write an effective one, for example. It takes all three. Competence is judged by two criteria—effectiveness (fulfilling set goals for an interaction) and appropriateness (right for the interpersonal relationship and context).[32] A well-formatted resumé packed with relevant data might net a job interview, but it would not be appropriate to lie about one's qualifications to achieve that end.

Communicating in Organizations

Internal and External Communication

To stay in business and be successful, today's companies must communicate with two main audiences: the organization's internal audience—employees and owners—and its external audience—customers, government officials, suppliers and other businesses, and the general public. **Internal communication** stays within an organization and involves the back-and-forth sharing of ideas and information among superiors, co-workers, and subordinates. Although the speed, instantaneousness, interactivity, and relative informality of e-mail make it the most popular and logical choice for use within a company, internal communication also occurs via memos, department reports, in-house newsletters or magazines, face-to-face conversations, group meetings, cloud-based messaging platforms, intranet sites, opinion surveys, speeches, and telephone conversations. Together, they provide the means for organizations to detect and solve problems, coordinate activities, foster decision-making and policy-setting, introduce and explain procedures, and persuade employees and managers to accept change.

Through **external communication**, organizations establish themselves in the marketplace, foster good public and media relations, and keep their operations functional, efficient, and productive. Some of the functions of external communication are to influence consumer decisions through advertising and promotion, process orders and collect payment, answer customer service inquiries and handle complaints, respond to government agencies, and carry out purchase transactions. External communication can take a variety of forms, such as newsletters, e-mail, social media blogs and messages, press releases, financial and corporate responsibility reports, information about products and services posted to company websites, and letters and direct mailings on company letterhead. Regardless of form, an externally directed message carries its company's reputation and corporate values. Today's businesses recognize the importance of using external communication with outside stakeholders as an opportunity to build prestige and a favourable public image by fostering goodwill and establishing solid business relationships. While the general functions of business communication are to

- **inform,**
- **persuade, and**
- **promote goodwill and create a favourable impression,**

it is the third of these functions that has increasing importance in external communication.

Essential Skills for Workplace Communication

Performing basic business functions well requires effective speaking, writing, reading, and listening. Later chapters will provide more specific suggestions and strategies for improving your skills in these four areas, but here we will take a brief look at the complementary skills of reading and listening.

Reading. On the job, you may spend almost as much time reading as you do writing. Well-developed reading and comprehension skills enable you to absorb and analyze masses of sometimes complex and technical written information quickly, even when

internal communication
Communication that takes place within an organization.

external communication
Communication with audiences who are part of an external environment.

faced with distractions. Effective responses start with knowing and understanding what you are responding to.

Active listening. There is a big difference between hearing—an auditory function—and listening—the act of decoding and interpreting a sound message. Learning to listen effectively requires knowing the difference between *passive listening* and *active listening*. Polite, passive listening is a kind of mechanical listening that doesn't involve real responses, just a pattern of pre-formulated statements and counter-statements. Active listening requires a much higher and more sustained level of interaction between the speaker and the listener, not to mention greater concentration and openness. Asking questions, anticipating what will be said next, reviewing and paraphrasing points that have already been made, and tuning in to non-verbal cues are active-listening techniques that let you focus on the speaker's main idea and essential message. (For more on active listening, take a look at the "Participating in a Meeting" tips in Chapter 13.)

> **active listening** Listening that demands both close attention to a message's literal and emotional meaning and a level of responsiveness that shows the speaker their message was heard and understood.

The most important thing a listener can do is pay close and respectful attention to everything that is said, not just a portion of the message, and to synthesize that information in his or her own words so it is both memorable and manageable. Part of this process involves overcoming the tendency to immediately reject a message that does not fit with your personal values or beliefs. It may be necessary to be mindful of the emotional filters—e.g., strong opinions about the subject or the speaker—that prevent you from understanding a message.

Informal and Formal Channels

Formal and informal pathways of communication operate both inside and outside the organization. Generally, the more an organization grows and expands, the greater its need for instituted systems that formalize and regulate its communications. With the purpose of enhancing efficiency, productivity, and overall performance, a **formal communications network** defines how messages such as letters, memos, reports, and proposals are sent according to a company's organizational structure or chain of command. This hierarchical structure is often laid out in the form of a chart. Once mapped out, an effective communication system establishes lines of communication—how certain types of messages flow within the company hierarchy and at what level each message should be aimed.

> **formal communications network** A system of communication sanctioned by organizational management.

Managers whose objective is to achieve business goals by putting these systems in place may also recognize that communication can be channelled through an **informal oral network**. Commonly known as grapevines, these informal internal communication channels develop when individuals socialize by talking about work—chatting around the water cooler, trading unofficial news in the coffee room, or exchanging gossip over lunch. Passed from one person to the next according to a pattern of serial communication, a message that travels through the grapevine spreads quickly but may not be entirely accurate or reliable. Regardless, informal oral networks are a major source of information in most workplaces, helping to alert managers to problems with morale, allowing them to test opinions, and informing employees about upcoming changes such as layoffs or restructuring. Though most employees prefer to learn important information through formal channels, astute managers may choose to use the grapevine to their advantage by placing someone with reliable information within the network or issuing the official version before a dangerous rumour has a chance to spread.

> **informal oral network** Unofficial internal communication pathways, also known as grapevines, that carry gossip and rumours—sometimes accurate, sometimes not.

Informal oral networks, or "grapevines," are not always reliable sources of information, but they can provide employees with a comfortable space to express their frustrations and network with co-workers.

The Flow of Information

formal communication channels Official internal communication pathways that facilitate the flow of information through an organization's hierarchy.

upward communication flow The movement of information from subordinates to superiors.

downward communication flow The movement of information from superiors to subordinates.

Among workers within an organization, information flows through **formal communication channels** in three directions: upward, downward, and horizontally.

Upward communication flow. Communication that takes this route, from subordinates to superiors, can be enormously beneficial to organizations that take it seriously enough to foster a climate of openness and trust in which opinions and ideas can be voiced freely. Whether in the form of solicited feedback or unsolicited suggestions, this kind of communication can help insulated upper management to stay in touch with workplace realities and give subordinates a valuable opportunity to provide input. While subordinates may feel they are part of a company team, they may also find that differences in status make it more difficult to communicate.

Downward communication flow. Directives are sent downward from top decision-makers via the chain of command to subordinates. This route is used to clarify corporate strategies, explain policies, outline job plans, and give performance feedback. Sometimes the downward flow strategy takes on the added purpose of instilling loyalty and improving the morale of employees. Downward communication is serial, travelling from person to person through various levels of an organization. As with most forms of serial communication, the longer the chain, the greater the chance the message will undergo distortion, develop flaws, or change meaning in transmission through a simplification, reordering, or rephrasing of its details. Unless messaging is properly monitored, this reinterpretation and resulting distortion may occur several times, as the message passes through the proper formal channels, from the CEO to managers and from managers to employees.

Wavebreak Media Ltd/©123RF.com

Horizontal communication flow. Also called lateral communication, horizontal flow involves people at the same organizational level. Conducted by e-mail, by telephone, or through personal contact, it has a variety of functions: to share information, to solve problems, and to coordinate and harmonize activities so each department knows what the other is doing in order to avoid duplication of initiatives. Companies with "flattened" hierarchies, in which there are fewer levels of management, need to make the most productive use of horizontal communication.

> **horizontal communication flow** The movement of information that enables individuals at the same organizational level to share ideas and exchange information.

Cross-Cultural Communication

Communicating in a Global Economy

The pace of business has increased rapidly in recent decades. New technologies, economic globalization, and international media have made it not just possible but also necessary for us to communicate and do business globally. Furthermore, market borders and boundaries are now less significant than they once were. Canadian companies, for example, may become partners in a global economy and expand through acquisitions, alliances, and mergers. They may look beyond home to an international marketplace, relying on the import and export of goods and services and conducting business with suppliers, customers, and distributors around the world. In today's business environment, Canadians may work for homegrown multinational corporations, such as McCain Foods, or for Canadian branches of multinational organizations headquartered in other countries; they may also work abroad or through internationally distributed virtual work teams.

The need for interconnectivity demands that employees learn to communicate effectively, in spite of the obstacles presented by differences in culture and language. To alleviate the latter, Business English has become the vernacular of this new global economy. BELF (Business English as a Lingua Franca) is a variety of English for specific task-related purposes, learned as a second or even third language worldwide. It is simple, clear, and free of idioms but anchored in a serviceable business vocabulary.

Diversity in the Workplace

The internationalization of Canada's workforce is another significant trend impacting business communication. It is common to work with people of many different ethnic, national, and religious backgrounds. Statistics Canada predicts that by 2031, between 11.4 million and 14.4 million people living in Canada (approximately one-third of the country's population) could belong to a visible minority group.[33]

Diversity is a strategic force that influences communication on the job. The ability to communicate with people from different cultures, backgrounds, and minority groups has internal and external benefits. Because culture has the power to influence behaviour, it also has the potential to create clashes and misunderstandings in the workplace. Learning to resolve differences and close cultural gaps is therefore essential. Successful businesses capitalize on the strengths of a diverse multinational workforce and reduce misunderstandings in order to benefit consumers, promote harmony, forge high-performance work teams, and gain a competitive edge.

Understanding Cultural Differences

culture The shared values, customs, and patterns of behaviour of a particular group or society, including its rules, beliefs, language, and structures.

Culture—the shared system of values, beliefs, attitudes, norms, and practices established and used by a group—is something that we learn. Although it provides us with our identity and sense of self, culture is not part of our genetic code. It is something dynamic, constantly changing, and passed from one generation to the next. What we value, how those values influence our behaviour, how we perceive the world, and even how we communicate are all determined by the culture in which we grow up and in which we live as adults. So, too, are our thinking and reasoning patterns and our approaches to problem-solving.

Because people from different cultures encode and decode messages differently, there is always the potential for misunderstandings and, consequently, antagonisms to occur across cultural boundaries. Part of the challenge of communicating across cultural differences is to recognize and defy **ethnocentrism** (the belief that one's own culture is superior), which intensifies cultural misunderstanding and makes communication difficult. Cross-cultural competence—the ability to communicate effectively with people from different cultural groups based on cultural knowledge, understanding, skill, and attitude—is a learned skill that is becoming increasingly important in today's workplaces.[34]

ethnocentrism The belief that one's own cultural or ethnic group is superior to others, leading to false assumptions.

Defining Intercultural Communication

Intercultural communication (or *cross-cultural communication*) refers to the management of messages between people and groups of different cultural backgrounds. It is guided by principles for understanding those cultural differences and exchanging meaningful information in a clear, unambiguous way that upholds mutual respect.

The field and practice of intercultural communication developed in the 1950s and 1960s as multinational businesses looked for ways to overcome miscommunication and resolve the difficulties that resulted from how different cultures perceived reality. People soon discovered there are multiple things to consider before communicating across cultures.

First, cultures tend to differ in several important respects:

- attitudes to individualism and collectivity
- reliance on logic and feeling
- the relative directness of their communication styles
- attitudes to the relational role of communication in business transactions
- attitudes to the elderly, life partnerships, and gender roles
- time orientation
- propensity for risk and uncertainty
- the degree of formality and protocol that governs social interactions
- interpretations of non-verbal communication and body language

Of these, social psychologist Geert Hofstede[35] identified five key "dimensions" of culture—or the ways in which cultures differ from one another.

1. **Power distance**, or the degree to which less powerful members of a group expect and accept that power is distributed unequally. For example, an employee new to Canada

might be so used to the top-down chain-of-command decision-making system in his or her country of origin that he or she may be uncomfortable in taking the initiative when asked to do so, even viewing this sort of behaviour as insubordination.

2. **Uncertainty avoidance**, or a society's tolerance for ambiguity and comfort level with situations that are new, unstructured, or unknown. Differences in the need for rules, for example, may lead to a dispute or misunderstanding between a customer and the business owner who, in his or her birth country, sealed an agreement with a handshake rather than a written contract.

3. **Individualism vs. collectivism**, or the degree to which people are integrated into groups and expected to take care of others. For example, a new employee recently arrived from Iraq might decide to miss an afternoon of work to escort several female members of his extended family from the airport.

4. **Masculinity vs. femininity**, not about individuals but related to the societal distribution of emotional roles and values between genders. Masculine societies are more openly gendered and endorse competition and the use of force. For example, a female employee trying to maintain a life–work balance might ask to leave work early to attend her daughter's ballet recital but be refused by her male supervisor, who is intent on completing the department's project ahead of schedule.

5. **Short-term vs. long-term orientation**, or the degree to which societies are future-focused (long-term orientation) or anchored in the past or present (short-term orientation). For example, a Japanese manufacturer, part of a short-term-oriented culture where social spending is significant and customary, may insist that a Canadian certification inspector accept lavish gifts.

High- and Low-Context Communication Styles

Another important way cultures differ from one another has to do with how much they value context when delivering messages. The distinction between **high-context cultures**, in which most of the information of a message is inferred from the message's context, and **low-context cultures**, which depend on explicit verbal and written messages, sheds light on cultural differences according to the beliefs, practices, and communication styles of each particular group. Developed by Edward T. Hall, this system serves as a useful analytical tool when preparing for cross-cultural interactions. It is also useful as a means of making broad assessments of national styles of communication and negotiation. As such, Hall's model has special relevance to any dialogue and correspondence you conduct with international vendors, suppliers, and operators.[36] High- and low-context cultures certainly value different styles of communication, and this is true not only for the words and nuances of verbal communication but also for the facial expressions and gestures of non-verbal communication. Knowing about high- and low-context cultures can help you adapt your perspective and keep up with the demands of communicating in multicultural and cross-cultural environments.

Low-context cultures. Communicators in low-context cultures convey their meaning exclusive of the context of a situation. Meaning depends on what is said—the literal content of the message—rather than how it is said. Low-context communicators can say "no" directly. They don't need to be provided with much background information, but they do expect messages to be professional, efficient, and linear in their logic. Low-context cultures value individualism and self-assertion, which they regard as the means to achievement and success.

high-context cultures
Cultures in which communication depends not only on the explicit wording of a message but also on the message's context.

low-context cultures
Cultures that favour direct communication and depend on explicit verbal and written messages exclusive of context.

iStock.com/metamorworks

Canadians doing business in Tokyo, Japan, and other places where high-context communication is the norm must pay careful attention to how non-verbal cues and context influence the meaning of what is said and agreed upon.

High-context cultures. In high-context cultures communication relies heavily on non-verbal, contextual, and shared cultural meanings. In other words, high-context communicators attach great importance to everything that surrounds the explicit message, including interpersonal relationships, non-verbal cues, and physical and social settings. Information is transmitted not through words alone but also through non-verbal cues such as gestures, voice inflection, and facial expression, which can have different meanings in different cultures. Eye contact, for example, which is encouraged in North America, may have ambiguous meaning or be considered disrespectful in certain high-context cultures. Meaning is determined not by what is said but by how it is said and by how social implications such as the communicator's status and position come into play. For high-context cultures, language is a kind of social lubricant; it eases and harmonizes relations that are defined according to a group or collectivist orientation and where "we" rather than "I" is the key to identity. Because directness may be thought of as disrespectful, discussions in high-context cultures can be circuitous, circling key issues rather than addressing them head-on. Communicating in high-context cultures, especially in a business context, can require you to focus on politeness strategies that demonstrate your respect for readers and listeners. Doing business internationally can also involve a higher degree of formality and strict adherence to rules of social etiquette.

Communicating Interculturally

Communicating interculturally is something you may do in many settings:

- in multicultural organizational work teams or in interactions with individuals
- in multinational teams when working with partnered organizations

- in international audiences when working on assignments overseas, in global leadership, or in cross-cultural negotiations

In these contexts, written, spoken, visual, and non-verbal communication can require you to rethink the ingrained habits that govern how you express yourself. It demands cultural intelligence,[37] which is an individual's ability to function and manage effectively in culturally diverse settings. Adapting successfully to diverse audiences and situations also requires knowledge, motivation, enhanced awareness, and changes in behaviour. Showing respect for your readers and listeners and learning whatever you can about their cultural expectations are the first steps toward achieving clarity and mutual understanding in your communication.

Oral Messages: Speaking

1. **Pay attention to non-verbal behaviours.** "Listen" to what is not being said and interpret what silences communicate. Look for eye messages—raised eyebrows, loss of eye contact—and facial gestures indicating that listeners are not following what you say. Keep in mind that the degree of comfortable eye contact varies by culture and even by individual. For many Indigenous Peoples, for example, maintaining eye contact may not be expected in conversations as a sign of courtesy.[38]
2. **Use simple English, and enunciate clearly.** Opt for familiar, unpretentious words and avoid idioms (e.g., *up to my ears*, *two cents' worth*) and slang. Deliver your message at a slower pace than you would use for an audience of first-language English speakers, but do not speak so slowly as to be condescending.
3. **Adjust the level of formality to what is considered culturally acceptable.** Addressing someone on a first-name basis and being direct may be acceptable in certain cultures but undesirable in others where reserve, deference, ceremony, and social rules play a big role in business communication.
4. **Be mindful of cultural expectations and protocols.** If you are communicating with members of an Indigenous community, learn how to spell and pronounce the name of their territory and people before you initiate communication. Do some preliminary research to learn about their community and how to respectfully address Elders and elected officials.
5. **Excuse misunderstanding.** If your audience doesn't understand your message, take the time to make it clear without causing embarrassment.
6. **Encourage feedback and test your audience's comprehension.** Pause from time to time to ask if your listeners would like you to clarify any points. Confirm their comprehension by inviting them to sum up your message in their own words.

Oral Messages: Listening

1. **Don't interrupt.** Be patient and allow the speaker to finish a thought. Don't be too ready to jump in and offer to elaborate.
2. **Practise active listening.** Concentrate on the speaker's message. If necessary, ask questions or restate the message to focus your listening.
3. **Be sensitive and patient.** Don't assume that a person who can speak English will automatically comprehend every word you say. Recognize the challenges the speaker may face communicating in an adopted language.

Writing for Culturally Diverse Audiences

1. **Adopt formats that are used in the reader's country.** Study the communication you receive and, as much as possible, adapt your own correspondence to the formatting preferences of your audience. Use appropriate diacritical marks (the symbols added to letters to indicate their pronunciation), especially for proper names (e.g., *Dubé, Müller, Métis*).

2. **Carefully consider forms of address and pronouns.** In cultures where formality is still highly valued (e.g., in Japan), using first names in a direct address is usually too informal for international correspondence, especially in an initial contact. Use a personal or professional title such as *Ms.* or *Director* with a surname. Businesses in many parts of the world must now refer to trans people by their preferred non-binary gender-neutral pronoun, usually *ze* (for *he* or *she*) or *they* (for singular and plural references).

3. **Use only terms that can be found in English-language dictionaries.** Slang, jargon, idioms, and/or colloquialisms are usually specific to one context or country and don't necessarily translate well to others. Readers whose first language is not English—and even English speakers in another country—may not know what you mean if you use *suits* to refer to business executives or *the 411* to refer to information. Similarly, it is best to avoid unnecessary jargon, idioms (e.g., *blue moon, fruits of your labours*), unusual figures of speech, abbreviations, and sports references (e.g., *it's a slam dunk, a ballpark figure*). If possible, try to avoid words with double meanings.

4. **Keep sentences as direct and simple as possible.** Communicate using complete but not complex sentences, arranging your thoughts in short, coherent paragraphs. Add relative pronouns (e.g., *that, which*) for clarity, and check for correct pronoun reference (readers should be able to judge what the relative pronoun refers to). Avoid contractions.

5. **Use correct grammar.** Never insult your reader's intelligence by writing in overly simplified English. Instead, use language that is literal and specific.

6. **Include politeness strategies where they are required.** Show courtesy by thanking the reader and by using the words *please* and *thank you* when it makes sense to do so. An indirect approach, which delays a direct request, gives you the chance to establish goodwill and build a business relationship.

7. **Avoid humour, irony, and sarcasm.** These features rarely translate well across cultural contexts and can lead to miscommunication.

8. **Use international measurement standards.** Using these standards, such as the metric system, ensures that the majority of your audience will understand your references.

Checklist

Intercultural Communication and Workplace Diversity

There are several ways to bridge the gap between different cultures, whether you are writing for an international audience or just helping to make diversity work for everyone in your workplace. Gaining awareness, building knowledge, and adjusting your behaviour are fundamental to meeting this challenge.

- ❑ **Show respect.** Acknowledge respect for each other's languages, values, and behaviours. Realize that differences do not inevitably lead to conflict. View them simply as differences, not as matters of right or wrong.

- ❑ **Gain knowledge and develop awareness.** Become aware of your own thinking and assumptions. Educate yourself: seek information about other cultures as a means to overcome prejudice and stereotypes and take advantage of the diversity-training programs your company may offer. Be conscious of values, norms, languages, and beliefs of other cultures when approaching others and initiating communication. Recognize the richness available to you through other cultures and the synergy of different viewpoints.

- ❑ **Avoid negative judgements.** Do not express damaging assumptions or views based on your own cultural heritage. Suspend judgement until enough information becomes available about the other person in a cross-cultural interaction. Consider the perspectives of other cultures, be open to developing a sympathetic understanding while upholding your own ethical values, and attempt to understand how your own cultural conditioning or ethnocentrism has the potential to influence your behaviour. Curb any impulse to let negative opinions or defensive attitudes dictate your conduct and communication.

- ❑ **Cultivate a work environment that values diversity.** Make sure the diverse voices, cultures, and expertise in your workplace are heard and valued. Values of tolerance and sensitivity, if given enough emphasis, can allow your organization to foster harmony among employees and build high-performance international and multicultural teams.

- ❑ **Ask questions.** Foster openness in your communications and encourage feedback and constructive dialogue. Exercise sensitivity in the ways you ask others about themselves. When communicating globally, research your intended audience's culture to determine acceptable usage and style elements.

- ❑ **Prepare to be flexible.** When speaking, adjust your tone, volume, rate of speaking, and use of pauses and silences. Alter your non-verbal behaviours and facial expressions to suit the needs of the situation when communicating face-to-face. Make allowances for simpler, idiom-free vocabulary choices and shorter sentences when the interaction requires it.

- ❑ **Seek common ground.** Where there is potential for intercultural conflict, look to what you share by emphasizing compromise and solutions. Being adept at cultural understanding does not mean that you have to adopt the cultural norms and expectations of others; rather, it shows that you are open to meeting others halfway and making necessary adjustments.

- ❑ **Tolerate ambiguity and uncertainty.** Communicating with someone from another culture can create uncertainty and sometimes make you uncomfortable. Accept that you may face difficulties in communicating and face rather than avoid uncertainty.

- ❑ **Listen to others, not to the voice of your ethnocentrism.** Pay attention to the situation and rely on feedback from multiple cues to monitor an individual's understanding.

- ❑ **Bridge.** Live the values of greatest importance to you and those you share with others through consideration and sensitivity.

- ❑ **Encourage your employer to commit to a harassment- and discrimination-free workplace.** If such a commitment has not been made, a human-rights policy and set of procedures can be instituted to resolve problems related to diversity issues quickly and fairly.

Checklist

Chapter Review

- ❏ What is communication? What is communication theory?
- ❏ What are the primary elements of the transactional communication model? How does the communication process work?
- ❏ What types of barriers can occur in the communication process? How can those barriers be overcome?
- ❏ Name the five communication contexts. How do they differ and what specific skills are required for each?
- ❏ What is interpersonal communication and what competencies does it require? How can it be improved?
- ❏ What is non-verbal communication? What are the three domains of skills and abilities that lead to non-verbal competence?
- ❏ What are the five roles of non-verbal communication cues?
- ❏ What are the four components of non-verbal communication?
- ❏ Define the terms *internal communication* and *external communication*. Give examples of each.
- ❏ Which skills are most essential for effective workplace communication?
- ❏ What are the ways in which information can flow in organizations? What impact can information flow have on organizational culture?
- ❏ What is culture? Cultural intelligence? Cross-cultural competence? Ethnocentrism?
- ❏ What is intercultural communication?
- ❏ What are the dimensions of cultural difference?
- ❏ What are the best practices for speaking, listening, and writing interculturally?
- ❏ What are the characteristics of high- and low-context cultures?

Exercises, Workshops, and Discussion Forums

1. **Analyzing Barriers to Communication.** Working in large groups, play a variation of the game broken telephone. Nominate a group leader to compose a message of no more than 12 words. The group leader will then whisper this message to the person seated to his or her immediate left or right, who will in turn pass it on to his or her neighbour, and so on. Once the message has made its way through the entire group, ask the last person to say the message aloud. Repeat the process, only this time have two messages circulating at once. If you complete the process a third time, use a written message and a verbal message at once. What happened to each message in the course of its transmission? What barriers to communication made it difficult to deliver and react to each message? How did they impact your understanding of the message?

2. **Analyzing Interpersonal Interactions.** Make a list of one-to-one conversations and one-on-one online interactions you have had over the past 48 hours. What is your relationship to each participant? What level (high, medium, or low) of trust, control, and intimacy-distance applies to each one? How did your communication style and level of self-disclosure differ as a result?

3. **Observing and Analyzing Non-Verbal Cues.** Record a five-minute video of a conversation between yourself and a partner. When you watch the video, decide whether the non-verbal signs are voluntary or involuntary and note the non-verbal cues that repeat, contradict, substitute for, complement, or accent each partner's spoken messages. Note any discrepancies between your verbal communication and your non-verbal communication and whether the non-verbal signs were aggressive or caused discomfort. Variation: Watch a short speech, business presentation, or political speech online. Note the speaker's use of non-verbal cues and discuss how they contradict or enrich each other or the message.

4. **Experimenting with Proxemics.** In a classroom with moveable furniture, work in a group and re-arrange the furniture in the following positions:

   - in a circle and half-circle
   - in standard classroom style, with all chairs facing one direction
   - in a random formation

   Continue the class. How do the dynamics of the group change depending on the seating arrangement?

5. **Experimenting with Personal Space.** For this activity, first work with a partner and then repeat the activity in a small-group session. Determine the dividing line between comfortable and uncomfortable distance by saying "continue" or "stop" as your partner or group members move toward you, starting from a distance of three metres. See if your spatial tolerance changes if you imagine your partner is a co-worker, friend or family member. Keep a log of your reactions, according to what is an allowable distance between you and your group members. At what point did you begin to feel uncomfortable? Were your reactions different from your peers'?

6. **Taking Stock of Non-Verbal Communication.** Working in a small group, spend one minute identifying as many ways of communicating non-verbally as you can, then get more specific by identifying examples of non-verbal communication (paralanguage, gestures, facial expressions) that typically express each of the following emotions, sentiments, or actions:

happiness or celebration	admiration
anger	sympathy
sadness	praise
shame	hello or goodbye
hailing a cab	disbelief
showing respect	"good luck"
"come here"	agreement
"over there"	disagreement
"this one"	like
friendship or warmth	dislike

To what extent do group members agree on the meaning of each gesture or expression? Are any of the gestures universal? Which ones have a place in business communication?

7. **Experimenting with Eye Contact.** For this activity, work with a partner and note and compare your reactions to the length and intensity of eye contact. Begin by maintaining eye contact for two seconds, increasing by increments of two seconds up to a total of 20. At what point does your partner's gaze become unsettling and intrusive? Try the experiment again, this time by looking away (for up to 15 seconds) before you hold and increase your gaze. What is the effect of interrupting your gaze or increasing its duration?

8. **Improving Your Active-Listening Skills.** In a small group, have each person perform a one- or two-minute introduction that covers such subjects as that person's program of study, career goals, school- or job-related interests, and technological proficiencies. When every group member has spoken, take a few minutes to record what you can remember of each person's introduction. Compare your observations and recollections with those of other group members. Discuss what makes the difference between poor and effective listening. Variation: Choose a partner to interview about his or her program of study and interests. Based on what you have learned, deliver a one-minute introduction to the class.

9. **Establishing Guidelines for Communicating Interculturally.** In a small group, imagine that you and your fellow group members work for a medium-sized Canadian business that has recently signed its first overseas business contract. The contract requires a number of employees to work closely with representatives from a manufacturing

firm in South Korea. Your group has been asked by management to develop guidelines for all employees to follow when communicating with stakeholders in South Korea and, more generally, in all intercultural business settings. Draft a concise list of guidelines based on what you have learned in this chapter.

Writing Improvement Exercises

1. **Assessing Barriers to Communication.** Recall a recent event or situation that made you angry (e.g., a parking ticket, a missed transit connection, or a ruling or school/government policy with which you strongly disagreed). Write two messages, each seeking restitution or settlement of the problem. In the first message, vent your grievance and sense of frustration according to what you felt in the heat of the moment. Allow several hours to elapse before you write your second message. Compare the messages on the basis of tone, content, and coherence. Discuss how emotional barriers affect the communication process.

2. **Identifying Your Communication Channels and Choices: Always On.** Linguistics professor Naomi S. Baron claims that online and mobile technologies such as instant messaging, cellphones, Facebook, blogs, and wikis are transforming how we communicate, creating an environment in which we are "always on" one technology or another.[39] These technologies offer users the power to control who they communicate with—with the option of blocking incoming IMs, creating alter egos in virtual worlds, and screening calls. Analyze the percentage of your day you devote to communications and estimate the amount of time you spend on each of the following:

   - face-to-face and phone conversations, e-mail, and texting (communicating with individuals)
   - social networking (presenting yourself to others)

   In a few paragraphs or as a brief e-mail to your instructor, outline your communication preferences and describe how your communication style, behaviour, and self-presentation change according to the technology or channel you use.

3. **Analyzing Your On-the-Job Communication.** If you currently have a job or have recently been employed, analyze your on-the-job communication by answering the following questions:

   a) What channel(s) do you principally use to communicate?
   b) How important is communication to the duties you must perform?
   c) In what direction does your communication primarily flow—upward, downward, or horizontally? With whom do you primarily communicate internally and externally?
   d) What types of messages/documents do you typically create or generate? What types of messages/documents do you receive?
   e) What barriers to communication exist?
   f) How does your organization facilitate communication in the workplace?
   g) How formal or informal is it necessary to be when communicating?
   h) Is the grapevine in your organization accurate?

   When you have written out your answers to these questions, draw a diagram that illustrates the flow of information in your workplace.

4. **Analyzing Non-Verbal Cues.** Although it is sometimes difficult to interpret gestures, body language, and other non-verbal signals, consider what each of the following scenarios communicates:

   a) Olivia Visconti, human resources director, places visitors' chairs across the room from her desk and arranges a coffee table in front of the chairs.
   b) Bev Saunders places her hands on her hips as she conducts a training session.
   c) Goran Garabedian, while being interviewed for a job, crosses his arms over his torso and looks at the floor.

5. **Identifying Communication Competencies.** Imagine that you are fulfilling a lifelong dream of launching a small business. You have expertise but realize you cannot do everything on your own and must hire and train a small staff to ensure your business is a success. The problem is you don't have the funds to cover your workforce needs and related training right now. You learn from a government of Canada website and from friends who have launched businesses of their own that you are eligible to apply for government business workforce development grant. Preparing a grant application (a formal request for funding) isn't something you have done before. You've heard from your friends that it involves filling in an online form with a description of your business and its goals, the need for staff, a plan and timeline for implementing your hiring and training, and an estimated budget. Learning to write a grant and actually writing one involves competencies and different types of knowledge, some of which you may already have and some you may need to develop. Many first-time grant-writers, like yourself, learn by doing and by asking experienced writers and grant officers for guidance. For now, before you actually write a grant, your task is to determine which of the following competencies you are confident of and which ones you might need to work on.

- Language competence: Can you make your case for funding clearly, informatively and persuasively?
- Genre knowledge: Do you know what a grant is and basically what it consists of?
- Procedural knowledge: Do you know what to do to get started? Where can you find information and answers to FAQs?
- Context-sensing competence: Do you know the right/appropriate way to ask for funds? How does the grantor and the projects it has funded in the past influence the writing of your grant?
- Digital and technological competency: Do you have the skills to be able to access and fill out the grant and search for additional support?

6. **Communicating with Competence I: Knowledge, Skill, and Motivation.** For the following examples, identify (i) the challenge to each individual's communication competence (lack of knowledge, lack of skill, lack of motivation) and (ii) what could each person do to become more competent.

a) Drew has a graduate degree in communication and submitted the best resumé and application letter the corporate hiring committee had ever seen, but on the job he is always the last to answer a group e-mail and sometimes ignores his e-mail entirely.

b) Manaz is a fan of TEDTalk videos and self-help public-speaking apps. She is always the first to volunteer to make a pitch to clients. When it comes to actually speaking in front of a group, however, she is terrified. Her pauses are lengthy and she prefers to look at the floor rather than her audience.

c) Memengwaa is a Gen Z college graduate with a BA in the natural sciences, background in Ojibway storytelling, and 10,000 Instagram followers. On the strength of her social media and storytelling skills, she is offered a position in corporate communication, an area in which she has no formal training. She takes the job because she has a passion for continuous learning, something the job ad promised to new hires, but once on the job she realizes the company offers nothing in the way of mentorship or training.

7. **Communicating with Competence II: Effectiveness and Appropriateness.** In each of the following situations, consider whether the communication is (i) effective, (ii) appropriate, or (iii) both. How could the communicator be both effective and appropriate?

a) Kevin writes a polished and professional proposal that is successful in securing funding for the development of a new app he claims is unlike anything currently available; however, he hides the fact that an identical app is already on the market.

b) Tamoor has to write a rejection letter to a top job prospect he interviewed but was unable to hire. The letter is overly polite and never mentions that he cannot hire the candidate. The candidate has to contact the company to ask about the hiring decision.

c) Wei is a persuasive speaker. At a benefit dinner attended by noted investors, she makes a compelling elevator pitch to get funding for her new startup but she makes claims about its projected impact and reach without the benefit of market research.

8. **Identifying Forms of Internal and External Communication.** Distinguish between the following types of communication according to whether the message is internal or external (or both):

a) a response to a request for proposals (RFP) that tenders a bid on a plumbing contract for a municipal housing project

b) a group e-mail to staff members who have signed up for a series of telecommuting training sessions

c) an announcement of changes to the company pension plan

d) a press release announcing the hiring of a corporate legal representative

e) an annual report for shareholders

f) an adjustment letter settling a claim against your company

g) a formal report on the outsourcing of human resources functions

9. **Assessing the Flow of Communication.** In each of the following situations, consider whether communication is channelled through an upward, a downward, or a horizontal flow:

a) an e-mail message to a co-worker in your department asking for clarification of the latest sales figures

b) a recommendation report to the president of your company suggesting the development of a staff incentive or awards program

c) a text to a trainee explaining how to prepare a press release

d) discussions with co-workers over revisions to a report written collaboratively

e) a bank regulatory compliance document that helps frontline employees, such as bank tellers, understand new banking regulations

Write a paragraph discussing the special demands of each message.

10. **Recognizing Cultural Differences.** Large multinational corporations, such as McCain Foods and Tim Hortons, create websites for every country or region in which they operate. Visit the following sites and note the similarities and differences in language, content, and design. Write a memo that summarizes and analyzes those similarities and differences, including differences in values and belonging related to individuals and communities, differences in site design, and differences in how products are presented and described (with a clear message that is typical of low-context cultures, or implicitly, which is more typical in high-context cultures). Include URLs of the applicable sites.

McCain Foods Worldwide: *www.mccain.com/information-centre/mccain-foods-worldwide/* (covering sites for the Americas, Africa, Asia Pacific, and Europe)
Tim Hortons English Canada: *www.timhortons.ca*
Tim Hortons US: *www.timhortons.com*
Tim Hortons UK: *www.timhortons.co.uk*
Tim Hortons Spain: *www.tim-hortons.es*

11. **Connecting with Other Cultures.** Describe your experience of eating out to try an international cuisine, visiting a country in a different region or hemisphere, or watching an international, foreign-language film (one with subtitles).

12. **Intercultural Communication: Proxemics and Personal Space.** How much personal space do you need to be comfortable? In a small group compare your preferences. Do women in your group prefer more or less personal space than men do? Together conduct an online search for guidelines, especially ones based on research findings, that allow you to compare contact cultures (South America, the Middle East, Southern Europe) and non-contact cultures (North America, Asia, Northern Europe). What other contextual features might affect a degree of acceptable personal space?

13. **Improving Intercultural Communication.** The following message is intended for a reader in another country. Make it more reader-friendly by

eliminating any colloquial expressions and slang, inflated language, and acronyms. Simplify sentence structures that are too complex, and add pronouns where they are needed for clarity.

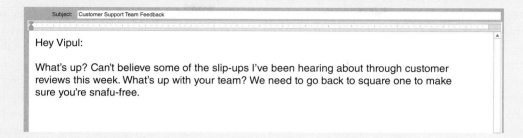

Subject: Customer Support Team Feedback

Hey Vipul:

What's up? Can't believe some of the slip-ups I've been hearing about through customer reviews this week. What's up with your team? We need to go back to square one to make sure you're snafu-free.

Case Study Exercises

1. **Intercultural Communication: Religious Acceptance and Accommodation.** Masood is an observant Muslim who is working on a one-year contract as a corporate trainer for an established mid-sized Canadian company. Although the employee-base is diverse, at company events he is conscious of being the only Muslim trainer and has come to understand that management is somewhat inflexible, skirting human rights guidelines, when it comes to accommodating special requests from employees. Masood is concerned, despite his legal rights, that his contract might not be renewed if he asks for what other employees might perceive as concessions. Neither the company intranet nor the corporate HR page offer information on accommodations for religious observance, including for Ramadan. Because Masood is fasting during the day and does not intend to break for lunch but instead will use part of that time for prayer, he asks his manager, without telling him the reason, if he can start work an hour early and leave an hour early. Access to the building very early in the morning is restricted, and his request is denied. His manager, Gunther Platt, insists that all training sessions, including the ones Masood conducts, begin on time and run without unexplained delays, interruptions, or unscheduled breaks. When Masood avoids mandatory working lunches and makes a habit of starting sessions late, complaints follow, and Gunther calls Masood into his office for a tense conversation about job expectations and business goals, lecturing him on punctuality and workplace engagement. Masood still can't bring himself to explain why his work practices were different this month but privately he feels his manager is being intolerant and unfair.

   a) What caused conflict between Masood and Gunther and led to a deterioration of their working relationship?
   b) What could Masood, Gunther, and the organization have done differently? What strategies could they use to improve understanding and build successful working relationship?

2. **Intercultural Communication: Job Interview Misperceptions.** Jacinta Valera and Todd McCormack are expanding their Peterborough, Ontario,-based eco-tourism business to northern Ontario and hiring three guides to conduct sustainable canoe and hiking tours each June through September. Indigenous band councillor Gary Mashquash applies for one of the positions and comes highly recommended as an expert guide with extensive knowledge of the Temagami region and northern ecosystems, along with a strong work ethic and commitment to customer safety and experience. Jacinta and Todd have little experience interviewing Indigenous applicants, but Gary is at the top of their candidate list. They have many interviews to conduct in a short time and rattle off their questions quickly. Finding their approach brusque and pushy but determined to interview well, Gary answers slowly and pauses for a long time before each answer. His answers are focused but not as detailed as Jacinta and Todd had hoped, and he rarely makes eye contact. When

Gary follows up by e-mail to thank Jacinta and Todd for the interview and express his strong interest in the job, Jacinta is surprised. "At the interview it seemed like he wasn't interested. He hardly looked at us. I had trouble adjusting to the way he spoke—some double negatives, 'tanks' rather than 'thanks,' 'I seen dese' rather than 'I saw these.'" Todd, who has worked extensively in northern Ontario communities, responds, "I think he was speaking a dialect called Aboriginal English. Our customers shouldn't have any trouble with it. He's the most experienced candidate by far. We'd be missing out if we didn't hire him." Jacinta remains unsure.

a) What is the basis for misunderstanding?
b) How could Jacinta and Todd have prepared to ensure better grounds for assessing Indigenous candidates?

For additional background, see:
Indigenous Corporate Training, Inc. 9 Tips for Doing Business with First Nations: *https://ictinc.ca/blog/9-tips-for-doing-business-with-first-nations*
Canadian Construction Association Indigenous Engagement Guide: *https://cca-acc.com/wp-content/uploads/2016/03/IndigenousEngagementGuide.pdf*

3. **Intercultural Communication: Working in Dubai.** Former classmates Yohanna Nemerian and Jeremy Stahl are experienced Vancouver-based videographers and photographers who have worked outside of Canada extensively and have now been hired on one-year contracts by Aleaqarat.com, a UAE real estate database and marketing company based in Dubai. The company prides itself on its friendly environment and advises in its job postings that "When we hire someone, it should be taken as a privilege." Yohanna's work visa is delayed. Jeremy travels ahead to Dubai and is introduced to the company president and members of the Emirati videography team. They are friendly and welcoming, and they offer him tea, which he refuses—"I never did like that stuff." Over dinner they show genuine interest in him and ask him questions about his background, which he refuses to answer because it makes him uncomfortable. He has never enjoyed socializing with work colleagues and now is no exception. He would like to start training as soon as possible and get to know the rules he must work by. English is the lingua franca, so there is no language barrier. At the first department meeting he attends, Jeremy has creative differences with the team over the handing over of filming responsibilities to assistants and directs his concerns in front of the group to his manager, Abdullah Aziz, who is tight-lipped and seemingly resentful of what Jeremy believes was an honest attempt to improve quality and optimize viewers' experience of their database. After that, an older member of the team who had begun to advise Jeremy becomes increasingly distant. Jeremy texts Yohanna that he believes their decision to work in Dubai, as beautiful as it is with its beaches and vibrant nightlife, was a mistake. When Yohanna arrives in Dubai, she is surprised that Mr. Aziz does not extend his hand to her in greeting. None of the predominantly male staff will sit next to or talk to her in the company lounge, and her isolation worsens after she wears shorts to work one day. Jeremy and Yohanna look for termination clauses in their contracts and discuss whether they can pull out of their contracts early and return to Canada.

a) What are the reasons for Jeremy's growing social exclusion from his work colleagues? For background, read Sharon Schweitzer's short article: "Dubai: 3 Cross Cultural Tips for Business Success." *www.huffpost.com/entry/dubai-3-cross-cultural-tips-for-business-success_b_58a25803e4b0cd37efcfec78*
b) What are the reasons for Yohanna's negative experience? Research business etiquette guidelines for women working in Dubai.
c) How could Jeremy and Yohanna have better respected Emirati cultural norms and found their way into this new organizational culture?
d) What are the positive and negative aspects of being part of a global workforce?

4. **Intercultural Communication in Practice: International Student Support.** Imagine that you are a student volunteer with International Student Support services at your college or university. Your role is to mentor students from around the world, help them transition to the campus and community, and enrich their social lives and cultural experiences while they are in Canada. You will work to support a number of activities: collaborating on a "What to Pack/What to Buy" list, mentoring in the support centre once a week, planning a series of peer social events, developing wayfinding resources so they can make their way around and off campus, and planning an event to support refugee awareness.

You have been assigned three students from South Korea to mentor, but none of them is fully proficient in English or has visited Canada before. Your first task is to send each one a personal e-mail welcoming them and getting their post-secondary experience off to a positive start. Take a look at the online resources available for International Students on your institution's website, but don't try to summarize all the information you find there. Your goal is to connect with them and start a conversation that you can eventually carry on by text or via social media with some human perspective on what makes your institution a special place and its academic experience unique.

Online Activities

1. **How Well Do You Read Other People?** View the 20 headshots provided online to identify the emotion conveyed in each and measure your emotional intelligence.

   http://greatergood.berkeley.edu/ei_quiz/

2. **Leading with Emotional Intelligence: A *Harvard Business Review* Quiz.** From Annie McKee, a senior fellow at the University of Pennsylvania, this 25-question quiz focuses on core competencies. Complete the quiz to learn more about your emotional intelligence.

   https://hbr.org/2015/06/quiz-yourself-do-you-lead-with-emotional-intelligence

3. **Are You Fluent in Body Language?** This 10-multiple-choice-question quiz from the Guardian newspaper in the United Kingdom helps you discover how to read non-verbal signs and communicate non-verbally in business relationships.

   www.theguardian.com/small-business-network/2016/mar/04/quiz-fluent-body-language-business-success-relationships

4. **Body Language Activities.** These exercises are designed to help you tune in to the subtleties of body language. Along with warm-up exercises, you will find activities that involve mirroring the body language of others.

   http://truecenterpublishing.com/tcp/bodylang.html

5. **Active-Listening Skills Quiz.** This online quiz presents 14 statements to help you assess your active-listening skills.

   www.mindtools.com/pages/article/listening-quiz.htm

6. **Active-Listening Games and Exercises.** Test Quest: Active Listening is a web page maintained by Northeastern Educational Television of Ohio. On it, you will find quick-reference listening tips as well as links to online listening games and exercises.

   http://westernreservepublicmedia.org/testquest/listen.htm

7. **The Business Culture in Other Countries.** Select a region and then a country from the menus on the Centre for Intercultural Learning website. Note the political, economic, and cultural considerations for doing business in that country.

   www.intercultures.ca/cil-cai/countryinsights-apercuspays-eng.asp

8. **Cultural Differences in Professional Communication.** Watch international business professor Erin Meyer's presentation "How Cultural Differences Affect Business." What did Meyer learn from her experiences in Japan? How could you apply what she learned more broadly to other intercultural business settings?

   www.youtube.com/watch?v=zQvqDv4vbEg

9. **Cultural Stereotypes in Fashion Marketing: The Case of Dolce & Gabbana.** In November 2018, the luxury fashion house Dolce & Gabbana faced accusations of racism and a backlash for promoting cultural stereotypes in a video ad campaign. The outrage, which D&G sparked by depicting a Chinese model struggling to eat Italian food with a pair of chopsticks, intensified when racist messages from brand co-founder Stefano Gabbana were leaked on Instagram (which he later claimed were the result of a hacking). Soon the brand was shunned by Chinese celebrities, the label was dropped by online Chinese retailers and social-media engagement dropped by 98 per cent. An apology by the co-founders (see the video below) did little to undo the damage. Watch the video and the apology, identify the missteps, and suggest how they could be remedied.

www.youtube.com/watch?time_continue=2&v=Jfzy-_jDyeo

www.youtube.com/watch?time_continue=4&v=7Ih62lTKicg

3 Getting Started: Planning, Writing, and Revising Business Messages

Chapter Preview

This chapter covers the steps involved in planning, producing, and refining business messages. You'll learn how to get ready to write focused, purposeful messages that respond to both the needs of your readers and the specifics of a situation. You'll be introduced to strategies to help you overcome writer's block, organize facts and ideas, and find the best way to transmit your message. You'll also learn best practices for both collaborative writing projects and providing feedback to peers.

Learning Objectives

1. Recognize the four key concepts of the writing process.
2. Consider contextual factors and genre differences when you write.
3. Identify the steps in the writing process.
4. Plan a message according to its purpose, scope, audience, medium or channel, design, and content.
5. Use prewriting techniques to generate content and gather ideas.
6. Describe types of detail and narrative used in business messages.
7. Organize business documents with informal and formal outlines.
8. Apply strategies for overcoming writer's block and writing under pressure.
9. Employ guidelines for revising and editing your messages and critiquing others'.
10. Use methods for effective group communication, including collaborative writing.

Case Study

Pressmaster/Shutterstock.com

Employers consistently look for strong communication skills—including the ability to prepare effective written materials—when hiring and promoting employees.

Most people know a good letter, report, or e-mail message when they read one, but saying what makes it work or writing one themselves can be a different story. Getting the words onto the page takes skill, planning, and problem-solving. Any message is, after all, a structure of logical relationships. Merging words, sentences, and paragraphs into a comprehensible and focused statement that achieves its goals and meets the needs of readers demands serious thought. These days, the use of computer-equipped workstations and mobile devices means business professionals assume greater responsibility for their messaging and for writing they do collaboratively in online shared environments.

A Conference Board of Canada study reported that 30 per cent of employers rated new workforce entrants with a four-year degree as deficient in written communication.[1] This deficiency can affect both an employee's and an organization's success. For Elizabeth Short, a major events and show manager for some of the world's best-known brands, "one ill-conceived e-mail can spell disaster for contract negotiations, equipment orders or client expectations."[2] Organizational and communication skills, as well as attention to detail, are crucial in Short's business. Indeed, in many businesses taking a casual approach can have unintended side effects, such as appearing unprofessional and inexperienced. Effective communication skills in fact ranked with leadership skills as the most important competencies identified by 845 business executives in a national management education survey published by Leger Marketing in association with the Schulich School of Business and other Canadian business schools.[3]

The Communications Policy of the Government of Canada is a good place to look for the qualities and practices of effective communication. This document generally applies to all types of professional communication and to the multiple considerations of the writing process—providing timely and accurate information, considering readers' concerns, working collaboratively—that we will explore in this chapter.

Writing in Context: Four Key Concepts

From first considerations to the confidence earned by knowing how to communicate in many forms and in meaningful ways, understanding the following concepts can help you develop targeted writing plans, become a stronger writer, and better reflect on the practice of writing.

Contextual Factors

Communication never takes place in a vacuum. It is embedded in and emerges in response to specific situations and is linked to what members of an organization must feel, know, or believe in order to accomplish their goals.[4] Though much writing in the workplace is done independently, writing overall involves and shapes social interactions. Power conflicts, collaborations, and the give-and-take of negotiations can therefore be expected.[5] **Contextual factors** such as the writing situation, an organization's procedures, and the document's readers influence the writer's decisions at every step.[6] Writing theorists Lisa Ede and Andrea Lunsford describe writing as "socially constructed."[7] In other words, it is the product or by-product of human choices. Writing effectively is thus a matter of making logical and strategic choices in a given situation.

> **contextual factors** Elements of a writing task, such as the situation, the organization's procedures, and the readers, that influence the writer's choices.

Genre and Register

Genres are agreed-upon forms of writing that develop in response to recurrent situations. For instance, the resumé, with its distinctive formatting, categories of information, and conciseness, was an answer to applicants' and employers' needs in the job-search and hiring process.[8] Developed and made coherent over time, genres tend to differ in format (the visual or spatial design of the document) and structure (the arrangement of topics). Genres allow things to get done. They are tools used in certain situations that let users act purposefully in a particular activity.[9] Learning about business genres and the situations in which each one applies is an important step in managing the challenges of workplace writing.

> **genres** The agreed-upon forms of writing that develop in response to recurrent situations and that allow users to act purposefully in a particular activity.

   Register refers to the level of formality used for a specific purpose and social setting. A register can be formal, casual, or a mix of both.

> **register** The level of formality gauged to a specific purpose and social setting.

- **Formal register.** A board of directors' or annual general meeting typically calls for a formal register. This means using complete sentences, technical or academic vocabulary, and no slang or contractions. For example, *Unprecedented growth of 27 per cent realized in the fourth quarter. By any measure, this was a spectacular finish to the fiscal year.*
- **Casual register.** Messages exchanged among friends typically call for a casual register. Greater intimacy and reduced social distance leads to informal conversations full of colloquialisms and slang. For example, *Hey, talk about revenue. 27 per cent in Q4. We're smokin' this year! Way to go!*

Chapter 4 provides further details on how to use the right register for your message.

Discourse Communities

No matter what position, responsibilities, or profile you have in your organization, you start gaining expertise as part of one or more "discourse communities" the moment you write or speak on the job. A **discourse community** is a group of communicators who share a goal or an interest in adopting a way of participating in a public discussion.[10] These ways, known as discursive practices, involve using particular genres, registers, and terminology. Depending on your career path, you will find yourself part of many discourse communities of varying size and specialization. For example, you might be a contributor to a corporate blog, an editor of a medical journal, or part of a group of municipal government representatives working to establish green-living guidelines. Workplace practitioners may belong to several discourse communities at the same time, sometimes requiring them to write in many different ways as part of a day's work. According to genre theorist John Swales, discourse communities have six defining characteristics:

- communal interest and a common public goal
- a forum or means for participation and intercommunication between members (e.g., meetings, e-mails, texts, and blog postings)
- exchange of information and feedback
- genre development (based on group expectations about the appropriateness of topics and how elements of the genre are placed and what function they serve)
- specialized terminology (e.g., community-specific abbreviations, acronyms, and in-jokes)
- expertise (a good ratio of experts to novices ensures members can become experts on content and discourse)[11]

iStock.com/IPGGutenbergUKLtd

Every profession involves its own set of contextual factors, genres, and discourse communities. For example, a judge writes case decisions, a teacher completes lesson plans, and an industrial worker fills out work orders, invoices, and union forms.

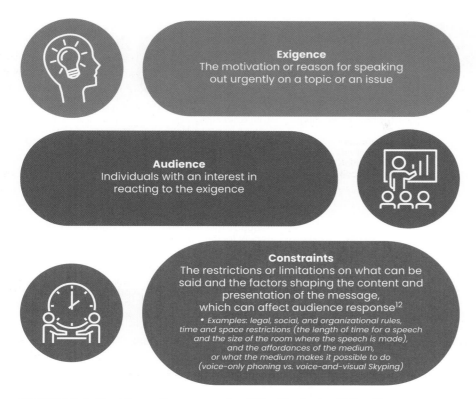

FIGURE 3.1 The Three Components of the Rhetorical Situation

Rhetorical Situations

Rhetoric has many meanings, but at its most basic level it describes the effective use of language to achieve certain, often persuasive, goals. Rhetoric can also refer to an awareness of the choices made in writing. Writing to change opinions, attitudes, or behaviours requires special thought to what theorist Lloyd Bitzer has called "the rhetorical situation," or the circumstances in which individuals communicate. There are three components of the rhetorical situation—**exigence**, **audience**, and **constraints** (Figure 3.1).

Being able to analyze a rhetorical situation can make your writing stronger, more organized, and more reader-friendly.

Not all situations are rhetorical, however. For instance, natural phenomena, such as droughts or storms, are not rhetorical situations because they cannot be changed or prevented through rhetoric. But what can be altered is the human response to or preparation for such disasters. A rhetorical situation, then, could be an insurance agent writing a letter to remind and convince a client to renew a policy before it expires.

Steps in the Writing Process

The most reliable route to a successful finished product is a process for generating, organizing, and translating ideas into text. This process involves several overlapping parts or stages that can be repeated multiple times (Figure 3.2).

Prewriting	Organizing and Outlining	Drafting	Revising	Editing and Proofreading
Assessing the purpose, audience, and most appropriate channel for the communication.	Mapping out the most strategic and logical arrangement of ideas and details.	Writing the actual message by choosing the precise wording, the style, and the organization that delivers information most strategically.	The process of reading over and reassessing your draft with a critical eye to ensure its information, wording, sentences, paragraph structure, audience focus, organization, and layout or design make sense and come together to form a clear, concise, and readable message that is right for the context and accomplishes your goals. After this stage, your draft will begin to resemble the final product.	A last chance for improving the look and sound (or "tone") of your draft, these steps usually involve more than just getting rid of mistakes in spelling, punctuation, and mechanics. In this stage, you evaluate your revised draft from your readers' point of view, making sure that it is complete, coherent, accurate, consistent, concise, well-organized, properly formatted, and professional in its appearance.

FIGURE 3.2 The Five Overlapping Steps of the Writing Process

These steps are generally thought of as recursive rather than as part of a locked-in system. That is, writers are free to return to and repeat an earlier stage at any point. In revising, for example, a writer may find the need to brainstorm additional content or re-think their readers' needs. Leaving out any of these steps or taking too many shortcuts can lead to miscommunication that causes misunderstandings and yields poor results.

Making this five-step process part of your regular writing routine can simplify communication tasks and reduce the time it takes to complete them. After all, there is more to writing than just keying in a document or jotting down whatever crosses your mind. While all writing involves the making of decisions, effective writing involves the making of *informed* decisions. It also requires giving serious thought to how your document will be used and what changes might result from it. Thinking ahead allows you to catch problems before they become insurmountable and to size up the context in which your communication will be received. This extra effort will ensure that your communication is more likely to have an impact and accomplish what it is meant to do. Reviewing what you have written enables you to check that your communication meets requirements, maintains the standards of professionalism demanded by you and your organization, and doesn't include mistakes that could cause problems for others. Perhaps the best part of learning this process is that the skills you acquire can be applied to other forms of communication, such as oral presentations and deliverables (see Chapter 13).

The Importance of Message Planning

In writing a document or making a presentation, you usually have only one chance to get your message across. There are no chances to correct mistakes or misunderstandings, no opportunities to "get it right" the second time. Planning and preparation are forms of risk prevention—your best insurance against miscommunication. Planning contributes to business communication that is purpose-driven, audience-focused, and concise (Figure 3.3).

As you begin to plan your document, create a rough schedule that indicates how much time you expect to spend on each stage of the writing process. Set aside roughly half of the time you have for planning—prewriting, organizing, and outlining—and be sure to leave enough time at the end for editing and proofreading.

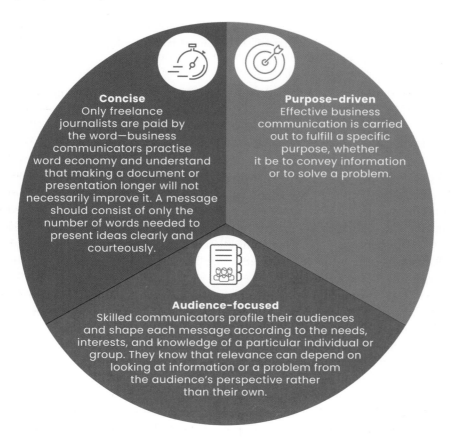

FIGURE 3.3 **Purpose-Driven, Audience-Focused, and Concise Business Communciation**

As you estimate how long it will take you to complete each stage of the writing process, plan to devote roughly half of the time you have to planning (prewriting, organizing, and outlining). Planning your message will save you time later when you draft and revise your work.

Prewriting

The longer and more complex a message, the more that can be gained from proper preparation and planning. Thinking a message through is the best thing you can do to simplify the communication process. Thinking critically about your subject, the reason for your communication, and the intended audience brings the greatest benefits to written correspondence and reports, but it also applies to any sizable oral presentation. **Prewriting** involves analyzing the writing task—its purpose, scope, audience, context, channel, and other details—before you start writing. Each time you write, take a few seconds to analyze the context in which your message will be received:

prewriting The process of gathering ideas and establishing the purpose, scope, audience, channel, and other details for a message.

- Identify the primary purpose of the document.
- Estimate the scope of the subject you must cover.
- Determine your audience's needs.
- Select the medium or channel that is most appropriate for your message.
- Choose the most effective design or layout.
- Collect the information you plan to exchange.
- Develop supporting points (evidence and examples).
- Craft a story or stories that will help you get your message across and appeal to your audience's needs.

Doing these things will help you adapt your message to the situation and tailor it to readers' needs.

Purpose

purpose Your reason for communicating and the objectives your message is meant to achieve.

Business communication is purposeful and results-oriented. For every rhetorical situation, including any time you write, speak, or present data in a visual form, you must first understand your **purpose**—your reason for communicating and the objectives your message is meant to achieve. Once your purpose is clear, you will have an easier time organizing and composing your message as well as shaping how people will receive it. Forgetting the purpose for your communication increases the chance that a message will fail. For example, the writer of a claim letter may describe poor service or a faulty product but forget to ask for an adjustment.

Most business communication has only one of two broad purposes: to inform (the most common purpose) or to persuade. Commonly, messages have multiple purposes—a primary and a secondary. An e-mail message informing customers of a new store location, for example, can also be used to convey goodwill and encourage future business. In business and organizations, people communicate with each other for one or more of several reasons (Figure 3.4).

In defining the reason for writing or speaking, consider what you want your receivers to gain from your message and what their purposes for reading or listening may be (for instance, to receive instruction or notice or to evaluate). How will they use the information? Is there a particular result (e.g., a general response, a specific action, a change in attitude,

FIGURE 3.4 **Reasons People Communicate at Work**

approval for an initiative, or a decision) you are seeking from your audience? Keep these things in mind when you define the purpose of your message.

Scope

Any form of communication comes with constraints, or the limitations placed on you as the sender of the message. These constraints may be related to organizational norms and expectations, time, the physical environment, or the technologies you're using to compose a message.

Scope refers to the expected breadth and depth of detail in a document relative to the subject it covers. Understanding the scope of your message can help you weed out irrelevancies that can bore receivers and bury important information. Having a clear sense of the scope of your message can also help you avoid covering too many ideas or using too much detail. After all, why write a four-paragraph e-mail when what the receiver really expects is a few compact but informative sentences? Too little detail, on the other hand, can make for a trivial or pointless message. Determining the scope of your message makes the writing task more manageable and the resulting message more responsive to receivers' needs. Here are some tips on achieving the right scope:

scope The depth or breadth of a document's coverage.

- Limit your scope as much as possible while maintaining a balance between the number of ideas or main points you present and the amount of detail and number of supporting points you provide for them. In general, the more ideas you include, the less receivers will expect you to write about each one.[13]

- Familiarize yourself with the level of detail that is normally considered acceptable for similar documents or deliverables in your workplace.
- Carefully follow through on instructions and be mindful of corporate and industry standards while taking into account the receiver's expectations about length, format, and visual elements.
- Consider the ethical dimensions of your message and confine yourself to information you can legally disclose or to which you legally have access.
- Keep the scalability of messages in mind; for example, you may be asked to write a short investigative report for now, but that report could form the basis of a more detailed recommendation report later on.
- Use overview or preview statements, when needed, to prepare receivers for the level of detail to expect, and use headings to segment your document and make it more navigable.

Changing technological environments have shifted standards for the scope of certain types of documents and deliverables. For example, content marketers must now consider mobile e-mail approaches, such as scalable or responsive design, to best deliver impactful content with mobile-friendly layouts. Scope, now more than ever, has design implications.

Audience Profile

audience The receivers and decoders of a message.

Audience refers to the receivers and decoders of a message. Acts of communication are performed with an audience in mind, and we design our messages in order to connect with them. In business today, it is common to communicate with people you may never meet face to face and about whom you can only make a series of informed assumptions. Even so, it is important to focus your message by thinking about your audience beforehand and evaluating their needs within the context of their organizational culture (what they do and where they work) and cultural environment (what their backgrounds are). No other single factor can have such an impact on the success of written or oral communication as giving serious thought to an audience and its needs and resources in the context of the rhetorical situation.[14] Even in routine communication, audience analysis is essential because it informs other decisions you make as you create your document, including your choice of channel, design, content, word choice, and tone.

According to Corinne LaBossiere, editor and writer at Toronto-based CGL Communications, "Visualizing who you're writing to will give you a clearer idea of what information to include and what language and tone to use. . . . When it's a group of people, visualize a person who best represents this audience."[15] Speakers have the advantage of having their audience right in front of them, but writers have to "construct" their audiences based on what they know or assume to be true about them. While you should guard against false assumptions, you can make a few educated guesses based on your experiences with people who fit into your target audience, and based on your knowledge of the professional positions and responsibilities your audience members are likely to have. Applying this analysis and adapting your message to your audience can influence how a message is received and increase its chances for success, especially if you are able to put yourself in the receiver's place and see beyond your own perspective. In fact, knowledge of an audience's needs, beliefs, expectations, and attitudes is essential to successful writing.[16] An audience-focused message has immediate and unmistakable relevance. It demonstrates that a message has been tailor-made and is responsive to an audience's needs.

iStock.com/monkeybusinessimages

As you write, keep in mind your target audience. Thinking about their needs, beliefs, expectations, and attitudes will help you decide what information to include, what channel to use, and what tone to apply to get your message across most effectively.

Audience analysis and adaptation is sometimes done unconsciously, almost out of habit, but in other cases it may require serious consideration to determine what your receiver is like. Asking the following questions may help:

> **audience analysis and adaptation** The process of assessing the needs and knowledge of readers and listeners and adapting messages accordingly.

1. **What are the receiver's responsibilities and position?** Understanding the receiver's responsibilities will help you determine how the information you pass on will be used. Also ask yourself if you are communicating with a superior (for instance, a supervisor), a subordinate, or a co-worker. Considering the receiver's position relative to your own can help you select the appropriate level of formality and cultivate a tone that balances deference and authority. A message to a long-time business associate may be more easy-going and familiar in its tone and language, but using the same style in a memo to your supervisor may risk offence through the lack of respect it conveys.

2. **What are the receiver's attitudes, interests, and questions?** Think about the level of importance the receiver will assign to the message. A lack of interest on the receiver's part may require you to compensate by giving additional emphasis to key points, highlighting the relevance in a subject line, or making the action the receiver is supposed to take easier to understand. Shaping a message to the receiver's needs can also involve anticipating the questions that the person might ask.

3. **What is your experience with the receiver?** Based on personal or professional experience you or your colleagues may have had with the receiver, you can predict possible areas of need or conflict that you should take into account when shaping your message. Consider the situational and organizational influences on your receiver. When you must communicate with someone who views you or

your organization negatively, it may require extra effort on your part—and careful control of tone and emphasis—not to let reciprocal hostility or defensiveness interfere with your ability to get the message across tactfully and professionally.

4. **How much does the receiver know about the subject?** The reader's level of knowledge will determine the amount and type of detail, background, and explanation that you should include in the message. Estimating exactly what to include can be difficult, as it carries the risk of patronizing, confusing, or annoying the receiver. Receivers bring differing levels of knowledge and understanding to a given subject, depending on whether they are laypersons, managers, or experts. Refrain from telling receivers with technical expertise or specialized knowledge too much of what they already know (for example, don't define key terms they use daily). The same applies to managers, who may have a low tolerance for technical details but a general concern for findings and recommendations. On the other hand, avoid overestimating the knowledge receivers may have and failing to define key terms or concepts or neglecting to interpret specialized information they will need to follow instructions. Build on the knowledge the receiver may already have by linking it with new facts.

5. **What is the receiver's likely response?** Anticipate what the receiver's reaction to your message will be—neutral, receptive, or resistant. If the receiver is unlikely to agree with you, be prepared to use persuasive strategies or structure your message according to an indirect pattern that presents an explanation before the main message.

6. **What words define your relationship with the receiver?** Be deliberate in your choice of pronouns (e.g., *I*, *you*, *we*), as these words can define or change your relationship with the receiver. Pronouns can also make a significant difference to your tone. Consider the point of view that represents the most effective way of addressing or appealing to the receiver.

7. **Is there more than one receiver?** Receivers with whom you must communicate to achieve your purpose are your **primary audience**. Primary audiences are key decision-makers, usually managers, team members, or clients. Anyone else who may, indirectly, happen to read or listen to your message forms your **secondary audience**. Secondary audiences include

> **primary audience** The intended receiver of a message; the person or persons who will use or act on a message's information.
>
> **secondary audience** Anyone other than the primary audience who will receive a message and be affected by the action or decision it calls for.

- employees who need to know how changes brought about by managerial decisions will affect them
- people removed from or without authority to make final decisions but with some influence over or input into them
- gatekeepers (individuals, institutions, or organizations) who may control the flow of information, decide what information will go forward, and inevitably regulate knowledge and influence people's understanding of what is happening around them

Because electronic messages can be forwarded and documents can be called as evidence in legal cases, there is no way to know for certain where the messages you send may end up. For this reason, it makes good sense to uphold ethical and legal standards in all communication.

8. **Do you need to adapt your message for an international receiver?** Consider what you need to take into account about the receiver's background, environment, and beliefs.

9. **Does the receiver have particular expectations?** The receiver may intend to use the document in a particular way, which will influence his or her expectations about the document's length and form. Consider how and for what purpose the receiver will use the document and what the receiver must be able to do, decide, or understand after reading it. Give thought to how the receiver will learn from or interact with the text or how it can be used in problem-solving. Adjusting sentence length, grouping information, changing the organization and level of detail, adding or omitting information, inserting headings, strengthening transitions, and amending word choices are all options for making your document more user-friendly.

To make the task of answering these questions easier, imagine your readers sitting across from you as you write. Performing audience analysis can help you define the **reader benefits** of an informative and/or persuasive message by uncovering what will motivate readers.

Going beyond profiling an audience to fostering audience affinity is a growing focus in areas such as social media marketing and fundraising. Fostering affinity encourages audience members to identify with a group (e.g., fans, customers, subscribers, donors), which makes it more likely that they will like or buy a product or support a cause. More generally, an audience's perception of you and your organization influences its receptiveness to your message and willingness to accept and act on information. **Credibility** is the root of strong professional relationships and the core of professional identity and organizational image. Your credibility is a measure of how much you are viewed as believable, based on your professional competence, ethical character, and capacity to care for others.

Credibility is something you must build with new audiences—people who don't know you. Once established, credibility must continue to be maintained, as it can keep relationships with audiences positive. Mistrust, on the other hand, breeds uncertainty, and where there is uncertainty communication often fails. Credibility can help you be influential, an important skill.

Knowing how to reach and hold a specific audience is vital for today's organizations on many different levels, including marketing. Content marketing, for example, is "all about your audience."[17] Audiences in the world of social media have become particularly valuable targets for marketers. Attracting and engaging the right audience on digital platforms where competition for attention is high is fundamental to innovative marketing strategies such as influencer marketing, where visibility for a product or service comes from the rapport and trust followers already have for a niche blogger or celebrity. The question isn't just who an audience is but where they are and how to listen to them.[18] Savvy marketers who specialize in writing persuasive messages know the importance of researching online behaviour and understanding where audiences and potential consumers for their products and services spend their time online.

The power of social media for businesses and organizations is, according to Robin Grant of the social media agency We Are Social, the "ability to build an audience over time that you speak to on an ongoing basis."[19] More broadly, audience is an important dimension of all forms of professional communication.

Medium or Channel

The **medium** or **channel** is the vehicle of transmission for a message. Given that several channels may often suit your needs, choosing the best one depends on its appropriateness to both your purpose and the context—for example, to solve a problem, collaborate,

reader benefits The advantages the reader stands to gain by complying with what the writer is proposing (e.g., by following a policy, endorsing an idea, or using a service).

credibility The extent to which you are viewed as believable, based on your competence, ethical character, and caring for others.

medium or **channel** The physical means by which a message is transmitted.

Chinnapong/Shutterstock.com

Choosing the best channel for a specific message requires you to consider the reach and capabilities of the channel, the specifics of the situation, your purpose in communicating, the content of your message, and the preferences of your audience.

pass on information, or establish rapport. It also has to do with how well you understand the receiver's preferences and what technological constraints will enable you to communicate. You have a choice of traditional channels such as memos and letters, face-to-face meetings, and telephone calls as well as electronic and digital media such as e-mail, voicemail, text messaging, and video conferencing. Organizations may differ in their adoption of certain types of channels, particularly as new technologies are introduced to the marketplace and implemented for specific purposes, so it's always best to familiarize yourself with your company's practices before choosing a channel.

Digital media offers communicators a particularly diverse array of options for reaching an audience. Video-sharing platforms such as YouTube offer communicators the ability to convey complex information to a wide audience in a visually and audibly stimulating way. Evolving 360-video and VR (virtual reality) platforms provide for an immersive experience that encourages audience members to connect with and develop an affinity for content providers.[20]

To assess which channel is best for your purpose, consider the following factors:

- **Accuracy.** Is the channel susceptible to technical difficulties, or can you count on its reliability? Think back to your most recent bad cellphone connection for an example of how misunderstandings can result from channel barriers.
- **Speed.** Does the message have to reach someone quickly? Telephone, text message, e-mail, and voicemail are good options in time-sensitive situations.
- **Cost.** You should be able to justify the cost of transmitting a message according to its importance and urgency.
- **Need for a permanent record.** Instructions, policies, and legally binding agreements must be recorded and archived for future reference.

- **Detail.** If your message is complex or highly detailed, you should avoid channels such as telephone or voicemail, which cannot accommodate a high level of detail or precise wording. Written communication is better for this purpose.
- **Importance.** Certain channels project more authority and command more respect than others do. For an initial contact, a formal business letter may communicate a company's professionalism in a way that an e-mail does not.
- **Privacy.** Not all channels deliver the same degree of privacy or security, so consider a channel's vulnerabilities to keep your data safe. E-mail, for example, is an unsuitable means to transmit confidential information or private messages.
- **Channel capacity and constraints.** Whether by design or convention, the quantity of information a channel allows you to transmit can be restrictive. Instant Messaging (IM), for example, isn't suited to highly detailed messages.
- **Audience size and location.** Channels such as e-mail are effective for communicating with a large, dispersed audience. When travel is impractical, video conferencing can bring together people who are spread out geographically and allow them to both see and hear one another.
- **Formality.** Consider your relationship to the receiver and your purpose when choosing a channel.
- **Immediacy of feedback.** Some channels, such as the telephone or a face-to-face conversation, allow for immediate feedback. Other channels, such as voicemail, a hard-copy letter, or e-mail, feedback will be delayed, so be prepared to wait for it.
- **Level of control over the message.** If you must word your message carefully, use hard-copy letters, e-mails, and voicemails. Telephone and face-to-face conversations require you to think on your feet.
- **Richness.** **Richness** refers to the quantity of different types of cues—verbal and visual—from which meaning can be inferred. A rich medium is better for building rapport. If you have to deliver bad news, the tone of voice and facial expressions you use in a face-to-face conversation can convey an empathy and sensitivity that cannot be so easily expressed in an e-mail message.
- **Organizational preferences.** Learn your employer's policies as soon as you can and follow them closely.

richness The quality of containing plentiful types of cues by which meaning can be derived from a message.

The medium or channel you choose can influence how your message is interpreted. Each channel has its own advantages and drawbacks, and each is better suited to certain purposes than to others (see Table 3.1).

Design or Layout

Well-designed messages create positive impressions of the sender and the sender's organization. An effective design conveys professionalism, priming receivers, even before they read the document, to be more receptive to the message. On the other hand, an ineffective design—for example, one that contains inconsistent formatting or poor use of space—may lead receivers to question the sender's competency or intentions. Designs that make a good impression have

- an uncomplicated appearance, with clean lines, an appropriate amount of open space, and no unnecessary decorative elements
- consistent formatting and alignment of headings, columns, paragraphs, lists, borders, and other components

- wide, even margins
- consistent line spacing
- fonts that are easy to read and consistent in size, treatment, and colour
- sufficient contrast between text colour and background colour
- headings that are well-worded and well-placed
- adequate labels, appropriate sizes, and a clear purpose for all tables, photos, illustrations, and other visuals

TABLE 3.1 Communication Channels and Their Best Uses

CHANNEL	BEST USES
Report or proposal	Delivering extensive data internally or externally
Letter on company stationery	Initial contacts with customers, suppliers, and outside associates, or when you need a written record of subsequent correspondence with them
Memos	Internal communication; when you need a written record to issue reminders, outline policies, explain procedures, or gather information
E-mail	Less formal communication replacing letters and memos, when you need fast delivery and response (e.g., to ask for feedback, solicit opinions, start discussions, or collect data) and/or you need to send a digital file; useful for communicating with large, decentralized groups; not appropriate for sending private or emotionally charged information
An organization's intranet	Sharing important documents and information that employees will need to reference repeatedly (e.g., letter templates, HR policies) but are not intended for the public
Telephone call	Gathering or sharing information quickly, or for negotiating and clarifying contracts when it is impossible to meet in person; for meeting with three or more participants via conference call as a less expensive alternative to a face-to-face meeting
Voicemail message	Brief, uncomplicated messages—a question, an answer, a request, or a confirmation—to which the receiver can respond when it is convenient
Social media	Supporting and facilitating participation, interaction, engagement, and awareness; for reaching dispersed audiences; for linking to online content and simultaneously sharing content; useful for building communities, learning about audiences, and increasing traffic to websites
Messaging and chatting	Brief messages containing time-critical or routine information; useful for obtaining answers to questions, confirming purchases, or offering customer service support
Face-to-face meeting	Establishing initial contact and rapport with clients, customers, and associates; for negotiating, brainstorming, problem-solving, or any other group communication where consensus is required
Face-to-face conversation	Delivering a personal message or negative news, or for communicating persuasively
Video conferencing, videotelephony, and video chatting (e.g., Skype)	Meeting when travel is impractical and participants are dispersed; useful when participants need to both see and hear each other
Blogging	Providing news and announcements, sharing knowledge, and positioning yourself as an expert to a broad audience; useful for building communities, increasing web traffic, and developing influential relationships
Podcasting	Distributing audio content; reaching listeners on the move; useful for providing valuable information, motivation, entertainment, and sometimes business training
Photographs, videos, graphics, and other visuals	Conveying complex information at a glance

Formatting should facilitate the receiver's understanding of a message, not act as a barrier to comprehension. It should draw the receiver's eyes to the meaningful elements and indicate the sequence in which the material should be processed.

Content Generation

Good content contributes to effective communication. Collecting all the information you need before you start to write, whether by researching data or simply generating ideas, is essential. Keep in mind that the facts you gather should warrant your efforts and your readers' attention. Formal research methods, required for formal reports and presentations, are detailed in Chapter 12. Many types of business messages (e.g., routine memos and e-mails) require only informal idea-generation strategies, such as the following:

1. **Brainstorming.** **Brainstorming** is a free-association exercise that stimulates creative thinking, unlocks ideas, and reveals hidden connections. If you reached a point of stalemate in planning your document, brainstorming can put a fresh perspective on a stubborn topic. Start with a blank computer screen or sheet of paper and write down your topic. Set aside ten uninterrupted minutes and, while suspending judgement about how good or bad your ideas are and without stopping, jot down any thoughts that come to mind. When the ten minutes have elapsed, sort through and analyze what you have recorded, saving only your best ideas and discarding the rest. If a single attempt doesn't yield enough ideas, repeat the process. Next, group the items that are related or arrange them in logical order according to the purpose of your document and the needs of your reader. This process will yield a preliminary outline. A further brainstorming session can help you fill in any omissions and correct any weaknesses. For an example of brainstorming, see Figure 3.5.

   brainstorming A method of generating content by listing ideas as they come to mind.

• overstuffed inboxes	• poorly written messages
• shouting	• mistakes in grammar, spelling, and punctuation
• flaming (angry messages)	• rambling, poorly formatted messages
• rampant cc-ing of bosses and colleagues	• incorrect address
• poorly written messages	• overly telegraphic style
• overly telegraphic style	• misleading/inaccurate subject lines
• grammar mistakes	• overstuffed inboxes
• spam	• rampant cc-ing of bosses and colleagues
• lack of e-mail protocol	• spam
• inappropriate and/or offensive messages	• unnecessary/irrelevant messages
• unnecessary/irrelevant messages	• lack of e-mail protocol
• rambling messages	• shouting
• misleading/inaccurate subject lines	• flaming (angry messages)
• incorrectly addressed messages	• inappropriate and/or offensive messages
• lack of formatting	
• incomplete information	

FIGURE 3.5 A Brainstorming Example on the Topic of Problems with Office E-mail | The initial list of ideas (left) is refined into a list grouped in a logical order (right).

2. **Mapping or clustering. Mapping**, also known as **clustering**, is a form of brain-storming that involves visualizing a topic and its related classifications and sub-topics. A cluster diagram is useful for defining the relationship between ideas. Start with a fresh sheet of paper and put a keyword that best characterizes your topic in a circle at the centre of the page. Draw lines, like spokes radiating from the hub of a wheel, to connect your topic word with related ideas. Circle each new idea you generate and allow each subtopic to stimulate additional subtopics. Con-tinue the process, without stopping to critique yourself, until you have exhausted your ideas. The resulting map will show clusters and subclusters of ideas grouped around the central concept. Figure 3.6 provides an example of mapping.

3. **Asking questions.** The five *Ws*—*who*, *what*, *why*, *when*, and *where*—not to mention *how*, are productive **journalistic questions** to ask about your topic and its major ideas, especially if you intend to write a clear and compelling document.

Information can be gathered in-house, from digital media, and from traditional sources. Although research strategies for complex documents, such as reports, are ex-plored in Chapter 12, not every project or message requires formal research. In fact, some simple strategies for locating and assembling information may be all you need.

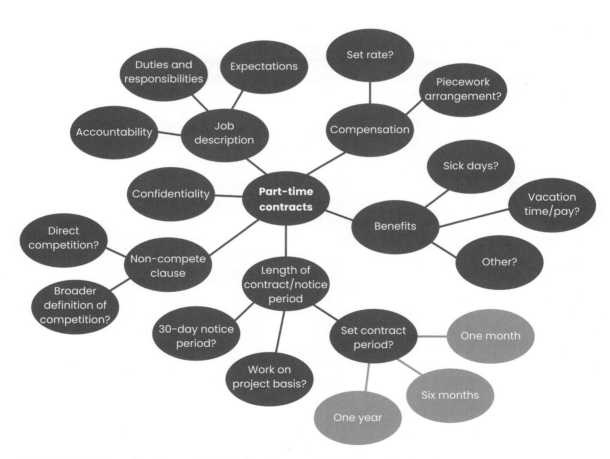

FIGURE 3.6 Mapping Example: Defining Terms of Part-Time Contracts

- **In-house.** Archived company records, documents, and files such as financial statements, business and marketing plans, project proposals, budgets, annual reports, sales and marketing reports and projections, investigation and project reports, recorded presentations, customer surveys, newsletters, and press releases may contain information pertinent to your message or document. Such documents are often accessible in digital form through a company's intranet or knowledge management system (KMS), a repository for "living information inside the organization" to which everyone in an organization has access.[21]

- **Digital (new) media.** A generation ago, the Internet revolutionized how people find information. Since then, the changing digital landscape of the information age has continued to alter how we find, consume, and share information. Social media, apps, websites, personalized services and recommendations, blogs, podcasts, and online video can all provide information quickly, easily, and economically.

- **Traditional published sources.** More traditional resources such as published books, research studies, and statistics are also useful for capturing certain types of data. In particular, the information they provide can be helpful for understanding trends related to economic conditions, labour, imports and exports, product markets, and demographic characteristics.[22]

In some cases, you may need to conduct **market research** to find the information you need. For many businesses, market research is a crucial stage in the planning process that lays the foundation for important decisions about growth, innovation, and the pricing, placement, and promotion of products and services.[23] General market research may involve sorting through data from a third-party organization that specializes in conducting public surveys (e.g., the Conference Board of Canada or Statistics Canada). For targeted results, business can arrange surveys, questionnaires, interviews, or even focus groups for which they specify the questions and topics of discussion; larger businesses often choose to conduct such research through an external agency that provides market research services for a fee (e.g., Ipsos-Reid). While conducting this sort of targeted market research can be expensive, it is often well worth the cost.

> **market research** The process of gathering information about how people will react to current or proposed products and services.

Supporting Points: Evidence and Examples

Major points that anchor each paragraph of a message can usually be established through associative techniques such as brainstorming, **freewriting**, or mapping. Major points, however, sometimes cannot stand entirely on their own. They often require amplification or explanation—in other words, details. A product, once introduced, may need to be described to help receivers fully understand its features and benefits. Similarly, an announcement of new procedures will need to be explained so receivers will know when they go into effect, what to do, and what will change as a result. Supporting evidence and examples provide the details and context receivers need in order to grasp major points and accept or reflect on a message, act on it, or make a decision based on it. Supporting information can be provided in various formats and through various rhetorical approaches.

> **freewriting** A method of generating content based on unstructured writing and the recording of ideas as they come to mind.

- **Numerical, statistical, and factual data.** Because businesses are commercial enterprises concerned with profits, losses, and expenditures, accurate facts and figures related to expenditures, timelines, results or outcomes, projections and estimates, analyses, and terms of agreements are essential to operations and decision-making. Stakeholders need to know such things as how much time a project will take and how much it will cost.

- **Visual and graphical elements.** Charts, numerical and word tables, infographics, photos, and videos make complex data easier to understand and remember.
- **Appeals to authority.** Quoting or paraphrasing experts supports and validates claims and builds credibility, especially when the authority is well respected or the quotation comes from a properly cited scholarly journal.
- **Narratives.** In business, narratives, often with the support of statistical and numerical data, can be useful in providing detailed, chronological accounts of past events, conversations or agreements, problem investigations and resolutions, and the progress of a project. Stories can be told and transmitted textually, visually, or orally, or through a combination of media. They can be told about the past, the present, or the future, and they can go deeper into a problem to root out causes and identify potential solutions.[24]
- **Descriptions.** Business professionals are often required to describe an object, a site, a product, or a process to someone who has less experience or knowledge of it. Effective descriptions make concepts and artifacts more tangible to the audience by providing specific details about colour, dimensions, parts, materials, and functions.

Storytelling and Corporate Narrative

A story is a "series of logically and chronologically related events that are caused or experienced by actors," or people in the story.[25] Stories and the telling of them are fundamental to human experience. Stories not only convey information and promote learning but also have the power to cement social bonds, inspire, warn, and bring about change. The receiver's identification with what is being told can serve as a springboard to understanding, something that facts and statistics alone cannot always promote. Stories, after all, make information tangible and memorable.[26] Corporations and non-profits are increasingly capitalizing on this dynamic communication tool, making the ability to tell stories well a sought-after skill.[27]

In business communication, stories offer many advantages because they

- help audience members remember key details
- provide pathways to problem-solving
- show patterns and connections
- provide audience members with the feeling of having experienced an activity or a process[28]
- drive emotional engagement

To be effective, stories used in business communication should

- be fairly brief
- be believable, familiar, true, and authentic
- be told from one perspective
- focus on a problem or a dilemma
- give hope or present a positive or purposeful ending
- preserve confidentiality
- matter

- say something about who you are or what your company does
- win over the audience, issue a call to action, or close a deal[29]

According to primatologist and conservationist Jane Goodall, good stories engage their audience on an emotional level: "With storytelling you have to get to people's hearts. It's not about engaging them intellectually."[30] Stories that elicit a strong emotional response are particularly useful as fundraising tools for charitable campaigns. For example, stories that describe social problems but leave room for hope build empathy for those in need, as exemplified by the stories appearing on the website of War Child Canada (warchild.ca). Also effective for fundraising purposes are stories that make the donor the hero or involve the donor in the story,[31] as illustrated by the Movember Foundation's annual campaign that asks men to "grow and groom their moustache for 30 days to become walking, talking billboards for men's health."[32]

The emotional connection that stories help to build is also useful in telling corporate narratives and establishing brand identities. Such stories may follow one of several basic plots or represent archetypal themes; for example, they may involve

- rebirth or journeys of transformation
- the overcoming of threats or obstacles
- quests for perfection
- a progression from rags to riches—starting with nothing, ending with success
- comedy or tragedy[33]

The story of the Hudson's Bay Company is the story of Canadian heritage. Dove's story takes up the issue of "real beauty."[34] When designing campaigns, companies consider the longevity of the story of their brand—what they are, what they do, what they stand for[35]—and how well the new campaign will fit with and re-tell this story.

Keeping in mind the story you want to tell—as well as your organization's overarching corporate narrative—throughout the prewriting stage will give you a solid foundation for the next stage in the writing process: organizing and outlining.

Organizing and Outlining

Once you have gathered your material, it needs to be structured in a coherent way so readers will understand it. You can accomplish this task through **organizing and outlining**. Based on your purpose and your readers' needs, select a method of development that orders your subject from beginning to end. There are four main methods:

- **sequential development**
- **chronological development**
- **general-to-specific development**
- **cause-and-effect development**

Not all business documents require **outlines**, but those of any length, importance, or complexity do. An outline is a skeleton or framework of the document you are going to write. Preparing an outline helps to ensure your document is complete and also helps you detect errors in logic and coherence. It plots out your document from beginning to end and gives you the opportunity to experiment with the arrangement of ideas before you

organizing and outlining
The process of arranging information for clarity and impact.

sequential development A method of organization that describes the arrangement of steps in a process.

chronological development A method of organization that describes events in the order in which they occurred.

general-to-specific development A method of organization that begins with general information on a topic followed by specific details.

cause-and-effect development A method of organization that links events with the reasons for them.

outline A framework for a document, showing its divisions and elements.

commit them to the written page. Once you begin to write, the work of deciding how to organize your document will have already been done, leaving you to concentrate on tone, word choice, sentence structure, and accuracy. A short, basic topic outline, such as the one below, includes concise phrases that describe the breakdown of your topic's presentation, arranged in the order of your primary method of development.

    I.   Primary Research
   II.   Secondary Research
  III.   Research Strategies

Usually an outline breaks the topic down into three to five major categories that can then be divided into smaller segments that represent minor points and supporting evidence.

    I. Primary Research
       A. Direct observations
       B. Interview   Classification
       C. Surveys and questionnaires
       D. Social media and YouTube videos
   II. Secondary Research
       A. Books, e-books, articles, and reports
       B. Websites and web documents   Classification
       C. E-mail discussions
  III. Research Strategies
       A. Conducting library and online searches
       B. Evaluating resources   Sequential
       C. Taking notes

For more complex documents, use alphanumeric and decimal outline templates, which can be found in most word-processing software. You can find examples of these outlining systems in Chapter 11. In Chapters 6 to 9, which cover the most frequently written types of messages, you will learn basic writing patterns for receptive and unreceptive audiences—sometimes known as good-news and bad-news patterns—for business correspondence.

Drafting

drafting The preliminary writing of a document.

When you write for business, you cannot always wait for inspiration. In fact, **drafting** a message is a task best viewed as a necessary means to an end, like any other business function. Rely on good preparation to get the job done and begin by expanding your outline without worrying too much about creating a perfect copy on your first try. Remember, you can usually refine your language and make corrections later. Write continuously, not stopping once you have gained some momentum. You may want to begin with the part of the message or document that seems easiest to write. In longer documents, the introduction serves as a lens to focus the detailed information that follows. If you are writing a sizable document, such as a report, you may want to write your introduction last so it will more accurately reflect the overall content. In shorter routine messages, the opening may either reveal the primary purpose for writing or prepare the reader for the details to come. The type of content you generate depends largely on the requirements of the message and your receiver.

Overcoming Writer's Block

Eventually, even the best and most confident writer will experience **writer's block**—the temporary inability to formulate and express one's thoughts because of a lack of inspiration. The good thing about writer's block is that it usually doesn't last; it is just a short-term halt in the writing process. The bad thing about writer's block is that it can strike at any time, when you least expect it and—worst of all—when you are up against a deadline. Feeling rushed can intensify feelings of communication anxiety and turn procrastination into paralysis. The results can be missed deadlines, a breakdown in the communication process, and decreased productivity. Though potentially serious, writer's block is entirely curable and doesn't have to become chronic. Experimenting with a few simple strategies may be all you need to do to banish writer's block:

> **writer's block** A psychological state of being unable to begin or continue the process of composition out of fear or anxiety over the communication task.

1. **Start early.** Give yourself enough time to think through a writing task and complete it according to your goals. Remember that good writing is easier to produce when you are relaxed.

2. **Talk it out.** Many people may be able to articulate their thoughts more fluently in spoken as opposed to written language. Verbalizing your ideas or dictating them into a voice recorder can help you get your thoughts down in some form. Ask yourself, *What am I trying to say here?* and answer the question as directly as possible. Ease up on self-criticism—there will be time to polish and perfect your draft later. What you want to do at this stage is capture the essence of what you mean. If you work in a crowded office, you can internalize your verbalizations and make this strategy work for you in silence. Just write down your thoughts once they are fully formed.

3. **Skip around.** Don't feel you have to start at the beginning of a document and work your way through to the end. Capitalize on your inspiration by starting with the section you feel most comfortable about. Leave the section you are unsure about until you've had a chance to build your confidence.

4. **Take a break.** Obviously, if you are at work, you won't want to fritter away company time, but switching to another activity—filing, tidying up your desk, answering a telephone call, listening to voicemail—can give you the objectivity you need to return to the writing task refreshed.

5. **Practise freewriting.** Freewriting is an exercise in dedicated, non-stop writing. Basically, it involves forcing yourself to write on a particular subject for a period of ten uninterrupted minutes so that ideas can be unlocked and translated to the page. Not everything you write will be useful, but you may want to keep some parts of the draft. Repeat the process until you have accumulated enough material on which to base your document.

6. **Adopt a positive attitude to writing.** Practise writing regularly and ask colleagues and bosses for feedback. Through interaction you can learn about the corporate culture in which you are writing and determine exactly what readers expect and what certain situations demand. Think of writing as a means toward achieving your professional goals and be positive in thinking that those goals are achievable.

Writing under Pressure

Business documents are usually produced quickly in response to demands and deadlines. It can be difficult to keep up with the volume of daily messaging, let alone generate formal reports and documents on which the bottom line depends. Producing error-free, results-oriented documents in time-sensitive situations requires a cool head and a little preparation. The following process can help busy communicators cope under pressure:

1. **Allocate your time.** Consider how much time and energy you need to invest in writing your message relative to its purpose and importance. Spending an hour drafting a brief e-mail may not make sense if you have 50 more messages to write that day. Develop a mental timetable for accomplishing your writing tasks.

2. **Keep distractions to a minimum.** Tune out office banter and organize your writing area by setting out all the tools and resources you will need.

3. **Get the most from word-processing software.** Use the outline feature to brainstorm and organize an outline, then cut and paste to organize alternative ways of presenting information.

4. **Take a few seconds to plan the structure.** Every document has a beginning, a middle, and an end. Quickly select a method of development to keep your information under control (see pg. 99).

5. **Remember your reader.** Visualize your reader. Explain difficult concepts by relating them to what is familiar and already known to your reader.

6. **Go with the flow.** Start with the section of your document that is easiest to write and resist the temptation to take a break once you have momentum. Plan to reward yourself in some way—with a break or a coffee—once you have finished your task.

7. **Leave refinements for revision.** Your copy doesn't have to be perfect until it is time to send it.

Revising, Editing, and Proofreading

revising The process of reviewing and making changes in a draft document—adding, deleting, reorganizing, or substituting—to transform it into a finished document.

editing The process of checking a writing draft to ensure it conforms to standards of good English, style, and accepted business-writing practice.

proofreading A process of checking the nearly final copy of a document for errors and inconsistencies.

Revising a document involves adding, deleting, reorganizing, and replacing the words, sentences, or paragraphs of a final draft. **Editing** is the fine-tuning of the revised draft—a final correction of spelling, grammar, punctuation, and consistency problems. **Proofreading** involves reading through the nearly-final draft to catch and correct any remaining typos or formatting errors. Together, revising, editing, and proofreading represent the now-or-never phase of document production—the point at which final changes and refinements can make or break a piece of writing. Even a document that looks fine at first glance can usually do with a few last-minute adjustments, some gentle tweaking, or even some major rethinking. At this stage, you become your own impartial critic, deciding if your document measures up to the goals you set out for it, correcting potential weaknesses and spotting areas for improvement. Always keep your prewriting goals in mind so you won't be tempted to either ignore the revision process or be so hard on yourself you feel you must start over. Your goal should be to make the document better, continuing until it is satisfactory.

Before you start the revision process, take a break to ensure that you can look objectively at the document you have written. Clear your head by doing something different for a few minutes or a few hours (whatever the time frame for your document and its deadline allow for). For brief, routine letters or e-mails, you can usually carry out a quick but careful proofreading on the spot or revise onscreen as you go, checking for effective organization, appropriate style and tone, and accurate language and content.

For all other documents, especially for important external or upwardly directed communication, the revision process needs to be taken very seriously. Follow a few basic strategies:

1. **Work from a saved document or printed copy of your draft.** Print out your document. You will want to have a record of what you originally wrote in case you decide that the first version was preferable. Mark up the copy (which is best double-spaced to make room for comments) using standard proofreaders' symbols (see Figure 3.7). Alternatively, use your word-processing program's editing functions (e.g., Word's "Track Changes" feature) to mark-up, delete, and add text.

2. **Reduce your reading speed.** It is unlikely you will find any errors if you speed-read. Take your time.

3. **Look at your document from the reader's perspective.** Put pride aside and pretend you didn't author your document, remembering that it is always easier to find errors in someone else's writing. Give yourself credit when you find an error; it means you are doing your job well.

4. **Make several passes over the draft.** No matter how careful and scrupulous you are, you won't be able to spot every error or analyze every need for global revision on a single reading. Simplify the editing task by reading for one specific set of problems at a time. Use the content-organization-style (COS) method to polish your document in three stages of editing:

   a) **Content.** Focus first on editing for content. Consider whether your document is complete and clearly expresses its main points. If its purpose is persuasive, your concern is whether you are using enough of the right types of evidence to convince your reader and whether the appeal you use—one based on logic, emotion, credibility, or a combination of the three—will have the right effect on your reader.

   b) **Organization.** At this stage, organization and your document's main message are your focus. Check that the main message is clear and has a logical relationship to other parts of the document. Consider whether your document is structured in a consistent and strategic way for readability and follows the structure you established at the beginning.

   c) **Style (line editing and proofreading).** At this stage, sentence style and format are your focus. Check that the tone of your document is formal/informal enough to suit the situation, and review each sentence for correct grammar, punctuation, and a smooth and coherent style.

5. **Read your draft aloud.** Errors and awkward phrasings are detected more easily when you hear them spoken. Making a recording and playing it back is sometimes a useful method for clearing up problems with sentence structure, tone, and fogginess in documents that have to be perfect.

6. **Use spell- and grammar checkers, but respect their limitations.** Diagnostic software has great capabilities, but it may not flag every error. Sometimes, it may isolate a proper noun and suggest an incorrect spelling for it or fail to detect a misspelled technical term, so look carefully at each highlighted word and be prepared to use your own judgement. Unless your organization tells you to do otherwise, ensure that your spell-check program is set for Canadian English. If you opt for US English, be sure to use its distinctive spellings consistently. There is no substitute, however, for reading the document yourself, even if you have to do it two or three times.

Mark in Margin	Instruction	Mark in Margin	Instruction
∧	Insert	*rom*	Set in roman type
ℓ	Delete	*sp*	Correct spelling/Spell out
stet	Let stand	¶	Start paragraph
‿	Close space	run-in	No paragraph
cap	Capitalize	⊙	Insert period
lc	Make lowercase	⋏	Insert comma
ital	Italicize	ˇ/ˇ	Insert quotation marks

FIGURE 3.7 Proofreaders' Symbols

A critical read-through requires that you pay close attention to the following factors, many of which are discussed in Chapters 4 and 5 and which can be grouped into three steps:

Step One

- **Completeness.** Ensure that your document achieves its purpose and meets readers' needs. Adequate information should be provided without causing information overload. Check that essential material enables readers to take action, make a decision, or know what to do when they are finished reading the document.

Step Two

- **Structure and coherence.** The elements that make up your document should be organized logically according to the rhetorical purpose you wish to achieve. Related ideas should be linked through logic and appropriate transitional devices.

Step Three

- **Accuracy.** Verify the accuracy of the information you present. Look for inaccuracies and ensure your information is free of distortion. Compare names and numbers with their sources.
- **Conciseness.** Delete clichés and redundancies to create a lean, reader-friendly document.
- **Sentence and paragraph construction.** Look for awkward sentences. Use the active voice and replace weak verbs and noun phrases with precise, forceful verbs.
- **Consistency and format.** Check for lopsided formatting by making sure your document is balanced on the page. Look for problems with lettered items, headings, bulleted and numbered lists, capitalization, underlining, bold print, and italics.
- **Readability, word choice, and ethics.** Decide if the document's level of difficulty is appropriate for the readers. Replace vague or pretentious words with

specific and familiar ones. Keep biased language out of your document and ask yourself whether you would mind if someone other than the intended receiver read your document.

- **Grammar, spelling, and punctuation.** Check for grammar errors that can undermine the professionalism and readability of your document. Scan for spelling mistakes and punctuation errors that can make your document look sloppy.
- **Typographical errors.** Check for any inadvertent errors (e.g., transposed letters and misplaced punctuation) that may have crept into your draft.

Revision becomes easier with practice. Make the most of the constructive feedback you receive from instructors and always use it to help you evaluate the success of your communication relative to your goals. Review the advice and comments you receive and assess the types of faults and errors most common to your writing. From this assessment, devise a customized checklist you can refer to when revising and proofreading your documents. The end of Chapter 5 offers additional tips on proofreading.

Checklist

Revising, Editing, and Proofreading

Checklists and rubrics can serve as helpful guides in the final stages of producing a document. Making several passes over the document can help you focus on one specific issue at a time.

Content

Focus

- ❏ Is the purpose of the document stated unambiguously? Is it clear what the main idea is?
- ❏ Is no more than one main idea developed in each paragraph?
- ❏ Is the focus appropriate for the primary audience? Does the information satisfy the audience's needs?
- ❏ Are actions to be taken stated clearly and completely? Will the audience know what to do or think?
- ❏ If a subject line is used, does it clearly state the focus of the message?

Support

- ❏ Do supporting points relate logically to main points? Are supporting points appropriately grouped together or separated?
- ❏ Is there enough evidence to fully support claims?
- ❏ Are the types of evidence used relevant and appropriate to the writing task and situation?
- ❏ Is the evidence accurate, logical, and relevant, and is the amount of it appropriate for the scope of the document (not too much or too little)?
- ❏ Is your use of supporting evidence credible and ethical (drawn from reliable sources, properly credited, complete, not distorted or taken out of context)?

(Continued)

❑ Is the document free of factual errors?

❑ Will the audience have enough information to act on, make a decision, or follow-up by contacting you?

❑ Do visual elements (e.g., tables, figures, photographs) clearly support important points? Are they placed where they will have the greatest impact?

❑ For digital documents, are links active and have attachments uploaded properly?

Organization

❑ Does the message follow an identifiable writing pattern or approach (direct/indirect)?

❑ Is the organization strategic according to your purpose, the type of information conveyed (positive/negative/persuasive), and your relationship to the audience? Does the organization support your objectives?

❑ Does the organization of the document help the audience understand, accept, remember, and act on the information? Does it reduce resistance and help receivers be more receptive?

❑ Is the most important information easy to identify and extract?

❑ Has the information been grouped logically into paragraphs?

❑ Are sentences organized coherently? Do supporting sentences relate to topic sentences? Do transitional expressions show logical relationships between sentences? Is there a logical sequence of ideas, continuity, and flow?

❑ Is the organization of the message supported by its formatting? Is there adequate white space between paragraphs? Are multiple questions numbered, lists bulleted, and subheads inserted, if needed, to guide the audience or signpost subtopics? Is the message easy to skim?

❑ Is the layout appropriate to the type of document and the means of transmission? Does it prevent distortion?

Grammar, Spelling, Punctuation, Style, and Format

❑ Are grammar, spelling, punctuation, and typography correct? Have you looked closely for errors in grammar and style?

❑ Have you avoided unnecessary shifts in person or tense?

❑ Is your message as concise as it could be? Have you eliminated wordy constructions, fillers, and redundancies?

❑ Have you used a mix of sentence style and length (short, medium, and long)?

❑ Have you eliminated awkward constructions, mismatched pronoun references, and multiple *that*, *which*, and *who* clauses?

❑ Is the register or level of formality appropriate for the situation, audience, and channel?

❑ Is your word choice idiomatic, gender neutral and inclusive, and free from inappropriate jargon?

❑ Is the tone appropriate to the writing situation and the audience?

❑ Have you identified yourself and signed off appropriately? Are your receivers addressed appropriately? Is the document dated appropriately?

❑ Is the formatting of your message consistent with your organization's standards? Are margins, paragraph breaks, alignments, and special characters formatted correctly? Are page numbers, headers, and footers problem-free?

❑ Is the font attractive, of readable size, and consistent with company or industry standards?

❑ Are tables, figures, photographs, and other visuals clearly labelled, and have you provided source lines for them where necessary?

❑ Have copyright notices and/or references been included where necessary?

❑ For mobile messages, have you double-checked to make sure the autocorrect feature has not miscorrected a word?

Collaborative Writing

Most successful businesses rely on teamwork to bring their projects and initiatives to fruition. Teamwork, though, is possible only when a spirit of co-operation exists in the workplace and when individuals are willing to share responsibilities and decision-making. Employers screen applicants partly on the basis of their ability to work as a team. This important skill has increasing application to **collaborative writing** projects, whose size or time constraints may demand that two or more writers work together to produce a single document. A project may involve multiple areas of expertise that no single person is able to supply on their own. Responsibility for these projects doesn't rest on a solitary writer but on the ability of a group to communicate, build loyalty, reach consensus, and both accept and give criticism objectively. In North America, close to 90 per cent of business professionals engage in collaborative writing.[36] A lack of competency in this area can therefore be costly. In fact, 83 per cent of knowledge workers report losing or wasting time on document collaboration issues.[37]

collaborative writing The process of writers working together to create finished reports, proposals, and other important documents.

Political, social, and logistical challenges can interfere with the process of collaborative writing. First, collaboratively written documents generally take longer to write, revise, and edit than individual documents, partly because they require a high level of coordination. Second, participants may have different writing styles, leading to inconsistencies and the need for harmonization in the final edit, which can be time consuming—especially if participants are not clear on what is expected from them and have not agreed upon procedures for resolving disputes.[38] Finally, a lack of sensitivity and/or diplomacy, poor personal communication, and personal conflicts arising from differences in power and status can interfere with participants' receptivity to each other's ideas. This can lead to control issues and an unequal ability to add, edit, and remove text.

Understanding the pitfalls and challenges of collaborative writing before you start can help you avoid them and make the process a rewarding one, where mutual support and respect, motivation, clear goals, and timely and valuable feedback allow participants to learn from each other and produce a well-received, high-quality document.[39] Engagement, involvement, and the feeling that each writer can contribute and make a difference are key to a successful collaboration.

That said, not all collaborative writing occurs in the same way. Consultation between team members may or may not take place during planning, draft preparation, revision, or final editing.

In fact, researchers on collaborative writing in the workplace note various strategies for approaching the task (Figure 3.8).

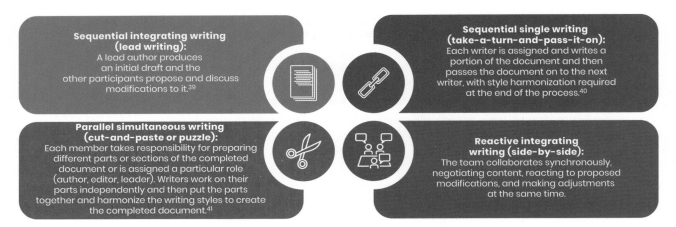

Sequential integrating writing (lead writing):
A lead author produces an initial draft and the other participants propose and discuss modifications to it.[39]

Sequential single writing (take-a-turn-and-pass-it-on):
Each writer is assigned and writes a portion of the document and then passes the document on to the next writer, with style harmonization required at the end of the process.[40]

Parallel simultaneous writing (cut-and-paste or puzzle):
Each member takes responsibility for preparing different parts or sections of the completed document or is assigned a particular role (author, editor, leader). Writers work on their parts independently and then put the parts together and harmonize the writing styles to create the completed document.[41]

Reactive integrating writing (side-by-side):
The team collaborates synchronously, negotiating content, reacting to proposed modifications, and making adjustments at the same time.

FIGURE 3.8 Collaborative Writing Strategies

Here are some key points to keep in mind when working and writing collaboratively:

- **Practise active listening.** Take other viewpoints seriously and consider them impartially and open-mindedly. Be attentive to nuance and make sure you understand what you've heard before responding.
- **Designate a team coordinator.** This person may not have authority over the entire project but can coordinate planning and activities. They will keep track of progress on the document and consolidates draft segments into a master copy.
- **Do up-front planning.** Meet to discuss the document before anyone begins to write. Brainstorm ideas for the project, conceptualize the document, evaluate its content, and create an outline, documenting the planning process as you go. Create a schedule that accommodates all group members' work commitments and that notes due dates for drafts, revisions, and final versions.
- **Agree on writing style standards.** Establish the style points and formats writers are expected to follow. This step will help to diminish differences in individual writing styles.
- **Make the most of technology.** An initial face-to-face meeting can help group members get to know each other and build group loyalty. After that, e-mail, file-sharing sites, virtual meeting software, and collaborative writing tools can help members work together over distances.
- **Determine who is responsible for each segment of the document.** Equalize workloads as much as possible. Allow group members to work according to their strengths or where they will learn the most. Each member is responsible for researching and writing a segment but should not hesitate to ask for help.
- **Foster a spirit of co-operation.** Everyone should feel that they are making a contribution and can be heard. To do this, you may have to compromise. Even when you check your ego at the door, expect a certain level of disharmony. However, creative differences can be a good thing; under the right conditions, divergent viewpoints gradually meld into productive consensus.
- **Harmonize writing styles.** Exchange and review writing segments while remaining diplomatic in your criticism. Let the group's best writer or editor to

do a final check for consistency and integration of writing styles. The final copy should read in one voice and have a continuous style, not look as though sections have simply been pasted together. Ask several people to check the document to make sure all the parts are properly integrated and error-free.

Collaborative Writing Tools

The ability to collaborate is now "a driver of value creation."[43] TELUS, for example, has put collaboration at the core of its values and of how employees work and interact. This telecommunications company has implemented an array of easy-to-access, user-friendly technologies that allow employees to collaborate with one another.[44] Collaborative writing tools (Figure 3.9) allow group members to co-author documents in real time, keep track of individual members' contributions, review and comment on other members' progress, ask questions and make suggestions for revisions, and track changes to existing text without overwriting the original copy. (Figure 3.10 shows a draft message with changes tracked; note that the colleague who has made the comments offers constructive feedback on the content, style, and organization of the message. Figure 3.11 shows how the original writer incorporated his colleague's comments to improve his original message.)

A number of tools, platforms, and systems exist to help dispersed writers organize their activities and achieve their common goals through continuous workflow.

The best collaborative writing tools are easy for users to use and access, allowing activity to be fast and spontaneous.[45] They also enable multiple people to make changes from

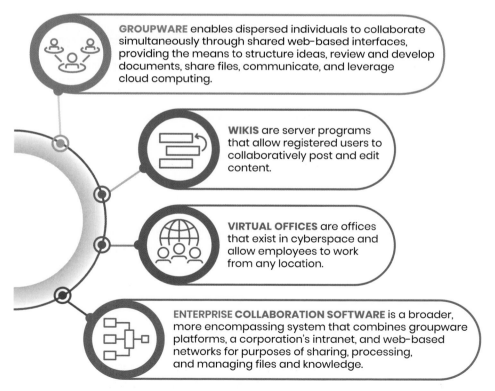

GROUPWARE enables dispersed individuals to collaborate simultaneously through shared web-based interfaces, providing the means to structure ideas, review and develop documents, share files, communicate, and leverage cloud computing.

WIKIS are server programs that allow registered users to collaboratively post and edit content.

VIRTUAL OFFICES are offices that exist in cyberspace and allow employees to work from any location.

ENTERPRISE **COLLABORATION SOFTWARE** is a broader, more encompassing system that combines groupware platforms, a corporation's intranet, and web-based networks for purposes of sharing, processing, and managing files and knowledge.

FIGURE 3.9 Collaborative Writing Tools

Dear Rada Chase,

Re: Your WALKERCOM Account 839221743

~~We must inform you that~~ the promotion you enjoyed has ended. When you get your next bill on or after October 20, 2020, the monthly rate for CMNTV will go up by $5.00 per month to $52.95<u>, plus taxes</u>. ~~And, added to that, you will also have to pay applicable taxes.~~ All other aspects of your ~~amazing~~ WALKERCOM service will rem<u>a</u>in the same. ~~If you want to complain about this letter or i~~<u>I</u>f you have questions<u>;</u> <u>or</u> concerns or decide to cancel your service plan or maybe ~~just change it,~~ <u>would like</u> to explore new low-cost Digital TV options, with up to 15 per cent savings, <u>please</u> give us a call at 1-888-WALKER1. We take your loyalty and business ~~really~~ <u>very</u> seriously. Over the last 5 years, the price of your CMNTV has not gone up. During this ~~period of~~ time, though, we've had ~~a lot of~~ <u>to cover many</u> programming costs from our network provider in order to <u>ensure your access to hit</u> ~~let you watch. Hit~~ series like *Martian Rangers* and Big Prairie. ~~We're sure you understand that h~~<u>H</u>igher costs make for quality programming and enhanced service. ~~Our corporate re-organization has seen WALKERCOM weather difficult times.~~ Thank you for doing business with us.

Thank you for choosing WALKERCOM.

Sincerely,

Sidney Cioran

Comment [MW1]: The focus should be on the reader. The tone is too negative. Could you try to make the tone friendlier and place less emphasis on the negative news?

Comment [MW2]: The phrases "added to that" and "have to" reinforce the reader's loss. What do you think about adding the information, in brief, to the end of the previous sentence?

Comment [MW3]: Word choice is exaggerated, making the tone inconsistent.

Comment [MW4]: This assumes the reader will be angry. We don't want to encourage complaints!

Comment [MW5]: Too wordy. Try to make it more concise.

Comment [MW6]: Sentence fragment. I've suggested linking it with the previous sentence, but you may be able to find a smoother option.

Comment [MW7]: Don't assume the reader will understand.

Comment [MW8]: Keep the explanation to the essentials. Avoid risking customer confidence.

Comment [MW9]: Too repetitive. Is there a way to vary the sentence structure to make this sound more natural?

FIGURE 3.10 Draft Message with Changes Tracked

Dear Rada Chase,

Re: Your WALKERCOM Account 839221743

At Walker.com, we take your loyalty and business seriously. That's why for two years the price of your CMNTV service has not increased. We've continued to provide you with the same high-quality programming, including hit series such as Martian Rangers and Big Prairie, for the same low price. Rising programming costs from our network provider and investments in service enhancement, however, mean that special promotional pricing can't be extended. Your October 17, 2020, bill will show a monthly rate increase of $5 per month to $52.95, plus applicable taxes. Although the promotion has ended, you will still enjoy the same high standard of service and 40 new digital channels. Please call us at 1-888-WALKER1 to find out more about our low-cost Digital TV packages, which offer one-year savings of up to 15 per cent.

Thank you for choosing WALKERCOM. We look forward to serving you in the future.

Sincerely,

Sidney Cioran

FIGURE 3.11 Revised Message

a distance at the same time. Live collaboration, with real-time co-authoring and typing as well as the ability for pairs of collaborators to see each other's presence, is now standard in systems such as Microsoft Office.[46]

Critiquing Others' Writing

Critiquing is a pathway to improved writing. Feedback from a peer is especially beneficial during the revision stage of the writing process. Peer feedback can help a writer improve the organization of a document, check that meanings are clear, and ensure that the message will meet its audience's needs. The act of critiquing others' work also benefits the person giving the feedback by helping her or him build confidence, powers of critical reflection, interactive and negotiation skills, empathy, and sensitivity.[47] It is possible, too, to learn more about writing and to become better at self-assessment through critiquing others' work.[48] When you evaluate others' writing, the usefulness of your feedback depends on your being thorough in your review and your understanding what the writer needs or wants from your feedback.[49] Critiques can have different purposes, for instance to reinforce learning or organizational standards or to motivate the group or an individual.

A few general principles help lay the foundation for giving and receiving feedback productively:

- Build a safe environment where people can give feedback honestly and receive feedback comfortably.
- Be an attentive and responsive listener.
- Stick to any guidelines that have been set or follow a rubric (if one is provided) to ensure that criteria are met.
- Know when to be candid and open with your feedback and when to give feedback in private or defer negative comments to spare the writer embarrassment.
- Avoid criticism that could suppress further responses.[50]
- Keep in mind that the skills learned through peer assessment are also applicable to self-assessment.

Checklist

Chapter Review

☐ Consider contextual factors, genre differences, your discourse community, and the rhetorical situation when you are writing.

☐ Approach the writing task as an achievable process consisting of five overlapping and repeatable stages: prewriting, organizing and outlining, drafting, revising, and editing and proofreading.

☐ Plan for a message that will be purpose-driven, audience-focused, and concise.

☐ Make prewriting part of your writing routine by first identifying the purpose, the scope of your message, the audience and its needs, the most logical and time-appropriate channel, the most effective design, and the required content.

☐ Organize content by creating an outline that shows topics according to order and level of importance.

☐ Draft the message by using techniques to reduce writer's block.

☐ Revise, edit, and proofread your document carefully, paying attention to content, organization, grammar, spelling, punctuation, style, and format.

☐ Recognize the benefits and challenges of collaborative writing and prepare for them by understanding the different types of collaboration, applying strategies for effective group communication, and using collaborative tools.

☐ When critiquing writing by peers, identify the purpose of the critique, be sensitive in your communication, and follow any pre-set guidelines.

Exercises, Workshops, and Discussion Forums

1. **Selecting the Most Effective Communication Channel.** Decide which communication channel would be most effective in each of the following situations. Be prepared to defend your choice in each case and discuss why the options you rejected would be ineffective.

   a) Your manager has just rewarded you for a job well done with two tickets to tonight's baseball game. The first pitch is in 90 minutes and you would like to invite a colleague in another department to go with you. How do you contact him?

      i. Call his desk phone and leave a brief voicemail.
      ii. Write a detailed e-mail in case he checks his inbox before heading home.
      iii. Send a text message because you know he is never without his smartphone.

   b) As a departmental manager, you have just received a directive from the company CEO advising you of a new and very detailed sexual harassment and discrimination policy that will go into effect shortly. Which method do you use to explain the policy's terms to your department?

      i. Call a fifteen-minute meeting and tell all staff members that they are responsible for recording details of the policy.
      ii. Write a detailed departmental memo clarifying every aspect of the policy and offering to address potential questions and concerns.
      iii. Post an announcement of the new policy on the departmental message board and tell department members to read it when they have a chance.
      iv. Talk the new policy over when you meet department members in the break room.

   c) Although you hold a junior position in your company, you have a few suggestions to improve the efficiency of operations and would like to run your ideas by the COO. How do you approach her?

      i. Prepare an informal recommendation report in which you outline your ideas based on evidence you have gathered from company documents.
      ii. Tap her on the shoulder when you pass her in the hallway and ask if you can bend her ear.
      iii. Book an appointment with her to discuss your ideas in a face-to-face meeting.

2. **Picturing Channels for Workplace Communication.** For this activity, work with a small group (three to four members). Using a smartphone, take a series of four to six photos or record a one-minute video that depicts communication channels that you currently use and will use in your career. Post your photos or video to a social media site or a learning management system, or incorporate them into a slide presentation. Discuss your reason for including each image and, if you have time, share your work with your class.

3. **Revising.** Working in a group, read the excerpted press release on page 114 and consider how it can be improved through revision and editing. Keep in mind the factors for successful revision summarized on pages 105–107.

4. **Writing Collaboratively.** Assemble a group of up to eight classmates and appoint a team leader. Assume that you have been asked to design three new college or university courses for programs in which you are now studying. Meet to brainstorm ideas, establish style preferences, and assign responsibilities (e.g., researching current courses, identifying potential needs, establishing course outcomes and outlines, writing course descriptions, revising and polishing draft material). Once each member has completed his or her portion of the draft, meet again to discuss problems and harmonize writing styles. When you are satisfied with the final version, submit it to your instructor for feedback. Each team member should then write a brief one-paragraph assessment of the collaborative writing process. What were its benefits and advantages? What were its drawbacks?

5. **Peer Editing.** Drawing on your worst hotel or restaurant experience, write a social media message similar to the kind found on sites such as TripAdvisor. Exchange messages with another student

FOR IMMEDIATE RELEASE

For More Information Call
Susan Sullivan

WINNIPEG, MANITOBA, MAY 10, 2020 . . . Gordon Wong has joined Superior Plastics as vice president—marketing. Superior Plastics, headquartered in Winipeg, produces polymer tubing and coils. Since 1991 Superior also been producing tubing for U.S. distribution through the firm of Reliable Plastics, Chicagoe. Wong will coordinate overseas distribution through, the company's Jakarta office. Wong will travel extensively in the Far East while developing marketing channels. For Superior.

Formerly, Wong was director of services at Big Name Marketing Associates, a consulting group in Montreal. While at Big Name, he develop a computer-based marketing centre that link textile firms in Hong Kong, Poland and Portugal. He graduate from the Rotman School of Business. Wong was chosen out of a pool of 350 applicants that included well-known marketing executives such as Peter Farnsworth and Livy Cohen.

(either through a direct exchange or through a platform such as Blackboard). Following the guidelines for peer critique outlined in this chapter, provide feedback to your classmate. Review the feedback you receive and apply the aspects that will most help you improve your message.

Writing Improvement Exercises

1. **Analyzing Your Genre Knowledge.** Compile a list of genres you use on the job or at school. Which ones are most familiar to you? Which ones are you learning about? How do they differ?

2. **Belonging to Discourse Communities.** Compile a list of the discourse communities to which you belong. What goals, genres, interactions, and terminology do the groups share? (Hint: Start by considering your most frequented social media platforms and whom or what you follow, what deliverables you produce for school and community service, and how you communicate on the job, for hobbies, and for other activities.)

3. **Discussing Topics in Discourse Communities.** Different discourse communities have various ways of discussing the same topic. Consider how each of the following groups or individuals would discuss the topic of water pollution:

   a) members of an Indigenous community dealing with a boil-water advisory
   b) your province's ministry of health
   c) oil industry executives
   d) parents and parent groups
   e) environmentally aware YouTube personalities
   f) non-profits or NGOs devoted to environmental causes
   g) small, committee-run green energy companies
   h) town councils of communities whose air quality has been negatively affected by nearby industrial polluters

4. **Identifying the Purpose.** For each of the following examples, identify the primary purpose—to inform, persuade, or convey goodwill.

a) a newspaper editorial
b) a corporate year-end report
c) a request to a charitable organization for a grant or donation
d) a set of operating instructions for the departmental photocopier
e) a congratulatory e-mail
f) a sales letter for a low-interest-rate credit card
g) a tweet from a customer service representative in response to a customer complaint

5. **Assessing the Receiver.** Assume that you must write to each of the following individuals to ask for a favour:

a) your bank manager (to ask for a loan)
b) your course instructor (to ask for a review of a grade you believe is unfair)
c) a friend, sibling, or other close family member (to ask for help moving to a new apartment)
d) a former employer (to ask for a reference on short notice)
e) a company vice-president (to ask him or her to take part in your college's career day)

Consider the receiver's needs in each case and create a reader profile based on your assessment. Indicate what your approach might be in each case.

6. **Analyzing Messages.** For each of the following writing situations, devise an audience analysis.

a) an unsolicited sales letter promoting life insurance to university alumni
b) an application for a job posted on an employment website (your qualifications are a close match for the position)
c) a letter from the municipal waste department explaining the introduction of a mandatory composting program
d) an e-mail to a fellow electrical engineer outlining the technical specifications for a new circuitry panel

e) an e-mail to your departmental manager suggesting the introduction of an internship program
f) a letter to members of a municipal board asking that the height restrictions on a multi-storey condominium project your company is currently developing be lifted
g) an e-mail to a supplier in Hong Kong requesting textile samples to be used in your new clothing line

7. **Analyzing the Audience: YouTube Video.** Select a YouTube video that offers tips or instruction. Based on its content and level of detail, identify its audience in terms of demographics (e.g., the age of the typical viewer the video would appeal to), attitudes (e.g., how the typical viewer might react to the video), and knowledge (e.g., how much the video appeals to newcomers, novices, and experts according to how much information it provides).

8. **Analyzing Your Social Media Audience: Facebook.** Log in to your Facebook account and review your recent posts. What assumptions do you make about your Facebook friends when you are deciding what content to post? In particular, what do you assume about their knowledge, attitudes, and demographics?

9. **Analyzing Social Media Audiences: Influencers.** Select a social media influencer and analyze one or two of their posts and how their audience responds to them. What sort of sentiments do audience members express? Are the comments generally favourable or unfavourable to the influencer's posts? How do the influencer's posts demonstrate an awareness of their audience's needs, priorities, and/or dispositions?

10. **Choosing Functional and Appropriate Communication Channels.** Analyze each of the following situations and select the most and least appropriate communication channels: face-to-face conversation, phone call, voicemail, e-mail, hard-copy memo, text message, or formal letter.

a) cancelling a business lunch at the last minute
b) confirming attendance at an upcoming meeting
c) informing a claimant of the advantageous terms of a settlement

d) notifying a long-time, soon-to-be terminated employee of the company's decision to downsize

e) convincing a long-time customer to purchase a new line of software your company is launching

f) presenting findings and recommendations related to your organization's need for a new health insurance provider

g) notifying five department members of a training seminar scheduled for two weeks from now

h) apologizing for offensive comments made by your company's well-known CEO on a nationally broadcast radio show

i) promoting a new product to a demographic consisting largely of millennials

j) convincing millennials to donate to a national or global charity

k) convincing senior citizens to continue to donate to a local charity

11. **Freewriting.** Select one of the following tasks and freewrite about it for ten minutes.

a) Explain the registration procedure at your college.

b) Describe the technical requirements for your current job.

c) Describe the communication skills required in your current job or in your program of study.

d) Describe the communication skills required of a successful social media influencer or YouTube star.

When the time has elapsed, stop and analyze what you have written. If the exercise has not helped you uncover at least three to five major ideas, repeat the process. Use the points you generate as the basis for an outline. Has the process helped you uncover new ideas?

12. **Creating a Cluster Diagram.** Assess a problem you have encountered on campus or at your workplace—inadequate or faulty equipment, inefficient or understaffed services, or inconvenient scheduling. Prepare a cluster diagram to explore the problem and analyze possible solutions. Use the diagram as the basis for a three- to five-point outline.

13. **Creating an Outline.** Assume that a friend is interested in your program of study and has asked you to write a letter or an e-mail describing its prerequisites, annual cost, and course requirements. Create an outline for your message.

Online Activities

1. **Business and Professional Writing Quiz.** This online quiz, from Thompson Rivers University, tests your knowledge of business writing by asking you to answer a series of questions as if you were a member of the business community. Enter your numeric choice, then click to check your answer.

   www.tru.ca/disciplines/biz.html

2. **Types of Evidence.** Examine a corporate or non-profit web page. Analyze the types of evidence used (e.g., facts, statistics, stories). How does each type of information contribute to your knowledge of the company or non-profit? What is each type of information used for? How do these different forms of information shape your response?

3. **Organizational Storytelling.** Work in a small group and begin by watching one of the research story videos listed on the website of the Social Sciences and Humanities Research Council of Canada. Using this video as a model, create your own video about a research study or community project being undertaken at your university or college. Enter your video in the contest.

   www.sshrc-crsh.gc.ca/society-societe/storytellers-jai_une_histoire_a_raconter/index-eng.aspx

4. **Non-Profit Storytelling.** Sharing personal stories allows people to connect and engage on a deeper level. Analyze how one of the following non-profit organizations uses stories on Facebook. What information does the story convey more effectively than statistics could have conveyed? How did the story change your perception of the cause or its beneficiaries? Did it help you identify with the organization or the beneficiaries?

Save the Children
www.facebook.com/savethechildren

Charity: Water
www.facebook.com/charitywater

Business Style: Word Choice, Conciseness, and Tone

4

Chapter Preview

In this chapter, you will learn strategies for effective word choice to ensure your messages are understood easily by diverse audiences in a range of business contexts. You'll be introduced to plain style and techniques for keeping your messages brief, to the point, and powerful. You'll also learn to control the tone of your messages to project confidence, frame information positively, and make receivers more receptive to your messages.

Learning Objectives

1. Use plain, precise, and familiar language to make your point, prevent misunderstanding, and write with impact.

2. Identify and eliminate problem words that do not convey your meaning clearly and directly.

3. Choose appropriate words for constructive, inclusive, reader-oriented, and ethical messages.

4. Identify strategies for writing concise messages.

5. Develop a conversational and confident tone and adjust it to suit a range of writing purposes, professional situations, and readerships.

6. Differentiate between personal and impersonal styles.

Case Study

iStock.com/AlexRaths

Complex documents such as user agreements, instruction manuals, and mortgage applications can benefit from a plain language approach. With its emphasis on simplicity, directness, and clarity, plain language allows businesses to make complicated information accessible to their customers and clients.

Business style is constantly evolving. A few decades ago, legal contracts regulating business were written in a formal style full of twisted sentences and difficult language (called *legalese*) that often made key concepts, obligations, and rights nearly impossible to understand. In Canada, banking and insurance industries were at the forefront of the transition from this type of writing to a plain language style.[1] In 1979, Royal Insurance of Canada produced the first plain-language insurance policy and Scotiabank worked with lawyer Robert Dick to redesign and rewrite its loan forms. Through the mandate of the Canadian Bankers Association (CBA), Scotiabank has maintained its commitment to plain language: "We know that plain language makes sense for our customers. And it also makes sense for us—saving time by eliminating confusion and improving communication within our organizations and with our customers."[2] The Government of Canada, through its 2018 Content Style Guide (www.canada.ca/en/treasury-board-secretariat/services/government-communications/canada-content-style-guide.html) and Directive on the Management of Communication (www.tbs-sct.gc.ca/pol/doc-eng.aspx?id=3068) continues to champion plain language by mandating communications products and activites that are "clear, timely, accurate, accessible and written in plain langauge."

Developing an effective business writing style is the key to reaching your readers and conveying your message. Style comprises the rules, conventions, registers, and options you need to consider whenever you write. These considerations apply to the words you choose and combine to form sentences that are correct, factually well-supported, and context-specific.

Effective business style also involves thinking about how words "sound" and how your readers are affected by the words you use. Good style creates a good impression, not just of you but of the company you represent. By paying attention to the language you use, you can eliminate the frustration caused by communication that is hard to read, confusing, or uninformative and thereby build and sustain business relationships. Savvy communicators know that a clear, factual, concise, and adaptable style can simplify everyday tasks and make information manageable. An effective writing style matches your meaning with your intentions; makes it easier for audiences to understand facts, claims, and proposals; and shows readers that you have thought through what you have proposed and why you have proposed it. In the long term, good writing supported by an effective business style is a major contributor to career growth and a vital factor in building personal and corporate credibility.

Word Choice

Plain Style

The need for clear, understandable, concrete language is not unique to the age of high-speed communication. Centuries ago, when people first began to write for science and business and industry, demands were heard for the kind of simplicity and economy that is now the hallmark of **plain style** or **plain language**. Plain style makes it acceptable for you to write in the same everyday language that you use when you speak and helps you to reach your readers instead of putting your audience at a distance. One of the aims of plain style is to banish dead and empty words in favour of lively, expressive ones that readers connect with and remember. Because it saves time, puts readers first, and makes ideas and information meaningful, plain language is good for business. For example, note the difference in the following sentences:

> I will be responsible for undertaking a prioritization of my commitments in terms of my daily scheduling.

> I will arrange my daily schedule.

The case for putting plain language into wider practice continues to gain momentum. In recent decades, the international plain-language movement—dedicated to presenting information so it makes sense to most people and can be acted upon after a single reading—has gained the endorsement of government agencies, businesses, professions, and industries alike. Plain style, with its pared-down, keep-it-simple approach, is characterized by a few common-sense principles:

- **Use common, everyday words, except for necessary technical terms.** Language should be familiar and accessible, not pretentious.
- **Use reasonable sentence lengths.** Aim for 20 words or fewer to avoid padding or needlessly overloading sentences.
- **Use the active voice and phrasal verbs.** Verbs in the active **voice** show who or what performs an action. **Phrasal verbs** are simple and informal, combining verbs and prepositions to deliver their meaning (for example, *work out* instead of *devise*). (See Chapter 5, pg. 134.)
- **Place the subject as close as possible to the verb.** The meaning of a sentence relies on the clear relationship between its subject and verb. Long modifying phrases that separate the subject from the verb create tangled, confusing sentences.

plain style or **plain language** A style of writing that values simplicity, directness, and clarity.

voice A term that describes a verb's ability to show whether the subject of a sentence acts or is acted upon.

phrasal verb A verb that combines with one or more prepositions to deliver its meaning.

pronouns Words that replace or refer to nouns.

ambiguity Obscure or inexact meaning.

vagueness A lack of certainty or specificity in meaning.

- **Use personal pronouns:** *I*, *you*, and *we*. Personal **pronouns**, used in moderation in all documents except formal reports, let you say what you need to say with minimal awkwardness.
- **Use clear, unambiguous language.** Sometimes the words you use may not completely or accurately describe a thought, or the thought itself may defy easy expression, or the thought itself may not be fully formed enough to be expressed and understood. **Ambiguity** refers to an inexact expression that has multiple meanings and is therefore open to interpretation (for example, does *Ricardo likes boring classmates* mean that Ricardo likes to bore classmates or that he likes classmates who are boring?). Ambiguity is characterized by uncertainty; it is difficult to decide which meaning is the correct or intended one. When given a choice between two ambiguous options, people have been shown to prefer the less ambiguous option.[3] **Vagueness** is similar to ambiguity but makes it difficult for readers to form *any* sort of interpretation (e.g., *The report is due soon.* When, exactly, is it due?). Good communicators do their best to prevent ambiguity and vagueness from creeping into their writing.

Some writers worry plain style will make their writing dull or simplistic, but such fears are unfounded. Quite the opposite is true: an effective plain style gives daily communication energy, impact, and precision that sustains readers' interest and helps them grasp complicated ideas and activities.

Word Choice Step 1: Use Familiar Words

A plain style relies on familiar, accessible language—common, everyday words of one or two syllables. Difficult words tend to be longer, with three or more syllables. In long sentences they can make even the most routine message dense and unreadable. Writers

iStock.com/andreusK

Just as an out-of-focus photograph blurs the image it represents, so too does ambiguous and vague language muddy the message it means to convey. To be effective, business writing must be sharply focused and clear.

usually resort to long, pretentious words for the wrong reasons—to appear experienced, to intimidate, to impress, or to express authority. Pretentious words can be tempting status symbols and smokescreens, dressing up or hiding your intended meaning, but they usually alienate readers instead of impressing them. Readers often skip over unfamiliar words or only partly grasp their meaning. The consequences of not opting for plain language can be seen in the following rewording of a well-known saying:

Pretentious:	It is preferable to effect the adoption and implementation of precautionary measures than to embark on a regrettable course of action.
Plain:	It's better to be safe than sorry.

Pretentious **jargon**-filled business language invites ridicule and is hard to take seriously. If you suspect your own writing is more pretentious than plain, use a readability index (such as Robert Gunning's fog index) to measure its level of difficulty. Alternatively, consult a list of words to avoid (e.g., *Forbes*'s "Most Annoying Business Jargon" or Wikipedia's "Glossary of Business and Management Terms") to help you identify overly pretentious language.

> **jargon** (1) The specialized terminology of a field. (2) Outdated, unnecessary words used in a business context.

The following tips will help you avoid common word traps:

1. **Curb your use of words ending in -*ize* and -*ization*.** Verbs ending in -*ize* and nouns ending in -*ization* may sound rich and sophisticated, but they can also lead to an inflated, heavy-handed style that grinds comprehension to a halt. Some words that fit this category (such as *privatize*, *hospitalize*, *unionize*, *maximize*, *authorization*, and *specialization*) are common enough to use without compromising readability. However, many other words ending in -*ize* or -*ization* (as well as some ending in -*tion*, -*ment*, -*ate*, or -*ism*) can boggle the mind. Remember that bigger isn't always better. The chart below offers some simpler substitutes for bigger, more difficult words:

Plain English	-*ize* Verb	-*ion* Noun
make communal	communalize	communalization
use	utilize	utilization
make best use of	optimize	optimization
make real	actualize	actualization
develop a business	corporatize	corporatization
finish	finalize	finalization

2. **Use words derived from French sparingly.** Words borrowed from French can add formality to your writing when they are used sparingly. If overused, though, they can sound contrived and affected when compared with simpler English alternatives.

Plain English	French Derivative
talk, have a conversation	converse
tell, inform	apprise
begin, start	commence

3. **Avoid foreign words and phrases.** Phrases such as *ad hoc* (meaning "for a particular purpose") and *pro bono* (meaning "for free") are used in legal documents

and formal writing, where they are part of an established idiom. Otherwise, use foreign expressions only when absolutely necessary.

Plain English	Foreign Word/Phrase
reason for being	raison d'être
genuine	bona fide
for each day	per diem
exchange, substitute	quid pro quo

4. **Use only job-related jargon.** Jargon is the special vocabulary for a group, trade, profession, or sphere of activity. This terminology is sometimes essential for conducting business and concisely describing sophisticated concepts and activities. Certain types of jargon once thought of as specialized—such as computer jargon—are now the stuff of common knowledge. Once-ordinary words such as *import*, *export*, and *cookie* have taken on meanings specific to computing, which in turn have come to be understood by almost everyone. Similarly, many business-related terms, such as *intangible assets*, *scalable technology*, and *buyback* describe actions and concepts that cannot be summed up easily in any other way.

   Jargon is permissible when it is purposeful and transparent. Because it is a private language of the "inner circle," you must be sure that it will be universally understood by your audience. Before using jargon, size up your audience and define any special terms you may have used in documents intended for a broad readership.

buzzwords Fashionable technical, business, or computer jargon.

5. **Bypass buzzwords.** Buzzwords are fashionable, often technical-sounding pieces of jargon. Known as trendy attention-getters, buzzwords sound fresh, current, and suitably corporate. Their trendiness is part of their appeal, but it is also a large part of their drawback because they tend to go out of style quite quickly, often through overuse. Some better-known buzzwords include the following:

Buzzword	Definition
synergy	co-operative or combined action
globalize	make or become global
paradigm shift	a fundamental change in approach or philosophy
solutioning	the process of creating a solution
blue-sky thinking	brainstorming unhindered by concern for limitations

Communications professionals are split on whether buzzwords are a feature of good writing. Clunky corporate "doublespeak" can kill meaning and be a smokescreen, camouflaging financial problems or poor performance—that is why readers distrust it. In fact, "straight-talking companies" have been shown to outperform "non-straight-talking companies."[4] Screening documents, especially external ones, for buzzwords demonstrates reader awareness and concern for fair dealing that helps build confidence in your organization.

A final thought about familiar words: use simple language for getting simple, time-sensitive messages across. Save sophisticated vocabulary for types of writing that require greater finesse or formality. On the job, pay attention to and learn about language preferences in co-workers' documents and consult your organization's style guidelines, if available, to help you make effective vocabulary choices.

Word Choice Step 2: Use Fresh and Current Language

To stay competitive, today's businesses explore and implement progressive approaches and technologies. It makes sense, then, for them to use contemporary language that reflects and reinforces those aims and creates a corporate image that is modern and up to date.

1. **Replace clichés. Clichés** are descriptive expressions that have been drained of meaning through overuse. Unless a cliché adds uniqueness or, by way of analogy, sums up something that is otherwise impossible to describe, replace it with fresh and direct language. Here are some of the better-known business clichés:

tighten our belts	needless to say
true to form	address the bottom line
all over the map	explore every avenue
rest assured	with all due respect
a change for the better	protect the bottom line
going forward	get your fiscal house in order
without further delay	to be perfectly honest
outside the box	push the envelope

   > **clichés** Overused, tired expressions that have lost their ability to communicate effectively.

2. **Retire outdated business expressions.** Many commonly used business expressions have outlasted their usefulness, such that modern readers see them more as artifacts than as communicative tools. Unless your organization recommends a very formal or traditional style, replace stiff, outmoded business expressions with modern phrases, especially if you want to project a modern, contemporary image for your organization and yourself.

3. **Eliminate slang. Slang** is the term for colourful, highly informal words or figures of speech whose meanings are specific to a particular era, locality, or occupation. Words that fit this category may be new words or familiar words used in new and sometimes humorous ways (for example *pony up*, which means "to hand over a sum of money"). Most slang has a short shelf life and may have meaning for only a small audience.

   > **slang** Coined or existing words that are informal and have meanings specific to particular groups or localities.

Slang	Translation
greenback	US dollar
schlepp	carry, haul
suit	a business executive
blow off	disregard, ignore
confab	a conversation
slugfest	an intense quarrel

   Slang is unsuitable for most professional communication because of its extravagance and informality; it can shock readers who are unprepared for it. An exception is slang that is specific to business and management, including widely accepted terms such as *phone tag*, *team player*, *walk* (resign from a job), and *spot* (a radio or TV commercial). Less common slang terms such as *tire kicker* (a prospective customer who demands a lot of attention but doesn't buy anything) may be too informal for general use.

4. **Consider the implications of using instant messaging abbreviations, emoticons, and emojis outside of informal digital contexts.** The popularity of e-mailing, texting, and social media has brought about a new lexicon specific to high-speed

communicators. At the same time, the popularity of instant messaging (IM) and work-place communication tools for informal discussion, such as Slack, and their use by businesses as productivity tools are having implications for business style. Features of IM style—e.g., incomplete sentences, deliberately misspelled words, e-friendly abbreviations, and **acronyms**—make typing dialogue in real time quicker and easier but do not translate well to formal documents.

acronym A pronounceable word formed from the initial letters of other words (e.g., NATO).

Abbreviation	Plain English
idk	I don't know
b4	before
any1	anyone
yw	you are welcome
btw	by the way
lol	laughing out loud

Our way of using visual elements such as emojis in our writing and reading of messages signals a shift away from the linear information processing[5] we are accustomed to with alphabetic forms of writing to a mode that is more imaginative and multi-modal. **Emoticons** and **emojis** came about to make up for a lack of nonverbal cues in digital communication by providing a way for the sender to signal emotion to the receiver.[6] Emoticons and emojis generally have positive effects in social e-mails, but in formal social settings and work e-mail emoticons such as smileys lose their effect—they do not increase perceptions of warmth the way that actual smiles do and can decrease perceptions of competence, an effect that can undermine information sharing.[7] Emoticons work better in less-formal work settings where they do not affect perceptions of competence and can actually help to show warmth.[8] In digital service-provider and marketing interactions, the nature of the customer-marketer relationship dictates how appropriate and meaningful emoticons will be. In one-to-one service provider-customer interactions emoticons such as smileys generally work well because they are directed to one person and elicit good feelings. On a social media webpage, designed for a large audience, however, the same smiley would not be recognized as being personally directed to any one receiver and would lose its value and authenticity as an emotional expression.[9] The interpersonal context and the formality of the interaction therefore matter when it comes to using emoticons and emojis to signal emotion and meaning. Emojis aren't universal and can have unintended negative consequences.

emoticon A symbol consisting of a sequence of keystrokes that produce a sideways image of a face conveying an emotion.

emoji A digital pictogram that expresses a strong emotion in electronic communication.

Stephen Plaster/Shutterstock.com

In certain contexts, emojis can humanize digital platforms, attracting customers and making them feel more at ease. However, their cartoonish and informal nature makes them inappropriate for most serious business communication.

Word Choice Step 3: Keep Language Specific, Precise, and Functional

Novelist Mark Twain once wrote, "the difference between the right word and almost the right word is the difference between lightning and the lightning bug." Words that are almost right tantalize but ultimately frustrate readers by hinting at an intended meaning without actually delivering it. When reading involves guesswork, readers cannot act on instructions, accept decisions, or give new ideas serious thought. Imprecise wording puts writers in a bad light too because poor word choice can be mistaken for fuzzy logic or unclear thinking. The more exact your word choice is, the more persuasive and informative your message will be. Every word you write should be clear and purposeful. Here are some tips for writing with precision:

1. **Provide specific details that help readers act on information and requests.** **Concrete nouns** (things knowable by the senses—*computer, annual report, resumé*) are easier to grasp than **abstract nouns** (intangible things knowable through only the intellect—*integrity, loyalty, justice*). Use concrete language to support and explain abstract words and show readers exactly what you mean. Because the language of business is full of intangible abstracts—*security, prestige, profitability, leadership*—data can often make difficult concepts meaningful to readers.

Abstract:	Our company demands loyalty.
Abstract/Concrete:	Our company demands employee loyalty to corporate policy.

2. **Quantify facts and avoid vague qualitative statements.** Tell readers how much, how many, or what type you mean; specify when something happened, happens, or will happen; and identify by title or name the agents and recipients of particular actions.

Vague:	They received some complaints about it some time ago.
Specific:	Our customer service representatives received 36 complaints about Model G500 in 2015.

   Terms such as *soon, later, good, bad, nice, numerous, substantially,* or *a majority* are often used out of politeness as hedging devices to make things sound less harsh and demanding than specific words

Vague:	A majority of employees indicated they would sign the agreement soon.
Specific:	Close to 75 per cent of employees indicated they would sign the agreement by Friday.

Vague:	The stock is performing poorly.
Specific:	Shares of Grocerynet.com lost 15 per cent of their market value in 2019.

3. **Avoid ambiguous and non-idiomatic expressions.** Ambiguous statements can be confusing. For instance, a sentence such as *She said on Thursday she would drop by the office* can mean two things—either that the statement was made on Thursday or that the visit would occur that day. As you compose your draft or write your message, check for potential multiple meanings and remember that readers like consistency, so avoid using two or more names for the same thing.

   Using idiomatic expressions can also reduce confusion. **Idioms** are word groupings that "sound right" to a typical reader and have special meaning distinct

concrete nouns Things knowable through the senses.

abstract nouns Things not knowable through the senses.

idiom A word or phrase that has a meaning different from its literal meaning.

from their literal meaning: *hand in* (submit) or *look up* (search for information). Used correctly, these phrasal verbs add punch to your writing, but they can also be difficult for anyone new to English to decipher. Idiomatic usage also applies to the pairing of prepositions with adjectives (*different from*) and nouns (*use for*). For instance, the phrase "to have confidence *in*" is correct but "to have confidence *on*" is not. When you need to know which preposition to pair with a particular word, it is always wise to refer to a college-level dictionary or an idiomatic dictionary.

4. **Use comparisons and analogies to clarify.** An analogy explains something unfamiliar or complex by likening it to something familiar. In fact, the business world is full of descriptive **analogies** that make fuzzy concepts clear and tangible. When there is no other way to explain a concept, a comparison can help to bring it into sharper focus. (See also Appendix A, pages 535–556.)

> **analogy** An explanation of the unfamiliar in familiar terms.

Word Choice Step 4: Practise Factual and Ethical Communication

How you communicate on the job is a reflection of your ethical standards and those of your organization. With this in mind, it is important to follow ethical practices in your workplace communication. Recall the tips for ethical business communication discussed in Chapter 1 (Figure 4.1):

① Be reasoned, factual, and moderate in your judgements.

Keep personal biases out of your workplace communication and use only inclusive, non-discriminatory language.

② Consider the impact your communication has on others as well as yourself.

Make sure the actions you endorse are legal and that your communication would reflect well on you if it were disclosed publicly.

③ Consult qualified colleagues.

Seek out experienced co-workers to help you navigate ethical minefields and find feasible solutions to the wording of important messages and documents

④ Avoid libellous language.

Common law protects every person against libel (printed character defamation). Harmful and potentially libellous words include *drunk, lazy, crazy, crooked, corrupt, incompetent, stupid, maniac, drug addict,* and *thief.*

⑤ Be timely and accurate in your communication.

Avoid unjustified delays in replying or processing information. Retain print or electronic copies of important documents.

⑥ Avoid untrue, deceptive, or misleading statements.

It is a good policy to back up any generalization qualified by *entirely, completely,* or *always* with supportable facts and evidence.

⑦ Know what you can and cannot disclose to certain parties.

Familiarize yourself with corporate disclosure practices and confidentiality agreements and handle your organization's intellectual property with care.

⑧ Distinguish between fact and opinion.

Let readers know the difference between unsubstantiated belief or conjecture and verifiable fact. Passing off an opinion as a fact is misleading and unethical.

⑨ Don't claim authorship of documents you have not written.

The consequences of plagiarism are serious. Always acknowledge your sources through notes or citations, and never take credit for ideas that aren't your own.

FIGURE 4.1 Tips for Ethical Business Communication

> ## Checklist
> ### Word Choice Guidelines
> For effective writing on the job, opt for language that is:
>
> - ❏ **Plain and familiar:** Use short and common words that are meaningful and easily understood.
> - ❏ **Fresh and current:** Match your language to the image of your profession and organization, avoiding stale and outdated expressions.
> - ❏ **Specific and functional:** Show readers what you mean through specific details and precise wording, and key language to your readers' understanding.
> - ❏ **Factual and ethical:** Avoid angry, exaggerated, irresponsible, and libellous statements.

Achieving Conciseness

It may come as no surprise that the origin of the term *business* is *busy-ness*. Time constraints and pressing deadlines are the norm for most business people. Therefore, readers expect to receive workplace documents that get to the point directly. A modest amount of time spent crafting a concise, easy-to-read, well-organized message is time saved for your readers. In turn, time saved translates not just into money earned or saved but into goodwill from the busy people you communicate with on a regular basis. Compare the following messages—think about how long it takes to read each one and how the choice of words affects coherence and readability:

> **Original:** This is just a very brief memo to inform you that it is the opinion of the employee council that at the present time it is expedient to undertake an investigation of the possible institution of a proposed on-site fitness centre. Kindly be advised that any time up to August 31 you should make your views known to your employee council representative.
>
> **Revised:** The employee council invites your input on the proposed creation of an on-site fitness centre. Please contact your employee council representative before August 31.

While conciseness is a virtue in business communication, being *too* concise leads to messages that sound uneven, blunt, or rude. A little terseness or even abruptness is usually excusable, but readers may bristle at a writing style that is so telegraphic that there is not enough detail or development to make a message clear and complete. After all, readers should not be expected to fill in missing words or information.

Conciseness means using the fewest words possible to say what you need to accurately and completely. Weighing the need for conciseness against similar concerns for completeness and politeness is important once you pass the draft phase, where wordiness is understandable.

> **Wordy:** Please note that you are requested to read and offer your comments on the attached file.
>
> **Terse:** Read this. Get back to me.
>
> **Concise and polite:** Please review and comment on the attached file.

Politeness strategies sometimes work at cross-purposes to editing techniques, but it is still relatively easy to write concise messages that have the right level of courtesy. Editing documents for conciseness is really a form of precision revision. You can start by eliminating anything that does not add meaning to your message: long lead-ins, noun conversions, padded and redundant expressions, needless relative pronouns, and excess modifiers. Getting rid of sentence padding and achieving conciseness requires only a little extra time, so avoid falling into the same trap as French mathematician Blaise Pascal, who once admitted to a friend, "I made this letter longer than usual because I lack the time to make it short." Here are nine ways to keep your messages concise:

1. **Eliminate long lead-ins.** Baseball pitchers warm up in the bullpen before they head to the mound. Many writers prefer to "limber up" in the same way by starting their sentences with an introductory phrase or two before they get to the point. While softening a message in this way is a common politeness strategy, lead-ins are mostly unnecessary because they add nothing to a sentence except for information that is already obvious (e.g., *This message is to inform you that . . .*). Readers in a hurry want information conveyed to them as directly as possible. Unless extreme politeness is required, delete any opening phrases ending in *that* or *because*. In brief messages, such as routine e-mail, make sure you get to the point before a count of three.

   Wordy: I am writing to inform you *that* parking lot C will be closed for maintenance Monday, September 30.

   Concise: Parking lot C will be closed for maintenance Monday, September 30.

2. **Revise noun conversions.** Each type of word has a different purpose. **Verbs** are "doing" words that convey actions, conditions, and states of being. **Nouns** name people, places, things, and abstract concepts. When verbs are converted into nouns, often with the addition of a *-sion*, *-tion*, or *-ment* ending, they lose their power and agency and in turn require weak supporting verbs to convey their actions. *Noun conversions* focus on things, not actions—*establishment* over *establish*, *approval* over *approve*, and *decision* over *decide*. As you review the chart below, note how affected and formal noun conversion phrases sound in comparison with the verbs from which they derive:

Noun Conversion Phrase	Verb
reach a conclusion	conclude
make the assumption	assume
conduct an investigation	investigate
engage in consultation with	consult
give consideration to	consider

   Noun conversions may sound impressive, but they will also make your writing weak and wordy, so it is best to avoid using them.

   Wordy: The company **undertook a revision** of its full-year earnings forecast.

   Concise: The company **revised** its full-year earnings forecast.

verbs Words that describe actions, occurrences, or states of being.

nouns Words that name people, places, things, and abstract concepts.

noun conversions or **nominalizations** Verbs that have been converted into nouns, often with the addition of *-sion*, *-tion*, or *-ment* endings.

Wordy: Leading economists **made a prediction of** a stronger Canadian dollar.

Concise: Leading economists **predicted** a stronger Canadian dollar.

Wordy: City council **brought about an amendment** to the bylaw.

Concise: City council **amended** the bylaw.

3.   **Eliminate redundancies. Redundancies** are word pairs that express the same meaning twice. Avoid the following "doubled-up" expressions by eliminating the italicized word:

> **redundancies** Unplanned repetitions.

absolutely essential	*necessary* imperative
past experience	*mutual* co-operation
reiterate *again*	*exactly* identical
refer *back*	each and every (use *each* or *every*)
enter *into*	

4.   **Eliminate or revise empty words and phrases.** Rid your sentences of imprecise, inexact language and trim padded expressions.

Replace	With
am of the opinion that	believe
at a later date	later
at this point in time	now, currently, at present
despite the fact that	although, though
due to the fact that	because (of), since
during the course of	during, in
during the time that	when, while
for the purpose of	to
for the reason that	because, since
in light of the fact that	because
in the amount of	for, of
in the event that	if
in the process of	now, currently
in spite of the fact that	even though
in view of the fact that	because (of), since, as
it has been brought to our attention	we have learned
it is probable that	probably
I wish to call your attention to	note, please note
make the necessary inquiries	look into, investigate
the question as to whether	whether
with the exception of	except, except for

Articles such as *the*, *a*, and *an* are sometimes overapplied. Omit *the* before plural nouns expressing generalizations.

Unnecessary article: The human resources specialists review the applications.

Articles omitted: Human resources specialists review applications.

5. **Use strong verbs.** Opt for clear, precise, instructive verbs rather than extended verb phrases.

Wordy:	The learning centre placed an order for materials for the courses.
Concise:	The learning centre ordered course materials.

Eliminate the need for intensifiers and qualifiers—such as *really, extremely, incredibly, definitely, rather*—by finding a verb that exactly fits the meaning you wish to deliver.

Wordy:	We were **really incredibly thrilled** to hear of the partnership.
Concise:	We were **delighted** to hear of the partnership.

Avoid poorly defined, ambiguous verbs whose meanings are open to interpretation.

Weak Verb:	Buying market share in foreign markets **affected** profits. (*affected* how?)
Precise:	Buying market share in foreign markets **increased** profits **by 10 per cent**.

Replace weak verbs, such as *have* and *be* (*am, is, are, was, were*), when they occur alone, with strong ones.

Weak Verb:	The CEO **is of the opinion** that the company will survive the current crisis that **has to do with** market instability.
Precise:	The CEO **believes** the company will survive the current crisis **caused by** market instability.

Weak Verb:	It **is necessary** for him to complete the application.
Precise:	He **needs to** (or **must**) complete the application.

Replace *could*, *would*, and *should* with strong verbs when you do not need to show that an action is conditional.

Weak Verb:	In her previous job, she **would write** to charitable foundations.
Precise:	In her previous job, she **wrote** to charitable foundations.

active voice A writing style in which the grammatical subject of a sentence performs the action.

passive voice A writing style in which the grammatical subject of a sentence is acted upon.

prepositional phrase A phrase beginning with a preposition and functioning as a modifier.

As much as possible, write in the **active voice** (as opposed to the **passive voice**; see Chapter 5).

Passive Voice:	The script of the speech should be edited and double-spaced.
Active Voice:	Edit and double-space the script of the speech.

6. **Revise wordy prepositional phrases.** Prepositions—common words such as *but, in, to, at, of, after, with, between*—combine with other words to form **prepositional phrases**. These modifying phrases show relationships in time and space, indicating how, when, where, or how long something happens. The wordiness of some prepositional phrases can make sentences sound awkward and overwritten. The phrase can usually be replaced with a single-word modifier.

Wordy:	An **error in computation** was discovered in **the report from last spring**.
Concise:	A **computational error** was discovered in **last spring's report**.

Prepositions break up long chains of nouns used as adjectives and clarify relationships so readers can tell which nouns are modifiers and which nouns are being modified.

growth management executive training → growth management training for executives

petroleum diesel replacement fuel → replacement fuel for petroleum diesel

climate change mitigation technologies → technologies to mitigate climate change

7. **Eliminate fillers.** Avoid beginning sentences with empty filler words such as *there is/are* and *it is/was* (when *it* has not been defined). **Expletive constructions**, as they are called, only make sense only when extreme politeness or emphasis is called for. Otherwise, delete the expletive and craft a straightforward sentence that begins with the subject and is followed closely by the verb.

> **expletive construction**
> A phrase such as *there is/are* or *it is/was* at the beginning of a clause, delaying the introduction of the subject.

Wordy:	**There are** three bids **that** the board is considering.
Concise:	The board is considering three bids.

Wordy:	**It is** paying down debt **that** is our priority.
Concise:	Paying down debt is our priority.

8. **Shorten multiple *that/which/who* clauses.** Too many clauses introduced by *that*, *which*, and *who* create a clumsy stop-and-go sentence flow. In many cases, you can drop *that*, *which*, or *who* as well as the verb that immediately follows it. Sometimes an entire clause can be reduced to a single word by making this simple change.

Wordy:	His company, **which is reputed to be a leader in employee satisfaction**, hosts regular events for employees **who have retired**.
Concise:	His company, **a reputed leader in employee satisfaction**, hosts regular events for **retirees**.

Wordy:	We offer prices **that are competitive**.
Concise:	We offer **competitive prices**.

9. **Combine multiple short sentences and reduce clauses and phrases.** Use pronouns (*that, which, who*, as well as personal pronouns) to combine shorter related sentences and eliminate monotonous repetition. Reduce sentences to clauses, clauses to phrases, and phrases to single words.

Wordy:	She is a sales representative. She specializes in commercial real estate.
Concise:	She is a sales representative who specializes in commercial real estate. (second sentence reduced to a clause)
Concise:	She is a sales representative specializing in commercial real estate. (second sentence reduced to a phrase)
Concise:	She is a commercial real estate sales specialist. (second sentence reduced to descriptive words)

Keep in mind that for certain types of documents, such as reports and even social media posts, information can be communicated visually as well as textually. Photos, illustrations, graphs, and other visuals can allow you to provide a large amount of data in a concise, impactful way.

Checklist

Conciseness

❑ Have you used as few words as possible to make your point?

❑ Have you eliminated long lead-ins and sentence fillers?

❑ Have you replaced noun conversions (and *-ize* words) with strong verbs?

❑ Have you eliminated redundancies, empty words, and empty phrases?

❑ Have you replaced prepositional phrases with single-word modifiers?

❑ Have you shortened clumsy *that/which/who* clauses and combined short, related sentences?

❑ Have you considered replacing text with visual elements?

Tone

Read between the lines of almost any business message and you can detect the writer's frame of mind, emotions, and attitudes from arrogance or modesty to indifference or concern. When we read, we often make snap judgements about the writer, especially a writer we have never encountered before. Our judgement of others is based on two fundamental perceptions—(i) their *warmth*, based in perceived personal traits such as trustworthiness, kindness, friendliness, and (ii) their *competence*, or perceived capacity to make good on goals and intentions based on traits such as skill, confidence, intelligence, and ability to get the job done.[10]

tone The implied attitude of the author to the subject and the reader, as reflected by word choice.

Impressions we form of the writers of messages we read are partly a product of **tone**. Tone refers to the mood of a message—the writer's implied attitude toward the subject and readers. In the absence of vocal inflection and visual cues such as body langauge, tone in written communication creates an impression based purely on the words that are used and the length and structure of sentences the writer happens to choose.

The tone of a message should support its content and remain fairly consistent from beginning to end. A wide range of tone is possible in workplace communication, meaning that a casual tone appropriate for an e-mail message to an associate will be unacceptable in a formal report, which demands a more serious and professional tone. Ultimately, much depends on the writing situation, purpose, and channel of communication. Once you have determined the tone you want to use, it should remain consistent throughout a document, mainly because erratic, "Jekyll-and-Hyde" shifts in tone give mixed messages that unsettle readers and leave them confused about your attitude and intentions. Make sure the tone you establish supports your content and creates the right impression.

Tune in to Word Connotations

Words with similar or overlapping meanings, like the synonyms in a typical thesaurus entry, rarely mean exactly the same thing. The way a word affects the reader helps to differentiate it, even subtly, from other words with similar or overlapping meanings. This is due to the difference between **denotation** and **connotation** (Figure 4.2):

> **denotation** A word's literal or dictionary definition.
>
> **connotation** A word's implied or associative meaning, often coloured by emotion.

Denotation:

The literal, dictionary definition of a word

- cheap, inexpensive, cost-effective, low priced, thrifty, economical
- artificial, faux, synthetic, sham, fake, imitation, mock
- flexible, changeable, fickle, adaptable, compliant, resilient

Connotation:

The implied, associated meaning of a word; distinct in terms of the positive or negative emotional response the word provokes

FIGURE 4.2 **Denotation vs. Connotation**

Connotation has the power to shape perceptions, which accounts for why a "pre-owned" vehicle may sound like a better investment than a "used" or "second-hand" car, even though the products these terms label may be the same. Being aware of words' connotations can help you anticipate your reader's reaction. Often, the right words may be the ones with the most appropriate connotations.

Keep Your Style Conversational

Formality or "register" involves observing style rules and conventions and thinking about language use in a particular social context for a particular purpose. Formality is on a sliding scale of style. Levels of formality depend on word choice, sentence length, and sentence structure. Most business writing, with the exception of formal reports, meets the needs of a wide audience with a mid-level style that is fairly conversational and moderately informal. Writing conversationally is as easy as imagining yourself sitting across from your reader and expressing yourself as you would in an ordinary face-to-face discussion or meeting. Try to resist the temptation to be chatty or to repeat yourself. The result should be unforced and natural, not stiff or stuffy. Keep sentence length manageable, use correct grammar, and edit to eliminate awkwardness. A written style that is too informal or casual—with noticeable slang, colloquialisms, or grammar abuses—can give the impression of carelessness and even suggest poor work habits. Writers have some freedom to vary their level of formality from document to document, but a mid-level style is typical of business letters, memos, informal reports, and most print journalism. Its elements are summed up in the checklist below:

> **formality** The level of writing; using the appropriate register based on writing rules and conventions.

- ☑ even-handed, efficient, conversational tone
- ☑ mix of familiar words and business terms

☑ correct grammar and standard punctuation

☑ manageable sentence structure (one to three clauses per sentence)

☑ single-word verbs and phrasal verbs (*look into* instead of *investigate*; *throw out* instead of *discard*)

☑ occasional contractions (*I'm*, *she's*, *we're*, *it's*, *can't*, *isn't*, *who's*)

☑ personal pronouns and limited forms of personal address

☑ absence of slang, legalisms, long words, and outdated language

Examples: I am pleased to submit the enclosed report.
              Please have a look at the enclosed report.

Select the Right Level of Formality: Personal and Impersonal Styles

personal style A style of writing that seems warm and friendly based on its use of first- and second-person pronouns.

impersonal style A style of writing that seems objective and detached based on its use of third-person pronouns.

Within the acceptable range of business style, you might be more or less formal and more or less personal. A **personal style** puts you and/or your readers into your sentences through the free use of first- and second-person pronouns (*I*, *me*, *we*, *us*, *you*). The impression it gives is one of warmth, friendliness, and candour, helping to build rapport and engage readers. Because facts are either delivered from the writer's perspective or targeted specifically at readers, this style sometimes seems biased or slanted, even when it is not. An **impersonal style** uses only third-person pronouns (*he*, *she*, *it*, *one*, *they*). It sounds detached yet objective, emphasizing facts and concepts rather than the writer's perspective. For this reason, impersonal style is commonly used for announcements and policy statements.

Personal Style
• Uses short sentences • Uses personal pronouns • Uses first names and personal references • Use of the active voice throughout

Impersonal Style
• Uses a mix of sentence lengths, including long sentences • Does not use personal pronouns • Does not use first names or personal references • Includes legitimate use of the passive voice

Personal style: I recommend that the company reschedule its annual general meeting.

Impersonal style: The company should reschedule its annual general meeting.

Personal style: Please let me know if you have any questions.

Impersonal style: Employees should submit all inquiries to their supervisors.

Be Positive

Is the glass half empty or half full? The answer to this question separates the optimists from the pessimists. Readers usually like to think of their glasses as half full, which means they are more receptive to good news or neutral news that is free of negativity. Although you should never knowingly distort facts or ideas just for the sake of putting a positive spin on them, it is worth remembering that positive wording makes messages reader-friendly and inviting. Unless you are issuing a warning meant to stop or deter certain actions, it is useful to emphasize what the reader can do instead of what the reader can't.

Negative attitude: You cannot use the online training system until you have been issued a password.

Positive attitude: You may begin using the online training system once you receive your password.

Avoid negative wording for positive or neutral ideas:

Negative wording: You will never be sorry you purchased a three-year extended warranty.

Positive wording: Your three-year extended warranty covers all parts and on-site repairs.

Weigh the impact of blatant or hidden negatives such as *unfortunately*, *allege*, *careless*, *regret*, *mistake*, *oversight*, *overlook*, *negligence*, *neglect*, *unable*, *reject*, *deny*, and *fail(ure)* before you use them. Used the wrong way, these can be harsh, inflexible words that antagonize readers by painting them as adversaries or inferiors.

iStock.com/C0rey

Is this glass half empty or half full? Taking a positive approach to conveying messages—and focusing on what can be done rather than what can't—will make readers more receptive to your message.

Negative words:	By failing to park in your assigned space, you caused our visitors a terrible inconvenience.
Positive words:	Parking spaces adjacent to the entrance are reserved for visitors.

Sometimes, you will need to reduce negativity and depersonalize unfavourable facts. In these cases, use dependent clauses and the passive voice (see Chapter 5).

Negative:	We cannot extend credit to you at this time.
Less negative:	Although credit cannot be extended to you at this time, we look forward to serving you on a cash basis.

Stress Reader Benefits and Relevance

Occasionally, everyone reads a message only to ask, *What does this have to do with me?* Relevant, reader-focused messages never provoke this reaction. Instead, readers can easily see how information concerns them or how they stand to benefit.

When readers feel that their opinions matter and have been taken into consideration, they are more likely to follow instructions and comply with requests. To write in a reader-focused style, edit your messages with the following suggestions in mind:

1. **Present meaningful content.** Avoid sending trivial or unnecessary messages, as they might cause your reader to overlook the seriousness of future, more important messages.

you-attitude A writing style that focuses on the reader rather than the writer.

2. **Develop a positive you-attitude.** Make the readers part of your message by presenting your information from their point of view rather than your own whenever possible:

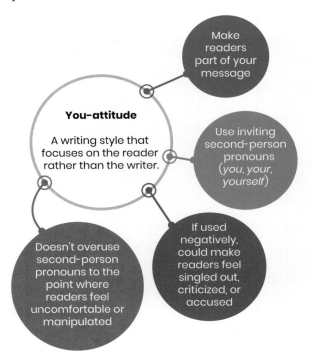

You-attitude

A writing style that focuses on the reader rather than the writer.

Make readers part of your message

Use inviting second-person pronouns (*you, your, yourself*)

If used negatively, could make readers feel singled out, criticized, or accused

Doesn't overuse second-person pronouns to the point where readers feel uncomfortable or manipulated

Writer-centred:	I am hosting a private reception at the Royal York Hotel on December 15 and am inviting all senior managers to attend.
Reader-focused:	As a senior manager, you are cordially invited to a private reception at the Royal York Hotel on December 15.
Negative you-attitude:	Your failure to observe safety guidelines will result in a mechanical shutdown.
Neutral attitude:	The machine automatically shuts down whenever a safety infraction occurs.

You can also involve readers by writing with a **we-attitude**:

we-attitude A writing style that focuses on the shared goals and values of the writer and reader(s).

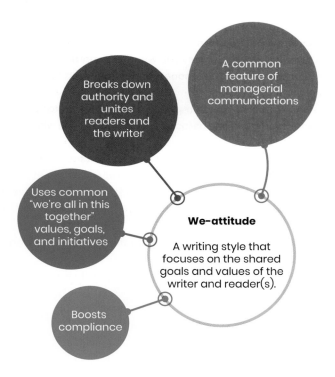

Writer-centred:	We ask that all customers complete the enclosed questionnaire so that we may assess the effectiveness of our technical support services.
Reader-focused:	To ensure you receive the highest standard of technical support, please complete the enclosed quality-control questionnaire.

3. **Emphasize benefits to readers.** Put yourself in your readers' place. Appeal to readers and their interests by indicating what they stand to gain. This may be all the incentive or motivation necessary to encourage a favourable, action-oriented response. This technique is especially well suited to service-oriented messages.

Be Polite

Politeness involves ways of using language to show consideration for those we communicate with and to avoid giving offence or hurting interactants' self-esteem. It is all part of building rapport and relationships and ensuring we follow norms for communicating appropriately. Business writing involves request making, negotiation, and task fulfilment. Strategies for politeness contributes to the success of these activities.[11] Politeness creates a humane environment of mutual respect and consideration where work gets done more easily. Rudeness, pushiness, sarcasm, and abruptness—whether actual or perceived—can alienate readers. Being courteous involves more than just adding a simple *please* or *thank you* to brief or routine messages: courtesy is a mindset with zero tolerance for sarcasm, condescension, presumptuousness, or anger. Emotional language can provoke hostile reactions, so avoid phrases that belittle or talk down to readers.

Rude:	Obviously, if you had the slightest idea of our policies you would have known that, unless you want to be fired, you should never use company-issued cellphones for personal calls.
Polite:	Please reserve your company-issued cellphone for business calls so that customers and associates may contact you without delay.

Extreme politeness, on the other hand, can be mistaken for coldness or insincerity. It can also undermine your assertiveness or authority, especially if you suppress or censor what you need to say for fear of sounding impolite. Do your best to strive for a courteous tone that sounds natural, friendly, and unforced.

Too polite:	Kindly be advised that, if even the smallest question arises, we will be only too happy to help.
Polite:	Please contact us if you have any questions or concerns.

Some essential politeness strategies include:
- Positive politeness strategies (showing friendliness)
  - Balancing criticism with compliments
  - Using politeness markers (*please*, modal verbs such as *would*, *could*)
  - Finding common ground and using in-group language
  - Showing interest
- Negative politeness strategies (showing deference instead of imposing)
  - Asking questions (rather than asserting)
  - Presenting disagreements as opinions
  - Using hedges (words such as *perhaps*) and modal verbs (such as *could* and *would*)
  - Being indirect and avoiding imposition[12]

Use Inclusive Language

Not only unacceptable but also against the law, discrimination involves the making of unjust and prejudicial distinctions. The Canadian Human Rights Commission (CHRC) defines discriminatory treatment on 13 prohibited grounds: age, sex, sexual orientation, gender identity or expression, religion, race, colour, national or ethnic origin, marital status, family status, physical or mental disability, genetic characteristics, and pardoned criminal conviction. Through enacted protection for gender diversity, gender expression, and the transgender community, the Government of Canada has made it illegal to discriminate on the basis of gender identity. Discriminatory and gender-biased language, even when it is unintentional, demeans and offends readers, leaving them hurt and unreceptive. Such language is actionable, opening the way for harassment suits and legal proceedings. Using inclusive, bias-free language that treats all groups equally and fairly shows sensitivity, consideration, and respect, all of which build goodwill and better business relations.

1. **Don't make discriminatory comments.** Avoid prohibited references that draw unnecessary attention to any of the 13 grounds identified by the CHRC when writing about groups and individuals. Such references, even when made in a positive spirit, are irrelevant and can contribute to negative stereotypes.

   - ☒ Hassan fasts throughout the day during this month's observance of Ramadan, but he will nevertheless be available to answer your questions.
   - ☑ Hassan will be available to answer your questions.
   - ☒ Sondra, who uses a wheelchair, is the new social media manager.
   - ☑ Sondra is the new social media manager.

2. **Use only gender-neutral job titles and salutations.** Most occupations aren't defined by gender; nevertheless, it's important to avoid suggesting occupational gender bias. Substitute correct and gender-neutral job titles—ones that do not suggest that only men or only women can hold a particular job—for more traditional, gender-specific ones:

Gender-Biased	Gender-Neutral
salesman	salesperson, sales representative
spokesman	spokesperson, company representative
businessman	business person
chairman	chair, chairperson
workman	worker
man-hours	work-hours
female manager, male nurse	manager, nurse
man and wife	husband and wife, spouses, partners
deliveryman	courier, delivery person

Avoid sexist **salutations** such as *Dear Sirs* and non-binary unfriendly salutations such as *Ladies* and *Gentlemen*. Better options include *Dear Colleagues, Dear Guests, Dear Participants*, or another similar salutation that includes a generic group descriptor.

salutation A greeting at the beginning of a letter (e.g., "Dear Ms. Gill").

   Revise any sentences containing sexist terms and automatic gender assumptions about jobs:

- Account managers are invited to bring their ~~wives~~ spouses/partners.
- The ~~girls in bookkeeping~~ bookkeepers will correct the error in your account. *Or* Aruna Sharma and Joyce Fitzgerald in bookkeeping will correct the error in your account. (Whenever possible, refer to people by their names.)
- ~~Each secretary reports to her supervisor.~~ Secretaries report to their supervisors.

3. **Use gender-neutral pronouns.** Avoid following the old grammatical rule of "common gender" using masculine pronouns (*he, his, him, himself*) to refer to groups of people or individuals of unknown gender. Consider the exclusionary nature of the following sentence, in which all executives are assumed to be male: *Each executive has his own parking space.* It is difficult to avoid using pronouns, but can you be sure you are using one that is non-discriminatory? A best practice is to share your pronoun at the beginning of a business relationship or interaction (e.g., the gender expansive *they/their, he/him, she/her*) and to avoid making assumptions when it comes to the pronouns employees, colleagues, and customers use. By leading with the pronoun you use, others may respond in kind. It is a matter of courtesy to get pronouns right and show care in how you address people you interact with, something that can be done as simply as asking a polite questions or saying "I was just wondering how you would like me to address you."[13] Organizations are currently preparing for a gender non-binary employment and customer experience in a number of ways: financial services company TIAA recommends client-facing employees share their pronouns in introductions; the Association for Business Communication asks conference registrants to note their pronouns for name tags through the online registration system; United Airlines gives passengers the option to identify as Gender X when booking a flight.[14] Including pronoun use in the signature line of e-mails is a practice many organizations now recommend. There are several ways to make your writing gender-neutral when it comes to pronoun use:

- ☑ **Replace the gendered pronoun with an indefinite article (a, an):** *Every executive has a parking space.*

- ☑ **Recast the sentence, making the singular pronoun plural:** *All executives have their own parking spaces.*

- ☑ **Use *they* and *their* as singular pronouns:** Although some people still insist on using *they* and *their* only in their traditionally plural senses, these pronouns are now widely accepted as singular as well as plural: *Every lawyer has their own parking space.*

- ☑ **Use *their* for greatest inclusiveness:** *Every executive has their own parking space.* Use these gender-neutral pronouns in cases when you have not yet learned the pronoun and individual uses.

If you are referring to a specific person, use the pronoun that person uses when referring to themselves. If you're unsure, politely ask the person which pronoun to use.

4. **Use respectful, accurate language.** In cases where you need to identify a person's or a group's nationality or ethnicity, disability, gender identity, or sexual orientation, always use the terms most commonly preferred by members of the group. These terms may change frequently, so it's best to research those preferences beforehand. Here are some examples:

- ☑ Generally, the term *Indigenous Peoples* is preferable to *Aboriginal Peoples* or *Native Peoples*. Note that both *Indigenous* and *Peoples* begin with capital letters.

☑ Remember that *Inuit* is a plural noun meaning "the people," so *the Inuit* translates to *the the people*. Use *Inuk* as the singular noun and *Inuit* as the plural noun.

☑ The Métis are a culturally distinct people with their own language, traditions, and practices. If you are referring to a person or people who are Métis, verify how they define themselves, and how they refer to themselves, for example as *Métis*, *Michif*, or another alternative.

☑ When referring to specific First Nations or groups, use the spelling and terminology they use to refer to themselves. You can usually find this information on their websites. This is important if you are writing to or about a specific band or council that is part of a larger confederacy or nation alliance—you must make sure you use the right names, spellings, and characters. For example, *The Boston Bar First Nation, which is a member of the Nlaka'pamux Nation Tribal Council* (correct) versus *Boston Bar First Nation, which is in British Columbia* (incorrect).

☑ Generally, *Indigenous Peoples in Canada* is preferable to *Indigenous Canadians*.

☑ Use person-first language—especially when referring to people with disabilities.

For example, use *a person with a disability* rather than *a disabled person*, or *a person with epilepsy* rather than *an epileptic person*.[15]

☑ The acronym *LGBTQ2S* (short for *lesbian, gay, bisexual, transgender, queer, and two-spirit*) is generally preferable to less inclusive alternatives such as *gay* or *queer* on their own. You may also see *LGBTQ2SIA*, with the *I* and *A* referring to *intersex* and *asexual*, respectively.

The best way to keep current on rapidly changing terminology is to continuously check in with the groups with and about whom you're communicating.

iStock.com/kroach

Always use gender-neutral pronouns to refer to groups of people or individuals of unknown gender, and never make assumptions about other people's gender.

Write with Confidence

A confident tone encourages readers to accept your decisions and opinions rather than question them. When you need to express yourself firmly and decisively, apply the following strategies:

1. **Use definite, forward-looking language.**	• Give priority to strong, deliberate verbs, precise nouns, and vivid adjectives. ⊗ *Although I might not have as much experience as the other applicants, I did take a few courses in risk management while trying to complete the requirements of my MBA.* ⊘ *Two courses in risk management for my recently completed MBA degree will allow me to contribute to your mutual funds division.*
2. **Don't make unnecessary apologies.**	• Apologies for routine requests weaken your perceived authority. • Understand when apologies are needed (i.e., when something has gone wrong) and when they are not. ⊗ *I am so sorry to have to ask you to confirm the time and location of our next meeting.* ⊘ *Please confirm the time and location of our next meeting.*
3. **Use strong, assertive phrasing.**	• Deferential and well-intentioned phrases such as *I hope* and *I trust* can sometimes sound weak and tentative. • With overuse, phrases such as *perhaps, if you have time maybe, if it's not too much trouble, if you could possibly,* or *I find it probable that* can slowly drain the power and assertiveness from your writing. • Other hedging words to watch for include *tend, in some ways, perhaps, seems, seemingly,* and *possibly.*[16]
4. **Be knowledgeable and informative.**	• Know your subject well enough to make it intelligible to the reader. • Well-presented data and meaningful information help reduce readers' uncertainty and allow them to take action and make sound decisions.
5. **Guard against overconfidence.**	• Too much confidence can make you sound egotistical, affecting your credibility and turning readers off. ⊗ *You will undoubtedly agree that my marketing genius makes me more than qualified for the job.* ⊘ *My experience in marketing and additional background in public relations have prepared me for this challenging position.*

Checklist

Tone Guidelines

❑ **Select the right level of formality.** Decide how formal or personal you want to be and choose words in the right register.

❑ **Be positive.** Use constructive language and avoid dwelling on negatives.

❑ **Stress reader benefits and relevance.** Cultivate a sincere you-attitude, and interpret facts and information to appeal to the reader's point of view.

❑ **Be polite.** Show courtesy and consideration.

❑ **Use inclusive language.** Don't discriminate. Use only bias-free terms.

❑ **Write with confidence.** Be firm and decisive but never arrogant.

Checklist

Chapter Review

❑ Use plain, precise, and current language to make your message clear and meaningful to your reader.

❑ Be ethical and purposeful in your choice of words to reflect good public relations for your company and good human relations with colleagues.

❑ Use as few words as possible to express your thoughts and pass on information.

❑ Use a style (personal or impersonal) that's appropriate to the type of message you write.

❑ Make your messages constructive, relevant, reader-focused, and inclusive.

❑ Adopt a tone that's conversational, confident, and courteous.

Exercises, Workshops, and Discussion Forums

1. **Tuning in to Word Choice and Tone.** In each of the following exercises, compare the sentence options and identify what makes one sentence preferable to the other(s).

    a) Which style is more readable?

        i.   When new safety measures for plant employees go into effect March 1, machine operators will be required to wear protective goggles at all times in the assembly facility.
        ii. The March 1 effectuation of amended plant employee safety measures institutes a requirement applicable to all machine operators who will be expected to wear protective eyewear devices whether or not they are engaged in machine operation in the assembly facility.

    b) Which writing style is clearer?

        i.   A prestigious consulting firm reached the conclusion that a specially formed committee should undertake an investigation of corporate asset mismanagement.
        ii. A prestigious consulting firm concluded that a special committee should investigate the mismanagement of corporate assets.

    c) Which sentence is more positive?

        i.   Our systems will be down until 4:00 p.m. today.
        ii. Our systems will be operational as of 4:00 p.m. today.

    d) Which sentence makes a better impression on the reader? How would you describe the tone of each?

        i.   Please let head office know of your travel plans in advance so that suitable arrangements can be made for you.
        ii. If you fail to notify head office of your travel plans, you will terribly inconvenience all concerned.

    e) Which writing style is more likely to win over a potential customer?

        i.   We are proud to be opening our new location, with the largest square footage of any of our five stores.
        ii. Come celebrate the opening of our new location in Bonaventure Mall and enjoy tax-free shopping on Friday, October 18.
        iii. You are invited to our convenient new location in Bonaventure Mall.

    f) Which writing style is more likely to attract the favourable attention of an HR job specialist?

i. Notwithstanding my lack of any full-time work experience and the fact that I am still trying to get my college diploma, I think I could be the "dynamic and progressive individual" for which your company advertised.

ii. With five years of part-time work experience in a related field and a soon-to-be-completed diploma in logistics management, I would like to be considered for the position of inventory specialist offered by your company.

2. **Social Media Buzzwords.** In a small group (three or four), brainstorm a list of social media buzzwords. Discuss which ones are most overused, which ones could have negative connotations, and which ones are most meaningless.

3. **Using (and Not Using) Slang.** Make a list of five slang words (not expletives) you use frequently or that are unique to your social world, peer interactions, or first language. Consider in what situations and with what social audience you would use and not use these words. Share your list and definitions of each word with members of a small group. Did you learn any new slang words? Is the meaning of these words transparent? When, if at all, would you use these words in a business context?

Writing Improvement Exercises
Recognize the Need for Plain, Precise, and Current Language

1. **Using Familiar Words.** Read the following sentences and replace long and unfamiliar words, jargon, and noun phrases with plain English equivalents.

   Sample: Please ascertain labour costs pertaining to the Corbin project.

   Revision: Please estimate labour costs for the Corbin project.

   a) It is incumbent on our organization to pursue radical debt reduction through the implementation of a corporate asset divestment program.
   b) Please acquaint yourself with the plans for the optimization of plant-level information systems.
   c) In lieu of a full refund, might we suggest a suitable quid pro quo or pro bono service?
   d) By formulating a timeline, we will facilitate production and accomplish our goals more expeditiously.

2. **Using Fresh and Current Language: Eliminating Slang and Clichés.** Revise the following sentences by replacing slang and updating old-fashioned business expressions.

   Sample: Here's the 411 coming down the pike on our latest corporate meltdown: everyone's gonna be sacked unless the top guns upstairs pony up and come up with some megabucks.

   Revision: The workforce will be downsized unless management secures new funding.

   a) Don't knock the head honcho: he may not have deep pockets but he never loses his cool.
   b) Hey paper pushers, check out this sweet report.
   c) Please rest assured that if we tighten our belts and stay true to form, we should see a change for the better.
   d) As per your request and for your perusal, please find enclosed our newest home ownership saving plan brochure.

3. **Using Specific and Functional Language.** Revise the following sentences by replacing vague words and abstract nouns with purposeful, concrete details.

   Sample: Please contact me sometime soon.
   Revision: Please call me tomorrow.

   a) Five of our current top salespeople are young.
   b) Our real-estate brokerage firm has low commission rates.
   c) A majority of shareholders think a hostile takeover bid will affect share prices substantially.
   d) Our high-speed Internet service is really fast.

Identify Strategies for Concise Messaging

4. **Achieving Conciseness by Eliminating Clutter.** Edit and revise the following sentences by eliminating noun conversions, long lead-ins, expletive constructions, prepositional phrases, and relative clauses.

> **Sample:**   The company undertook action that was decisive despite the fact that the resources it had were limited.
>
> **Revision:**   The company acted decisively despite its limited resources.

a) It was a clerk from accounting who located the spreadsheets that had been missing.

b) A senior engineer will complete an inspection of the safety requirements and, if necessary, make changes to them.

c) By and large, it is our assumption that share prices have been sagging due to the fact that there is by all accounts weakness in this particular sector.

d) In response to your letter of August 16 that was received August 18, we cannot act in accordance with your express wishes in making a refund due to the fact that the warranty of the product you purchased from us has expired.

e) For each and every customer who is dissatisfied, there isn't only a sale that is lost, there is a lifetime value of that customer that is lost as well.

5. **Achieving Conciseness by Eliminating Redundancies and Repetition.** Revise the following sentences to eliminate obvious statements and unnecessary repetition.

> **Sample:**   Her sister is a woman who works as an investment advisor at Forest Financial.
>
> **Revision:**   Her sister is an investment advisor at Forest Financial.

a) If you refer back to the final section of the report, you will see that the recommendations suggest we should continue on with the current profit-sharing plan.

b) In view of the fact that your freight has not arrived as scheduled, we have asked our supervisor of shipping to make the necessary inquiries.

c) During the course of the meeting, the need for mutual co-operation was brought to our attention.

Differentiate between Personal and Impersonal Styles

6. **Writing Conversationally and Informally.** Rewrite the following sentences in a less formal, impersonal style.

> **Sample:**   Subscription rates have increased by less than 5 per cent.
>
> **Revision:**   I am sorry to tell you that subscription rates have increased by less than 5 per cent.

a) Those interested in volunteering for the United Way fundraising committee should inform human resources at their earliest convenience.

b) Supervisors should discipline brokers who use discriminatory language when communicating with clients and co-workers.

c) The customer service department should continue to monitor all calls for purposes of quality control.

7. **Writing Informally.** Lessen the formality of the following e-mail message.

It is most important to note that, as of today, advertisements for departmental job openings must be routed through the human resources department. This improvement is made in accordance with the company's commitment to efficiency and operating expenditure reduction. Following this new procedure will save employees work and enable human resources to help employees fill their openings more quickly.

Create Constructive, Inclusive, and Reader-Oriented Messages

8. **Being Positive.** Revise the following sentences to create a positive impression.

> **Sample:** Because you failed to provide us with your postal code, we could not send you the estate-planning package you requested.
>
> **Revision:** Please tell us your postal code so that we may send you your estate-planning package.

a) We never fail to offer our GIC investors the most highly competitive rates.

b) In your e-mail to our customer service department, you allege that our Dependability-Plus model printer is defective.

c) Aren't you being unreasonable in asking for your vacation at this time of year?

d) It is categorically impossible for us to obtain model A311, which is no longer in production. Only model A312 is available.

9. **Stressing Reader Benefits and Relevance.** Revise the following sentences so that they reflect the reader's viewpoint.

> **Sample:** We charge our guests only $175 per person for one night's accommodation at our deluxe resort, a full spa treatment, and dinner at our award-winning restaurant.
>
> **Revision:** For only $175 (per person), you can enjoy a night's accommodation at our deluxe resort, a full spa treatment, and dinner at our award-winning restaurant.

a) I will allow you to take your vacation during the last two weeks of August.

b) We are currently seeking individuals to be part of our highly focused and dedicated team.

c) We are pleased to announce a new rewards program that guarantees discounts on future purchases.

d) I am enclosing Form C52, which must be completed before we can reimburse you for your educational expenses.

10. **Being Polite.** Revise the following sentences to make them courteous.

> **Sample:** You had better get moving on that draft proposal.
>
> **Revision:** Please begin work on the draft proposal as soon as possible.

a) If you honestly expect me to meet the November 21 deadline, I need the latest sales figures and I need them now. Can you at least hand them over?

b) We have far better things to do here at Apex Industries than speak with customers who could easily find the same information on our website.

c) Have the decency to let me know how the meeting went.

d) Since you're the team leader, motivating team members is your problem, not mine.

11. **Using Inclusive Language.** Revise the following sentences so that they are bias-free, gender-neutral, and non-discriminatory.

> **Sample:** John is the best disabled IT specialist we've ever had.
>
> **Revision:** John is one of the best IT specialists we've ever had.

a) The suspension of mandatory retirement means that old folks can stay in their jobs as long as they like.

b) Jennifer suffers from bouts of clinical depression, but she still gave a great presentation yesterday.

c) All executives and their wives are invited to our annual Christmas party. Every executive will have his choice of seating arrangement.

d) Our director is committed to improving service provision for Aboriginal Canadians. Our new program also has options for Inuit people and the Métis.

Develop a Conversational and Confident Tone

12. **Writing with Confidence.** Revise the following sentences to eliminate doubtful tone and tentativeness.

Sample: I'm sorry to have to ask you when we might receive our new software.

Revision: Please tell us the delivery date of our new software.

a) Perhaps you could send me the latest figures sometime, that is, if it's not too much trouble for you.
b) I hope you won't find fault with my investigation.
c) Apparently, the missing laptop you asked about doesn't seem to be on our premises.
d) In some ways, decentralization is possibly the best thing we have ever tried to do.

Online Activities
Recognize the Need for Plain, Precise, and Current Language

1. **Learning about Plain Style.** Select three examples from the Plain Language website and make a list of tips for writing in this style. Share the list with your class.

   www.plainlanguage.gov/examples/index.cfm

2. **Tracking Plain Language Trends.** Review the Twitter feed of the Plain Language Association InterNational (PLAIN) and review posts to identify three trends in language change and the adoption and use of plain style.

   https://twitter.com/PLAIN_Lang_Intl

3. **Identifying Elements of Effective Plain Style.** The Center for Plain Language sponsors the Clear-Mark Awards, an annual contest that recognizes the best plain language communication written for consumers. Review two or more of the wining submissions and the judges' comments on them. Compile a list noting the features that make for a winning plain style.

   http://centerforplainlanguage.org/awards/clearmark/

   http://english.glendale.cc.ca.us/roots.html

4. **Identifying Buzzwords.** Visit *The Wall Street Journal*'s business buzzwords generator. Select a phrase by clicking on "New phrase," then use the button on the right to replace the buzzwords in the sentence. Compile a list of buzzwords you recognize and understand and ones you don't. How does replacing the buzzwords change the meaning of the sentence? Write a one-paragraph analysis of business buzzwords and how they communicate—or fail to communicate.

   http://projects.wsj.com/buzzwords2014

5. **Revising Abbreviations for Readability.** Visit Better-English.com and complete the interactive abbreviation exercises by correctly identifying the abbreviation in each case. In a small group, discuss how recognizable each abbreviation is and consider its suitability for professional communication.

   www.better-english.com/vocabulary/abbreviations.htm

6. **Eliminating Slang and Clichés.** Visit Better-English.com and complete the interactive online exercise on business idioms by filling in the blanks for each question. The results will feature business slang and clichés. Suggest fresher, more professional alternatives and discuss your choices with your classmates.

   www.better-english.com/vocabulary/busids.htm

   writing2.richmond.edu/writing/wweb/cliche.html

7. **Identifying Business Jargon.** The Plain English Campaign's Gobbledygook Generator allows you to click on a button to generate a random piece of business jargon. At the page listed below, click on the button, identify the jargon in the sentence, and propose a clearer replacement. Repeat this exercise until you've compiled a list of ten or more jargon terms and their plain language equivalents.

   www.plainenglish.co.uk/gobbledygook-generator.html

Identify Strategies for Concise Writing

8. **Writing Concise Sentences.** Visit Purdue University's Online Writing Lab and examine the "Eliminating Words" examples. Revise each "wordy" sentence or phrase, then compare your revision with the site's "concise" version. Compare and discuss your revisions with your classmates.

   https://owl.purdue.edu/owl_exercises/sentence_ style/eliminating_wordiness_test/eliminating_ wordiness_exercise_1.html

9. **Tweeting Your Way to Conciseness.** Using a class hashtag provided to you by your instructor, write a tweet that succinctly states your thoughts on the following:
   a) What you hope to achieve after graduating from your program
   b) What your college or university could do to improve food services
   c) The best part of college or university life
   d) The best way to deal with stress during exam time

10. **Analyzing Brand Tone Tweets.** Brand tone of voice—the language style a company uses to communicate its unique personality–is aligned to organization values and vision as well as to brand persona.[17] Select a two or more of the following companies and analyze the text in their tweets from the past week. Focus on their language and style strategies and how they keep their content compelling while also keeping it concise. What is the tone of each brand's tweets and how does tone reflect brand personality and connect to a buyer persona? What category of customers is the brand tone meant to attract?

Arc'teryx:

https://twitter.com/Arcteryx

Aritzia:

https://twitter.com/ARITZIA

Mountain Equipment Co-op:

https://twitter.com/mec

TenTree:

https://twitter.com/tentree

Create Constructive, Inclusive, Reader-Oriented Messages

11. **Writing with Inclusive, Respectful Language.** Visit the website for Termium Plus, the Government of Canada's style guide. In what ways does Termium Plus capture the need to write with inclusive, respectful language? Is there anything discriminatory about its language? Work with a small group to discuss these questions and, if there is time, discuss your answers with the class.

   www.btb.termiumplus.gc.ca/tpv2guides/guides/ wrtps/index-eng.html?lang=eng&lettr=indx_catlog_ g&page=9tZXuAe4oZYs.html

   www.btb.termiumplus.gc.ca/tcdnstyl-chap? lang=fra&lettr=indx_catlog&info0=4.11 &info1=14.12

12. **Recognizing Word Connotations.** Go to Thesaurus.com and enter three of the following words: *ambitious, intelligent, careless, advanced, aggressive.* Compare the synonyms of each one and, in groups of three or four, discuss their connotations and suitability for business messages.

   www.thesaurus.com

13. **Accentuating the Positives.** Read the online tutorial from Purdue University, scroll down to "Effective Use of Space," and evaluate the examples to determine whether they present negative information favourably.

   https://owl.purdue.edu/owl/subject_specific_ writing/professional_technical_writing/ accentuating_the_positives.html

14. **Writing for the Brand: Voice, Tone and Word Choice.** Most successful brands have brand books and guides that catalogue design and content features. Brand books help to ensure everyone associated with marketing and broadcasting the brand is on the same page and can deliver consistent messaging for stakeholders to interact with the brand through a variety of channels. Review the following brand books and read the instructions for creating messages that reflect brand tone and personality. Identify the qualities that define each brand, making it recognizable and unique, and describe how each brand voice "sounds." How do tone and word choice contribute to the distinctive brand voice? Now imagine that you work for these organizations and engage with the public through customer service, marketing, or donor relations. Follow the brand guidelines for messages as described in the brand books and use each distinctive brand voice to write a short (1–3 sentence) message.

Charity: water (see pp. 25–30)

https://d11sa1anfvm2xk.cloudfront.net/media/downloads/brandbook-2016.pdf

I Love New York Brand Guidelines (slide 13)

https://issuu.com/lukaszkulakowski/docs/8278452-i-love-new-york-brand-guide

Alienware Brand Book (pp. 8–9)

https://issuu.com/design.st.ch/docs/alienware_brand_guide_2016_pages

15. **Perceptions of Warmth and Competence: Adapting Tone.** The following e-mails were written by a new hire and sent to their assigned project team leader-colleague whom they have never met. One pair of messages concerns the cancellation of a scheduled group project team meeting. The other pair concerns the cancellation of an informal after-work social gathering for project team members. What is your perception of the writer's warmth and competence in each of the e-mails?[18] Discuss your perceptions with your classmates.

a) Hey Sheila!
Nice to meet you ☺! Heard something about our project team meeting being cancelled ☹. Am I right? See you around I guess.

b) Hi Sheila,
I'm new to the project team and excited to be working on the product redesign.
I understand this Friday's meeting has been cancelled. Is there anything I can help out with ahead of our next meeting?
Looking forward to meeting you and rest of the team!

c) Good Morning, Sheila!
Let me introduce myself. I'm Tess, the newest member of your team.
It seems our get-together isn't happening this week. Having a chance for all of us to meet outside of work is a nice idea. Please count me for the next gathering.

d) Dear Sheila,
Just heard about this week's shindig—bummer ☹. Après-work soirees aren't really my scene but if they're expected and a regular thing count me in. When's the next one anyway?

16. **What is Your Brand: Defining Your Personal Brand Tone.** A personal brand is marketing of yourself and your career as an authentic, relatable, and goal-oriented brand. Imagine that you are launching your own personal brand as a company. (You don't need to have a specific product to sell or a service to offer—you are the product.) Consider your values, personality traits, story and approach to life, goals, and vision for the future and how they link to you as a professional. Being a brand also means you have a value proposition: the unique benefit or problem-solving ability you offer to a specific group of people. How could you project everything that you are, do, and stand for through the tone of your written message? Write

a 1–3 sentence brand statement that projects your personal brand voice.

Example: I give non-profits maximum impact by reaching out to untapped donors through the power of interactive mobile giving.

17. **Using IBM Watson AI Tone Analyzer to Understand Tone.** Companies increasingly rely on the ability to analyze emotion and tone in what people write online. The IBM Watson Tone Analyzer uses linguistic analysis to detect emotions of joy, fear, sadness, and anger and tones of confidence and tentativeness found in text. This technology benefits companies wishing to better understand the emotions and communication styles of their customers in social listening and customer service contexts. Pit your skills against Watson's by opening the Tone Analyzer demo and first analyzing the sample tweets, online review, and e-mail message (do not attempt to enter your own text). To start your analysis, copy the sentences and messages from the demo textbox into a separate document and use colour highlighting to flag each tone:

- Blue = analytical
- Red = anger
- Purple = confident
- Green = fear
- Turquoise = tentative

Once your analysis is complete, return to the Tone Analyzer Demo and under "Tone" click on each option to reveal Watson's analysis. Note how your analyses differ from those of Watson. What words and phrases were harder to associate with a specific tone?

https://tone-analyzer-demo.ng.bluemix.net/

18. **Gender-Decoder for Job Ads.** Do job ads implicitly dictate who "belongs" in a job according to subtleties of language? This tool was inspired by a research study by Danielle Gaucher Justin Friesen of the University of Waterloo and Aaron C. Kay[19] of Duke University to test reader perceptions of subtle gender-coding, and therefore perceptions of bias, in job ads. (Note: no non-binary people were included in this research and the tool does not code for this). Find a job ad for an internship or paid position of interest to you related to your field. Read it thoroughly, paying attention to tone and word choice, and consider your own perceptions of bias (or lack of bias) in the ad. Next, go to the website below, and paste the ad into the analysis field and click on "Check this ad." Compare your perceptions to the tool's coding and share the results with your classmates.

http://gender-decoder.katmatfield.com/

19. **Best Practices for Sharing Pronoun Use.** In a small group, conduct an online search for the guidelines your college or university provides on pronoun use. Extend your search to find out what 1–2 businesses recommend when it comes to sharing pronouns and establishing forms of address. Together, propose human rights-compliant strategies and phrasing for asking about and articulating pronoun use.

5 Business Style: Sentences and Paragraphs

Learning Objectives

1. Recognize the basic types of sentences.
2. Improve sentence variety by matching sentence style and length to purpose.
3. Phrase basic types of questions effectively.
4. Improve sentence clarity.
5. Use parallelism to write with consistency and impact.
6. Emphasize important facts and ideas; minimize less important ones.
7. Distinguish between active and passive voice.
8. Identify and eliminate sentence errors that impair clarity and unity.
9. Develop logical, coherent, and focused paragraphs.

Chapter Preview

This chapter provides strategies for improving the clarity, correctness, and impact of your sentences and paragraphs. You'll learn to adjust and vary your sentences according to their length and type to emphasize ideas, convey your purpose, and hold the reader's interest. You'll also learn about the concept of voice, the secret to achieving a strong and direct style and to breaking unfavourable news tactfully. You'll explore options for creating focused, cohesive paragraphs with logical flow and organization. Finally, you'll learn to identify common sentence errors and how to eliminate them.

Case Study

Accuracy and clarity are particularly important for legal contracts. Ambiguously worded or poorly punctuated contracts can lead to costly, lengthy legal disputes.

In the high-stakes world of business, seemingly minor writing errors can cause serious misunderstanding and be extremely costly. The case of the million-dollar comma is one example. The story first grabbed headlines in 2006, when telecommunications leaders Rogers and Bell Aliant clashed over the meaning of a single sentence in a 14-page contract. Rogers believed that it had an ironclad five-year deal to rent utility poles in New Brunswick, with an option to extend the agreement another five years. However, Bell Aliant raised its rates and attempted to cancel the agreement a year early. The placement of a comma in a crucial clause of the contract allowed Bell Aliant to justify its actions. Rogers protested, saying that it would never have signed such an agreement. The Canadian Radio-television and Telecommunications Commission (CRTC) settled the dispute by referring to the French version of the agreement, which stated that the contract could not be terminated early.[1] Similarly, a missing comma in legislation governing overtime pay cost Portland, Maine-based Oakhurst Dairy $5 million in a 2018 payout to three truck drivers claiming years of unpaid overtime.[2]

As this case shows, correct grammar is important in business communications. In the workplace, clear, error-free, and context-specific sentences and coherent paragraphs not only accelerate the exchange of information, they also demonstrate your writing abilities and other professional skills, ensuring readers associate you with precision and ease of communication.

Effective Sentences

Your ability to express your thoughts depends largely on how well you can craft sentences. While there isn't exactly a scientific formula to sentence construction, there is a simple logic to it. The next sections explain the building blocks and types of sentences you need to write effectively.

The Building Blocks of Complete Sentences: Phrases and Clauses

The tools of any writer's trade are groups of related words—better known as phrases and clauses. Understanding what they are and how to put them together helps you write in complete sentences and adds to your range of expression as a communicator.

A **phrase** is a group of words containing a **subject** or a **verb** but not both. Phrases function as parts of speech—as nouns, verbs, and **modifiers**—but they do not express complete thoughts, so pay attention to how they're used. In the example below, the segments in bold are phrases.

> **After negotiations**, the company offered a new bonus plan to its employees. **By contacting our customer service representative**, you may learn more **about this program**.

A phrase punctuated like a complete sentence is a sentence fragment, a potential source of confusion.

A **clause** is a group of words containing a subject and a verb. There are two types:

Independent Clauses	Dependent Clauses
• Grammatically complete and can stand on their own as sentences *The program cost more than expected.*	• Grammatically incomplete and reliant on independent clauses for their meaning • Begin with a dependent marker (*if, as, because, since, or although*) or a relative pronoun (*that, which, or who*) • Any combination of subject and verb loses its grammatical completeness with the addition of a dependent marker or relative pronoun. ***Although*** *the program cost more than expected, it has improved company morale.* *The program,* ***which*** *cost more than expected, improved company morale.*

Clauses and phrases are the building blocks of sentences; therefore, make sure that you combine and punctuate them carefully.

phrase A group of words containing either a subject or a verb, which cannot stand on its own as a complete sentence.

subject The word or group of words in a phrase, clause, or sentence that performs the action of a verb.

verb The word or group of words in a phrase, clause, or sentence that describes an action, an occurrence, or a state of being.

modifier A word or group of words that describes or gives more information about another word in a sentence.

clause A group of related words containing a subject and a verb; a clause can be either independent or dependent.

independent clause A clause that functions as an independent grammatical unit.

dependent (or **subordinate**) **clause** A clause that cannot function as an independent grammatical unit.

Types of Sentences

A sentence is not just a group of words but a method for full and accurate communication. To be complete and effective, a sentence must have two things: a subject and a complete verb, which carry the core of your meaning. For a group of words to qualify as a sentence, these elements must make sense together and express a complete thought.

The way ideas are linked affects your reader's understanding of the relationship between and among those ideas and their relative importance. There are four types of sentences, each with its own distinct purpose:

Sentence Type	Consisting Of	Example
Simple	one independent clause	We will discuss the issue.
Compound	two or more independent clauses	John will present his report, and we will discuss the issue.
Complex	one or more dependent clauses and one independent clause	When we meet Thursday, we will discuss the issue.
Compound-complex	one or more dependent clauses and two or more independent clauses	When we meet Thursday, John will present his report, and we will discuss the issue.

simple sentence A sentence containing one independent clause.

Simple sentences are straightforward and emphatic. The shorter they are, the more emphasis they have. There are two potential drawbacks to using simple sentences, however. First, without the connecting words typical of other sentence types, a simple sentence may not fully show relationships among ideas. In addition, a string of simple sentences can be flat and monotonous:

> Tax season is approaching. I would like to update you on some details. These details relate to allowable deductions.

compound sentence A sentence containing two or more independent clauses joined by one or more coordinating conjunctions.

Compound sentences join related sentences with coordinate conjunctions: *for*, *and*, *nor*, *but*, *or*, *yet*, and *so*. Compound sentences stress the equivalence or equal value of the ideas they express. It is important to use this connecting technique—known as coordination—only for related sentences. Over-coordinated sentences skew logic and lack unity:

> **Over-coordinated sentence:** You may choose from a number of investment options and I look forward to our next appointment.
>
> **As two sentences:** You may choose from a number of investment options. I look forward to our next appointment.
>
> **As related clauses:** I look forward to our next appointment, when you may choose from a number of investment options.

complex sentence A sentence containing one or more dependent clauses and one independent clause.

compound-complex sentence A sentence containing one or more dependent clauses and two or more independent clauses.

Complex and **compound-complex sentences** are best at showing the relative importance of ideas and encompassing details. Any of the following subordinate markers lessen the grammatical value of the word groupings they're added to:

Subordinate Conjunctions	
• Although	• If
• Though	• If only
• Whereas	• Unless
• As soon as	• Because
• Until	• As
• When	• As if
• Since	• Since
• While	• Even if
• Before	• Even though
• Where	• Whether
• Even	

Relative Pronouns	
• That	• Whoever
• Who	• Whichever
• Whose	• Which

A clause introduced by a subordinate marker won't make sense on its own and must rely on an independent (or stand-alone) clause in the same sentence for its meaning.

Dependent clause: **Although** tomorrow's e-business seminar has been cancelled,

Complex sentence: **Although** tomorrow's e-business seminar has been cancelled, you will have another opportunity to learn about e-business issues at a series of lectures scheduled for April.

Keep in mind that the longer your sentences are and the more clauses they have, the harder it is to find the subjects and verbs essential for delivering meaning. Sentences with more than three clauses can be difficult and confusing to read.

Checklist

Sentence Completeness

Make sure every sentence you write passes the "completeness" test:

❑ Is there a verb?

❑ Does the verb have a subject?

❑ Do the subject and verb make sense together and express a complete thought?

❑ If the sentence contains subordinating words—relative pronouns (*that, which, who*) or subordinate markers—does the sentence also contain an independent clause?

Improving Sentence Variety and Length

Good writing relies on a mix of sentence styles and lengths; however, you do not need to constantly shape and reshape sentences just for the sake of variety. Let the patterns of normal, everyday speech guide your writing. The following tips will help you break sentence monotony and create useful distinctions between ideas:

1. **Vary the rhythm by using short and long sentences.** Sentences of 10 or fewer words have the greatest impact and readability; however, sentences of up to 20 words also have a high rate of reader comprehension. Beyond that point, readers' ability to easily grasp a sentence's meaning falls off sharply. The example below does a nice job of varying sentence length while still being easy to grasp:

   Please complete and return the enclosed survey [short sentence]. Your answers to our questions will help us review our current practices so that we may provide the highest standard of customer service [long sentence]. By completing the entire survey, you will also receive a 25 per cent discount coupon that you can apply to your next purchase [long sentence].

2. **Turn a clause into a prepositional or a participial phrase.** Prepositional and participial phrases act as modifiers to describe something else in a sentence. They can be useful for combining short, simple sentences. A **prepositional phrase** is a group of words beginning with a preposition (a word such as *with*, *at*, *to*, *of*, *by*, *against*, *toward*, *from*, *above*, *on*, or *in* that relates a noun or pronoun to another word in the sentence).

   > **prepositional phrase** A phrase beginning with a preposition that sets out a relationship in time or space.

Two independent clauses:	The plan has the support of upper-level management. It will include extended health benefits.
Sentence with prepositional phrase:	**With recent support from upper-level management**, the plan will include extended health benefits.

   A **participial phrase** contains a verbal, which is a word that looks like a verb but doesn't actually function as one. Verbals generally take the form of a present participle (e.g., *working*), an infinitive (e.g., *to work*), or a past participle (e.g., *worked*).

   > **participial phrase** A phrase beginning with a participle that modifies the subject of the attached clause.

Sentence with participial phrase:	**Supported by upper-level management**, the plan will include extended health benefits.

3. **Turn an independent clause into a relative clause.** Another way to convert two or more sentences into one is to use a sentence builder known as a **relative clause** (a clause beginning with *that*, *which*, or *who*). The new clause, which replaces an entire sentence, acts like an adjective by adding information to define or describe a particular word or group of words.

   > **relative clause** A dependent clause beginning with *that*, *which*, or *who* that acts as an adjective to modify another part of a sentence.

Sentence with relative clause:	The plan, **which has the support of upper-level management**, will include extended health benefits.

4. **Convert a sentence defining or describing something into an appositive.** Use commas (or, for extra emphasis, dashes) to set off an **appositive**—a descriptive noun or noun phrase that renames a neighbouring noun—from the rest of the sentence.

Two sentences: Frederica Schmidt is a senior social media manager. She is a frequent speaker at conferences.

Single sentence: Frederica Schmidt, **a senior social media manager**, is a frequent speaker at conferences.

Phrasing Basic Types of Questions

Declarative sentences—sentences that make statements—are useful for relaying facts and decisions, but what if your goal is to get information? Asking questions is an important part of doing business, but there is more than one way to go about it. The type of question you ask depends on the type of response you seek. Asking the right type of question is the first step in getting the information you need. Here are three types of questions you can ask:

appositive A word or group of words that renames or restates the noun that it follows or precedes.

declarative sentence A sentence that makes a statement.

closed question A question with a limited number of possible responses.

open question A question with an unlimited number of possible responses.

hypothetical question A question that poses a supposition.

Closed questions can be answered with a simple "yes" or "no" or, when you are fact-checking or seeking verification, one or two words.

Closed questions follow inverted word order and do not feature question-forming words such as *why*, *what*, and *how*.

Can you ship our order today?

Are the new sales figures ready?

Will you attend tomorrow's meeting?

Open questions call for a fuller, more thoughtful response than is possible with just a single word.

How can we reduce production costs?

In what way will deregulation affect the industry?

Why do you support this initiative?

Hypothetical questions ask readers to suppose that circumstances are different from what they actually are. These "what if" scenarios are useful for brainstorming and contingency planning.

If you were given creative control of this project, what would you do?

The way you phrase a question suggests the amount of information you expect in response. The question words *why*, *what*, and *how* indicate open questions and typically demand the most detailed responses.

A well-phrased question will elicit a useful response without making readers defensive or causing confusion.

Improving Sentence Clarity

Occasionally, sentences may need a sharper focus for their exact meaning to be clear. Here are a few tips for revising fuzzy, ambiguous sentences:

1. **Avoid broad references using *this*, *that*, and *it*.** When you use *this*, *that*, and *it* by themselves, make sure the reader understands what the pronoun renames and replaces. Check that the **pronoun reference** isn't ambiguous (i.e., that the pronoun couldn't refer to more than one thing). If necessary, repeat the noun after *this* or *that*, or replace *it* with the noun.

   pronoun reference The relationship between a pronoun and the antecedent to which it refers.

   Vague pronoun reference: She helped to negotiate the recent settlement and **this** makes her an asset to the organization. [*This* could refer to either the negotiations or the settlement.]

   Clear pronoun reference: She helped to negotiate the recent settlement, and this experience makes her an asset to the organization.

   (See also Appendix B, pages 576–577.)

2. **Avoid embedding dependent clauses.** Put dependent clauses at the beginning or end of a sentence, not in the middle where they can come between the subject and verb. Choppy sentences formed in this way are difficult to read. Opt for more fluid sentence patterns that mimic natural thought processes.

Embedded clause:	The recycling facility, **although it was originally intended for use by only one municipality**, is now shared with neighbouring townships.
Revision:	**Although the recycling facility was originally intended for use by only one municipality**, it is now shared with neighbouring townships.

3. **Limit multiple negatives.** Multiple negatives are sometimes used for rhetorical effect or as euphemisms, but their range of meaning may result in confusion.

Unclear:	He was **not un**happy about **not failing** to meet the criteria.
Clearer:	He was pleased he met the criteria.

Writing with Consistency

Sticking to certain grammatical principles and patterns is another good way to banish awkward, unreadable sentences. Readers like the predictability of sentences that stay consistent in the following ways:

1. **Number.** Don't switch from singular to plural or from plural to singular when referring to the same thing.

   Women have made considerable strides in **their** [not **her**] chosen fields.

   > **number** A term that refers to whether a word is singular or plural.

2. **Person.** Don't shift the frame of reference from first person (*I*) to second person (*you*) or third person (*he, she, it, they, one*).

   Before **you** apply for a permit, **you** [not **one**] must show proof of Canadian citizenship or landed immigrant status.

   > **person** A term that describes who or what is performing or experiencing an action: first person (*I, we*), second person (*you*), or third person (*he, she, it, they, one*).

3. **Verb tense.** Show time changes only when logic requires them.

   When the CEO **entered** the auditorium, the crowd **applauded** [not **applauds**] wildly.

   > **verb tense** The form of a verb that shows time (past, present, or future).

4. **Voice.** Don't shift unnecessarily from active to passive voice.

   Financial analysts expect continued growth in the third quarter **but anticipate weakness in the tourism sector** [not **weakness in the tourism sector is anticipated**].

Writing Balanced Sentences: Parallel Structure

Parallelism involves delivering similar content in a similar way. The consistency of a repeated pattern helps readers absorb and remember information. Balanced constructions—matching nouns with nouns, verbs with verbs, and phrases with phrases—have a rhythmic appeal that makes sentences more forceful and compelling.

Unbalanced:	Britannia Capital's chief analyst proposes three strategies for debt servicing: **slowing** spending, **issuing** equity to pay down debt, and **to sell** assets.
Parallel:	Britannia Capital's chief analyst proposes three strategies for debt servicing: **slowing** capital spending, **issuing** equity to pay down debt, and **selling** assets. [parallel construction matches *-ing* verbals (nouns)]
Unbalanced:	We anticipate expansion into **underserviced regions**, **border areas**, and **markets that are located overseas.**
Parallel:	We anticipate expansion into **underserviced regions**, **border areas**, and **overseas markets**. [parallel construction matches nouns]
Unbalanced:	Our priorities are to **improve** employee morale, **reduce** absenteeism, and **encouraging** professional development.
Parallel:	Our priorities are to **improve** employee morale, **reduce** absenteeism, and **encourage** professional development. [parallel construction matches verb infinitives]
Unbalanced:	To qualify for funding you must submit an application and **three letters of reference must also be provided.**
Parallel:	To qualify for funding you must **submit an application and provide three letters of reference**. [parallel construction matches active voice with active voice]

Parallelism also applies to comparative statements. It is important to balance these constructions for readability and rhetorical force.

Unbalanced:	This is a time not for restraint but boldness.
Parallel:	This is a time not for restraint but for boldness.

Writing for Emphasis

Office information is often exchanged and processed quickly, sometimes without time for methodical word-for-word readings. Make sure your most important information gets the attention it deserves by using **emphasis**. Emphasis makes important facts stand out and is a matter of mechanics and style. The approaches below can be used on their own or in combination.

Use Eye-Catching Mechanical Devices, Punctuation, and Formatting
Mechanical devices, punctuation, and formatting can enhance the visual appeal of the written word:

Mechanical Devices

- Mechanical treatments used for emphasis include the following:

<u>Underlining</u>   ALL CAPS

Boldface   Colour

Italics   Text boxes

modified font sizes

Punctuation

- Dashes—the most emphatic of all punctuation marks—can be used in place of commas and parentheses when introducing or enclosing facts that demand special attention.

Formatting

- Make important details stand out by formatting them in horizontal or vertical lists.
- Vertical lists in particular give extra emphasis to important ideas through their distinct formatting.

> The newly created Employee Integrity Website has links to several vital resources:
> - Haskell Networks Employee Code of Conduct
> - Professional development seminar information
> - Citation guides

These strategies are effective as long as they are used in moderation. If overused, such devices can be distracting. A message typed in all caps, for example, is hard to read and "shouts" its information. (This heavy-handed practice is actually known as ***shouting***.) In addition, too many bolded or italicized letters, fonts, or font sizes can make a serious document look crude and amateurish, like a cut-and-paste ransom note.

shouting The largely unacceptable practice of typing an entire message in uppercase letters.

Add Emphasis through Style

Style adaptations for emphasis require planning but are generally worth the effort in terms of their impact on readers. Techniques for creating emphasis through style involve three basic principles:

Placement
- For maximum impact, put important facts first or last.

Sentence Length and Structure
- Use short, simple sentences to spot-light key ideas.

Word Choice
- Use tags and labels to flag important ideas.
- Use specific words to identify the main point.
- When necessary or helpful, repeat key words for rhetorical effect.

Here is a closer look at stylistic techniques that give power to your writing through emphasis:

1. **For maximum impact, put important facts first or last.** The most emphatic placements are first and last in a sentence or paragraph. Avoid creating an "information sandwich" that hides crucial facts and details in the middle of a sentence or paragraph.

Unemphatic:	A new deadline of **March 18** has been set for all funding applications.
Emphatic:	**March 18** is the new deadline for all funding applications.

Unemphatic:	**No one can deny** that the bear market has had a substantial impact **on pension funds**.
Emphatic:	Undeniably, the bear market's impact on pension funds has been substantial.

   Generally, placing the subject word at the beginning establishes a focus for the remainder of the sentence. Changing the subject allows you to change the intended emphasis of a sentence.

Focus on _survey_:	The survey indicated that most employees support the adoption of staggered work hours.
Focus on _employees_:	Most employees support the adoption of staggered work hours, according to the survey.
Focus on _adoption_:	The adoption of staggered work hours is supported by most employees, according to the survey.

2. **Use short, simple sentences to spotlight key ideas.** The fewer words there are in a sentence, the more impact each word is. Short, uncluttered sentences reward readers instantly with information.

Long and unemphatic:	The on-site fitness centre opens next Wednesday, at which time all employees will be invited to try out top-quality equipment that includes exercise bikes and rowing machines.
Short and emphatic:	The on-site fitness centre opens next Wednesday.

3. **Use tags and labels to flag important ideas.** Simple word-markers such as _most important(ly)_, _most of all_, _above all_, _particularly_, or _crucially_ alert readers to an idea's significance.

4. **Use precise and specific words to identify the main point.** Avoid generalization and obfuscation and use specific language to identify and describe your main point.

Vague:	The conference was good.
Specific:	The conference was lively and informative.

5. **Repeat key words in a series for rhetorical effect.** Advertisers and marketing specialists sometimes rely on repetition to persuade customers of the value of a product, concept, or service. However, this technique can easily induce boredom and does not necessarily work well in other, subtler forms of writing.

> Look how far **we've** come. **We were the first** Canadian company to receive the Gold Award from the International Customer Service Association. **We were among the first** in the world to introduce service breakthroughs like voice dialing and 1X technology. **We simplified** the prepaid world by making cellphone minutes available at bank machines, and **we simplified** the banking world by facilitating cellphone transactions. **We're working hard** to continue to earn your business.

De-emphasize Unpleasant Information Through Style

You can de-emphasize news that is unfavourable or less significant by applying principles opposite to those used for emphasis. Here are a few simple tips to follow:

1. **Use complex sentences to de-emphasize bad news.** Complex sentences have a dual advantage: their independent clauses emphasize while their subordinate clauses de-emphasize. Capitalize on these strengths by putting the bad news in the opening subordinate clause and using the independent clause that follows for better news.

Bad news emphasized:	Although the quality of the applications has never been higher, the number of applications is down.
Good news emphasized:	Although the number of applications is down, the quality of the applications has never been higher.

Multiple smartphone and tablet apps are specifically designed for writing and editing documents. Pages and TinyMCE Editor, for example, allow you to customize fonts and colours; use boldface, italics, and underlining; and insert images, tables, and text boxes.

2. **De-emphasize unpleasant facts by embedding them.** Unfavourable information is less harsh and less noticeable when buried mid-sentence or mid-paragraph. Use this technique sparingly, however, as it can make your sentences long and difficult to understand.

> **Mid-sentence de-emphasis:**   Our best-selling global positioning device, **though currently out of stock**, will be reissued in a new deluxe model next month.

Applying Active and Passive Voice

The voice of a verb tells you whether a sentence's subject acts (active voice) or receives an action (passive voice). Voice often accounts for why one message or document can sound lively and direct, while another can seem impersonal or flat. The active voice should be your first choice for business messages, but you should also make room for legitimate uses of passive-voice constructions.

The active voice is energetic, forceful, and direct. In the active voice, the question of "whodunit" is always clear because the grammatical subject "acts" by performing the action of the sentence: *The supervisor* [ACTOR] *approved* [ACTION] *the changes* [RECEIVER]. Use the active voice in the following situations:

1. **To state good and neutral news clearly and directly.**

   Active: John completed his expense report before the April 1 deadline.
   Passive: John's expense report was completed (by John) before the April 1 deadline.

2. **To emphasize the doer of an action.** The active voice tells the reader where actions originate and who is responsible for them.

   Active: Belinda authorized the purchase.
   Passive: The purchase was authorized (by Belinda).

3. The passive voice is less vigorous and forthright. To some readers, it sounds evasive because it is not always clear who or what performs the action of the sentence. Passive constructions invert the order of the active voice: *The changes* [RECEIVER] *were approved* [ACTION] *by the supervisor* [ACTOR]. Emphasis falls on the action itself, not on who or what performs it. Look for three common elements to check for passive constructions:

   the verb TO BE (*am, is, are, was, were, be, been***) + past participle + *by . . .***

The term *institutional passive* refers to the practice of concealing the performer of an action (by omitting the word or words after *by*). Use the passive voice in the following situations:

1. **To conceal the doer of an action when that information is unimportant, unknown, or harmful.** The active voice assigns responsibility for actions; the passive voice does not. In certain cases, such an omission can seem evasive or

even dishonest. The passive voice should not be used to cover up facts, weasel out of agreements, or manipulate readers.

Active: The executive committee delivered the development plan on schedule.
Passive: The development plan was delivered on schedule.

2. **To de-emphasize negative news.** The passive voice depersonalizes sentences by taking actors out of the picture. It is therefore useful in situations where you need to soften negatives or avoid accusations. The passive voice emphasizes a refusal or denial, not the individual(s) responsible for that decision.

Active: We cannot release specific salary information.
Passive: Specific salary information cannot be released.

3. **To show tact and sensitivity.** The passive voice is one of many "politeness strategies" in business writing. Its natural "weakness" is an alternative to the bluntness of the active voice and allows you to pass on information without allocating blame, finding fault, or making readers feel singled out.

Active: You must return all materials to the resource centre.
Passive: All materials must be returned to the resource centre.

4. **To reduce intrusive first-person pronouns.** Writing in the passive voice is a way of eliminating the multiple *I*'s and personal pronouns of the active voice. The passive voice is appropriate when it is already clear from the context that you are responsible for an action. Use this technique sparingly.

Active: I did extensive market research for this study.
Passive: Extensive market research was done for this study.

5. **To maintain consistency or avoid awkward shifts in focus.** Stick with the passive voice if a shift to the active voice results in awkwardness.

Active: When the new shipment arrived, the sales associates unpacked it.
Passive: When the new shipment arrived, it was unpacked by the sales associates.

Diagnostic grammar-checking software flags passive-voice constructions, but keep in mind that not all instances of the passive voice make for ineffective writing.

Eliminating Grammar Errors and Awkwardness

Sentence errors detract from the professionalism of your messages and reduce readers' confidence in what you have to say. Writing under pressure can increase the possibility of errors, so recognizing the types of errors you tend to make is the first line of defence. Here is a guide to some of the most common grammatical errors:

1. **Sentence fragments.** Phrases or dependent clauses punctuated like complete sentences—called **sentence fragments**—create ambiguity and distortion. To correct this error, join a fragment to the grammatical unit that completes it.

sentence fragment
A portion of a sentence that is punctuated like a complete sentence but does not deliver full meaning.

Fragment: We will discuss the Orkin account. **Which has been experiencing problems lately.** [relative clause punctuated as a complete sentence]

Revision: We will discuss the Orkin account, which has been experiencing problems lately.

Fragment: Sales figures for the year were strong. **Even though there was weakness in the third quarter.** [subordinate clause punctuated as a complete sentence]

Revision: Sales figures for the year were strong even though there was weakness in the third quarter.

Fragment: The company has experienced numerous setbacks. **For example, the failure of its light industrial division.** [The example cannot stand on its own as a sentence.]

Revision: The company has experienced numerous setbacks—for example, the failure of its light industrial division.

fused (or run-on) sentence
Two or more independent clauses erroneously run together without the use of required punctuation or coordinating conjunctions.

2. **Run-on (fused) sentences.** Run-ons, or **fused sentences**, combine two or more independent clauses without adequate punctuation (a semicolon) or without a connecting element (a comma followed by a conjunction). You can either separate the run-on sentence into two shorter sentences or add correct punctuation and/or a conjunction:

Run-on: Most companies reported moderate growth this year some anticipate similar growth next year.

Revision: Most companies reported moderate growth this year, and some anticipate similar growth next year.

Revision: Most companies reported moderate growth this year. Some anticipate similar growth next year.

comma splice The error of connecting two independent clauses with only a comma.

3. **Comma splices.** In a **comma splice**, independent clauses are strung together with only a comma. To eliminate the splice, add a conjunction or change the comma to a period or semicolon.

Comma splice: I decided against purchasing an extended warranty, however when my credit card statement arrived this month I noticed an extra $149 charge from Info Service, Inc.

Revision: I decided against purchasing an extended warranty; however, when my credit card statement arrived this month, I noticed an extra $149 charge from Info Service, Inc.

4. **Misplaced modifiers.** Modifying words that end up where they do not belong can make your meaning ambiguous and your sentences unintentionally funny. To eliminate **misplaced modifiers**, position modifiers as close as possible to the word or words they describe. Do this by asking yourself what goes with what.

misplaced modifier
An incorrectly placed descriptive word or phrase that attaches its meaning illogically to a word it is not meant to modify.

Misplaced modifier: The changes in personnel taking place recently affected productivity. [*Recently* could refer to when the changes in personnel took place or when those changes affected productivity.]

Revision:	Recent personnel changes affected productivity.
Revision:	Changes in personnel recently affected productivity.

5. **Dangling modifiers.** A dangling modifier occurs when modifying words do not clearly apply to another word in the sentence—when *what* the words modifies is either absent or disconnected. This problem often occurs with introductory verbal phrases containing a past participle (e.g., *informed*), an infinitive (e.g., *to inform*), or a present participle (e.g., *informing*) but no subject. Verbal phrases can enhance the flow of your writing, but make sure the subject being described in the introductory phrase comes immediately after the phrase itself. Otherwise, convert the dangling phrase into a dependent clause using the technique shown in the second revision below.

> **dangling modifier**
> A phrase that does not clearly modify another word in the sentence.

Dangling phrase:	Sent by overnight courier, you will receive your package by 9:00 a.m. the next day. [This sentence says *you are sent by overnight courier*.]
Revision:	Sent by overnight courier, your package will arrive by 9:00 a.m. the next day.
Revision:	When a package is sent by overnight courier, you will receive it by 9:00 a.m. the next day. [In this case, the dangling phrase has been converted to an initial dependent clause.]

Generally, the more formal the document, the less excusable dangling modifiers are. Sometimes a dangling modifier results from misuse of the passive voice:

Dangling phrase:	To qualify for our points program, your mother's maiden name must be provided. [This sentence says *your mother's maiden name will qualify for the program*.]
Revision:	To qualify for our points program, you must provide your mother's maiden name.
Revision:	To qualify for our points program, please provide your mother's maiden name.

6. **Faulty elliptical constructions.** *Ellipsis* means "omission." An **elliptical construction** leaves out words that have already appeared in a sentence because their meaning is inferred from the context. Don't automatically assume that a word appearing elsewhere in the sentence will stand in for the omitted word in the elliptical construction. The implied word has to be exactly the same as the one already used for the construction to be correct:

> **elliptical construction** A sentence structure that deliberately omits words that can be inferred from the context.

Word omitted:	The new treatment was intended and administered to patients who had not responded to conventional therapies.
Word added:	The new treatment was intended **for** and administered to patients who had not responded to conventional therapies.

7. **Faulty predication and mixed constructions.** Mixed-construction sentences pair mismatched elements that do not logically fit together. In a sentence with **faulty predication**, there is sometimes an illogical pairing of subject and verb.

> **faulty predication** An error involving the illogical combination of subject and verb.

Faulty predication:	The solution to this problem was remedied when Johnson proposed splitting company stock. [Solutions don't need to be remedied; problems do.]
Revision:	This problem was remedied when Johnson proposed splitting company stock.

8. Faulty predication often arises in connection with the combinations *is when* and *is where*. To fix a sentence featuring an *is when* or *is where* construction, drop *when* or *where*, add a classifying word, or substitute another verb for the verb *to be*:

Faulty predication:	Direct channel **is when** you sell and distribute products directly to customers.
Revision:	Direct channel is a marketing term for selling and distributing products directly to customers.
Revision:	Direct channel refers to selling and distributing products directly to customers.

9. Faulty predication also results from use of the expression *the reason . . . is because*. *This combination* is redundant (akin to saying *because . . . because*) and can be replaced with *the reason . . . is that* or *because*:

Faulty predication:	**The reason** he can't travel overseas **is because** he has family obligations.
Revision:	The reason he can't travel overseas is that he has family obligations.
Revision:	He can't travel overseas because he has family obligations.

mixed construction The error of pairing mismatched grammatical structures in the same sentence, resulting in unclear or illogical meaning.

10. In a sentence of **mixed construction**, the sentence starts in one grammatical form then shifts to another. Common culprits in mixed construction sentences are introductory phrases such as *The fact that*:

Mixed construction:	**The fact that** more job seekers submit their résumés electronically than they do by more traditional methods.
Revision:	The fact **is** that more job seekers submit their résumés electronically than they do by more traditional methods.
Revision:	More job seekers submit their résumés electronically than they do by more traditional methods. [drops troublesome opening phrase]

11. A mixed construction can also arise from an illogical sentence subject:

Mixed construction:	By reviewing job performance on a semi-annual basis was how we aimed to increase productivity. [*By reviewing* cannot function as the subject of a sentence.]
Revision:	By reviewing job performance on a semi-annual basis, we aimed to increase productivity.
Revision:	Reviewing job performance on a semi-annual basis was how we aimed to increase productivity.

Checklist

Sentences

❑ Does each sentence express a complete thought?

❑ Is every sentence clear and grammatically complete? Does every one have a complete verb and a subject?

❑ Does your style reflect a mix of sentence types and lengths suited to your purpose?

❑ Have you used parallelism effectively?

❑ Have you used emphasis for important ideas?

❑ Are most of your sentences in the active voice? Have you used the passive voice legitimately?

❑ Is every sentence error-free? Have you eliminated run-ons, comma splices, faulty predication, mixed constructions, pronoun shifts, and dangling and misplaced modifiers?

Effective Paragraphs

A **paragraph** is a group of sentences that introduces a main idea and makes one or more points about it. Paragraphs are the building blocks of effective writing; the white space that separates them alerts the reader to a change in subject, paving the way for new ideas and mapping out information so it is easy to understand and remember.

paragraph A group of sentences that develops one main idea.

Paragraph Length

There is no ideal paragraph length. The length is regulated by what you need to say and how you need to say it. For most types of business messages, though, short paragraphs are usually best because they promise easier reading and retention. Long, overloaded paragraphs form uninviting blocks of text that are visually intimidating.

A well-constructed message usually relies on a natural mix of paragraph lengths to match your purpose and support your content. Different types of paragraphs are suited to different types of messages:

Single-Sentence Paragraphs
- Single-sentence paragraphs (or paragraphs of up to two sentences) are common message openers and closers.
- Brief and serviceable, they are also useful for lending emphasis to especially important facts or ideas and have a special place in e-mail.
- A series of single-sentence paragraphs, however, can be mistaken for point form, robbing your message of coherence and development.

Short Paragraphs (5–6 sentences)
- These are standard in most types of business messages.

Long Paragraphs (up to 8 sentences)
- Longer paragraphs belong in reports, where the complexity of the material merits full and thorough development.
- Beyond the eight-sentence limit, consider regrouping sentences into smaller, more manageable units.

Topic Sentences

Most paragraphs benefit from having a **topic sentence** that announces the paragraph's main idea. Usually the first sentence of a paragraph, a topic sentence previews the paragraph so readers can decide on the relevance and usefulness of what follows. Documents that feature topic sentences are easy to scan because their most important information is front-loaded. Once it is clear that a sentence in the grouping is no longer related to the first one, it is time to start a new paragraph.

> **However substantial, the rights of authors to receive compensation for their efforts are limited by the doctrine of fair use.** According to law, fair use gives writers a limited right to use brief sections of copyrighted material without asking for permission. For instance, quoting a single sentence from a magazine article is considered fair use, whereas quoting a page or more is not.

Topic sentences are recommended for paragraphs that define, describe, classify, or illustrate.[3] They are less suited to paragraphs that reveal bad news, where it is important to first explain or justify a negative decision. Revealing the bad news first risks alienating readers, who are less likely to accept unexpected and unwelcome news. In paragraphs of comparative or persuasive purpose, you might delay the topic sentence to allow for an opening statement of contrast or concession.

Readers appreciate writers who produce well-structured, coherent, error-free documents that present information clearly and logically, with emphasis on the most important points.

Gaudilab/Shutterstock.com

Paragraph Development

Identifying your subject and purpose are the first steps in writing a clear, effective paragraph. A paragraph's form often depends on your purpose. Here are some examples of common paragraph purposes:

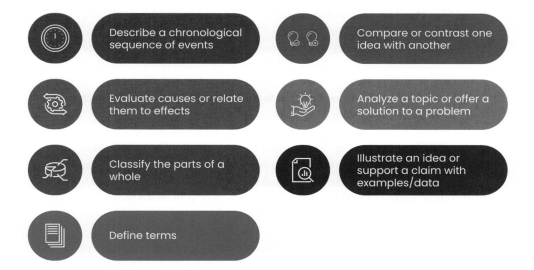

- Describe a chronological sequence of events
- Compare or contrast one idea with another
- Evaluate causes or relate them to effects
- Analyze a topic or offer a solution to a problem
- Classify the parts of a whole
- Illustrate an idea or support a claim with examples/data
- Define terms

All except the shortest paragraphs require supporting sentences that explain and amplify the main idea in the topic sentence. A typical paragraph should follow a logical pattern that builds and expands on the topic sentence in a relevant and meaningful way.

Paragraph Coherence

Good "flow"—the free and continuous movement of sentences from one to the next—is a quality many writers strive for. Flow is really a matter of **coherence**: the sentences in a group have to make sense in sequence and sound as though they belong together. Coherence is lost when logical gaps and unrelated sentences appear within a paragraph. To make your sentences fit together seamlessly, focus on linking and bridging techniques that enable you to guide your readers through a paragraph from beginning to end.

> **coherence** The logical and semantic links between sentences.

Creating Logical Coherence
Develop a paragraph game plan: know your line of reasoning and order your ideas accordingly. Anticipate where your sentences will lead and what readers will expect. Consider if a sentence is meant to show a cause-and-effect relationship or consequence.

> Despite an increase in revenue, the company showed a decline in profit.

The climactic order of this sentence leads to the main idea—decline in profit—at the end. If the paragraph were to continue, the next sentence would offer reasons for the decline or a statement of its degree.

Creating Coherence through Word Choice

Fluid, unified writing is easily achieved through a few simple techniques:

1. **Carry over a topic from sentence to sentence.** To prevent redundancy, use synonyms to stand in for the sentence subject or put a phrase or clause in front of the sentence subject to reduce its impact. An especially effective technique is to connect an idea at the end of one sentence to an idea at the beginning of the next.

2. **Use pronouns to carry over a thought from a previous sentence.** For clarity, combine *this*, *that*, *these*, and *those* with the single word to which each refers. Other pronouns, such as *some*, *they*, and *it*, can be used alone when they clearly refer to the nouns they replace. The following paragraph combines methods 1 and 2 to improve coherence:

   > Their company offers an outstanding **flexible payment plan**. **This plan** permits deferred payments of up to two years. **Its** payment schedule can be customized to suit the needs of individual **clients**. **Customers** can choose from a range of payment options. **Some** may even decide to make their payments online with just a few simple keystrokes.

3. **Use transitional words and phrases to segue from sentence to sentence.** Because **transitional expressions** show logical, temporal, and spatial relationships, they act as helpful signposts, preparing readers for what comes next and guiding them through your train of thought. Use them in moderation as comprehension aids, and ensure they don't become unwelcome distractions from your message. Adding them where they don't belong can lead to gaffes in logic and non sequiturs. Transitional expressions can play a number of roles:

transitional expressions Words and phrases that show logical, temporal, and spatial relationships and connect ideas to create coherence.

Role	Examples
To add a point	also, and, as well, besides, for the same reason, in addition, likewise, similarly
To illustrate	for example, for instance, in fact, in particular, namely, to be specific
To show cause and effect (or explain a previous point)	as a result, because, in this way, since, meaning that
To show contrast or reversal	although, at the same time, but, in contrast, however, instead, still, whereas, while
To show similarity	in the same way, likewise, similarly
To summarize or conclude	altogether, consequently, for this reason, hence, in short, so, therefore, thus
To concede a point	certainly, granted, naturally, of course
To show time sequence	at this point, currently, during, finally, first, last, meanwhile, now, once , then

4.   The following paragraph highlights some of these transitional expressions:

> **Once** a drug patent expires, generic competitors usually introduce copies that retail at a fraction of the price, **meaning that** brand-name manufacturers' share prices can be hit hard. **For example**, Biotex Corp. has declined from over US$55 a share in early 2001 to less than US$20 recently **because** its patent on the blood pressure drug Ambutroxin expired last May. **Altogether**, patents on brand-name drugs with about US$40 billion a year in sales will expire over the next three years. **As a result**, even fund managers have trouble picking pharmaceutical stock.

Checklist

Paragraphs

- ❏   Is your paragraph clear and intelligible on the first reading?

- ❏   Is there only one main idea per paragraph?

- ❏   Have you combined related short paragraphs and divided those that cover multiple topics?

- ❏   Have you included a topic sentence where required? Is it supported by sufficient detail?

- ❏   Do your sentences show clear relationships among ideas? Have you clustered related points? Is there logical development from one sentence to the next?

- ❏   Are paragraphs arranged coherently? Is there logical development throughout the entire document?

Proofreading

It is important to get in the habit of proofreading messages before sending them. Effective proofreading involves reducing your reading speed, reading word for word, and gaining the objectivity you need to spot errors before they cause you embarrassment. The point is to read what is actually written on the page or screen, not what you *think* you have written. To give you the objectivity you need to read impartially and analytically, it always helps to have a "cooling period" between composing and proofreading. The time and energy you devote to proofreading depends on the length and importance of the document. It may be necessary to make several passes over an especially significant document or message, each time reading for potential problems in one or two areas:

- Accuracy of names, facts, and figures: Double-check important facts for accuracy; compare figures with source material to eliminate typographical errors; transcribe names and addresses correctly.

format A term for the parts of the document and the way they are arranged on a page.

- Appropriateness of **format**: View page-layout options or print a document to see if it appears balanced and uncluttered and conforms to style guidelines.
- Correctness of grammar: Use the sentences checklist on page 162. Remember that diagnostic grammar-checking software will not catch all grammatical mistakes and may incorrectly flag grammatically correct constructions as incorrect. Consult Appendix B for more on grammar and usage.
- Correctness of spelling: Spell-checking software is good but nowhere near perfect. It may not always detect errors in usage, such as the transposition of commonly confused words (e.g., accepted and excepted). It may also flag proper nouns that are spelled correctly. Choose the proper spelling setting (e.g., Canadian, British, or American) so words spelled correctly (cheque and check) won't be flagged unnecessarily.
- Correctness of Punctuation: Follow the basic rules of comma usage and watch for misplaced terminal punctuation responsible for sentence fragments.

Checklist

Chapter Review

For effective sentences and paragraphs, practise these guidelines:

- ❏ Follow standard sentence structure.
- ❏ Aim for a natural mix of sentence styles and lengths matched to your purpose.
- ❏ Use parallelism and other techniques to write with consistency.
- ❏ Emphasize important facts and ideas with visual devices, punctuation, and the order of words and phrases.
- ❏ Use the active voice as much as possible.
- ❏ Eliminate grammar errors and awkward constructions.
- ❏ Limit paragraph length.
- ❏ Rely on coherence-building techniques that show relationships between ideas.
- ❏ Develop proofreading strategies for different kinds of messages and documents.

Exercises, Workshops, and Discussion Forums

1. **Grammar- and Spell-Checking Software: Help or Hindrance?** The following message contains multiple faults and errors. In a small group, flag and count the errors and then correct them to improve the message's overall accuracy and precision. Type the original and your revision on a computer equipped with grammar- and spell-checking software. What errors did you miss that the software flagged? Has the software inadvertently labelled correct usage as incorrect? Discuss how useful diagnostic software is for improving writing proficiency.

   During the last several months. Our company, after we undertook extensive market research and considered many different diversification options, had a new gourmet food category launched. The reason we are embarking on this new cross-merchandising venture is because the annual turn rate for food is far above the industry average of two times a year.

Wanting you to attend an information session and see the new line of products, the information session will be next Monday from 7:00 in the evening to 9:30 at our downtown location. Come and sample such delicacies as caribou pate, pepper jelly, chili-infused olive oil, and cherries that have been infused with amaretto. From several gourmet food purveyors, we will have representatives on hand to answer questions about their products. A product and price list is on line.

2. **Assessing Writing Apps.** In a small group, research English-language writing-enhancement platforms Grammarly and Ginger, discuss their potential advantages and pitfalls, and write one paragraph summarizing the benefits and disadvantages of using writing-enhancement software.

Writing Improvement Exercises

Recognize the Building Blocks of Sentences

1. **Building Sentences.** Combine each list of words to create a logical sentence, inserting punctuation where necessary.

   a) turned
      into
      the merger
      two companies with two specialty channels each
      one company with four

   b) studied
      business school
      Connie
      the
      risk management
      CFO
      at

Improve Sentence Variety by Matching Sentence Style and Length to Purpose

2. **Improving Sentence Variety.** Revise the following paragraphs by varying the sentence structure and reducing the prominence of personal pronouns.

   a) I joined R.H. Rayburn's marketing team in 2013. I provide marketing information for companies that make consumer-packaged goods. I have had several responsibilities. I collected point-of-sale data from stores, analyzed the data, and then passed the information on to corporate clients. I have learned that employees are key to strong revenue growth.

   b) We maintain an ongoing relationship with our clients. We train one or two client staff members. They train the rest of the staff. They provide immediate on-site assistance on routine matters. They can contact us when they need help with more complicated matters.

Phrase Basic Types of Questions Effectively

3. **Recognizing Types of Questions.** Identify the following questions according to type: open, closed, or hypothetical.

   a) How must we improve our product so that it meets CSA specifications?

   b) If we were to improve our product, what modifications would you suggest?

   c) Will CSA approve our newest model before production is scheduled to begin?

   d) In what way is our competitor's product better than our own?

e) How many similar products has CSA approved in the past five years?

f) Have you considered seeking approval from Underwriters Laboratories in the United States?

4. **Asking Questions.** Imagine that you must do research for an upcoming report. With your research task 80 per cent complete, you must make an unscheduled out-of-town business trip related to another high priority project, leaving you no time to complete the remaining research you promised your team. Draft several questions—closed, open, and hypothetical—to determine how to best ask your team members to help you complete your research.

Improve Sentence Clarity

5. **Improving Sentence Clarity.** In the following sentences, correct problems such as vague pronoun reference, embedded dependent clauses, and multiple negatives that interfere with clarity.

a) The proposed changes, while they do not entirely solve our personnel shortage, will help to improve morale.

b) We do not doubt that borrowing from home equity is not an unrealistic way for seniors to source extra cash.

c) Courtney is familiar with debt-reduction initiatives. That is her primary focus.

d) The committee recommended the adoption of a cost-cutting plan, but this has not been implemented.

e) The plan, when he first opened his doors six years ago, was to, in part, pitch their services to small businesses.

Use Parallelism to Write with Consistency and Impact

6. **Writing Balanced Sentences.** Revise the following sentences to improve parallel structure.

> **Sample:** I believe that employee satisfaction drives client satisfaction, which the satisfaction of shareholders is in turn driven by.
>
> **Revision:** I believe that employee satisfaction drives client satisfaction, which in turn drives shareholder satisfaction.

a) Renovating our current location is less expensive than to buy or rent a new property.

b) Japanese and Korean carmakers are gaining in every market segment with products that offer reliability, performance, designs that are alluring, and prices that are competitive.

c) Fabiola Cortez, of our R&D division, will now head our Regina facility; and our head office in Toronto will now be managed by Lu Huang, former chief of our consulting department.

d) Good security is based on a combination of three types of identifying information: something you know, usually a password or PIN; something you have, such as a plastic card, key, or security token; and what you have on your person.

e) Most biometric systems are expensive to buy and using them is awkward.

f) A radio spot will air contest details, where promotional events will be held, and what products are new.

Emphasize Important Facts and Ideas; Minimize Less Important Ones

7. **Writing with Emphasis: Sentences.** Assess the following sentences.

a) Which sentence is more emphatic?

i. Our banking services are good for your business.

ii. We offer highly competitive commercial rates and 24-hour online services to meet all your business needs.

b) Which sentence is more emphatic?

   i. We reduced inventory by 40 per cent.
   ii. We reduced inventory substantially.

c) Which sentence is more emphatic?

   i. Alberta's workforce is smaller than Ontario's.
   ii. Alberta's workforce is half the size of Ontario's.

d) Which sentence is more emphatic?

   i. His supervisor was able to take decisive action.
   ii. His supervisor acted decisively.

e) Which sentence puts more emphasis on the date of the meeting?

   i. On August 30, a meeting will be held to discuss stock options.
   ii. A meeting will be held on August 30 to discuss stock options.

f) Which sentence places more emphasis on risk management?

   i. Risk management is a primary concern for investors.
   ii. Investors are primarily concerned about risk management, although other concerns may enter into their choice of funds.

g) Which sentence de-emphasizes the job refusal?

   i. We filled this position months ago. Our company cannot offer you employment at this time.
   ii. Although our company cannot make an offer of employment at this time, we wish you success in your future career.

8. **Adding Emphasis.** Revise the following sentences to emphasize key facts and concepts.

   a) Emphasize the date:
      The deadline is March 31 for requesting transfers to the Toronto sales office.

   b) Emphasize individual departments:
      Three departments, namely Marketing, Sales, and Distribution, are participating in the pilot project.

   c) Emphasize the appointee:
      Our current operations manager, John O'Reilly, will now head up our Montreal office.

9. **Writing with Emphasis: A Short Document.** Revisit the memo you wrote for the first Writing Improvement Exercise in Chapter 1, and revise it to emphasize the most important information. Apply what you've learned in this chapter, especially in terms of using mechanical devices, punctuation, formatting, style, sentence length and structure, and paragraph construction to draw readers' attention to the most important points.

Distinguish between Active and Passive Voice

10. **Using the Active Voice.** Convert the following sentences to the active voice. Add subjects if necessary.

> **Sample:** Substantial career rewards are provided by this challenging position.
>
> **Revision:** This challenging position provides substantial career rewards.

   a) It was found by the committee that profits had been affected by the new industry guidelines.
   b) Credit derivatives are used by banks to offload troubled loans.
   c) The pack is led by heavy-parts manufacturers who show innovation.
   d) A recommendation was made that all advertising and promotion must be handled by senior marketing specialists.
   e) After approval was sought, the new site was approved by city building inspectors.
   f) Your personal information is not sold or otherwise marketed to third parties.

11. **Using the Passive Voice.** Convert the following sentences to the passive voice. Decide whether to omit the subject.

> **Sample:** Last year, the township issued an advisory on the illegal disposal of yard waste.
>
> **Revision:** Last year, an advisory was issued on the illegal disposal of yard waste.

a) When the hiring committee has concluded its search, we will notify you.

b) Tiffany over-budgeted for the team-building retreat in Muskoka.

c) If you do not remit your full term premium by July 25, we will cancel your insurance coverage.

d) Marjorie, Tom Chrysler's assistant, has re-scheduled tomorrow's meeting to Friday.

e) We have added the following exclusions to your policy.

Eliminate Sentence Errors that Impair Clarity and Unity

12. Eliminating Common Sentence Errors. Fix fragments, comma splices, and run-ons in the following sentences.

> **Sample:** Our new line of high-resolution copiers is affordably priced it will be introduced in the fall.
>
> **Revision:** Our new line of high-resolution copiers is affordably priced. It will be introduced in the fall.

a) All our branches have extended hours, some even offer weekend banking.

b) Before the Internet was developed and before it began to have such an impact on market research. One of the most effective techniques for building mailing lists was sweepstakes.

c) The president and CEO embarked on a spending spree. Resulting in a higher debt load.

13. Correcting Misplaced and Dangling Modifiers. Correct dangling and misplaced modifiers in the following sentences.

> **Sample:** Her co-worker told her on the first day no one eats in the cafeteria.
>
> **Revision:** On the first day, her co-worker told her no one eats in the cafeteria.

a) A shipment was forwarded from the warehouse that cost more than $12,000.

b) Mouse pads were given to conventioneers featuring the company logo.

c) The computer was returned to the manufacturer that was defective.

d) To apply for this position, an updated résumé and the names of three referees must be submitted.

e) Outsourcing its printing jobs, substantial amounts of money were saved by the company.

f) Complaints from customers must be taken seriously by all sales associates, regardless of their triviality.

14. Eliminating Mixed Constructions, Faulty Predication, and Over-Coordination. Correct the following sentences.

> **Sample:** One reason spam e-mail is unpopular is because most people find it time-wasting.
>
> **Revision:** One reason spam e-mail is unpopular is that most people find it time-wasting.

a) The purpose of the program was established to reduce job dissatisfaction.

b) When the demand for industrial goods increased was an indication to expand our operation.

c) We look forward to speaking with you and you'll find additional information in the enclosed booklet.

d) We're proud of our services and you should call when you need help.

e) The main reason that supervisors are concerned that staff members consider the request to be an invasion of privacy.

Develop Logical, Coherent, and Focused Paragraphs

15. Adjusting Paragraph Length. Revise the following memo by dividing it into several manageable paragraphs.

Please answer the questions below about the possibility of instituting an in-house daycare at Resource Management Plus. Many employees and some managers have inquired about the possibility of providing company-sponsored daycare services on the premises. In my opinion, on-site facilities, similar to the recently opened fitness centre, increase job productivity, morale, and job satisfaction. Employees are at ease knowing their toddlers and preschoolers are close at hand and well cared for in a fully accredited and supervised facility. They enjoy the convenience of dropping off and picking up their children with no additional commuting time. On the other hand, an on-site daycare facility might be a distraction from business. Your answers to the following questions will help us make an informed decision on the issue.

16. Paragraph Coherence: Using Transitional Expressions. Add transitional words and phrases to improve the coherence of the following paragraphs.

a) Our Small Parts Division needs to improve its quality control. Complaints so far have been few. Spot inspections revealed serious defects that could have an impact on long-term contracts and result in legal liability. We need to hire more quality control specialists. We need to foster better work habits.

b) We will soon introduce a new procedure that will allow us to project resource costs more accurately. Team members will be required to complete weekly time sheets and submit them to the project manager. The time sheets will be used to update the forecasts. A monthly, consolidated report will be presented to the directors for review. The new procedure will not improve efficiency immediately. It will allow us to take advantage of current methods in project management.

17. Paragraph Coherence: Identifying Transitional Expressions. Find a short (approximately 200 words) newspaper or magazine article. Highlight and list the transitional expressions. Would the article make sense without the transitional expressions? Why or why not?

Strategies for Proofreading Different Kinds of Messages

18. Proofreading Checklist: Correcting Sentence Errors. Draft a list of your ten most frequent writing errors (look for feedback on your previously graded assignments). Before handing in your next three assignments, refer to your customized checklist as you proofread. When your graded assignments are returned to you, see if using a checklist has helped you achieve greater writing proficiency. Work to gradually reduce the number of items on your list.

Online Activities

Recognize the Building Blocks and Types of Sentences

1. Recognizing Dependent Clauses and Types of Sentences. Before you try this interactive quiz from Capital Community College, click on the link for a review of dependent clauses. Then, go back to the quiz and make your choice for each question.

You will receive immediate feedback on the accuracy of your answer.

http://grammar.ccc.commnet.edu/grammar/ quizzes/niu/niu5.htm

2. **Understanding Sentence Structure.** Visit the University of Ottawa's HyperGrammar site to sharpen your skills in identifying different types of sentences.

   https://arts.uottawa.ca/writingcentre/en/ hypergrammar/building-sentences

3. **Gaining Practice in Sentence Structure.** The BBC's Skillswise website offers a unit on sentence structure, complete with instructional videos and games. Watch the one-minute video then select one or more games that help you hone your sentence style and competency.

   www.bbc.co.uk/skillswise/topic/sentence-structure

Use Parallelism to Write with Consistency and Impact

4. **Parallel Structure: Writing Balanced Sentences.** At the URL below, first click on the link for a review of parallelism, then go back and complete the quiz on parallel structure provided by Capital Community College.

   http://grammar.ccc.commnet.edu/grammar/ quizzes/niu/niu10.htm

Eliminate Sentence Errors that Impair Sentence Clarity and Unity

5. **Eliminating Sentence Fragments.** Test your knowledge of complete sentences with this exercise from Purdue University's Online Writing Lab. Edit these examples from student papers, then check your answers using the link at the bottom of the page.

   https://owl.purdue.edu/owl_exercises/sentence_ structure/sentence_fragments/sentence_fragments_ exercise_1.html

6. **Improving Modifier Placement.** Try this interactive exercise from Capital Community College for practice in identifying sentences with effective modifier placement. In groups of three or four, discuss your answers and compare results.

   http://grammar.ccc.commnet.edu/grammar/ quizzes/niu/niu9.htm

7. **Combining Sentences.** Complete these quizzes from Capital Community College by combining groups of sentences into effective single sentences containing only one independent clause each.

   http://grammar.ccc.commnet.edu/grammar/ quizzes/combining_quiz1.htm

   http://grammar.ccc.commnet.edu/grammar/ quizzes/combining_quiz2.htm

Develop Logical, Coherent, and Focused Paragraphs

8. **Improving Logical Coherence in Paragraphs.** Visit the following page from the Using English for Academic Purposes (UEfAP) website and complete the four interactive exercises that require you to reorganize sentences for logic and coherence.

   www.uefap.com/writing/exercise/parag/paragex5. htm

9. **Improving Paragraph Structure.** Re-order the sentences provided in this activity from GramR TutR to produce a clear, coherent paragraph. If you have difficulty unscrambling the sentences the first time, repeat the exercise until you feel confident in your ability to construct well-structured paragraphs.

   www.gramrtutr.net/writingParaScrambleGame.htm

6

Memorandums, E-mail, and Routine Messages

Learning Objectives

1. Recognize the characteristics of memorandums and e-mail.
2. Apply formatting rules and writing plans for memorandums and e-mail.
3. Format horizontal and vertical lists for clarity and conciseness.
4. Eliminate common e-mail problems and etiquette gaffes.
5. Recognize steps in processing and managing e-mail.
6. Develop correct e-mail style and tone.
7. Write memorandums and e-mails that inform, request, respond, convey goodwill, and follow up.

Chapter Preview

This chapter introduces you to routine computer-mediated business messages. You will discover strategies for formatting and writing memos and e-mail for specific purposes and learn how proper e-mail etiquette can maximize readability and reader-responsiveness to your messages. You will also be introduced to best practices for managing your inbox and communicating via instant messaging.

Case Study

iStock.com/jacoblund

An effective internal communications strategy encourages open dialogue, promotes employee engagement, and helps to foster a sense of community among co-workers. Employees who feel engaged and valued at work are more likely to do their jobs well and to project a positive image of their organization when they communicate with customers and clients.

An effective internal communications strategy is one of the touchstones of a highly engaged workforce. Esther Huberman, communications consultant at Pal Benefits, believes that employers should develop and implement an internal communications strategy right from the start: "Inaccurate information may have a negative impact on employees' perceptions, which may spill over into what they communicate to customers and other audiences."[1] With so many options—e-mail, the Internet, intranet, video, webcasts, podcasts, interactive portals, social media, and so on—asking employees for their preferences is important, according to Huberman. Kim McMullen, principal of KMcMullen Communications, adds that a delivery method should support an organization's goals. She recommends that organizations align their internal communication strategy with their external brand and mission and transmit the same message in a variety of ways to accommodate employee needs.[2]

Even with the clearest and most specific of communication protocols, however, employees may still be confused about where to draw the line between using e-mail as a productivity tool and using it as a channel for personal conversations. Management consultant Michael Marmur says that most people have regretted sending at least one e-mail at some time and "need to be reminded of what's appropriate and what's inappropriate."[3] It is also important to remember that employers can monitor their staff's e-mail messages; employees have no expectation of privacy when using company networks.

Certain e-mail mistakes can impact a company's image and productivity. In 2015, an employee at Thomson Reuters, a Canadian mass media and information firm, accidentally sent an e-mail to 33, 000 of his colleagues. Soon after the initial message, hundreds of Thomson Reuters employees began using the "reply all" function to angrily request they be removed from the e-mail thread. Hundreds of e-mails, each sent to over 33, 000 recipients, began slowing down the company's servers as employees took to social media to post about what became called "#ReutersReplyAllGate."[4] This large-scale misuse of the "reply all" function—from the original message to the hundreds of follow-ups—speaks to the importance of using e-mail correctly, effectively, and with respectful tone and style.

Memorandums

Memorandums, more commonly known as **memos**, can be many things—reminders, instructions, records of actions and decisions, data-gathering tools, and aids to problem-solving. Memos are a fast, efficient way of informing people inside your organization and getting answers. The paper memo was once the primary means of inter-office communication. Its distinctive style and structure has left its mark on **e-mail**, the channel for both internal and external messaging that has essentially replaced it. E-mail brings the best of memo style to internal and external communication, using its time-saving format and straightforward approach while eliminating printing.

Memos and e-mail are the workhorses of business communication, indispensable aids to gathering, sharing, and analyzing information about products, day-to-day operations, services, stakeholders, and personnel. Bringing corporate levels together, memos and e-mail are the most common ways for managers to inform employees of policies and decisions and for employees to stay informed and offer their input. Writing them well can win kudos for employees eyeing the road to advancement. It therefore pays to perfect the e-mail style through which your managers and co-workers will come to know you and to always review your messages before you send them.

The advantage of a typical memo is its simplicity. It is designed to be read quickly, even when it is organized like a report or conveys vital information. Usually less formal than a standard letter, a well-written memo opens with its purpose—the main idea or primary action—and is presented so that it makes sense even to secondary readers. Any hard-copy or electronic memo should be clear, concise, and informative, sharing the following common traits:

1. single-topic focus
2. brevity
3. two-part structure, consiting of a **header** (*Date*, *To*, *From*, *Subject* guide words) and message (divided into an opening, body, and closing)

Because corporate e-mail systems vary and style guidelines are constantly evolving, there is some variation in the way writers treat e-mail and in the form some messages may take. Some writers use salutations; others don't. In some instances, a complex or critically important memo might be more than a page, or an e-mail message might fill more than a single screen. However, the longer or more complicated a message happens to be, the more it requires additional formatting techniques such as the use of **headings**, subheadings, **boldfaced** elements, **italics**, **bullets**, and lists.

Memo Format

A memo has a no-fuss, two-part structure. The *Date*, *To*, *From*, and *Subject* headings or fields tell readers exactly what they need to know about a message's content and distribution. In replacing standard letter elements such as the inside address, salutation, and complimentary close, these guide words save time and make formatting easy. They can appear in horizontal or vertical format, and their standard order can be altered to suit a company's needs.

memo A specially formatted document sent to readers within an organization.

e-mail Messages distributed by a computerized mail service.

header A block of text appearing at the top of a document.

headings Visual markers consisting of words or short phrases that indicate the parts of a document and signpost its organization.

boldface A thick, black typeface used for emphasis.

italics Sloping letters used for emphasis or to distinguish foreign words.

bullets Visual cues, usually large dots or squares, that set off items in a vertical list or emphasize lines.

It is common practice to type guide words in capital letters, leaving a blank line between headings and three blank lines before the body of the memo. The fill-in information following each guide word should be aligned, usually two to three spaces following the longest guide word ("SUBJECT"). Many companies provide memo templates, as do "wizards" in most word-processing programs, that simplify the tasks of formatting and alignment.

Each heading in a memo serves a particular purpose:

DATE:	Provides the complete and current date. To reduce confusion, follow company practice in choosing between North American (May 1, 2018) and European (1 May 2018) styles.
TO:	Identifies the destination or the person(s) to whom the message is addressed. The job title and department of the addressee are optional, except when the name alone isn't enough to ensure that the message reaches its destination. Courtesy titles (e.g., Ms., Mr.) and professional titles (e.g., Rev., Dr.) may also be omitted unless you are addressing a superior. Dispense with surnames only if you are on a first-name basis with the addressee. If your memo is directed to several people, list their names alphabetically or in descending order of importance in the company hierarchy. Crowded address lines can be avoided by simply using a group designation ("Claims Processors," "Marketing Group," etc.).
FROM:	Identifies the author or origin of the message. Your job title and the name of your department can be used if your name alone is not sufficient to identify you as the writer. Courtesy titles generally aren't used because they're too formal to suit this relatively informal mode of communication. The practice of initialling the end of the line applies to hard-copy memos only.
SUBJECT:	Identifies the topic and/or purpose of the message for reading and filing. The more old-fashioned "RE" (from the Latin for "about" or "concerning") is sometimes also used to designate the content of the message. Ideally, the subject description should not exceed one line. It does not have to be a complete sentence and can be abbreviated (leaving out articles—*the*, *a*, and *an*). Nevertheless, it must be specific enough to give readers a full and accurate idea of what follows (e.g., instead of "Estimate" write "Cost Reduction Estimate") or how they are to act on your information (e.g., "Cost Reduction Estimate for Review").
CC:	This abbreviation stands for "carbon copy," an obsolete term for the generic "copy." Insert the name(s) of anyone who will receive a copy of the message but is not an addressee. In the case of e-mail, avoid unnecessary copying, especially if sending the memo electronically, so as not to that will clog receivers' inboxes and e-mail systems. Learn what others want and need to be copied on.

Memo Organization

Even though memos tend to be short and informal, they still require forethought and planning. Before you begin to write, consider the facts and issues you must cover and anticipate your readers' needs. Then, choose a writing plan that meets those requirements. Most positive and neutral messages conveying routine or non-sensitive information can be organized in the following way:

opening The first paragraph of a memo; contains the most important information regarding the subject matter, the purpose for writing, and/or the action required by the reader.

Opening

Use the **opening** for your most important information, purpose for writing, or required action.

Don't mechanically restate the **subject line**; fill in the *who, what, where, when, why,* and *how.*

Get to the point as quickly as possible. One to three sentences are usually sufficient to summarize your central idea.

Include a few words of context telling readers why they need to know the information you're sharing:

> *"To maintain productivity levels during power outages, our company has leased an on-site power system from Energy Now."*

Body

In the **body** of the memo, move on to more detailed information. Expand on, discuss, or explain the problem, assignment, request, or required action.

Include only the details your readers must know to act on your information.

If you are relaying a sequence of actions or several requests, put them in a grammatically parallel list prefaced by a summary statement that gives readers an overview or glimpse of the "big picture."

Points may be presented:
1. chronologically
2. in order of specificity (most to least or vice versa)
3. in order of importance (most to least or vice versa)

Make sure the body provides sufficient background and clearly identifies deadlines and people involved.

Closing

In **closing**, summarize your request or call for action, clearly indicating who should do what, by when, and for how long.

If compliance isn't assured, point out alternatives or benefits to readers.

It may be appropriate to end-date requests, cite reasons for them, invite feedback, provide contact information, tell readers where they can get more information, or state what happens next.

Avoid canned or mechanical phrases that do not suit the situation, and show courtesy and appreciation as the situation merits.

Double-spacing between paragraphs visually separates topics and reinforces good organization. Graphic highlighting techniques can help emphasize key information, but be aware that some e-mail systems may not allow you to use features such as boldface or italics. For memos longer than a page, open with a summary statement (a condensed version of the memo highlighting purpose and action sought), and organize the rest of your information under headings. Even basic headings such as "Problem," "Situation," and "Solution" can help readers understand and act on your ideas and initiatives. To simplify messaging and ensure uniformity, some companies provide templates for different kinds of memos: ones delivering information, asking for action, or demanding urgent action.

subject line The part of a memo or an e-mail that indicates the document's title, topic, purpose, and importance.

body The middle paragraph(s) of a memo; provides necessary background and more detailed information about the subject matter.

closing The final paragraph of a memo; summarizes the content and indicates next steps, invites feedback, offers further resources, and/or provides contact information.

list A group of three or more logically related items presented consecutively to form a record or aid to memory.

When you must deliver bad news or write persuasively, start with the evidence. Readers are more likely to accept a decision, even a negative one, when they are prepared for it and know it is logical and well justified.

Formatting Lists for Memos and E-mail

A **list** is a group of three or more logically related items. Ideally, lists in memos and e-mails should be between three and eight points. The purpose of a list is to order and emphasize important information—breaking up solid blocks of text, sequencing events and actions, and making concepts easier to understand, remember, and reference. Using similar phrasing for each item, where every item begins with the same part of speech, reinforces the similarity of the list's content.

To be effective, a list must have these features:

- a lead-in introducing, explaining, and putting the items that follow in context
- parallel phrasing for every item
- semantic and grammatical continuity between the lead-in and items (every item must read grammatically with the lead-in)
- adequate transition to the sentences that follow after the list

Lists are formatted in two ways: horizontally (or in-sentence) and vertically (with points preceded by bullets, numbers, or sometimes letters). Horizontal lists give minimal emphasis but are less intrusive:

> We will discuss the following items at next Monday's meeting: the need for new quality control measures, the performance of our customer service hotline, and the proposed switch to voice-recognition phone technology.

> As director of commercial real estate finance, you will monitor market trends, provide information and support on our lending programs, and recommend refinements to existing programs.

A colon is required before a list if the lead-in forms a complete sentence (as in the first example above). For additional impact, individual items can be introduced with a letter or number enclosed in parentheses.

> Please bring the following items with you on retreat: (1) walking shoes, (2) a raincoat, and (3) sunscreen.

If your list has more than four or five items, a vertical list is a better choice.

With their high visual impact, vertical lists break up imposing blocks of texts into manageable "bite-sized" segments. Introduce a list with a strong explanatory lead-in that reads logically and grammatically with each point that follows. If your introduction is complete, you will not need to repeat explanatory details in each point. Punctuate the lead-in with a colon if it is a complete sentence; use no punctuation if the lead-in depends on the point that follows to complete its meaning.

☒ Our company
- has one segment that deals with investing
- has another segment that takes care of mortgages
- also has leasing operations

☑ Our company has three key business segments:
- investing
- mortgage operations
- leasing operations

Use numbers or letters to indicate chronological sequence or importance, especially if you plan on referring to an item later. Numbers are useful for indicating priority. Bullets, on the other hand, suggest that all items are equally important.

When each point forms a complete sentence, capitalize and punctuate each item as you would a sentence. If you are giving instructions or issuing directives or polite commands, begin each item with an action verb:

To ensure fairness in the evaluation process, please follow these instructions:
- Distribute evaluation forms to seminar participants.
- Remind participants that their responses will remain confidential.
- Ask for a volunteer to collect and mail completed forms.
- Leave the room.

Try not to mix clauses and sentences that require different terminal punctuation. Any item expressed as a complete sentence or as a phrase that completes the lead-in requires terminal punctuation, as does any item consisting of two or more sentences.

Apply the principles of **chunking**—a yardstick for list design—to determine how many items a vertical list can accommodate. The average person's short-term memory can store seven pieces of data, plus or minus two, depending on the complexity of the information. If your list has more than eight items, it can lose its focus and purpose. In such cases, it is best to find a way to subdivide points and consolidate them under appropriate lead-ins.

> **chunking** The grouping of related items together so they are remembered as a unit.

Paper Memo vs. E-mail

You do not always have to opt for electronic transmission over paper-based messaging. There are instances where a hard-copy memo is preferable, when legality, confidentiality, or document integrity (preserving the layout or formatting features that e-mail systems cannot accommodate) are primary concerns. Traditional paper memos do without the informal salutations and complimentary closes sometimes used in e-mails.

Figure 6.1 shows a memo that functions as a letter of transmittal accompanying and explaining other hard-copy documents.

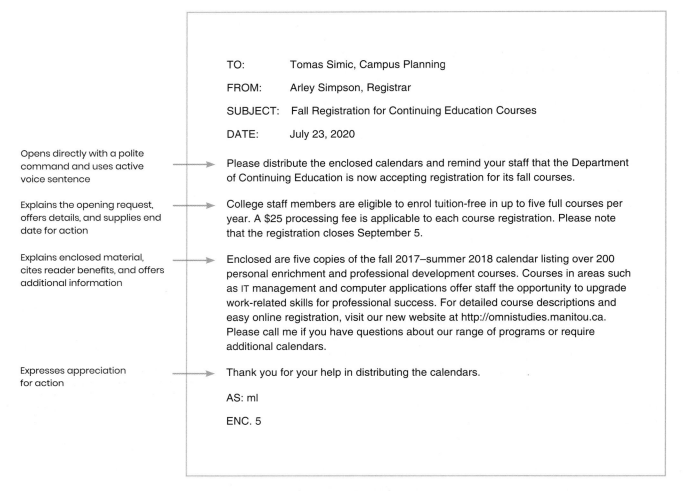

Opens directly with a polite command and uses active voice sentence

Explains the opening request, offers details, and supplies end date for action

Explains enclosed material, cites reader benefits, and offers additional information

Expresses appreciation for action

TO: Tomas Simic, Campus Planning

FROM: Arley Simpson, Registrar

SUBJECT: Fall Registration for Continuing Education Courses

DATE: July 23, 2020

Please distribute the enclosed calendars and remind your staff that the Department of Continuing Education is now accepting registration for its fall courses.

College staff members are eligible to enrol tuition-free in up to five full courses per year. A $25 processing fee is applicable to each course registration. Please note that the registration closes September 5.

Enclosed are five copies of the fall 2017–summer 2018 calendar listing over 200 personal enrichment and professional development courses. Courses in areas such as IT management and computer applications offer staff the opportunity to upgrade work-related skills for professional success. For detailed course descriptions and easy online registration, visit our new website at http://omnistudies.manitou.ca. Please call me if you have questions about our range of programs or require additional calendars.

Thank you for your help in distributing the calendars.

AS: ml

ENC. 5

FIGURE 6.1 Sample Paper-Based Memo

Checklist

Memos

- ❏ Fill in appropriate information, including a strong subject line, after headers.
- ❏ Be brief.
- ❏ Follow the style guidelines of your organization.
- ❏ Be direct and begin with your most important point when relaying routine news or information.
- ❏ Provide only as much background or evidence as your reader needs to act on your instructions or information.
- ❏ Itemize supporting details, related questions, and additional requests in bulleted or numbered lists in parallel form.
- ❏ End courteously with a request for specific action, reason for the request, and deadline.

E-mail

Few technologies have had such dramatic impact on the business world as e-mail has in recent years. E-mail is now the most common means of transmitting workplace documents and files. Its advantage—and ironically its disadvantage—is that messages can be produced easily and quickly and transmitted instantaneously. E-mail's versatile capabilities and wide availability make it an ideal productivity tool—a cheap and convenient way to access, exchange, and process information; collaborate; and communicate with staff and customers. One of the advantages e-mail has is that it is not public. Thus, many businesses encourage dissatisfied customers to contact them by e-mail, where their concerns can be dealt with discretely. Dealing with customer service complaints in this way rather than through more public forums (e.g., social media platforms) prevents complaints from damaging a company's reputation or hurting future business.

The widespread use of smartphones and tablets has meant that employees can access their workplace e-mail at any time and from almost any location, leading many to work remotely beyond set office hours.

E-mails can also be a source of corporate embarrassment—a smoking gun that can offer incriminating and permanent proof of companies' wrongdoing. Because e-mails can end up anywhere and compromise confidential and classified information, many organizations have been forced to clamp down on e-mail use and to regulate and monitor it closely, even going as far as requiring employees to save their messages for several years as proof of ethical conduct.

While e-mail has certainly changed the way companies do business, many of the e-mail practices that are meant to boost efficiency can result in poor, lazy behaviours that waste time and energy and leave recipients frustrated and vexed by unwanted messages. Not surprisingly, e-mail has its own special set of problems: clogged inboxes; indiscriminate distribution lists; serious privacy violations; uncooperative servers; unsolicited, sloppy, inflammatory, or undeliverable messages; and difficult-to-follow "thread" e-mails. The urge to check for incoming messages or to hit the "Send" button without first reviewing a message can strike even the most disciplined e-mail user. An ever-increasing portion of a typical day at or even away from the office involves the necessary but sometimes tedious work that e-mail demands. The fact that it is possible to access e-mail almost anywhere at any time has created a round-the-clock virtual workday. A 2015 survey conducted by Angus Reid revealed that 41 per cent of Canadians who use technology at work check their work e-mail outside of office hours.[5]

Although some users may love the technology, they should also stop to consider e-mail's relevance and suitability to a given task. Because e-mail is a hybrid form of speaking and writing, users sometimes have trouble deciding exactly what it replaces—an informal chat or a formal hard-copy letter—which accounts for the range of e-mail styles and quirky tonal variations that characterize today's e-mail traffic.

Some organizations have come to the rescue by instituting e-mail guidelines regarding what their employees can say and how to format that information. Though these guidelines vary from organization to organization and though e-mail style varies from document to document, savvy communicators recognize the value of smart e-mail practices. Knowing your **netiquette** and being proactive in managing your messaging makes e-mail a channel that is fast, functional, and efficient.

netiquette The informal code of conduct governing polite, efficient, and effective use of the Internet.

General E-mail Guidelines

Keep in mind some general considerations for successful electronic communication:

1. Keep it brief.

- A short message is most likely to be read fully. Long messages may end up being skimmed, marked to be read later, or simply forgotten.
- Consider using attachments or breaking up longer text (e.g., with headings) to visually highlight key messages.[6]
- Include only as much information as recipients need to take action and make decisions.

2. Remember that e-mail is not your only option.

- Strive for a balance between technology and human contact.
- Don't use e-mail simply to avoid face-to-face contact, especially if you wish only to distance yourself from conflicts, arguments, or bad news.
- Match the situation to the correct communication channel.

3. Compose crucial messages offline.

- This allows you to review messages and reduces the chance that they will be lost after technical issues.

4. Follow organizational rules for e-mail.

- Some companies have standardized procedures for e-mail; some have only unwritten or loosely applied guidelines.
- If rules haven't been established, allow the most effective messages you receive to guide you.

5. Don't use company e-mail for personal communication.

- Your organization's resources shouldn't be used to shop or send personal photos or personal messages.
- Though some companies allow their employees "reasonable personal use" of e-mail, others prohibit it. Sending personal e-mails and using the Internet for matters unrelated to business is risky and may have professional repercussions for you.

6. Aim for a balance of speed and accuracy.

- E-mail readers are generally more tolerant of writing errors, but there are limits to allowances for incorrect spelling, poor grammar, and misused punctuation.
- Ensure that your spell-check software is set to the correct language, and review your messages to catch errors in spelling, grammar, and punctuation before you hit "Send."
- Give important, non-routine e-mails with many recipients close and careful reading, and employ the same kinds of strategic planning and range of writing skills as you would for non-electronic documents.
- Because e-mail involves the rapid exchange of information, let your readers' needs be your guide, but don't double or triple your composition time by putting every single word under the microscope. After all, e-mail should boost your productivity, not reduce it.

7. Keep your messages professional.

- Only use emoticons and emojis in cases where you are mimicking the style of the person you're communicating with, and even then use them only if the situation and your audience's expectations truly call for them[7].
- Instead, state your business plainly in standard English. Use *please* and *thank you* for the sake of politeness, and adjust your tone if you want to sound friendlier.
- Use your e-mail system's settings to add an electronic signature containing your name, professional title, and, if you like, other contact information or even a photo. Decide if you want different signatures for different situations

8. Understand that e-mail is not guaranteed to be private.

- Even deleted e-mail can be retrieved, providing a permanent record of actions and decisions. It can be saved, archived, forwarded, and even used as legal evidence. Some companies even monitor employee e-mail.
- Avoid sending gossipy, incriminating, disparaging, or inflammatory messages. Refrain from making jokes, sarcastic jabs, or facetious remarks.
- Don't write anything in an e-mail that you wouldn't want published in the company newsletter.

9. Don't "write angry".

- Avoid electronic aggression and **flaming**—firing back and venting anger via e-mail. Instead, communicate contentious matters and sensitive is sues through other channels, preferably ones with visual or tonal cues.
- If you have to deal with an angry e-mail, give yourself enough time to cool down and consider your response before you reply. If an immediate response is not required, save the draft overnight, review the document the next day, and then decide whether to trash or revise it.

10. Don't send unnecessary messages.

- Don't send trivial messages or ones that say merely "thank you" or "you're welcome." Respect your fellow e-mail users by putting a stop to time-wasting messages.
- With some exceptions, for example when a message just can't wait, avoid sending e-mail late in the day or on weekends if it means the receiver's time will be infringed upon without justification.
- Review the **distribution list** before sending an e-mail to ensure that it has been properly updated and that your message will reach only those recipients to whom it is relevant.

11. Protect yourself and your company.

- Be aware of ownership and copyright issues and safeguard your organization's intellectual property. Add a copyright symbol (©) to all corporate material intended for Internet posting.
- Keep your password and user ID confidential to ensure secure applications aren't compromised.
- Fight **spam** by using anti-spam software that blocks unwanted messages and by not posting your e-mail address on web pages, where it can be easily copied by spammers.
- Exercise caution in opening any file attachment you suspect has been corrupted. Computer malware and viruses can have a devastating impact on data security, with implications for the entireorganization.

flaming The act of sending out an angry e-mail message in haste without considering the implications of airing such emotions.

distribution list A group of e-mail recipients addressed as a single recipient, allowing the sender to e-mail many users without entering their individual addresses.

spam An advertising message—electronic junk mail—sent widely and indiscriminately.

In October 2015, professional networking site LinkedIn settled a class-action lawsuit in which users accused the organization of repeatedly spamming their contacts with requests to join the site. LinkedIn agreed to pay $13 million in compensation as part of the settlement.

Reading and Processing Incoming Messages

Manage your e-mail and maintain professionalism by following a few common-sense principles:

1. **Schedule time for reading and writing e-mail.** While urgent messages may require an immediate response, you can effectively deal with most e-mails by setting aside a few times a day to read and respond. Be systematic, first scanning for important messages from stakeholders and superiors and leaving personal messages for last. Check for incoming messages regularly, especially before sending out anything significant, just in case a new incoming message necessitates a reply different from the one you had in mind. After long absences, open your most recent mail first, then scan for earlier messages from critical stakeholders and superiors.

2. **Do regular inbox clean-ups.** Learn what your company expects you to file or archive, then get rid of the clutter by deleting unwanted, irrelevant, or outdated messages and checking for ones that may have escaped your attention. Assign messages you want to save to project files. Update your e-mail address book.

3. **Scan all new messages in your inbox.** Read all current messages before writing follow-up responses.

4. **Use filtering options and anti-spam software.** Ensure the mail you get is the mail you want. Most companies make ample provision for this in their e-mail systems.

5. **Properly store e-mail messages.** Follow your organization's guidelines for the secure management and storage of your messages.

Formatting and Writing E-mail

As you prepare to write, follow these tips to ensure your message stays on target and gets the attention it deserves:

1. **Type the e-mail address correctly.** Rely on your electronic address book if you routinely leave out or mistype characters. Determine distribution and mailing lists beforehand so you can tailor messages to recipients' specific needs. Add "CC" (copy feature) and "BCC" (blind copy feature) addresses accordingly. Send copies only to people who have a legitimate need for your information, and keep some e-mail addresses anonymous if recipients are likely to object to their circulation.

2. **Compose an action-specific subject line.** Subject lines help readers decide how relevant, important, and urgent a message is. Labels such as "URGENT" can be used from time to time when companies approve of them. Subject lines should be descriptive, relate logically to the message, and strategically set the tone. Be specific—for example, instead of "New Statement" (too general) write "Revised Quality Assurance Statement." If an action is needed, use a verb (e.g., "Complete Attached Survey"). Be sure to revise reply subject lines when they no longer reflect the content of the message. E-mails without subject lines are most likely to be deleted without being read.

3. **Design messages for clarity and readability.** Apply reader-friendly formatting to make your e-mail visually appealing and quickly scannable. Use a standard, professional font (e.g., Arial, Calibri). Use headings, boldface, lists, and other formatting techniques to break up larger blocks of text into manageable segments. Do not write messages in all caps. If you use bold, italics, or underlining, be aware that some platforms won't accommodate them. In such cases, use asterisks (*) around a word to show italics and underscores (_) to show underlining.

4. **Keep paragraphs and sentences short.** You should aim to keep text shorter than in regular word-processing documents. Use double-spaced paragraph breaks for emphasis and readability. Smart organization means less reading time per message, helping readers cope with the ever-increasing volume of inbound e-mail.

As you begin to compose your message, keep in mind the following strategies for shaping its content:

1. **Use appropriate greetings to soften messages.** When you know the recipient well, include an informal **salutation** (e.g., *Hello*, *Hi*, or *Greetings*), either on its own or followed by the recipient's first name. Memos omit greetings, and quick, routine messages may not require a greeting but can sound impolite or abrupt without one. For external e-mail, salutations are recommended, but avoid the "one-size-fits-all" approach and make sure the greeting you choose fits the context. Use *Dear Ms.* or *Mr.* (plus the recipient's last name) when you aren't on a first-name basis with the recipient and *Dear* (followed by the recipient's first name) when you know the person well.

> **salutation** The greeting in a letter, used to address the person being written to.

2. **Get to the point immediately.** Begin by asking for action, information, or a reply or by providing an overview if your message runs longer than one screen. A strong opening that identifies issues, people, products, or services is vital to a message's success.

3. **Use lists without overloading them.** Divide material into short, manageable segments or into lists with bullet points or numbers.

4. **Sign off with a complimentary close when appropriate.** Your closing should maintain the tone of your greeting and of your message as a whole. If nothing too formal is required, a simple *Regards* or *Thanks* will do. Reserve *Sincerely* for messages where you need to show deference. Use *Cheers* only if the message is cheerful. Drop the **complimentary close** in quick routine messages where politeness isn't a concern or in messages that function as memos.

5. **Tell people who you are.** For external e-mails in particular, set up an automatic signature. Recipients will then know (as listed vertically) your first and last name, (optionally, degrees held), job title and company affiliation, contact information including company website and international prefixes for contact numbers. Your signature might also include clickable-icon links to your professional social profiles, a photo, meeting booking link, call-to-action, pronouns (e.g., "She/Her," "They/Their"), and territorial statement.

6. **Edit your text and run a spell-check.** Readers won't expect absolute perfection, but the more correct your e-mail is, the more professional and credible you will seem.

7. **Follow common-sense rules for attachments.** Before you create an **attachment**, consider if its contents could be put in the text of the message. Label attachment documents so they can be easily recognized, and summarize their contents in your e-mail. Identify the application you are running as well as its version, and ask permission before sending large attachments, or multiple attachments, to make sure your recipient's system or device can handle them.

8. **Don't be impatient for a reply.** Be patient and allow a reasonable amount of time for a response. If you need an immediate answer on a pressing matter, make a quick telephone call instead of sending an e-mail.

complimentary close A formulaic closing, usually a word found after the body of a letter and before the signature.

attachment An independent computer file sent with a regular e-mail message.

Many of the above tips also pertain to e-mail replies, but Figure 6.2 describes a few more guidelines to consider when writing responses.

E-mail Style and Tone

The style and tone of your e-mails make a statement about your personal and professional image. If you keep in mind what your e-mail replaces—a face-to-face conversation, a telephone call, a hard-copy letter, a traditional proposal—you will begin to understand how informal or formal your style and tone should be.

E-mail is so flexible and adaptable that it accommodates a range of styles. Semi-formal or conversational style applies to most e-mail messages, especially routine communication. It resembles the proceedings of a well-conducted meeting. Personal pronouns, contractions, and active-voice constructions make this style crisp and accessible. E-mail tends to be less formal than other forms of communication; however, a telegraphic style marked by abrupt shifts in topic and omitted subject words is not recommended for most e-mail messages.

Reply as promptly as possible.

- Develop a response game plan, deciding how best to juggle this and other tasks. If you can't reply immediately or are unsure of how to reply, write a quick message indicating that you will send a full reply later.

- If you anticipate conflict or must deliver bad news, consider other channels—the phone, Skype, or a face-to-face conversation.

Modify your distribution list.

- If you receive a group e-mail, you may need to send your response to the entire group or only a few members. Think twice before you automatically hit "Reply All."

- Prune the distribution list so that only individuals who have a legitimate need for your message receive it.

- Indiscriminate use of "CC" and "Reply All" tops the list of e-mail users' biggest complaints, so take a few seconds to decide who needs the contents of your reply and who doesn't.

Don't automatically include the sender's original message with your reply.

- When determining how much of the original message to incorporate in a reply, consider the context in which your reply should be placed. For short, routine messages, the original can be included with your reply, but be sure to put the latter at the top so readers don't need to scroll down.

- If you decide not to return the sender's message, provide a reply full enough (not just "OK" or "No problem") for readers to know exactly what you're referring to. For engthy or complex messages, type your response next to the relevant portions of the original message, but always make sure the distinction between your words and those of the original is clear.

Avoid indiscriminately forwarding e-mails.

- Consider whom the message is relevant to and who really needs the information.

Make provision for your absences from the office.

- Use automatic out-of-office outgoing messages to let people who are trying to reach you know you are out of the office, when you will return, and whom they can contact in your absence.

Protect and respect authorship.

- Select a read-only status for critical documents that could subsequently be altered without your knowledge and retain a time-stamped copy of the original.

- Always credit the original author of forwarded documents. The rules of plagiarism apply equally to electronic communication.

FIGURE 6.2 Additional Guidelines for Writing E-mail responses

Tone is hard to control in e-mail because of the rapid and informal way most messages are written. For many e-mail users, the prime concern is simply getting their point across clearly and not how a message sounds. This may make people sound cold, impersonal, or rude to those who know them through only their e-mail, leading to anger, resentment, or impatience. To avoid such misunderstandings, think of your recipients, their needs, and how they might respond in a conversation. Then read your message back to detect inappropriate tonal cues, and make adjustments where necessary.

Routine Messages: Positive and Informative Memos and E-mail

informative memo A brief message conveying information to which the reader will react neutrally.

Informative memos and e-mail convey announcements, company policies, guidelines, instructions, and procedures. Informative messages must be clear and direct in order for readers to put directives into practice and carry through on initiatives. A clearly worded subject line, direct opening, clear explanation, follow-up instructions (often in a numbered list), good closing, and positive emphasis all support an informative aim.

Figures 6.3 and 6.4 are two versions of a message explaining the adoption of new ordering procedures for office catering services. In Figure 6.3, numerous faults reduce the effectiveness of the message, whereas in Figure 6.4, the message is specific, descriptive, clear, and informative. Figure 6.3 begins with a vague subject line that doesn't accurately describe the message's purpose or content. Its negative opening puts a complaint

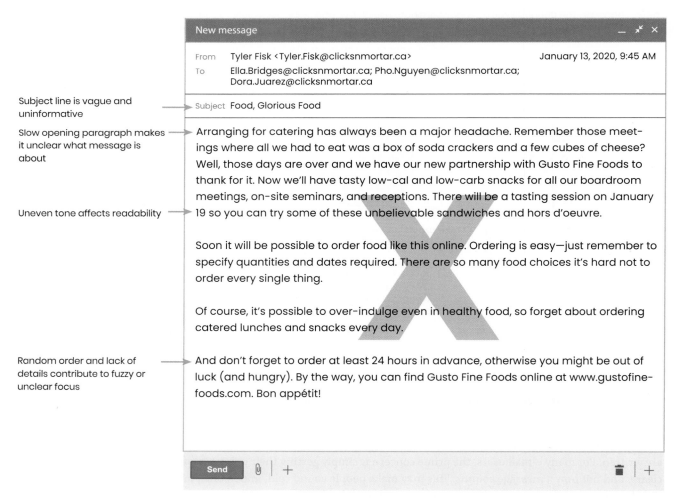

Subject line is vague and uninformative

Slow opening paragraph makes it unclear what message is about

Uneven tone affects readability

Random order and lack of details contribute to fuzzy or unclear focus

New message

From   Tyler Fisk <Tyler.Fisk@clicksnmortar.ca>   January 13, 2020, 9:45 AM
To   Ella.Bridges@clicksnmortar.ca; Pho.Nguyen@clicksnmortar.ca; Dora.Juarez@clicksnmortar.ca

Subject Food, Glorious Food

Arranging for catering has always been a major headache. Remember those meetings where all we had to eat was a box of soda crackers and a few cubes of cheese? Well, those days are over and we have our new partnership with Gusto Fine Foods to thank for it. Now we'll have tasty low-cal and low-carb snacks for all our boardroom meetings, on-site seminars, and receptions. There will be a tasting session on January 19 so you can try some of these unbelievable sandwiches and hors d'oeuvre.

Soon it will be possible to order food like this online. Ordering is easy—just remember to specify quantities and dates required. There are so many food choices it's hard not to order every single thing.

Of course, it's possible to over-indulge even in healthy food, so forget about ordering catered lunches and snacks every day.

And don't forget to order at least 24 hours in advance, otherwise you might be out of luck (and hungry). By the way, you can find Gusto Fine Foods online at www.gustofine-foods.com. Bon appétit!

Send

FIGURE 6.3 Ineffective Informative E-mail Draft

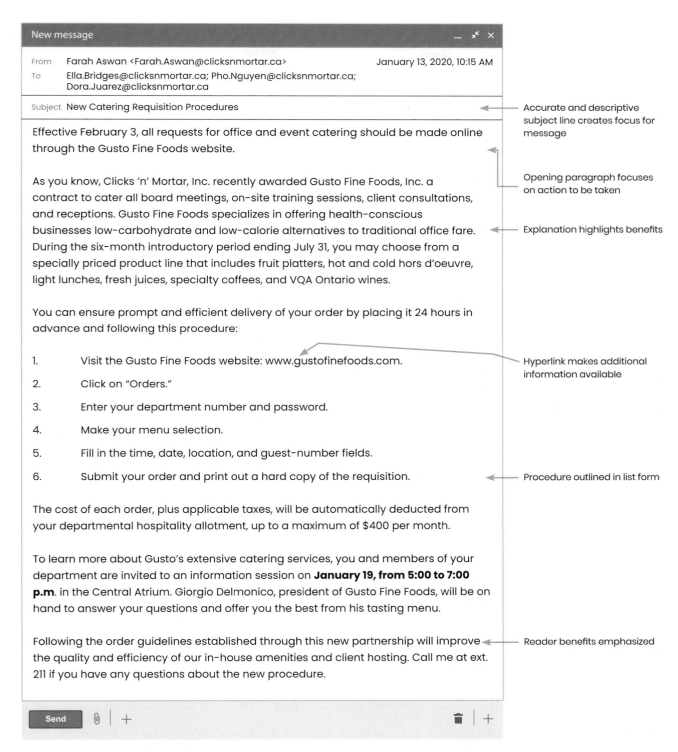

New message   — ⤢ ✕

From   Farah Aswan <Farah.Aswan@clicksnmortar.ca>   January 13, 2020, 10:15 AM
To   Ella.Bridges@clicksnmortar.ca; Pho.Nguyen@clicksnmortar.ca; Dora.Juarez@clicksnmortar.ca

Subject   New Catering Requisition Procedures   ← Accurate and descriptive subject line creates focus for message

Effective February 3, all requests for office and event catering should be made online through the Gusto Fine Foods website.   ← Opening paragraph focuses on action to be taken

As you know, Clicks 'n' Mortar, Inc. recently awarded Gusto Fine Foods, Inc. a contract to cater all board meetings, on-site training sessions, client consultations, and receptions. Gusto Fine Foods specializes in offering health-conscious businesses low-carbohydrate and low-calorie alternatives to traditional office fare.   ← Explanation highlights benefits
During the six-month introductory period ending July 31, you may choose from a specially priced product line that includes fruit platters, hot and cold hors d'oeuvre, light lunches, fresh juices, specialty coffees, and VQA Ontario wines.

You can ensure prompt and efficient delivery of your order by placing it 24 hours in advance and following this procedure:

1.   Visit the Gusto Fine Foods website: www.gustofinefoods.com.   ← Hyperlink makes additional information available

2.   Click on "Orders."

3.   Enter your department number and password.

4.   Make your menu selection.

5.   Fill in the time, date, location, and guest-number fields.

6.   Submit your order and print out a hard copy of the requisition.   ← Procedure outlined in list form

The cost of each order, plus applicable taxes, will be automatically deducted from your departmental hospitality allotment, up to a maximum of $400 per month.

To learn more about Gusto's extensive catering services, you and members of your department are invited to an information session on **January 19, from 5:00 to 7:00 p.m.** in the Central Atrium. Giorgio Delmonico, president of Gusto Fine Foods, will be on hand to answer your questions and offer you the best from his tasting menu.

Following the order guidelines established through this new partnership will improve   ← Reader benefits emphasized
the quality and efficiency of our in-house amenities and client hosting. Call me at ext. 211 if you have any questions about the new procedure.

Send   0   +   🗑   +

FIGURE 6.4 **Effective Informative E-mail**

first, well before important information, so it isn't immediately clear what the message is about. Random, out-of-sequence steps aren't itemized, making the instructions difficult to follow. The tone is alternatively breezy and accusatory, creating incoherence, and many key details are left out—the effective date of the new ordering procedure, the time and location of the tasting session, and contact information.

Figure 6.4, however, creates a focus for the message with a specific and descriptive subject line. The direct opening tells readers exactly what the message is about, and the second paragraph indicates why the new procedure must be implemented and explains its advantages. The numbered list shows the steps in the new procedure in sequence, simplifying instructions for easy reference. The hyperlink to the catering company's website allows readers to access information that can't be provided in a short message. To encourage compliance, the writer reminds readers of the new procedure's benefits and invites their questions by offering contact information in the final paragraph. Readers are left knowing when the new procedures go into effect and what they are supposed to do.

The purpose of an informative message can also be to confirm a change in plans or schedule or to acknowledge receipt of materials. Writing an acknowledgement is usually a matter of courtesy and requires no more than one or two sentences.

Routine Messages: Request Memos and E-mail

request memo A message that asks the reader to perform a routine action.

If you seek routine information or action, always use the direct approach. **Request memos** and e-mail stand a greater chance of gaining compliance when readers know by the end of the first paragraph what you are asking for and what action they must take. This directive is usually expressed as a polite command (e.g., "Please explain the procedure for ordering a transcript of one of your broadcasts") or a direct question (e.g., "How may I obtain a transcript of one of your broadcasts?"). Multiple requests can be introduced by a summary statement and then listed as numbered or bulleted questions. For ease of response, readers can be invited to reply within the original message. Explanations and justifications belong in the body of the message. While politeness is key to gaining compliance, citing a reason for the request, reader benefits, and an end date can build goodwill and help to ensure a useful and timely response. A consistent tone that's not too apologetic or demanding reduces the chance readers will overlook or be resistant to your request. See Figure 6.5 for an example of an effective request message.

Requests that make sizable demands on the reader's time and resources should follow the indirect plan (see Chapter 8) that includes a reason for the request. If you think the reader may not readily comply, reduce resistance by persuading with reasons and justifications.

Routine Messages: Reply Memos and E-mail

response A message that answers a request or query.

Like requests, **responses** are crucial to the day-to-day operation of organizations. Response messages deliver specific information itemized in the order that the requests were made. Using the direct approach (see Chapter 8), you can write an effective response that is complete, focused, and well organized. Open by announcing the most important fact or answer (often by referring to the previous message), sharing good news, or introducing

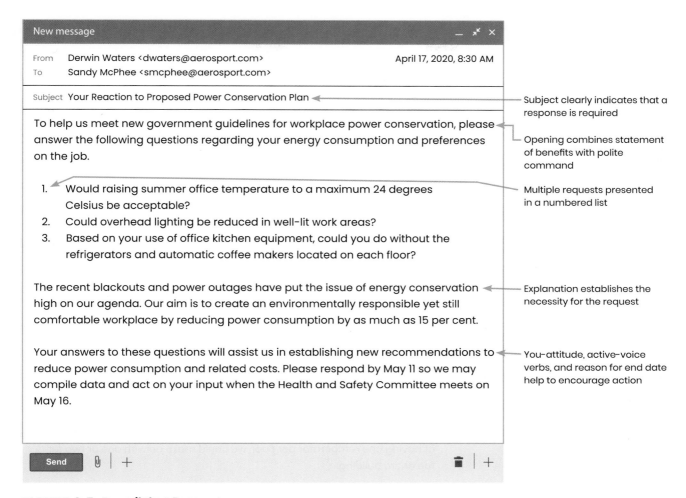

FIGURE 6.5 E-mail that Requests

multiple responses by way of a summary statement. Arranging these responses according to the order of the original request saves time and increases coherence. You can use bolded headings or catchphrases to summarize the focus of each response. It may be appropriate to provide additional information relevant to the original request. The closing sums up your response or offers further assistance. A prompt reply indicates both efficiency and a willingness to help. The e-mail in Figure 6.6 is a reply to the message in Figure 6.5.

Goodwill E-mails

In putting good wishes ahead of business transactions, **goodwill messages** help reinforce the professional and personal bonds between writer and reader. Thank-you messages express appreciation for help, invitations, hospitality, interviews, recommendations, past business, favours, emergency services, and special duties performed. Congratulatory messages recognize special achievements or milestones—career promotions, job appointments, awards, or special honours. These types of messages first identify

goodwill message A message that enhances the value of a business beyond its tangible assets by creating a bond of friendship and establishing trust and mutual understanding between the writer and the recipient.

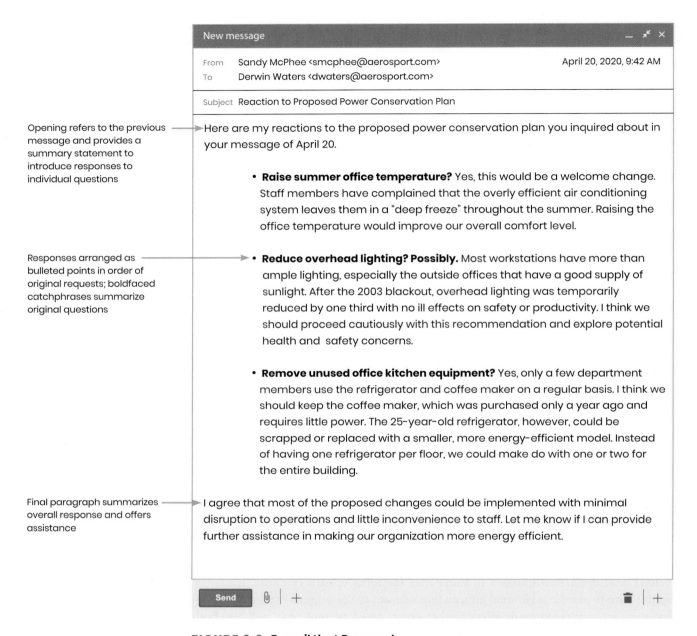

Opening refers to the previous message and provides a summary statement to introduce responses to individual questions

Responses arranged as bulleted points in order of original requests; boldfaced catchphrases summarize original questions

Final paragraph summarizes overall response and offers assistance

New message

From   Sandy McPhee <smcphee@aerosport.com>   April 20, 2020, 9:42 AM
To   Derwin Waters <dwaters@aerosport.com>

Subject   Reaction to Proposed Power Conservation Plan

Here are my reactions to the proposed power conservation plan you inquired about in your message of April 20.

- **Raise summer office temperature?** Yes, this would be a welcome change. Staff members have complained that the overly efficient air conditioning system leaves them in a "deep freeze" throughout the summer. Raising the office temperature would improve our overall comfort level.

- **Reduce overhead lighting? Possibly.** Most workstations have more than ample lighting, especially the outside offices that have a good supply of sunlight. After the 2003 blackout, overhead lighting was temporarily reduced by one third with no ill effects on safety or productivity. I think we should proceed cautiously with this recommendation and explore potential health and safety concerns.

- **Remove unused office kitchen equipment?** Yes, only a few department members use the refrigerator and coffee maker on a regular basis. I think we should keep the coffee maker, which was purchased only a year ago and requires little power. The 25-year-old refrigerator, however, could be scrapped or replaced with a smaller, more energy-efficient model. Instead of having one refrigerator per floor, we could make do with one or two for the entire building.

I agree that most of the proposed changes could be implemented with minimal disruption to operations and little inconvenience to staff. Let me know if I can provide further assistance in making our organization more energy efficient.

Send

FIGURE 6.6 E-mail that Responds

the situation, include a few reader-focused details, and end pleasantly, often with a forward-looking remark. Avoiding trite, wooden expressions allows you to come across as spontaneous and sincere. Figure 6.7 shows a goodwill e-mail that conveys appreciation for participation in a business-related charity event.

Because e-mail is informal and spontaneous, it has become a common means of transmitting quick or impromptu goodwill messages. If you need to be deferential and reserved, consider sending a more formal typed or handwritten letter.

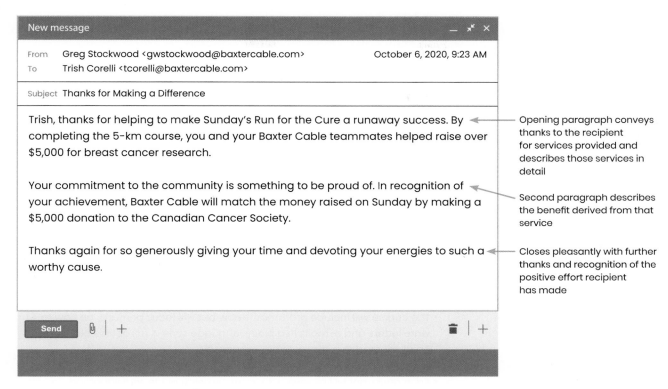

New message   _ ⤬ ✕

From   Greg Stockwood <gwstockwood@baxtercable.com>   October 6, 2020, 9:23 AM
To   Trish Corelli <tcorelli@baxtercable.com>

Subject Thanks for Making a Difference

Trish, thanks for helping to make Sunday's Run for the Cure a runaway success. By   ◀── Opening paragraph conveys
completing the 5-km course, you and your Baxter Cable teammates helped raise over   thanks to the recipient
$5,000 for breast cancer research.   for services provided and
                                                                                          describes those services in
                                                                                          detail

Your commitment to the community is something to be proud of. In recognition of   ◀── Second paragraph describes
your achievement, Baxter Cable will match the money raised on Sunday by making a   the benefit derived from that
$5,000 donation to the Canadian Cancer Society.   service

Thanks again for so generously giving your time and devoting your energies to such a ◀── Closes pleasantly with further
worthy cause.   thanks and recognition of the
                                                                                      positive effort recipient
                                                                                      has made

[Send]   📎 | +   🗑 | +

FIGURE 6.7 Thank-You E-mail Message

Follow-Up Memos and E-mail

A **follow-up** is a more specialized type of informative message, one that reflects good business practices. As the memory of a conversation or meeting fades, a follow-up message serves as a record confirming the time, place, and purpose of a meeting. The follow-up also serves as a reminder of basic facts and major directives, decisions, and issues—from the names and titles of participants to the terms of a verbal agreement or the roles of a working relationship. Because others may not remember a conversation exactly as you do, make allowances for differing accounts by using phrases such as "As I recall" or by inviting feedback that verifies the information you have passed on (e.g., "Please reply if you agree that this message accurately reflects our conversation"). Writing follow-up messages lessens the chance of later retractions, falsifications, or broken commitments. The more important an oral agreement is, the more vital it is to have proof in the form of written confirmation. For especially crucial or sensitive agreements, print out a copy of your follow-up e-mail or send a hard-copy letter. See Figure 6.8 for an example of an effective follow-up message.

follow-up message Provides a record of a meeting, including its time, place, purpose, and any agreements that may have been made.

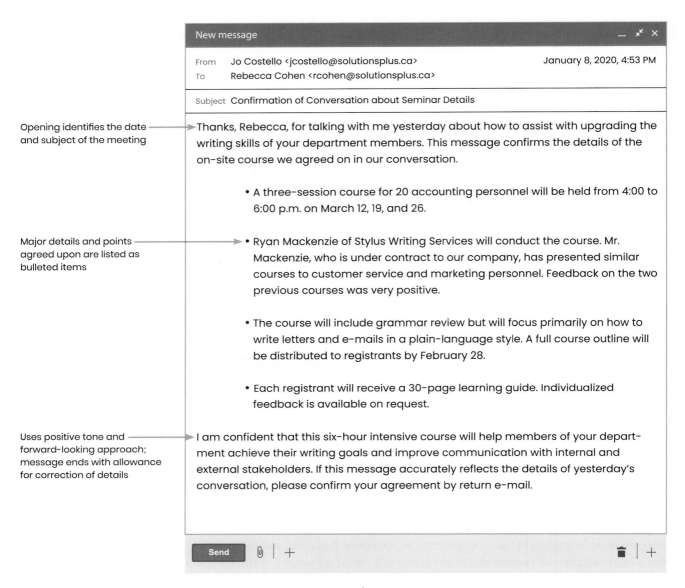

Opening identifies the date and subject of the meeting

Major details and points agreed upon are listed as bulleted items

Uses positive tone and forward-looking approach; message ends with allowance for correction of details

New message

From   Jo Costello <jcostello@solutionsplus.ca>   January 8, 2020, 4:53 PM
To   Rebecca Cohen <rcohen@solutionsplus.ca>

Subject   Confirmation of Conversation about Seminar Details

Thanks, Rebecca, for talking with me yesterday about how to assist with upgrading the writing skills of your department members. This message confirms the details of the on-site course we agreed on in our conversation.

• A three-session course for 20 accounting personnel will be held from 4:00 to 6:00 p.m. on March 12, 19, and 26.

• Ryan Mackenzie of Stylus Writing Services will conduct the course. Mr. Mackenzie, who is under contract to our company, has presented similar courses to customer service and marketing personnel. Feedback on the two previous courses was very positive.

• The course will include grammar review but will focus primarily on how to write letters and e-mails in a plain-language style. A full course outline will be distributed to registrants by February 28.

• Each registrant will receive a 30-page learning guide. Individualized feedback is available on request.

I am confident that this six-hour intensive course will help members of your department achieve their writing goals and improve communication with internal and external stakeholders. If this message accurately reflects the details of yesterday's conversation, please confirm your agreement by return e-mail.

Send

FIGURE 6.8 Follow-Up E-mail Message

Instant Messaging (IM)

instant messaging (IM) The exchange of messages over the Internet between two or more users who are online simultaneously.

Some organizations support the adoption and integration of **instant messaging (IM)** into their businesses; some take steps to ban it. While there is no consensus among IT managers that instant messaging maximizes productivity and profitability, many users claim they can't do business without it. Moreover, business relationships that begin with e-mail often develop further via IM, especially for networking purposes. IM combines features of synchronous, real-time communication (face-to-face meetings, telephone calls) with traits more commonly identified with e-mail. Many of the guidelines for using e-mail also apply to IM (Figure 6.9).

1. Understand when IM is appropriate.

Assess your audience and its needs carefully. IM may be appropriate for a simple exchange of information or when a question or responses urgent. However, certain types of information, such as negative news, require a more formal channel.

2. Limit abbreviations.

IM abbreviations such as idk ("I don't know"), imo ("in my opinion"), and btw ("by the way") may confuse individuals who are unfamiliar with these terms, and may appear too casual or familiar.

3. Use a natural mix of uppercase and lowercase letters.

Try to make your messages as readable as possible by using proper capitalization and avoiding practices such as SHOUTING.

4. Keep conversations to a few people at a time.

More than four or five participants in a conversation can make for an interactive free-for-all.

Notify participants before distributing the contents of a thread or conversation.

5. Inform people about your availability.

Set status flags to "away" or "busy" if you don't wish to be engaged.

6. Be specific.

IM's short, rapid exchanges make it essential for you to be concise in conveying your message and to tell readers exactly what information you need from them.

7. Keep messages brief.

If you need to send detailed information, break it up into two or more messages rather than one to avoid long messages.

8. Use clear, consistent wording.

Keep in mind that messages can lose context as IM discussions progress. Make your word choice consistent to reinforce the connection of one message to another.[8]

9. Be cautious in using IM with groups and managers.

Group members may have differing attitudes and technology aptitude, so a message may not be understood the same way by all. Managers may view IM as too informal and unprofessional for interactions with employees.

FIGURE 6.9 Guidelines for Using IM

Checklist

E-mail and Instant Messaging

Netiquette

❑ Be an effective e-mail manager, checking your inbox at regular intervals, responding promptly, and filing messages for easy reference.

❑ Adopt good e-mail practices (pruning distribution lists, using anti-spam software, resisting the urge to "flame," and using company e-mail only for business purposes).

❑ Make every message count by avoiding unnecessary replies and blanket messages.

❑ Create a functional and descriptive subject line for every message you write.

(Continued)

Composition

- ❏ Put your main message in a strong opening so readers won't have to scroll down to find it.
- ❏ Remember that e-mail is permanent and public—be careful what you write.
- ❏ Write with speed and accuracy by obeying the rules of good writing but not agonizing over every character or line.
- ❏ Be conversational.
- ❏ Insert responses into the original message when doing so would make your responses clearer and easier for the recipient to navigate.

Checklist

Chapter Review

- ❏ Use hard-copy memos sparingly; use e-mails for internal and informal external communication.
- ❏ Apply correct formatting rules and writing plans for memos and e-mails by using accurate headers, providing clear subject lines, and organizing messages with an opening, main body, and closing sentence or paragraph.
- ❏ Incorporate horizontal and vertical lists for clarity and conciseness.
- ❏ Eliminate common e-mail problems by avoiding dubious practices and observing proper netiquette.
- ❏ Follow common-sense steps in processing and managing e-mail.
- ❏ Use the direct approach for most memos and e-mails that inform, request, respond, convey goodwill, and follow up.

Exercises, Workshops, and Discussion Forums

1. **E-mail Round-Table Discussion.** In groups or as a class, answer the following questions, propose solutions to some of the most pressing problems and dubious practices, and create a list of general e-mail guidelines based on your discussion. Decide which rules would help you to use e-mail most effectively.

   a) How many e-mails do you receive daily?

      i.   fewer than 10
      ii. 10–25
      iii. 26–50
      iv. more than 50

   Is your inbox manageable, or do you suffer from e-mail overload?

   b) How many e-mail messages do you write each day?

      i.   5 or fewer
      ii. 6–10
      iii. 11–25
      iv. 26–50
      v.   more than 50

   If your answer was "5 or fewer," what forms of communication do you use more frequently?

   c) If you use e-mail to communicate at work, how much of your workday is spent writing or answering e-mail? Does e-mail create more work or help you do work?

   d) How long is your average message?

i. one or two sentences
ii. one or two paragraphs
iii. one screen
iv. more than one screen

If your answer was "more than one screen," what techniques do you use to break your message up into more manageable parts?

e) How does e-mail make you feel? What types of messages do you most dislike or look forward to and why? How difficult or easy is it to communicate emotional or sensitive issues by e-mail?

f) What bothers you most about communicating by e-mail? Have you ever received an e-mail you couldn't understand? What aspects of the message made it difficult to understand? Have you ever misinterpreted an e-mail? If so, what caused you the most confusion?

g) How does your use of e-mail compare with the frequency of your texting?

2. **E-mail Style: Bending the Rules of Usage.** Identify faults and weaknesses in the following routine message. How do its flaws reduce readability? Are errors in spelling, grammar, usage, and punctuation ever permissible in e-mail? Why or why not?

> Subject: Meeting
>
> Date: June 18, 2020
>
> To: All Concerned
>
> FYI, we have alot of problems with our shipping proceedures, idk how were supposed to fix it. May be it'd be a good idea to discuss it. hoping to workout some solutions, a meeting will be held. A meeting to discuss shipping proceedures will take place next Tuesday, if that's o.k. with u. Their are three items we need to discuss. ☺ . . . k see u at the meeting.

3. **E-mail Privacy: Expectations and Illusions.** In March 2013, Harvard University's administration searched the e-mail accounts of 16 resident deans to learn who had leaked an internal memo about a student-cheating scandal to the media. According to Harvard policy, e-mail accounts can be searched for purposes of internal investigations, but the account holder must be notified before or soon afterward. In this case, only one dean was told of the search, after it had occurred. The administration had apparently felt entitled to search these accounts because resident deans are classed as employees rather than faculty members, who have more protection under the university's electronic media policies. However, the resident deans are considered by many to be faculty. (More information on this story is available at www.bostonglobe.com/metro/2013/03/10/harvard-university-administrators-secretly-searched-deans-email-accounts-hunting-for-media-leak/tHyFUYh2FNAaG2w9wzcrLL/story.html.)

In small groups, discuss the Harvard case and answer the following questions: Should the resident deans have had any reasonable expectation of privacy? Was Harvard administration justified in their actions? What actions do you think would have been just, reasonable, and appropriate under the circumstances?

4. **Emojis: Trendy Slang or New Language?** Is the use of emojis a passing fad, or is it forever altering the way we communicate? In a small group, discuss how you use emojis and what you like or dislike about it. Is its inability to express verb tense and lack of plural nouns, linking words, and personal pronouns a serious drawback? Are its disadvantages cancelled out by its ability to project tone of voice into digital communication? Do you think it is a linguistic innovation that is here to stay? Why or why not?

Writing Improvement Exercises

Recognize the Nature and Characteristics of Memos and E-mail

1. **Evaluating Memo Subject Lines.** Mark each of the following subject lines as *V* for vague or *S* for specific.

a) Holiday Celebration
b) Cancellation of Holiday Celebration
c) Casual Dress
d) Proposed Casual Dress Day Program
e) Complete Attached Questionnaire
f) Questionnaire
g) Your Request for Information on Corporate Media Relations

h) Media Article
i) Customer Service
j) Introduction of Customer Service Hotline

2. **Writing Subject Lines for Memos and E-mail.** For each of the following scenarios, write a focused and action-specific subject line.

a) You are writing to all employees to ask them to complete an attached questionnaire on proposed changes to the pension plan.

b) You are writing to all employees to announce a diversity awareness seminar that your company will be holding on June 9. The purpose of the seminar is to promote a more positive and inclusive work environment. Attendance is mandatory.

c) You are writing to all employees to announce changes to the company dress code. The changes are necessary because many staff members wear clothing inappropriate for the workplace, including midriff-baring tops, micro minis, and T-shirts with offensive slogans. The new dress code will take effect on July 2.

d) You are writing to your manager to communicate your progress on an ongoing online marketing initiative. Your manager has asked you to send her updates on a weekly basis.

3. **Getting to the Point.** Unscramble the following memo so that it starts with the main message and reserves the explanation for the body. Eliminate unnecessary details.

Trespassing and vandalism have become increasingly serious problems for our organization. Following three reported security violations in the past month, we have hired Garrison Safety Consultant Services to redesign building access and entry procedures. Garrison Safety Consultant Services has a proven track record and over 40 years' experience in the industry. The altered procedures Garrison has recommended will go into effect September 15 and help ensure a safe working environment and the protection of company property. Please access the building by the Wilcox Street entrance and present your photo ID badge for security inspection at the reception desk. All other doorways will remain locked from the outside and are to be used only in the event of emergency evacuation. Visitors will be issued security badges and must sign in and out at reception. While on premises, all personnel must wear their photo ID badges.

4. **Composing Strong Memo Openings.** Revise the following paragraphs to front-load and summarize the main message.

a) Many of our employees have indicated that they favour adjusted work hours throughout the summer. After careful consideration, we have decided that new hours will go into effect from June 2 to September 2. The new hours are 8:30 a.m. to 4:30 p.m.

b) Our association holds its annual conference in August, and we are interested in your hotel and conference centre as a possible venue for this year's event. We require a hosting facility to accommodate our 500 members from August 17 to August 18, 2020, and need information about cost and availability.

c) We have recently received numerous complaints from points program members indicating that they have been prevented from applying their accumulated bonus points for discounts on recent purchases. I am asking customer relations to conduct a study of and make recommendations on the efficiency of the points program.

d) We have noticed recently a steady decline in the quality of our high-speed Internet service. Because our contract with our current provider expires next month, I am asking you to investigate the rates and service records of its chief competitors.

Format Horizontal and Vertical Lists for Clarity and Conciseness

5. **Creating Effective Lists.** Reorganize the following information into list form, tabulating steps and supporting points. Compose a lead-in that suits each item.

   a) Please follow these packaging procedures to ensure that all shipped items arrive undamaged. First of all, ensure that the item does not exceed weight restrictions for the type of packaging used. Fragile items should be shipped in special protective packaging. Larger items should be shipped in customized crates and containers. Always ensure that the package is properly sealed.

   b) Setting up your new HT printer involves only a few steps. You should start by plugging the unit in and making sure the printer cable is connected to your computer. Then you should follow printing software instructions and align print settings, but before you commence your first print job, you should run a test sample in case settings need adjustment.

   c) The new direct-deposit payroll system has several advantages. Employees will no longer have to wait in bank lineups to deposit their cheques, and there is no risk that paycheques will be lost or stolen. Employees can enjoy the added security of knowing that their salaries go directly into their bank accounts on bi-monthly paydays.

Eliminate Common Problems and Dubious Practices in E-mails

6. **Extinguishing "Flaming."** Revise the following message to neutralize its angry tone and improve its professionalism.

   I absolutely have to have the latest sales figures by Friday—no ifs, ands, or buts. I find it difficult to understand why so simple a request goes unnoticed until the deadline has passed, especially when the survival of our retail clothing division depends on ongoing analysis of this important data.

Develop Correct E-mail Style and Tone

7. **Adopting a Conversational Style and Tone in E-mail.** Revise the following message between two long-time co-workers to eliminate stiffness and undue formality.

   Dear Mr. Harry Singh:

   Please be advised that you are instructed to review the revised procedures for sending courier packages to the United States. Please find attached a copy of the revised procedures for your perusal. Substantial savings will be realized if all personnel comply with the new procedures and I would be most grateful if you complied with them as well.

   Respectfully,
   Paula Wittington

8. **Maintaining a Professional Style and Tone in E-mail.** Revise the following message between an employee and her manager to ensure the message is not too informal. Fill in missing information where appropriate.

   Hey,

   Here's the report you wanted. It took me ages to talk to everybody and get the info. Better late than never, right? Give me a shout if you need anything else.

   TGIF,
   J.

Case Study Exercises

Write Memos and E-mails that Inform, Request, Respond, Convey Goodwill, and Follow Up

Analyze the following scenarios and select relevant details to include in your messages.

1. **E-mail that Informs.** As an assistant buyer for Space One, a new Vancouver-area furniture and home accessories store, write a message to Marcella Ponti, proprietor and chief buyer, summarizing the top trends at the Interior Design Show. Marcella is currently on a buying trip in Italy and has sent you to the show in her place. The Interior Design Show in Toronto is Canada's largest residential design show, attended by 8,500 design professionals and over 50,000 visitors every year. Its exhibits and presentations by designers from around the world showcase innovative products and trends in furniture, textile, and home accessories design, residential interior design, and landscape architecture. In your three days at the show, beginning with Trade Day, you noted many new trends but were most impressed by the innovative use of materials in furniture design. Standouts included a collection of ottomans and chairs in leather, fur, and chrome priced in the $1,000 to $2,000 range from the Montréal design team Verité. "Clear" was another hot trend in furniture and accessory design, seen in an array of glass, Lucite, and acrylic products and best exemplified by Philippe Starck's interpretation of a classic Louis XV armchair and the use of glass tile and countertops in kitchens and bathrooms. In textile design, the most noticeable trend was toward textural and richly embellished fabrics in silk and synthetic blends, notably in a colour palate of golds, browns, and corals. Having carefully reviewed product literature and pricing information, you believe a strong case could be made for stocking several Canadian items that reflect Space One's design sensibility.

2. **E-mail that Informs.** As director of loss prevention for a small chain of grocery stores, write an e-mail to store managers advising them of a surge in the use of counterfeit e-mail coupons. In recent months, the problem has grown more serious. In July, for example, retailers were hit with a flood of bogus coupons promising free ice cream bars from Häagen-Dazs, a brand represented in Canada by Nestlé. With this in mind, advise store managers to monitor the situation closely and warn cashiers to closely inspect coupons offering free or heavily discounted items and to decline coupons without bar codes and expiry dates. Of course, you realize that some bogus coupons are difficult to detect because technophiles can easily alter manufacturers' coupons or create their own from scratch with the right tools. The Food Marketing Institute, an international association based in Washington, DC, estimates that frauds cost the sector up to US$800 million annually. Make it clear to your readers that the cost of these downloaded forgeries is a cost you prefer to avoid.

3. **E-mail that Informs.** As your company's office events coordinator, write an e-mail to all employees informing them of a retirement dinner party for Gerald Dwyer. Gerald joined the company in 1977, first working as a mail clerk and steadily earning promotions to become manager of operations. Known as a team player, he spearheaded the company's United Way fundraising drive for five record-breaking years and streamlined office procedures for greater efficiency. Retirement parties are usually dreary affairs, but you'd like this one to be different. Include information about when and where the party will be held, how formal it will be, what type of food will be served, whom to contact for tickets, cost per ticket, whether guests are permitted, additional charges for a gift, and venue parking and accessibility details (consider using a hyperlink for this final item). Use appropriate formatting techniques for easy readability.

4. **Goodwill E-mail.** As a colleague of Gerald Dwyer (see the previous scenario), write Gerald a congratulatory e-mail conveying your best wishes on his retirement. Gerald was your supervisor when you first joined the company ten years ago. Although you found his attitude somewhat paternalistic,

you appreciated his fairness and guidance, both of which contributed to your career advancement. A long-standing family commitment prevents you from attending his retirement dinner.

5. **E-mail that Informs.** As a student volunteer for the international exchange program at your college or university, write an e-mail to groups of students coming to your institution from Japan and Taiwan that advises them how to dress for the winter and describes campus life, specific challenges, classroom experience, and other details of what to expect. Your secondary aim is to foster goodwill and make the students feel welcome. Consider using a list form to ensure details are well-organized.

6. **E-mail that Requests.** As associate vice-president for information technologies at Kelso Community College, compose an e-mail to faculty asking them for their feedback on a proposed WLAN (wireless local area network), part of the college's comprehensive e-strategy. For you, the advantages of "going wireless" are obvious. Instructors will be able to manage their course workloads, schedules, and students' needs online, leaving more time for them to be actively engaged in research. Students will be able to access grades more easily, e-mail assignments to instructors, and interact with fellow classmates. You would like to know if faculty members agree that wireless technology will create a more effective way of teaching and a more efficient way of learning. Will it make their work easier? Do they have the skills—for example, basic computer literacy—to make good use of the new technology? Can students be relied upon to bring their laptops to class and use them consistently? Do they have other concerns?

7. **E-mail that Responds.** As chair of the Early Childhood Education Program at Kelso Community College, respond to the associate vice-president for information technologies' message regarding the proposed WLAN (see the previous scenario). Having heard that most other academic institutions have adopted wireless technologies, you would like to see Kelso gain a similar "electronic edge," but you have a few reservations. Primarily, you are concerned about anti-virus security and related privacy issues. Would students' marks be secure? What would happen if the system crashed? Another issue that concerns you is student access to laptops and available funding for those unable to meet the technological requirements. Many of your students cannot afford to buy a laptop, so you would like to see funding set up before such a program is implemented.

8. **Memo that Informs.** As marketing coordinator of your company, write to members of the marketing division advising them of the venue change for the team-building retreat scheduled for August 8 to 10. The sudden closure of Cedarcrest Resort and Conference Facility because of a health alert has left your division without a venue. Rather than cancel the event, you have negotiated with the resort operator, Riverwood Inc., to move the event to Huntingwood, a nearby luxury resort in the Riverwood chain. The health alert has not affected Huntingwood, nor is it expected to. The aim of the retreat remains the same: to foster better relations among your sometimes-combative team members. The program of events is also unchanged. From 8:30 a.m. to noon each day, the group will make presentations and discuss marketing strategy. From 1:00 to 4:00 p.m., the group will participate in fun and challenging team-building exercises such as three-legged races and obstacle courses.

9. **E-mail that Follows Up.** As coordinator of your organization's newly established intramural sports program, write a message to Garinder Singh, vice-president of human resources, confirming the details worked out in a meeting several days ago. Since it is your responsibility to organize events for the upcoming winter–spring season, you want to be sure that you and Garinder agree on the terms of participation and the structure and membership of the teams. The program has been established to promote friendship, co-operation, and healthy lifestyles among employees. Six co-ed teams will be open to employees only and will offer them the opportunity to participate in non-body-contact hockey, soccer, and softball. Everyone is welcome to participate in more than one sport and will be notified by e-mail of game dates and cancellations. Registration will commence immediately and end one week prior

to the season-opening games. You will be responsible for notifying team members of game dates and cancellations and for booking arenas and diamond times. To ensure employee safety, Garinder has asked you to arrange for volunteers with refereeing experience who in turn could be offered a small gift or honorarium for their services. A $20-per-person rink fee applies to hockey participants to cover booking and rental charges.

Hockey players are expected to provide their own equipment, including sticks, skates, helmets, and mouthguards. Softball players must come to games equipped with gloves and appropriate footwear. All other softball and soccer equipment will be provided. During the program's inaugural season, teams will play every two weeks. There will be prizes for winning teams and certificates for players who attend throughout the season.

Online Activities

Recognize the Nature and Characteristics of Memos

1. **Reviewing Memo Guidelines.** Take the quiz created by the El Paso Community College to test your knowledge of memos.

   http://start.epcc.edu/Student/Tutorial_Quizzes/ Writing_quizzes/memo_quiz.htm

2. **Writing Memos.** Visit the Web Writing that Works! "Challenges" web page and complete the exercises. For each of the four paragraphs, also add a subject line and introductory statement.

   www.webwritingthatworks.com/ eGuideScan2dChallenges.htm

Recognize Steps in Processing and Managing E-mail

3. **Writing E-mail Subject Lines.** Visit the Royal Melbourne Institute of Technology's Study and Learning Centre website and complete the subject-line exercise:

   www.dlsweb.rmit.edu.au/lsu/content/4_ WritingSkills/writing_tuts/business_%20english_ LL/emails/subject_line.html

4. **Reducing Spam.** Review the spam you receive over a two- or three-day period, then visit the Spamhaus Project, a database on the history and methods of spammers. Discuss ways to reduce and eliminate spam.

   www.spamhaus.org

Analyzing Trends in Electronic Communication

5. **Analyzing Websites.** Use the questions to evaluate one or more of the following Canadian retail websites:

   www.roots.com/ca/
   www.chapters.indigo.ca
   www.leevalley.com
   www.canadiantire.ca
   www.thebay.com
   www.marks.com
   www.tentree.com
   www.canadagoose.com
   www.lululemon.com

6. **Analyzing Emojis for Business Purposes.** In 2015, General Motors published a press release entirely in emojis. The press release promoted the 2016 Chevy Cruze. Use the link below or search online for #ChevyGoesEmoji and read the press release. How much are you able to translate into English? Based on your answer, write a paragraph analyzing when and how emojis should be used for business along with their associated risks and benefits.

   https://media.chevrolet.com/media/us/en/ chevrolet/news.detail.html/content/Pages/news/us/ en/2015/jun/0622-cruze-emoji.html

7

Routine and Goodwill Messages

Chapter Preview

This chapter focuses on strategies for sharing good news and neutral information. Both types of information are so essential to business that handling and managing them are considered routine—key competencies expected of employees on a daily basis. You'll see how the adaptable direct writing plan can be applied for specific purposes to different types of routine messages. As formal business letters are still the preferred way to communicate important information, you'll discover their essential elements and standard approaches to their format.

Learning Objectives

1. Use a direct writing plan for routine business messages.
2. Request general information and claims adjustments.
3. Order services and merchandise.
4. Respond positively to requests for information, purchase orders, and claims adjustments.
5. Write messages confirming contracts and arrangements.
6. Compose messages of appreciation, congratulations, and sympathy.
7. Write announcements, cover (or transmittal) letters, and instructional letters.
8. Format formal letters in a variety of ways.

Case Study

OMER MESSINGER/EPA-EFE/Shutterstock.com

As customer service moves online, routine communications through social media can become a way to build goodwill not just with individual customers, but with the wider public.

Drew Bomhof had been working as a communications manager at Samsung Canada for just three months when he received an unusual message via the company's Facebook page. Shane Bennett, a loyal Samsung customer, had sent a playful request for a free Galaxy S III smartphone and attached a Microsoft Paint drawing of a dragon to boost his chances. Bomhof declined, but softened the refusal with his own drawing of a kangaroo riding a unicycle. Bennett posted the thread to Reddit, where it quickly went viral. The interaction drew so much positive attention to the company that Bennett was invited to the launch party for the Galaxy S III and even given his free phone—customized with his dragon. Then-Samsung Canada president James Politeski personally congratulated Bomhof for his social media management, and the communication manager's good-natured response continues to be used as one of the best examples of how social media can be used to boost a company's profile through fun customer interactions.

Direct Writing Plan

Good news messages, which inspire positive reactions from readers, establish rapport all on their own. Readers are always receptive to good news and are eager to learn key information. The same applies to routine and informative messages, to which readers react neutrally. Good news and informative messages are the mainstays of business correspondence. When it comes to these messages, don't make readers wait. Take the direct approach and make your point right away.

direct-approach message
A message that presents the main point in the first paragraph.

A **direct-approach message** makes your purpose clear from the start, stating the main point in the first sentence before moving on to details. At first glance, readers can tell if you are asking for or supplying information, requesting or granting credit, or making

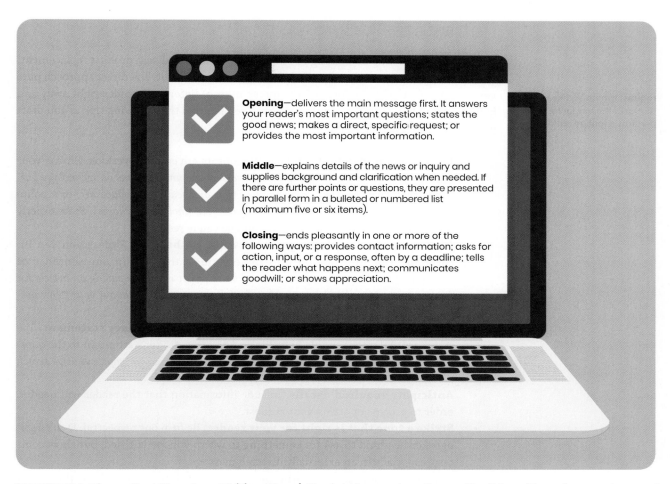

FIGURE 7.1 Three-Part Structure Writing Plan | Straightforward and versatile, this writing plan can be used for most routine correspondence, including requests and responses.

or settling a claim. You can count on the direct approach to speed the flow of information and expedite purchase orders, credit applications, and claims adjustments. A three-part structure (see Figure 7.1) helps guide readers through a direct message approach.

Direct-approach messages are the norm in North America, but not every culture responds to direct correspondence in exactly the same way. In high-context cultures—such as those in China, Japan, and Arab nations—directness is considered rude. In such cases, it is important to establish rapport before citing a problem or making a request and even then to suggest or ask rather than demand. In Japan, where formality is important, it is customary to embed a request and to soften it with preliminaries and other politeness strategies. On the other hand, people in Western cultures consider a lack of directness to be a waste of their time. When you are communicating cross-culturally, weigh your reader's tolerance for directness before you launch into your request or response. Familiarize yourself with local preferences. Making directness work for you means avoiding a one-size-fits-all approach to messaging.

Requests

The first step in getting something you need—data, merchandise, a product replacement, a refund, an action, or assistance—is knowing how to ask for it. The direct approach puts your request (often in the form of a **request memo**) before the reader right away and helps to speed the exchange of information. Keep in mind the following tips as you draft your direct-approach requests:

- **Put the main idea first.** Embedded requests are easy to overlook. Phrase your request as a question (*Will you please provide recommendations on technology purchases that would help reduce turnaround time on document production?*) or a polite command (*Please provide recommendations on technology purchases*). State exactly what you want—vague requests encourage vague responses.
- **Give a reason for the request or state its benefit.** Unless you can incorporate this information into the opening paragraph in one sentence or less, put it in the second paragraph: *Please assist me in preparing an article for* Accountants Monthly *by answering the following questions about your CPA work-study program.*
- **Introduce multiple requests or questions with a summary statement.** The summary statement should be polite and draw the reader's attention to the questions that follow: *Please answer the following questions about your executive search services.*
- **Anticipate required details.** Include information that the reader will need in order to process or act on your request.
- **Strike a tone that is right for your reader.** Be firm but respectful. Don't apologize or be afraid to ask for something to which you are entitled, but show courtesy, especially in an externally directed message.
- **Keep minor points to a minimum.** Unnecessary information blunts the impact of your request. If you want to give your reader additional information, enclose supporting documents.
- **Use a layout that focuses attention on your request.** Incorporate bulleted or numbered lists, surround specifics with white space, and boldface or italicize key points for emphasis.
- **Close in a courteous and efficient way.** Focus on the action you want the reader to take and use positive language to communicate goodwill and show appreciation. Avoid closing with canned expressions, such as *Thanking you in advance.*

Requests for Information or Action

An effective request for information or action lets the reader know at the beginning exactly what is required, what should be done, or what compliance you seek. A common fault of both **information requests** (or **inquiries**) and **action requests** is that they are either too abrupt and demanding or too apologetic and deferential. Aim for a tone that is firm yet polite. To elicit as much relevant information as possible, pose open-ended questions. If appropriate, explain how you will use the information. If the reader is expected

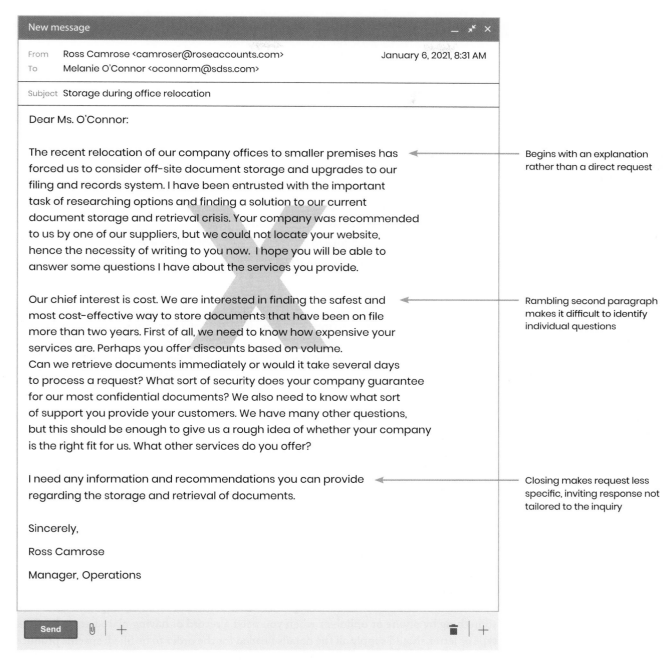

New message   — ⤢ ✕

From   Ross Camrose <camroser@roseaccounts.com>   January 6, 2021, 8:31 AM

To   Melanie O'Connor <oconnorm@sdss.com>

Subject   Storage during office relocation

Dear Ms. O'Connor:

The recent relocation of our company offices to smaller premises has ⟵ *Begins with an explanation rather than a direct request*
forced us to consider off-site document storage and upgrades to our
filing and records system. I have been entrusted with the important
task of researching options and finding a solution to our current
document storage and retrieval crisis. Your company was recommended
to us by one of our suppliers, but we could not locate your website,
hence the necessity of writing to you now. I hope you will be able to
answer some questions I have about the services you provide.

Our chief interest is cost. We are interested in finding the safest and ⟵ *Rambling second paragraph makes it difficult to identify individual questions*
most cost-effective way to store documents that have been on file
more than two years. First of all, we need to know how expensive your
services are. Perhaps you offer discounts based on volume.
Can we retrieve documents immediately or would it take several days
to process a request? What sort of security does your company guarantee
for our most confidential documents? We also need to know what sort
of support you provide your customers. We have many other questions,
but this should be enough to give us a rough idea of whether your company
is the right fit for us. What other services do you offer?

I need any information and recommendations you can provide ⟵ *Closing makes request less specific, inviting response not tailored to the inquiry*
regarding the storage and retrieval of documents.

Sincerely,

Ross Camrose

Manager, Operations

Send   📎 | +   🗑 | +

FIGURE 7.2 Ineffective Information Request (extract)

to perform an action, citing the benefits can encourage a more favourable reply. End with a paragraph specific to the reader and the request. Make a point of refocusing your request, end-dating it if necessary, and expressing appreciation for compliance.

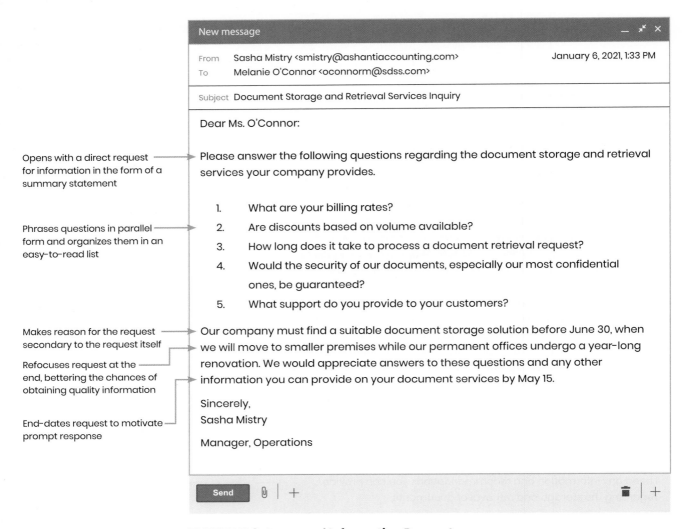

Opens with a direct request for information in the form of a summary statement

Phrases questions in parallel form and organizes them in an easy-to-read list

Makes reason for the request secondary to the request itself

Refocuses request at the end, bettering the chances of obtaining quality information

End-dates request to motivate prompt response

New message

From   Sasha Mistry <smistry@ashantiaccounting.com>   January 6, 2021, 1:33 PM
To   Melanie O'Connor <oconnorm@sdss.com>

Subject Document Storage and Retrieval Services Inquiry

Dear Ms. O'Connor:

Please answer the following questions regarding the document storage and retrieval services your company provides.

1.   What are your billing rates?
2.   Are discounts based on volume available?
3.   How long does it take to process a document retrieval request?
4.   Would the security of our documents, especially our most confidential ones, be guaranteed?
5.   What support do you provide to your customers?

Our company must find a suitable document storage solution before June 30, when we will move to smaller premises while our permanent offices undergo a year-long renovation. We would appreciate answers to these questions and any other information you can provide on your document services by May 15.

Sincerely,
Sasha Mistry

Manager, Operations

FIGURE 7.3   Improved Information Request

Order Requests

order request A request for merchandise that includes a purchase authorization and shipping instructions.

You may decide to write an **order request** for merchandise when it isn't possible to order something by phone or online or when you need a record of having placed an order. This type of letter should supply all the details needed for the order to be filled: specific product names and descriptions, quantities, order numbers, units and total prices, desired method of shipment, preferred date of delivery, and method of payment. Don't forget to factor in applicable taxes and specify the delivery address if it is different from the billing address. Careful formatting of the message can make the order faster and easier to process:

1.   **Authorize the purchase and specify the preferred method of shipment.** Merely expressing interest in certain merchandise may not communicate your intention to purchase it. Your request should be explicit rather than implied. Indicate the source of merchandise information, especially if you lack a current price list.

ASHANTI ACCOUNTING ASSOCIATES
418 Grafton Street, Brampton, ON N9C 2G8

January 6, 2021

Practically Everything Office Supply
6315 Haliburton Boulevard
Oshawa, ON L4K 2M9

RE: RUSH PURCHASE ORDER ◄———— *Subject line identifies purpose of the message and emphasizes shipping instructions*

Please send by overnight courier the following items from your Fall 2020 catalogue. ◄————

Simplified style uses no salutation,

Opening authorizes purchase and indicates method of shipment

Quantity	Catalogue Number	Description	Price
10	X88900	Deluxe staplers	$215.00
15	X82270	Tape dispensers	150.00
50	X85540	60W fluorescent tubes	500.00
		Subtotal	$865.00
		Estimated taxes	60.55
		Shipping	$36.00
		Total	$961.55

Itemized list clearly identifies and quantifies order purchase

Our newly expanded tax preparation centre is scheduled to open January 20 and we would appreciate receiving these items promptly in preparation for that event. Please charge this order to our account no. 590 837 428. Should you ◄———— *Preferred method of payment included with special instructions* need to discuss any of these items, please call me at 905-751-2240.

Ashanti Achebe ◄———— *No complimentary close is used in simplified style letters*

Ashanti Achebe, CA

FIGURE 7.4 Sample Order Request (in simplified style)

2. **Itemize requested merchandise, using a list format.** Use tabulation, tidy columns, and white space to create a readable summary of details about multiple items. Align dollar figures (unit prices and totals).

3. **Close with special instructions and thanks.** State how you intend to pay for the merchandise—ask to be billed, refer to credit agreements, or enclose a cheque. Specify the date by which you expect to receive your order, and end with appreciation for the processing of the order.

Claim Letters

claim A demand or request for something—often a replacement or a refund—that is considered one's due.

When, as a customer, you seek a correction of a problem or compensation for losses incurred, the type of letter you write is called a **claim**. Filing a claim means you are writing as a customer about something that has gone wrong—merchandise has turned out to be faulty, goods haven't been delivered, a delivery has contained the wrong merchandise, a billing error has been made, or the service you received has been unsatisfactory. Your claim is justified and relatively straightforward if a product is still under warranty or a service is guaranteed. However, you must explain in a written letter why your claim is justified if you hope to receive a refund, a replacement, a correction, or an apology. Naturally, you may be angry about what has happened, but you should refrain from adopting a complaining or accusatory tone. Focus on providing details the company will need to

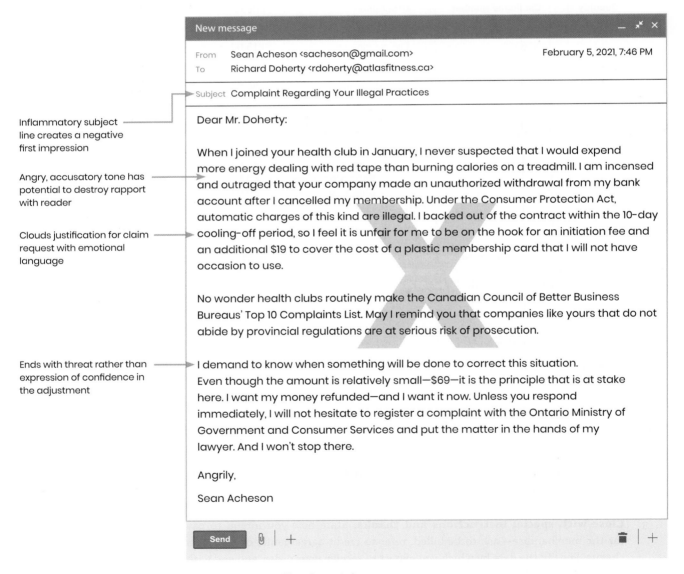

New message

From   Sean Acheson <sacheson@gmail.com>   February 5, 2021, 7:46 PM
To   Richard Doherty <rdoherty@atlasfitness.ca>

Subject Complaint Regarding Your Illegal Practices

Dear Mr. Doherty:

When I joined your health club in January, I never suspected that I would expend more energy dealing with red tape than burning calories on a treadmill. I am incensed and outraged that your company made an unauthorized withdrawal from my bank account after I cancelled my membership. Under the Consumer Protection Act, automatic charges of this kind are illegal. I backed out of the contract within the 10-day cooling-off period, so I feel it is unfair for me to be on the hook for an initiation fee and an additional $19 to cover the cost of a plastic membership card that I will not have occasion to use.

No wonder health clubs routinely make the Canadian Council of Better Business Bureaus' Top 10 Complaints List. May I remind you that companies like yours that do not abide by provincial regulations are at serious risk of prosecution.

I demand to know when something will be done to correct this situation. Even though the amount is relatively small—$69—it is the principle that is at stake here. I want my money refunded—and I want it now. Unless you respond immediately, I will not hesitate to register a complaint with the Ontario Ministry of Government and Consumer Services and put the matter in the hands of my lawyer. And I won't stop there.

Angrily,

Sean Acheson

Send

Annotations (left margin):
- Inflammatory subject line creates a negative first impression
- Angry, accusatory tone has potential to destroy rapport with reader
- Clouds justification for claim request with emotional language
- Ends with threat rather than expression of confidence in the adjustment

FIGURE 7.5 Ineffective Claim

assess your problem and motivating the reader to work on your behalf and grant you the **adjustment** you seek.

> **adjustment** A written response to a complaint that tells the customer what will be done about the complaint in terms of solving the problem, correcting an error, granting a refund, or adjusting the amount due.

1. **Make your request for an adjustment.** State what you expect the reader to do to solve the problem.

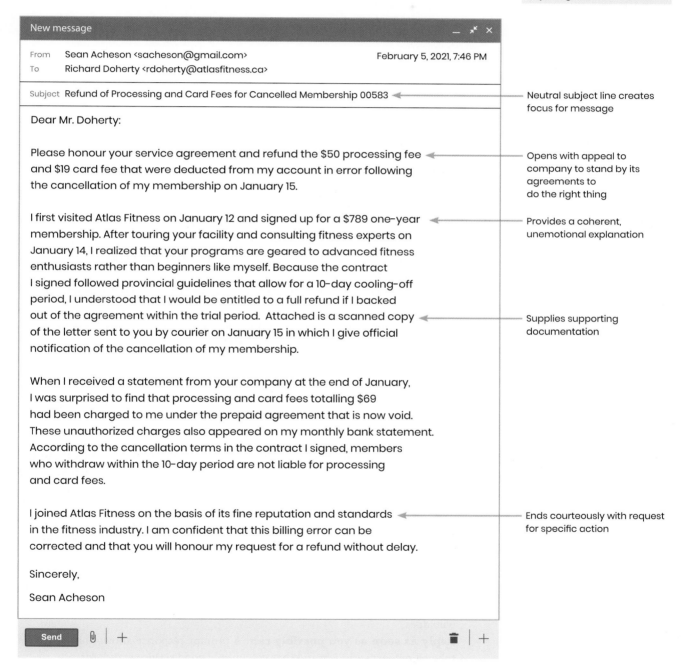

New message

| From | Sean Acheson <sacheson@gmail.com> | February 5, 2021, 7:46 PM |
| To | Richard Doherty <rdoherty@atlasfitness.ca> | |

Subject Refund of Processing and Card Fees for Cancelled Membership 00583 — Neutral subject line creates focus for message

Dear Mr. Doherty:

Please honour your service agreement and refund the $50 processing fee and $19 card fee that were deducted from my account in error following the cancellation of my membership on January 15. — Opens with appeal to company to stand by its agreements to do the right thing

I first visited Atlas Fitness on January 12 and signed up for a $789 one-year membership. After touring your facility and consulting fitness experts on January 14, I realized that your programs are geared to advanced fitness enthusiasts rather than beginners like myself. Because the contract I signed followed provincial guidelines that allow for a 10-day cooling-off period, I understood that I would be entitled to a full refund if I backed out of the agreement within the trial period. Attached is a scanned copy of the letter sent to you by courier on January 15 in which I give official notification of the cancellation of my membership. — Provides a coherent, unemotional explanation / Supplies supporting documentation

When I received a statement from your company at the end of January, I was surprised to find that processing and card fees totalling $69 had been charged to me under the prepaid agreement that is now void. These unauthorized charges also appeared on my monthly bank statement. According to the cancellation terms in the contract I signed, members who withdraw within the 10-day period are not liable for processing and card fees.

I joined Atlas Fitness on the basis of its fine reputation and standards in the fitness industry. I am confident that this billing error can be corrected and that you will honour my request for a refund without delay. — Ends courteously with request for specific action

Sincerely,

Sean Acheson

Send

FIGURE 7.6 Effective Claim

2. **Identify the faulty item or problem and explain logically and specifically why your claim is justified.** State what the reader needs to know to assess the situation and include pertinent details and documents. If you are uncertain about the cause of the problem, avoid guessing. Simply explain why the situation is a problem for you and work on the assumption that the company will want to do its best to retain you as a customer.

3. **End positively and pleasantly.** Restate the action you have requested and express confidence in the settlement of your claim. End-date your request if you require a speedy response. Keep a copy of your letter in a file with other documents related to your claim.

Checklist
Request Letter

❑ Have you phrased the request so the reader views it positively?

❑ Is your request straightforward and specific? Have you stated your purpose at the beginning rather than embedding it?

❑ If there are multiple requests, are they introduced with a summary statement and then presented individually in a numbered or bulleted list?

❑ Have you kept the number of questions to a minimum?

❑ Are the questions specific, concise, and phrased so the reader will know immediately what you are seeking?

❑ Have you selected details that will help the reader respond more promptly and completely?

❑ Have you told the reader how to and by when to respond? Will the reader know what to do? Have you provided contact information?

❑ Have you expressed appreciation to the reader for taking the trouble to respond?

Responses

response A message that answers a request or query.

A **response** is usually most effective when it is prompt, informative, and gets to the point. When you can respond favourably to a request for information or action, waste no time conveying the news; prompt responses build goodwill, make readers feel valued, and give a positive impression of you, your department, and your company. A routine response provides focused details of a decision, an answer, or an action so readers can make informed decisions, follow through, or know what happens next. Here are a few tips for writing a good response:

- **Determine if you are the right person to handle the response.** If you do not have the knowledge or authority to process a request, refer it to someone who does.

- **Reply as soon as you possibly can.** A prompt response shows that you have taken a request seriously and that you uphold good service standards.

- **Begin with good news or the most important piece of information.** When you can provide what the reader has requested, you should say so in the first sentence.
- **Design your response to be useful.** Anticipate information your reader may need.
- **Respond within your company's ethical guidelines.** Disclose only the information your reader has a right to know. Don't share legally sensitive, potentially contentious details in an effort to make your response absolutely complete. Your letter is, in effect, a legal contract, and all facts and figures contained within it must be accurate.
- **Make your closing work for you.** View your closing remarks as an opportunity to cement relationships if they are in need of reinforcement.

Information Responses

A response to an information request (or inquiry) should supply the requested information first without the need for an introduction.

Cluttered: Thank you for your letter of July 14, received July 17, in which you requested information on day trading.

Better: Here is a copy of our brochure, *Day Trading: A Beginner's Guide.*

Writing a complete and useful response may require you to interpret hard-to-grasp facts and statistics and to anticipate questions your readers still might have once their original inquiries are answered.

Thank you for your inquiry dated March 12. This is to advise you that we are now in receipt of this message. We are always glad to receive requests of this kind and are happy to assist you with the research for your article on employee recognition programs. I believe your specific questions relate to the impact of our program on employee morale. There are many issues to be addressed, but we will try to answer what questions we can.

Our program is good for our employees. We give rewards—some nominal, others quite substantial—for all kinds of initiatives, including good ideas and leadership. Since the program was established, many employees have seen their good work rewarded.

We are glad to have helped. Good luck with your research.

Annotations:
- Words of thanks should be saved for the main response or at the end, where they would help to build goodwill
- Opens by thanking the reader for inquiry and notifying them that the request has been received. Receipt of the inquiry is self-evident
- Language is stiff and formal. First paragraph padded with irrelevant details
- Second paragraph fails to provide concrete details. No evidence is offered to prove why the program is "good"
- Closing remarks sound insincere because little information has been offered

FIGURE 7.7 Ineffective Information Response (extract)

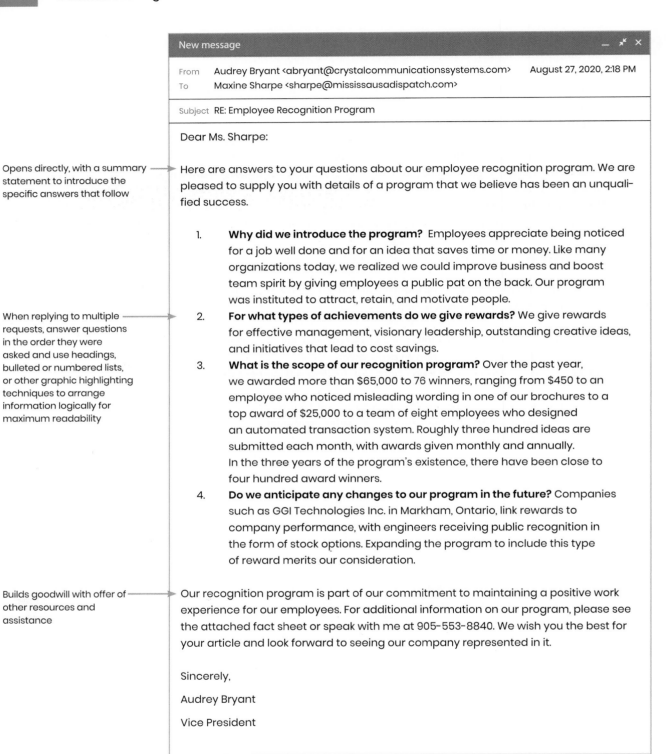

Opens directly, with a summary statement to introduce the specific answers that follow

When replying to multiple requests, answer questions in the order they were asked and use headings, bulleted or numbered lists, or other graphic highlighting techniques to arrange information logically for maximum readability

Builds goodwill with offer of other resources and assistance

New message   _ ⤢ ×

From   Audrey Bryant <abryant@crystalcommunicationssystems.com>   August 27, 2020, 2:18 PM
To   Maxine Sharpe <sharpe@mississausadispatch.com>

Subject RE: Employee Recognition Program

Dear Ms. Sharpe:

Here are answers to your questions about our employee recognition program. We are pleased to supply you with details of a program that we believe has been an unqualified success.

1. **Why did we introduce the program?** Employees appreciate being noticed for a job well done and for an idea that saves time or money. Like many organizations today, we realized we could improve business and boost team spirit by giving employees a public pat on the back. Our program was instituted to attract, retain, and motivate people.

2. **For what types of achievements do we give rewards?** We give rewards for effective management, visionary leadership, outstanding creative ideas, and initiatives that lead to cost savings.

3. **What is the scope of our recognition program?** Over the past year, we awarded more than $65,000 to 76 winners, ranging from $450 to an employee who noticed misleading wording in one of our brochures to a top award of $25,000 to a team of eight employees who designed an automated transaction system. Roughly three hundred ideas are submitted each month, with awards given monthly and annually. In the three years of the program's existence, there have been close to four hundred award winners.

4. **Do we anticipate any changes to our program in the future?** Companies such as GGI Technologies Inc. in Markham, Ontario, link rewards to company performance, with engineers receiving public recognition in the form of stock options. Expanding the program to include this type of reward merits our consideration.

Our recognition program is part of our commitment to maintaining a positive work experience for our employees. For additional information on our program, please see the attached fact sheet or speak with me at 905-553-8840. We wish you the best for your article and look forward to seeing our company represented in it.

Sincerely,

Audrey Bryant

Vice President

Send   📎 | +   🗑 | +

FIGURE 7.8 Effective Information Response

Personalized Form Letters

Personalized form letters allow you to deliver the same routine information without the inconvenience of retyping a message. Word-processing software enables you to customize a message so it applies to the reader. Simply merge your document with your mailing list and use variable data fields to insert names, dates, addresses, balances, or whatever information is specific to the message. A well-written form letter provides a way to save time and money when sending order acknowledgements, requesting action from customers and suppliers, and supplying answers to frequently asked questions (FAQs).

personalized form letter A standardized letter that can be sent to different recipients and that has adjustable fields for including the recipient's name, address, and perhaps other information, all of which may be stored in a database and merged with the form letter.

TOP FOOD

99 St. Elizabeth Avenue East
Toronto, ON M2A 8G5

{Current date}

{Title} {First name} {Last name}
{Street address}
{City}, {Province} {Postal code}

Dear {Title} {Last name}:

We appreciate your interest in the construction of our new Top Food Lakeview superstore. The enclosed brochure highlights the superior shopping experience that begins with our grand opening in June 2021.

Our new 5,500-square-metre facility will be our flagship store, offering customers the best in quality produce and the largest selection of brands in the Greater Toronto Area. Among the many amenities and conveniences you will find are a pharmacy, shoe repair, hot-meals take-away counter, flower shop, dry cleaners, and coffee bar. Our new location will be equipped with two hundred underground parking spaces and an express checkout.

Please drop by for our open house on {date} to tour the store, sample our newest product lines, and see for yourself the many ways in which we are committed to making your shopping experience enjoyable.

In the meantime, we invite you to continue shopping with us at our nearby Duchess Park location. Shuttle service from our Lakeview store departs daily at {time}.

We appreciate your patronage and look forward to offering you the best at our expanded superstores and our Lakeview location.

Sincerely,
TOP FOOD SUPERSTORES

Suzanne Wong

Suzanne Wong
Customer Service Specialist

Enclosure

FIGURE 7.9 Sample Form Letter

Order Acknowledgements

The ability to order online, by telephone, or by e-mail has increased expectations for prompt replies to requests for goods and services. Customers are eager to know when their transactions will be completed. An effective **order acknowledgement** is upbeat, efficient, and concise. The following template can be modified to send an acknowledgement or confirmation as a matter of courtesy:

1. **Begin directly.** There is no need to mention that you received an order. Readers are most interested in knowing that a shipment is on its way.

   Dear Mr. Vukovic:

   Your industrial air conditioning unit and invoice forms have been shipped to you by air freight and should arrive by April 2.

2. **Give details of the shipment and convince readers they have made a wise purchase.** As you specify individual items, refer to their features or confirm their popularity. Mention if products are currently unavailable or will ship later:

   The air conditioning unit you ordered features a humidity-control mechanism that allows you to regulate the amount of moisture in the air. Customers say that this dehumidifying feature has kept their offices and residences comfortably cool while helping them to reduce their summer energy costs.

3. **Use discretion in pushing additional products.** Gently suggest related products and emphasize their benefits, but avoid aggressive sales tactics:

   For your interest, we are enclosing a price list of Northwind Air Conditioning filter attachments. Customers who have already purchased a customized Northwind Air Conditioning unit from us receive an automatic 20 per cent discount on the purchase of any anti-allergen or aromatherapy attachment.

4. **Close pleasantly.** Express appreciation for the reader's business and include a forward-looking, personalized remark:

   We genuinely appreciate your order, Mr. Vukovic, and we look forward to serving you again.

Messages Confirming Contracts and Arrangements

A message of confirmation summarizes and clarifies any of the following:

- the terms of an agreement
- an action or a transaction that has taken place, including receipt of an invitation, resumé, or report
- a decision
- arrangements for a future event

The goal of a confirmation message is to confirm and explain details already established in a related document or to put an oral agreement into writing. A message confirming a contract helps to ensure that the meaning of an agreement is shared by all parties who enter into it, so that there is no confusion between the parties or any misunderstanding that could lead to disputes. Confirmation of an arrangement, including time-specific events such as travel, meetings, conferences, and appointments, keeps planners and participants onside so that they can properly coordinate their activities and ensure that those activities have the intended outcome.

A message of confirmation has several key functions:

- highlighting the key terms and conditions of a contract, including the offer, obligations, rules for acceptance, and effective date, or the details of an arrangement, including the date, time, place, nature or purpose, and length of the event
- showing appreciation to the reader for agreeing to participate in or helping to set up the event or arrangement
- specifying and delegating tasks to be completed and identifying administrative tasks
- providing clear wording that allows the reader to point out anything in the agreement that is contrary to what he or she thought it should be
- setting out actions the reader must take, such as signing and returning an agreement

Some letter agreements can have the legal effect of contracts, so it is always best to check with a lawyer to determine whether to use a contract or a letter of agreement.

Claims Adjustments

A claim response rights a wrong resulting from poor service, poor product performance, or a billing error. Its purpose is threefold: (1) to inform a customer that his or her claim has been successful, (2) to show how you intend to rectify the problem or resolve the complaint, and (3) to repair customer relations, rebuild goodwill, and restore confidence. A prompt response that reflects a thorough investigation of the problem and sounds happy about making the adjustment helps to promote favourable attitudes to your company.

A **claim adjustment** is damage control in action. The reader should be left with a sense of having been dealt with fairly—and have every reason to want to do business with your company again. When writing this type of response, keep the following guidelines in mind:

> **claim adjustment**
> A response to a claim letter telling the customer what a company intends to do to correct the problem.

1. **Grant the adjustment.** Avoid alibis, excuses, and especially admissions of negligence that could be used against your company in court.
2. **Explain how you intend to make the adjustment.** Give details of how you will comply—worded carefully to take into account legal issues and company policy.
3. **Close pleasantly.** Look forward to a continuing business relationship and build on the goodwill your explanation has already helped to re-establish.

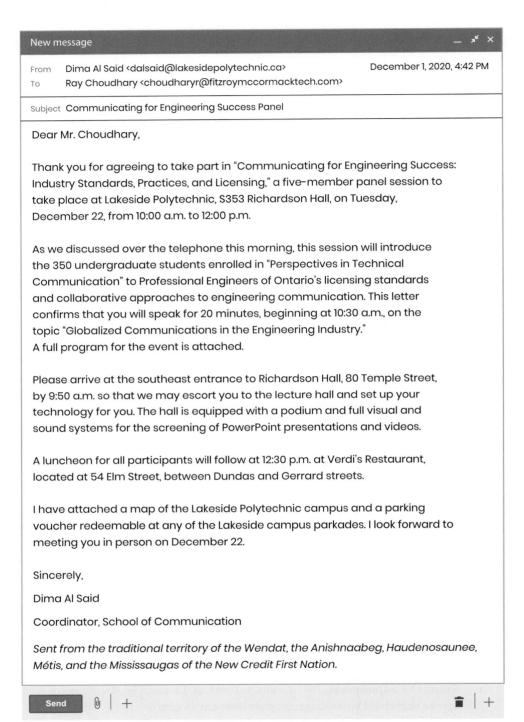

New message   — ⤢ ✕

From   Dima Al Said <dalsaid@lakesidepolytechnic.ca>   December 1, 2020, 4:42 PM
To   Ray Choudhary <choudharyr@fitzroymccormacktech.com>

Subject   Communicating for Engineering Success Panel

Dear Mr. Choudhary,

Thank you for agreeing to take part in "Communicating for Engineering Success: Industry Standards, Practices, and Licensing," a five-member panel session to take place at Lakeside Polytechnic, S353 Richardson Hall, on Tuesday, December 22, from 10:00 a.m. to 12:00 p.m.

As we discussed over the telephone this morning, this session will introduce the 350 undergraduate students enrolled in "Perspectives in Technical Communication" to Professional Engineers of Ontario's licensing standards and collaborative approaches to engineering communication. This letter confirms that you will speak for 20 minutes, beginning at 10:30 a.m., on the topic "Globalized Communications in the Engineering Industry."
A full program for the event is attached.

Please arrive at the southeast entrance to Richardson Hall, 80 Temple Street, by 9:50 a.m. so that we may escort you to the lecture hall and set up your technology for you. The hall is equipped with a podium and full visual and sound systems for the screening of PowerPoint presentations and videos.

A luncheon for all participants will follow at 12:30 p.m. at Verdi's Restaurant, located at 54 Elm Street, between Dundas and Gerrard streets.

I have attached a map of the Lakeside Polytechnic campus and a parking voucher redeemable at any of the Lakeside campus parkades. I look forward to meeting you in person on December 22.

Sincerely,

Dima Al Said

Coordinator, School of Communication

Sent from the traditional territory of the Wendat, the Anishnaabeg, Haudenosaunee, Métis, and the Mississaugas of the New Credit First Nation.

Send   📎 | +   🗑 | +

FIGURE 7.10   Sample Message Confirming Arrangements

Dear Alexis:

The failure of our sales staff to honour our famous price-matching policy is a common occurrence. Neverthe-less, we are extremely sorry for the inconvenience you must have suffered when you requested a discount at our Northridge Mall outlet. As a result of past abuses of this policy, our staff is sometimes over-scrupulous in demanding proof of our competitors' retail prices. Apparently, the advertisement you presented did not seem to meet standards that would qualify you for an in-store discount.

Despite the weakness of your claim—and because we want to keep you satisfied—we will allow you a refund of the price difference in this case. Incidentally, if you are in the market for a printer capable of meeting the needs of your small business, may we suggest the HP Deskjet 5150.

Let us say again how very sorry we are for this problem. We sincerely hope it doesn't happen again.

Addresses claimant on a first-name basis—too personal

Begins with admission of negligence—pointing to a chronic problem that has gone Opens with news of the favourable adjustment, using positive and reader-focused language

Questions the validity of the claim and sounds grudging in granting the claim

Introduces promotional information at the wrong time

Apologizes excessively and ends with a reminder of difficulty

FIGURE 7.11 Ineffective Claim Adjustment (extract)

Computer Central Ltd.
124 Fischer Street, Suite 601
Calgary, AB T3E 6A9
1-888-764-3333
www.computercentral.ca

February 11, 2021

Ms. Alexis Sorensen
525 Gosling Lane
Calgary, AB T3E 7M9

Subject: Enclosed Price-Matching Refund

Dear Ms. Sorensen:

The enclosed cheque for $158.85 demonstrates our commitment to our price-matching policy and our desire to offer our customers quality brand-name products at the lowest possible prices.

When we received your letter, we immediately contacted our store managers and asked them to review our price-matching policy with their sales associates. A few of our sales trainees, it seems, were not fully acquainted with our refund requirements, so we instituted a special training session and redesigned this portion of our website to make it easier for both our employees and our customers to find this information. We invite you to have a look the next time you visit us at www.computercentral.ca.

According to our guidelines, the advertisement you presented at the point of purchase should have immediately qualified you for a discount. We are of course happy to meet Computer Country's price of $2,199 for an Apatel XG package.

Please accept the enclosed cheque and our appreciation for bringing this important matter to our attention. We look forward to offering you continued discount pricing in the future.

Sincerely,

Meredith Anderson

Meredith Anderson
Manager, Customer Service

Enc.

Opens with news of the favourable adjustment, using positive and reader-focused language

Identifies how the company will prevent a recurrence of the problem, but does not admit fault or liability

Doesn't remind the reader of the problem; instead closes by conveying respect for the reader and expressing confidence in a renewed business relationship

Regains customer's confidence with positive language and an explanation of the claim investigation, resulting improvements, and claim settlement

FIGURE 7.12 Effective Claim Adjustment

> ## Checklist
>
> ### Response Letters
>
> - ❑ Do you have the knowledge and authorization to handle the response?
> - ❑ If you are the right person to answer a request, have you responded as promptly as possible?
> - ❑ If a request was referred to you to answer, have you notified the letter writer that the request has been forwarded? Does the first paragraph clearly state why someone else—not the original addressee—is answering the inquiry?
> - ❑ Does the first paragraph give the good news or answer the reader's most important question?
> - ❑ Is your response complete enough to meet the reader's needs? Have you included clarifying details?
> - ❑ Have you disclosed only what the reader has a right to know?
> - ❑ As much as possible, have you answered questions in the order they were asked?
> - ❑ As required, have you shaped the reader's attitude to the information or the organization by citing reader benefits?
> - ❑ Does your message reflect goodwill and good business practices?

Goodwill Messages

goodwill message
A message that enhances the value of a business beyond its tangible assets by creating a bond of friendship and establishing trust and mutual understanding between the writer and recipient.

Goodwill messages show that you are thinking of the reader and care about more than just your profit margin. They can say "thank you" to readers or show that you share their sorrow in loss and happiness in achievements. They satisfy basic human needs and recognize what it is to be human, even in the workplace. Sending them is not so much a matter of business but of good business etiquette. Such messages have the power to improve and solidify relationships with customers and co-workers. To be effective, goodwill messages should be

1. **Personal.** Individualized details make the difference between an impersonal greeting and a meaningful message. Address the reader by first name if you know the person well.
2. **Prompt.** Send goodwill messages immediately. The longer you wait, the less it can seem that you care.
3. **Spontaneous, short, and sincere.** Goodwill messages don't have to be long, but they should sound sincere. Avoid clichés; instead, imagine what your reader would like to hear.

Thank-You Letters

thank-you letter (or **letter of appreciation**) A message thanking someone for his or her help, hospitality, or business.

If you or your company has benefited from what another person or organization has provided, such as hospitality, business, a gift, or a favour, it is important to express your gratitude with a brief but sincere **thank-you letter**:

© GAC-AMC.

WBE Canada issued an open thank you letter to the Honourable François-Philippe Champagne, who became the first Minister of International Trade to attend the Women's Business Enterprise National Council (WBENC) National Conference in 20 years when he joined the delegation to Detroit in June 2018.

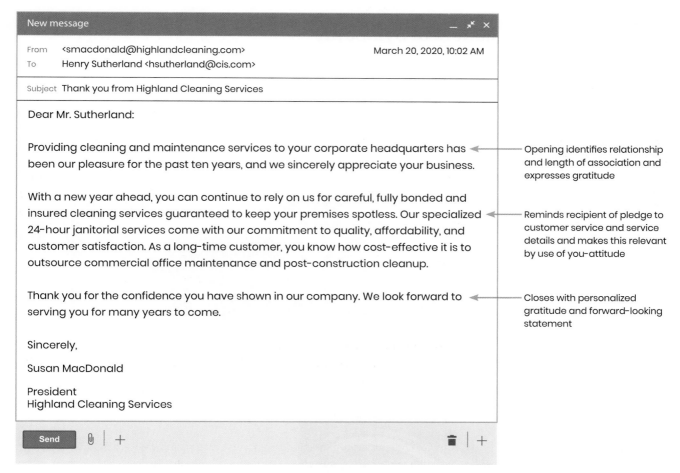

New message	— ⤢ ✕
From <smacdonald@highlandcleaning.com>	March 20, 2020, 10:02 AM
To Henry Sutherland <hsutherland@cis.com>	

Subject Thank you from Highland Cleaning Services

Dear Mr. Sutherland:

Providing cleaning and maintenance services to your corporate headquarters has been our pleasure for the past ten years, and we sincerely appreciate your business.

← Opening identifies relationship and length of association and expresses gratitude

With a new year ahead, you can continue to rely on us for careful, fully bonded and insured cleaning services guaranteed to keep your premises spotless. Our specialized 24-hour janitorial services come with our commitment to quality, affordability, and customer satisfaction. As a long-time customer, you know how cost-effective it is to outsource commercial office maintenance and post-construction cleanup.

← Reminds recipient of pledge to customer service and service details and makes this relevant by use of you-attitude

Thank you for the confidence you have shown in our company. We look forward to serving you for many years to come.

← Closes with personalized gratitude and forward-looking statement

Sincerely,

Susan MacDonald

President
Highland Cleaning Services

Send 📎 | +   🗑 | +

FIGURE 7.13 Appreciation for Business (E-mail)

1. **Thank the reader for what he or she has done, given, or provided.** Recall what it consisted of by identifying the situation or your purpose in writing.
2. **Include a few details.** Detail the benefits you derived and why you are grateful. If you are expressing thanks for hospitality, compliment your host on the food, company, or surroundings. If you are sending thanks for a gift, tell why you appreciate it and how you will use it. Express thanks for a favour by stating plainly what the favour means to you.
3. **Close with goodwill or a forward-looking remark.** Consider ending with a compliment, further thanks, or good wishes.

Letters of Congratulations

letter of congratulations A message conveying pleasure at someone's happiness or good wishes on someone's accomplishment.

A **letter of congratulations** expresses happiness at a reader's good fortune. It is important to avoid patronizing language that could sound like a put-down masquerading as praise (e.g., *it seems only yesterday you were a struggling young writer hungry for that elusive byline*) or that might suggest an honour isn't deserved. Show that you share in the reader's happiness by using words that correspond to the occasion.

Letters of Sympathy

letter of sympathy (or **letter of condolence**) A message expressing sadness at someone's bereavement and offering words of comfort.

Responding to loss is always difficult. A **letter of sympathy** should express your sadness at learning of the reader's loss, offer sympathy, and let your reader know that you are ready to offer support. The message should be handwritten and sent as soon as possible after you learn of the bereavement. Your first sentence should refer to the loss—and

YAKOBCHUK VIACHESLAV/Shutterstock.com

Handwritten messages can convey genuine warmth better than computer-generated ones, although letters set on company letterhead are always acceptable.

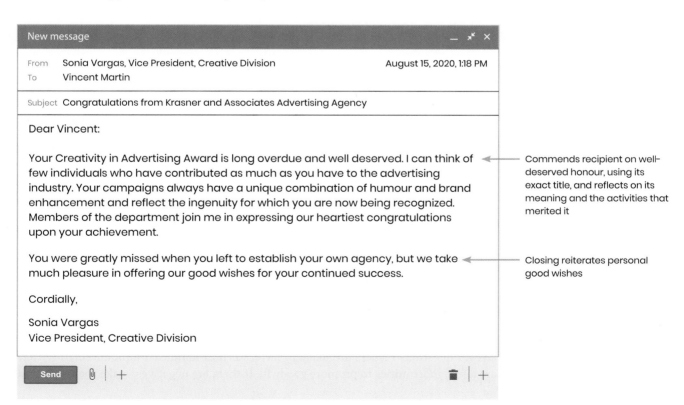

Fiona Dubois
14½ Brock Street
Guelph, ON
N2Y 2K9

May 14, 2021

Josephine Camarelli
128 Maplewood Avenue ←———————— Handwritten on personal
Guelph, ON N1L 6V4 stationery

Dear Josephine:

Paul and I want you to know how much we enjoyed the dinner you hosted for apprentice ←———————— Opening identifies the
CAs last Saturday. The evening was a welcome break from our exam preparations, and situation and describes it,
we were especially touched by the warm reception you gave us. Your superb Italian using personalized details
cookery and great dinnertime conversation definitely succeeded in taking our minds off enhanced by you
our studies for the entire evening, just as you had planned.

We are grateful for your kind hospitality and the chance to get to know you better. ←———————— Closing expresses warm
Thank you again for making the evening such a special one. appreciation for hospitality

Yours truly,
Fiona

FIGURE 7.14 Appreciation for Hospitality

New message   — ⤢ ✕

From   Sonia Vargas, Vice President, Creative Division   August 15, 2020, 1:18 PM
To   Vincent Martin

Subject Congratulations from Krasner and Associates Advertising Agency

Dear Vincent:

Your Creativity in Advertising Award is long overdue and well deserved. I can think of ←———————— Commends recipient on well-
few individuals who have contributed as much as you have to the advertising deserved honour, using its
industry. Your campaigns always have a unique combination of humour and brand exact title, and reflects on its
enhancement and reflect the ingenuity for which you are now being recognized. meaning and the activities that
Members of the department join me in expressing our heartiest congratulations merited it
upon your achievement.

You were greatly missed when you left to establish your own agency, but we take ←———————— Closing reiterates personal
much pleasure in offering our good wishes for your continued success. good wishes

Cordially,

Sonia Vargas
Vice President, Creative Division

Send   📎 | +   🗑 | +

FIGURE 7.15 Letter of Congratulations

Handwritten letter on personal stationery →

Immediately offers condolences; uses appropriate words →

Recalls positive attributes of the deceased →

Offers assistance →

John MacDougall
18 Parkland Terrace
Prince Albert, SK
S4N 1G7

May 10, 2020

Dear Miriam,

I was so sorry to hear of your loss. Please accept my deepest sympathies at this time.

Ben was a kind and talented individual whose knowledge and dedication contributed greatly to the success of our company. May you have the comfort of knowing how much he was respected by all in our organization and how much he will be missed.

Your many friends here at MacDougall & Kish join me in offering assistance. Please do not hesitate to let us know how we may help.

Sincerely,
John MacDougall

FIGURE 7.16   Letter of Sympathy

your reaction to it—in a tactful way. If you knew the deceased, recall positive attributes for which that person will be remembered. Offer personal help or business-related assistance. The reader may find it difficult to absorb a long letter, so keep the message brief and its sentiments sincere.

Informative Letters

informative letters
Messages that provide important and relevant information and to which the reader will react neutrally.

announcement A message that makes something known about a company policy, event, or change.

Informative letters have an explanatory purpose—to let readers know what something is or to keep them up to date on changing policies, personnel, or circumstances.

Announcements

Announcements inform readers about company policies, events, and personnel changes. When the news you have to deliver is positive or neutral, use the direct approach: give the most important news first and then move on to clarify details that answer questions readers are likely to have. Keep in mind that announcement letters are also opportunities to promote goodwill. If there are negatives, make them clear but present them as positively as possible. Explain any reader benefits of a new product or updated policy.

> Goldsmith Press is pleased to announce the appointment of Jocelyn Harwood as its director of marketing. Ms. Harwood has more than ten years' experience in the publishing industry and most recently worked as assistant marketing director at Manticore Publishing. She joins us as we expand our business publishing division and brings with her extensive experience in marketing texts to colleges and universities.

Cover or Transmittal Letters

A **cover** or **transmittal letter** accompanies something you are sending to someone inside or outside your organization—a report, proposal, or shipment of materials. It identifies what is being sent and the reason for sending it. The message serves as a permanent record of the exchange of goods or information. The more important your document or material is, the more essential it is to type a transmittal letter to accompany it.

Follow these steps when writing a cover letter:

> **cover letter** (or **transmittal letter**) An informative letter that accompanies materials sent from one person to another explaining why those materials are being sent.

1. **Identify what you are sending.** Your phrasing depends on how friendly or formal you want to be:

   > Enclosed is a proof copy of the article you recently wrote for us.

   > I am pleased to enclose a proof copy of the article you recently wrote for us.

   > Here is a proof copy of the article you recently wrote for us.

2. **Briefly summarize the attached document or describe the enclosed materials.** Call attention to sections of particular interest.

   > "Minding Your Periods and Commas" is a welcome addition to Vol. 7 of *Resources for Business Writers*.

3. **Point out important details.** Help the reader understand the document or give instructions on how to use the materials. Have all the items the reader requested been sent as promised? Is the document a draft or a final version? Will other documents or materials be forwarded later? Are there recommendations or findings the reader is likely to support?

   > The proof copy reflects minor editorial changes, including the abbreviation of some subheadings.

4. **Offer further assistance or tell the reader what happens next.** State what you will do or tell the reader what to do if you expect action or a response. Give a deadline if needed, then close in a friendly or helpful way.

Please examine your copy carefully to make sure it contains no typographical or factual errors. If you have changes to suggest, please call my office by June 4 so that we can begin production on June 6. You should expect to receive a copy of *Resources for Business Writers* in early July.

Instructional Letters/Memos

Instructions explain a process, activity, or operation for the average reader. Directives share important information about what employees must do as a result of changes in regulations, policies, or day-to-day procedures. Staying competitive and working responsibly involve keeping pace with changing regulations and technological developments, and instructions and directives help organizations ensure compliance with new procedures and the effective adoption of new technologies. Written as e-mail messages, memos, or letters, these routine messages promote legal, ethical, and safe work, and help avoid costly mistakes. Use a direct approach when writing instructions. See Figure 7.18 for key tips on writing good instructions.

Writing instructions that meet the guidelines in Figure 7.18 involve a systematic approach:

1. Be sure you understand the procedure well enough to explain it, either from having performed it yourself or from having seen an expert demonstrate it.
2. Assess your audience's familiarity with the procedure and determine the right levels of technicality and explanation. Think about the circumstances in which

Written instructions are useful for teaching employees how to use workplace equipment without damaging company property or injuring themselves. In addition to being clear and accurate, good instructions should be broken up into easy-to-understand steps, use the right level of technicality and explanation for the audience, and include visual representations where appropriate.

Good instructions are:

 Clear and accurate: There should be no guesswork in following the instructions. The order of the steps into which a procedure is divided should be clear and logical.

 Precise: Instructions should include no more and no less than what readers need to know. Exact times, amounts, and measurements should be used to quantify details.

 Complete: Missing or out-of-sequence steps can lead to non-performance, damage, or injury. Any warning or caution should be highlighted at the beginning or in the step to which it applies. Specialized terms must be defined. With effective instructions, the reader has no need to seek information from another source.

 User-friendly: Include basic information that a reader with no knowledge of the procedure would need to achieve the desired result. Lists and numbering make the steps easier to follow. In addition, positive phrasing that emphasizes what readers should do is easier to understand than negative phrasing.

 Action-oriented: The active voice and imperative (command) mood give instructions clarity and authority. Each step in the sequence should begin with an action verb. Parallel phrasing and similar structures focus attention on the actions readers must take, while transitions (*next, before*) help to keep steps in order.

Figure 7.17 Characteristics of good instructions

the instructions will be used and whether you must persuade readers that the instructions are necessary.

3. Include an introduction, a list of equipment and materials, a description of the steps, and a conclusion.

4. Explain the purpose (the *what* and the *why*) of the procedure in the introduction.

5. Organize your information in short, numbered steps, each beginning with an action verb and arranged in chronological sequence. Note relationships between steps and use transitional words where appropriate.

6. Use headings to divide long lists of steps into shorter sections.

7. Give warnings where mistakes can lead to damage or injury. Note the consequences of missing a step or performing a step incorrectly.

8. Use visuals to repeat or reinforce prose descriptions.
9. Put the procedure in perspective by commenting on the outcome it is meant to achieve.

Directives let employees know what to do—when an activity or a requirement takes effect, what it involves, and where it takes place. Figure 7.18 is an example of a group e-mail message that combines features of directives and instructions.

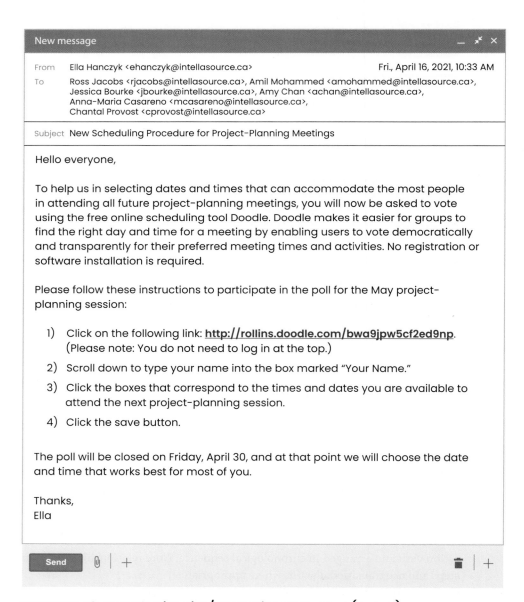

FIGURE 7.18 Sample Directive/Instructional Message (E-mail)

Checklist

Goodwill and Informative Messages

- ❏ Do you get to the point immediately?
- ❏ Does the first sentence summarize your key information or request?
- ❏ If the purpose of the message is to make a request, is the request specific rather than implied?
- ❏ Have you used lists when appropriate to organize details, prioritize questions, and sequence instructions?
- ❏ Have you supplied all details needed for the reader to act on information or a request?
- ❏ Have you disclosed only what the reader has a right to know?
- ❏ If follow-up is required, have you end-dated a request for action or information?

Letter Formats

The appearance of a document is a reflection of the professional standards of the writer and the organization to which that person belongs. Well-prepared letters are accurately typed and follow standard practices and conventions—many of them centuries old—according to how their elements are arranged and styled.

Letter Balance and Placement

A professional-looking letter is centred vertically and horizontally on the page, like a picture formed by blocks of text surrounded by an even frame of blank space. In word-processing programs, the standard default setting for margins—which create the blank frame—is 1 inch (2.54 centimetres), but you may have to widen your margins to give a fuller appearance to very short letters. Letters with "**ragged**," or **unjustified, right margins** are easier to read than justified margins. Before you print, check that your letter is well-proportioned by using the preview or full-page feature.

ragged right margins (or **unjustified, right margins**) Margins that end unevenly on the right side of the page.

Letter Styles and Layouts

The most common formats or styles for business letters are **full block**, **modified block**, and **simplified**. Figure 7.19 provides illustrations of these three formats. The choice of letter format is usually determined by the company, but it is important to be familiar with all styles so you can use them accurately when needed.

Letter Elements

Professional-looking business letters have multiple parts that are arranged in a conventional sequence. Properly used, each part has a specific function. For a letter that is balanced and easy to read, double space between elements and single space within:

Standard Elements	Optional Elements
Heading/return address	Delivery/confidential notation
Dateline	Reference line
Inside address	Attention line
Salutation	Subject line
Message	Identification initials
Complimentary close	Enclosure notation
Signature block	Copy notation
	Postscript (discussed in Chapter 9)
	Continuation page heading

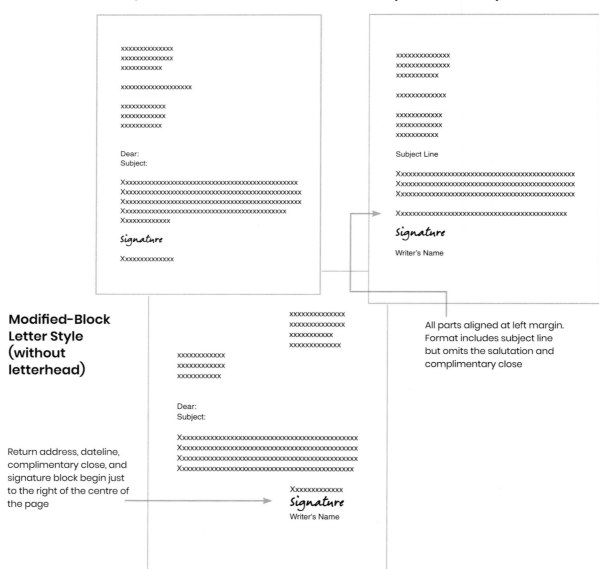

Full-Block Letter Style (without letterhead)

Simplified Letter Style

Modified-Block Letter Style (without letterhead)

Return address, dateline, complimentary close, and signature block begin just to the right of the centre of the page

All parts aligned at left margin. Format includes subject line but omits the salutation and complimentary close

FIGURE 7.19 Letter Formats

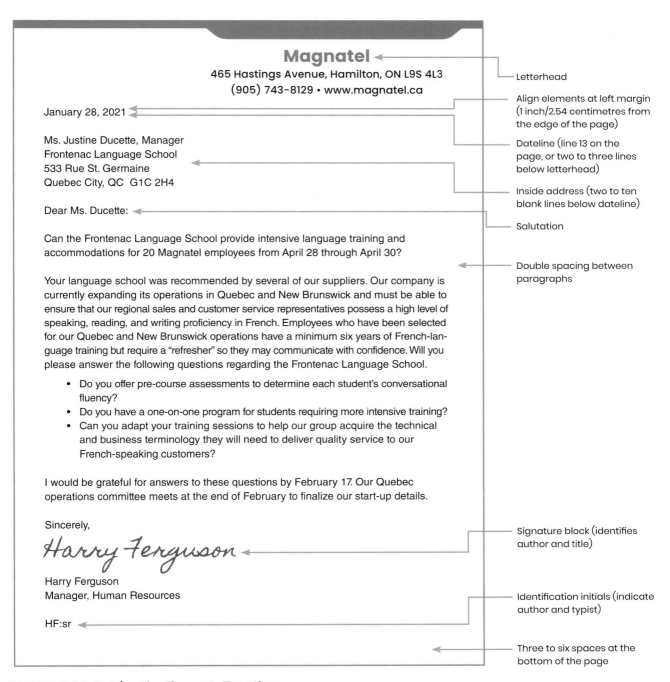

Magnatel
465 Hastings Avenue, Hamilton, ON L9S 4L3
(905) 743-8129 • www.magnatel.ca

Letterhead

Align elements at left margin
(1 inch/2.54 centimetres from
the edge of the page)

January 28, 2021

Dateline (line 13 on the
page, or two to three lines
below letterhead)

Ms. Justine Ducette, Manager
Frontenac Language School
533 Rue St. Germaine
Quebec City, QC G1C 2H4

Inside address (two to ten
blank lines below dateline)

Dear Ms. Ducette:

Salutation

Can the Frontenac Language School provide intensive language training and accommodations for 20 Magnatel employees from April 28 through April 30?

Double spacing between
paragraphs

Your language school was recommended by several of our suppliers. Our company is currently expanding its operations in Quebec and New Brunswick and must be able to ensure that our regional sales and customer service representatives possess a high level of speaking, reading, and writing proficiency in French. Employees who have been selected for our Quebec and New Brunswick operations have a minimum six years of French-language training but require a "refresher" so they may communicate with confidence. Will you please answer the following questions regarding the Frontenac Language School.

- Do you offer pre-course assessments to determine each student's conversational fluency?
- Do you have a one-on-one program for students requiring more intensive training?
- Can you adapt your training sessions to help our group acquire the technical and business terminology they will need to deliver quality service to our French-speaking customers?

I would be grateful for answers to these questions by February 17. Our Quebec operations committee meets at the end of February to finalize our start-up details.

Sincerely,

Harry Ferguson

Signature block (identifies
author and title)

Harry Ferguson
Manager, Human Resources

Identification initials (indicate
author and typist)

HF:sr

Three to six spaces at the
bottom of the page

FIGURE 7.20 Putting the Elements Together

Addressing Envelopes

Follow Canada Post guidelines for formatting envelopes:

- On envelopes without a pre-printed return address, the return address should be formatted in the same way as the destination address and located in the upper left-hand corner.

- In both the return address and the address block, the municipality, province or territory, and postal code should appear on the same line.
- Postal codes should be printed in uppercase, and the first three elements should be separated from the last three by one space.
- For international letters, adjust the content of the address as necessary (e.g., listing a state instead of a province or territory), and provide the full name of the country on a separate line at the end of the address block.
- Affix the stamp(s) in the upper right-hand corner.

Checklist

Chapter Review

- ❑ Use the three-step direct writing plan for positive and neutral messages that request, respond, convey goodwill, and inform.

- ❑ Begin request letters with a purpose statement, then introduce multiple requests with a summary statement, arrange your questions in list form, use details that will help the receiver respond, and close with an end-date, request summary, and appreciation.

- ❑ Determine if you are the right person to respond to a message; if so, answer promptly, begin with the most important information or a summary statement, answer each inquiry logically and fully in list form, include additional information based on an analysis of the receiver's needs, disclose only the information you can give, and show sincerity and goodwill in closing.

- ❑ Write goodwill messages to establish rapport and build business relationships by showing empathy, respect, and consideration.

- ❑ Make sure informative letters—including announcements, cover or transmittal letters, and instructional letters—provide a clear, concise, and complete explanation of the information they are intended to transmit.

- ❑ When writing formal letters, use a standard format (full-block style, modified-block style, or simplified style) and modify the style as necessary to conform with the preferences of your organization.

Exercises, Workshops, and Discussion Forums

1. **Applying the Direct Approach.** Rearrange the paragraphs in the following extract from a request letter according to the direct-approach writing plan.

My supervisor at KDS Laboratories has asked me to investigate car-fleet leasing options. Our sales representatives require reliable, low-maintenance, fuel-efficient sedans for servicing their territories throughout Ontario and Quebec. Our current lease expires August 31. We will require 20 vehicles.

I would be grateful for answers to these questions by July 15, when our transportation committee must meet to decide.

Please answer the following questions about car leasing options and vehicle features:

1.   What leasing packages does your dealership offer?

2.   What level of servicing do you provide?

3.   Do you offer flexible leasing payments?

4.   What model sedan provides the greatest fuel economy?

---

2. **Analyzing a Letter of Congratulations.** What mistakes does the writer of the following letter make? How would you feel if you received this message?

Dear Imogen:

Talk about overnight success! I find it hard to believe that someone who has been with the company for as little time as you have could rise through the ranks so quickly, putting us all to shame. It seems that only yesterday you were our eager office assistant, fetching us coffee from the local Starbucks. Well, times have changed—and it couldn't have happened to a nicer person. No doubt your pleasant smile and excellent telephone manner will help you with the many challenges that lie ahead in your new job as assistant district manager. I would like to know what a person has to do to climb the corporate ladder as fast as you have.

Cheers,

Larry, et. al.

Larry and the gang

---

3. **Analyzing a Request.** In a group, discuss whether the following extract meets the guidelines for an information request and how easy it would be to respond to this inquiry.

> What can you tell me about your banquet facilities? A few weeks ago, my boss asked me to find out as much as I could about upscale banquet facilities in the area. Our company is hosting an event to celebrate its twentieth anniversary. We expect that the event will be held the week of June 9–13, although June 10 is our preferred date. Any other week would be unsuitable. Of course, we are only interested in booking a facility if it is air-conditioned. Is your banquet hall air-conditioned? We anticipate having 200 guests. Do you have a banquet room that would accommodate 200 guests? I would also like to know if your banquet centre is wheelchair-accessible. Because our workforce is quite diversified, we would like to offer menu selections that appeal to many different tastes. Do you offer international menus? Thank you for any information you can provide.

4. **Revising an Announcement for Clarity.** What common errors make the message below ineffective? Rewrite the announcement, focusing on clarity.

> **<u>Announcement</u>**
> **<u>WRITE ON BUSINESS COMMUNICATIONS CONFERENCE</u>**
>
> The National Write On Association herewith wishes to inform you that it is seeking presentations concerning the impact of electronic communication on business writing efforts for its annual national conference scheduled for March 18th to 21st, 2021, in Halifax, Nova Scotia.
>
> Joining the NWOA in sponsoring the conference are the Canadian Jargon Association, the National Society for the Prevention of Obfuscation, the Stop Flaming Now League, and the Canadian Anti-Spam Federation. The last conference, held in 2020 under the sponsorship of the National Save the Comma Society, drew over 750 participants from every province with the exception of PEI and saw representation from various branches of industry, business, government, academia, industry, and business from across the country.
>
> Conference coordinators desire presentations that deal with documented case histories of e-mail abuse in business and industry. According to Dr. Lyle Mudd, the NWOA executive coordinator, "We are most interested in the impact of e-mail on standards of grammar and the corporate measures that have been implemented to redress existing problems. We are also seeking presentations on acceptable e-mail length and the introduction of corporate e-mail guidelines." Members wishing to give presentations on any of the aforementioned topics are advised to submit a two-hundred-and-fifty (250) word proposal.
>
> All proposals must be postmarked no later than November 1, 2020, and directed to the attention of Dr. Lyle Mudd, NWOA Executive, St. Sebastian University, Halifax, NS D4A 2E1.

5. **Changing Letter Style.** Rewrite the following full-block style letter in simplified style. When would a simplified style be appropriate?

Salmon Run Tackle and Fishing Supply
4 Timberline Avenue
Carlyle, BC W9G 2B1

July 26, 2020

North by Northwest Supply
28 Forest Avenue
Prince George, BC W5L 2K9

ATTENTION ORDER DEPARTMENT SPECIALIST

Dear order department:

SUBJECT: ORDER FOR GAS GENERATOR

Enclosed is a cheque for $1,682.98 in payment for the Deluxe Genron Gas Generator, item #7753 in your Winter 2020 catalogue.

As arranged, I will pick up this item at your Selkirk Road service depot when I am in Prince George on August 6.

Please enclose an updated price list with my order.

Sincerely,

Brad Hutchinson

Brad Hutchinson
Enc.

Phone: 304-590-8831   salmonrun@ccre.net   Fax: 304-590-8824

6. **Arranging Letter Elements.** Retype the following letter using your computer software's letter wizard and note the resulting changes in style and formatting.

Subject: Summer Outreach Tours

April 16, 2021
Mr. Jordan Fisher, Marketing Director
College Life Tours
1515 Aubrey Avenue
Toronto, ON M5S 2K1

18 Belgrave Street
Toronto, ON M9M 3H7

Dear Mr. Jordan Fisher:

Please answer the following questions about the student-outreach tour packages offered by your company this summer.

1. Can you recommend a tour of Central America that combines volunteer work with adventure vacationing?

2. Could such a tour accommodate a group of five travellers in June or July?

3. What is the approximate cost per person for a three-week package?

Along with a group of friends, I plan to tour Central America this summer. While there, my friends and I would like to contribute what we can to the communities we visit. We are therefore looking for a tour that would allow us to do volunteer work, similar to our past work for Habitat for Humanity, while also giving us the chance to pursue extreme sports and explore some of the region's best-known ecological preserves.

I would appreciate answers to these questions by May 30, when my friends and I will meet to discuss our summer travel destination.

Yours very sincerely,

Justin Littleton

Justin Littleton

Writing Improvement Exercises

1. **Revising Direct-Approach Openings.** Make the following openings direct, professional, and specific.

   a) Hello! My name is Wayne Dumont. I am a junior accountant at Hammond Financial and I have a number of questions for you to answer. Let me first explain that all of these questions have to do with import and excise taxes.

   b) It is my pleasure and privilege to write to you today to ask about your retirement-planning education programs. I am most interested in finding out if your educational package includes a focus section on financial planning for early retirement.

   c) Give me any information you can on your conference-hosting services. I need to know how much it costs to hold a half-day conference for 30 people at your conference facility.

   d) We always appreciate hearing from customers who have experienced problems with products under warranty and have the courage to ask for a refund. While your claim seems valid, and there doesn't seem to be a strong reason why we should not do as you request, let me first explain company policy on this issue.

   e) In response to your letter of inquiry, received September 29, in which you asked about the availability of price discounts on our web hosting services, I am pleased to tell you that the answer is yes.

   f) Pursuant to your letter dated August 28, we would like to advise you that you can take the PowerPoint projector with which you have apparently had so much trouble to Prism Servicing for inspection and, if necessary, free repair.

2. **Itemizing Parts of a Request or Response.** Improve the readability of the following request by organizing its various questions into a list.

   Please answer the following questions about your new line of high-nutrition sports snacks.

   First, I would like to know if individual food items are vacuum sealed. I conduct guided cycling tours of Prince Edward County and I need assurances that the products I supply to tour members will be fresh and appetizing, even at the end of a hot summer day. How long do products remain fresh after they have been opened? Is dietary information for each item printed on the packaging? I am also interested in finding out if you have any gluten-free and organic products. And are your snacks suitable for diabetics and people with food allergies? Of course, I would like to sample products from your new line before I commit to purchasing them. Can you send me some samples to try? I already have your price list.

   As an operator of tours for experienced cycling enthusiasts, I would like to offer complimentary premium sports snacks on my one- and two-day excursions.

   I would appreciate answers—in fact all the information you can provide—by April 15, when our tour planning committee meets to finalize purchasing details.

3. **Writing Subject Lines.** Below are opening sentences from request and response messages. Write a concise and specific subject line that corresponds to each.

   a) The enclosed cheque for $365 represents our quality commitment to our customers and our desire to earn their confidence.

   b) Please answer the following questions about the role of mediation service companies in the labour–management relationship. I am writing an article on this topic for *Business Weekly*.

   c) Here are answers to your questions about our corporate gift services.

4. **Revising Letter Closings.** Rewrite the following closings to make them more specific and polite.

   a) Please get back to me soon. My boss really needs this information and I don't want to get into trouble for missing our April 7 deadline.

b) Because we want to keep you satisfied and because we would like to resolve this problem
once and for all, we are offering you a complimentary repair on your automatic door. We
hope the inconvenience and minor injuries
your customers experienced as a result of our
malfunctioning door will not discourage you
from doing business with us in the future.

c) I trust that I have provided the information you
require. If you need information in the future,
I recommend that you direct your inquiry to
my assistant, who has time to handle minor
requests of this kind.

5. **Writing an Instructional Letter/Memo.** Write an
instructional letter or memo describing best practices for business writing. Direct your instructions
to your classmates. Base your instructions on the
advice given in this chapter and Corrine LaBossiere's article "The No. 1 Rule for Good Business
Writing? Get to the Point" (www.theglobeandmail.
com/report-on-business/careers/career-advice/
life-at-work/the-no-1-rule-for-good-business-
writing-get -to-the-point/article14607000/).

Case Study Exercises

1. **Information Request.** As assistant to the vice-president of Excelon Investments, you have been asked
to research business etiquette agencies. Your boss,
Francesca Franca, has noticed that many of your
company's top managers and investment counsel-
lors are conscious of the etiquette gaffes they make
while attending corporate functions and formal
dinners. Entertaining important clients is customary, but it is a part of the job that many talented
senior personnel seem reluctant to do. Which
fork is used for the fish course? Why is it wrong to
whistle for the cheque? Ms. Franca would like to
ensure that senior personnel know the answers to
these questions and, without causing them embarrassment, see to it that company representatives
have good table manners and can do business with
savvy while eating a meal. She has proposed that
an etiquette course be made available to interested
personnel. You have heard that Decorum Business
Etiquette Services offers a one-day seminar on
telephone manners, dining etiquette, and interpersonal skills for client retention. You are wondering
if Decorum could accommodate a group of up to 20
people. Because the social functions your employees attend include casual lunches and formal dinners, you would also like to know if students have
the opportunity to test their new skills in a supervised restaurant-style meal. Will students, for example, learn to use each piece of cutlery properly?
You would prefer that the training take place within
the next three weeks because senior employees are
set to attend the premier fundraising dinner next
month, an event for which Ms. Franca has already
booked two $10,000 tables.

2. **Information Request.** As a Ryerson grad and the
president/owner of Edgerton & Smith, a bricks-
and-mortar fashion retailer with five stores in the
GTA and a strong online presence, you are interested
in getting involved with the Ted Rogers School of
Retail Management's internship program. You are
considering providing at least one paid internship
for a third-year student in the upcoming summer.
You would like to be in a position to provide clear
expectations to students before they apply to and
accept the opportunities within your organization.
Having read the information on the program's
website, you understand that your company will
be facilitating the development of professionally
related skills, as defined by the Conference Board
of Canada. The school asks that you develop two
or three measurable goals by which to monitor and
evaluate internship progress, as well as a flexible
learning plan. You are not sure, however, how detailed the learning plan has to be. An internship
fair is scheduled to take place and, in advance of
this event, you will have to identify a supervisor/
mentor to coach each intern; however, you have
had some recent personnel changes and are wondering when this information has to be finalized.
A timeline would be helpful as you would also like
to know when internships could begin and end,
and when you would need to submit copies of your

internal application, recruitment, and selection schedules. As your company has a growing online presence, you are also wondering if students would have a background in social media marketing. You would like to have answers to your questions by the end of the month so that your management team can discuss options at an upcoming October meeting. Write to Elena Jacobek, Coordinator, TRSM Retail Internship Program, 55 Dundas Street West, Toronto, ON, M5G 2C3.

3. **Information Request.** You are the founder and owner of a small but growing start-up company. Your company is known for its community crowd-sourcing tool, HaveYRSay, which can be integrated into existing online communities for gathering, prioritizing, and executing ideas. Companies such as Coca-Cola use HaveYRSay to gather, prioritize, and act on consumer suggestions. You have just discovered that the college or university from which you graduated is having a part-time job fair next week. You understand that it is too late to be part of this upcoming event, but you would like to be able to tap into talent and recruit students for part-time employment through similar events in the future. To do so, you need to know more about the process, including how to register your company to participate, when future career fairs will be held, and what procedures are standard for interviewing candidates at the fair. You were unable to find much information online to help you act on this opportunity. Write a direct-approach request letter seeking information about these concerns, as well as any additional concerns you many have. Address the letter to the director of the career centre at your college or university. Use the following return address: [Your Name], Founder, HaveYRSay, 123 Innovation Street, Vancouver, BC, V5Y 2Z6. You may create letterhead if you wish.

4. **Order Request.** Rewrite the following order request so that details of each item are formatted for quick and easy reference. Clearly indicate the products you intend to buy, your planned method of payment, and how you would like your order shipped. Eliminate parts of the letter that detract from the effectiveness of the request.

My small home-decorating business has an account with your company. I am interested in several items that were featured on your website last week. Because your website is currently down, I have chosen to send my order by conventional mail. I hope this is acceptable.

I am most interested in the deluxe paint sprayer that was advertised as your monthly special. I believe it was manufactured by Craftline. Its unit price was around $175. I would need two of them. You also advertised a cordless sander manufactured by Precision Master. Its unit price was approximately $80. Please send me three sanders. Another item caught my eye—a virtual decor software program that would allow my customers to preview a room in a variety of colours and finishes. I would require the version for Windows 8. I believe it cost $95 and went under the name of Samtex Color Options.

By the way, my company's account number is 551H27. Please notify me if the prices you advertised are no longer in effect. Because we have many contracts to complete in the next few weeks, please ship my order as fast as you can.

5. **Order Request.** As marketing director of Ambiant, a new lighting design firm and retailer of electrical fixtures, you have been appointed to represent the company at a number of upcoming design and trade shows. Because the market for lighting products and services is extremely competitive, you would like prospective customers to keep your company in mind for their next lighting project. To help your fledgling business gain a foothold in the marketplace, you plan to distribute novelties bearing your company name and logo at the upcoming trade shows. You have heard that Your Name Here, a supplier of corporate gifts and novelties in Taiwan, can customize any item from a product line that includes LED flashlights, glow-in-the-dark pens, pen lights, and illuminated pens. Because your instructions are

detailed and involve a series of customizations, you have decided to draft a summary that can be pasted into the "Additional Instructions" field in the online form. You would like 50 mini LED flashlights, item number 62-J, in red if possible, listed at $9. You also want 200 glow-in-the-dark pens, item number 98-K, with black ink, listed at $2 per unit. Finally, you would like 100 pen lights, item number 55-R, again in red, listed at $4 per unit. You would like the company logo to be reproduced as accurately as possible, so you are attaching an enlarged sample. Each item should also be stamped with the slogan "Ambient—Lighting the Way" together with the web address, www.ambiantlighting.com. You would like to be invoiced for this purchase. Your Name Here's website provides no option for expedited delivery. However, because you need these items for a trade show to be held in ten days, you want this to be a rush order, with shipment by overnight international courier. You would like immediate notification if, for any reason, Your Name Here is unable to process the order as stipulated.

6. **Writing a Claim Letter.** Write a claim letter based on a problem you have experienced with a product or service that was under guarantee or covered by a warranty.

7. **Claim Request.** As office manager of Inukshuk Mining and Exploration in Yellowknife, NT, you have received a shipment of mismatched modular office components from Cubicle Junction of Vancouver. When you telephoned Cubicle Junction's customer service hotline to complain, you were told that the faulty components could be replaced, on condition that they be returned to the warehouse. However, Cubicle Junction could not promise to cover shipping costs—the charges for which would be passed on to you. You feel these charges are unwarranted and unfair, as Cubicle Junction was at fault for the irregularities in the original shipment. Write to Maya Sutcliffe, manager of customer service at Cubicle Junction, asking that the company cover the estimated $300 in shipping charges.

8. **Follow-Up Letter.** As owner of Get It Write, an editorial and tutoring service, write to Giacomo Giancarlo confirming the details of yesterday's telephone conversation. Mr. Giancarlo, a marketing expert with a high profile in the business community, is writing a series of articles for a business publication and is also working on a book-length manuscript that he plans to submit to publishers in Canada and the United States. He has asked you to review his writing and make necessary changes so his academic style will have broader popular appeal. You agreed on an hourly rate of $80 and discussed the type of style for which he is aiming. You also agreed to meet next week to discuss his projects in greater detail.

9. **Information Response.** When you graduated from high school, you volunteered for a mentorship program designed to help students in the next graduating class choose colleges and universities best suited to their needs and career objectives. You agreed to write briefly to your former guidance counsellor with details of academic programs, standards of instruction, student services, residence accommodations, extracurricular activities, and overall college life at the academic institution you attend. Although you prefer not to include personal information, you would like to record your impressions and provide helpful details that supplement what prospective students can find on your college's or university's website. Write to your guidance counsellor with brief comments on the topics listed above. Offer to greet a small group of students from your former high school when they tour your college or university next month.

10. **Order Response.** As sales director of Your Name Here, you have just received Ambient's order (see Case 5). The only negative element you must include in your message is that the mini LED flashlights ordered are available in black only because of high demand. A new shipment of red mini LED flashlights is expected in one week. Although you cannot guarantee that the red LED flashlights will be ready for the company's first trade show, you would like to offer to fill the order partially or fully with black LED flashlights, available at a substantially discounted price of $5 per unit. All other items on order can be customized as requested and shipped immediately. Write a response to Ambient outlining this information.

11. **Claim Response.** As Maya Sutcliffe, manager of customer service at Cubicle Junction, respond to the letter from Case 7 and grant the request to waive $300 in shipping costs. In reviewing the customer service records, you immediately determined that the problem with the prefabricated office system resulted from the inclusion of five mismatched panels in the shipment. The bolts provided were compatible only with the ordered panels, not with those shipped in error, making it impossible for the parts to be assembled correctly. When only a few components require replacement, your company policy is to simply ship the replacement parts free of charge, not to demand the return of the entire order at the customer's expense. In investigating the cause of the problem with the shipment, you discovered that a changeover to new software had temporarily disrupted inventory control at the time the order was processed. By bringing the matter to your attention, the customer has allowed you to implement a backup system so problems of this kind will not recur. The customer can expect to receive the new shipment in one week and can find technical support at www.cubiclejunction.com or at 1-888-288-4853.

12. **Letter of Appreciation.** As a coordinating assistant, you have been asked to draft thank-you letters to sponsors following the completion of the second annual Indigenous Fashion Week Toronto (https://ifwtoronto.com/). The director asked that the letters thank sponsors for their contributions to the success of the festival, and specifically mention how each sponsor helped to support the mission and mandate of the event. Choose a sponsor from the IFWTO website and draft a letter of appreciation that thanks the sponsor for their contributions, and encourages their ongoing support of the event.

13. **Letter of Appreciation.** As the president of the student union for your program, draft a letter to be sent to members of the union executive committee at the end of the year thanking them for their service and participation. Be sure to mention the support they provided for important activities and events, including orientation for first-year students, a panel discussion with industry leaders, and a mid-year social mixer. Also mention their role in overseeing student competitions, including a t-shirt design competition and a winter e-card design competition, and running a student-life Instagram page and blog. The letter is important because committee members can include it with future job applications as evidence of their commitment to extracurricular activities, not to mention the experience they gained through work on behalf of students and through interactions with college or university administration and the public.

14. **Letter of Appreciation.** Think of a charity or community event you have organized or participated in, or one that you are interested in organizing or participating in. Assume the role of the event organizer, and draft a letter to volunteers identifying and describing the event and its outcome and thanking them for their commitment and hard work.

15. **Message of Congratulations.** Your co-workers Amy and Cameron have had a baby. They sent you an e-mail to let you know that their baby was born last weekend and that they've chosen a gender-neutral name, Taylor, for their child. They made it known at the office baby shower you and your co-workers hosted for them that they don't wish to disclose their child's sex or be asked about it. Write a congratulatory message that conveys your happiness and good wishes for them.

16. **Transmittal Letter.** As president of an architectural firm specializing in historical restoration, you have been asked by real estate developer Jay Delmonico to develop a proposal for restoring a heritage building his company is thinking of buying. Mr. Delmonico plans to convert the four-storey heritage property to a multi-purpose commercial space that will still retain its historical designation. Write a letter of transmittal to accompany the draft version of your proposal.

Online Activities

1. **Applying the Direct Approach to a Claim Request.** Look at the sample complaint letter on the Writing Business Letters website. Using the information provided, rewrite the letter so that it follows the direct writing plan.

   www.writing-business-letters.com/complain-letter. html

2. **Creating a Form Letter.** Watch the online video describing how to use Microsoft Word's "mail merge" function, then draft a form letter that makes use of this function. (If you do not have access to Microsoft Word, do a quick online search to find a similar tutorial for the word-processing program you use.)

   Word 2010: www.youtube.com/ watch?v=UusH-4DvFaw
   Word 2016: www.youtube.com/ watch?v=do9ujnZLIC4

3. **Using AI for Request Responses.** Chatbots and virtual assistants are taking over many of the more basic tasks of customer service and engagement. In this IBM Watson Assistant demo, engage with a virtual banking assistant in simulated scenarios, such as booking an appointment, choosing a credit card, and making a payment. Navigate down the page to "Ready to Get Started?'" and select "Try a Simple Chat" and "Try an Intermediate Chat." How does the experience of receiving customer service from a virtual assistant differ from the experience of providing and receiving customer service through standard e-mail?

   https://watson-assistant-demo.ng.bluemix.net/

4. **Analyzing Your Customer Service Experience.** Recall a time you complained online about an Amazon (or similar) purchase by interacting with a chatbot. In a small group describe your experience, give a break down of steps n your request, and rate your satisfaction with the complaints process.

8 Delivering Unfavourable News

Chapter Preview

This chapter explores the special demands of communicating information that is unfavourable to receivers. You'll revisit two standard writing plans that can be adapted and applied to communicate negative information while neutralizing its emotional impact and being respectful of receivers' needs. You'll be introduced to considerations for word choice, style, and tone that make a refusal, a denial, or an announcement of negative information easier for readers to accept. You'll also learn how and when to apologize, and you'll discover that sharing unfavourable news need not threaten business relationships.

fizkes/Shutterstock.com

Learning Objectives

1. Identify the special demands and characteristics of bad news messages.
2. Apply direct and indirect writing plans for bad news messages.
3. Organize bad news messages with a direct plan.
4. Organize bad news messages with an indirect plan: writing buffers, citing reasons, and de-emphasizing the bad news.
5. Politely refuse requests, claims, and credit; turn down job applicants; announce bad news to employees; and decline invitations.

Case Study

In 2018, Canadian packaged meats company Maple Leaf Foods announced the construction of a new, more environmentally friendly plant in London, Ontario, which would necessitate the closure of three other plants across Ontario.

November 26, 2018, Maple Leaf Foods announced plans to build a $660-million fresh poultry facility in London, Ontario, set to open in 2021. This announcement via corporate press release was framed as a good-news story. Maple Leaf Foods President and CEO Michael McCain said that that the new facility would "incorporate leading edge food safety, environmental and animal care technologies." The plant would also create 1,450 new jobs.[1]

The bad news? The new plant would necessitate the closure of three other plants in Toronto, Brampton, and St. Marys, meaning that the new plant would actually result in a net loss of 300 jobs in Ontario. This announcement came close to the holiday season, with no prior notice, leaving current employees shocked and anxious about their employment prospects and—in the case of St. Marys—the future of their town.[2]

Clearly, organizational change, as this announcement and its aftermath show, can meet with resistance and have a massive impact on employees and the wider public and so must be disclosed and managed with care and sensitivity. Although Maple Leaf provided affected employees with at least three years to transition into different employment and promised to help interested employees move into new roles at the London plant, the union representing workers at the three plants said that they would have liked earlier notice of the closures.[3] Maple Leaf made both sound and less clear choices in delivering news of the plant closures. Maple Leaf took care in providing compelling reasons for the closures, made strategic language choices, and emphasized the benefits of the new plant, all strategies for mitigating bad news. How could it have improved? The timing of Maple Leaf's announcement was less-than-opportune, causing shock and uncertainty. The announcement raised the prospect of alternative employment options for plant workers without getting union guarantees.[4] The top-down approach of the press release made employees feel the change was done to them and reduced the opportunity for early consensus building and buy-in. All but the final paragraph of the message is directed to one of its two primary audiences—investors—and its second primary audience, employees, are addressed, with more limited attention, only at the end.

Goals of Negative Messages

Delivering bad news is an unavoidable fact of doing business, and a task that is often more difficult than just saying no. Whether it involves turning down a job applicant or denying an insurance claim, the communication is more complex because the sender and receiver are in conflict: one denies what the other wants, leading to a loss of co-operation. Breaking bad news can make even confident writers reluctant to the point of distancing themselves from the news they have to share (the so-called Mum effect)[5] while leaving recipients defensive, disappointed, shocked, or angry. No one enjoys provoking these emotions, let alone experiencing them. When the bad news is serious or significant, receivers may end up feeling wronged and powerless, which can impact their behaviour. Often, when the reader cares strongly about the situation, these bad feelings can result in a loss of goodwill and future business with the company.

Readers may stop reading a message once they detect negativity in the form of a problem, refusal, or criticism, especially when they haven't been prepared for unpleasant information and have no way to adjust to it. Often, the anger provoked by a message can spill over into antagonism toward the writer, particularly if the bad news has been trivialized, exaggerated, or stated too bluntly. This acting out on the part of readers when they feel limits have been unfairly imposed on them and their freedom—a phenomenon known as psychological reactance—is a common result when bad news is handled poorly or tactlessly. Writers who routinely antagonize their readers get reputations for being thoughtless and insensitive, a perception that can damage relationships with colleagues, suppliers, customers, and other stakeholders. Writers therefore need to take care and

Primary Goals

- To give the bad news in a clear, brief, and respectful way, and state it only once
- To help readers accept the bad news by showing the fairness and logic of the decision, offering an explanation when it is possible to do so, and eliminating unnecessarily negative language
- To maintain and build goodwill toward the reader and the reader's organization despite the unpleasant facts the message must communicate
- To get your purpose across the first time, without ambiguities that may create a need for clarification, follow-up correspondence, or ongoing dispute resolution

Secondary Goals

- To balance business decisions with sensitivity to readers by putting yourself in their position
- To reflect promptness, accountability, and due consideration—factors that reduce impatience and potential hostility—by delivering the bad news at the right time
- To protect yourself and your organization from legal liability

FIGURE 8.1 Goals for Communicating Bad News

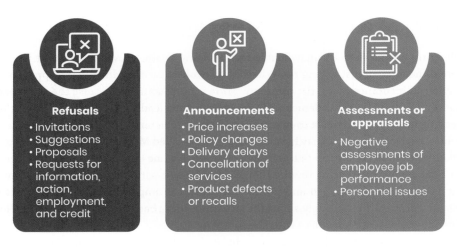

Refusals
- Invitations
- Suggestions
- Proposals
- Requests for information, action, employment, and credit

Announcements
- Price increases
- Policy changes
- Delivery delays
- Cancellation of services
- Product defects or recalls

Assessments or appraisals
- Negative assessments of employee job performance
- Personnel issues

FIGURE 8.2   Three Categories of Bad News Messages

strategize to preserve the organization's good image and brand when communicating un-favourable information.

Communicating unfavourable news doesn't have to result in bad feelings. Strategic **negative messages** are unique in their special attention to content, structure, context, and tone. These elements work together to preserve goodwill and ensure that the recipient finishes reading the message and accepts the bad news without feeling bitter, hostile, or resentful. Figure 8.1 shows some important goals to keep in mind when communicating bad news.

negative message A message that communicates negative information that may upset or disappoint the reader

Tone in Bad News Messages

Tone is important in bad news messages. A tactful, neutral tone tailored to the situation puts readers in a receptive frame of mind and lowers their psychological resistance to a refusal. Avoid phrasing that is harsh, defensive, and accusatory, which can intensify readers' feelings of anger and inadequacy. The following are a few tips for maintaining an even, reader-friendly tone:

- Don't plead with the reader (*please understand*) or resort to name-calling.
- Beware of mixed messages, for example, by expressing an unwillingness to comply when it is within your power to do so (*I am sorry that we have chosen not to*).
- Avoid statements based on assumptions that the reader will accept the bad news (*you will certainly agree/understand/appreciate*).
- Stick to facts and keep your language jargon-free.
- Avoid statements of opinion that can expose you and your company to legal liability.
- Edit timid or overly apologetic statements that may weaken the reader's confidence in your decision (*I am afraid that we cannot*).
- Avoid unnecessarily writer-centred remarks (*we cannot afford to/we must refuse/disappoint/reject*).
- Use expressions of sympathy (*sorry/I regret/unfortunately*) carefully to avoid hinting at the bad news.

A positive emphasis, as long as it doesn't mislead readers into expecting good news, can compensate for the sense of limitation a reader may feel in being denied. Sincerity and politeness are the best ways to let readers down gently and help them adjust to negative information.

The subject line sets the tone for a message. For negative responses, you can simply reply with the original subject line. If you are writing a letter, you can drop the subject line altogether if it is too blunt. You will need to type a new subject line if the negative information you pass on is crucial to action-taking and decision-making. Select the type of subject line that best suits your purpose:

- **Positive subject lines** highlight solutions in problem-oriented messages and persuade readers of the benefits of potentially unpopular policies or changes. However, a subject line should never overstate positives to the point of misleading readers. The following subject line is from a message announcing an increase in monthly deductions for employee benefits:

  Subject: Upgrading Employee Benefits Package

- **Neutral subject lines** signal the topic but without referring to the bad news. Use them in routine memos to peers and subordinates, especially when the bad news is minor or expected.

  Subject: Water Shut Off Sunday, October 5
  Subject: Subscription Rate Increase, Effective March 31

- **Negative subject lines** are can be used to command attention for serious internal problems and issues that might otherwise be ignored. They sometimes headline brief e-mails alerting readers to situations for which the readers are not at fault.

  Subject: Error in Q3 Sales Data [when the error is your own]
  Subject: Downgrade to AA Credit Rating

Closings should be in keeping with the balance of your message. Readers who have just been let down can be upset by an upbeat complimentary close such as *Cheers*, mistaking its friendliness for sarcasm or flippancy.

Organizing Bad News Messages

There are two writing plans for structuring negative messages: direct and indirect. Knowing which plan to use is a matter of analyzing the context and the message's anticipated effect on the reader. Audience analysis is therefore an important step in writing an effective bad news message. There are several important factors to consider before you write:

- how well you know the reader
- what position the reader holds relative to you in the company hierarchy
- how much information you can disclose to the reader without compromising privacy or commercial (intellectual property) concerns

- how prepared the reader is for the bad news
- how much resistance you anticipate
- how adversely the bad news will affect the reader
- what readers, especially of internal messages, are accustomed to

No plan is complete without equal consideration of channel choice. In one research study, participants judged e-mail to be more comprehensible, while they viewed voicemail as more persuasive and better for maintaining a personal customer relationship.[6] Choosing the right channel will help communicate bad news clearly and limit the impact on a continuing professional relationship.

Indirect Writing Plan for Bad News Messages

Using the Indirect Approach

The indirect strategy is a more traditional way of delivering unfavourable news. By opening with the explanation before stating the decision, the writer can gain an advantage of greater tact and diplomacy. These benefits are supported in communications research that has indicated that recipients of bad news consider messages written with an indirect strategy more agreeable and easier to understand, think of the writer as more emphatic and competent, and are more inclined to comply when the explanation is presented first.[7]

Use the indirect approach when:

- you don't know the reader well
- the bad news isn't anticipated by the reader
- you anticipate a strong negative reaction from the reader

indirect writing plan A method of organizing a document so that the main message is delayed and presented toward the end.

Instead of beginning with a blunt announcement of the bad news, the approach of an **indirect writing plan** gradually eases the reader into the news and thereby reduces its impact. The main message is embedded—delayed until the reader has been prepared for it. This unique organization makes the message readable and easy to tolerate from beginning to end. The advantage of sucha a plan is clear: a reader who grasps the reasons for a negative decision or assessment is less likely to react negatively, toss the message aside, or take the bad news personally. Figure 8.3 shows a four-part formula for indirect messages, and can be modified depending on the specific type of message and how sensitive you need to be: the next sections offer a closer look at each of these four elements.

Bad News Buffers

buffer A meaningful, neutral statement that cushions the shock of bad news.

The **buffer** (one to three sentences) is a first defence against toxic messaging that puts the reader in a more agreeable frame of mind, helping to neutralize the bad news when it is finally revealed. It is a meaningful, neutral statement that establishes rapport with the reader without forecasting the bad news, and is particularly useful in messages intended for superiors, customers, or job applicants. A buffer can be an expression of agreement, appreciation, or general principle or a chronology of past communications (see Table 8.1). Avoid connotatively negative language (e.g., *no, not, cannot, refuse, deny, unfortunately,*

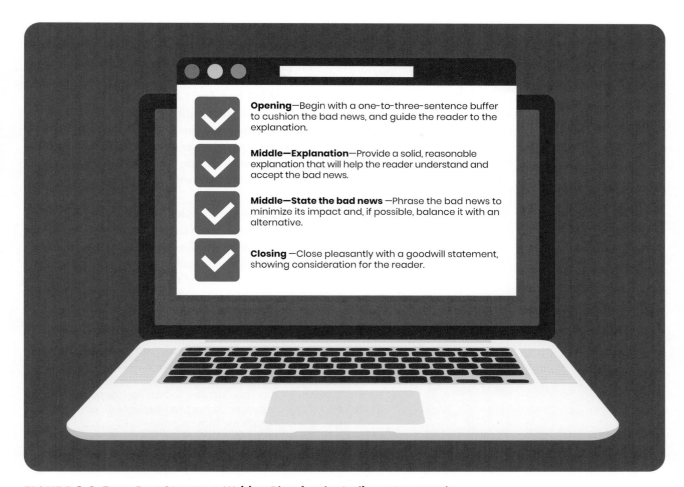

Opening—Begin with a one-to-three-sentence buffer to cushion the bad news, and guide the reader to the explanation.

Middle—Explanation—Provide a solid, reasonable explanation that will help the reader understand and accept the bad news.

Middle—State the bad news—Phrase the bad news to minimize its impact and, if possible, balance it with an alternative.

Closing—Close pleasantly with a goodwill statement, showing consideration for the reader.

FIGURE 8.3 Four-Part Structure Writing Plan for the Indirect Approach

regrettably, and the prefixes *un-* and *non-*). An effective buffer never misleads the reader into thinking that positive news will follow. Instead, it guides the reader toward the explanation, often by planting a keyword that carries over to the next paragraph. Internal messages on routine matters may not require buffers, but messages intended for superiors, customers, or job applicants benefit from the sensitivity this device helps to show. Writing a good buffer can be difficult, so let the situation govern the type of buffer you use.

Explaining the Bad News

An explanation of the bad news is the most important part of a negative message because it prepares the reader for the refusal or denial. Whether you choose to justify or explain negative information, you need to be objective and let readers see that the unfavourable decision is based on valid, legitimate reasons, not snap judgements or weak excuses.

1. **Stick to the facts and avoid editorializing.** Focus on your strongest reason or reasons for saying no, being careful not to divulge confidential, legally sensitive information that may be damaging to you or your company. Avoid expressing a personal opinion that might be mistaken for the view of your organization or

criticism of its policies (e.g., *I know how senseless this policy must seem, but it must be enforced*), and statements that imply you doubt a reader's honesty (*you claim that, you state that, we are surprised at your request*). Your goal is to clarify your or the company's decision put it in perspective briefly and tactfully.

2. **Refer to company policy as needed but don't hide behind it.** Unless you want to distance yourself from negative information by using an official tone, avoid mechanically restating company policy to justify your decision (*Our company policy forbids the conversion of lease payments to purchases*). Instead, tactfully point to the reason why the policy is reasonable, fair, or beneficial (*As our company is committed to keeping rates low, conversion of payments toward a purchase is not an available option*).

3. **Use positive or neutral words.** Present your explanation in a constructive way to make the reader more receptive. Edit out words that are known to create resistance: *impossible, unable, unacceptable, unwise, unwilling, difficulty, inconvenience, unwarranted, unreasonable*. Your explanation should sound humane, transparent, and helpful. Also avoid phrases such as *please understand* and *you surely understand* that beg the reader to agree with you. Show respect by taking the matter seriously.

TABLE 8.1 Types of Bad News Buffers

CONTEXT	CONCERNED WITH . . .
Appreciation	Thanks readers for their inquiries, contributions, applications, business, feedback, or interest: *Thank you for your application for the position of accounts executive at Pendleton Management.* Avoid expressions of gratitude that might seem illogical, especially if the opening remark is connected to a request you are about to refuse. If you have no intention of complying with a request, saying *we were very pleased to receive your request* sounds insincere.
Good or neutral news	The "first the good news, now the bad news" approach wins over readers, but only if the good news is relevant and meaningful. Don't struggle to find something pleasant to say unless it is related to the main message.
General principle or fact	Outlines organizational policies or practices. For example, a memo announcing a reduction in paid release time for corporate fundraising events can open by reminding readers of the "big picture" that won't change as a result of the bad news: *Our company has shown a long tradition of support for employees in their fundraising activities for local charities.* A message announcing the cancellation of an employee service can be buffered by a statistic illustrating that the service is under-subscribed: *Consumption of coffee in our complimentary Grab-a-Java program has dropped in the past year. More than 90 per cent of the staff now say they prefer to purchase their coffee off the premises.*
Chronology of past communications	Retraces events or correspondence relevant to the current situation. In responding to a claim that must be refused, for instance, you may begin by recapping what has happened so far: *When we last spoke, on October 7, I agreed to review our shipping procedures for perishable goods.*

Statement of agreement or common ground	Refers to a relevant view shared by the writer and reader. In rejecting a proposed method of expenditure reduction, you could begin with an endorsement of the general principle: *We both agree on the importance of operational expenditure reduction.*
Apology or statement of understanding	Expresses sympathy or regret for what has happened or what the reader has experienced as a result of a decision. An apology may be necessary in cases where the reader suffered severe or unreasonable difficulty or financial loss. Otherwise, apologies can lead to legal liability, so they should be issued with care. It is important not to overdramatize an error. If you are in doubt about what to say, consult your organization's legal department. Tailor the apology to the situation and make sure it is sincere and genuine: *Please accept our apologies for any inconvenience caused by the temporary malfunction of our automatic transit turnstiles.*
Compliment	Praises the reader's efforts without resorting to false flattery. Avoid beginning with an ego-booster that it raises hopes for good news or builds a reader up only to let the person down. The compliment should take into consideration noteworthy achievements, actions, conduct, or overall performance: *Your attention to detail and your thorough research are commendable. Once again, you have prepared a complete and cogent proposal.*

Revealing the Bad News

Withholding the bad news until after the explanation is fundamental to the indirect strategy. However, delaying tactics alone may not make disappointing or upsetting news any easier to accept. It helps to remember that saying no or revealing disappointing information doesn't necessarily mean being negative. You can take the sting out of unfavourable news by using one or more de-emphasizing techniques that lessen its grammatical presence and impact. Even with these techniques, it is still essential to state the bad news clearly and unequivocally, so readers will understand it the first time and won't need to ask for clarification.

1. **Put the bad news in a dependent clause.** Dependent clauses de-emphasize what they convey because of their grammatical incompleteness. Readers are less likely to linger over clauses beginning with *although, as, because, if, since, while,* or *whereas* and more likely to focus on the independent clause in a complex sentence.

2. **Suggest a compromise or an alternative.** Readers like solutions. Alternatives emphasize what you or your company *can* do and show you are focused on solving the problem. Alternatives help to lift the sense of limitation readers may feel on receiving bad news. Give the alternative maximum impact by putting it in an independent clause in a complex sentence or in an independent clause on its own. Provide enough information for the reader to be able to act on the suggestion.

   Although your printer could not be repaired, we would like to offer you a 15 per cent discount and free extended warranty on your next purchase of a printer in our Laser-best 5000 series.

Although we cannot disclose individual salaries, we can provide you with a fact sheet listing the salary range of our senior managers.

3. **Use the passive voice.** Passive-voice verbs allow you to describe an action without identifying who performed it. Facts stand out; personalities and their conflicts fade into the background. Use passive-voice constructions alone or as part of a dependent clause.

Although a refund cannot be granted at this time, we can offer you free shipping on your next order.

4. **Use long sentences rather than short ones.** Put the bad news in a sentence containing more than 15 words—long sentences tend to de-emphasize content.

5. **Use positive language.** Readers are more receptive when you present the glass as being half full. It is never advisable to make unrealistic promises or use overly effusive language, but you can avoid words and phrases that readers may perceive as antagonistic: *we must refuse/reject/deny your request/disappoint you.* The statement *we refuse to accept applications after March 15* seems more severe than *applications will be accepted until March 15.*

6. **Avoid spotlighting the bad news.** Embed the bad news in the middle of a sentence or paragraph where it is less noticeable. Beginning with the bad news increases its shock value; ending with it encourages readers to dwell on it. Don't let the bad news sit by itself in a single, high-emphasis paragraph; combine it with an explanation or alternative.

7. **Imply the refusal.** For this technique to be effective, the explanation must be clear and thorough. Here is an implied refusal for a request for software training for a group of 30 people:

Our on-site training facility can accommodate a group of up to 20 people.

8. However, implied refusals backfire if readers don't grasp the negative information, putting you in the awkward position of having to send a second letter that states the news more directly.

Goodwill Closing

The closing is the last chance to repair goodwill and normalize relationships so that business can continue. A **goodwill closing** must be consistent with the overall tone and content of your message—never so canned or mechanical that it seems tacked on, sounds insincere or so cheerful as to make the reader think you are happy about delivering bad news. It must normalize business relationships using positive, you-centred remarks and, as required, express confidence that those relationships will continue.

> **goodwill closing** The part of a message that draws attention away from the bad news and toward a positive and continuing relationship with the reader.

1. **Don't repeat the bad news, remind the reader of past problems, or hint at future difficulty.** Words and phrases such as *problem, difficulty, error, mistake, trouble, unfortunate situation,* or *inconvenience* renew the bad feelings you have

worked so hard to dispel. Instead focus on the problem's resolution and look ahead to a continuing business relationship.

2. **Do offer your good wishes to the reader.** This step is more important when declining job applications and invitations or writing to customers. Your comments should sound genuine and conciliatory, not overdone (*Thank you for the interest you have shown in our research and development program. I wish you every success in your future career.*)

3. **Don't invite further correspondence unless you sincerely want contact.** If the matter isn't open to debate or discussion, don't encourage the reader to believe your decision isn't final by signing off with a suggestion of further contact (*please feel free to contact me if you would like to discuss this matter*). Readers who won't take no for an answer will interpret such a statement as an invitation to pursue the matter further. A goodwill closing should be the final step in encouraging the reader to accept the bad news and closing the door on further correspondence.

4. **Don't apologize for having to say no, especially at the end of your message.** A brief, sincere apology may be appropriate at the outset if the situation merits it, but unnecessary apologies later on can undermine your perceived authority and weaken your explanation. Apologies can sometimes expose organizations to legal liability, so exercise caution or seek legal counsel before issuing them.

5. **Don't take credit for helping the reader unless you have actually provided assistance.** Even brief statements that are meant to boost the reader's mood—such as *I hope this information has been useful to you*—ring false if you have done nothing for the reader.

Indirect-Approach Message

The following message announces a substantial increase in membership dues for a professional association. Because higher dues could mean a substantial drop in membership, the message has a strong persuasive component. It begins by expressing appreciation to members for their contributions and by stressing, through the keyword *services*, the benefits of membership. News of the increase is minimized by the helpful suggestion to pay immediately and save. The closing conveys goodwill with a forward-looking emphasis. Typical of some bad news messages, the purpose of this letter is also persuasive in encouraging readers not just to note but also to accept the bad news.

The Canadian Association of Business Management values the ground-breaking initiatives and active participation of its members. Thanks to a strong collective effort, the array of services and events now available to members has helped make our group the fastest-growing professional association in Canada.

Our mentorship program matches young members with those possessing years of experience in the industry. This program has been a success. Membership now includes a quarterly publication with the latest trade information and access to websites and online resources, including hundreds of trade publications. Although the cost of these services has led to an unavoidable increase in annual dues, we now offer a three-year membership for only $230—a $50 saving over the one-year membership rate.

To take advantage of this special rate, please complete and return the attached renewal form before December 31. We thank you for your past support and look forward to your continued participation in our organization.

Limitations of the Indirect Strategy

The indirect strategy does have its drawbacks. When readers fail to find good or neutral news in the first few sentences, they may see through the delaying or "hedging" tactics of the buffered opening and explanation and suspect the true purpose of the message. When this happens, readers may see the lack of directness as manipulative rather than polite. Messages organized according to this pattern also tend to be longer, making greater demands on the reader's time and patience.

Checklist

Indirect-Strategy Messages

- ❑ Have you buffered the bad news with an opening that is relevant, focused, and neutral?
- ❑ Have you explained the circumstances of the situation or the facts leading to the refusal or bad news?
- ❑ Have you presented reasons that will help the reader understand and accept the negative information as a logical conclusion?
- ❑ Have you stated the bad news as clearly and tactfully as possible? Have you used appropriate techniques to de-emphasize it?
- ❑ Have you closed by re-establishing goodwill?

Direct Writing Plan for Bad News Messages

Using the Direct Writing Plan

It is not always necessary to break the bad news gently by using the special delaying strategies that characterize the indirect writing plan. Some readers prefer directness. Some messages demand it. In many situations it is possible to level with the reader and begin with the main message. Use the direct approach to deliver bad news in the following situations:

- when you know that the reader expects or prefers conciseness and immediacy in their messages and may not have the time or patience to read a lengthy lead-in
- when the bad news is expected or related to a known problem or minor delay
- when critical information might otherwise escape notice (organizations commonly use the direct approach to announce price increases, disruptions in service,

or changes in policy; if you embed this information somewhere in the middle of the message, you may not succeed in bringing it to the reader's attention)
- when the bad news is not serious, significant, or detrimental to the reader
- when it is company practice to write all internal messages straightforwardly
- when you intend to terminate a business relationship

The direct writing plan for delivering bad news has one notable difference from that used for good-news messages: it follows up the explanation with the offer of an alternative (whenever possible). See Figure 8.4 for a four-part approach when writing a direct bad news message.

Limitations of the Direct Approach

The direct, up-front approach is all business. The impression it gives is of no-nonsense decisiveness. However, an overly brief message constructed according to this plan can sometimes seem cold and brusque. To make your message polite without adding to its length, focus on using a tone that conveys respect and courtesy.

Opening—Begin with a simple, well-phrased statement of the bad news. Give the bad news only once.

Middle—Explanation—Provide a brief, clear explanation that the reader can reasonably accept.

Middle—Alternative—Offer an alternative if it is possible to do so. Promise only what is legally and realistically allowable for you or your company to do.

Closing—Close with a goodwill statement that doesn't refer to the bad news.

FIGURE 8.4 Four-Part Structure Writing Plan for the Direct Approach

Opening expression of sympathy also announces the bad news

> Dear Registrants:
>
> Unfortunately, the course you registered for has been cancelled.

Gives no reason for the cancellation and does not identify the cancelled course, Offers no alternative—another course or possible rescheduling

> It looks like we may not be able to make this course available to employees for at least another few months.

Closing an afterthought that reminds readers, somewhat facetiously, of their disappointment

> We hate to disappoint our registrants, but I am sure you understand our budgetary constraints.

FIGURE 8.5 Ineffective Direct-Approach Message (extract)

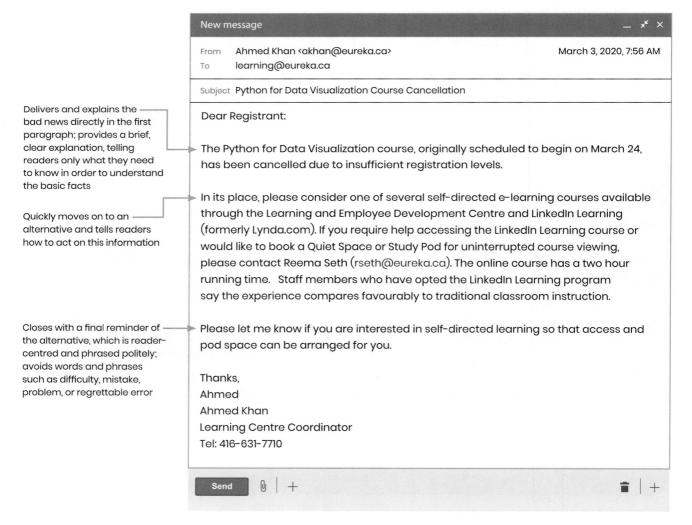

Delivers and explains the bad news directly in the first paragraph; provides a brief, clear explanation, telling readers only what they need to know in order to understand the basic facts

Quickly moves on to an alternative and tells readers how to act on this information

Closes with a final reminder of the alternative, which is reader-centred and phrased politely; avoids words and phrases such as difficulty, mistake, problem, or regrettable error

New message

From   Ahmed Khan <akhan@eureka.ca>   March 3, 2020, 7:56 AM
To   learning@eureka.ca

Subject Python for Data Visualization Course Cancellation

Dear Registrant:

The Python for Data Visualization course, originally scheduled to begin on March 24, has been cancelled due to insufficient registration levels.

In its place, please consider one of several self-directed e-learning courses available through the Learning and Employee Development Centre and LinkedIn Learning (formerly Lynda.com). If you require help accessing the LinkedIn Learning course or would like to book a Quiet Space or Study Pod for uninterrupted course viewing, please contact Reema Seth (rseth@eureka.ca). The online course has a two hour running time.   Staff members who have opted the LinkedIn Learning program say the experience compares favourably to traditional classroom instruction.

Please let me know if you are interested in self-directed learning so that access and pod space can be arranged for you.

Thanks,
Ahmed
Ahmed Khan
Learning Centre Coordinator
Tel: 416-631-7710

Send

FIGURE 8.6 Effective Direct-Approach Message

Apologies in Bad News Messages

The first decades of the twenty-first century have been called the age of apology.[8] Apologies from celebrities, politicians, and corporations abound on the Internet, particularly on social media platforms. Apologies play a key role in managing impressions from customers, stakeholders, followers, and the general public. They are also essential to restoring the reputations of individuals and groups by explaining and making amends for an offence, whether that offence involves errors of judgement, acts of negligence, or wrongdoings causing suffering, loss, or humiliation to others. People who have been wronged expect justice, and an apology can be the first step in offering those affected by a mistake or wrongdoing a measure of justice.[9]

Apologies are common in bad news messages on many platforms and channels, but they are not standard in every message of this kind. Apologies can have several functions:

- restoring dignity and a sense of justice
- expressing fairness
- reducing the effects of anger
- providing a convincing explanation for the offence
- giving assurances that the same unpleasantness won't occur in the future[10]

Apologies consist of several elements, not all of which may be used for every apology:

- acknowledgement of the offence
- explanation of factors contributing to the offence
- show of remorse
- offer of repair or restitution
- commitment to reform

At the highest levels of management, some companies may choose not to apologize, even for big mistakes, out of fear that their words may be taken as an admission of guilt or may have a negative impact on employees not responsible for the mistake. In other cases, apologizing, sometimes with advice from a lawyer, is a first step in recovering from a setback and moving on. Knowing when and how to apologize is fundamental to business interests. Saying sorry shows you care, rights wrongs, and helps to fix problems. A poorly worded apology, however, can be misinterpreted—all the more reason to handle apologies with care. For an apology to work, it must seem sincere and unambiguous, qualities that are sometimes hard to establish in written texts. For instance, consider United Airlines CEO Oscar Munoz's tone-deaf apology for a passenger being forcibly removed from an overbooked flight in April 2017 miss the mark. PR experts pointed out that Munoz failed to recognize the feelings of others by apologizing only for de-boarding a passenger, not for having seriously injured him[11]—a move that plunged the company into a PR crisis:

> This is an upsetting event to all of us here at United. I apologize for having to re-accommodate these customers. Our team is moving with a sense of urgency to work with the authorities and conduct our own detailed review of what happened. We are also reaching out to this passenger to talk directly to him and further address and resolve this situation.[12]

THE CANADIAN PRESS/Sean Kilpatrick

Prime Minister Justin Trudeau delivers a formal apology in 2019 for the federal policy on tuberculosis in the mid-20th century. While some see the Canadian government's formal apologies as an attempt to whitewash its ongoing role in perpetuating injustices, others see these acts as key to normalizing the relationship between the government and historically oppressed groups, as well as an important teaching tool for other Canadians.

Here are four main points to remember about apologies:

- **Don't apologize for minor errors that have been promptly corrected or when there is nothing to apologize for.** The reader has to care for there to be a true need for an apology. When you have done your absolute best to correct a problem or delay resulting from circumstances beyond your control, provide an explanation in place of an apology. Unnecessary apologies—apologizing for the sake of apologizing— weaken your perceived authority and erode confidence in your decisions.

Unnecessary apology: I am so sorry to have to tell you that our Get It Fresh or It's Free policy does not apply to reduced-for-quick-sale items.

Positive explanation: To guarantee our customers a high standard of food quality and freshness, our Get It Fresh or It's Free policy applies only to regularly priced or nationally advertised sale items.

- **Do apologize for any serious trouble or inconvenience for which you or your company are responsible.** Issue a brief, sincere apology as early in the message as you possibly can, without overdramatizing. An apology left to the end can seem like an afterthought and remind readers of their difficulty. Acknowledge the wrong done to the injured party. Be aware, however, that apologies not only convey regret or sympathy, but they can be taken as admissions of responsibility or negligence. If you think an apology could admit liability, refer the matter to an experienced colleague or company-affiliated legal expert.

Apologetic: I'm sorry that the order for 500 embossed folders won't be ready by September 12.

Explanatory: Due to shipping delays related to customs inspections, the embossed folders you ordered will not be ready by September 12. Would you like to keep this order or would you prefer to look at the enclosed samples of comparable products from other suppliers?

- **Craft apologies that fit with and extend your company's narrative.** Apologies often reflect the values of the companies they come from. Consider apologies as part of a larger corporate story. Help to control that narrative by asking colleagues for advice on how they handle apologies for different types of issues.
- **Control the tone of your apology.** Aim to strike a balance by registering remorse without sounding weak or defensive. Restore confidence for serious wrongs or errors by making receivers feel they are in capable hands.[13]

Types of Bad News Messages

Refusing Requests for Information, Actions, and Favours

When refusing requests from people outside your organization, you can say no tactfully by using the indirect writing plan that buffers, explains, and softens the bad news. Putting reasons before the refusal shows you are sensitive to the reader's concerns. It also prepares the reader for unwanted news—namely that a request for information, action, credit, or a favour must be turned down. A direct writing plan is workable only when you know the reader well or when politeness is not essential to maintaining a business relationship.

1. **Buffer the opening.** Writing a buffer can be difficult, so concentrate on information that is relevant to the message as a whole but isn't so positive that it misleads the reader.
2. **Give reason(s) for the refusal.** Limit your explanation to the main reason for refusing the request, focusing on what you can rightfully disclose in order to help the reader accept your decision. Be brief and make it plausible.
3. **Soften or subordinate the bad news.** Avoid harsh, negative phrasing and use one or several de-emphasizing techniques to cushion the bad news. Your refusal should be unequivocal. Implied refusals, however tactful they may be, may not say no clearly enough.
4. **Offer an alternative or a compromise if a good one is available.** Is there something that you *can* do in response to the reader's request? Provide an alternative or a compromise only if it's a viable one.
5. **Renew goodwill in closing.** A sincere, forward-looking ending can renew good feelings, but it is unlikely to succeed if it sounds sarcastic, clichéd, or forced. Ending with *we are happy to have helped in this matter and look forward to providing more information whenever we can* is illogical if a company has just refused to help. Keep the closing pleasant and focused on the reader by maintaining a sincere you-attitude or making a comment that reduces the sense of limitation imposed by the bad news.

The message in Figure 8.7 politely turns down a request for volunteers to participate in a local charity's fundraising event. It opens by offering praise for the event but also sets the stage for a refusal by setting limits on participation. The policy on which the refusal will ultimately be based is explained, rather than simply stated, so that readers

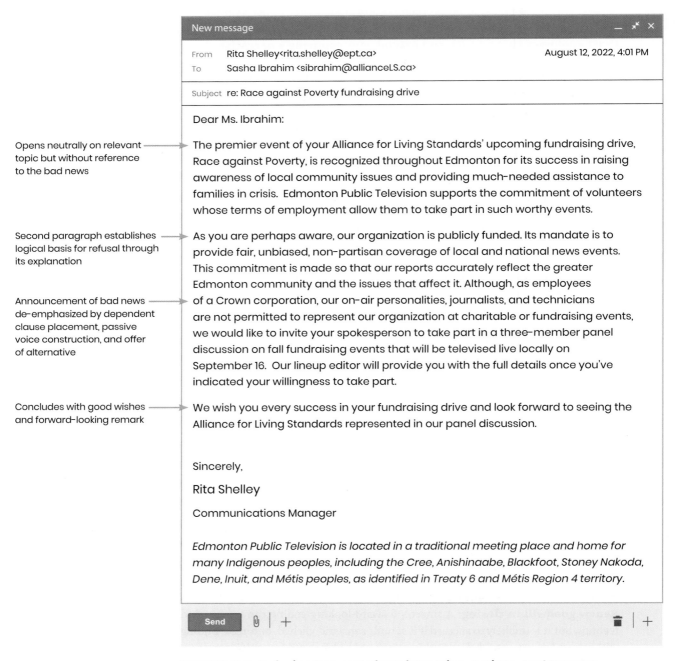

Opens neutrally on relevant topic but without reference to the bad news

Second paragraph establishes logical basis for refusal through its explanation

Announcement of bad news de-emphasized by dependent clause placement, passive voice construction, and offer of alternative

Concludes with good wishes and forward-looking remark

New message

From　Rita Shelley<rita.shelley@ept.ca>　　　　　　　　August 12, 2022, 4:01 PM
To　　Sasha Ibrahim <sibrahim@allianceLS.ca>

Subject　re: Race against Poverty fundraising drive

Dear Ms. Ibrahim:

The premier event of your Alliance for Living Standards' upcoming fundraising drive, Race against Poverty, is recognized throughout Edmonton for its success in raising awareness of local community issues and providing much-needed assistance to families in crisis. Edmonton Public Television supports the commitment of volunteers whose terms of employment allow them to take part in such worthy events.

As you are perhaps aware, our organization is publicly funded. Its mandate is to provide fair, unbiased, non-partisan coverage of local and national news events. This commitment is made so that our reports accurately reflect the greater Edmonton community and the issues that affect it. Although, as employees of a Crown corporation, our on-air personalities, journalists, and technicians are not permitted to represent our organization at charitable or fundraising events, we would like to invite your spokesperson to take part in a three-member panel discussion on fall fundraising events that will be televised live locally on September 16. Our lineup editor will provide you with the full details once you've indicated your willingness to take part.

We wish you every success in your fundraising drive and look forward to seeing the Alliance for Living Standards represented in our panel discussion.

Sincerely,

Rita Shelley

Communications Manager

Edmonton Public Television is located in a traditional meeting place and home for many Indigenous peoples, including the Cree, Anishinaabe, Blackfoot, Stoney Nakoda, Dene, Inuit, and Métis peoples, as identified in Treaty 6 and Métis Region 4 territory.

Send

FIGURE 8.7　Refusing Requests for Information, Actions, and Favours

can understand how it is beneficial and fair. Rather than hiding behind policy, the writer shows that the refusal is based on legal obstacles, not on staff's unwillingness to participate. A good-news alternative helps to balance the refusal, and the message ends with good wishes and a forward-looking remark.

Refusing Claims

Not all claims are valid or reasonable. Some are the result of an honest mistake or misinformation on the part of the claimant. A rare few are fraudulent. Saying no to someone who is already dissatisfied enough to make a claim can be difficult. In refusing a claim, you may find yourself in the middle of an upsetting or a hostile situation that can easily deteriorate. Using the indirect approach allows you the tact to let the reader down gently. Its emphasis on an explanation helps you communicate the desire to be fair and encourages the reader to believe that the claim has been given thorough and serious consideration. The dual purpose of a claim response, even a negative one, is to put the matter to rest while retaining the goodwill and patronage of current customers.

1. **Begin with a statement of appreciation, common ground, or understanding.** Opening with a refusal is enough to shock an unprepared reader. Instead, open neutrally, even if it is just to thank the reader for bringing the matter to the company's attention:

    We appreciate your taking the time to write to us regarding your purchase, and we welcome the opportunity to explain our price-matching policy.

    We can understand your concern when you received an invoice for an amount substantially higher than you had anticipated.

    Your purchase of an Exacta product comes with a 20-year record of quality assurance.

    The XBJ software you purchased recently is the only software in its price range with superior graphics capability.

    I can appreciate your need for a dependable air-conditioning system, especially during the summer months.

    Don't raise false hopes or mislead readers into believing they're entitled to something they're not with a statement such as *you were absolutely right in bringing your problem to our immediate attention.*

2. **Provide a concise, factual explanation.** Use emotionally neutral, objective language to review facts of a sale or dispute and explain why a claim must be refused. To show a desire to be fair, acknowledge any correct assertion by the claimant, and avoid assigning blame (e.g., avoid responses such as *if you had read the instructions carefully you would have realized your claim is invalid*). Remind the

claimant pleasantly about a company policy but don't use it as a smokescreen. Briefly show how the policy is reasonable by emphasizing its purpose or benefits in the current circumstances. Avoid negative language that conveys distrust—*you claim that, you failed to*—and edit long-winded explanations that can leave readers feeling patronized or hoodwinked.

3. **Don't apologize for saying no.** Apologize only if the situation truly warrants it and, even then, keep the apology brief. Hedging your refusal can give readers the false impression that your decision isn't final. A firm yet helpful refusal tells a potentially persistent claimant that the matter isn't open to further discussion. Implied refusals are workable, but only if the claimant can fully grasp that the answer is no.

4. **End in a friendly, confident, conciliatory way.** Don't close by reminding the claimant of the refusal or by using language that implies the claimant will be dissatisfied with your decision and therefore stop being your customer. Assume the role of problem-solver. When a full adjustment is not possible, consider if you can offer the claimant the next best thing—an alternative or a compromise, perhaps in the form of a substitute service, minor repair, or replacement product. If it is in your company's best interest to do so, provide information about where the claimant can seek help with the problem or go for servicing on a product. If a claim has been denied only for lack of supporting documentation, suggest that the claimant resubmit the request for adjustment. Otherwise, do not invite the claimant to try again.

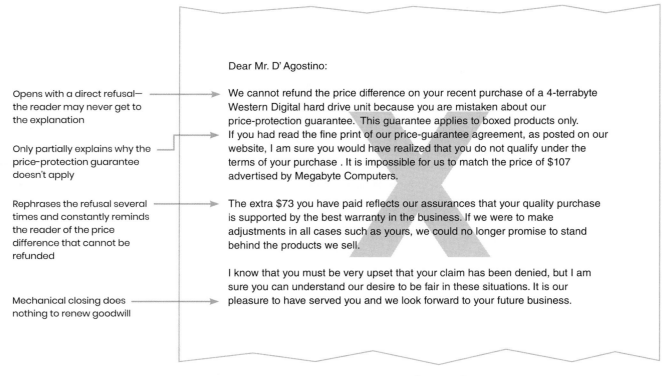

Dear Mr. D'Agostino:

Opens with a direct refusal— the reader may never get to the explanation

We cannot refund the price difference on your recent purchase of a 4-terrabyte Western Digital hard drive unit because you are mistaken about our price-protection guarantee. This guarantee applies to boxed products only.

Only partially explains why the price-protection guarantee doesn't apply

If you had read the fine print of our price-guarantee agreement, as posted on our website, I am sure you would have realized that you do not qualify under the terms of your purchase . It is impossible for us to match the price of $107 advertised by Megabyte Computers.

Rephrases the refusal several times and constantly reminds the reader of the price difference that cannot be refunded

The extra $73 you have paid reflects our assurances that your quality purchase is supported by the best warranty in the business. If we were to make adjustments in all cases such as yours, we could no longer promise to stand behind the products we sell.

Mechanical closing does nothing to renew goodwill

I know that you must be very upset that your claim has been denied, but I am sure you can understand our desire to be fair in these situations. It is our pleasure to have served you and we look forward to your future business.

FIGURE 8.8 **Ineffective Claim Refusal (extract)**

New message   — ⤢ ✕

From   Ryan Tan <ryant@computergiant.com>   March 26, 2021, 2:22 PM
To   Don D'Agostino <ddagostino@gmail.com>

Subject Re: 4-terabyte Western Digital hard drive unit query

Dear Mr. D'Agostino:

For top-quality computer merchandise at the lowest possible price, thousands like ◄——— Opens neutrally with a
you have come to rely on Computer Giant. Our confidence in the computer products   statement of company policy
we sell prompted us to establish our price-protection guarantee.   and philosophy; last sentence
                                                                                       foregrounds main topic of the
                                                                                       claim response

This guarantee applies to all factory-sealed equipment and entitles our customers to
the lowest advertised price on identical items. In other words, we'll match the price as
long as the model number matches. To qualify for an immediate point-of-purchase ◄——— Offers factual explanation in
discount or a refund within 30 days, a customer need only produce verified proof of   neutral language and makes
purchase or a copy of an advertised price listing.   important distinctions that lead
                                                                                        to a logical conclusion

Because we not only sell for less but also promise to stand behind everything we sell, ◄
we must be able to back each product's warranty. When an item comes to us
unsealed from the factory, it is sold as an OEM (original equipment manufacturer)
product. The lack of packaging means an OEM product is more susceptible to damage
during shipping. The extra care Computer Giant takes in bringing OEM products to you
is reflected in a slightly different cost structure when compared with retail boxed
products. Because we wanted our customers to be aware of this
important difference, we adopted the slogan "Packaged Products, Better Prices."

The 4-terabyte Western Digital hard drive unit you purchased from us for $180 is an ◄—— Refusal de-emphasized by
OEM product. It comes with a three-year warranty and our pledge to you of high   dependent clause and
performance and reliability. This hard drive unit is, as you rightly pointed out, available conciliatory offer of
for less elsewhere. The Computer Giant price reflects our assurances to you that your   next-best alternative
quality product comes with the best warranty in the business. Although our
price-protection guarantee does not apply in this case, we would like you to accept
the attached coupon redeemable for a 20 per cent discount on your next retail boxed
purchase at Computer Giant. This coupon can be used in store or online in
conjunction with our price-protection guarantee.

We value your business and look forward to offering you packaged products at better ◄—— Closes by expressing
prices.   confidence in a continued
                                                                                           business relationship

Sincerely,

Ryan Tan

Communications Manager

Send   📎 | +   🗑 | +

FIGURE 8.9 Effective Claim Refusal

Refusing Credit

Refusing credit can cause hard feelings, with consequences for future business. Given the sensitive nature of this type of message, most companies prepare carefully worded, lawyer-reviewed credit refusals (often as templates) for use by credit managers and their departments. These letters can vary in content depending on the source of negative information.

In all cases, the goal is to draft a sensitive, respectful refusal that says no without criticizing applicants for their low cash reserves, debts, or poor credit records—and without raising false expectations of future credit. Being careful in handling third-party information from credit agencies about an applicant's record reduces the chance of litigation. It is sometimes in a company's best interest to give no reason for the denial but to simply refer the applicant to the credit agency on whose information the decision is based. A courteous, respectful tone and, if appropriate, a cheerful reminder that orders can still be filled on a cash basis help keep the letter as positive as possible despite current circumstances.

Follow these steps when writing credit refusals:

1. **Buffer the opening.** Begin by referring to the credit application and expressing appreciation for the customer's business.
2. **Use discretion in explaining the reason for the refusal.** Be careful in disclosing third-party information from credit agencies. Business clients often provide financial information directly to suppliers. Only in these circumstances are you free to state your reasons straightforwardly, and even then you must exercise tact to avoid offending anyone.

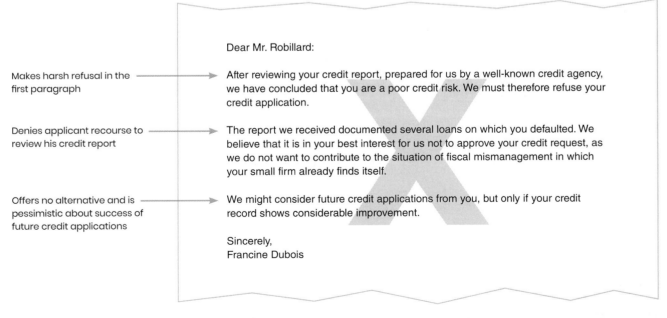

Makes harsh refusal in the first paragraph

Denies applicant recourse to review his credit report

Offers no alternative and is pessimistic about success of future credit applications

Dear Mr. Robillard:

After reviewing your credit report, prepared for us by a well-known credit agency, we have concluded that you are a poor credit risk. We must therefore refuse your credit application.

The report we received documented several loans on which you defaulted. We believe that it is in your best interest for us not to approve your credit request, as we do not want to contribute to the situation of fiscal mismanagement in which your small firm already finds itself.

We might consider future credit applications from you, but only if your credit record shows considerable improvement.

Sincerely,
Francine Dubois

FIGURE 8.10 Ineffective Credit Refusal (extract)

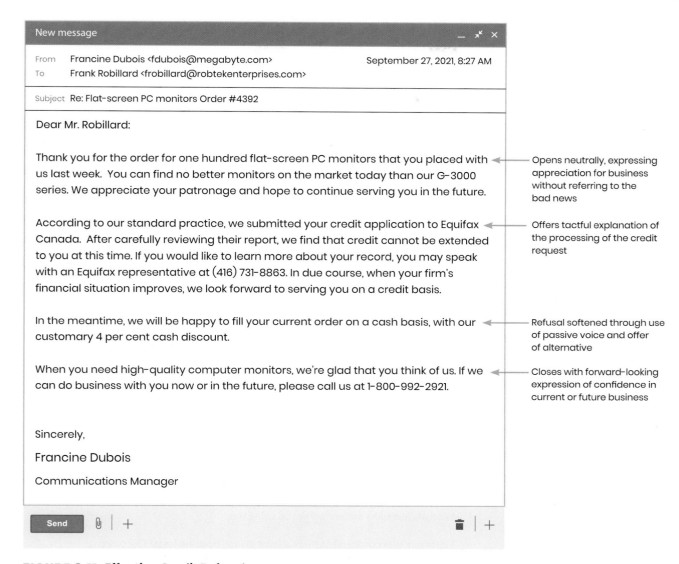

FIGURE 8.11 Effective Credit Refusal

The email content reads:

> New message
>
> From Francine Dubois <fdubois@megabyte.com>   September 27, 2021, 8:27 AM
> To   Frank Robillard <frobillard@robtekenterprises.com>
>
> Subject Re: Flat-screen PC monitors Order #4392
>
> Dear Mr. Robillard:
>
> Thank you for the order for one hundred flat-screen PC monitors that you placed with us last week. You can find no better monitors on the market today than our G–3000 series. We appreciate your patronage and hope to continue serving you in the future.
>
> According to our standard practice, we submitted your credit application to Equifax Canada. After carefully reviewing their report, we find that credit cannot be extended to you at this time. If you would like to learn more about your record, you may speak with an Equifax representative at (416) 731-8863. In due course, when your firm's financial situation improves, we look forward to serving you on a credit basis.
>
> In the meantime, we will be happy to fill your current order on a cash basis, with our customary 4 per cent cash discount.
>
> When you need high-quality computer monitors, we're glad that you think of us. If we can do business with you now or in the future, please call us at 1-800-992-2921.
>
> Sincerely,
>
> Francine Dubois
>
> Communications Manager
>
> Send

Annotations:
- Opens neutrally, expressing appreciation for business without referring to the bad news
- Offers tactful explanation of the processing of the credit request
- Refusal softened through use of passive voice and offer of alternative
- Closes with forward-looking expression of confidence in current or future business

3. **Soften the refusal with a passive-voice construction.** A refusal such as *credit cannot be extended to you at this time* is less likely to cause bad feelings than *we cannot extend credit to you* or *your credit application has failed.*
4. **Offer incentives to sustain business.** Point out the advantages of doing business on a cash basis.

Turning Down Job Applicants

A single job advertisement can net hundreds of applications, but only one person will eventually land the job. Sending written notification to every unsuccessful candidate is often impossible, so many job advertisements now state that only candidates selected for an interview will be contacted. LinkedIn emphasizes that creating a positive rejection process, in part by handling bad news to candidates carefully and consistently, builds a positive impression of the company and keeps the communication pipeline open for future applications.[14]

For companies that do have the resources to draft a rejection letter to communicate bad news to job applicants, the indirect approach is widely preferred, although the direct approach is increasingly common. A job rejection has to be courteous and respectful, subordinating the bad news to a message of good luck and encouragement. Insensitive rejection letters not only damage applicants' egos, but also earn the organization a reputation for treating applicants badly. Effective employment refusals leave the applicant's self-esteem intact so that the rejection is less likely to be taken personally, which helps to ensure there are ready applicants for the next job opening.

Because time and resources are often at a premium, form letters are a common way of notifying a sizable applicant pool. The "mail merge" feature in word-processing software can be used to personalize a standard letter. A personal letter is a must for applicants selected for interview but not hired.

1. **Open by cushioning the refusal.** To avoid breaking the bad news too harshly, thank the applicant for applying or politely express appreciation for his or her interest. A general comment on the overall standard of applications is another common way to begin (*We were very impressed by the applications we received*). A well-intentioned opening should never mislead the applicant into thinking he or she got the job.

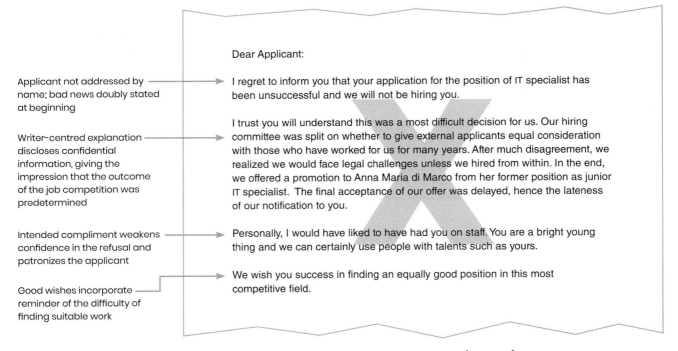

Applicant not addressed by name; bad news doubly stated at beginning

Writer-centred explanation discloses confidential information, giving the impression that the outcome of the job competition was predetermined

Intended compliment weakens confidence in the refusal and patronizes the applicant

Good wishes incorporate reminder of the difficulty of finding suitable work

Dear Applicant:

I regret to inform you that your application for the position of IT specialist has been unsuccessful and we will not be hiring you.

I trust you will understand this was a most difficult decision for us. Our hiring committee was split on whether to give external applicants equal consideration with those who have worked for us for many years. After much disagreement, we realized we would face legal challenges unless we hired from within. In the end, we offered a promotion to Anna Maria di Marco from her former position as junior IT specialist. The final acceptance of our offer was delayed, hence the lateness of our notification to you.

Personally, I would have liked to have had you on staff. You are a bright young thing and we can certainly use people with talents such as yours.

We wish you success in finding an equally good position in this most competitive field.

FIGURE 8.12 Ineffective Employment Refusal (extract)

2. **Give reasons for the company's selection, if it is possible to do so.** Without going into specifics or mentioning an applicant's personal deficiencies, briefly explain the basis for your selection. Take care to protect the confidentiality of decision-makers. Never disclose details of the selection process or legally sensitive information that could embarrass your organization or invite litigation. Volunteering too much information or expressing a personal opinion (for example, *if it were up to me, I'd hire you*) can be risky and hurtful.

3. **Quickly move on to the bad news.** State the bad news only once, using appropriate de-emphasizing techniques and a personal, humane tone.

4. **Gently encourage the applicant.** Offer a positive message of good luck expressed with sincerity, not false flattery. Point to future employment possibilities if you are interested in hiring the applicant when there is a suitable opening (for example, mention that the application will be kept on file.)

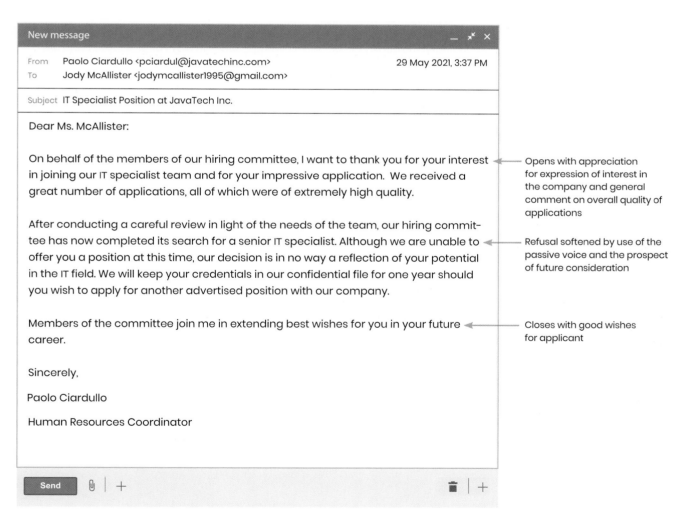

FIGURE 8.13 Effective Employment Refusal

Announcing Bad News to Employees

Bad news is often handled differently when the audience in question is within an organization rather than outside it. Announcements of setbacks (e.g., lost contracts, rising benefit costs, declining profits, and public relations crises) and reminders of unpopular policies or altered procedures (e.g., reduced benefits, cutbacks, and reductions in raises) have the potential to affect employee morale and performance. Information on these issues has to be communicated skilfully—in a way that motivates employees to comply with new measures and accept less advantageous circumstances. From a managerial standpoint in

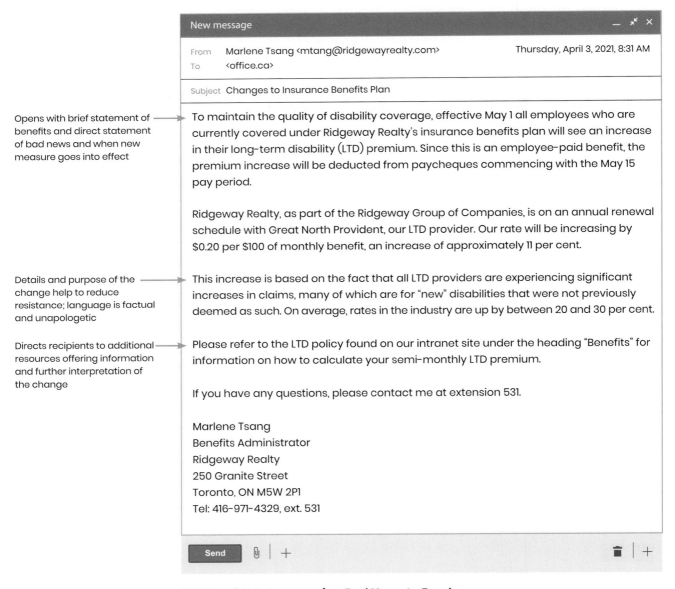

FIGURE 8.14 Announcing Bad News to Employees

particular, it helps to be able to explain why a change is necessary and how it relates to business objectives. In particular internal CEO messages are meant not only to inform but to motivate, contributing to internal employee relationships, promoting a positive sense of belonging, developing awareness of changes in the work environment, and developing understanding of the need for the organization to evolve.[15] Motivating language in such messages has several functions: to clarify goals and instructions to reduce uncertainty, forging a bond through empathy, and transmitting norms and expectations.[16]

Individual organizations pass on unfavourable news to their employees in different ways. Some organizations use a direct approach for all internal messages, no matter if the news is good or bad. Others use the indirect approach if the negative information is new or surprising. Usually, the more serious the bad news is, the more readers benefit from an explanation that helps them take stock of the situation and put it in perspective. Your knowledge of your organization—based on its size, values, goals, and openness of communication—can help you communicate bad news more effectively. Before you write, you should have firm answers to the following questions:

- Why has the decision forcing the announcement of bad news been made?
- What is the purpose of the change?
- How does the bad news affect employees?

AP Photo/Paul Sakuma, file

On September 6, 2011, Yahoo CEO Carol Bartz sent an e-mail to employees, telling them that the company's chairperson had fired her over the phone. How does this situation compare with the guidelines offered in this chapter, both in regards to the method of dismissal and the informing of the staff?

Declining Invitations

Invitations are an integral part of business life. They offer valuable opportunities to network, learn, and promote your organization. When you must decline an invitation to speak at or attend an event, how you communicate your regrets depends on how well you know the reader and how much your attendance is expected. For large-scale events where your absence is unlikely to cause disappointment, it is possible to send brief regrets along with an expression of thanks for the invitation. When turning down an invitation from an important client or superior, you must ensure your refusal won't seem like a personal rebuff by adopting a warm tone and focusing on something positive about the situation.

1. **Express appreciation for the invitation or pay the reader a compliment.** Recognize the significance of the event, event sponsor, or organization.
2. **Express your regret at not being able to attend and, if appropriate, explain why you are unavailable.** Briefly offer a valid reason for not accepting—not a weak or trivial excuse that might belittle the event or its hosts or organizers. Use the passive voice or keep the reason vague if you need to soften a refusal that might be taken too personally.
3. **Propose a constructive alternative if one is available.** Name someone to speak in your place or express interest in attending a future event.
4. **End by renewing goodwill.** Close on a friendly note with good wishes for success, a word of thanks or praise, or a forward-looking remark. Don't backtrack to the refusal. Tact and courtesy will earn your readers' respect and keep you on their guest lists.

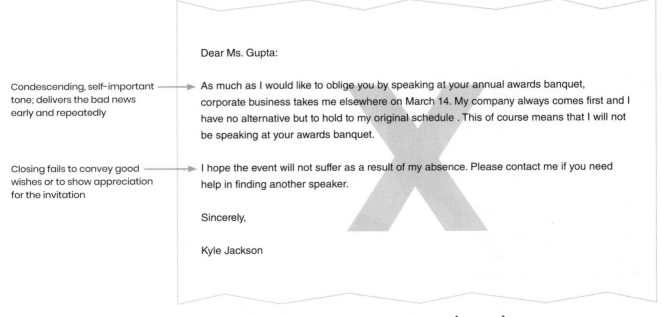

Dear Ms. Gupta:

Condescending, self-important tone; delivers the bad news early and repeatedly →
As much as I would like to oblige you by speaking at your annual awards banquet, corporate business takes me elsewhere on March 14. My company always comes first and I have no alternative but to hold to my original schedule . This of course means that I will not be speaking at your awards banquet.

Closing fails to convey good wishes or to show appreciation for the invitation →
I hope the event will not suffer as a result of my absence. Please contact me if you need help in finding another speaker.

Sincerely,

Kyle Jackson

FIGURE 8.15 Ineffective Refusal of Invitation (extract)

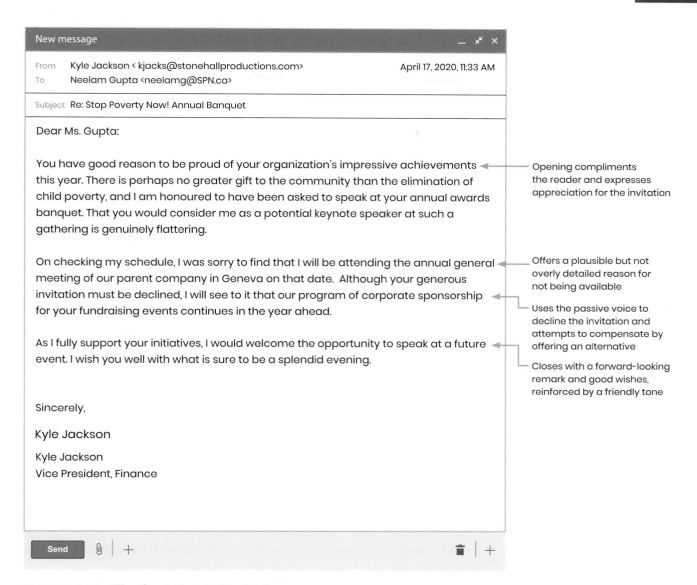

The email message shown reads:

New message

From: Kyle Jackson < kjacks@stonehallproductions.com>
To: Neelam Gupta <neelamg@SPN.ca>
April 17, 2020, 11:33 AM

Subject: Re: Stop Poverty Now! Annual Banquet

Dear Ms. Gupta:

You have good reason to be proud of your organization's impressive achievements this year. There is perhaps no greater gift to the community than the elimination of child poverty, and I am honoured to have been asked to speak at your annual awards banquet. That you would consider me as a potential keynote speaker at such a gathering is genuinely flattering. *(Opening compliments the reader and expresses appreciation for the invitation)*

On checking my schedule, I was sorry to find that I will be attending the annual general meeting of our parent company in Geneva on that date. Although your generous invitation must be declined, I will see to it that our program of corporate sponsorship for your fundraising events continues in the year ahead. *(Offers a plausible but not overly detailed reason for not being available)* *(Uses the passive voice to decline the invitation and attempts to compensate by offering an alternative)*

As I fully support your initiatives, I would welcome the opportunity to speak at a future event. I wish you well with what is sure to be a splendid evening. *(Closes with a forward-looking remark and good wishes, reinforced by a friendly tone)*

Sincerely,

Kyle Jackson

Kyle Jackson
Vice President, Finance

FIGURE 8.16 Effective Refusal of Invitation

Responding to Negative Messages on Social Media Platforms

Social media environments offer businesses extraordinary exposure and immeasurable opportunities for marketing and brand promotion, not to mention the chance to engage with and learn from their customers in ways that can help them build their business and their customer base. At the same time, the public nature of social media platforms means customer complaints and negative feedback have costlier and potentially longer-lasting consequences. Repeat and future business—especially future business from new customers who rely on online reviews and electronic word-of-mouth when making purchasing decisions—may hang in the balance.[17] Companies are vulnerable to attacks that can spiral out of control, as negative comments can spread very far very quickly in online environments. Responses to negative reviews (RNRs) therefore play an important role in handling dissatisfied customers and recovering clients, maintaining trust and loyalty, achieving service recovery, and protecting a brand and company image.[18] As online business messages go, RNRs are fairly flexible in terms of content but the steps of acknowledging feedback, dealing with the complaint, and concluding the message are most essential.

- Salutation: "Dear + reviewer's name"
- Acknowledging feedback: expressing gratitude/valuing feedback/expressing regret, concern or apology: *Thank you for your review. Your feedback is important to us and we were disappointed to learn that your recent experience did not meet your expectations.*
- Brand positioning aimed at building and maintaining a positive image by referring to company commitment or standards
- Dealing with the complaint by showing a willingness to handle it, explaining the incident's causes or source of trouble, reporting an investigation result or taking responsibility for the incident or mistake with a genuine apology, all of which build credibility and help in regaining trust.

Concluding remarks vary by situation and may include thanking the reviewer, soliciting direct contact, promising to improve products or services or giving proof of action to prevent problem recurrence,[19] and looking forward to and welcoming future business. Semi-formal signoffs (*Best regards*) and the responder's job title and contact information are commonly included.[20]

A few best practices apply when responding to unfavourable social media posts:

- **Be strategic and swift in responding.** Reach out promptly and express concern. Attentiveness through a conversational human voice and timely, empathetic interaction between the organizational representative and the customer is important.
- **Avoid using defensive, threatening, or coercive language.** Be careful not to say anything that could escalate the conflict. Instead of responding to negative messages in-kind, formulate a thoughtful, positive response.
- **Discreetly move the conversation to a less public forum.** If possible, send the complainant a private message, offering to address his or her concerns in a private chat, an e-mail correspondence, or a one-on-one phone conversation.[21] Companies may go a step further in overcoming threats to their brand from negative electronic word of mouth by using image repair and impression management strategies: gaining approval by emphasizing positive traits and perceptions of the company (*bolstering*), offering something of value to the customer (*compensation*, such as a money, goods, or a discount on future purchases), preventing the problem from happening again (*corrective action*), and asking for forgiveness (*mortification*).[22]

Checklist

Chapter Review

- ❑ Apply the direct or indirect approach according to the type of bad news and its audience.
- ❑ Never mislead the reader by implying that the purpose of the message is to deliver good news.
- ❑ Use an appropriate subject line.
- ❑ If you use a buffer, make sure it is neutral and relevant, not simply a delaying tactic.
- ❑ Limit the explanation of the bad news to relevant facts and details arranged in a logical order. Make sure your reason is clear, complete, and airtight.
- ❑ Avoid hiding behind company policy; instead, show how the policy is reasonable by explaining its purpose or benefits.
- ❑ State the bad news only once, clearly.
- ❑ For direct-approach messages, begin with a concise statement of the bad news, followed by a brief explanation, an alternative, and a goodwill closing.
- ❑ For indirect-approach messages, buffer, explain, and de-emphasize the bad news and close with expressions of goodwill.
- ❑ Offer a counter-proposal or alternative if a good one is available and provide enough information for the reader to act on that alternative.
- ❑ Use neutral, respectful, and non-accusatory language to maintain goodwill. Avoid a condescending, patronizing, know-it-all tone.
- ❑ End positively with a goodwill-building statement not related to the bad news while avoiding clichés or remarks that suggest your decision isn't final.
- ❑ Don't invite further correspondence unless you truly want it.

Exercises, Workshops, and Discussion Forums

1. **Revising a Bad News Message.** Analyze the following excerpt from a letter delivering unfavourable news and list its faults and weaknesses. Using the chapter review checklist as your guide, make a plan for revising it.

> I regret to inform you that it is impossible for us to admit children under the age of six to our Junior Trekker summer camp program. Our camp policy does not allow us to make any such exceptions, no matter how precocious or mature a child may seem. To allow children of that age to participate in full-day activities that even a ten-year-old might find challenging would endanger all campers and put our operation at risk.
>
> Thank you for understanding our position. Call us when your child is older. We take pride in offering safe and fun activities for children of many ages.

2. **Assessing Direct and Indirect Approaches to Bad News Messages.** In a small group, discuss the advantages and disadvantages of direct and indirect approaches to delivering unfavourable news. In what circumstances would you prefer to receive bad news directly? What types of situations merit a softer, less direct approach?

3. **Analyzing Corporate Apologies.** The Twitter-sphere offers many examples of corporate apologies. The reasons for these apologies vary. Some respond to criticism for weak performance, poor treatment of customers, or product or service flaws. Others respond to public accusations of poor business practices, errors in judgement, mismanagement, or wrongdoing. Still others result from public backlash to products or marketing materials found to be offensive. For this small-group activity, go to the following link, analyze the components of each apology, and discuss whether the apology makes up for the wrong or harm done.

   www.forbes.com/sites/blakemorgan/2018/10/24/10-powerful-examples-of-corporate-apologies/#6688194340de

4. **Advice on Responses to Negative Reviews.** Companies such as TripAdvisor, Canadian online retailer Shopify, and Google offer guidance on responding to negative reviews and feedback. In a small group, have each member explore a different company advice page (from the list below) to identify tips and approaches most helpful and relevant in strategizing RNRs. Follow by discussing each company's philosophy regarding negative reviews and their purpose in responding to them. Share specifics of the company advice you explored. Together, write a memo summarizing best practices for writing RNRs.

   TripAdvisor—Respond to Travellers on TripAdvisor:

   www.tripadvisor.com/TripAdvisorInsights/respondreviews

   Shopify—Replying to Reviews in the Shopify App Store:

   www.shopify.ca/partners/blog/reply-to-reviews

   Google—Read and Reply to Reviews (Negative Reviews):

   https://support.google.com/business/answer/3474050?hl=en

5. **Cancelling an Event.** The customer experience team for Eventbrite, an event management and ticketing website, offers advice on how to communicate with attendees when cancelling an event.

   a) Read the advice Eventbrite offers in "How to Gracefully Cancel an Event." What impact can an event cancellation have on a brand? What implications can that have for how the news of the cancellation is communicated? What practices does Eventbrite recommend for communicating a cancellation?

   b) Read the cancellation e-mail Eventbrite provides as an example. What writing strategy (direct or indirect) is used? What reasons might explain the choice of this strategy? What are the main components or 'moves' of the message? What is the tone of the message and what specific word choices establish that tone?

   www.eventbrite.com/blog/gracefully-cancel-event-ds00/

6. **Complaints and Responses to Negative Reviews.** For this activity, visit the travel site TripAdvisor (or a comparable travel or restaurant review site) and select a negative review by looking for a one-star review of a property of your choice. Together, in a small group, read the review and the response to it. Discuss the writing strategy used in the response and identify the various parts or sections that make up the message. Is the company in its response engaging in constructive dialogue? Based on the message and the way it is written, is there a reasonable chance of service recovery and customer retention? What aspects of the message work toward that goal?

7. **Apologizing to Customers Discussion Forum.** In 2017, an Indigenous healing and wellness coordinator visited a Walmart store in Niagara Falls, Ontario, and took a photo of a sleeper that bore text reading "I still live with my parents" along with graphics that included an arrow and two teepees. She subsequently posted the photo on

her Facebook and Twitter accounts, where it was retweeted hundreds of times and drew outraged comments citing Walmart for its insensitivity in selling a product that referenced the residential school system and its damaging legacy. Following complaints, Walmart Canada pulled the product from sale and its senior manager of corporate affairs offered this apology: "We thank our customers for bringing this matter to our attention. The graphic on this item does not represent Walmart's beliefs and has no place in our stores. We are removing the product immediate and sincerely apologize for any unintended offence this has caused."[23]

a) Does the apology Walmart Canada offered suffice? Does it respond to what the incident called for?
b) When a company apologizes, how likely are you to forgive an offence it has committed? Are there circumstances in which more than an apology is required?

Writing Improvement Exercises

1. **Evaluating Subject Lines.** Revise the following subject lines from negative messages to make them more reader-centred and neutral.

   a) Insurance Premiums Going Up
   b) Layoffs Possible
   c) Privacy Nightmare! Anyone Can See Your Google Calendar!!!
   d) Compliance Failure a Costly Mistake
   e) Customer Dissatisfaction Rate At All-time High

2. **Choosing a Direct or an Indirect Approach.** Identify which writing plan—direct or indirect—you would use for the following messages.

   a) A memo to employees announcing the cancellation of a lunchtime lecture series.
   b) A letter informing a customer of a six-week postponement of on-site software training.
   c) An e-mail turning down a student for a sought-after internship.

3. **Evaluating Buffer Statements.** Analyze the strengths and weaknesses of the following openings for bad news messages.

   a) We were very happy to receive your recent request for a refund of the purchase price of your new XJL copier, the model *Consumers Annual* ranked top for efficiency and customer satisfaction.
   b) We are so sorry that we won't be repairing your poorly functioning air-conditioning system.

   c) You honestly can't expect us to investigate a claim for a product that is no longer under warranty.
   d) We at Timberline Tire and Auto make every effort to provide our customers with high-quality products at the lowest possible prices. We are committed to finding ways to make shopping at our stores more convenient for you.

4. **Softening the Bad News with Subordinate Clauses and the Passive Voice.** Use dependent clauses and/or passive-voice constructions to de-emphasize the bad news in each of the following statements.

   a) We cannot extend credit to you at this time but we invite you to fill your order on a cash basis.
   b) We cannot waive service charges on chequing accounts.
   c) We cannot substitute a more expensive item for the one you purchased, but we are sending you a complimentary upgrade kit.

5. **Evaluating Bad News Statements.** Discuss the weaknesses of the following statements and revise them as needed.

   a) It is utterly impossible for us to ship your order before November 10.
   b) How can you honestly expect us to act on your complaint more than three years after your purchase?
   c) We cannot provide you with the information you requested because doing so would violate

agreements with our employees and expose us to legal action.

d) We don't accept credit cards.

6. **Evaluating Closings.** Analyze the weaknesses of the following letter closings and revise them as needed.

a) We thank you for understanding our position and hope to see you in our store very soon.

b) I am sorry that we were forced to refuse your application, but I wish you the best of luck in finding employment when there is so much competition for the few jobs that are available.

c) Although we must turn down your request for a refund, we usually do issue refunds if merchandise is undamaged and returned within ten days of the date of purchase.

d) If we knew the answer to your question, we would be only too happy to provide you with the information that you are seeking. Perhaps we will able to help you with a future inquiry.

Case Study Exercises

1. **Refusing a Request.** Editors of the monthly publication *National Business* have asked you, a consultant with Brandwise Solutions, to write a brief case study article for their magazine. In particular they are interested in your response to the rebranding of Goliath Groceries, Canada's fourth-largest supermarket chain, which commands a 14 per cent market share. Goliath has recently merged its distribution network, switched over to large-format stores, and repositioned itself as a whole foods and express foods retailer in order to gain a market niche distinct from recently arrived US rivals such as Stars and Stripes of Arkansas. Although you would like to offer your opinions on the subject, you fear a possible conflict of interest because your consulting firm advised on the branding and redesign of Goliath's low-price chain, Save-a-Buck. You are also scheduled to leave this evening for a three-month overseas consulting job. Write to the editors declining their request but leaving the door open for future writing opportunities.

2. **Refusing a Claim.** Your company, Ergolab, manufactures and sells ergonomic, sustainably designed, made-in-Canada modular office furniture. One of the things that sets your company apart is its generous 90-day return policy. As long as the components are undamaged and returned in their original packaging, a full refund and coverage of return shipping costs are guaranteed. A few days ago, in your role as social media manager and manager of customer service for your small company, customer Joseph Heywood initiated a live chat through your company's customer service software. From the few details he shared, you understand he purchased five standing desks and a suite of conference room furniture for his tech startup five months ago and now claims the price was too high and wants to return the items even though he has discarded the packaging. Before you could resolve the issue, Joseph ended the chat but immediately took his complaint to Twitter, where he wrote that your products were "ridiculously expensive" and that returns are "a nightmare." "If you want a deal, shop somewhere else," he tweeted. You will attempt to redirect the conversation to private e-mail, where you hope to resolve the matter; however, Joseph was more than two months' late initiating the return and your company policy regarding refunds after the deadline, as noted on all receipts and your company website, is firm. According to your understanding, the quality of the Ergolab furniture he purchased was not the reason for his wanting to return it. Your company will automatically replace any defective item and send its troubleshooting team onsite to problem-solve setup and configuration issues. Your products are manufactured in Canada, not overseas, to LEED-certified standards superior to those of your closest competitors and your company has won numerous awards for sustainable design, which accounts for the difference in price. The task of service recovery and the resolution of Joseph's claim will involve two steps:

a) Respond to Joseph's tweet to redirect the conversation to private e-mail.

b) Write to Joseph via your company e-mail and refuse his claim while managing the potential threat of negative word of mouth and repair the relationship with the cusomter to keep the door open to future business.

3. **Refusing Credit.** As credit manager at Concept Office Furniture, you must turn down a credit application from Alan Medwell of Discount Realty. Mr. Medwell has placed a sizable order for modular office furniture, asking for 120-day credit terms. Though Discount Realty has been a good customer in the past, a review of its financial statement and information supplied by credit references has led you to conclude that the firm is in financial difficulty. Refuse Mr. Medwell's request for credit while encouraging his business now or in the future.

4. **Announcing Restaurant Closure.** As co-owner of Wiik, a 26-seat restaurant serving Indigenous cuisine, you are proud to have joined chef and fellow owner Benjamin Adawish in realizing his dream of bring the full range of flavours from the Wiikwemkoong Unceded Reserve on Manitoulin Island to downtown Toronto. Your restaurant was an instant hit, rated 4.8 on TripAdvisor, awarded a TripAdvisor certificate of excellence, and showered with adjectives such as "genius" and "a new standard in Indigenous cuisine" in important food-review publications. One of the positives of the neighbourhood you chose for your restaurant was its low rent, which left you with more money to cover the high cost of sourcing the elk, venison, and foraged delicacies you serve, but in a short time the area gentrified, with new condo developments appearing on your doorstep, and rents tripled. You tried to negotiate with the property owner, to no avail, and each month had more difficulty making your skyrocketing rent. Even though almost every table was booked each night, you and Benjamin finally had to make the decision to close, at least temporarily, until you could find new, more affordable premises. Your task is to analyze how the closure will affect various stakeholder groups and communicate the news of the closure to them using a channel that best suits their needs and your relationship to them:

a) Employees
b) Customers
c) Silent/angel investors
d) Suppliers (many of them in Northern Ontario)

5. **Announcing Bad News to Employees—Loss of Best Client.** Your public relations firm, Applause, has a reputation in the industry for staging successful retail pop-ups and events. Your expertise in supporting Indigenous fashion designers and retailers is unrivalled in the Greater Vancouver Area. You were surprised when you received a text yesterday from your best client, Colleen Kuyass, that she had lost faith with your company and was now working with another PR firm. This is a major blow to your small company but you sense that Colleen's unhappiness had something to do with the recent departure of Tarah Setso, who managed Colleen's account but left three months ago to take a position with the Council of the Haida Nation. Although Edward Nunez did his best to step into Tarah's shoes, he and Colleen never really connected and you later realized he lacked experience in supporting Indigenous clients and had given her account less attention in preference to newer clients. As a result, Applause fell behind in planning events to launch Colleen's new line of sustainable winter clothing. While you don't wish to cast blame, you need to inform your employees of the loss of this important client.

6. **Announcing Bad News to Customers—Privacy Breach Preparedness.** You and your two partners are seeking additional seed financing from angel investors for your startup, FireLine, a business that will provide comprehensive end-to-end First Nations online and mail-in voting management services along with First Nations membership and financial reporting tools aimed at wealth creation and the lifting of impediments for benefit and entitlement access. You already have pilot customers and strategic partnerships in place. Investors are intrigued but what they ask about most often is possible risks related to proprietary data and users' personal information, and how privacy breaches would be handled. What they would like to see, as part of the privacy-breach response plan

highlighted in your pitch slide deck and presented in your prospectus, is a message template that could be used in the event of a privacy breach. You are well-acquainted with the Breach of Security Safeguard Regulations that went into effect in 2018 (for a recap of this, see "The risk society" in Chapter 1). Prepare a one-page e-mail message that could be used in the event of such an incident. More information about reporting breaches can be found at the link below.

www.priv.gc.ca/en/privacy-topics/business-privacy/ safeguards-and-breaches/privacy-breaches/respond- to-a-privacy-breach-at-your-business/gd_pb_ 201810/

7. **Announcing Bad News to Conference Goers.** As a member of the organizing committee for New Horizons in AI, a prestigious North American conference on AI and NeurIPS (artificial intelligence and neural information processing systems) to be held next month in Montreal, you share responsibility for planning, program design, conference marketing, and communication with invited researchers and keynote speakers to ensure they have been issued the visas necessary to enter Canada. You encouraged invited speakers to begin the visa application process early, especially as 150 of them are African nationals or of African descent living and completing PhDs in the United Kingdom, United States, and Europe. You are alarmed when they begin to get back to you to say their visas have been denied or are still unprocessed. You immediately contact Immigration, Refugees and Citizenship Canada to find out what went wrong and are told that the visa candidates were evaluated according to standard criteria but that there were concerns the applicants lacked stable employment and that their invitations to the conference were fakes. You predict that over 50 per cent of your program speakers could be affected by visa denials. You and the rest of the organizing committee are angry and dismayed, to say the least. With only a few weeks to go, it is too late to find replacements for the invited researchers, all of who are field leaders. At this point your only option is to bring the speakers in remotely via live streaming and telepresence technologies,

something for which you hadn't budgeted but which you may be able to implement using the recoupable funds from cancelled travel expenses. Still, the purpose of the conference is to bring researchers from all over the world together to share their findings, synergistically engage in dialogue, and connect with the tech industry. Your fear is that many registrants will withdraw, demanding refunds, and that future AI conferences will bypass Canada due to visa issues. You can't help feeling that harm has been done to the advancement of research in AI and that tech development in Canada will be the worse for it. Now the work begins of having to revise the conference program and inform registrants by preparing messages for the following platforms and channels:

a) an e-mail to registrants
b) an announcement to be posted on the conference website
c) an announcement

8. **Responding to Negative Social Media Posts.** As the assistant manager of the Grand Superior Hotel, you are responsible for monitoring social media feeds and responding to both complaints and positive feedback. This morning, you came upon the following review, and you must now respond appropriately. The Grand Superior is a boutique hotel, not part of a chain. The manager insists that complaints be dealt with on a case-by-case basis.

★☆☆☆

The Grand Superior . . . not grand, not great

I had a disappointing stay here three days ago. I'd expected a lot better service and facilities—the free WiFi I'd been promised, a state-of-the-art business centre, a swimmable pool, and a fully equipped gym. At check-in I was told there'd been a problem with my reservation. I showed them my booking confirmation on my phone guaranteeing me a conference rate $50 less than the standard rate. Apparently, the guaranteed-rate room was gone. I ended up paying over $200 more than I'd expected for the 4-night stay. No apologies from the staff. I was told that this was the last room at the hotel—take it or leave it. There were other issues. The WiFi password I got didn't work. I went to the Business Centre but it closed at 4 p.m. If it hadn't been for a colleague there, who let me use the WiFi in his room, I would have been stuck and forced to cancel my presentation.

I was stressed at that point. A workout would have been nice, but both the gym and the pool were closed for repairs. I hadn't heard about this when I registered. Because of the mix-up with my reservation no one knew about my dietary restrictions. I ended up eating a scallop (I'm allergic to seafood) and that meant a trip to the emergency room. I managed to give my presentation but the conference was a washout because of how sick I felt. All the front desk staff could suggest was taking some antacids. I hoped I might get a rebate or refund when I checked out but no such luck. The beds are comfortable here and the rooms have spectacular views but I'm glad this is the only time I'll ever have to stay here.

9. **Announcement of Startup Failure.** When fledgling companies, such as startups, fail, confirmations of shutdown follow. Analyze the language use, tone, and organization of each of the following statements:

a) Statement from drone startup Airware confirming shutdown after losing $118 million

History has taught us how hard it can be to call the timing of a market transition. We have seen this play out first hand in the commercial drone marketplace. We were the pioneers in this market and one of the first to see the power drones could have in the commercial sector. Unfortunately, the market took longer to mature than we expected. As we worked through the various required pivots to position ourselves for long term success, we ran out of financial runway. As a result, it is with heavy heart that we notified our team, customers, and partners that we will wind down the business.[24]

b) Halo Smart Labs says goodbye

It is with our sincere apologies that we must let you know that Halo Smart Labs is closing its doors. You may have noticed a lack of available product and support responses, and we apologize for taking so long to let you know what is going on. While we are proud to have created a best-in-class product, it takes more than a great product to make a great business. Despite the best efforts of our team, ultimately the resources required to continue making and supporting Halo products were beyond our reach.[25]

Online Activities

1. **Rules for Delivering Bad News.** Read Calvin Sun's "Delivering bad news: 10 tips for doing it right":

www.techrepublic.com/blog/10-things/10-tips-for-delivering-bad-news/

Then watch the two videos listed below. The first is a video of Maple Leaf Foods President and CEO Michael McCain as he spoke in the wake of the 2008 listeria outbreak that was linked to deli meats sold by his company. The second is a video of Lululemon founder Chip Wilson apologizing for inappropriate comments he made about women's bodies on national television:

www.youtube.com/watch?v=zIsN5AkJ1AI

www.youtube.com/watch?v=7oJ8dFlOfVU

To what extent does each speech uphold the principles outlined in Sun's article? Which apology is more effective?

2. **Varieties of Bad News Messages—Product Recalls.** Product recalls are a form of crisis communication that alert consumers and other stakeholders to health and personal safety dangers arising from the use of a commercial product (e.g., a brand of bottled water that contains glass fragments, an infant car-seat with defective harness fasteners). Go to Health Canada's Consumer Product Recalls and Safety Alerts site and choose

a recall or an alert notice for one product. What types of information are included? Use the link to the firm's website and compare the government advisory with the company's recall notice.

www.healthycanadians.gc.ca/recall-alert-rappel-avis/index-eng.php

3. **Analyzing Apologies—Westjet CEO Apologizes.** In May 2018, WestJet CEO Ed Sims apologized in front of a media scrum, something that is rare for corporate leaders in Canada who more often record their statements when they need to apologize. The reason for Sims' apology was a company program that had asked frequent flyers to record their experiences aboard WestJet and its rivals. Video-recording of flight attendants, however, was in direct violation of privacy rules and angered Union officials. Watch Sims' apology. In a group discuss how well it reduces negative perceptions and restores corporate legitimacy.

www.cbc.ca/news/canada/calgary/westjet-ceo-ed-sims-apologizes-unreservedly-to-airline-employees-1.4654044

9 Persuasive Messages

Chapter Preview

Persuasion involves providing the motivation for people to act in specific ways, including ways that require them to change their behaviour. In any profession, knowing how to be persuasive is a vital skill. In this chapter, you'll be introduced to strategies for motivating readers to change their attitudes, beliefs, or behaviours or to take action according to the arguments and benefits you present. You'll see how two standard writing plans can be adapted to fit any situation to help readers overcome their resistance and how establishing rapport and making strong arguments can be key to gaining acceptance and influencing readers.

Learning Objectives

1. Identify the need for persuasive communication.
2. Use the indirect writing plan to persuade.
3. Apply persuasive appeals.
4. Ask for favours and action persuasively.
5. Gain support for new ideas in persuasive memos.
6. Make contestable claims successfully.
7. Convince debtors to pay their bills promptly.
8. Compose effective sales letters and fundraising messages.
9. Identify how to harness the power of social media to influence people.

Case Study

While persuasive message techniques continue to evolve and become more sophisticated in our increasingly digital age, persuasion still involves influencing your audience's attitudes and behaviors and motivating individuals to act. The more attractive you can make your message, the more persuasive it will be.

Today there is hardly a time when we are not exposed to persuasion. Social media, e-mail, and mobile technologies in addition to print and billboard ads, electronic banners, and other media deliver a steady stream of messages designed to influence us to buy, believe, and act in certain ways.

Persuasive messaging has changed in the hyperconnected digital age as we constantly interact with web content. Now more complex and sophisticated, persuasion takes place across multiple contexts (business, political, government) and often takes the form of psychological mass persuasion involving not only opinion leaders such as influencers, but analysis of web users' digital footprints.[1] Because persuasive appeals are more effective when they are targeted to individuals, data mining and analysis of data such as Facebook likes, Tweets, and search engine histories enable marketers to use a big-data advantage to glean insights, predict preferences, and tailor their appeals to a person's psychological characteristics and according to other metrics such as language, location, and interests. Psychological and target audience analysis leverage a big-data advantage to take the guesswork out of understanding what customers want; however, they carry both opportunities and risks for web users. Customized content and individualized recommendations may help web users make better-informed buying decisions linked to their core needs. But web users may also fall prey to deceptive practices (including fake news and toxic content) and be encouraged to act against their own best interests.[2] A consequence is that many are now social media skeptics who distrust what they read online.[3] A 2019 Ipsos international survey found that one in four people do not trust the Internet. This insight has implications for companies using algorithms to target customers, a business model that according to former federal Public Safety Minister Ralph Goodale leads to profits, but which also "entices people down some very dark and dangerous pathways."[4] The age-old requirement for persuasion and marketing practices to be ethical has intensified in the digital age.

Best practices for persuasion are top of mind for savvy Canadian retailers, business leaders, and market researchers as traditional forms of advertising are rivalled by electronic word-of-mouth (e-WOM) and the driving of conversations that make consumers into influencers through rapidly diffused feedback, brand buzz, and customer reviews. Brands are built and engagement with them is nurtured through strategies such as persuasive storytelling. Jennifer Aaker, General Atlantic Professor of Marketing at Stanford Graduate School of Business, says that "Research shows our brains are not hard-wired to understand logic or retain facts for very long. Our brains are wired to understand and retain stories. A story is a journey that moves the listener, and when the listener goes on that journey they feel different and the result is persuasion and sometimes action."[5] Creating authentic, empathetic narratives that are compelling to consumers and shareable through a range of channels fosters emotional engagement. For instance, Canada Goose, with its chronicles of everyday-hero "Goose People"—such as Indigenous artist and activist Sarain Fox and Indigenous leader and former NHL player Jordin Tootoo—have turned customers into brand champions who drive sales. Through the persuasive force of stories, customers associate the brand with a satisfaction of their needs.[6] Leadership communication also taps into strategic storytelling, especially when opportunities or internal and external threats force companies to drive or manage change and in order to overcome resistance and secure the buy-in of employees and other stakeholders.[7]

Writing Persuasively

Persuasion (the attempt to influence opinion) works at changing attitudes, beliefs, and behaviours. Persuasive communication motivates readers to accept recommendations and act on requests. It gradually breaks down resistance and establishes rapport with readers by appealing to their needs, interests, values, and powers of reason. It doesn't coerce or *make* readers do something; it respectfully makes them *want* to do it. Reasonable propositions, well-framed arguments, and vivid supporting evidence—along with the effort to establish credibility and rapport in a way that makes the message relatable— are key to convincing people.

> **persuasion** The process of gradually influencing attitudes and behaviours and motivating the audience to act.

The ability to write persuasively is a valued workplace skill with endless applications. Any message that encourages action requires persuasion: favour requests, contestable claims, collection letters, sales and fundraising letters, and job application letters (see Chapter 10). In the small groups that compose today's work environments, persuasive skills help to make things happen both inside and outside of traditional hierarchies.

Preparing to Write Persuasively

The following are some points to remember when writing persuasive messages:

- **Know your purpose and what you want your reader to do.** Make your request reasonable and beneficial to the reader.

- **Understand what motivates your reader.** Analyze your audience's goals and needs and tap into them. Organizational psychologist Abraham Maslow defined these motivating factors in terms of an ascending **hierarchy of needs**, from the most basic at the bottom to the abstract at the top (see Figure 9.1). How does your pitch for a product, service, or action answer that need in benefitting the reader by saving them money, solving a problem, or helping them achieve an objective?
- **Consider design and layout.** Opinions are often formed before a message is read, based on its appearance alone. A proper layout—one that conveys non-verbal messages through proper proportioning, typography, and use of white space—will make your message attractive and professional.
- **Be positive and accurate.** Use a sincere, confident tone and reader-centred language. Match your phrasing to your relationship with the reader and avoid giving the impression that you are handing out orders or coercing them. Stick to the facts—don't distort information just to get your way.
- **Anticipate objections and plan how to deal with them.** An effective persuasive message is also informative. Collect data that will help you overcome resistance and allow readers to follow up easily.

Persuasion is necessary whenever you expect resistance or preference for the status quo. Overcoming resistance depends on swaying readers in three processes of influence:

- compliance (through rewards/benefits or punishments)
- identification (commonality)
- internalization (affirmation of goals and values)[8]

Consider why readers might object to what you have to say and be prepared to offer clear and compelling counter-arguments to refute the opposing view. Overcoming resistance is best done in non-threatening ways (through rewards rather than punishments). Readers are more receptive to change when their viewpoints are respected. Try to frame your persuasive request as a win–win proposition. A concession statement can let you acknowledge those objections in a non-judgmental way before you offer a rebuttal that logically supports a needed action (e.g., *Although the new system may cause some disruptions at first, it will speed processing dramatically and give us access to all relevant company-wide databases*).

To counter resistance and gain compliance, present your request in light of one of the following arguments:

- Short-term pain for long-term gain: small sacrifices or inconveniences now will result in the achievement of greater long-term objectives.
- The advantages outweigh the disadvantages.
- Money and/or time spent now is money and/or time saved in the long run.
- Investment of time or money will bring other benefits.

Deal with serious objections early, but don't give trivial objections a false importance by spending too much time on them.

Self-actualization is the highest level of need, met when people use their talents and problem-solving skills to serve humanity and live up to their potential.

Esteem is first among what Maslow termed "growth needs." The need for status, appreciation, and recognition leads people to strive for status symbols, work promotions, positions of authority, or good reputations.

Love and a sense of belonging are at a slightly higher level of need. Most people seek acceptance, companionship, and group identity. They don't want to be alone—they need to be needed.

Safety and security represent the next level of need. People are often motivated by the fear of not having a comfortable standard of living, a good health insurance or pension plan, reliable investments, job security, home security, or a pleasant work environment. They want to hold onto the money and resources that give them a sense of security.

Physiological needs include basics such as food, shelter, clothing, medical care, and a safe working environment.

FIGURE 9.1 Maslow's Hierarchy of Needs: **When writing persuasively, it's important to analyze your audience in terms of its goals and needs. Organizational psychologist Abraham Maslow defined these motivating factors in terms of an ascending hierarchy of needs, from the most basic at the bottom to the abstract at the top. Tapping into one of these motivational needs will make your message more persuasive.**

Maslow's hierarchy of needs Identified by Abraham Maslow, a specific order of needs—physiological needs, safety and security, love and a sense of belonging, esteem, and self-actualization—that motivate humans.

Persuasive Appeals

Persuasive messages appeal to the reader's reasoning, emotions, or sense of what is right and credible. The success of your communication depends on the strength of the case you build. Because not all audiences or persuasive tasks are alike, messages that must convince can rely on single or combined **appeals**.

appeal An attempt to persuade.

- **Appeal to reason:** With so much at stake, business decisions must be logical and well-justified. Effective reasoning based on evidence in the form of non-numerical facts, expert opinions, statistics, examples, or analogies allow you to show the merits of your claim. Clear, logical development in the way these facts are presented encourages readers to agree with your conclusion and support the action you propose. A cause–effect, problem–solution, or chronological pattern can help an appeal make more sense. Take care to eliminate unsound reasoning—errors in logic called **logical fallacies**, such as circular arguments (which restate rather than prove an opinion instead of backing it up), personal attacks, mistaking coincidence for cause, and begging the question (sidetracking)—which can rob your appeal of its persuasive power.

logical fallacy An error in logic that weakens a persuasive argument. Among the most common logical fallacies are *post hoc ergo propter hoc*, circular arguments, begging the question, and false analogy.

- **Appeal to emotion:** Emotions are powerful persuasive tools. When facts alone fail to convince, an emotional appeal can create a desire that motivates people to act and respond. The reader not only sees the logic of doing something but also actually *wants* to take action. Tapping into emotions such as pride, hope, honour, pleasure, respect, and fear is a leading strategy and catalyst in marketing, sales, and leadership communication that helps people connect with brands through positive associations and motivates them to act and adapt in times of change. If an appeal to emotion is excessive or not handled skillfully, however, it can backfire. Readers may see it as inauthentic, overhyped, and manipulative, especially if they believe they are being prevented from considering your argument logically or the emotions you are trying to evoke don't resonate with them for cultural or other reasons.[9] Poorly calculated appeals to emotion can turn readers off or cause a backlash, which in turn can have implications for ethics and credibility, with risks to company or brand reputation. A balanced approach that combines an emotional appeal with a logical one is a more reliable approach. Emotional power comes from language, such as the use of words like *deserve*, *special*, *safe*, *new*, or *free*. Stories, concrete examples, and sensory descriptions are also effective. The following are two examples of appeals to emotion:

    1. A memo that asks for safer working conditions may play on a sense of responsibility and pride in a company's reputation (*Our company has always maintained a level of safety above industry standards*).
    2. The final letter in a series of collection letters or payment-past-due notices may arouse fear at the consequences of not paying immediately (*If we do not receive payment immediately, we will be forced to turn your account over to an attorney for collection. Such action will damage your previously good credit rating*).

- **Appeal to ethics.** If you want to influence people based on ethics, it is important to establish your credibility. See Figure 9.2 for four key sources of credibility.

Finally, if you want people to trust you, avoid sarcasm and hostility, and keep your focus on reader benefits, not on what you have to gain personally.

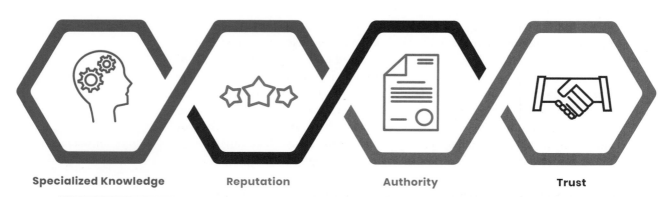

| Specialized Knowledge | Reputation | Authority | Trust |

> **Credibility refers to how believable, responsible, and ethical you, your company, and your statements are perceived to be. Personal credibility is based on your knowledge, reputation, position of authority, and familiarity with your reader.**

FIGURE 9.2 Four Key Sources of Credibility

A company's ability to build and maintain credibility can help it attract, retain, and persuade loyal customers. In 2019, the University of Victoria's Gustavson Brand Trust Index ranked Mountain Equipment Co-op (MEC) as the most trusted corporate brand in Canada (www.uvic.ca/gustavson/brandtrust).

Indirect Writing Plan for Persuasive Messages

The purpose of an indirect persuasive strategy is to break down resistance and prepare readers for a request or proposal that could easily fail if made directly. A gradual approach allows you to earn trust and show readers how they will benefit from what you're asking them to do. This three-step plan is an effective way to overcome resistance and indifference:

1. **Obtain interest.** In a short paragraph, define a problem, identify common ground, cite reader benefits, ask a pertinent question, or state a related fact that stimulates interest. Use an attention-getting technique that is relevant to your audience and purpose.
2. **Prove your proposal or product can benefit the reader.** Capitalize on the interest you have generated by explaining how what you propose or sell meets a particular need. Benefits may be direct (e.g., receiving an income tax deduction as a result of making a charitable donation) or indirect (e.g., the satisfaction of knowing that your donation will help someone else). Give readers the information they need to act on your request and deal with any objections they might have.
3. **Ask for action and link it to reader benefits.** Close with a specific and confident request that motivates readers to act immediately.

This basic pattern can be modified to deliver a variety of persuasive messages.

Types of Persuasive Messages

Favour and Action Requests

Small favours are easy to ask. However, when you make greater demands on readers by asking them to donate money or volunteer their time and expertise, you can expect resistance. An indirect strategy allows you to gain acceptance for invitations, requests for volunteer services, and appeals for any kind of unpaid help. The direct benefits of performing such favours are usually small or non-existent. An explanation focusing on the indirect benefits of complying (see the second point below) reassures readers that they are doing the right thing.

1. **Gain favourable attention.** Catch readers' attention with a genuine compliment or a fact that awakens their social conscience.
2. **Persuade the reader to accept.** Help readers view the request positively by associating it with one of the following:

   » the chance to assume a leadership role or showcase talents
   » the chance to network, develop professional contacts, or gain exposure for their views
   » the chance to help others or bring about positive change in their workplace or community

   Specify exactly what the favour involves by referring to dates, times, and locations.
3. **Ask for action.** Express your request with confidence and courtesy to encourage acceptance.

Opens with an apology and offers reader a convenient excuse to say no

Fails to build interest in the event and doesn't provide readers with details of how the money raised will be spent and who will benefit

Offers no details about the fundraising event and doesn't mention direct and indirect benefits (e.g., the chance to have fun and help others)

Bullies readers into buying tickets and doesn't mention how the tickets can be ordered

Dear Dr. Rhynold,

I'm sorry to bother you during what I understand is a very busy time of year, but I hope that you will consider supporting the Children's Aid Foundation by purchasing a $250 family package for our "Be a Kid Again" fundraising event, which will be held at Canada's Wonderland on Saturday, August 22, 2020.

We guarantee that this money will be put to good use. The amount we raised last year certainly was.

If you have any questions about this event, you should phone me at 519-331-8693. Remember to buy your tickets—the kids are counting on you. Don't make them suffer.

Hoping you'll get back to me,

Fiona Walsh

Regional Councillor

FIGURE 9.3 Ineffective Favour Request (extract)

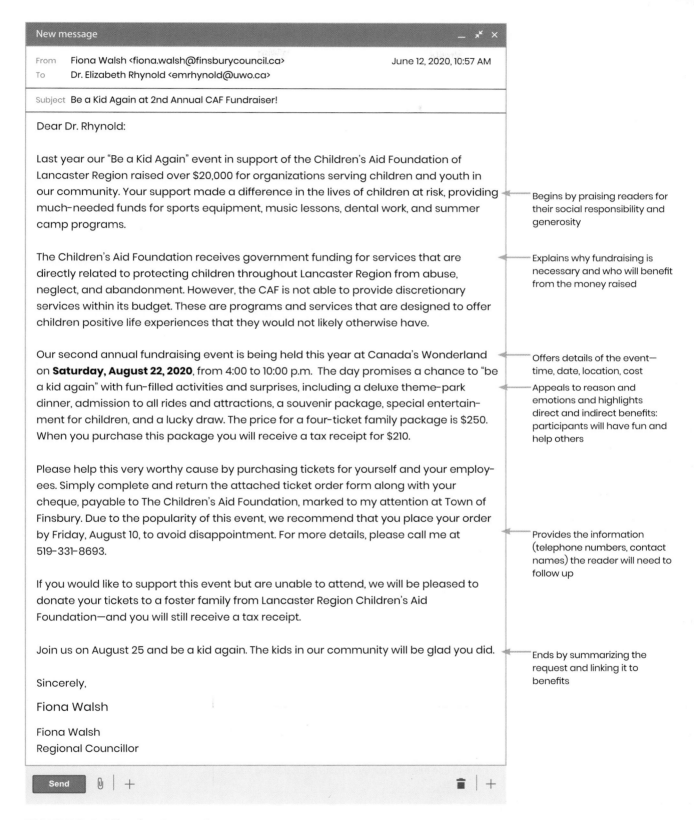

New message   _ ⤢ ✕

| From | Fiona Walsh <fiona.walsh@finsburycouncil.ca> | June 12, 2020, 10:57 AM |
| To | Dr. Elizabeth Rhynold <emrhynold@uwo.ca> | |

Subject Be a Kid Again at 2nd Annual CAF Fundraiser!

Dear Dr. Rhynold:

Last year our "Be a Kid Again" event in support of the Children's Aid Foundation of Lancaster Region raised over $20,000 for organizations serving children and youth in our community. Your support made a difference in the lives of children at risk, providing much-needed funds for sports equipment, music lessons, dental work, and summer camp programs.

> Begins by praising readers for their social responsibility and generosity

The Children's Aid Foundation receives government funding for services that are directly related to protecting children throughout Lancaster Region from abuse, neglect, and abandonment. However, the CAF is not able to provide discretionary services within its budget. These are programs and services that are designed to offer children positive life experiences that they would not likely otherwise have.

> Explains why fundraising is necessary and who will benefit from the money raised

Our second annual fundraising event is being held this year at Canada's Wonderland on **Saturday, August 22, 2020**, from 4:00 to 10:00 p.m. The day promises a chance to "be a kid again" with fun-filled activities and surprises, including a deluxe theme-park dinner, admission to all rides and attractions, a souvenir package, special entertainment for children, and a lucky draw. The price for a four-ticket family package is $250. When you purchase this package you will receive a tax receipt for $210.

> Offers details of the event—time, date, location, cost

> Appeals to reason and emotions and highlights direct and indirect benefits: participants will have fun and help others

Please help this very worthy cause by purchasing tickets for yourself and your employees. Simply complete and return the attached ticket order form along with your cheque, payable to The Children's Aid Foundation, marked to my attention at Town of Finsbury. Due to the popularity of this event, we recommend that you place your order by Friday, August 10, to avoid disappointment. For more details, please call me at 519-331-8693.

> Provides the information (telephone numbers, contact names) the reader will need to follow up

If you would like to support this event but are unable to attend, we will be pleased to donate your tickets to a foster family from Lancaster Region Children's Aid Foundation—and you will still receive a tax receipt.

Join us on August 25 and be a kid again. The kids in our community will be glad you did.

> Ends by summarizing the request and linking it to benefits

Sincerely,

Fiona Walsh

Fiona Walsh
Regional Councillor

Send   📎 | +   🗑 | +

FIGURE 9.4 Effective Favour Request

Persuasive Memos

How can you successfully lobby for safer working conditions, persuade staff to accept a new computer system, or justify the expense of a new program? A persuasive memo uses an indirect problem–solution strategy, describing a problem to management or colleagues before presenting a solution that ends in a related proposal or request. The way it is organized gains attention and gradual support for an action that requires approval before it can be implemented. Because a persuasive memo communicates facts and benefits before it pushes for action, there is less chance the initiative it endorses will be misunderstood or rejected prematurely. The memo ultimately succeeds when it puts words and ideas into action to overcome resistance and wins support for a well-defined and workable solution to a problem. Here are the steps to follow when writing a problem-solving memo that gives limited chance for readers to say no:

1. **Summarize the problem.** Identify the cause or source of a problem while suggesting that the problem is solvable. To stimulate interest, begin with a subject line that focuses on positive results and benefits.
2. **Explain how the problem can be solved.** Establish a logical foundation for your later request, citing statistical evidence, facts, and figures while also outlining benefits.
3. **Minimize resistance.** Anticipate possible objections (e.g., too expensive, too time-consuming, or a threat to someone's authority, professional status, or the status quo). Because there is more than one way to solve a problem, including a solution your reader prefers, be prepared to offer convincing counter-arguments to prove how yours is better.
4. **Ask for a specific action.** Be firm but polite. Set a deadline for readers to act or respond as long as it won't seem aggressive, and offer incentives (e.g., time or money saved) if you require action promptly..

Persuasion for Managing Change and Motivating Performance

Organizations are often confronted by change: change they actively seek and change that is imposed on them that may not come easily. Managers and other decision makers

Vague subject line fails to highlight benefits or focus on positive results

Opens with negative, accusatory language

Pushes for action before it fully communicates the reasons for that action; offers no statistical evidence to back up explanation of the problem

Aggressive closing

Subject: Switching to Satellite Training

Lately, training costs have gone out of control. The real problem is covering the travel expenses of employees and trainers, who must travel between local branches and national headquarters. For this reason, I strongly urge you to meet with representatives from Finance Vision, operator of an interactive television network, and see their demonstration on satellite training. The cost for a half-day training session is just $10,000. I hope you will agree with me that this is the best possible solution.

Please get back to me as soon as possible. We will need to liaise with Finance Vision soon if we hope to use this technology for our RRSP training season.

FIGURE 9.5 Ineffective Persuasive Memo (extract)

Bothwell and Associates, Inc.

Interoffice Memo

FROM: River Simons, Training Coordinator

TO: Malcolm Reynolds, Human Resources Manager

DATE: April 17, 2020

SUBJECT: Reducing Training Program Costs ◄——————— Subject line focuses on positive results and benefits

Last year, the cost to send trainers on the road and to bring employees from across the country to training events at our national headquarters exceeded $1.8 million. Mounting travel costs accounted for the dramatic increase in training expenses. According to projections, by 2021 it will cost over $2.5 million to maintain training programs at current levels. ◄——————— Opening gains attention by describing problem and quantifying it with statistical evidence

With advances in satellite delivery methods, however, it is now possible to conduct nationwide training more cost-effectively in virtual classrooms equipped with satellite dishes, television sets, and interactive handsets. Satellite presentations have several distinct advantages over conventional methods:

1.   Everyone receives the same information at the same time from keynote speakers and slide and video presentations. ◄——————— Explains how the problem can be solved and lists advantages for greater emphasis
2.   Employees can interact with each other and share ideas just as they would if they were sitting side by side. They can ask questions, take multiple-choice tests by keying responses into interactive handsets, and be polled by the presenter.
3.   Nationwide training programs that normally take months can be conducted in a matter of days.

While computer-based training is an option, test groups often complain that this delivery method isn't engaging enough. Satellite training can be expensive, with the cost of in-house setups averaging $10,000 to $15,000 per site. However, by outsourcing the service to an interactive television network such as Finance Vision, it is possible to offer a half-day seminar to an unlimited number of sites at approximately the same price. Finance Vision operates from 40 hotels across Canada, all fully equipped and staffed by technicians. ◄——————— Minimizes resistance by acknowledging counter-arguments and potential drawbacks

Please allow me to arrange for a demonstration from Finance Vision so that we can learn more about how a satellite training program can help us reduce our training costs. ◄——————— Politely asks for action and connects action to benefits

FIGURE 9.6 Effective Persuasive Memo

show their leadership by helping employees adapt to change and in the process reduce push-back and encourage buy-in. Using plain language for easy comprehension, making the same message understandable in several ways, and even using stories to build trust are strategies in managers' persuasive toolkit for managing change and overcoming uncertainty through communication.[10]

Internal corporate communication has four goals: (i) encouraging internal relations and commitment, (ii) promoting a positive sense of belonging, (iii) developing employees' awareness of change and of (iv) the need to evolve. Part of a manager's role is to stimulate employees' desire to commit to the job, motivate worker performance, and increase job satisfaction, all of which indirectly benefit work outcomes. Skilled leaders are adept at combining informational and motivational goals in their messages and using motivating language:

- Direction-giving and uncertainty-reducing language clarifying goals and duties
- Empathetic language that encourages and inspires the workforce and shows gratitude
- Meaning-making language outlining norms and expectations (strategic storytelling and references to teams)[11]

Claim Requests

Straightforward, well-justified claims can be made directly. However, if a warranty has lapsed, if a term of a contract has been contravened, or if a product is no longer under guarantee, a claim may be judged questionable—and fail—unless persuasive strategies are used. This means you must first prove the legitimacy of your claim with a clear line of

Begins negatively and offers the reader a reason for not granting the adjustment

Doesn't specify the type of membership, indicate when it was taken out, or refer to the terms of the contract

Doesn't provide a chronology, supporting data, or a strong reason for granting the adjustment

Ends angrily without asking for a refund

Dear Manager,

The health club industry has a poor track record when it comes to responding to membership complaints. Now I hope you will prove this perception wrong by allowing me to cancel my membership even though the 10-day cooling-off period has now elapsed.

When I took out a membership, I thought it would guarantee me full access to every class and facility. As it turned out, all the classes I went to were full and I was turned away even though I had signed up in advance. I think this is a poor way to treat paying members, don't you?

If you don't do something about this situation, I will have no alternative but to contact the Canadian Council of Better Business Bureaus, the Ontario Ministry of Government and Consumer Services, and my lawyer. Then we'll see what happens.

Angrily,

Francesca Auola

FIGURE 9.7 Ineffective Persuasive Claim (extract)

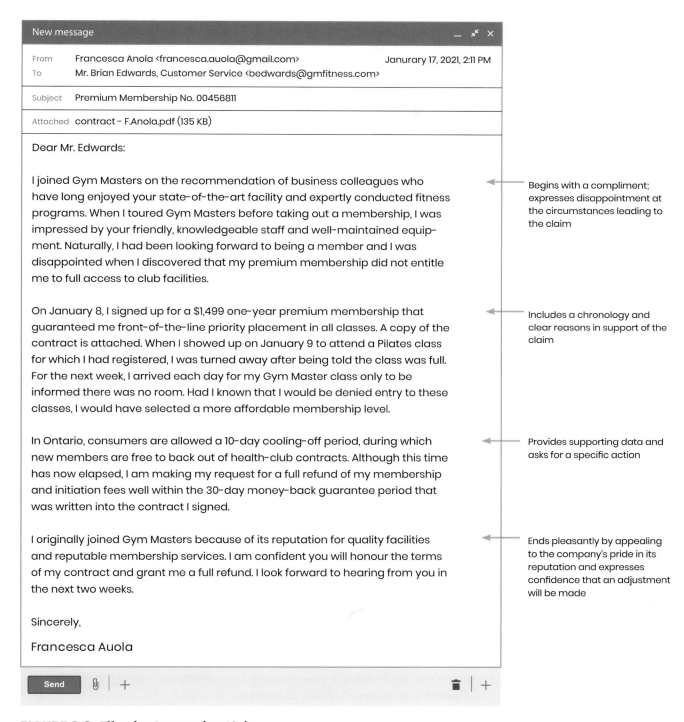

New message   — ⤢ ✕

From   Francesca Anola <francesca.auola@gmail.com>   Janurary 17, 2021, 2:11 PM
To   Mr. Brian Edwards, Customer Service <bedwards@gmfitness.com>

Subject   Premium Membership No. 00456811

Attached   contract - F.Anola.pdf (135 KB)

Dear Mr. Edwards:

I joined Gym Masters on the recommendation of business colleagues who have long enjoyed your state-of-the-art facility and expertly conducted fitness programs. When I toured Gym Masters before taking out a membership, I was impressed by your friendly, knowledgeable staff and well-maintained equipment. Naturally, I had been looking forward to being a member and I was disappointed when I discovered that my premium membership did not entitle me to full access to club facilities.

Begins with a compliment; expresses disappointment at the circumstances leading to the claim

On January 8, I signed up for a $1,499 one-year premium membership that guaranteed me front-of-the-line priority placement in all classes. A copy of the contract is attached. When I showed up on January 9 to attend a Pilates class for which I had registered, I was turned away after being told the class was full. For the next week, I arrived each day for my Gym Master class only to be informed there was no room. Had I known that I would be denied entry to these classes, I would have selected a more affordable membership level.

Includes a chronology and clear reasons in support of the claim

In Ontario, consumers are allowed a 10-day cooling-off period, during which new members are free to back out of health-club contracts. Although this time has now elapsed, I am making my request for a full refund of my membership and initiation fees well within the 30-day money-back guarantee period that was written into the contract I signed.

Provides supporting data and asks for a specific action

I originally joined Gym Masters because of its reputation for quality facilities and reputable membership services. I am confident you will honour the terms of my contract and grant me a full refund. I look forward to hearing from you in the next two weeks.

Ends pleasantly by appealing to the company's pride in its reputation and expresses confidence that an adjustment will be made

Sincerely,

Francesca Auola

Send 📎 | +   🗑 | +

FIGURE 9.8 Effective Persuasive Claim

reasoning before you can ask for an adjustment. A weak or questionable claim can usually be strengthened with expressions of confidence in a company's integrity and fairness and appeals to its pride in its products and reputation, if only because successful businesses want customers to be satisfied.

Your challenge is to show that the company or receiver is responsible for the problem while maintaining a moderate tone. If you succumb to anger or irrational threats and accusations, you risk antagonizing the person handling your claim. You will likely be communicating with a claims adjuster or customer service representative with no prior knowledge of the complaint or difficulty. If you present yourself as fair and easy to deal with and show your disappointment without expressing anger, your claim will stand a better chance of being granted promptly. Here are some steps to follow:

1. **Gain positive attention.** Open with a compliment, a point of shared interest, a review of action taken to solve the problem, or your original reason (if favourable) for buying the product or service.

2. **Prove your claim is valid.** Describe the problem in a calm and credible way. Give a chronology to explain what happened and what you have done to resolve the problem. Provide supporting data to help the reader assess the situation such as order numbers, delivery dates, method of shipment, servicing locations, and descriptions of the items in question. Go with your strongest reasons to prove your claim is worthwhile. Take steps to defend yourself against possible blame (*I carefully reviewed the owner's manual before I attempted to install the new unit*). Attach supporting documents (sales receipts, invoices, shipping orders) that will help the reader investigate your claim. Your line of reasoning should lead the reader to conclude that responsibility rests with his or her company, not with you.

3. **Ask for a specific action.** State how the claim can be resolved and what you expect the company to do (make a refund, offer a replacement, or apologize). End positively, expressing confidence in the company's ethical standards.

Collection Letters

collection letters A series of increasingly persuasive appeals to a customer asking for payment for goods and services already received.

The purpose of a **collection letter** is to collect an overdue bill (a month or more past due) while preserving the customer relationship. Collection letters, usually written in a series of three to five letters, put polite yet persistent pressure on readers, persuading them to promptly pay debts owing for goods already received or services already rendered. Usually, the longer a bill remains unpaid, the more demanding and urgent the collection letters become. The forcefulness of a collection demand also depends on the relationship between the creditor and the debtor. When a customer usually pays on time, the chances of collecting on a current bill are good, making courtesy all-important to preserving a friendly customer relationship. For customers with records of unreliable payment, it may be necessary to adopt a firmer approach, reinforced by a no-nonsense tone that is direct but still polite. Adapting your messages to the type of debtor you are dealing with can help you recover the money owed to your company faster—without risking future business.

Collection letters generally follow three stages:

reminder letter A collection letter that informs a customer in a friendly way that a payment has not been received.

1. **Reminder:** First messages work on the assumption that the customer intends to pay but has simply forgotten and fallen behind. This stage calls for a friendly **reminder letter** that mentions the customer's good credit record (if there is one), alerts the customer to the problem, and asks for a response. In place of a personalized letter, it is also possible to use a form letter or to send a copy of the original invoice, stamped "Second Notice" or "Past Due."

2. **Inquiry:** Messages at this stage are firmer and more direct, but they work on the assumption that the customer has a legitimate reason for not paying—a cash-flow problem, out-of-town absence, or similar circumstance. The **inquiry letter** summarizes the situation, expresses concern over non-payment, and asks for an explanation or immediate payment. This request is reinforced by positive appeals to one or more of the following:

- **fairness**—emphasize the customer's fairness in completing a transaction by paying for goods and services already received
- **reputation**—emphasize the benefits of debt payment to a company's or person's good name
- **sympathy**—express concern while reminding the customer that prompt payment is crucial to your operations
- **self-interest**—show that prompt payment removes risks to credit ratings and keeps interest charges low

If the customer is unable to pay the whole bill immediately, you have the option of offering to negotiate an instalment payment plan. Make it easy for the customer

> **inquiry letter** A collection letter that attempts to determine the circumstances that are preventing payment and asks for payment.

Portfolio Electronics

520 Wellington Street
London, ON N6A 1J7

www.portfolio.com
1-800-667-8384

February 4, 2021

Mr. Wesley Denisof
12 Adelaide Street East
London, ON N4S 7R9

Dear Mr. Denisof:

You have been sending your monthly instalments to us promptly for over a year. However, we find that your payment of $3,558.77 for December has not yet arrived. Please send us a cheque in this amount now to avoid the buildup of interest charges and ensure uninterrupted service in the months ahead. If you have already paid, please accept out thanks and disregard this notice.

We value your business very much and look forward to serving you again soon.

Sincerely,

Alexander Foster

Alexander Foster
Accounts Payable

Opens politely, reminding customer of good credit record

Mentions problem; uses neutral language

Makes a polite request for payment in terms of benefits of paying on time

Closes with appreciation for business

FIGURE 9.9 Sample Collection Reminder Letter

to respond by including a toll-free phone number, fax number, postage-paid envelope, or web address for convenient credit card payment.

3. **Demand:** The last letters in a collection series are unequivocal demands for immediate payment. The **demand letter** usually takes the form of an ultimatum, urgently asking for payment and warning of the penalties for non-payment (including legal action, garnishment of wages, or referral of the account to a collection agency). Refer to previous collection notices that have been ignored. This will show how reasonable you have been and will strengthen your case should you eventually launch legal proceedings. Your tone should still be courteous, expressing reluctance at having to take action but determination to do so if the customer

demand letter A collection letter that makes a firm and unequivocal request for immediate payment and attempts to convince the debtor to pay the bill within a stated time by raising the possibility of legal action.

Portfolio Electronics

520 Wellington Street
London, ON N6A 1J7

www.portfolio.com
1-800-667-8384

May 6, 2021

Mr. Wesley Denisof
12 Adelaide Street East
London, ON N4S 7R9

Dear Mr. Denisof:

Our records indicate that your account is now three months overdue. We are very concerned that we have not heard from you even though we have already sent you two reminder notices.

We are requesting that you pay your balance of $3,558.77 immediately so that you can preserve your excellent credit record with us and avoid further accumulation of interest charges. Because you are one of our best customers and have always paid your account promptly in the past, we are sure you will want to retain your good reputation by paying your bill now.

Please use the enclosed envelope to send your cheque today. If a problem is preventing you from making this payment, please call 1-800-667-8384, toll-free, to discuss your account or details of a mutually satisfactory payment plan.

Sincerely,

Alexander Foster

Alexander Foster
Accounts Payable

Annotations (left margin):
- Opening summarizes facts of overdue account and expresses concern over non-payment; mentions previous correspondence
- Makes direct request for payment and reminds customer of benefits of immediate compliance
- Shows sympathy and fairness and appeals to customer's self-interest
- Makes it easy for the customer to respond
- Closes positively by expressing confidence in a solution

FIGURE 9.10 Sample Collection Inquiry Letter

Portfolio Electronics

520 Wellington Street
London, ON N6A 1J7

www.portfolio.com
1-800-667-8384

June 10, 2021

Mr. Wesley Denisof
12 Adelaide Street East
London, ON N4S 7R9

Dear Mr. Denisof:

This is the fourth time we have called your attention to your long-overdue account. So far, we have received neither your payment nor the courtesy of an explanation. Because we value your business, you have already received a generous extension in time, but we cannot permit a further delay in payment. Now we are counting on you to meet your obligation.

Unless you pay your balance of $3,558.77 by June 30, we will be forced to turn your account over to a collection agency, resulting in certain damage to your previously good credit rating.

We would prefer to mark your account paid than to take this unpleasant action, so please send your cheque today.

Sincerely,

Alexander Foster

Alexander Foster
Accounts Payable

Opening makes unequivocal demand for immediate payment

Delivers an ultimatum, clearly stating the consequences of non-payment, and sets deadline for compliance with request

Tone in closing is polite yet firm

FIGURE 9.11 Sample Collection Demand Letter

doesn't pay. Impose a time limit for payment, usually 10 days, and be explicit about the follow-up action you intend to take.

Pre-authorized payment and the practice of phoning customers to notify them of overdue accounts have lessened the need for this type of communication.

Sales Messages

Among the types of persuasive messages, **sales messages** are unique. They are rich in details orchestrated to make readers want a product or service. Sales messages can be composed one by one or as form e-mails, sent out in mailings of hundreds or even thousands.

sales message A message that promotes a product, service, or business and seeks prospective customers or additional sales.

In large organizations, specialists oversee market research and promotional writing. In smaller organizations, these areas are handled by individual employees or are outsourced. Successful sales people are usually effective communicators:

- They know that sales messages help build a business by advertising a product or service directly to individual customers or business accounts.
- They rely on direct-mail marketing, using market research to adapt their sales messages to the needs, preferences, and demographics of targeted groups and to create mailing lists to ensure that sales messages reach the people most likely to be interested in particular products and services.
- They realize that most sales messages are unsolicited and frequently ignored, so they avoid hard-sell pitches, empty hype, and deceptive product claims that turn readers off. They minimize risk for buyers by providing product information, indicating how buyers will benefit, and building confidence in the product's value and performance. Only at the end do they push for a sale.
- They use appropriate persuasive appeals and incentives to create desire for products and services. The aim is to translate that interest into sales and an ongoing relationship of trust with customers.

Even if your job doesn't involve sales and promotions, sales writing has broad applications. Knowing how to do it well can help you sell not just your company's products, mission, and values but also your own ideas and skills. As you will see in Chapter 10, job application letters are closely related to sales letters.

Aiming to Make a Sale: Analyzing the Product and Audience

An effective sales message delivers specific facts to a specific audience. Careful planning is essential, so start with the following preliminary steps:

1. Study the product or service. Keep the problem it solves top of mind. Become an expert on its design, construction, composite materials, manufacturing process, and operation. Be prepared to vouch for the product's ease of use, performance, durability, efficiency, warranty, availability of colours and finishes, and arrangements for servicing. Analyze its special features, especially its central selling point—the thing that gives your product an edge over the competition—and compare its price with that of other products in its class.
2. Learn as much as possible about the target audience.
3. Ensure an ethical sales pitch.
4. Consider the timing, presentation, personalization, and tone of your message.

Writing Plan for Sales Letters

A typical sales letter involves a four-step writing process.

Step 1: Gain Attention

A strong, concise opening captures attention before the reader has a chance to lose interest. Weak openings turn readers off, so avoid obvious statements, questions with obvious answers, and stories that take too long to get to the point. This is especially important when your sales message is unsolicited or uninvited. Choose from the following devices:

- **a thought-provoking fact or statement**

  Over 20,000 vehicles are stolen every year in this city.

- **good news that makes the reader feel important or unique**

  You're **pre-approved** for the Ultra Platinum Card. This exciting credit card is yours to help you achieve the best in life.

- **a special offer or bargain**

  The cheque below is yours to cash toward your Ultra Card Registry service! It's a special way to introduce you to the protection and peace of mind that Ultra has provided to Canadians for over 20 years.

- **a product feature that makes a difference to the reader**

  Ultra is the first platinum card that allows you up to 15 days of out-of-province travel medical insurance—absolutely free!

- **a question**

  Have you ever wondered if you paid too much for an all-inclusive resort vacation?

- **a story**

  I am pleased to write to you today to tell you an alumni success story about Janet and Steve, who may not be very different from you. They work hard and invest their money wisely to build a bright future for their family. Although they know they can't predict the future, they have protected it by investing in the Alumni Term Life Insurance Plan. With low rates for alumni, they protect themselves, their family, and everything they have worked so hard for.

For extra emphasis, some of these devices can be bolded or underlined, in whole or in part, or incorporated as captions and headlines.

Step 2: Introduce the Product

Once you have gained attention, the next step is to forge a link between the need you have identified and how the product you are selling meets that need. The following example ties a product to the sample story given above:

> You too can take advantage of the Alumni Term Life Insurance Plan and provide the people you love with the same security that Janet and Steve did for their family.

Step 3: Make the Product Desirable

Your challenge is to make readers want the product and understand the need it meets. Describe the product from the reader's point of view. Instead of listing flat details, suggest what it is like to use and benefit from the product. Rather than saying *our vacuum has a 6-metre cord*, interpret details so they are meaningful to readers:

> The Power Vac's 6-metre cord allows you to vacuum even the largest rooms from a single outlet.

If necessary, balance and dispel possible doubts with clear reminders of product benefits:

> If you ever worried that a home security system might mean a loss of privacy, we want to reassure you that our monitoring system is activated only when the alarm is triggered.

Build product confidence by using hype-free language and risk-reducing inducements such as a warranty, money-back guarantee, special offer, free trial, or sample. Rely on statistics and testimonials—even stories about how the product was developed—to counter resistance and provide assurances of satisfaction. If the product is affordable, emphasize the price by mentioning it early. Otherwise, omit it or de-emphasize it in one of the following ways:

- Mention it only after you have created a desire for the product.
- Break the price down into smaller units (monthly instalment payments, cost per day or issue).
- Make the product a bargain by calculating the cost after discount or rebate.
- Show savings over a competitor's product or, for subscriptions, over the per-unit purchase price.
- Link the price with benefits.

Dear Computer Owner,

Opening suggests the product already owned is satisfactory, making a replacement unnecessary → If you think the computer system you're using now is good, you should see the desktop PCs and notebooks from Micro-Genius. We think you should check out our new A50 and R40 series. We think you'll be pleasantly surprised.

Does not specify how fast, powerful, and affordable the product is; muted language ("quite satisfied") fails to create desire for the product → Our computers are fast, powerful, and affordable. Our customers say that overall they are quite satisfied with their performance. Now, for a limited time, you can get an additional 500 gigabytes of hard drive space and no-charge shipping when you purchase any system included in our special promotion.

Closing action is conditional and doesn't provide enough information for easy follow-up → We have some real beauties in stock right now. If you think Micro-Genius might have a computer for you, give us a call. Micro-Genius computers aren't just good, they're very good.

FIGURE 9.12 Ineffective Sales Message (extract)

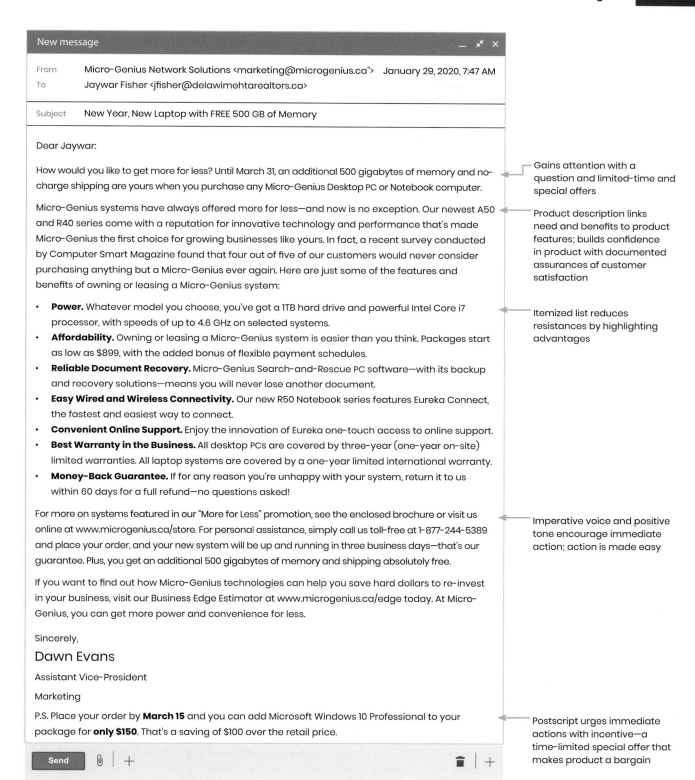

New message   _ ⤢ ✕

| From | Micro-Genius Network Solutions <marketing@microgenius.ca">   January 29, 2020, 7:47 AM |
| To | Jaywar Fisher <jfisher@delawimehtarealtors.ca> |

Subject   New Year, New Laptop with FREE 500 GB of Memory

Dear Jaywar:

How would you like to get more for less? Until March 31, an additional 500 gigabytes of memory and no-charge shipping are yours when you purchase any Micro-Genius Desktop PC or Notebook computer.

> *Gains attention with a question and limited-time and special offers*

Micro-Genius systems have always offered more for less—and now is no exception. Our newest A50 and R40 series come with a reputation for innovative technology and performance that's made Micro-Genius the first choice for growing businesses like yours. In fact, a recent survey conducted by Computer Smart Magazine found that four out of five of our customers would never consider purchasing anything but a Micro-Genius ever again. Here are just some of the features and benefits of owning or leasing a Micro-Genius system:

> *Product description links need and benefits to product features; builds confidence in product with documented assurances of customer satisfaction*

- **Power.** Whatever model you choose, you've got a 1TB hard drive and powerful Intel Core i7 processor, with speeds of up to 4.6 GHz on selected systems.
- **Affordability.** Owning or leasing a Micro-Genius system is easier than you think. Packages start as low as $899, with the added bonus of flexible payment schedules.
- **Reliable Document Recovery.** Micro-Genius Search-and-Rescue PC software—with its backup and recovery solutions—means you will never lose another document.
- **Easy Wired and Wireless Connectivity.** Our new R50 Notebook series features Eureka Connect, the fastest and easiest way to connect.
- **Convenient Online Support.** Enjoy the innovation of Eureka one-touch access to online support.
- **Best Warranty in the Business.** All desktop PCs are covered by three-year (one-year on-site) limited warranties. All laptop systems are covered by a one-year limited international warranty.
- **Money-Back Guarantee.** If for any reason you're unhappy with your system, return it to us within 60 days for a full refund—no questions asked!

> *Itemized list reduces resistances by highlighting advantages*

For more on systems featured in our "More for Less" promotion, see the enclosed brochure or visit us online at www.microgenius.ca/store. For personal assistance, simply call us toll-free at 1-877-244-5389 and place your order, and your new system will be up and running in three business days—that's our guarantee. Plus, you get an additional 500 gigabytes of memory and shipping absolutely free.

> *Imperative voice and positive tone encourage immediate action; action is made easy*

If you want to find out how Micro-Genius technologies can help you save hard dollars to re-invest in your business, visit our Business Edge Estimator at www.microgenius.ca/edge today. At Micro-Genius, you can get more power and convenience for less.

Sincerely,

Dawn Evans

Assistant Vice-President

Marketing

P.S. Place your order by **March 15** and you can add Microsoft Windows 10 Professional to your package for **only $150**. That's a saving of $100 over the retail price.

> *Postscript urges immediate actions with incentive—a time-limited special offer that makes product a bargain*

| Send | 🖇 | + | 🗑 | +

FIGURE 9.13 Effective Sales Message

The following example combines several of these approaches:

> When you calculate what you could save with benefits such as Out-of-Province Travel Medical Insurance and Auto Rental Collision Insurance, you'll be pleasantly surprised that the fee for the Ultra Platinum Card is only $79 a year (with a current annual interest rate of 17.5 per cent), which is actually less than $7 a month.

Step 4: Ask for a Simple Action

After you have created a desire for the product, use a positive emphasis combined with the imperative voice to tell readers how easy it is for them to purchase it and urge them to take action without delay (discouraging procrastination). Make the action simple by providing a toll-free order number, giving a website or an e-mail address, or enclosing an order form or postage-paid envelope.

> Say yes to your Pre-Approved Acceptance Certificate today! Simply complete and mail it to us in the postage-paid envelope provided or give us a call at 1-877-553-0123.

Encourage the reader to act promptly with perks and incentives such as a time-limited offer, special offer, bonus, or rebate. If you cannot offer incentives, remind readers that the less they delay the sooner they will benefit from the product (*As quantities are limited, act now to avoid disappointment. Purchase your Zodiac watercraft today and enjoy it all summer long*).

Postscripts

Postscript lines are more common in sales letters than in any other type of message. Postscripts are high-impact sentences, attracting attention as soon as the letter is opened. They are useful for spotlighting free offers, for summarizing the central selling point, or for making a final appeal to readers, urging them to act promptly.

> P.S. If you're concerned about workplace stress, make mindfulness part of your work routine through MindSet's five-session Resiliency-Plus training program. Sign up today to learn from an accredited MRSR professional and feel the difference mindfulness can make.

Sales Follow-Up

Although not specifically a persuasive message, a sales follow-up confirms to customers that they have made the right decision by purchasing a product. Its expressions of appreciation for an order reinforce goodwill and promote future business. A follow-up may also confirm details of a sale or offer further services.

CHECKLIST

Effective Sales Messages

- ❑ **Opening:** Does the opening command attention? Is the attention-getting technique suited to the product, audience, and type of appeal? Does the opening provide a strong and logical lead-in for the rest of the message?

- ❑ **Product Description:** How is the product introduced? Have you used only concrete language to describe the product? Does the description help the reader picture what it is like to use and benefit from the product? Have you offered proof to back up your claims about the product?

❑ **Selling Points:** Does the message identify and emphasize the product's central selling points?

❑ **Persuasive Appeals:** What type of appeal have you used? Does it respond to the reader's needs? Have you created a desire for the product?

❑ **Resistance:** Have you dealt with questions and objections the reader might have?

❑ **Price:** Have you introduced the price strategically?

❑ **Closing:** Does the closing tell the reader exactly what to do? Does it motivate the reader to take action quickly? Does it make the action easy?

❑ **Postscript:** If a postscript is included, does it recap and give extra emphasis to a special offer or product feature or spur to action?

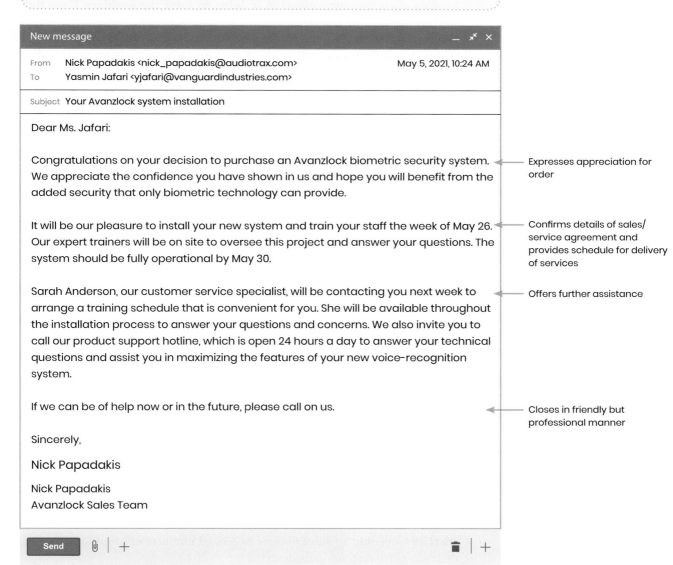

FIGURE 9.14 Sales Follow-Up

Fundraising Messages

A variation on a sales letter is the fundraising appeal. Readers in this case are asked not to spend money but to donate it to a worthy cause. Their support and generosity depends on how well you show how a problem could be solved or alleviated with a donation that will be put to good use. A fundraising letter should make readers feel good about giving.

To write an effective fundraising message, follow these steps:

1. **Identify an important problem.** Explain why the reader should care about it.
2. **Show that the problem is solvable.** If a problem seems insurmountable, readers will naturally feel incapable of doing anything to help. Hold out hope for even a partial, short-term solution. Link a need to your organization's ability to respond to it.
3. **Explain what your organization is doing to solve the problem.** Prove that funds will be going to a good cause, not just to the cost of fundraising. Outline past accomplishments and future goals, citing facts and statistics. An attached brochure or a link to an article about your organization can supply potential donors with useful background information.
4. **Ask for a donation.** Explain deficiencies in public funding that make private donations necessary. Put the gift in terms that the reader will understand by indicating what it will buy. If appropriate, suggest amounts in descending order, propose a monthly pledge, or suggest other ways (volunteering, writing letters) readers can lend their support.

The sample favour request (see Figure 9.5) shares certain characteristics with a typical fundraising letter. A fundraising package will usually include an appeal for a donation, a reply form, and a postage-paid envelope.

Persuasion through Social Media

Digital persuasion through social media channels is now an essential component of most businesses' online marketing strategies. It is also an important driver of support for causes and social good, which are more likely to be supported through social media than through traditional offline methods.[12] Social media persuasion is measured by the degree to which one's voice is "heard, repeated, and valued,"[13] and it can be achieved through the following techniques:

- **reciprocation**—mirroring or responding in kind to another person's post
- **social proof**—finding out what matters to other people and creating value for others through engaging content
- **liking**—establishing commonality by complimenting, making positive comments, or liking, sharing, or retweeting posts
- **authority**—establishing oneself as an expert (even if one's expertise is perceived rather than actual)
- **scarcity**—opening up subscriptions to limited numbers of people and making their access to you more exclusive[14]

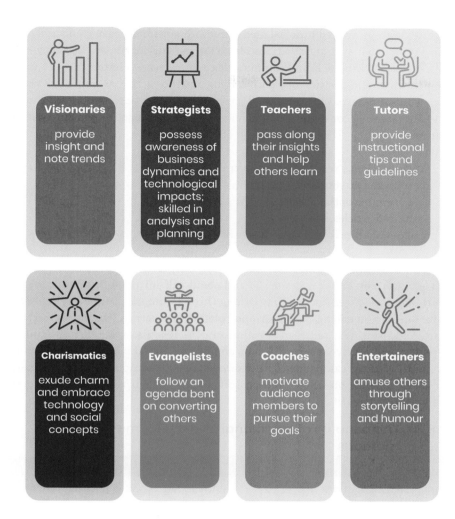

FIGURE 9.15 Influencers can be identified according to eight basic archetypes. Do you follow any influencers on social media? What archetype do they best fall under?

Adapted from Barry, J. (2015, March 16). Which of 8 archetypes fits your social influence? LinkedIn. www.linkedin.com/pulse/marketing-4-types-influencers-jim-barry

Marketers and social media brand managers actively seek out social media **influencers**, whose endorsements have tremendous value because of the solid relationships of trust they build with their followers. Thought leadership is one of the most visible forms of persuasion in the new economy.

Traditional vs. Digital Marketing

Social media environments have empowered consumers: facilitating their participation, connection, formation of online brand communities, and production of user-generated content. As a result, how brands and customers are managed and how sales and marketing communication is conducted have undergone massive change.[15] Marketing

influencers Third-party endorsers who have built relationships and earned trust with specific audiences or communities and who shape audience attitudes through tweets, blog entries, and other social media postings.

messages that are circulated in social media environments have been compared to balls in pinball games that encounter various obstacles, namely consumers who may help or hinder a message.[16] Online brand communities can co-create a brand and add value to it,[17] influencing brand decisions by encouraging a sale or acting as detractors through negative word-of-mouth. With advantages such as campaign-automation and advanced analytics for targeting consumers, digital marketing has exploded in popularity. It takes many forms:

- explainer videos describing a product or service,
- social media promotions,
- Search engine optimization (SEO),
- optimized articles,
- mail newsletters featuring exclusive offers.[18]

Forbes claims that digital marketing is no longer about products, but about "buying a better version of yourself . . . and about self-initiated communities, word-of-mouth trust, micro-influencers, branding through human stories, and messaging that stands for something."[19] Traditional offline marketing (through direct mail, billboard and print ads, radio and television commercials, and telemarketing) has its place. It can still drive results often by amplifying digital marketing through integrated, multi-channel campaigns. The choice between traditional and digital marketing methods depends on where your customers spend their time and consideration of each method's benefits:

TABLE 9.1 The benefits of traditional and digital marketing methods

Traditional/Offline	Digital
Resonates with older audiences	Advanced targeting and automation
Event-marketing allows for in-person and real-time engagement to build brand awareness	Enables instant interactivity
Proven success rate	Produces measurable results
	Delivers better return on investment (ROI)
	Increases brand loyalty
	Drives online sales[20]

Promotion and Self-Promotion in Social Media

"Promotion" is another way of thinking about persuasion in professional settings.[21] What we now promote through social media are not simply brands or services, but also ourselves, through strategic self-branding. The way that we persuade is increasingly subtler and more implicit, persuading without seeming to persuade. A big part of this is strategic marketing approach known as digital content marketing (DCM), which involves creating, distributing and sharing relevant, compelling and timely content to attract and engage a clearly defined group of customers when they are considering a purchase, keeping them engaged, and converting their interest to sales.[22] DCM content can be distributed through a variety of online platforms, including brand websites, podcasts, webinars, blogs, social media, and e-mail. DCM best practices include the following:

- Establish goals for your content marketing: to create brand awareness, build engagement, convert interest to sales, or promote community and interaction among audience members
- Identify your audience: who can your content help or benefit?
- Develop a unique and compelling brand story
- Create desirable quality informative content about your product or service and keep it fresh by constantly updating it to make it relevant, salient, inspire social media shares, and attract and engage your audience. Opt for innovative choices and multimodal content (e.g. videos, podcasts) to appeal to a wider audience and consider preparing your content for voice search to make it more accessible.[23]
- Interact and listen by using platforms that enable dyadic, two-way communication and feedback and facilitate real-time conversation with customers. Identify and celebrate brand champions who voluntary support the brand concept[24] and value them their ability to broadcast the brand.
- For business-to-business interactions, show knowledge, helpfulness, and the ability to solve problems.[25]

The content that companies create themselves is generally better perceived than sponsored content and more controllable than user-generated content. Amazon founder Jeff Bezos is noted as saying "your brand is what people say about you when you aren't in the room."[26] In the new digital and reputation economies, self-branding, or what Tom Peter has called "the brand called you," is part of employment at all levels in all industries, including for creatives, entrepreneurs, job-seekers, and contract and gig workers.[27] Strategic self-promotion involves managing impressions and adapting your self-presentation to each social platform and creating authentic, business-targeted and context-specific self-brands by

- creating a professional profile that builds trust and speaks to your work's impact,
- curating content and updating it frequently,
- interacting with colleagues and clients.[28]

Checklist

Chapter Review

- ☐ Have you begun your message by capturing the reader's interest? Have you made the message immediately relevant to the reader's concerns? Have you put the request in a positive light? Have you provided enough incentive for the reader to read on?
- ☐ Have you chosen the right appeal or persuasive strategy to help you connect with your reader? Is the persuasive strategy an ethical one your company condones?
- ☐ Have you overcome the reader's resistance?
- ☐ Have you built credibility with your audience?
- ☐ Have you justified the request with a clear explanation of its reasons, details, and benefits?
- ☐ Have you inspired the reader to act? When necessary, have you provided incentive for the reader to act promptly? Have you provided sufficient information so that the reader will know what to do next?

Exercises, Workshops, and Discussion Forums

1. **Identifying Types of Appeals.** Note the ads that appear on your social media feeds or websites that you visit. What types of products are advertised on each platform? What types of appeals are used in each case? What, if any, connection exists between the platform, type of product, and the appeal that is used?

2. **Analyzing a Sales Message.** Using the effective sales messages checklist on pages 310–11 as a guide, analyze the strengths and weaknesses of a sales message you or a friend received recently. Did the message grab your attention? Did it make you want to buy the product? Why or why not?

3. **Analyzing Fundraising Appeals.** Fundraisers use a variety of appeals to motivate potential donors. In a small group, review each of the following fundraising appeals and identify the appeals being used.

   a) **@charity:** water: Giving shouldn't be scary. We believe your impact should be as transparent as the ghost at your door asking for candy, which is why we prove each project with photos and GPS coordinates—44,007 projects and counting! See all of them here: https://www.charitywater.org/our-projects/completed-projects...

   b) **@sickkids:** Weekend plans? We're gaming for 25 hours STRAIGHT with @ExtraLife4Kids & @ExtraLifeTO! 🎮🕹 Join us on Saturday, November 2nd - Sunday, November 3rd for 25 hours of family friendly gaming fun—donations support top-priority needs at SickKids. More info ➡ https://www.facebook.com/events/2460199977598715/...

   c) **Save the Children:** For the past seven years, a Syrian child refugee has no place to call home. This child lives in constant fear, uncertainty and instability. Where will the next meal come from? Where will they sleep? Where will they live? And worst of all, what if loved ones are lost and a child is left all alone? For this child, basics like going to school, reading and playing are distant memories and the future is a dream.
   Save the Children is doing whatever it takes to ensure every child has a place to call home, a childhood and a future to believe in. Join us. Start a Fundraiser.

   a) Does the charity present logical arguments? What types of evidence are used? What types of evidence help the charity present its cause and its case most strongly?

   b) Are emotional appeals used? Does the emotional appeal strengthen or weaken the charity's case for support?

   c) How does the charity establish credibility?

   d) How does the website present information: by text, image, and/or sound?

   e) Which website is most persuasive? If you had $100 to donate, how much would you give to each charity? How much do you identify with each cause?

4. **Evaluating Fundraising Appeals.** As a group, collect three or four fundraising messages you have received and compare the types of appeals and approaches they use. Evaluate opening and closing statements and decide if each message has provided you with enough information to encourage you to make a donation. Write a brief report on your analysis of the letters, e-mails, texts, or social media posts.

5. **Refreshing a Fundraising Campaign.** Many world humanitarian crises continue for months and even years. As memory of the precipitating crisis fades, donors may become uninterested in continued calls for donations, creating a challenge for fundraisers in keeping a cause relevant and urgent. For this small group activity, identify a humanitarian crisis and learn more about it and fundraising campaigns through a web search. Discuss how to reignite interest in the crisis and need for humanitarian aid through strategies such as expanding the audience for your fundraising appeals, using new or a mix of channels to reach those audiences, changing the type of appeal (logical/emotional), and using stories and visual

content to raise awareness and financial support in the form of donations. Provide a one-paragraph summary of your brainstorming points or plan.

6. **Comparing Social Media Influencers: Persuasion in Practice.** Form a small group, and ask each member to identify (i) a prominent social media influencer, (ii) the archetype associated with that influencer (e.g., teacher, coach, entertainer, charismatic), and (iii) the brand(s), organization(s), or cause(s) associated with that influencer. As a group, discuss the source of each influencer's appeal and the means that person uses to exert influence over her or his followers to persuade them as individuals and consumers.

7. **Exploring Social Marketing Plan.** Social marketing involves the use of commercial marketing strategies to try to address and solve health and social problems for social change. In a small group, share your ideas for new solutions to a health problem or social problem (e.g., campus food insecurity) and develop a one-paragraph outline for a campaign that includes the issue, how you plan to bring about change, and the strategies and channels (such as social media) you would use.

8. **Analyzing Persuasion on Kickstarter.** Kickstarter is a crowdfunding platform that helps bring creative projects to life by seeking backers through tailored persuasive appeals. Go to Kickstarter Canada and select a project. Review the project page and take an inventory of the content elements you find there. How does the project campaign it persuade you visually? What role does storytelling play in presenting the project and pitch-making? Consider how the elements work together to persuade you. Prepare a brief one-paragraph summary of your findings and share it with the rest of the class. What elements and characteristics contribute to a persuasive Kickstarter campaign?

www.kickstarter.com/discover/countries/CA

9. **Creating and Presenting a Kickstarter Campaign.** For this activity, work with a small group (3–5 people) to create two basic elements of a persuasive Kickstarter campaign. Imagine that you and your team are launching a small arts-based project in your community or a creative project with wider distribution for which you require funding from backers on Kickstarter. Start with an idea for an eligible project (art, comics, crafts, dance, design, fashion, film & video, food, games, journalism, music, photography, publishing, technology, and theatre). Draft a one- or two-paragraph story about your project (who you are, what you are planning to make, where they idea came from, what your budget is, and why you are passionate about your project, and why others should care). Drawing from a bank of copyright-free images (such as Pixabay), select "strong" imagery linked to your project that will persuade visually. Present your campaign to your classmates (sharing your story and screening images) and ask each person to back your campaign (identifying the amount on a paper slip or via your class discussion board). Calculate the total amount pledged to your campaign and ask your classmates for feedback on its persuasiveness and their motivation to support your project.

Kickstarter Creator Handbook
www.kickstarter.com/help/handbook

Kickstarter Rules
www.kickstarter.com/rules

Kickstarter Story
www.kickstarter.com/help/handbook/your_story?ref=handbook_started

Pixabay
https://pixabay.com

10. **Making a Pitch with Persuasive Storytelling.** For this activity inspired by the research of Jennifer Aaker, a ground-breaking professor of marketing research at Stanford's Graduate School of Business, form a small group in which each member will develop a one-minute pitch for a product or service of their choice.[29] Half of the group members will use facts and figures in making their pitch. The other half of the group will use stories. Take 10 minutes to research and write your pitch, leaving an additional 5 minutes to deliver the pitches. After all group members have been heard from, invite them to write down what they remembered about each pitch. Discuss the elements of each pitch that were most memorable and to draw conclusions about whether facts and figures or stories are most memorable. How could you use both data and story in your pitch to make it more effective?

Writing Improvement Exercises

1. **Analyzing Subject Lines.** Identify the most persuasive subject line.
   a) Subject: Donations Required
      Subject: Can You Spare $10 for a Good Cause?
      Subject: Meeting Our Target for the United Way Campaign
   b) Subject: Suggestion
      Subject: Improving Security with Better Passwords
      Subject: Have You Changed Your Password Lately?
   c) Subject: Reducing Absenteeism and Low Morale
      Subject: On-Site Fitness Centre Required
      Subject: Couldn't You Use Some Time on a Treadmill?

2. **Analyzing Persuasive Openings.** How persuasive are the following openings?

   a) **Favour request:** With the support of businesses like your own, Project Outreach has counselled over 2,500 at-risk high-school students and helped them realize their dreams of post-secondary education.
   b) **Collection letter:** You owe us $5,048.00—so pay up!
   c) **Sales e-mail:** Lead your employees to excellence by attending this transformative one-day leadership conference. Learn the empathetic and innovative strategies of 10 world-renowned leaders. Register now for Leaders at Heart.
   d) **Sales letter:** For a limited time only, get a transatlantic flight for free when you purchase a Mediterranean cruise.

3. **Writing Clear and Concrete Descriptions.** Revise each of the following product descriptions from sales letters by making the language more positive, concrete, appealing to the senses, and reader-focused.

   a) Our chocolate products, which sell for as little as $15 a box, are made from fair trade cocoa imported from Ecuador and they taste good.
   b) Our Wind-Turbo Vacuum runs 20 minutes on a single charge.

   c) We think discerning customers, like you, will be pleasantly surprised by the luxurious selection of imported linens on which we pride ourselves.

4. **Citing Benefits.** For each requested action, cite one or more potential benefits.

   a) Call us today and for just $9.99 a month you can enjoy a smart home monitoring system.
   b) Please give me authorization to purchase handheld scanners for each of our 20 project team members.
   c) Use code GTWAY to book a mid-winter break in Barbados for as little as $899.
   d) Visit us soon at one of our five convenient Calgary-area locations to book your mid-winter getaway to sunny Barbados for as little as $899 a week.

5. **Analyzing Persuasive Closings.** Do the following action closings motivate readers to act quickly? Is the action made clear and easy in each case?

   a) **Favour request:** We really must have our list of speakers finalized, so try to respond by July 3, if not sooner.
   b) **Claim request:** If I don't hear from you by May 15, I will assume you have rejected my claim, and I will have no alternative but to seek legal action.
   c) **Sales letter:** Unless you act quickly, you'll be out of luck and won't qualify for the 10 per cent discount.
   d) **Sales letter:** I cannot urge you strongly enough to place an order now by calling 1-800-625-8771 and, when prompted, asking for Donald. To qualify for a 5 per cent discount, you must quote this reference number: 9312866B. Discounts do not apply to all products. For a list of exclusions, please see our website: www.easy_order.com.

6. **Making a Sale with Persuasive Appeals.** Imagine that you are part-owner of a small company that manufactures and sells a sustainably produced, quality-tested, Canadian-made high-performance

athletic shoe. You realize that the market is already saturated with consumer-favourites, most of which have instant brand recognition and come with endorsements from NBA players, but you believe your shoe is different. Your shoes are priced-competitively at $159 and have endorsements from top sports medicine professionals and a famous rapper (a recent convert to your brand). Additionally, your shoes are adaptable to each buyer's exact needs through custom-made orthotics created with 3D-printing technology. You now have pop-up shops in three major Canadian cities where prospective buyers can try-out a pair and be fitted for their orthotics. You offer a full money-back guarantee with a 30-day return. Create a pitch for your company by developing and using logical, emotional, and ethics appeals.

Case Study Exercises

1. **Persuasive Invitation Request.** Taking several Indigenous Studies courses has led you to volunteer for the organizing subcommittee for a two-day PowWow and Education Week hosted at your college's Centre for Indigenous Research and Creation. The PowWow has $20,000 in financial support from an Indigenous Arts and Culture grant. The programming you and the subcommittee of volunteers has planned for Education Week involves an Indigenous walking tour, an Indigenous medicine teachings workshop, an Indigenous treaty panel, a PowWow fitness class, and an Indigenous food practices and food sovereignty workshop (which the subcommittee hopes will include small-plate catering and a food education seminar). You have been asked to draft an invitation to chef Johl Whiteduck Ringuette of NishDish Marketeria and Catering, a business built on traditional Anishnawbe food (www.nishdish.com/) and food sovereignty education. The menu must cater to different appetites and dietary needs, including vegan and gluten-free dishes and game meats. A similar event last year had 40 attendees, but due to its popularity, you are expecting an even higher enrolment of 60 at your event. The budget for this event is generous but with 60 attendees, cost is a consideration. Because the organizing subcommittee envisioned this event taking place on Friday afternoon (12 pm–2 pm) of Education Week (held in the final week of March), when Chef Ringuette's Marketeria is open, you are hesitant to insist on that date and have asked the subcommittee to grant some flexibility in scheduling it earlier in the week. Your college's conference centre has full catering facilities for re-heating and food staging. Write to Chef Ringuette inviting him to lead and cater this important event.

2. **Favour Request.** Your aerospace company has recently responded to a request from Project Protégé, an educational mentorship program designed to help promising high-school students at risk of dropping out. Because you hire only college or university graduates and give preference to those with post-graduate degrees, you understand the importance of keeping teenagers in school. You would like your company to participate, but you realize this will require three volunteers from your firm to give up an entire Saturday to speak with students about career opportunities in the industry. As far as you know, mentors will receive no fee but will be invited to a year-end banquet in return for donating their time and services. Write a memo to staff, asking for their help.

3. **Persuasive Memo.** Identify a problem in need of a solution or a situation in need of improvement in your school or place of employment. Write a well-researched memo, identifying the benefits of what you propose and making a compelling case for change.

4. **Persuasive E-mail.** You are the manager of operations at Cancorant, a resource-management and consulting company based out of Ottawa. Your company employees a staff of over 100 and of them 75 travel frequently for business both within and outside of Canada. This travel often takes the form of transatlantic, North American, and domestic flights and long-distance road trips to remote locations. There is a high concentration of travel in the Windsor–Quebec City corridor. At meetings, conversations about your company's CO_2 emissions have become more frequent and

serious, so much so that you commissioned an analysis of your company's carbon footprint. You discover that your company's travel program is the source of 50 per cent of your company's entire CO_2 emissions. Based on this research and further consultations, management has voted unanimously to support a series of strict new measures to curb emissions by 40% by 2024. You know these measures will be expensive (funnelling funds away from other projects) and unpopular (due to substantial increases in travel time), but the alternative is facing public scrutiny and living with the uncomfortable knowledge of your company's outsized contribution to climate change. Among the planned changes are replacing one-day trips with virtual meetings and webinars, switching to off-peak road travel in a greener fleet of eco-friendly hybrid vehicles, opting for train travel over air travel when possible, and booking only accommodation pledged to water and energy conservation. A fee will also be levied on departments that exceed emission targets. You know you may need to do further research to provide a compelling picture of related benefits. This initiative will require you to write a series of related messages:

a) Write a persuasive memo to all staff encouraging their buy-in to this new proposal.

b) Prepare a brief one- or two-paragraph summary for use on your corporate website's Corporate Social Responsibility and Sustainability page that highlights this initiative and persuades the general public, customers, and shareholders of Cancorant's commitment to fighting climate change through reduction of the company's carbon footprint.

c) For additional background, refer to Chapter 14, then prepare engaging social media content (e.g. one-three tweets) that build corporate legitimacy and create a persuasively positive impression of the initiatives and their impact.

5. **Persuasive E-mail.** You work for a noted Canadian fashion retailer, Maison Nord, with destination stores in major cities across the country. In addition to stocking, promoting, and merchandising Canadian and international luxury brands, your company, as a signatory of the G7 Fashion Pact pledging to improve sustainability standards across the retail industry, has recently undertaken a partial rebranding to promote and sell mid-priced sustainable fashion, new labels from global street-inspired fashion startups, and fashion from a growing number of Indigenous designers. This initiative is a positive step forward, but it has fallen short. In your work as an assistant marketing and communications coordinator, you share responsibility for Maison Nord's social media management and the production of its ad copy, in-store promotions, fashion shows, and promotional events. You are also responsible for the production of a printed, wide-circulation catalogue included as an insert in a national newspaper. You report to the manager of marketing and communications who has worked effectively for more than 15 years with the same reliable photographers and talent from a well-regarded modelling agency. The problem is that Maison Nord's social channels, catalogue, and the models—the overall visual representation of the brand—come nowhere near to reflecting current Canadian diversity. An Indigenous model whom you worked with in your previous job complained, "if we look at the fashion industry beyond Native fashion, it's still white-dominated and Euro-centric. It's incredibly inaccessible. To some extent, this inaccessibility is probably what makes fashion so fascinating to so many people, but problems arise when we think about the lasting effects."[30] At the other extreme you are wary that a drive for diversity can also bring charges of tokenism and commodification or representing of diverse, non-Western fashion as a passing trend. These are missteps Maison Nord should avoid at all costs. You have researched several modelling agencies with pools of experienced Indigenous models and are in a position to recommend two of them: Write to your manager Manon Albright and make a case to her for hiring diverse models, including Indigenous models, and seeking further consultation to bring to Maison Nord an approach to fashion informed by Indigeneity.

6. **Claim Request.** As co-owner of a small graphics design firm, you recently hosted a one-day

business retreat for all staff at the Ocean View Inn, a conference facility you have long counted on for its excellent catering and technical services. One month in advance, you made an $800 deposit on the room booking and catering costs. The remainder of the total $4,000 cost (which includes all applicable taxes) was to be paid after the event. The retreat was a success, but you were surprised when you received a new invoice for $3,550. The additional charges were for a $100 user's fee and a $250 booking fee. You feel that these charges, because they were not part of the original agreement, are either unwarranted or erroneous. The Ocean View Inn, you have just discovered, is under new management, which may account for the discrepancies. Write to manager Kaleigh Smith, requesting an adjustment.

7. **Collection Letter Series.** You are the owner of a general contracting business that undertook extensive renovations on a property owned by Arnold Levitt. Work valued at $17,000 was completed on schedule three months ago, and the property subsequently passed inspection. Because Mr. Levitt has always paid you on time for all previous contracts, you are somewhat surprised that all but the original $1,700 deposit remains unpaid. There is some urgency to your request for payment because you must settle your own accounts with electrical and plumbing subcontractors who worked for you on the project. Mr. Levitt travels frequently, so you have been unable to reach him by phone. Your voicemail messages have gone unanswered. Write a collection series.

8. **Sales Letter.** As owner of Swiftcycle Courier Services, write a sales message to prospective customer Florian Heinz, president of Frontier Equity Mutual. Your ten-year-old company provides bicycle courier services at highly competitive rates to a large number of businesses, including six other tenants of First Canadian Place in downtown Toronto's financial district, where the head office of Frontier Equity Mutual is located. For the next three months, you are offering an introductory special to new clients, which entitles them to a 15 per cent discount on all envelope and small-package courier services. Your radio-dispatched delivery personnel are fully bonded and are experts at time-critical delivery. Online ordering is also one of the services you offer. Size up your prospect, then write a letter to Florian Heinz. (Make up any additional details you require.)

Online Activities

1. **Identifying Logical Fallacies.** The following interactive website defines 24 types of logical fallacies. Hold your cursor over each icon to pull up a definition, then write a sentence that exemplifies the logical flaw. Where have you seen a similar type of logical fallacy? How could it be harmful to the logic of a persuasive appeal?

    https://yourlogicalfallacyis.com/

2. **Analyzing Persuasion through Social Media and E-mail Brand Engagement.** For this activity, revisit a social media brand post or retrieve a brand promotion e-mail from your inbox.

a) What is its purpose (to engage you and build connection or to entice you to buy a product)?

b) What types of appeals, if any, are used (logical, emotional, ethical)? Provide an example of the appeal(s) that are used.

c) Which of the following strategies discussed on page 312 are used: ❑ Reciprocity ❑ Liking ❑ Authority ❑ Commitment ❑ Scarcity ❑ Social Proof ❑ Unity?

d) How does the post persuade you (textually, visually)? How much of the message is anchored in the text?

10 Communicating for Employment

Chapter Preview

Communicating for employment involves a targeted application of persuasive skills with the aim of showcasing your qualifications and accomplishments according to how they meet the needs of a prospective employer. This chapter offers a roadmap to the job application process, beginning with the identification of career objectives and competencies through self-analysis. You'll discover traditional, social media, and AI resources for networking, carrying out a job search, and applying for positions. You'll be introduced to a variety of options for designing a resumé and ensuring your resumé leads to an interview. Finally, you'll learn how to prepare for a job interview and what types of questions to expect.

iStock.com/AndreyPopov

Case Study

Natee Meepian/Shutterstock.com

Most recruiters today recognize that posting job notices on social media sites such as LinkedIn, Twitter, and Facebook is an effective way to reach a diverse range of smart, qualified, tech-savvy candidates. Many also use social media to investigate potential recruits and to arrange interviews with applicants.

Effective interpersonal communication, networking and relationship building are key to a successful job search, job fit, and satisfying employment. Brenda LaRose, founder of Higgins Executive Search specializing in the recruitment of Indigenous professionals for board-level positions, recounts an experience that proves keeping lines of communication open can ultimately change lives by enabling well-qualified professionals to seize opportunities. LaRose had been referred to a First Nations chartered account who at that time was working in Japan for a top international accounting firm. LaRose approached her contact, who wasn't interested in the certified public accounting role she was working on but indicated he would change jobs if the right position became available in Vancouver. LaRose and her employment prospect stayed in touch for the greater part of a decade, sending occasional e-mails to each other. "Then all of a sudden a position became available which was exactly what he wanted. I reached out to him," recalls LaRose. "The company initially interviewed him by Skype and flew him out to Vancouver and interviewed him again. He got the job. Just as he accepted the role, the accounting firm he had been working for in Japan went out of business, so he would have lost his job anyway." LaRose and the successful hire stayed in touch, a practice LaRose extends to the many candidates she has placed over the years. "They give us referrals, they refer candidates to us, they hire because they're running companies and they need senior people on their team," reflects LaRose. "It's all about communication. If we didn't communicate we wouldn't do well in business."[1]

The mission to reach Indigenous talent and attract them to company employment opportunities is behind RBC'c Purse Your Potential (PyP)—Indigenous Persons program.[2] Similar to its PyP—Persons with Disabilities program, it is voluntary and complimentary to applying for a role in the company and aimed at helping Indigenous Peoples build successful careers. Being successful in a job search is a process that requires a cluster of complementary and interrelated skills: research, analysis, organization, oral and written communication, persuasion, and, increasingly, social networking. While maintaining an engaged and professional presence on social media can help you attract the attention of recruiters, posts, or comments that show you in a negative light could attract the wrong kind of attention, and even jeopardize future employment.

Employers' use of social media to collect information on current or prospective employees is a new, and somewhat grey, legal area—Newfoundland and Labrador's privacy commissioner, Donovan Molloy, recently advised employers not to include social media accounts in a prospective employee's background check without their explicit consent.[3] However, as companies increasingly turn to social media as a recruitment tool, job seekers should be mindful of how their accounts may appear to prospective employers. In this chapter, you'll find tips on how to develop an online presence that will showcase your expertise and professionalism for future employers.

Analyzing Your Career Goals and Qualifications

Finding a job you can grow and succeed in starts with knowing your values, goals, preferences, qualifications, and competencies. The term *competency* describes the ongoing development of integrated knowledge, skills, attitudes, and behaviours required to perform work successfully. Competencies are measurable and observable and relate to work and work experience; therefore, they are important in evaluating performance.[4] Some professional stock-taking and personal soul-searching can guide you to the right career path. Self-assessment involves considering what you enjoy doing, identifying personality traits that apply to your work style, and learning from earlier work experiences. Answering questions in the following categories can help you decide what type of work is best for you.

Assessing Your Skills and Values

- Who are you? What are your values, interests, and marketable skills?
- What drew you to your program of study?
- What are you good at? What are you most interested in doing?
- Are you willing to acquire new skills or retrain for the sake of advancement?
- Where, realistically, do you see yourself in five or ten years?
- What trade-offs are you willing to make for job satisfaction? Do you live to work or work to live?

Assessing Your Work Preferences and Personality

- Are you an introvert or an extrovert?
- Do you prefer to work in a large organization with a big hierarchy or a more informal, small one?
- Do you enjoy working with people, materials, ideas, or data?
- Do you best succeed when working in a group or alone?
- Do you prefer to take a leading role or a supporting one? How much freedom do you need?
- Do you appreciate and apply feedback?

- Do you like work that is fast-paced or slow-paced? What type of work do you find most interesting?
- Are you looking for challenges and risks, even if they make your job less secure?
- Would you rather be a specialist or a generalist?
- What do you want from your job in terms of rewards?

Assessing Your Work History

- What accomplishments are you most proud of?
- What is the best praise you've received for your work? Why is that praise meaningful to you?
- What work tasks, experiences, and relationships have you found most satisfying?
- What work experiences have you most disliked?
- How well do you communicate and learn on the job?
- What hard and soft skills can you offer a prospective employer?

Enter into the job search and application process with clear thought not only to your qualifications and past employment but also to your competencies and "soft skills" and how you can demonstrate and prove them through the following means:

- approach to work (including flexibility and resourcefulness)
- knowledge and quality of work
- organization and time/task management
- client service orientation and social sensitivity
- communication and interpersonal skills
- leadership, team work, and team skills
- analytical thinking/problem-solving/decision-making
- result achievements and ability to cope with responsibility
- professional development and interest in lifelong learning[5]

Look for a position that allows you to play to your strengths and develop skills in a career area that fits your personality and qualifications. Be prepared to change jobs every few years to learn from experience—Canadians change jobs four to five times in their lives—and adapt to fluctuations in the job market and economy by building your marketable skills.[6]

Job-Hunting

Very few job offers materialize as if by magic. Job-hunting requires time, effort, and perseverance. The more information you have about employment opportunities, the greater your chance of getting the job you want. A successful search campaign begins with the following steps:

- studying the job market (by gathering information from published articles, blogs, other social media sources, career services offices, instructors and mentors, and job fairs)
- building professional networks that can be a source of information and insight (by joining professional associations or groups, volunteering, or interning)

- identifying sources of employment (by paying attention to channels and platforms including print, web, social media, and personal word-of-mouth communication)
- learning about the organizations you would most like to work for (by reading industry and trade publications, corporate and CEO blogs, and company websites, or by following or liking companies of interest on social media)
- establishing an online presence to build your professional brand
- matching your skills and training to the most suitable positions

The automation of talent acquisition, predictive hiring algorithms, and the use of artificial intelligence and "smart" e-recruitment technologies are changing the ways jobs are advertised and filled, altering human tasks in the process of acquiring talent.[7] A job search can involve several different types of activities and technologies, many of which are rapidly evolving and redefining the job-search landscape. Adapting to new recruitment and application technologies is key.[8] To get results from this process, follow these steps:

1. **Tap into the full potential of social media.** A growing trend among job-seekers is looking for employment opportunities through social media platforms such as LinkedIn, Twitter, Facebook, Google+, Pinterest, Instagram, Tumblr, and blogs. Deciding which sites to use depends on where members of your industry engage online and which sites are most compatible with your personal brand. For example, LinkedIn is popular with marketing professionals, while Instagram and Pinterest have a natural alignment with visual artists and graphic designers.[9] (For more on using social media in your job search, see the next section.)

2. **Master electronic job-search techniques.** Employers often post positions on general job-bank websites (such as Indeed and Workopolis), niche or industry-specific job sites (such as Idealist.org for non-profit job opportunities), and their own company websites. Most job-bank websites allow you to post your resumé online, browse through thousands of ads by occupation or geographic area, and set up alerts that will notify you when a new job listing in your area of interest has been posted. A 2019 Glassdoor survey found that 58 per cent of Glassdoor users, from every labour market sector, search for jobs on their mobile devices, though desk jobs attract fewer mobile seekers.[10] Applying via mobile devices is not without its challenges, many having to do with poor mobile experience: application difficulty may be higher, it may take longer to apply on mobile devices, and lower-income jobs may have more difficult applications. Employers continue to build more mobile-friendly features into the application process, but for now a few best practices can make applying by mobile more efficient:

   - Save the job and apply by computer
   - Save your resume to your phone or to the Cloud to access it quickly when you need to apply
   - Leverage integrated application methods (e.g., Glassdoor's Easy Apply) to access materials you have used for previous applications[11]

3. **Read the career pages, classified ads, and financial sections of newspapers, trade and professional journals, and business magazines.** To monitor these publications for free, check out the periodical section of your local or school library. Join professional and trade associations that will send you regular

TABLE 10.1 Select Online Job Banks, Aggregators, and Career Resources

WEBSITE	DESCRIPTION
CanadianCareers.com	This site provides information on all facets of careers and employment, including internships for Canadians under 30.
CareerBuilder.ca	This site allows you to search and apply for jobs across Canada.
Eluta.ca	This site lists new job announcements posted on employers' websites across Canada.
Indeed.ca	This aggregator site allows you to search job sites, newspapers, associations, and company career pages.
Jobpostings.ca	This site is Canada's largest student job network, especially helpful for finding internships and co-ops.
Monster.ca	This popular site offers thousands of job listings and a full range of interactive career tools, including advice on resumés and cover letters, job-hunt strategies, salaries and benefits, and career development.
Job Bank (jobbank.gc.ca)	This site allows you to search by occupation and location, explore careers, and investigate trends in the job market.
Government of Canada Jobs (canada.ca/en/services/jobs/opportunities/government.html)	This site allows you to search for federal public service jobs across Canada.
SimplyHired.ca	This popular site allows you to search for job opportunities across Canada.
Workopolis.com	This site allows you to search jobs by keywords, location, date of posting, and job category and to access articles and advice. Registration is not required to search the jobs, but you can register for free to save searches and set up a career-alert e-mail service.

listings of job openings. Read articles on expanding companies and business sectors to help you to predict where new jobs will be created. Specialized newsletters for job-seekers in specific industries—such as the MaRS Startup Career Newsletter, which focuses on tech startups—can identify and delivery harder-to-find opportunities to your inbox.[12]

4. **Learn to decode job advertisements.** Job ads are packed with information such as job title and position status (full-time, part-time), position number, salary and benefits, qualifications and job duties, company image, mission and domain, company initiatives and growth potential, and opportunities for employee learning and development.[13] The ad may also provide subtler hints through its phrasing about expectations and what is it looking for from a successful candidate:

- "Demonstrated" and "commitment to" are words that imply the need for evidence of accomplishments in a resume or an example or amplification in a cover letter.
- "Potential for" may be more difficult to prove but requires reflection on your skills and commitment to professional development.
- "Preferred" applies to qualifications that are most important for a candidate to have.[14]
- Read the ad carefully, paying close attention to key phrases and keywords and incorporating the exact same keywords in exactly the same way in your resume

and cover letter. Note special instructions for applications, including deadlines to apply, and criteria, such as number of years of experience, certification requirements, or location, that can put you into or out of contention for a job.

- An ad's tone can be a clue to organizational culture (informal startup vs. established company).

For all the details an ad provides about a vacancy, it may still be unclear what it is like to work for the company and whether its work environment, culture, and values are what you prefer and whether the requirements of the job are realistic. A company's social media pages and website (including CSR and annual reports) can reveal more about a company's health, initiatives, commitment to sustainability, corporate citizenship, and how it treats its employees and customers. News stories (searchable online) and word-of-mouth including peer-review sites such as Glassdoor that feature job satisfaction reviews are sources for checking that the company is reputable and has good growth prospects.

5. **Assess Job and Organization Fit.** Are you right for a job and company and are the job and company right for you? Career commitment, job performance, and job satisfaction can depend on matching values—yours and those of a prospective employer.[15] Person-organization fit is a matter of compatibility between a job-seeker and an organization based on shared characteristics and how they meet each other's needs. Factors that figure in person-organization fit include:

- organizational justice: perceptions of fairness in the treatment of employees
- organization-wide job characteristics
- the psychological contract: how organization regulate activities
- intrinsic motivation
- rewards
- leadership
- working relationship quality[16]

Person-job fit refers to the match between a person's abilities and the demands of a job.[17] These congruences between an individual and their work environment influence involvement and career commitment.[18] Fit with organizational culture is a primary focus in job interviews.[19] Companies such as Google and Marriott Hotel have experimented with gamification (MyMarriottHotel) to immerse would-be applicants in the culture of the organization.[20] Assessing person-job fit helps you decide whether to apply; the references named in your resume who vouch for you in your application (former employers, community-and-volunteer-project supervisors, teachers and academic advisors, and colleagues) will assess the same question of your person-job fit as will screeners, so target vacancies with the closest fit.

6. **Learn to network.** Networking is an essential business tool that involves meeting new contacts and cultivating relationships that could lead to professional success. Become involved in community and volunteer activities and attend networking events or professional conferences regularly. Get involved in mentorship programs and professionally-related societies offered by your college or university. Join professional societies linked to your career focus once your credentials enable you to do so. Conduct online networking through professionally-related Facebook groups and Eventbrite career networking. Don't be afraid to ask your personal and professional contacts for advice, especially people who are knowledgeable about

your field. For tech startup jobs, get to know startup recruiters and attend startup connectors like the one Toronto innovation hub MaRS hosts, Startup Open House, that connects prospects with startups actively seeking employees.[21] Here are some additional strategies to enhance your networking effectiveness:

- **Networking business cards and post-event communication.** Printed business cards have waned in popularity but remain a quick and inexpensive way to exchange contact information with "old school" audiences, provided cards are not shared indiscriminately. Have a supply of well-formatted good-quality business cards on hand that include your name, credentials, contact details, LinkedIn profile, website or portfolio link information, and, optionally on the front or reverse, a tagline that summarizes what you bring to a company or a list of three-five skills that define what you do. After a networking event, use a business card scanner app and your smartphone's camera to save contacts to your phone or a secure server (but make privacy and the security of your contact list a priority). Follow up during or after the event by sending lead contacts a brief message, connecting via LinkedIn, or following each other on social media; however, make sure new contacts are comfortable with and okay requests to connect via Facebook or Instagram.[22] It is useful to also create a digital business card.

- **Elevator pitches.** Elevator pitches are high-stakes 30-second sound bites for impression management that introduce you and your value proposition to prospective employers and influential contacts. Although a pitch is a prepared statement, it should sound authentic and spontaneous, never canned. Delivering it takes roughly the time of an average elevator ride, so it is important to get to the point. As a job seeker meeting employers for the first time, introduce yourself, identify your school, degree focus and when you will graduate, highlight skills unique to your value proposition, career goals, and the qualifications that will help you achieve them. Despite the formulaic quality of a pitch, you can be more or less creative depending on the industry you work in and the nature of the work you seek.

  > *Hi, my name is Mitra Bismilla and I'm graduating from Hudson University this spring with a Bachelor of Science in Environmental Management. I've just completed a three-month Climate Positive Development program internship here in the GTA. I'm committed to using my expertise in soil reclamation to help communities and development corporations reuse and redevelop industrial lands.*

- **Informational interviews.** Informational interviews are an important networking tool. Talking to knowledgeable people such as recruiters and professionals engaged in the work you hope to do can yield valuable insights on career paths and open the door to internships and other opportunities. Set up an interview by stating your purpose (why you are reaching out and how you identified the person you are reaching out to), suggesting a date, time, and location (ideally the professional's place of work) for the interview and specifying the length of time for your conversation and what career or work aspects you would like to ask about. The questions you ask are not aimed at getting employment, but at finding out about the industry's work culture, tasks, and responsibilities involved in the job; what to expect of an entry-level position and up the career ladder; and the education level, contacts, and resources you need to be successful. An interview is never fully complete until you have sent note of thanks.[23]

- **Optimize your online professional brand.** Anyone you meet while networking can research you online to confirm or re-evaluate the impressions they already have of you. What we do and say online fundamentally reflects perceptions of who we are, so HR and talent acquisition managers commonly use network data to screen and better understand attributes of applicants.[24] Find out what they can learn about you from your digital footprint (what you actively share through social media comments, Skype calls, and other online activity) and digital shadow (the information that is shared about you without your knowing about it).[25] Search yourself on Google and check your social media privacy settings to be certain that what you want to be private stays private. Keep your social media and online presence fresh with frequent and consistently-voiced content updates that get you favourably noticed in your online communities and earn you followers.

7. **Use the hidden job market. Only a small percentage of jobs are advertised**. To find out if a company might have an unadvertised job opening, you can write an unsolicited letter of application and send it to the company along with your resumé. You can also make **cold-call** inquiries to companies and set up informational interviews with individuals who are prepared to talk with you, even for a few minutes, about skill requirements, job duties, and hiring prospects. Have several specific questions in mind when you call so you won't waste the prospective employer's time. Another way to scout for unadvertised jobs is to sign up for interviews when company recruiters visit your school. Job recruitment fairs, including online ones, may also yield the big break you have been looking for.

8. **Visit career centres or employment agencies.** Take advantage of the job placement services at your college, university, or government **employment agencies** by registering early. Check out job notice boards and ask about counselling services offered by the centres.

9. **Think ahead.** Look into the possibility of getting a summer internship or co-op job while you are still a student. Non-salaried employment can help you gain valuable experience that gives you an edge once you graduate. Plan to devote as much time as you can to your job search and be persistent.

10. **Polish your interpersonal and communication skills.** Make sure your oral and written communication skills are first-rate. Your ability to communicate can make or break your first contact with a company.

cold call An unsolicited telephone call in which a job-seeker introduces himself or herself and asks about job openings.

employment agency An organization that matches job candidates with jobs, sometimes for a fee.

Using Social Media to Attract and Impress Potential Employers

Social media sites give you the opportunity to build social capital and network within communities to attract employers to you. Here are some tips to help you make the most of social media as you search for a job and build your career:

- **Create quality, business-oriented social profiles.** Make sure that all photos you include in your online profiles portray you in a positive, professional light and that your statements are well thought out, grammatically correct, and free of typos.

- **Get to be known as an expert.** Demonstrate knowledge of your chosen field and suggest how you might be a positive asset to a potential employer.
- **Show that you are a team player.** Emphasize your social connections and your ability to work well with others, and show yourself as "we" rather than "me" oriented.
- **Be engaged.** Network and connect with people in your professional community and sign up for subscriptions that show you are interested in keeping up with the latest developments in your field.

Using LinkedIn and Twitter to Establish an Online Presence

LinkedIn

Launched in 2002, LinkedIn was the first social media site to allow users "to create, manage and share their professional identities online."[26] LinkedIn helps businesses find you and, as a persuasive image-management tool, helps others see you as a leader and a desired employee.[27] Membership in LinkedIn groups can give you access to discussions with industry professionals outside your immediate network.

Create an attention-grabbing LinkedIn profile by following these steps and examples:

1. **Include a photo and preliminary information.** Upload a professionally taken headshot of yourself against a neutral background and looking business-ready (no selfies). Provide your name; a professional headline that can be a specific job title, your career goal or focus, or your current industry status; your geographic location, and your industry. According to Harvard University research, the headline is one of two core components of a LinkedIn profile.[28]
2. **Complete the intro section of your public profile.** This includes your name, location, a link to your contact info, and a headline. LinkedIn automatically fills in the headline with your current job and company, which it asks you to provide during signup. But you can edit your headline, so consider changing it to a brief statement that accurately and energetically describes who you are as a professional.

Tegan Shaw

Experienced professional communicator and team leader | Passionate about social media

Toronto, Ontario, Canada ● Contact info

3. **Make connections.** Search for people you know on LinkedIn and invite them to join your network. Make as many first-degree connections as possible in order to build a strong network.
4. **Provide details of your experience and education.** Your experience and education should be presented in much the same way as they would be in a standard resumé. You can also add specific skills to your profile, keywords that will highlight areas of expertise. Because these skills can be endorsed by your connections, make sure that the ones you choose are accurate.[29] Continuing with our example, here is what Tegan Shaw's more detailed profile looks like:

Experience

Associate Manager, Social Media Communications

TD Bank Group

November 2019–Present (2 years, 4 months) | Toronto, Ontario, Canada

Social Media Specialist

Tim Hortons Inc.

July 2018–November 2019 (1 year, 5 months) | Toronto, Ontario, Canada

Social Media Specialist

Canadian Tire Corporation, Limited

July 2017–July 2018 (1 year, 1 month) | Toronto, Ontario, Canada

Special Events Assistant

The Liberty Grand

November 2017–July 2017 (9 months) | Toronto, Ontario, Canada

Skills & Endorsements

Online Community Management

Digital Strategy

Social Media Marketing

Social Media Sponsorship Marketing

Media Relations

Corporate Communications

Marketing

Communications

Public Relations

Education

Western University

Bachelor of Arts, Media and Public Interest

2012–2016

Activities and Societies:

Vice-President, University Student's Council; Faculty of Information & Media Studies Students' Council; Students with Disability Commissioner; Theatre Western

Humber College

Graduate Certificate, Public Relations

2016–2017

Honours & Awards

Western University Students' Council

Leadership Award 2014

5. **Provide a thorough, compelling "About" summary.** Think of the "About" section as a commercial for yourself.[30] Demonstrate your expertise and include industry-related keywords. Consider including a note on what opportunities would interest you.

6. **Follow steps that will enable your profile to rank higher in search results.** Customize the public profile address that directly links to your full LinkedIn profile with your name. You can then add it to other documents, such as business cards, cover letters, resumés, and brochures. You can even include this custom URL in your e-mail signature.

7. **Enrich your profile with visual content.** LinkedIn supports visual content that can aid your professional storytelling. Upload a recent PowerPoint presentation or video that relates to your work, or add a link to a website with relevant visual content.

8. **Solicit endorsements and recommendations.** These can be drawn from a pool of individuals best positioned to judge your work accomplishments: co-workers, supervisors, and career mentors.[31]

9. **Update your profile to reflect fresh achievements and professional development.** Keep in mind that current employers may interpret frequent updates as a sign that you are looking for a new position. You can disable the "Share with Network" option so that your connections are not directly notified while you're making updates (just remember to turn it back on later).

Twitter

Twitter is another popular job-search tool. Think of your Twitter account as an online business card[32] and describe yourself in concrete terms, providing your professional title or area of expertise, company and/or industry, and a notable achievement or career aim (e.g., Social Media Youth Brand Marketer at Sport Chek). Use a professional headshot for your profile picture—not a cartoon or a selfie. Link to your blog or website, if you have one. Unless your hobbies relate directly to your career or soft skills, create separate profiles to showcase extensive extracurricular interests. To make your Twitter account stand out more and to align it with your personal brand, you can also customize the header with an eye-catching photo.

Once you've set up your account, start following people and institutions that are most relevant to your career. Use the "Advanced Search" and "Who to Follow" options to find people and organizations according to industry or location. Explore new topics through hashtags. If you follow many Twitter accounts, use lists to separate them into different categories, making those lists either public or private.[33] Gain attention that can bring you news and opportunities in return by posting content and retweeting what you find most intriguing. Direct message mentors and others you admire. Finally, if you restrict your tweets to professionally related topics, you can link your account to your LinkedIn profile.

Writing Persuasive Resumés

A **resumé** is a one- to two-page personal marketing tool that tells prospective employers about your education, employment experience, and skill sets. This document itemizes these details as specific blocks of information organized under easy-reference headings, arranged strategically to play up your strengths and provide a compelling picture of your hard skills, soft skills, and professional values (e.g., accountability, teamwork, punctuality). At the top of the page, it supplies contact information (full mailing address, telephone number, and e-mail address) so that interested parties can reach you. A resumé represents you and your best work on paper, providing evidence that will help prospective

resumé A persuasive written document in which job applicants summarize their qualifications and relate their education, work experience, and personal accomplishments to the needs of a prospective employer.

employers decide whether you qualify for interviewing. An effective resumé gets your foot in the door, giving you the chance to win over interviewers in person. Because your resumé is the first proof employers may have of your ability to communicate in writing, it should reflect your professionalism in its neatness, accuracy, and careful formatting and persuade prospective employers of your ability to add value to their company. A list of qualifications and experience can easily exceed two pages, so start by creating a fully-complete master resume recording your entire work history which you can then use as a jumping-off point and resource for each 1–2 page resume you create. From there, optimize your resume by customizing it for each position you apply for. Use keywords and phrases from the advertised job description once or twice in ways that make sense to ensure the employer's applicant tracking system (ATS) can scan and find them.

How Employers Use Resumés

Resumés help employers to gather standardized data to screen applicants. Few resumés are read word for word; faced with reviewing hundreds of resumés for a single position, HR specialists spend a minute or less perusing each one. They may enter electronic resumés (or scans of printed resumés) into an electronic job-tracking system. Only applicants whose resumés contain keywords matched to job requirements may pass to the next stage of the job competition, so you must prepare your resumé for easy skimmability and scannability (see "Preparing a Scannable Resumé" later in this chapter).

Resumé Writing Style

Because resumés deliver information quickly through lists and phrases, resumé writing requires a tight, clipped, action-oriented style that focuses on results. The reader will already understand that details in the document pertain to you, so there is no need to use *I*. Telegraphic phrases that begin with action verbs (see Table 10.2) take the place of complete sentences.

Conventional style:	I designed and coordinated two marketing campaigns that resulted in a 15 per cent increase in sales over one year.
Resumé style:	• Designed and coordinated two marketing campaigns. • Increased annual sales by 15 per cent.

As much as possible, these phrases should quantify details and incorporate keywords that relate your qualifications to those being sought. Here are a few more tips to help you produce a perfect final copy:

- Use capitals and/or boldface for headings only.
- Use consistent indenting.
- Leave space between sections to make information stand out.
- Proofread to catch errors.

Parts of a Standard Resumé

Resumés commonly contain the following sections, usually in the order given. Categories marked with an asterisk (*) are optional.

Name and Contact Information (do not use a heading)
*Objective/Career Profile
*Summary of Qualifications/Profile
Education
Experience
*Skills and Capabilities
*Awards/Honours and Activities
*References

TABLE 10.2 Action Verbs for Resumés

acted	estimated	prepared
adapted	expanded	presented
advised	facilitated	processed
analyzed	formulated	produced
arranged	founded	programmed
assembled	guided	promoted
assisted	handled	provided
built	harmonized	purchased
carried out	headed	raised
catalogued	identified	recommended
collaborated	implemented	recorded
collected	improved	redesigned
completed	increased	reorganized
computed	initiated	repaired
conducted	inspected	represented
conserved	installed	reviewed
constructed	instituted	revised
consulted	instructed	saved
controlled	introduced	scheduled
co-operated	investigated	selected
coordinated	launched	serviced
counselled	led	set up
created	made	sold
dealt	maintained	started
decided	managed	streamlined
decreased	monitored	supervised
delivered	negotiated	supplied
designed	operated	supported
determined	ordered	trained
developed	organized	unified
directed	performed	upgraded
distributed	pioneered	
established	planned	

Alternative headings may also be used, depending on your field of expertise:

> Publications
> Advanced Training
> Licences and Accreditations
> Language Proficiency/Foreign Languages
> Presentations
> Professional Affiliations/Memberships

You have some flexibility in how you arrange this information. Without distorting facts, you can shape your resumé to relate your education, work experience, and personal accomplishments to the needs of prospective employers. You can also emphasize your most impressive selling point—for instance, specialized training, an advanced degree, or strong work experience—by customizing the standard resumé templates supplied by your word-processing software. Simply vary the standard order and put important material toward the top, where it commands the most attention. Your most noteworthy qualification should come first. Any weaknesses can be de-emphasized by their placement.

Contact Information

No heading is needed for the contact information section. Type your full name (first name and last) at the top of the page, followed by your e-mail address (depending on the template you use, on the same line or the next line below). Include phone numbers you routinely use to receive and check messages. For privacy reasons, it is best not to include your permanent address (and/or your local campus address) or other personal information such as your date of birth, social insurance number, or age. As an alterative to your address, a city and a provincial abbreviation can be used to indicate to employers if you are currently living near the place of employment, something that can either help of hinder your application. If applicable, a link to your webpage or professional online profile URL can also be included.

Career Objective

An optional section, your career objective is a short, assertive summary that identifies your main qualifications and anticipated career path. It helps you target a specific job by enabling you to match your qualifications with key requirements. If you decide to make your career objective part of your resumé, you should revise it for each new application. Use descriptive phrases and minimal punctuation. Depending on your strategy, you can highlight the position you desire, a professional goal, the type of field you want to work in, your main qualifications, or a combination of all four.

- To utilize my [qualifications] as a [position title]: To utilize my working knowledge of maintenance techniques as a maintenance reliability supervisor.
- [Position title]: Marketing position with opportunity for growth and development.
- To [professional goal]: To assist low-income families in finding housing and support services.

Summary of Qualifications/Profile

As an alternative to the career objective section, a summary of your qualifications is a high-impact statement that provides an overall picture of you in relation to the job you are applying for. This section, consisting of one or two sentences, is useful if your experience has been varied or accumulated over a number of years.

Education

The education section—always of interest to employers—supplies information about your schooling and academic training, providing proof of your ability to do the job effectively. You should list all undergraduate and graduate degrees, diplomas, and certificates you have earned or are about to earn. Begin with your most recent or most relevant degree. Using commas to separate elements, list the following details:

- the degree, diploma, or certificate
- academic honours (for any degree earned with distinction, magna cum laude, summa cum laude, or with high distinction, italicize or bracket this information)
- the name of the institution that granted the degree
- the location of the school
- your major field of study, concentration, or specialization
- dates of attendance and/or date of graduation

Use the same style for every degree or diploma you list. Some job applicants also choose to list courses they have taken that are relevant to a current application. If you decide to do this, you should list courses by short descriptive title (not course code) and organize them under a subheading such as "Courses Related to Major" or "Courses Related to [position for which you are applying]." If you have an exceptionally high grade point average (3.5 or better), you might want to mention it; otherwise, withhold this information.

Work Experience

Information about work experience is key, especially for recent graduates new to the job market. Employment history is given in reverse chronological order (beginning with your present or most recent job). In addition to listing full-time and part-time jobs, you should include unpaid jobs, internships, volunteer work, and self-employment if these work experiences contributed to your set of relevant skills. Provide only minimal details of high-school jobs, but do indicate significant or relevant jobs concurrent with your post-secondary studies. For each position, list the following:

- job title(s) (indicating promotions)
- the company and its location (city and province)
- dates of employment (including month and year), significant duties, activities, context, details and quantified metrics of accomplishments and achievements, and promotions (use phrases introduced by strong action verbs to describe these details)

Use the present tense for the job you are in now; use the past tense for a job you no longer hold. Because each description serves as an advertisement for your skills, deal in specifics rather than generalities—quantifying accomplishments and activities—and incorporate dynamic verbs that help to portray you in a positive light and accent your most impressive qualifications.

Vague:	Responsible for social media marketing.
Specific:	Supervised over 40 social media marketing campaigns to increase SSov and applause rates by 45 per cent.

If there are gaps in your work history or frequent job changes, consider using a format that de-emphasizes employment dates. For example, you could place these dates after the job title rather than tabulating them or setting them in boldface. In functional resumés, work can be organized according to the type of work or skill rather than by positions held.

Skills and Capabilities

The skills section outlines the abilities and proficiencies that make you more employable. It gives you the opportunity to spotlight your technical training—your mastery of computer programs, interfaces, applications, special communications skills, or operating procedures for office equipment—as well as your fluency in foreign languages.

- Experienced with e-mail, MS Word and Excel 2016.
- Proficient in PowerPoint, Drupal, and Adobe Photoshop.
- Keyboard 80 wpm accurately.
- Trained in technical writing, including proposals and documentation.
- Fluent in French.

Awards/Honours and Activities

If you are a recent graduate or are re-entering the workforce, you can benefit from including an awards and activities section, reserved for academic awards and scholarships, volunteer experiences, special projects, leadership positions, professional memberships, and university and community service positions. This information shows you are a well-rounded person, with commitment, initiative, team spirit, or problem-solving ability. Include the date of involvement in an activity or the date of an award.

Personal Information

A resumé is not the place for personal information. By law, employers are not allowed to ask for personal information relating to country of origin or religious affiliation. Human rights legislation protects job applicants from discrimination. Your resumé should not include details about your age, marital status, or health.

References

As a job candidate you can wait until a recruiter shows interest before you give the names of references. Stating "References will be supplied on request" is sufficient, and saves space on your resumé. You can then prepare a separate reference list (entitled "Reference Sheet for [Your Name]"), which can then be submitted to employers at the time of your interview. However, if you do include references on your resumé, give each person's

According to LinkedIn, over 40 per cent of hiring managers "consider volunteer work equally as valuable as paid work experience when evaluating candidates".[34] Volunteering can also help job-seekers expand their network and learn about job opportunities within the organization(s) they assist.

full name and title, professional affiliation or company, address, phone number, and e-mail address. List this information in parallel form. Always contact references in advance and ask permission to use their names. Doing so will ensure that they are prepared to discuss your qualifications.

Resumé Length

The debate over resumé length is never-ending. The general rule is to keep it to one page as long as there is enough white space, as crowded resumés are hard to read. Recent graduates can easily stay within the one-page limit if they eliminate filler and consolidate headings; applicants with extensive work history and advanced training may require a second page to represent their qualifications adequately. Be sure to check the job advertisement for application instructions and details on resumé preferences.

Resumé Styles and Layouts

There is a resumé style to suit every applicant, from the rookie job-seeker with little experience to the seasoned veteran with an armload of honours and achievements. Because writing a resumé allows for some flexibility, you can choose a style that will help you look as good on paper as you are in person. The most widely used resumé styles are the chronological, the functional, and the combination. Each style has its own distinctive character, ranging from the fairly conventional to the more innovative.

Chronological Resumé

chronological resumé A document in which a job applicant's work experience, education, and personal achievements are presented in reverse time sequence, with the most recent experience in each category listed first.

The **chronological resumé** is considered the standard style. It tells employers what you have done professionally, organizing details in chronological order. It presents information under categories that recruiters have come to expect and can review quickly: "Objective," "Education," "Work Experience," "Special Skills," "Honours and Activities," and "References." The chronological style works well for applicants who have work experience in their field of employment and show sustained career growth. The chronological style is less suited to younger applicants with limited experience, or anyone with a negative or irregular work history, because its arrangement by employment dates makes gaps in employment more obvious.

Functional Resumé

functional resumé A document in which a job applicant's qualifications are presented in terms of notable achievements and abilities rather than work experience.

This skills-based resumé style emphasizes work-related skills and competencies, marketing relevant attributes and accomplishments that will be of value to the company. It works well for applicants who are about to redirect their careers or for anyone who has limited work experience but untold ability. The **functional resumé** is a good choice for accenting skills gained through volunteer experience. Its customizable categories allow for greater flexibility: "Objective," "Summary of Qualifications/Profile," "[Type of Work] Experience," "[Type of] Skills/Areas of Expertise," "Education," and "References." Skills can be arranged according to several types, bringing to light hidden strengths. However, some recruiters may view the omission of a job history as a weakness.

Combination Resumé

combination resumé A document that combines characteristics of chronological and functional resumés.

A cross between the chronological and the functional resumé, the **combination resumé** draws together the best of each style. It highlights capabilities at the same time as it provides a complete record of employment. This style works well for recent graduates who may or may not have experience, but do have the skills to gain employment. Its headings are borrowed from chronological and functional styles: "Objective," "Skills and Capabilities/Special Skills," "Experience," "Education," "Honours and Activities," and "References." A combination resumé is a more risky choice for anyone applying for jobs in traditional fields such as accounting, law, or banking, and the formatting should be strategic so that the combination of styles is not confusing.

General Tips

1. **Tell the truth.** A resumé is a legal document. It is fraudulent to lie on a resumé and unethical to tell half-truths. Companies routinely do background checks and these practices are grounds for disqualification or, if discovered after hiring, dismissal.

2. **Keep your resumé up to date.** Schedule regular resumé updates. Last-minute efforts at revision can result in sloppy formatting and typos.

3. **Create different versions of your resumé.** Have one that can be scanned into a resumé database and one that you can e-mail to company contacts.

4. **Fine-tune your resumé for each new application.** Revise your career objective statement to link it to the job for which you are currently applying.

5. **Avoid gimmicks.** Print your resumé on good quality, standard 8½– by 11–inch white paper. Use enough white space to make your resumé easy to read.

MITRA DAS

253 Elderwood Crescent

Brampton, ON N5L 2S9

(905) 862-5540

mdas@rogers.ca

Name is bolded, capitalized, and centred to help it stand out; as an alternative, it could be set in a slightly larger point size

OBJECTIVE   To assist a fashion retail chain in providing superior customer service while managing merchandise efficiently and maximizing store sales in an entry-level management position

Emphasizes professional goal in relation to the advertisement for the position being sought

EDUCATION   **Ryerson University**, Toronto, Ontario

Working toward a Bachelor of Commerce in Retail Management

Degree expected June 2011

Major courses: • Managerial Accounting

• Advanced Retail Management

• Organizational Behaviour

Places education first for emphasis, as degrees and diplomas of this young candidate relate directly to position being sought

Seneca College, Toronto, Ontario

Diploma in Fashion Merchandising (Co-op Education Program), 2019

Major courses: • Fashion Retail Entrepreneurship

• Retail Organizational Management

• Retail Human Resources Management

EXPERIENCE   **Assistant Manager** (part-time), Skylark Fashions, Vaughan, Ontario

May 2019 to present

• Assisted in directing, training, and motivating store sales team of eight in order to provide a high level of customer service and increase profits by 15 per cent

• Improved inventory-control procedures to reduce stock surpluses by 20 per cent

Describes work experience, quantifies specific achievements, and uses action verbs

Fashion Intern (work term), Shoe Depot Inc., Toronto, Ontario

January 2019 to March 2019

• Assisted district manager in coordinating store programs and events

• Created and managed seminars and team-building exercises to enhance customer service

• Maintained and updated client mailing lists

Visual Merchandiser, Suzy Shier, Dufferin Mall, Toronto, Ontario

September 2018 to December 2018

• Oversaw store signage, pricing, and visual displays

Sales Associate, Roots Canada Inc., Toronto, Ontario

May 2017 to September 2017

• Handled cash and credit transactions

• Worked with sales team to deliver excellent customer service

SKILLS   • Proficient with MS Word, Excel, PowerPoint, and Outlook

• Superior time-management and organizational skills

Mentions some skills commonly requested by employers

FIGURE 10.1 Chronological Resumé

Troy Ng   109 Ludlow Avenue, Regina, SK S4M 0A1

306-567-7783
tjng@gmail.com

OBJECTIVE

Position as assistant manager of front desk operations with opportunity for growth and development

PROFILE

College graduate with Global Tourism and Marketing Diploma and experience in the hotel industry

RELEVANT SKILLS AND QUALIFICATIONS

Computer and Office Skills
- Knowledge of Sabre, Fidelio, and Opera
- Proficient with Windows, Word, Acrobat
- Type 60 wpm with accuracy
- Able to perform general office duties, including photocopying, filing, and scheduling

Organizational and Marketing Skills
- Scheduled events and arranged catering plans for groups of up to 300
- Provided concierge services to guests, including tours of hotel facilities
- Prepared advertising copy for summer resort
- Trained and supervised three desk clerks at Red Lily Lodge
- Responsible for individual reservations through telephone and central reservation system

Communication Skills
- Demonstrated friendly and courteous telephone etiquette in answering guest inquiries regarding rates, special packages, and general information
- Performed test calls to competition and Global Reservation Centre
- Polished speaking skills by giving talks to class
- Completed college communication courses with an A grade
- Fluent in Japanese and Mandarin

Interpersonal Skills
- Demonstrated ability to work independently with minimal supervision and to work co-operatively in the interest of better guest satisfaction
- Assisted front desk manager in conducting team-building activities

EDUCATION

Medicine Hat College, Medicine Hat, AB
Global Tourism and Marketing Diploma, 2019

Troy Ng

Page 2

RELEVANT EXPERIENCE

Reservations Agent (part-time), Medicine Hat Lodge, Medicine Hat, AB
January 2019 to March 2019

Front Desk Clerk, Red Lily Lodge, Regina, SK
May 2018 to August 2018

OTHER EXPERIENCE

Sales Clerk, Holinger Hardware, Regina, SK
Summers, 2015 to 2019

Annotations (left margin):

Includes profile statement to summarize strengths and capabilities

Highlights skills mentioned in advertisement by listing them first; uses strong action verbs to describe achievements and market capabilities

Mentions experience last to de-emphasize limited work history

FIGURE 10.2 Functional Resumé

KELLY MARACLE
21 Rockycrest Drive
North Bay, ON P1A 2H7
(705) 490-1166
E-mail: kjmaracle@gmail.com

SKILLS AND CAPABILITIES
- Type 90 wpm with accuracy
- Take symbol shorthand at 80 wpm with accurate transcription
- Produce effective legal documents in fast-paced environment
- Experienced with MS Office
- Comprehensive knowledge of legal procedures as they apply to the commercial real estate business
- Able to communicate in a professional manner with clients and lawyers

Highlights skills named in advertisement

EXPERIENCE
Legal Assistant, Real Estate Group, Ball LLP, Sudbury, Ontario
May 2018 to August 2020
- Performed clerical, administrative, and general office duties, including accounting, closing files, docketing, and billing
- Transcribed and typed legal documents, confidential letters, and reports in detail-oriented environment
- Scheduled meetings and initiated follow-up with clients

Experience reinforces skills already described for impact and emphasis

Office Assistant (part-time), Horizon Realty, North Bay, Ontario
Summer 2017
- Routed and answered routine correspondence
- Typed and proofread documents
- Produced advertising copy and coordinated 15 mass mailings

EDUCATION
Seneca College, Toronto, Ontario
Administration (Legal), 2018
Major courses
- Legal Procedures–Real Estate/Corporate
- Legal Word Processing
- Communications and Machine Transcription
- Spreadsheets

Education emphasizes major courses relevant to the job applied for

ACTIVITIES AND HONOURS
- Volunteer, Daily Bread Food Bank, 2012–present
- Student Council Representative, Seneca College, Fall 2014
- Silver Medallist, 400m Hurdles, Ontario Junior Track and Field Championships, 2010

Mentions activities that show leadership, achievement, and community involvement

References are available on a separate sheet to be left, if required, after interview

REFERENCES

KELLY MARACLE
21 Rockycrest Drive
North Bay, ON P1A 2H7
(705) 490-1166
E-mail: kjmaracle@gmail.com

Professor Anya Giles
Office Administration Program
Seneca College
2581 Finch Avenue East
Toronto, ON M3L 2E9
(416) 250-8641

Mr. Bill Yan
President
Horizon Realty Ltd.
880 North Shore Avenue
North Bay, ON P1C 7R7
(705) 641-3328

Mr. Jeff Ball, QC
Chief Partner
Ball LLP
80 Brady Street
Sudbury, ON P3A 2B2
(705) 555-2948

FIGURE 10.3 Combination Resumé

Preparing a Scannable Resumé

Before you send your resumé, it is a good idea to first find out if the recipient uses scanning software. A **scannable resumé** is a resumé that has high visibility in an electronic resumé-tracking system or electronic resumé database. A scannable resumé spotlights an applicant's pertinent experience with keywords that correspond to ones used to describe the ideal candidate in the job posting (see Figure 10.4). Placed after the main heading of your resumé or near the end and entitled "Keywords," this pool of up to 50 relevant, attention-getting words may include current and previous job titles, job-specific professional jargon and its synonyms, titles of software programs, marketable skills, and adjectives describing interpersonal traits. Here are a few examples:

accurate	efficient	planning ability
active	experienced	positive
adaptable	flexible	problem-solving
communication skills	innovative	productive
creative	leadership	results-oriented
customer-oriented	motivated	takes initiative
detail-oriented	organizational skills	willing to travel

Applicants with the highest percentage of matches are identified as good candidates for the job and stand the best chance of being interviewed.

To create a scannable resumé, adhere to these dos and don'ts:

☑ **DO**

- List your name and address at the top of every page of your resumé.
- Use reader-friendly a sans-serif font, such as Arial, in ten- to twelve-point size.
- Use white space as your main formatting tool, leaving blank lines around headings.
- Use as many pages as necessary to list your skills and experience.
- If you are required to submit a printed copy of your resumé, send a crisp copy printed on a laser printer.

☒ **DON'T**

- Use horizontal or vertical lines.
- Use unusual fonts.
- Use special characters, bullets, italics, underlined text, graphics, slashes, or page numbers.
- Print your resumé on coloured or textured paper.
- Fold, staple, or fax your resumé.

Creative or Non-Standard Resumés

In certain cases, an applicant may choose to submit a creative or non-standard resumé in place of a more conventional one. Creative resumés can take many forms—for example, a text-based summary of the applicant's achievements that incorporates graphics or photos; a website that outlines an applicant's career history and provides links to sample work; or a video in which the applicant describes and shows evidence of his or her work history and/or accomplishments.

CAMERON TUCKER
158 Gardenview Blvd.
Gander, NL A1V 2G5
Phone: 709-231-9976
E-mail: cameron.tucker@sympatico.ca

KEYWORDS

Public Relations. Marketing Communications. Event Marketing. Media Advertising.
Sales Promotion. Advertising Research. Visual Communication. Telemarketing. Advertising
Sales. MS Office Suite. Excel. Quark. Photoshop. Communication Skills. Organizational Skills.
Persuasive Presentation Skills. Bilingual. Ontario College Diploma. Georgian College.

OBJECTIVE

Motivated, fast-learning individual seeks advertising/marketing position utilizing
communication and organizational skills.

EDUCATION

Georgian College, Barrie, ON
Ontario College Diploma in Advertising, 2020

RELEVANT COURSEWORK

Advertising Computer Applications
Professional Writing
Marketing on the Web
Copywriting
Media Planning Computer Applications

CAMERON TUCKER
158 Gardenview Blvd.
Gander, NL A1V 2G5
Phone: 709-231-9976
E-mail: cameron.tucker@sympatico.ca

Page 2

EXPERIENCE

The Gander Beacon
June 2020 to present
Part-Time Advertising Sales Representative

Represent *The Gander Beacon* to assigned and potential advertisers.
Handle incoming advertiser calls.
Increase advertising revenue and expand client base by 15 per cent annually through
cold calls and outbound sales.
Provide clients with creative advertising solutions and implement sales strategies for
existing clients.

Part-Time Sales Associate
Greeted customers, demonstrated products, successfully served more than 50
customers daily.
Answered questions and solved customer problems.

SKILLS

Computer: Macintosh Applications, Microsoft Office, Web Publishing.
Interpersonal: Communicative, persuasive, team-oriented, fluent in English and French.
                       Able to follow through in fast-paced, deadline-driven environment.

FURTHER INFORMATION

References, university transcripts, and a portfolio of computer programs are available
upon request

FIGURE 10.4 Scannable, Computer-Friendly Resumé

In general, creative resumés are most acceptable in creative fields or in application for positions with a visual dimension, such as a graphic designer or a videographer. In such cases, creative resumés may better engage, draw interest, and reflect the applicant's qualifications. However, even in creative fields, employers seeking evidence of applicants' ability to perform specific tasks typically ask for a standard resumé accompanied by relevant work samples or a portfolio. (See the discussion of career portfolios and e-portfolios later in this chapter.)

Preparing a Persuasive Cover Letter

cover letter (or **application letter**) A letter that accompanies a resumé to summarize a job applicant's qualifications and value to a prospective employer.

A **cover letter**—also called an **application letter**—is essentially a sales letter. Usually no more than a page in length, but never skimpy, an application letter introduces you to a prospective employer and helps to make a good first impression. A cover letter interprets raw data from your resumé so readers may better understand how your skills and experience fit the requirements of a specific job. A cover letter can do what a resumé on its own cannot: tell prospective employers what you are prepared to do for their company and convince them that you are qualified for the job. You have just a few paragraphs to grab the reader's attention and leave a strong impression—leaving no room for errors in grammar, spelling, and typography.

General Tips for Cover Letters

1. **Camouflage *I*, *me*, and *mine*.** It is almost impossible to write an application letter without using *I*, but overusing first-person pronouns may make you sound egotistical or boastful. To make *I* less noticeable, avoid placing it at the beginning of consecutive sentences. Vary your style by embedding *I* in the middle of sentences instead. By showing and interpreting what you have done rather than praising your own efforts, you can convince the reader of the advantages your employment can bring.

2. **Use proper grammar and spelling.** Because most companies seek employees who are detail-oriented and efficient, small things mean a lot to the success of a cover letter.

3. **Use keywords from the job ad or posting.** Show that your skills are transferable and relevant to the job you are applying for.

4. **Use the same font that you used for your resumé.** This gives a unified look to your application.

5. **Avoid dense, overloaded paragraphs.** Your letter should be designed for ease of readability. Shorter paragraphs make your letter quick to review.

6. **Don't plead, apologize, or exaggerate.** Employers are seeking positive and self-confident personnel.

7. **Avoid a cookie-cutter approach.** A generic letter is less likely to gain interest, so work from a bulleted list of your qualifications, achievements, and educational credentials to prepare a new cover letter targeted to each job opening. Keep in mind the requirements outlined by the employer in the job ad.

8. **Strive for a tight, clear writing style.** The letter should be no more than a page but no less than half a page.

Solicited Application Letters

How you capture attention at the beginning of your cover letter depends on whether the position for which you are applying is solicited or unsolicited. When you know a company is hiring, you can respond to an advertisement by writing a **solicited application letter**. Its purpose is to ask for an interview, not for the actual job. The goal is to convince prospective employers that you are not only qualified for the job but are better than other candidates.

Here are some tips for writing a solicited application letter:

1. **Introductory paragraph: Gain attention.** Name the specific job for which you are applying and indicate where you learned about the job. Include job competition or reference numbers to ensure your application ends up in the right hands. Clearly state that you are applying for the job. Briefly show that you possess the major qualifications listed as requirements in the posting. Here are some examples of how you might begin your letter:

> **solicited application letter** A letter in which a job-seeker applies to an advertised position and asks for an interview.

Figure 10.5 Use this three-part writing plan for your cover letter

- **Summary + Request Opening**

  With five years' experience as an industrial designer, I would like to be considered for the position of design team leader currently advertised on your company's website.

- **Shared Values/Interest in the Company Opening**

  A recent survey of the Canadian industrial sector ranked Weir Services first in the repair and refurbishing of mechanical equipment. I am interested in joining the expert, customer-focused Weir sales team because I share your company's belief in quality and dependability. With a soon-to-be-completed degree in sales management and two years' experience in industrial service sales, I am prepared to be an immediately productive member of your sales team.

- **Request Opening**

  I wish to apply for the position of regional sales manager, as advertised in yesterday's *National Post* (competition #4368). As the attached resumé suggests, my experience in fashion retail has prepared me for the challenging and dynamic work environment offered by this position.

- **Name Opening**

  At the suggestion of Mr. Farouk Aziz of your Accounting Department, I submit my qualifications for the position of human resources specialist posted on Workopolis.

2. **Middle paragraphs: Show that you are qualified by relating your skills to what the company requires.** Using action verbs (*managed, designed, organized, upgraded*), describe the skills, schooling, achievements, and experience that would make you valuable to the company. Emphasize your strongest skills, especially the kinds that employers generally seek: the ability to communicate well, take responsibility, learn quickly, and work as part of a team.

   Three years as a sous-chef at Chez Tom taught me how to work under pressure and maintain high standards of food presentation and menu selection on a limited budget.

Does not clearly identify the job being sought or refer to the resumé →

Description of work experience is vague and does not specify skills or educational credentials →

Writer-centred approach reinforces what the company is supposed to do for the applicant, not what the applicant can do for the company →

This letter is an application for a position that I saw advertised online.

I have worked part-time for R.J. McCormack for a few months. I am looking for a full-time position, preferably as a senior legal assistant. I think you will agree that my qualifications are a good match for the requirements of the job. I have strong practical skills that will benefit your company. I will receive my diploma soon.

I think this job was made for me. If you agree that I could be the right person for the job you advertised, I could find time to meet with you to discuss my qualifications. To arrange an interview, just leave a message for me on my voicemail, but try not to call early in the day.

Figure 10.6 Ineffective Solicited Letter of Application (extract)

Amy Fulton
62 Robin Street
Toronto, ON M4D 2P3

March 6, 2021

Ms. Patrizia Chernienko
Rossiter, Fleet, and Lee, LLP
1220 Yonge Street, Suite 230
Toronto, ON L4T 5S7

Dear Ms. Chernienko:

Subject: Legal Assistant Position (Ref. No. 68146) ← Clearly identifies the position applied for

With a soon-to-be-completed diploma in legal office administration and high-level skills, I wish to apply for the position of legal assistant, as posted on Workopolis. As the enclosed resumé suggests, my intensive internship training has given me the ← Refers to accompanying resumé
necessary practical experience to be immediately productive in a prestigious legal firm such as Rossiter, Fleet, and Lee, LLP.

My courses in the legal office administration curriculum at Great Huron College have ← Gains attention with a concise summary of qualifications
provided me with background in all aspects of legal assistance, including legal transcription, word processing, legal procedures (real estate), and spreadsheets. Over six semesters I transcribed and processed more than 300 legal documents and mastered the proofreading skills necessary to ensure the kind of accuracy Rossiter, Fleet, and Lee would expect.

During my six-month internship in the offices of R.J. McCormack, I learned to ← Relates skills and background to requirements of position, incorporating keywords from the job ad and quantifying achievements
manage time effectively in a detail-oriented environment and to perform and prioritize office duties such as docketing and closing files while maintaining flexibility. Assisting the chief legal assistant with additional duties, including the reorganization of client files and overhaul of billing procedures, allowed me to demonstrate my knowledge of office procedures and commitment to expediting the flow of work within the firm. My recent internship experience and participation in school organizations have helped me develop my ability to communicate in a professional manner with clients and lawyers and build the interpersonal skills needed to work effectively as part of a team.

After you have reviewed my résumé for details of my qualifications, please call me at ← Asks for action courteously and provides information necessary for follow-up
(905) 661-9865 to arrange an interview at your convenience . I look forward to discussing with you ways in which I can contribute to Rossiter, Fleet, and Lee, LLP.

Sincerely,

Amy Fulton

Amy Fulton

Enclosure

FIGURE 10.7 Effective Solicited Letter of Application

Show what separates you from the other applicants—your course work, summer jobs and internships, and experience gained from skills—and leadership-building activities. Refer the reader to your resumé; a good cover letter will make the reader want to know more about you.

> As you will notice from my resumé, I hold a certificate in cosmetology from Pioneer College.

> Please refer to the attached resumé for a complete overview of my work and volunteer experience.

3. **Closing paragraph:** Ask for action by asking the recruiter to call you to arrange an interview or telling the employer that you will take the initiative to call. Your request should sound courteous, appreciative, and respectful. Here are a few suggestions for ending your letter:

> I would like the opportunity to discuss my background and qualifications with you in a personal interview. I look forward to hearing from you and to arranging a meeting in the near future.

> I hope that this brief summary of my qualifications and the additional information on my resumé indicate my interest in putting my skills to work for Goldcrest Investments. At your convenience, please call me at (905) 881-9776 to arrange an interview so that we may discuss the ways in which my experience can contribute to your company.

> After you have examined the details on the attached resumé, please call me to arrange an interview at your convenience.

Unsolicited Application Letters

Unsolicited letters of application, also called **job-prospecting letters**, are written on the chance that employers may have an opening for someone with your skills and qualifications in the foreseeable future even though no such position has been advertised.

unsolicited application letter (or **job-prospecting letter**) A letter in which a job-seeker introduces himself or herself and asks about job openings.

Salutation too general (if possible, research the name of the individual to whom inquiry should be sent).

Does not demonstrate knowledge of the company; fails to mention why job-seeker wants to work for the company; tone fails to communicate interest and enthusiasm; leaves out details about background and qualifications

Closing question makes it easy for hiring manager to say no

Complimentary close too familiar

Dear Human Resources Director:

Can you tell me when there might be an opening for an HR recruiter like me? I have read about your company and it sounds like an organization I would like to work for. I have many skills I feel you could use. In fact, hiring me would be good for your company.

Shall I drop by your office for an interview sometime next week?

Warmest regards,

Sheila Finch

FIGURE 10.8 Ineffective Unsolicited Letter of Application (extract)

Rob Milton
115 Verity Drive
Dartmouth, NS B2W 0H6

February 10, 2021

Mr. Bertie Kwinter
Director of Human Resources
Braintrust Solutions
240 Robie Street
Halifax, NS B3H 1M6

Dear Mr. Kwinter:

In a recent article on Canada's top emerging growth companies, Profit Magazine ranked Braintrust Solutions as number 1. As your company continues to attract new clients with its innovative web-based workforce-management software, you are likely in need of experienced HR recruiters with strong networking skills and proven records of recruiting and resourcing ERP and J2EE consultants.

Gains attention by demonstrating knowledge of and interest in the company

Links potential employment needs to the job-seeker's assets and skills

Here are three significant qualifications, summarized from the enclosed resumé, that I believe you will find of interest:

Refers to resumé; relates job-seeker's accomplishments to potential contributions

- Five years of formal training in business administration and HR recruitment, including a BA from Dalhousie University and a diploma in Business Administration HR from Sheridan College, with specialized courses in strategic marketing, recruitment and selection techniques, and negotiation strategies.

- Four years of practical experience as a Recruitment Partner at JSM Software where my responsibilities included conducting initial meetings with managers, developing and executing sourcing strategies, overseeing reference and offer processes, and conducting salary negotiations.

- Strong networking skills and a knowledge of HR resources and applicant tracking technology, with an ability to work and apply problem-solving skills in a fast-paced environment.

At your convenience, I would like to have the opportunity to meet with you to discuss how my track record and skills could be of value to your company. I will contact your office next week to schedule an interview.

Takes initiative for follow-up

Sincerely,

Rob Milton

Rob Milton

Enc.

FIGURE 10.9 Effective Unsolicited Letter of Application

Writing an unsolicited letter of application can be difficult because you do not have a list of job requirements and you must catch and hold the reader's attention right from the start. Among the best ways to do this are the following:

- Show some enthusiasm.
- Use the indirect approach (for persuasive messages).
- Do research that enables you to demonstrate your interest in and knowledge of the company (the products it manufactures, the personnel it seeks, and the challenges it faces).

From your letter, it should be clear why you want to work for the company, what you are prepared to do for it, and how your qualifications can bring benefits.

Personal Statements

A personal statement is a 250- to 500-word career-focused essay, required by some applications, that articulates essentials of your post-secondary program, qualifications, fit between the program and position, and your long-term goals.[35] Although a personal statement is informative, it persuades in part from the strength of your writing, its creativity, and how it reflects who you uniquely are. Duplication of other elements in your application—such as your cover letter, transcript, or resume—is best avoided. Instead use your personal statement as a way to interpret and reflectively reframe this information, putting it in the best possible light and enabling the employer to get to know you, your capabilities, and your career aspirations.

- **Introduction.** A personal statement opening can be catchy or calculated to make favourable impression right away. It is less formulaic than a cover letter. Readers will want to know why you are interested in the job, program, or organization and why you are applying.
- **Supporting paragraphs.** The slightly more generous length of personal statements leaves more room to give specific and relevant examples of how you have applied your skills or knowledge from your degree or to share an anecdote or story about your professional development or experience. Because a personal statement is essentially an essay, focus each paragraph on a particular aspect of your professional skillset (e.g., teamwork, ability to work independently, or interpersonal and communication skills) or reason for applying (e.g., fit with program or career) and begin each paragraph with a topic sentence for a logical flow.[36]
- **Conclusion.** The final paragraph in a personal statement draws together the strands of the supporting paragraph to draw the reader to a conclusion of how right you are for a program, internship or career.

When writing your statement, consider your audience and the specifications for program acceptance or the job. Keep in mind that employers and program directors are seeking individuals who show clarity of thought, enthusiasm, and have knowledge of the program, job, or organization. The content of your statement should demonstrate these qualities (and specific ones described in job advertisements) and explain why you are applying and what you can bring to the organization or program.

E-mailing Cover Letters and Resumés

Many employers and hiring managers prefer e-mail resumés. You can follow the same strategies given earlier in this chapter when composing cover letters and resumes that will be e-mailed to employers. However, care should be taken in how these documents are sent. Not every application transmitted by e-mail ends up in the right hands. There is always the risk that inboxes may be flooded after a job is posted online or that junk filters may keep resumés from reaching their destination. Here are a few tips to help ensure your application isn't ignored or lost:

1. **Read application instructions carefully.** Some companies advertise positions online but do not accept resumés via e-mail. Some companies may not accept file attachments and may even delete e-mails with attached resumés rather than risk exposure to viruses.

2. **Use keywords.** Your document may end up on a resumé database essential to the screening process. Study keywords specific to the job ad and your field and incorporate ones that match your qualifications and background.

3. **Include a cover letter.** Unless instructed to, do not send just your résumé. Include a cover letter in the body of your e-mail, and if you are attaching a résumé, include the same cover letter as the first item in the same attachment.

4. **Make your subject line specific.** If you are responding to an advertisement or job posting, put the job title and/or reference number in the subject line of your message.

5. **Submit attachments in the requested format(s).** If the posting does not specify a file format for attachments, convert your documents to PDF format. A PDF will ensure document formatting remains the same wherever the file is opened. If the posting forbids attachments, submit your cover letter and resume in plain-text format in the body of an e-mail, avoiding fancy formatting (no graphics, lines, italics, bullets, or special characters).

Job Application Round-Up: Some Additional Tips

1. **Keep track of the companies to which you have applied.** Having to ask a prospective employer what job you're interviewing for will make you seem disorganized.

2. **Ensure future contacts remain professional.** Make sure your e-mail address and voicemail greeting are acceptable by professional standards. If necessary, open an e-mail account specifically for the purpose of your job search. Using your work e-mail address may alert your current employer to your desire for better prospects, not to mention the fact that you are putting company resources to personal use.

3. **Consider privacy and confidentiality.** Be selective about where you post your resumé, sticking to sites that are password-protected and accessible only to legitimate employers. To reduce the risk of identity theft, give only an initial and surname and limit information to only those details an employer rightfully needs to know. Omit your street address and phone number when posting your resumé on the web.

4. **Ensure your application is delivered on time, in the appropriate way.**
    Check for instructions on the company's employment opportunities web page if
    the posting supplies the web address.

Career Portfolios and E-Portfolios

A portfolio uses samples to show how you are able to apply your knowledge, values, and
expertise in the products you create: brochures, presentations, marketing materials,
papers, studies, project descriptions, reports, and so on. A portfolio may also include
explanations or reflections to help readers interpret and understand the purpose of each
piece of work, as well as the following:

- statement of career goals
- summary of research projects (proposed, in-progress, or completed)
- details of professional development activities
- details of volunteer work and community service
- letter of recommendation
- references[37]

As the purpose is to persuade, the portfolio must be professionally designed and free of
typographical errors.

An e-portfolio or digital portfolio is a similar collection of information, evidence, and
supporting reflections in an electronic format that demonstrates development, skills, and
competencies.[38] Many applications for post-graduate programs now require an e-portfolio.

Job Application Videos

It is becoming more common for jobseekers to enhance their application with a video and
for HR managers to require this component, especially for customer-facing jobs. Videos
can take several forms: (i) a short pre-recorded video submitted with your application to
make an impact, stand-in for your resume, or give one-way interview answers to pre-set
questions; (ii) a live interview conducted from a self-selected location or the potential
employer's office via a platform such as Skype or Google Hangout. Although video submissions provide an opportunity to express individuality and personality, applicants' age,
ethnicity, and gender can be gleaned from them and due to legalities and perceived potential for discrimination some HR managers think of videos as risky.[39]

Here are some tips for creating a strong video application:

- Wear what you would wear on the job, opting for pattern-free, light-coloured
  clothing that will photograph well.
- Be conscious of your surroundings and what the camera and audio might inadvertently pick up: opt for a quiet space where you won't be interrupted (by other
  people or by background noise from traffic, machinery, building ventilation)
  and record yourself against a well-lit, neutral and single-coloured or surfaced
  background.

- Create a script; but use it only as a general guide. Reciting it word-for-word can stifle your delivery; looking at a script that is off-screen breaks your eye contact with the camera and hence your audience.
- There are no hard-and-fast rules, but the general length is between one and three minutes. Begin by introducing yourself and avoid merely listing your qualifications—make them meaningful through an example or two while maintaining a positive demeanour.[40]
- Use iMovie or free editing software to improve viewing experience by optimizing image and sound quality.

Job Interviews

A good cover letter, resumé, and portfolio can open the door to a **job interview**, but they cannot ensure your success in the meeting. It is up to you to meet the employer or recruiter face-to-face and talk about the skills, experience, and other qualifications that make you right for the job.

> **job interview** A structured, face-to-face conversation between one or more recruiters and a job candidate, in which the latter's qualifications for a position and potential performance are assessed.

Before the Interview

1. **Prepare in order to minimize job interview anxiety.** Do at least an hour of advance research on the potential employer and what the job entails. Learn about company values and goals from a quick review of the corporate mission statement

Be aware of your body language during a job interview. Closed body language, nail biting, hair twisting, finger drumming, and knuckle cracking can make you appear less confident and rob the interviewer of the chance to see your full potential.

Dean Drobot/Shutterstock.com

or "About Us" synopsis. Learn about its products, services, corporate structure, people, culture, awards, and customers. Check out the websites and social media of the company's competitors to gain a broader understanding of the industry.

2. **Become familiar with your non-verbal communication habits.** Presentation style and appearance are important at interviews. Closed body language (the tendency to cross your arms, for example) can send a message that you are cold or nervous. Fidgeting can be a sign of nervousness that draws attention away from what you have to say. Be aware of your posture, facial expressions, and gestures so you can work on controlling them.

3. **Dress for the job.** The way you dress should show that you understand the corporate culture. If you are interviewing for an office job, for example, wear a business suit. Good grooming and personal hygiene are essential. Use perfume and cologne sparingly, if at all. Your outfit should be professional—slightly more formal than what you would wear on the job—but comfortable enough that you can devote your full attention to the interview.

4. **Anticipate what questions you might be asked.** Consider how you would respond to typical interview questions such as (1) *What skills will you bring to the company that will help us meet our goals?* (2) *How would you describe your skills?* (3) *Why should we hire you when other applicants might have better credentials or more experience?* (4) *What attracted you to this position at our company?* (5) *Can you give me examples of where you have demonstrated the competencies you think will be key to performing well in this job?*

5. **Be prepared to talk about your experiences and how you handled problems.** Keep relevant work experience, significant work achievements, and proven successes in mind. You can prepare a script that covers this information, but do not memorize it if you want to sound spontaneous.

6. **Prepare several good questions to ask the interviewer.** Prepare insightful questions that will help you better understand the company. Job candidates are judged in part on the questions they ask. Preparing relevant questions can make you appear wise, interested, and informed.

7. **Practise. Rehearse what you can.** Film yourself answering typical interview questions and assess your performance. Nervousness is natural—fight it by reminding yourself of your enthusiasm for your work and having faith in your own self-worth. The more interviews you experience, the less nervous you will be.

Behavioural Interview Questions and How to Prepare for Them

Behavioural interviewing involves questions that require interviewees to explain their actions in specific work situations.[41] The answers to these questions help interviewers evaluate hard-to-measure qualities and abilities. Here are some examples of behavioural questions:

Give an example of a time when you had to solve a challenging problem. How did you respond to that challenge? (problem-solving)

Describe a situation where you had many projects due at the same time. (time management and stress management)

Give an example of a time when your organizational skills really paid off. (results achievement)

Give an example of a time when you had to persuade other people to take action. (leadership)

Tell me about a time when you were part of a team and one of its members wasn't pulling his or her weight. (teamwork and collaborative skills)

Give an example of a project you initiated. (creativity)

How do you normally go about achieving an assigned task? (achieving results, time management)

Use the STARS technique to develop your response: focus on outlining the *situation*, noting the *tasks* you had to perform, explaining the *actions* you took, stating the *results*, and classifying and reflecting on the *skills* you used.[42] As you prepare for your interview, select three or more examples of situations that you feel you handled well and that are relevant to the competencies and skills required for the job.

At the Interview

1. **Arrive on time or a little early.** Plan your route the day before your interview and estimate how much time you will need to get to the location. Being late creates a bad impression and inconveniences the people who have the power to hire you.

2. **Go alone.** Although you may think you need moral support, leave family and friends at home unless you require physical assistance.

3. **Bring an extra copy of your resumé, your portfolio, and a reference list.** The interviewer will have your resumé on hand at the meeting, but bring a copy for your own reference and your portfolio.

4. **Mind your manners.** Be congenial and courteous to everyone you meet before, during, and after the interview.

5. **Make a poised and confident first impression.** Greet interviewers with a firm but not crushing handshake. Extend your hand, make eye contact, and introduce yourself: *I'm pleased to meet you, Ms. Radko. I'm [your name]*. Smile in a genuine, unforced way. Make sure that any small talk avoids controversial subjects.

6. **Listen carefully to the interviewer's questions, and don't interrupt.** You are not just telling the interviewer about yourself; you are taking part in a two-way dialogue. Let the interviewer finish asking a question before you begin your response.

7. **Speak clearly and confidently.** The way you speak is evidence of your ability to communicate, deal with people, and build rapport. Answer by expressing your thoughts as clearly as you can, using a pleasant tone and as few *uhms*, *ahems*, *yups*, and *ahs* as possible. Avoid slang or mumbling. Avoid simple yes/no or one-word answers that might suggest you have little to say.

8. **Concentrate.** Use your body language to show interest, and avoid making any gestures or facial expressions that could suggest you are bored.

9. **Avoid being negative.** You are trying to show that you are bright, energetic, and capable. Avoid negative comments about yourself and others, especially former

employers, supervisors, and colleagues. Interviewers might assume from such remarks that you are a difficult employee with poor interpersonal skills.

10. **Make intelligent use of your research.** Demonstrate that you understand the business by slipping relevant tidbits into the conversation. Make sure your comments fit the context. Show that you are knowledgeable and interested in the company.

11. **Don't obsess over salary or benefits.** An interview is not the place for demands. Ask for information you require on these topics, but put your emphasis on what you can do for the company.

12. **Don't expect an immediate response.** Don't end the interview by asking if you got the job. Most companies want to interview all candidates before making a final decision. You can ask the interviewer when you might expect a decision. Be sure to show courtesy by thanking the interviewer.

After the Interview

1. **Send a thank-you e-mail.** Within 24 hours of the interview, write a brief, personalized message thanking the interviewer. (Thank-you messages are discussed in the next section.)

2. **Consider your options carefully.** Don't rush into accepting a job if you feel it is a bad fit. Express appreciation for the offer, and ask for a day or two to decide: *I'd like a little time to consider your offer. May I call you back tomorrow?* If you must decline the offer (because it does not offer the salary, benefits, and advancement opportunities you want or because of other reasons), turn it down tactfully.

Follow-Up Employment Messages

Follow-Up Message

follow-up message An informative message that summarizes the key points of a job interview.

A **follow-up message** can be sent if you have not received a response to your resumé or have not heard from an employer following an interview within a reasonable time. It lets the employer know you are still serious about working for the company. Briefly indicate the date you submitted your resumé or interviewed for a position, and emphasize why you are interested in the position and the company. Inquire if additional information is required, or provide an update.

Thank-You Message

A thank-you message is typically sent within 24 hours of an interview. It expresses appreciation to the interviewer for his or her time and the courtesy that was extended to you. A thank-you message can help you stand out from other applicants. Begin by referring to the interview date and the exact position you interviewed for. Mention what led you to believe you would fit the position well—a job-related topic that was of particular interest to you during your conversation or a skill or qualification that the interviewer was especially interested in. Remember to send a thank-you message to anyone who has provided a reference for you.

Job-Offer Acknowledgement

An acknowledgement should be sent immediately on receipt of an offer, especially if you require time to make your decision. Briefly state the title of the job and salary, express your thanks for the offer, and reiterate your interest in the company. Indicate the date by which you will make your decision.

Job-Acceptance Message

It is a good idea to put your acceptance in writing. Restate the title of the position, salary, and starting date, and clarify details or special conditions. If the employer has sent you forms to complete, indicate that they are attached. End by expressing appreciation and confirming your acceptance of the offer.

Job-Refusal Message

Politely decline the position, thanking the employer for the offer and the organization's interest in you. Being courteous ensures that future job opportunities—for you and fellow graduates of your school—will not be adversely affected.

Reference-Request Message

Choose your referees who think well of you and can speak knowledgeably about your skills and capabilities based on your academic, professional, or volunteer work. If you sense someone's hesitation to act as your reference, move on and ask another person. Be sure to ask for permission before you list anyone as a reference. In your request, be sure to do the following:

- mention the job for which you are applying, its requirements, and the deadline for applications
- update the reader on significant recent accomplishments
- review good experiences the referee might remember you by
- include a copy of your resumé

Checklist
Chapter Review

Resumé

☐ **Name and address:** Does your resumé supply adequate contact information, including a daytime telephone number and a campus and/or permanent address?

☐ **Objective:** Does your resumé include an employment objective? Does the objective match the position you are applying for?

☐ **Education:** Are details of your education arranged in parallel form?

(Continued)

- ❏ **Experience:** Does your work experience start with your present or most recent employment? Do you use action verbs, specific details, and parallel form to describe your duties, activities, and achievements? Does your resumé show how you contributed to the workplace during previous employment? Is information about your work experience arranged strategically to show you are a reliable employee with a steady work history?

- ❏ **Skills and activities:** Does the resumé include a section that describes your skills? Does it emphasize your mastery of software and computer applications?

- ❏ **Overall content:** Do the skill headings and statements help to present you as well qualified? Is the content shaped to target a specific job?

- ❏ **Format:** Does your document look well balanced and tidy? Is the spacing attractive? Is the format consistent throughout? Does it fit on one or two pages?

- ❏ **Accuracy:** Is your resumé free of typographical errors, faulty punctuation, misspelled words, and incorrect capitalization? Has it been proofread by someone who gave you constructive feedback? Will it be submitted to the employer according to instructions posted in the advertisement or on the job site?

- ❏ **Persuasiveness:** Is your product persuasive? Does it market your skills and qualifications to HR personnel? Does it accentuate positives and de-emphasize or eliminate negatives? Does it convince a prospective employer that you can make a strong contribution?

- ❏ **Edge factor:** Will your resumé stand out against the competition? Do its design and content give it an advantage?

Cover Letter

Opening

- ❏ Does the letter gain attention and clearly identify the position for which you are applying?

- ❏ Is it free of clichéd, overworked expressions?

- ❏ Does it give a brief summary describing how your qualifications fit the job requirements?

Body

- ❏ Does the letter build interest by showing how your experience and preparation fill the requirements of the job?

- ❏ Does it emphasize reader benefits and give a brief summation of your selling points?

- ❏ Does it provide examples of your accomplishments and quantify them?

- ❏ Do action verbs accurately describe your skills?

- ❏ Does it refer the reader to your resumé?

- ❏ Does it vary sentence structure to reduce the dominance of *I*?

Closing

- ❏ Does it ask for an interview? Does it supply contact information that will make it easy for the employer to reach you?

- ❏ Does it briefly recap your main qualifications and link them to contributions you could make to the company?

- ❑ Does it include a forward-looking remark or mention how you will follow up?
- ❑ Does it end courteously?

Overall

- ❑ Is the letter brief enough to retain the reader's attention (not less than two paragraphs and not more than one substantial page)?
- ❑ Is it free of typographical errors as well as errors in grammar, spelling, and punctuation?
- ❑ Is it addressed correctly to the appropriate person or department?
- ❑ Is its layout neat and balanced?
- ❑ Is its tone pleasant, positive, and professional?
- ❑ Does the typography match that of the resumé in order to unify the package?

Exercises, Workshops, and Discussion Forums

1. **Identifying Keywords.** Visit an online job bank and find a listing for a job you are or will soon be qualified for. Make a list of its keywords and place an asterisk (*) beside the skills you possess. Are you currently missing skills that would make you more employable?

2. **Preparing a Professional Data Record.** Evaluate your qualifications by compiling personal data relating to your education, work experience, skills, activities, awards, and references. Use action-oriented words to describe your skills and accomplishments.

3. **Researching Employment Prospects.** Record basic contact information and instructions on how to apply to five companies in your area. Take note of information (about corporate culture, size of the company, etc.) that might be used in a prospecting letter or help you compile a list of questions to ask at an informational interview.

4. **Revising a Resumé.** The resumé on page 360 contains numerous faults. Analyze its strengths and weaknesses and suggest how it could be improved. Working in a group of three or four, collaborate on a revision that will help Nadia Salerno obtain an interview based on the qualifications she lists.

5. **Creating a Chronological Resumé.** Using the data you developed in activity 2, create a standard chronological resumé.

6. **Creating a Scannable Resumé.** Take your current resumé and use its information to prepare a scannable resumé.

7. **Writing a Personal Statement.** Identify a job or program relevant to your career direction that attracts your interest. Imagine that the application requires you to prepare a 250-word personal statement. Refer to the application specifications, and prepare a targeted personal statement that highlights why you are applying and why you are a fit for this opening or opportunity.

8. **Revising Application Letters.** Working in a group of three or four, analyze the excerpts from application letters on page 363 What impression does each one make? How could their tone, professionalism, and overall expression be improved? List the major faults of each letter, and work together to revise each one.

9. **Writing Cover Letters.** Using details from your resumé, write solicited (ad-response) and unsolicited (prospecting) letters of application based on the following instructions.
   a) Write an application letter in response to the job listing you found for activity 1. Refer to your resumé, and identify your qualifications for the position.

NADIA SALERNO

54 Big Nickel Lane
Sudbury, ON
P5K 1H7

(706) 555-9841

E-mail: soccergirl@hotmail.com

247 Dunlop Street
Toronto, ON
M9A 2M1

(416) 555-554

CAREER OBJECTIVE   Work in child daycare facility

EXPERIENCE   **ECD Assistant**, Childcare Connection, Toronto, Ontario
May 2020 to present
- Play music for children.
- Write daily evaluations.
- Take care of children.

ECD Assistant (part-time), Play Well Daycare, Toronto

ECD Assistant (internship), Kids First Nursery, Toronto
September 2019 to May 2020

HONOURS AND   I enjoy playing soccer.
ACTIVITIES

EDUCATION

Humber College , Toronto, Ontario
Montessori Certificate

Seneca College, Toronto, Ontario
Diploma in Early Childhood Education, June 2020

Royal Conservatory of Music , Toronto, Ontario
ARTC (Piano), 2019

b) From the list of companies you prospected in activity 3, select the one you are most interested in and write an unsolicited letter.

10. **Creating a Career Portfolio.** Watch the video "Job Interview—Creating a Portfolio," available from MonkeySee on YouTube (*www.youtube.com/watch?v=hQhigdJ-xEk*). Based on the information and advice given in the video, put together a visually appealing portfolio that reflects your accomplishments, training, and experiences.

11. **Practising an Interview.** First, read Jacquelyn Smith's "How to Ace the 50 Most Common Interview Questions" (*www.forbes.com/sites/jacquelynsmith/2013/01/11/how-to-ace-the-50-most-common-interview-questions/#66fcf2784873*). Next, work in a group of three or four to simulate the interview process. One person should play the role of the interviewer, one should take the role of the applicant, and the other one or two should observe and evaluate the

I respectfully submit my strong application for the position of regional sales manager. I have attached my resumé. I have a great deal of experience in the fashion retail industry. I believe this position is tailor-made to my considerable skills and talents. I am more than ready to meet the challenges of this position. I believe I have earned the opportunity to work for a prestigious and well-respected employer such as Bryant McKay.

I hold a degree in business administration from Western University, where I was an outstanding student. I completed all of my marketing courses with top honours. I am now a great salesperson. My communication skills are much better than those of my peers. I take pride in my ability to work well with others in a managerial capacity. Although I do not have any public-relations experience, I am a quick learner and should be able to master core public-relations skills in no time. My only regret in my short career is that my previous employers did not value the tremendous contributions I made to their organizations.

It would be a shame if you were to miss out on the opportunity to hire me. I look forward to interviewing with you and to the possibility of earning $100,000 a year with your company.

Please be advised that this is an application for the job that was advertised recently. Although I have just part-time experience, I feel I could be the independent sales representative your looking for.

I will graduate soon. I am sure you will recanize that my education qualifies me for this job. My communication skills are real good and people say I get along with them real well.

Please telephone me and let me know when I should come in for an interview. Will I need to fill out an application?

---

applicant's performance. Repeat the process until everyone has had a chance to be the applicant. Interviewers should select and ask eight to ten of the questions listed in Smith's article, and applicants should refer to the career portfolio they created for activity 10. Afterward, discuss the strengths and weaknesses of each applicant's interviewing skills.

12. **Creating a Video Application.** Imagine that a requirement of a job application is creating a three-minute video. Create a video and upload it to your course management platform (or another platform your instructor uses for this activity). Screen each other's videos in class and provide feedback to your classmates from the perspective of a recruiter. What constructive criticism can you offer?

13. **Creating an Online or Digital Portfolio.** A digital profile shows projects and pieces of work you have completed to provide evidence of your talents, capabilities, and domain of expertise to prospective employers.

a) Compile a list of completed projects and pieces of work that best represent what you can do and will be able to do at the end of your program—ones you can add now and ones to add later as expected by future employers according to training for them to use to evaluate your knowledge and skills. Include freelance, volunteer-based, and, when allowable, relevant work projects you may have completed outside of your program. Next, find a job posting in your field. How would you edit the list based on the requirements of the job to amplify certain skills?

b) Write a sample overview for the projects or pieces of work you have already completed, along with reflective framing material (such as a personal statement).

c) Identify the social media and portfolio platforms where you want your portfolio to be seen and where it would have the most accessibility and views. Are some more advantageous than others based on the type of work you do?

d) Develop a succinct strategy for promoting your portfolio and marketing it to prospective employers.

14. **Composing a Thank-You Letter.** After completing the interview role-playing workshop (activity 11), write a letter of appreciation to the interviewer. Exchange letters and discuss what makes a thank-you letter most effective.

Writing Improvement Exercises

1. **Writing Objective Statements.** From a job site or the careers pages of a newspaper, select three advertisements for jobs that closely match your qualifications. For each one, write a one- to three-line objective statement targeted to the position.

2. **Describing Duties and Accomplishments in Resumés.** Rewrite the following descriptions of significant work duties and accomplishments in appropriate resumé style. Eliminate personal pronouns, begin points with strong and specific action verbs, make points concise, apply parallel structure, and quantify accomplishments where possible.

   a) Administrative Assistant Position:

   I was responsible for the reorganization of procedures and implementation of cost-containment policies. I also monitored the production of all printed materials and ordered supplies and maintained on- and off-site inventories. I also did many mass mailings.

   b) Sales Manager/Production Assistant Position:

   I did a study of automobile accessory needs of 50 car dealerships in Victoria. I was responsible for marketing and sales for a manufacturer of automobile accessories. I also developed new accounts and maintained existing customers. I headed a sales team that generated orders for sales of $3 million annually. In this capacity, I monitored and trained a sales staff of seven to augment a high standard of service and increase profitability. I also travel to off-road functions to promote products.

3. **Using Descriptive, Action-Oriented Language for Resumés.** Improve the following job descriptions by using more precise, action-oriented language.

   a) Gave advice to sales staff on meeting monthly sales quotas.

   b) Did all bookkeeping functions, including internal audits, once a month.

   c) Talked with regular clients all the time to do technical support.

   d) Did a study of cost–benefit to bring about the updating of PCs to make network integration for 200 users a lot better.

   e) Got together a team to train staff in new safety procedures.

4. **Writing a Letter of Application.** Using information from Mitra Das's resumé (Figure 10.1), write a cover letter that answers the advertisement on page 341.

Redferns Limited

Area Sales Manager

Toronto, Ontario, Canada

Style. Sophistication. Elegance. It is what you expect from Redferns, one of Canada's leading fashion and lifestyle retailers.

This position will assist the store manager by providing team direction to ensure the execution and achievement of corporate initiatives, projected sales goals, and exceptional customer-service levels.

Responsibilities:

- Demonstrate visible leadership.

- Achieve targeted department sales goals through selling the Redferns way.

- Provide supervision, coaching/training, and mentoring to team members and participate in performance assessment of sales staff.

- Develop and maintain a high level of product knowledge pertaining to merchandise.

- Ensure ongoing department clientele development.

- Maintain high standards of accountability for department operation, budgets, and shortage control.

- Control and monitor proper stock-to-sales ratio.

- Follow all health-and-safety guidelines.

Required skills:

- Supervisory/management experience

- Strong demonstration of leadership skills

- Excellent organizational and follow-up skills

- Positive attitude

A career with Redferns is one of the most exciting opportunities in Canadian retail and includes a comprehensive benefits package.

Interested candidates are invited to submit their resumés to careers@redferns.com.

Online Activities

1. **Online Career Test.** Take the career aptitude test offered by What Career Is Right for Me? Once you have your results, conduct an online search to explore one of the career options that appeals to you.

   www.whatcareerisrightforme.com/

2. **Auditing Your Digital Footprint and Shadow.** For this activity, consider your digital image or persona by Googling yourself and conducting a three-pronged online search of the following:

   a) your digital persona based on publicly available information you consciously created about yourself or used to express yourself (for instance, your social media profile)

   b) your digital persona based on information available about you beyond your control (what others say about you and private posts you had not assumed were public)

   c) your digital persona based on information that is inadequate or lacking (e.g., a missing LinkedIn profile)

   Write a paragraph summarizing the impression you have of yourself—one that might be shared by an employer and can further qualify you or disqualify you for a job. Did you find anything unexpected that might lead employers to form an unfavourable impression? Based on your audit, what best practices for shaping an employment-friendly online persona will you follow from now on?

3. **Analyzing a Job Ad.** Visit a job site such as Indeed.ca and use a job title linked to your career intentions to find a posting for a job of interest to you. Conduct an audit of the information that the ad provides. Write a paragraph describing the organizational culture and your person-job fit.

4. **Research Companies Online.** What can you find out about a company through its website or its Facebook presence? Visit the following corporate sites and prepare a brief fact sheet on each one. What distinguishes the companies in terms of size, corporate culture, products and the language, images, and stories it uses to represent and brand itself online?

Bombardier
www.bombardier.com
www.facebook.com/Bombardier.corpo/

Herschel Supply Company
www.herschel.ca/about
www.facebook.com/HerschelSupply

Sobeys
www.sobeys.com
www.facebook.com/Sobeys/

5. **Build a Twitter Network.** Set up a professional Twitter account and find pundits, commentators, organizations, and top business professionals to follow based on your existing knowledge of a specific industry. Check the "Who to Follow" section to find out who the people you follow are following. Start building relationships by retweeting the best tweets or writing to the authors.

6. **Build a LinkedIn Network.** Set up a LinkedIn profile and use the "Advanced Search" option to find people, using keywords such as the name of your industry, geographic location, or job title. Find at least ten people relevant to your career or studies to follow or connect with.

7. **Online Resumé Builder.** Visit the online resumé and cover letter builder provided by the Government of Manitoba, and follow the prompts to create a chronological, functional, or combination resumé.

   http://resume.manitobacareerdevelopment.ca/en/

8. **Understanding Recruitment and Talent-Acquisition Apps.** Preparing a resumé, identifying an appropriate job opening and submitting application are crucial steps in securing employment, but what happens once an application reaches recruiters? The IBM Watson Recruitment User Guide summarized at the link below provides a window on how candidates are evaluated. Review the page below and summarize and discuss the metrics the are used. Consider how what you have learned about the process and how it changes the way you might think about what goes into your resumé.

*www.ibm.com/support/knowledgecenter/en/
SS4T5W/IBM_Watson_Recruitment_User_Guide/
whatisibmwr.html*

9. **Gaining Practice with Job Interview Simulators.** Job interview simulators can have some limited usefulness in preparing for an actual job interview. Use this link or search for an interview simulator to gain practice in answering standard interview questions.

https://elc.polyu.edu.hk/cill/eiw/interviews/

10. **Gaining Personality Insights from Writing Style.** AI-driven systems and humans are adept at sensing personality through the stories people tell and the way they express themselves. Companies can now use services such as IBM Watson Personality Insights, which applies linguistic analytics and personality theory to make educated assumptions about applicants and their attributes based on how they write. Use the link below to analyze the sample tweets. You can then instruct the service to analyze one of your tweets to glean insights about your Twitter personality (note: authorization is required to access your Twitter account). How do Watson's insights different from your self-perception?

https://personality-insights-demo.ng.bluemix.net/

11. **Brainstorming Content for a Digital Portfolio or Personal Branding Site.** Based on what you know now about your future career and what you can find out about professionals already working in the field (via a Google search), create a one-page plan for the content and design for your digital portfolio or a personal brand site. Explain the content and design decisions you made.

11 Informal Reports

Chapter Preview

Reports organize information for specific purposes and audiences and are essential to organizational planning, management, and decision-making. This chapter explores characteristic and types of informal business reports, as well as standard formats and plans for organizing them. You'll learn how to write standard types of informal reports, apply different levels of headings within those reports, and use graphics to tell meaningful stories about your data.

Learning Objectives

1. Identify the characteristics of an effective business report.
2. Differentiate between informal and formal reports and between informational and analytical reports.
3. Identify standard report formats.
4. Apply direct and indirect writing plans for reports.
5. Organize reports according to their purposes and apply informative headings.
6. Identify steps in the report-writing process.
7. Create meaningful and interesting graphics.
8. Describe types of reports according to their purpose.

NYCStock/Shutterstock.com

In January 2019, Vancouver-founded tech company Slack reported that it had over 10 million daily active users[1] in companies that include 21st Century Fox, Dow Jones, and the NASA Jet Propulsion Laboratory.[2] Have you used Slack, or a program like it, in a workplace?

As more work moves online, the nature of internal communication continues to evolve with new technologies. One company at the forefront of changing business communication is Slack Technologies Inc., founded in 2009 by Canadian entrepreneur Stewart Butterfield in Vancouver. Slack is a workplace collaboration platform that allows co-workers to message each other and chat about work and the workplace on searchable, hashtagged "channels." Slack's friendly, easy-to-use interface has proven popular in many companies.

While many users know Slack as an office-based social media site that primarily serves as an alternative for e-mail, Slack can be used to deliver many forms of informal reports—including social engagement and web traffic reports—that help managers stay aware of metrics and key progress indicators.[3] In its promotional material, Slack promises to help businesses function more efficiently by offering an easy way to compile progress reports and stay up-to-date on ongoing projects.[4] As you develop your skills and knowledge of internal reports through this chapter, consider how your abilities to write clear, professional reports and produce meaningful graphics could transfer to platforms like Slack, and the kinds of data collection that they facilitate.

Introduction to Report Writing

business report A document in which factual information is compiled and organized for a specific purpose and audience.

A **business report** is an essential form of corporate communication that helps managers and co-workers stay informed, review opinions, plan for the future, and make decisions. The larger an organization is, the more essential clear, easy to read, and concise reports are to its successful operation and management. Reports help departments to coordinate initiatives and activities and help managers to stay in touch with and on top of changing circumstances. These documents let management see the big picture so they can respond quickly and decisively to minor personnel, business, and technical difficulties before they become major problems. Over the years, a company's reports form an extended and permanent corporate journal that tracks trends and includes accounts of incidents, actions, decisions, and policies. Reports are legal documents that can be used as evidence in court, and so they must be accurate, complete, and objective.

informal report A report using a letter or memo format, usually ranging from a few paragraphs to ten pages in length.

An **informal report** is usually under ten pages and often under one or two. Its style is relatively casual, using a personal tone and the occasional personal pronoun or

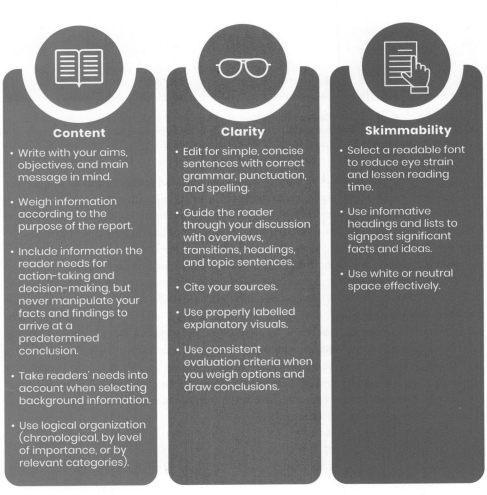

Content
- Write with your aims, objectives, and main message in mind.
- Weigh information according to the purpose of the report.
- Include information the reader needs for action-taking and decision-making, but never manipulate your facts and findings to arrive at a predetermined conclusion.
- Take readers' needs into account when selecting background information.
- Use logical organization (chronological, by level of importance, or by relevant categories).

Clarity
- Edit for simple, concise sentences with correct grammar, punctuation, and spelling.
- Guide the reader through your discussion with overviews, transitions, headings, and topic sentences.
- Cite your sources.
- Use properly labelled explanatory visuals.
- Use consistent evaluation criteria when you weigh options and draw conclusions.

Skimmability
- Select a readable font to reduce eye strain and lessen reading time.
- Use informative headings and lists to signpost significant facts and ideas.
- Use white or neutral space effectively.

FIGURE 11.1 The quality of a report and its effectiveness depend on three things that you, as a writer, need to control: content, clarity, and skimmability.

contraction. It is written as a letter or memo divided into subsections that are marked off by headings and, when required, subheadings. The informal report is the most routine of all reports and the type you will have to write most often. **Formal reports**, by contrast, tackle more complex and difficult problems and typically require five or six pages to do so, and sometimes as many as two hundred or more. Formal reports are discussed in detail in Chapter 12.

formal report A multi-page business document based on extensive research and following a prescribed format or pattern that includes elements such as a title page, transmittal or cover letter, table of contents, and abstract.

Distinguishing Features of Short Reports

Reports can vary in length, approach, and scope. They also differ according to their purpose, audience, and format (how they look and in what form their information is delivered). Here are a few ways of thinking of reports that will help to identify and differentiate them.

Purpose

There are two general kinds of informal reporting: informational and analytical/ recommendation. **Informational reports** answer questions and provide information without analysis. Informational reports may look into options, outline performance, or investigate equipment, but they never go so far as to offer recommendations. Readers of this type of report are in a neutral or receptive frame of mind: they want to know certain facts without being persuaded of anything. **Analytical** or **recommendation reports** go a step further by interpreting data and offering recommendations that may aid in problem-solving and decision-making. Because persuasion may be required in convincing readers that the proposed recommendation or conclusion is appropriate, greater thought has to be given to how readers might respond and to how the pros and cons of each alternative should be weighed, presented, and discussed. Writers of analytical reports need to present evidence in support of findings and establish criteria for any alternatives that are evaluated.

informational report A short report that collects data related to a routine activity without offering analysis or recommending action; its three parts are introduction, findings, and summary/ conclusion.

analytical report (or **recommendation report**) A report that interprets and analyzes information and offers recommendations based on findings.

Formats and Distribution

The following options for business reports range from least to most formal:

- **Memorandum report:** This format is appropriate for circulating data within an organization. **Memorandum reports** are under ten pages and use an informal, conversational style. These reports have the following features:
  » 1- to 1¼-inch (2.54- to 3.18-centimetre) side margins
  » the standard guidewords TO, FROM, DATE, and SUBJECT (usually the report's primary recommendation)
  » single-spaced paragraphs separated by two blank lines
- **Prepared-form report:** Time-saving forms with standardized headings are useful for recording repetitive data or for describing routine activities within an organization.
- **Letter report:** Letter format is often used for short, informal reports prepared by one organization and sent to another. A **letter report**, prepared on company

memorandum report A short, internal report presented in memo format.

letter report A short, external report presented in letter format.

stationery, contains all the elements usually found in a letter (date, inside address, return address, salutation, complimentary close). Descriptive headings can be used.

- **PowerPoint report:** A recent trend among business executives and consultants is the use of PowerPoint for short written reports, especially periodic reports such as progress reports. Because PowerPoint does not accommodate a high level of informative detail, it is best to use notes pages in a printed slide deck in order to provide adequate explanation of the text and graphics on each slide.
- **Formal report:** Formal reports are usually prepared in manuscript format and printed on plain paper. They have headings and subheadings.

Direct and Indirect Approaches

As you learned in chapters 7 to 9, the choice of a direct or indirect writing plan depends on the content of your letter or memo and the expectations your reader may have about it. The same general approaches apply to the organization of reports.

Direct Approach: Informational and Analytical Reports

Routine, non-sensitive information related to recurring activities and one-time situations is delivered most effectively when it is presented directly. Organizing an informational report comes with the expectation that readers will support or be interested in what you have to say and won't have to be persuaded. Because of its convenience, the direct approach is standard for most informational reports, in which sections are arranged in the following order:

- Purpose/Introduction/Background
- Facts and Findings
- Summary

You can also use the direct approach in analytical reports when you expect that the reader will agree with your recommendations without any persuasion. A direct-approach analytical report, which includes conclusions and recommendations, presents its information in the following order:

- Introduction/Problem/Background
- Conclusions or Recommendations
- Facts and Findings
- Discussion and Analysis

Indirect Approach: Analytical Reports

When you expect some resistance or displeasure on the part of the reader, an indirect approach works best. The more you need to persuade or educate your reader, the more you should consider using an indirect approach that builds gradual acceptance for the actions you endorse. The information is usually presented in the following order:

- Purpose/Introduction/Problem
- Facts and Findings
- Discussion and Analysis
- Conclusions or Recommendations

By mirroring the logical processes of problem-solving, this pattern works well when readers aren't familiar with the topic or problem.

Writing Style for Short Reports

Short informal reports use more personal language than long reports and may include personal pronouns such as *I* and *we* and even contractions, but they still must project an air of objectivity and professionalism so that readers will accept their findings and conclusions.

When you know the reader fairly well, your tone can be somewhat relaxed. When the reader is a stranger or a top manager, it is better to err on the side of caution and use a more impersonal style, one that is neutral but not overly stuffy. In all cases, avoid using any kind of language that may offend the reader, especially words that exaggerate or show bias.

Keep in mind that readers have to be able to decode the text when reading quickly. As you compose your report, take the time to check for ambiguous words and phrases. If in doubt, spell it out in specifics.

Headings

The longer a report, the more readers rely on **headings** to scan, skim, and navigate the document. Like signposts, headings guide readers through the text. Headings provide an outline or overview, a way of showing that the structure you have chosen for your report is clear and cohesive. Different heading levels (distinguished by size, colour, weight, underlining, and italics) can show which parts of the report belong together and the relative importance of each part. Short reports usually feature headings of the appropriate level before every section and subsection. Here are seven tips for using headings effectively:

heading Title or subtitle, usually a word or short phrase, within the body of a document that identifies its parts and gives clues to its organization.

1. **Use either functional or descriptive headings. Functional headings** are basic, generic headings (*Introduction*, *Findings*, *Summary*) that can be used in almost any report but are found most commonly in routine ones. **Descriptive** or **talking heads** are high-information headings that reflect the actual content of a report, making the report easy to skim (e.g., *Voicemail an Inappropriate Medium for Confidential Information*). Functional and descriptive headings can often be combined (*Recommendations: New Policy on Secure Messaging*).
2. **Keep headings short and clear.** Limit headings to eight words, but keep in mind that using a vague heading defeats the purpose of having a heading.

functional heading Each of a series of generic headings that, when taken together, show a report in outline.

descriptive head (or **talking head**) A heading that describes the actual content of a report and provides more information about it.

GaudiLab/Shutterstock.com

The writing style you use for a short report can be fairly relaxed, especially if you are writing the report for a colleague you know well. However, reports aimed at customers, clients, or top managers, regardless of their length, should be written in a more formal and professional style.

3. **Use parallel construction.** For the sake of consistency and readability, use balanced phrases and a parallel structure for subheadings:

Not parallel:	Improved Transmission of Sensitive Information
	How can we end e-mail errors?
	Voicemail problems
	Why we should change fax procedures
Parallel:	Improved Transmission of Sensitive Information
	Ending e-mail errors
	Eliminating voicemail problems
	Changing fax procedures

Functional Headings	**Descriptive Headings**	**Combination Headings**
• Background • Findings • Discussion and Analysis • Recommendations • Conclusion	• Watching Trends • How an On-site Paging System Could Benefit Us • Installation and Technical Issues	• Problem: Producing Memorable Corporate Functions Findings • Solution and Alternatives: Corporate-Event Management Companies

FIGURE 11.2 Types of headings with examples of each

4. **Ensure headings are clearly ranked.** Show the rank and relative importance of headings by formatting each level systematically. Here are a few suggestions on how to format three different levels of headings:

FIRST LEVEL

First-level headings can be typed in bold with all caps, centred. Text follows on a new line.

Second Level

Second-level headings can be typed in bold and run flush with the left margin. Only the first letter of each word is capitalized (this is also known as title case). Text follows on a new line.

Third level. Third-level headings can be typed in bold and run flush with the left margin. Only the first letter of the first word is capitalized. The heading is followed by a period and text follows on the same line.

5. **Put headings where they belong.** Don't use a subheading unless you plan to divide the material that follows into at least two subsections. Unless a heading or subheading will be followed by at least two lines of text at the bottom of a page, type it at the top of the next page.
6. **Don't enclose headings in quotation marks.** Bold type and capitalization are enough to distinguish a heading from surrounding text.
7. **Don't use a heading as the antecedent for a pronoun.** The line of text after the heading or subheading should not begin with *this, that, these,* or *those* alone because the reader may not know what you are referring to; instead, repeat the noun from the heading and add it to the pronoun (*This e-mail error . . .*).

Steps in the Writing Process

Like any task that involves time, effort, and resources, writing a report takes planning. It may help to think of your report as a process involving several achievable steps: planning, researching/analyzing information, composing, and revising.

Planning

Your first job is to define the boundaries of the project and think about any restrictions you may face in terms of time, finances, and personnel. The more extensive a report is and the more people there are involved in its production, the more necessary it is to create a work plan that includes a timeline. A work plan sets out the scope of the project, outlines how work will be done, identifies the amount and type(s) of research, and divides responsibilities according to each phase of the project.

Researching/Analyzing Data and Information

Before you begin your research, consider the various aspects of the subject of your informal report—how it can be divided into manageable sections, the larger issues related to it, and the changing trends or circumstances that may affect it—as this will give you a better idea about where to begin your search. Keep in mind that the information you collect should be current, valid, and reliable. Any data you use must meet these criteria, most of all statistics. For any figures you cite you must name their source, how they were derived, and how recent they are. Scrutinize survey results, paying close attention to the size of the sample group.

Because any report is only as good as the information that backs it up, it is essential to evaluate data to decide what portion of it is usable. You can extract pertinent facts from reams of raw data through a process of sorting and logical sequencing. In analytical reports, information-gathering goes hand in hand with analysis and tabulation—spotting trends and relationships among the facts and numerical data you have gathered, identifying logical patterns, and being prepared to back them up with illustrations. If you are working from raw numerical data consisting of a range of values, the following statistical terms may be of use to you as you attempt to describe and make sense of what you have assembled:

- **Mean** is the term for the arithmetic average calculated by dividing the total sum by the total number of units (e.g., the mean of 2, 5, 5, 5, and 13 is 6).
- **Median** is the term for the middle value of a series (e.g., the median of 2, 5, 5, 5, and 13 is 5).
- **Mode** is the term for the value that appears most frequently (e.g., the mode of 2, 5, 5, 5, and 13 is 5).
- **Range** describes the span between the lowest and highest value in a set.

No matter how compelling your data is, it won't have an impact unless it is first stored, tabulated, and managed effectively. Always keep track of where your data comes from, and establish a system for storing the information you collect. For each source, record the bibliographic details you will need when compiling a list of resources, including the following:

- the title of the document, web page, article, periodical, book, and/or other work from which it was taken
- the author's name
- the publisher/web address
- the publication date/web access date

alphanumeric outline
An outlining system that combines numbers and letters to differentiate levels of headings.

decimal outline (or **numeric outline**) An outlining system that uses a combination of numbers and decimal points to differentiate levels of headings.

Composing and Revising

Once you finish collecting data and drawing conclusions from it, your task is to communicate your findings in a logical and methodical way. Developing an outline, even a very brief one, can help you gain control over your material and smooth the flow of ideas and information. A working outline can be written in point form or complete sentences, and it can be organized as an **alphanumeric outline** (based on a combination of numbers and letters) or a **decimal outline**.

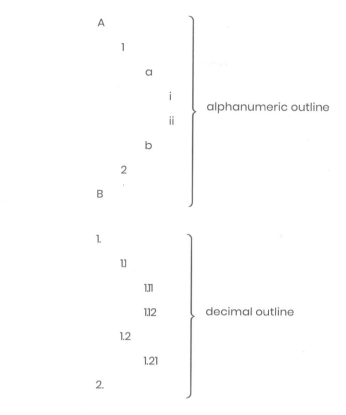

A
   1
     a
       i
       ii
     b
   2
B

} alphanumeric outline

OR

1.
  1.1
    1.11
    1.12
  1.2
    1.21
2.

} decimal outline

Outlines are particularly useful for lengthy, formal reports.

Until the final edited version is submitted, think of your report as a work in progress. Committing your facts and ideas to the printed page may require multiple drafts. Revising and editing your document may require cuts, additions, reorderings, and rewrites. Put yourself in the reader's place and ask, *Is all this detail really necessary? Are items logically linked? Could entire sections be removed without harming the report?*

If you have been working collaboratively, make sure each member of the group has read the report and is satisfied with the text of the final draft. Leave as much time as possible between completing the final draft and starting to edit. A day or two is optimal, but even an hour or so will give you the objectivity you need to read your document with a critical eye. Work from a printout or use the "track changes" option available in many word-processing programs. Once you are satisfied with the final version, leave time to proofread the document more than once, preferably making several passes over the document to read for content, spelling and grammar, tone, clarity, and coherence. Finally, cast your eye over the report to check for inconsistent or incorrect formatting.

iStock.com/Rawpixel

As you revise your report, try to look at the "big picture"—examine how each component contributes to the whole, ensure that your presentation of data and analysis is logical, and make certain that you've included enough detail for your reader to fully comprehend the report.

Elements of Informal Reports

Short, informal reports tell stories and share information in a logical and systematic way, grouping information in manageable, standardized elements from beginning to end. Any informal report has three major parts: an introduction that includes a statement of purpose, a findings section, and a closing summary or conclusion (with or without recommendations). Because there is no single right way of organizing a report, the headings you use are largely up to you and depend on the type of report you are writing, what you have to say, and whether your report contains recommendations.

Introductory Statement

introduction The first section in the body of a report, which provides readers with the information they need in order to understand and evaluate the report itself; it must include either the report's purpose or a statement of the problem the report addresses.

The introductory statement announces the report, indicating what it examines and providing any necessary background information. This section of the report is called the "**Introduction**" (or "Background"). Sometimes it simply states the purpose of the report, often in just a sentence: *This report examines the disposal of documents in our workplace.* In other cases, it may link that purpose with report recommendations: *This report on document disposal suggests ways to protect our intellectual property and client privilege.* It should specify the problem or technical question you will deal with and indicate the rhetorical purpose your report is aimed at achieving. An introduction may also preview key points (in the sequence in which they will be presented) or establish the limits of the report, either in the introduction itself or under separate headings immediately following it.

Findings

findings The most substantial part of a report, in which qualitative and numeric data is presented and organized by time, convention, order of importance, or component.

Also commonly called "Results" or "Facts," the "**Findings**" section is the most substantial part of a report. It offers details and relates results to circumstances. In a subsequent but related section called "Discussion/Analysis," findings are explained and made meaningful through analysis. Overall these sections reinforce logical connections between relevant facts and any conclusions or recommendations that are ultimately made.

The data can be organized under several subheadings written in parallel form. Use an appropriate method of organization to guide the reader through your discussion: (1) present facts chronologically, alphabetically, or in order of their importance; (2) draw comparisons, considering options one by one or developing point-by-point comparisons; and (3) divide or classify the topic, breaking it down into its component parts or applying consistent criteria in order to evaluate it.

Summary/Conclusions/Recommendations

summary The closing or second-last section of a report that briefly restates its main points.

conclusions and recommendations The closing section of an analytical or a recommendation report in which specific actions are proposed to solve a problem or aid decision-making.

Optional in informational reports (where it is called "**Summary**"), the concluding section is crucial to analytical reports, where it is called "**Conclusions and Recommendations**." The conclusions are the part of the report in which readers are often most interested. Though conclusions and recommendations are often found under the same heading and numbered for easy reference, they differ substantially in both purpose and phrasing. Conclusions present objective analysis directly related to the report's problem and findings (e.g., *Among forms of two-factor authentication, biometrics is the best method of ensuring secure online transactions*), whereas recommendations make specific suggestions for actions that will solve the problem (*Explore the possibility of using biometric fingerprint readers as the primary means of two-factor authentication*). Recommendations are typically phrased as commands, beginning with a strong action verb.

Only offer recommendations when you have been asked to do so, in which case you may also choose to explain how those recommendations can be implemented. In an analytical report, the recommendations section comes after the introduction (in direct-approach reports) or toward the end (in indirect-approach reports). When chances are good that readers will be receptive to your recommendation, it can be included in the title of the report—*Recommendation to Limit Fax Transmissions of Client Information*—and then repeated in the body of the report itself. In cases where there is more than one recommendation, the recommendations can be listed in order of their importance (from most important to least important).

Designed for simplicity, most informal reports do not include front and back matter such as covers, title pages, tables of contents, or lists of illustrations. Appendices, though rare, can be used to incorporate charts, supporting data, diagrams, or other documents needed to understand the recommendations.

Using Graphics and Visuals

A common feature of reports is the use of **visual aids**, which reflect the analysis of data and plot out the patterns and relationships you have found through your observations and research. They make numerical information meaningful to readers and clarify complex data. Visuals typically include tables, matrixes, pie charts, bar charts, line graphs, flow charts, organizational charts, and illustrations (see Table 11.1). To start creating professional-looking graphics, all you need is the assembled data and a computer program capable of producing the type of graphics you want (e.g., Excel or PowerPoint).

The most effective visuals meet several criteria:

- clearly titled and clearly labelled on each part or axis
- uncluttered, intuitive, and easy to understand

visual aids Materials such as charts, graphs, tables, and illustrations that present information in visually appealing ways to show trends and relationships, represent numbers and quantities, and make abstract concepts concrete.

TABLE 11.1 Commonly Used Graphics: Quick-Reference Chart

TYPE	USE
Table	To present exact figures concisely
Matrix	To present qualitative information concisely
Pie chart	To show a whole unit and the proportions of its components
Bar chart	To show how one item compares with others
Line graph	To show changes in numerical data over time
Flow chart	To map out a procedure
Organizational chart	To map out the structure or hierarchy of a company

- accurate, functional, and ethical (with clear attribution through source lines and no made-up or skewed data)
- included for a purpose
- integrated or placed where they make the most sense—near to where they are referred to in the text if they are important, or in an appendix if they are supplemental

Edward R. Tufte, author of *The Visual Display of Quantitative Information* and expert in the presentation of informational graphics, has summed up how graphs and charts may best be used: "Give the viewer the greatest number of ideas in the shortest space of time with the least ink in the smallest space."[5]

Tables

table A chart that presents data, usually numerical, in a compact and systematic arrangement of rows and columns.

The most common type of visual, a **table**, is made up of rows and columns of cells that can be filled with exact figures and values. Concise and compact, tables consolidate a lot of data in a small space while retaining detail. They are useful for drawing attention to specific numbers and drawing comparisons between them. It is easy to create tables using your existing word-processing software. Here are a few tips:

- Design your table so it fits on one page. If the table is too wide to fit across the page, change the page layout to "Landscape" rather than "Portrait."
- Apply a heading that includes the table number and an appropriate title/caption. Number your tables sequentially as they appear in your report and separately from figures. Only when an explanation immediately precedes the table can the heading be omitted.
- Label all parts clearly and identify units in which figures are given. Numbers and titles/captions go above the table. Any other information, such as a source line identifying where the data originated from, goes below.
- For long tables with many rows, improve readability by shading alternate lines or by increasing the height of the cells.
- Use N/A ("not available"), a row of dots, or a dash to acknowledge missing data.

Canada's Most Counterfeited Bills in 2018

Denomination	Number of Fakes
$20	8,601
$100	13,682
$5	3,345
$50	5,776
$10	1,466
Total Value	$ 1,870,000

Data source: RCMP

FIGURE 11.3 Simple Table

Foreign Exchange Cross Rates (July 11, 2019)

	Canadian Dollar	US Dollar	Euro	Japanese Yen	British Pound
Canadian dollar	–	1.3075	1.4718	0.0121	1.6395
US dollar	0.7649	–	1.1260	0.0092	1.2548
Euro	0.6795	0.8881	–	0.0082	1.1144
Japanese yen	82.8760	108.2900	121.9345	–	135.8823
British pound	0.6103	0.7969	0.8974	0.0074	–

Data source: Bloomberg Markets

FIGURE 11.4 Complex Table

Matrixes

A **matrix** is a word table that contains qualitative information rather than numerical data. Matrixes are used in reports and proposals to list instructional materials and consolidate complex information in a page or less. For example, a matrix could be used to describe the investment objectives and risks of different types of funds offered by a securities company.

> **matrix** A word table that presents qualitative information in a rectangular format or arrangement.

Canadian Equities	Target Weighing	Manager	Investment Objectives	Risk
Canstar True North Fund	11%	Canstar Investments Canada Limited	The fund aims to achieve long-term capital growth. It invests primarily in Canadian equity securities.	Main risk: • equity risk Additional risks: • credit risk
ACA Canadian Premier Fund	9%	ACA Exmark Investments Inc.	The fund seeks to generate long-term capital growth by investing in a diversified portfolio of Canadian equity securities.	• interest rate risk • small company risk • derivative risk • equity risk
St. Lawrence Enterprise Fund	6%	St. Lawrence Financial Corporation	The fund pursues long-term capital growth while maintaining a commitment to capital protection by investing in Canadian small-capitalization equity securities.	• liquidity risk • securities lending risk • smaller companies risk` • equity risk

FIGURE 11.5 Matrix

Pie Charts

A **pie chart** is a circular graph, showing different values as proportions of the whole. Each slice or wedge represents a percentage (usually identified with a horizontal label). The whole circle has to be equivalent to 100 per cent for the pie chart to make sense. Values in a typical pie chart start at 12 o'clock and with the largest percentage (or the percentage of greatest interest to your report). Pie charts are most useful for comparing one

> **pie chart** A circular chart divided into sections, where each section represents a numerical proportion of the whole.

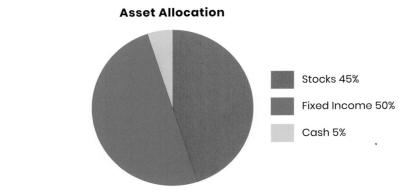

FIGURE 11.6 Pie Chart

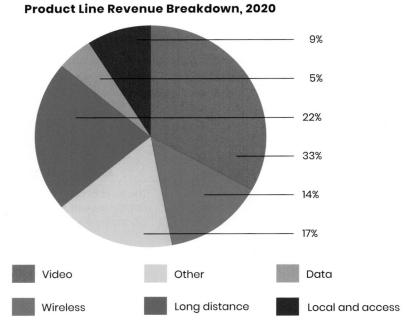

Data source: Telephone Services Annual Report 2020

FIGURE 11.7 Pie Chart

segment to the whole, by demonstrating, for example, a product line revenue breakdown, how a municipal tax dollar is spent, or how one fund compares against all others in an aggressive-growth investment portfolio.

Bar Charts

bar chart A visual consisting of parallel horizontal or vertical bars of varying lengths, each representing a specific item for comparison.

The purpose of a **bar chart** is to show how items compare with one another, how they compare over time, or what the relationship is between or among them. As the name suggests, a bar chart presents data in a series of bars or columns, drawn either horizontally (when labels are long) or vertically (when labels are short).

Arranged in logical or chronological order, bars can be segmented, divided, or stacked to show how the components of each add up. In this way, a **divided bar chart** (Figure 11.11) is much like a pie chart (Figures 11.6 and 11.7), but it can also be used to present complex quantitative information (Figure 11.12). A particular kind of bar chart called a **deviation bar chart** identifies positive and negative values, such as the year-by-year losses and gains of a dividend fund (see Figure 11.8). The data in all varieties

divided bar chart (or **segmented bar chart**) A visual consisting of a single bar divided according to the different portions that make up an item as a whole.

deviation bar chart A specific type of bar chart that shows positive and negative values.

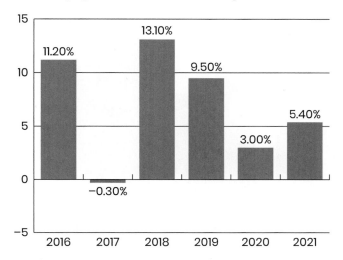

Mortgage Income Fund Year-by-Year Returns

FIGURE 11.8 Vertical Bar Chart

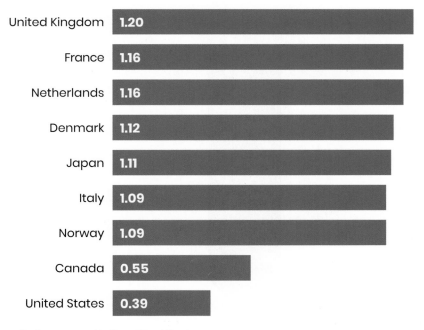

Gasoline Price per Litre (US dollars)

Data source: *National Post Business*

FIGURE 11.9 Horizontal Bar Chart

of bar charts should be properly scaled to fill the entire chart and not just squeezed into one corner. All bars should be the same width and close enough together to make comparison easy.

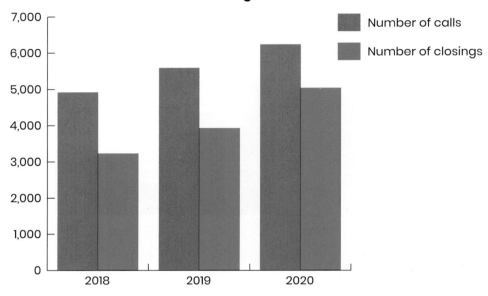

Annual Ratios of Sales Closings to Sales Calls

FIGURE 11.10 **Bar Chart Showing Comparisons**

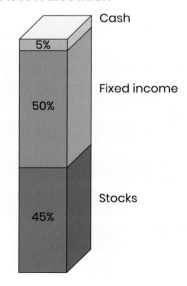

Asset Allocation

FIGURE 11.11 **Divided Bar Chart**

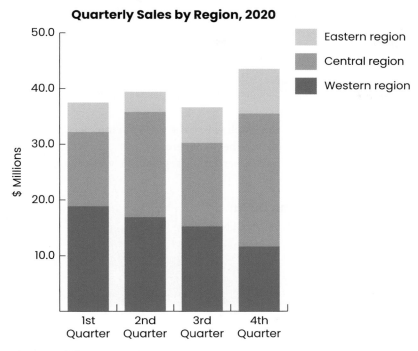

FIGURE 11.12 Divided Bar Chart

Picture Graphs

Looking a lot like bar graphs, **picture graphs** use pictorial symbols—for example, stick people, pine trees, or cars—to represent quantities of particular items. These symbols or images are arranged in bars that can then be labelled with the total quantity.

picture graph A visual that uses pictorial symbols to represent particular items.

FIGURE 11.13 Picture Graph

Line Graphs

line graph A visual that uses lines on a grid to show trends according to the relationship between two variables or sets of numbers.

grouped line graph A line graph that makes comparisons between two or more items.

Line graphs show the relationship between two variables on a grid, plotted by connecting the dots to form a continuous line. They are useful for showing trends, fluctuations, or progressions over a period of time. Below are some points to follow when devising a line graph or **grouped line graph**.

- Show the zero point of the graph where the two axes intersect. Insert a break in the scale if it is inconvenient to begin at zero.
- Quantities (e.g., litres, dollars, percentages) go on the vertical y axis; time always goes on the horizontal x axis.

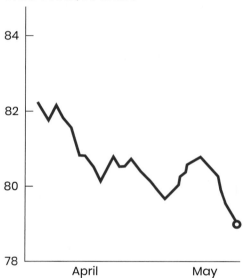

FIGURE 11.14 Line Graph

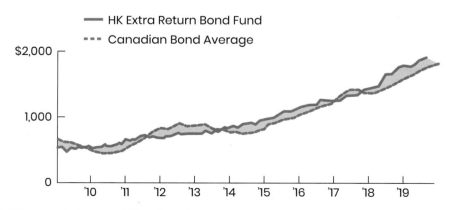

FIGURE 11.15 Grouped Line Graph

- If you want to draw attention to values, mark small dots at intersection points.
- If you want to emphasize the difference between two lines, shade between the lines.
- Handle the proportion of the horizontal and vertical scales carefully so that the presentation of data is free of distortion and all data is distributed equally over the graph.
- As needed, include a key that explains lines and symbols.
- If data comes from a secondary source, put a source line at the lower left corner of the figure.

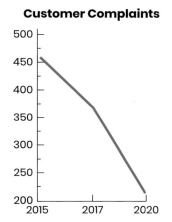

FIGURE 11.16 Ineffective Line Graph: Distorted Scale

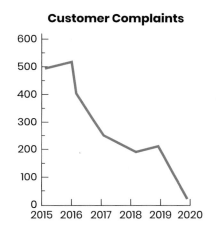

FIGURE 11.17 Effective Line Graph: Distortion Free

Gantt Charts

Named for its inventor, Henry Laurence Gantt, a **Gantt chart** is used for planning and scheduling projects. Its most useful application is blocking out periods of time to show, for example, what stage a project has reached or when staff will be on vacation.

Gantt chart A bar chart that is used to show a schedule.

Project Development Schedule

	September	October	November	December
Research	▬▬▬			
Planning		▬▬		
Recruitment			▬	
Training				▬▬

FIGURE 11.18 Gantt Chart

Flow Charts

flow chart A diagram that maps out procedures, processes, or sequences of movement.

A **flow chart** maps out a procedure, process, or sequence of movements diagrammatically using captioned symbols of different geometrical shapes (called ISO symbols) joined by lined arrows (for an explanation of these symbols, see Figure 11. 19). Each shape represents a particular stage in the process. Flow charts, even ones that use simple labelled blocks as in Figure 11.20, help to clarify procedures and make complex systems understandable.

FIGURE 11.19 ISO Flow Chart Symbols

Claims Adjustment Process

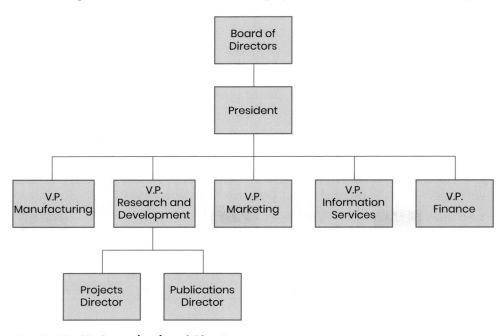

FIGURE 11.20 Flow Chart

Organizational Charts

organizational chart A diagram that shows how various levels or sectors of an organization are related to one another.

Looking much like a family tree, an **organizational chart** maps out the structure of a company, showing chains of command and channels of communication and making it clear who reports to whom, from front-line employees all the way up to senior managers.

FIGURE 11.21 Organizational Chart

Infographics and Data Visualizations

Infographics use visual displays to represent data and information in a quick, clear, and engaging way. While the term may be applied to describe the types of graphics outlined above, it is most commonly applied to visual representations that are more

infographic A visual display that conveys data or information in a quick, clear, and engaging way.

The most shared infographics have an average of 396 words

Average size is 3683 pixels tall by 804 pixels wide

Most popular color is blue (47% of infographics used it)

72.95% of infographics use an identifiable color scheme

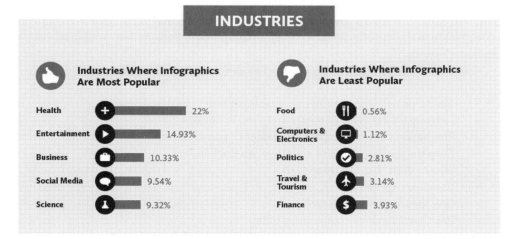

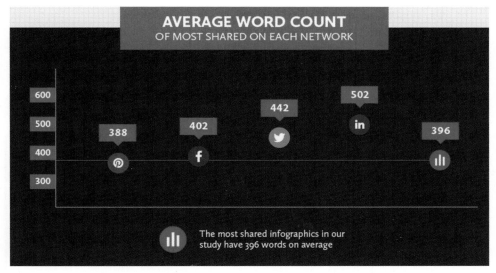

FIGURE 11.22 Sample Infographic

Source: Siege Media, "The Science Behind the Most Popular Infographics," by Ian Eckstein, pub. 11 April 2015, online at www.siegemedia.com/creation/infographics

elaborate in their construction. Infographics have many uses, but they are most effective for communicating complex information or data with many components to large, diverse audiences.[6] Thus, they are frequently used to disseminate critical information (e.g., information that explains why it is essential to vaccinate children or how to survive a natural disaster) to general populations. In addition, because they are good at drawing attention to connections and patterns among data, infographics can be useful for telling readers a story about the data or for simplifying complex relationships.[7]

When designing an infographic, keep in mind the principles of visual design: balance, proximity, alignment, repetition, contrast, and use of space. Consider how the reader's eye will be guided through the material, and the structure, patterning, and overall unity of the design. Unity can often be achieved through the repetition of elements within the design, such as a row of icons or a series of caption balloons. Bright colours draw viewers' attention, and the contrast between colours helps viewers differentiate components of the design. Blue is the most commonly used colour,[8] perhaps because most people tend to see blue as a favourable colour.[9] Considerations of visual complexity are also important, with low to medium complexity considered best for making a good first impression.[10] Ultimately, the effectiveness of an infographic depends on how well it serves its audience's needs.[11]

Consider the following best practices when designing an infographic:

- Aim to provide informative, shareable content.
- Leave space between elements and keep it simple.
- Emphasize the most important element to create a focal point.
- Keep the message concise and use plain English.
- Select a font that is easy to read.
- Use clear captions.
- Give visuals precedence over text.
- Use charts to show comparative data.
- Use line graphs to show trends.
- Use symbols or icons to stand for products and industries.
- Use groups of floating balloons to show percentages.[12]

A number of apps, many of them free to use, are available to help you design effective infographics. Examples include Piktochart, Easel.ly, and Venngage, all of which are easy to use and produce professional-looking results.

QUICK TIPS

Graphics

- Don't bury important information by overloading a graphic with too much data.
- Use a type of graphic that is appropriate to your message and objective.
- Use a scale that minimizes distortion. Figures 11.16 and 11.17, on page 387, show that compressed data emphasizes change while spread out data de-emphasizes change.

- Unless instructed otherwise, round off decimals to the nearest whole number (38 per cent or 38.2 per cent instead of 38.2431 per cent).
- Dollars in the millions can be simplified visually by adding (*$ millions*) or (*in millions*) to a table or graph heading.
- Don't distort data by omitting relevant information.
- Apply consistent style for titles, numbers, and sizing of graphs and charts.
- Tables of equal importance should be of equal size.
- Use a source line unless you collected the data yourself.

Commonly Used Short Reports: Informational and Analytical

Short reports can be either informational or analytical. Here is a brief look at some of the most frequently written categories of reports.

Informational Reports

As previously stated, informational reports have a specific purpose—to collect data and present it clearly and directly, without analysis, conclusions, or the need to persuade readers. These factual reports deliver routine information about different kinds of activities:

- **ongoing activities** (e.g., sales calls) that need to be monitored at regular weekly, biweekly, or monthly intervals
- **non-routine, case-by-case situations** (such as business trips or major projects) that must be accounted for and reported to management

Informational reports, such as progress reports, activity reports, trip/conference reports, and investigative reports, cover topics that readers are already familiar with. A brief opening provides the right degree of context, and a straightforward, business-like style with pared-down paragraphs, bulleted lists, and graphic highlighting techniques emphasizes important facts. Informational reports can be prepared in letter, memo, and e-mail formats; for frequently recurring situations, standardized templates and fill-in forms, and even PowerPoint, are sometimes used.

Informational reports fit into several categories, based on their purpose:

Periodic reports are written at regular intervals to describe recurring activities and outcomes (monthly sales figures, the volume of customer service calls, etc.). They assist in monitoring operations and keep management informed on the status quo.

Situational reports are written in response to two specific types of non-recurring situations: (1) business trips or conferences (see "Trip/Conference Reports," below) and (2) the progress of a continuing project (see "Activity Reports," "Progress Reports," and "Job Completion Reports," below).

Incident reports document problems or unusual events that affect a company's day-to-day operations. This type of report provides complete and accurate details of

incident report A short report that documents problems and unexpected occurrences that affect a company's day-to-day operations.

an incident, answering the questions *Who? What? Where? When? How?* and *Why?* It describes only what is known for certain happened, without speculation or inferences about supposed fault, cause, or liability. Incident reports spotlight areas of weakness in policy and procedure, helping to clear up trouble spots and prevent them from recurring.

investigative report A report written in response to a request for information about a specific problem or situation.

Investigative reports evaluate problems or situations and may or may not offer conclusions and recommendations. They are usually written in response to a one-time request for information. There are three basic parts in an investigative report:

- **Introduction**—states the purpose(s) of the report and defines its scope.
- **Body**—contains facts and findings arranged into several sections with descriptive headings. The topic can be divided into logical units according to importance, time, constituent elements, or criteria.
- **Summary**—may or may not offer conclusions and recommendations.

Compliance reports disclose information to governing bodies and government agencies in compliance with laws and regulations.

recommendation report An analytical report that recommends action, often in response to a specific problem.

justification report An analytical report that justifies the need for a purchase, investment, policy change, or hiring.

Recommendation reports investigate situations or actions, express a professional opinion about them, and recommend appropriate actions or interventions. Recommendation reports are commissioned.

Justification reports justify a purchase, an investment, a policy change, or a hiring, stating what is needed and why. They are prepared on a voluntary basis, not in response to a commission or request. Both recommendation and justification reports can be written with a direct or indirect approach, depending on how receptive readers will be:

- **Direct pattern**
  - » Introduce the problem briefly.
  - » Present the recommendation, action, or solution.
  - » Justify the recommendation by highlighting advantages and benefits and explaining it in more detail.
  - » End with a summary that refers to the action to be taken.
- **Indirect pattern**
  - » Introduce the problem and provide details that convince readers of its seriousness but do not reveal the recommendation.
  - » Discuss other measures or alternatives under descriptive headings, starting with the least likely and ending with your recommendation.
  - » Show that the advantages of your solution outweigh the disadvantages.
  - » Summarize the action to be taken and ask for authorization.

feasibility report An analytical report that evaluates whether a project or an alternative is advisable and practical.

Feasibility reports evaluate projects or alternatives to determine their chances for success by detailing project costs, staffing needs, scheduling, and potential problems and benefits. The process of writing a feasibility report generally breaks down into the following steps:

- Announce the decision to be made and list its alternatives.
- Describe the problem necessitating the decision.

- Evaluate positive and negative aspects of the project, including potential problems.
- Calculate costs and discuss the time frame.

Summaries compress longer information and condense it to what management needs to know: primary ideas, conclusions, and recommendations.

To-file reports provide a permanent written record of decisions, discussions, and directives. Left on file for future reference, they summarize decisions made and list the individuals involved in making them.

Proposals suggest ways of solving problems, presenting information about a plan or a project. Proposals may be competitive (a plan to secure new business or bid for corporate or government contracts) or internal (suggesting changes in policy or spending). Because they must establish credibility, proposals are substantial documents. (Look for more on proposals in Chapter 12.)

proposal A document presenting plans and ideas for consideration and acceptance by the reader.

Trip/Conference Reports

A **trip report** or **conference report** is an internal document that provides a record of what an employee learned and accomplished on a trip to client, supplier, or branch locations, conferences and conventions, or training and professional development seminars. A trip report, usually addressed to an immediate supervisor, allows an entire organization to benefit from information one employee has gained about products, services, equipment, procedures, laws, or personnel and operations management. Trip and conference reports may answer such questions as, Should our company consider purchasing equipment featured at the trade show? Should other employees attend this conference next year?

Trip reporting should be brief, with a maximum of five relevant and interesting topics used to organize your report. A writing plan for trip and conference reports includes the following elements:

trip report (or **conference report**) A short report that summarizes the events of a business trip or conference.

- **Subject line**—identifies the event/destination and the date(s) of the trip.
- **Introduction**—gives the event/destination, specifies exact dates, explains the purpose of the trip, and previews main points.
- **Body**—devotes a section to each main topic, event, or highlight that will be summarized. Headings may be used for each section.
- **Conclusion**—expresses appreciation and may make a recommendation based on the information in the report.

Because business travel can be expensive, managers look for proof that company travel dollars have been wisely spent. An expense report is often attached to the trip report.

The conference report in figure 11.23 is incomplete, supplying non-essentials details of little interest to management in place of specific information about events and accomplishments. In contrast, the trip report in figure 11.24 provides specific information that will be of value to managers and also offers a recommendation based on the writer's view of the event's value.

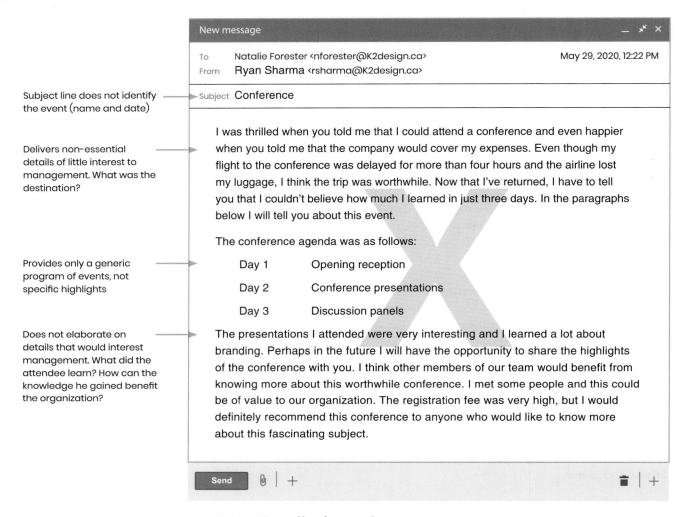

Subject line does not identify the event (name and date)

Delivers non-essential details of little interest to management. What was the destination?

Provides only a generic program of events, not specific highlights

Does not elaborate on details that would interest management. What did the attendee learn? How can the knowledge he gained benefit the organization?

New message

To   Natalie Forester <nforester@K2design.ca>   May 29, 2020, 12:22 PM
From Ryan Sharma <rsharma@K2design.ca>

Subject Conference

I was thrilled when you told me that I could attend a conference and even happier when you told me that the company would cover my expenses. Even though my flight to the conference was delayed for more than four hours and the airline lost my luggage, I think the trip was worthwhile. Now that I've returned, I have to tell you that I couldn't believe how much I learned in just three days. In the paragraphs below I will tell you about this event.

The conference agenda was as follows:

Day 1   Opening reception

Day 2   Conference presentations

Day 3   Discussion panels

The presentations I attended were very interesting and I learned a lot about branding. Perhaps in the future I will have the opportunity to share the highlights of the conference with you. I think other members of our team would benefit from knowing more about this worthwhile conference. I met some people and this could be of value to our organization. The registration fee was very high, but I would definitely recommend this conference to anyone who would like to know more about this fascinating subject.

Send

FIGURE 11.23 Ineffective Conference Report

Activity Reports

Activity reports, also called periodic or status reports, document the ongoing activities or projects of a division or department. These routine, recurring reports, typically prepared by supervisors, help middle and senior managers stay informed of activities and alert to unusual events that might negatively affect operations and therefore require swift solutions or changes in strategy. Activity reports can contain numerical data on sales volumes or product shipments or a more detailed discussion of key activities. They contain three main sections:

- **Summary**—briefly lists highlights of activities and projects carried out during the reporting period
- **Update**—offers an update on current problems and irregularities, including competition news of interest to managers of for-profit businesses
- **Needs/Plans**—overviews needs and forecasts plans for the next period

An activity report should deliver a complete, accurate, and objective account of events—both good and bad—that have taken place during the reporting period. This type

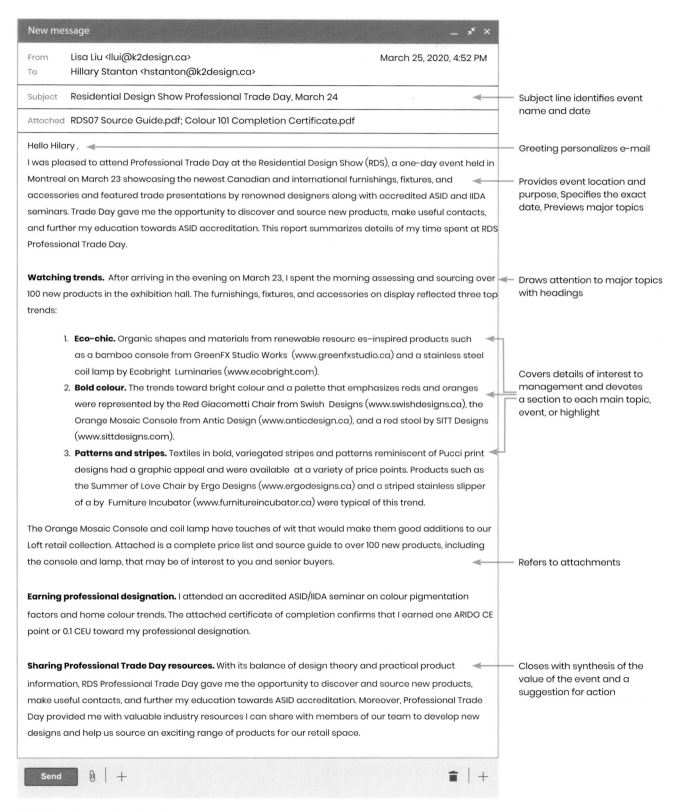

New message

From   Lisa Liu <llui@k2design.ca>   March 25, 2020, 4:52 PM
To   Hillary Stanton <hstanton@k2design.ca>

Subject   Residential Design Show Professional Trade Day, March 24   ← Subject line identifies event name and date

Attached   RDS07 Source Guide.pdf; Colour 101 Completion Certificate.pdf

Hello Hillary ,   ← Greeting personalizes e-mail

I was pleased to attend Professional Trade Day at the Residential Design Show (RDS), a one-day event held in Montreal on March 23 showcasing the newest Canadian and international furnishings, fixtures, and accessories and featured trade presentations by renowned designers along with accredited ASID and IIDA seminars. Trade Day gave me the opportunity to discover and source new products, make useful contacts, and further my education towards ASID accreditation. This report summarizes details of my time spent at RDS Professional Trade Day.

← Provides event location and purpose, Specifies the exact date, Previews major topics

Watching trends. After arriving in the evening on March 23, I spent the morning assessing and sourcing over 100 new products in the exhibition hall. The furnishings, fixtures, and accessories on display reflected three top trends:

← Draws attention to major topics with headings

1. **Eco-chic.** Organic shapes and materials from renewable resourc es–inspired products such as a bamboo console from GreenFX Studio Works (www.greenfxstudio.ca) and a stainless steel coil lamp by Ecobright Luminaries (www.ecobright.com).
2. **Bold colour.** The trends toward bright colour and a palette that emphasizes reds and oranges were represented by the Red Giacometti Chair from Swish Designs (www.swishdesigns.ca), the Orange Mosaic Console from Antic Design (www.anticdesign.ca), and a red stool by SITT Designs (www.sittdesigns.com).
3. **Patterns and stripes.** Textiles in bold, variegated stripes and patterns reminiscent of Pucci print designs had a graphic appeal and were available at a variety of price points. Products such as the Summer of Love Chair by Ergo Designs (www.ergodesigns.ca) and a striped stainless slipper of a by Furniture Incubator (www.furnitureincubator.ca) were typical of this trend.

← Covers details of interest to management and devotes a section to each main topic, event, or highlight

The Orange Mosaic Console and coil lamp have touches of wit that would make them good additions to our Loft retail collection. Attached is a complete price list and source guide to over 100 new products, including the console and lamp, that may be of interest to you and senior buyers.

← Refers to attachments

Earning professional designation. I attended an accredited ASID/IIDA seminar on colour pigmentation factors and home colour trends. The attached certificate of completion confirms that I earned one ARIDO CE point or 0.1 CEU toward my professional designation.

Sharing Professional Trade Day resources. With its balance of design theory and practical product information, RDS Professional Trade Day gave me the opportunity to discover and source new products, make useful contacts, and further my education towards ASID accreditation. Moreover, Professional Trade Day provided me with valuable industry resources I can share with members of our team to develop new designs and help us source an exciting range of products for our retail space.

← Closes with synthesis of the value of the event and a suggestion for action

Send   📎 | +   🗑 | +

FIGURE 11.24 Effective Trip Report

ENVIROWATCH

Working for a Greener Future

DATE: March 4, 2020

TO: Edward Shui, Director of Campaigns

FROM: Alex Scott, Sustainable Tourism Campaign Coordinator *AS*

SUBJECT: Activity Report for February 2020

Activity Summary

The following is an account of my activities for the period February 1–29:

Marketing Workshop Series. In partnership with the Northland Resort Association, I conducted the three-day event Workshop on Marketing Sustainable Tourism Products. Held on three consecutive Saturdays in Sudbury, the workshops identified the main challenges in the promotion of sustainable services and set out a three-step methodology to help tour, resort, and fly-in service operators integrate sustainability criteria into their business strategies and operations. More than 120 participants attended the workshops. Of these attendees, 25 requested French-language translations of our workshop publications.

Consultative Meetings. In Ottawa, on February 21, I met with representatives of Bike Ontario, the Green Trails League, and the Fresh Water Sports Association to discuss the promotion of bioregional tourism and a proposal to provide support to these associations through our newly launched Travelgreen.ca website.

Launch of Travelgreen.ca. Over 200 people, including colleagues and special guests, attended our reception on February 7 to launch the consultation phase of Travelgreen.ca. Provincial Environment Officer Lois Walsh paid tribute to the site as a platform for promoting co-operation for conservation in the tourism industry. Travelgreen.ca has already attracted more than 300 visitors and averages 11 comments a day from tourist operators interested in reducing ecological impacts in their industry.

Funding News

In the latest funding round, Green Now received a $50,000 grant from the Simcoe Foundation to raise public awareness of the fight against climate change. Although this is good news for the local conservation movement, the awarding of this grant may minimize the impact of our own grant proposal to develop a training package on sustainable tourism. We may wish to re-evaluate our proposal or target other funding opportunities.

Subject line identifies reporting period

Summarizes activities and events carried out during the reporting period, highlighting the status of projects

Because this is a non-profit organization, the writer provides an update on funding initiatives instead of sales competition

FIGURE 11.25 Activity Report

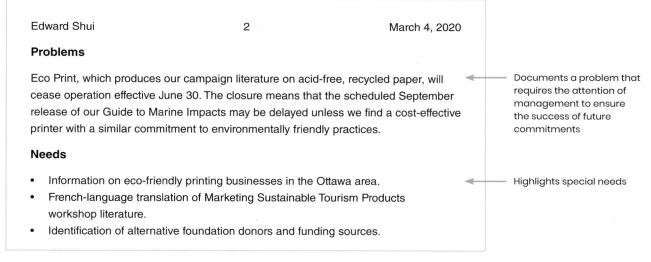

Edward Shui   2   March 4, 2020

Problems

Eco Print, which produces our campaign literature on acid-free, recycled paper, will cease operation effective June 30. The closure means that the scheduled September release of our Guide to Marine Impacts may be delayed unless we find a cost-effective printer with a similar commitment to environmentally friendly practices.

← Documents a problem that requires the attention of management to ensure the success of future commitments

Needs

- Information on eco-friendly printing businesses in the Ottawa area.
- French-language translation of Marketing Sustainable Tourism Products workshop literature.
- Identification of alternative foundation donors and funding sources.

← Highlights special needs

FIGURE 11.25 (continued)

of report represents a chance to check in with managers and inform them of problems that require their attention.

The monthly activity report in figure 11.25 highlights the status of projects and documents a problem that requires quick resolution to ensure the success of future commitments. Because this is a non-profit organization, the writer provides an update on funding initiatives instead of sales competition.

Progress Reports

Progress reports monitor a project at various intervals from start-up to completion. These reports indicate if a project is on schedule and if any measures need to be taken to correct problems or remove obstacles. Progress and activity reports help managers adjust schedules, allocate personnel and equipment, and revise budgets.

- **Opening summary** (no heading)—comments on the current status of the project in terms of the original schedule and goals.
- **"Work Completed" section**—describes what has been done since the last report and notes any problems and solutions.
- **"Work in Progress" section** (optional)—lists work currently being done.
- **"Work to Be Completed" section**—describes the work that remains and notes any foreseeable problems and likely solutions. A work schedule can be included in this section or under a separate heading.
- **Closing/Forecast** (no heading)—looks ahead to the progress that will be made between this and the next report and either expresses confidence that the project will be finished on time or discusses an extension of the project deadline.

Figure 11.26 shows an example of a progress report for a project that is underway.

Job Completion Reports

Job completion reports are last in a series of progress reports for a substantial project, or one-time reports arising from a short or small-scale project (See Figure 11.27 for an example of the latter). They put the project in perspective, ensuring a shared understanding about

Concise, descriptive subject line that creates a focus for the report

Opens with a summary statement describing the project and its proposed deadline for completion

"Background" establishes purpose and special requirements

"Work Completed" describes what has been done since the last report and mentions actions pending

"Work to Be Completed" describes work that remains and mentions deadlines for anticipated completion

"Anticipated Problems" looks ahead to conditions and circumstances that may alter the proposed plan

Closes with confirmation of delivery time of next report

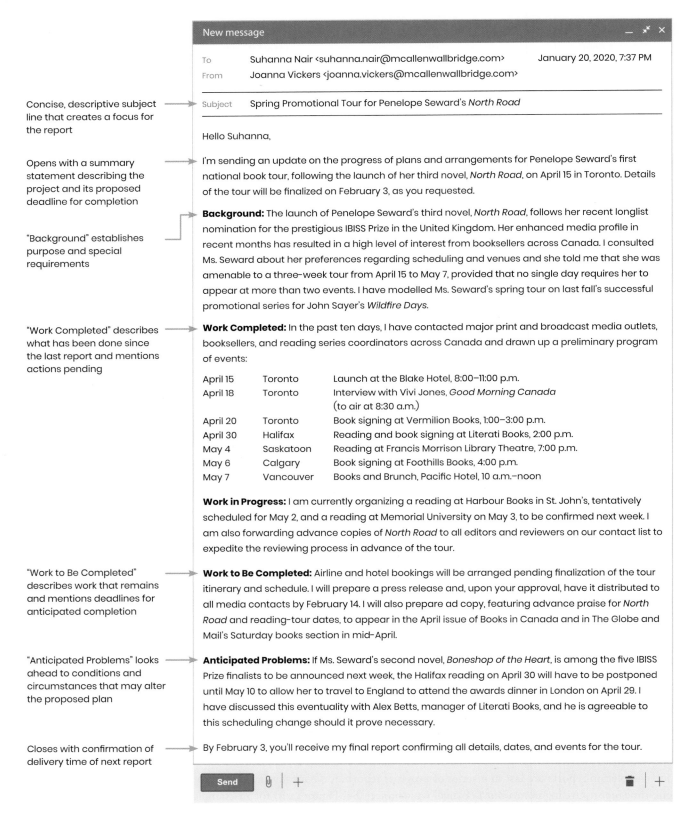

New message   — ⤢ ✕

To   Suhanna Nair <suhanna.nair@mcallenwallbridge.com>   January 20, 2020, 7:37 PM
From   Joanna Vickers <joanna.vickers@mcallenwallbridge.com>

Subject   Spring Promotional Tour for Penelope Seward's *North Road*

Hello Suhanna,

I'm sending an update on the progress of plans and arrangements for Penelope Seward's first national book tour, following the launch of her third novel, *North Road*, on April 15 in Toronto. Details of the tour will be finalized on February 3, as you requested.

Background: The launch of Penelope Seward's third novel, *North Road*, follows her recent longlist nomination for the prestigious IBISS Prize in the United Kingdom. Her enhanced media profile in recent months has resulted in a high level of interest from booksellers across Canada. I consulted Ms. Seward about her preferences regarding scheduling and venues and she told me that she was amenable to a three-week tour from April 15 to May 7, provided that no single day requires her to appear at more than two events. I have modelled Ms. Seward's spring tour on last fall's successful promotional series for John Sayer's *Wildfire Days*.

Work Completed: In the past ten days, I have contacted major print and broadcast media outlets, booksellers, and reading series coordinators across Canada and drawn up a preliminary program of events:

April 15	Toronto	Launch at the Blake Hotel, 8:00–11:00 p.m.
April 18	Toronto	Interview with Vivi Jones, *Good Morning Canada* (to air at 8:30 a.m.)
April 20	Toronto	Book signing at Vermilion Books, 1:00–3:00 p.m.
April 30	Halifax	Reading and book signing at Literati Books, 2:00 p.m.
May 4	Saskatoon	Reading at Francis Morrison Library Theatre, 7:00 p.m.
May 6	Calgary	Book signing at Foothills Books, 4:00 p.m.
May 7	Vancouver	Books and Brunch, Pacific Hotel, 10 a.m.–noon

Work in Progress: I am currently organizing a reading at Harbour Books in St. John's, tentatively scheduled for May 2, and a reading at Memorial University on May 3, to be confirmed next week. I am also forwarding advance copies of *North Road* to all editors and reviewers on our contact list to expedite the reviewing process in advance of the tour.

Work to Be Completed: Airline and hotel bookings will be arranged pending finalization of the tour itinerary and schedule. I will prepare a press release and, upon your approval, have it distributed to all media contacts by February 14. I will also prepare ad copy, featuring advance praise for *North Road* and reading-tour dates, to appear in the April issue of Books in Canada and in The Globe and Mail's Saturday books section in mid-April.

Anticipated Problems: If Ms. Seward's second novel, *Boneshop of the Heart*, is among the five IBISS Prize finalists to be announced next week, the Halifax reading on April 30 will have to be postponed until May 10 to allow her to travel to England to attend the awards dinner in London on April 29. I have discussed this eventuality with Alex Betts, manager of Literati Books, and he is agreeable to this scheduling change should it prove necessary.

By February 3, you'll receive my final report confirming all details, dates, and events for the tour.

Send   📎 | +   🗑 | +

FIGURE 11.26 Sample Progress Report

Sky Garden Design

June 18, 2021

Audra Holt, Senior Project Manager
Arden Lofts Property Development Ltd.
301 University Avenue, Suite 502
Toronto, Ontario M5J 1K6

Subject: Completion of "Green Roof" Project at Arden Lofts

Dear Ms. Holt:

Installation of a "green roof" at the Arden Lofts condominium property at 105–107 Grenville Street in Toronto is now complete. Work that was scheduled to start on February 1 and end on June 3 was extended by four days due to the delays in project start-up caused by a severe early spring ice storm. The roof garden is now ready to provide outdoor recreational space for tenants due to take occupancy in mid-July and to offer enhanced energy efficiency and storm-water management to this 14-storey, 450-unit complex.

Background

The City of Toronto's Green Roof bylaw applies to all new residential developments with a GFA of 5,000 square metres or greater. In compliance with this bylaw and its commitment to sustainable design, Arden Lofts Property Development Ltd. commissioned my company, Sky Garden Design Landscape Architects, to design and install a 500-square-metre extensive "green roof" at the Arden Lofts property at 105–107 Grenville Street.

The decision to install an extensive green roof was made to maximize the planting area without having to adjust the structural loading capacity of the building. The plan called for the creation of three accessible pathways, a deck, a dog-run, and two green roof plots, surrounded by approximately 1,000 square metres of decorative hard-surface concrete pavers. Project partner Fortex Roofing accommodated the extra weight of the green roof and rooftop recreational facilities by reinforcing the entire roof with steel girders. We then proceeded to incorporate a drip drainage/filtering system, quality waterproofing, root-repellency, engineered growing media, and plants.

53 Borden Street, Toronto, Ontario M74 2M9   Tel. 416 244-1480   Fax 416 244-2311
www.skygardendesign.com

FIGURE 11.27 Sample Job Completion Report

Ms. Audra Holt
June 18, 2021
Page 2

Project Highlights

The 500-square-metre green roof and corresponding 1,000-square-metre hard surface area were designed, supplied, and installed for just over $180,000, slightly below the $182,000 allocated for this project. Elements of Soprema's Sopranture green roofing system were used in the accessible extensive roof system. Sopraflor X, the growing medium, was selected for its ability to cling to plants in windy conditions. A total of 27 different species of plants native to Ontario were included in the design, among them pale-purple coneflower, woodland sunflower, and sedum, a succulent plant tolerant to extremes in temperature. All plants are under warrantee for one year from the date of purchase. The plants are now irrigated with a drip irrigation system, installed at a nominal cost of $15,000. Total expenditures are detailed in the enclosed budget.

Installation and Technical Issues

Our team of landscape engineers encountered two technical problems that had to be overcome: (1) transporting materials onto the roof of the 14-storey structure and (2) selecting plants that could withstand rooftop winds of up to 100 km/hr. As the building was still under construction, Sky Garden Design worked with contractors to arrange for the hoisting of growing medium, concrete slabs, and plants using the crane that was already on site. The use of day lily and other plants less resistant to wind and sun exposure, which the plan originally called for, was curtailed in favour of hardier plants such as sedum and alpine grasses.

Action

The green roof at Arden Lofts, having now passed all inspections, supports vegetation that helps to manage storm water, improve air quality, increase energy efficiency, enhance biodiversity, and provide outdoor recreational space in a high-density urban area with limited parkland. At present, no monitoring of the green roof has been proposed. The condominium association has the option to create a budget for the replanting and maintenance of the green roof that will ensure tenants enjoy this urban oasis for many years to come.

Sincerely,

Tom Battleford

Tom Battleford
Chief Landscape Engineer & Owner

FIGURE 11.27 (continued)

the work and any actions that are required. While typically not more than three pages long, a project completion report can be longer if the scope and magnitude of the project require lengthy analysis. The bigger the budget, usually the more substantial and detailed the report will be. This short, informational report uses the direct approach:

- **Opening**—provides a concise overview, naming the project and its client, confirming the completion of the project, briefly identifying major tasks or activities, and noting outcomes, successes, next steps, or special circumstances.
- **Background**—describes the job's purpose, what necessitated the project, who authorized or supervised it, what the original contract called for, who was involved, how much the project was budgeted at (optional), and who carried out the work. This section also identifies the start and completion dates (or schedule) outlined in the contract or original work plan.
- **Project milestones**—identifies all major accomplishments (work done, targets reached, and results achieved).
- **Variances**—notes deviations from the original plan, including problems encountered along the way that necessitated additional work outside the original scope of the project or work that had to be done differently in order for those problems to be solved. For each exception or revision to the original work plan, there should be an explanation of why it was necessary, how it addressed the problem, and how it affected the project overall.
- **Action**—restates the outcome and asks the reader to review the project, respond, sign-off, or follow-up.

Incident Reports

An incident or accident report helps an organization assess the problem, correct it, and make the changes necessary to prevent the problem from happening again. Fair and accountable business practices, not to mention occupational health and safety standards, demand that when trouble occurs in a workplace, the event be clearly and thoroughly documented. According to the Insurance Bureau of Canada, incident reports "serve as the basis for analyzing the causes of incidents and accidents and for recommending risk improvements to help prevent similar events in the future."[13] Workers' compensation claims, insurance claims, and lawsuits may hang in the balance, so it is important that reports of this kind be filed promptly, accurately, and with due diligence.

Incident reports are narratives, much like news stories, that present facts objectively and, at the same time, avoid assigning blame. Incident reports are usually submitted between 24 and 72 hours after the incident, and any delay in reporting must be disclosed and explained. Most incident and accident reports document internal matters, so they usually follow a simple memo format. Incident reports typically use forms or templates so they can be filed quickly. At minimum, they should contain the following information:

- names and contact information of the supervisor/reporter and any witnesses
- a detailed description of the event, including time, place, and names of individuals involved
- an objective assessment of the root cause of the event and recommendations to prevent a recurrence

Answering all applicable questions and using a direct writing plan, careful language, and factual details will result in a complete and thorough report (see figure 11.28).

When preparing an incident report, include the following sections:

- **Subject line**—identifies the precise or event and the date it occurred.
- **Opening**—provides a brief summary statement noting the incident/accident, the date it took place, who it primarily affected, and what the result was.
- **Body**—gives a precise description of the problem:
  - » What happened?
  - » Where and when did it happen?
  - » What was the exact sequence of events leading up to the incident?
  - » What type of equipment, if any, was being used? What materials, if any, were involved?
  - » Was anybody hurt?
  - » What type of injury occurred?
  - » What body part and which side of the body were affected?
  - » How severe was the injury? If known, what type of treatment was required?
  - » Was first-aid administered? Was a physician required?
  - » Did the injury result in lost time or a change/reduction in duties?
  - » Was there any property damage? What was the approximate value of material damage?
  - » Was there a work stoppage? How much time was lost?
  - » What were the contributing factors? While making it clear when you are speculating, what was the root cause of the event (e.g., unsafe equipment, lack of training)?
- **Conclusion**—follows through on the assessment by describing if the accident or incident was preventable and what has been, can be, or will be done to correct the problem and alter conditions that led to its occurrence.

Problem-Investigation Reports

Problem-investigation reports are written for two reasons: (1) to provide information or research that does not result in action or recommendation, as follow-up to a request, and (2) to document how a problem has been resolved. Figure 11.29 provies an example of a report written for the first reason. Investigation reports must clearly describe an issue that is up for study, whether that involves repairs, reorganization, the purchase and installation of new equipment to address old inefficiencies, the launching of a new project or initiative, or the allocation of people, space, or resources. The following plan outlines the organization of this type of direct-approach informational report. Descriptive headings (applied to each section except the opening summary) are most effective in helping to preview the organization of this type of report.

- **Summary of main points:** defines the problem, notes its cause(s) and resolution, and notes any further steps that should be taken.
- **Background or history:** establishes the report's purpose and sets out the circumstances in which the problem was discovered and the causes of the problem the report investigates.

National Precast Concrete

Inter-office Memo

To: Lucinda Harvey, Chief Officer
                Environmental Health & Safety

From: Scott Lisgar, Site Supervisor

Date: February 7, 2020

Subject: Skid-Steer Loader Accident on February 6, 2020   ← Subject line identifies the event and the date it occurred

The following report summarizes an accident that occurred on February 6, 2020, involving Joseph D'Alessandro (Employee #62651). The injuries he sustained resulted in three days of lost time and a one-hour work stoppage at a commercial construction site at 1119 Avery Boulevard, Oshawa.

← Opening provides a brief summary statement noting the incident/accident, the date it took place, who it primarily affected, and what the result was

Accident Summary

On February 6, 2020, Joseph D'Alessandro, a concrete truck driver employed for 12 years at National Precast Concrete's Oshawa facility, sustained injuries when he was struck and knocked down by a skid-steer loader. The accident occurred at 9:10 a.m. on a gravel section just outside the worksite trailer at the Maple Grove property development site.

← Body of the report gives a precise description of the problem

Accident Details

On the day of the incident, it was windy, with intermittent freezing rain. Mr. D'Alessandro had taken shelter inside the trailer as he waited for the arrival of a contract worker he was assigned to train that day. Mr. D'Alessandro, who suffers from a disability on the left side of his body, had just descended a set of wooden stairs leading out of the trailer when he stepped into the path of the skid-steer loader as it was backing up at a speed of approximately 15 km/hr.

← Describes precisely what happened, where and when it happened, the exact sequence of events leading up to the incident, and what type of equipment was being used and what materials were involved

The contract worker, Jeremy Grant, who was just arriving at the site, shouted at Mr. D'Alessandro and waved his arms to warn him that the skid-steer loader was backing up. Mr. D'Alessandro, who was wearing a hood and a heavy woolen hat and who had turned his head back toward the trailer to avoid a heavy gust of wind, later told co-workers Jack Yip and Victor Plavzik that he thought Mr. Grant was greeting him. A few seconds before impact, the sound of the skid-steer loader's motor alerted Mr. D'Alessandro to the approaching danger, but his limited mobility prevented him from moving out of the way completely. He was struck on the left side and knocked to the ground.

Skid-Steer Loader Accident Report, February 7, 2020

FIGURE 11.28 Sample Incident/Accident Report

When his head struck the gravel pathway, Mr. D'Alessandro suffered facial lacerations, later requiring 20 stitches, and lost consciousness for several minutes. The skid-steer operator, Mr. Adams, immediately dialed 911 and Pete Wurlitzer, a foreman equipped with a first-aid kit and defibrillator, checked Mr. D'Alessandro's pulse and respiration. Emergency medical services arrived at 9:20 a.m., within minutes of the phone call, and Mr. D'Alessandro was taken to the hospital where he was kept for observation overnight after complaining of headache and dizziness. He was diagnosed by consulting physician Dr. Alexandra Cho at Oshawa General Hospital as having suffered a mild concussion; he was advised not to return to work for three days.

Of the 10 employees and contract workers on site at the time of the accident, Mr. Grant, Mr. Yip, and Mr. Plavzik, whose contact information can be found in the company registry, were standing on the gravel pathway within 10 metres of the accident when it occurred and had unobstructed views of the collision. The information contained in this report is based on on-site interviews conducted with the three witnesses in the hours following the accident.

As there was property damage, the report details the approximate value of material damage

The worksite trailer sustained minor damage to its aluminum siding when the skid-steer loader went out of control after hitting Mr. D'Alessandro. Damage is estimated at under $100. On brief inspection, the skid-steer loader did not appear to be damaged, but it will be taken out of service until a full mechanical evaluation can be conducted. The initial inspection of the vehicle revealed that its backup alarm and electronic sensor were not functioning.

Records contributing factors and probably root cause of the event, while making it clear that writer is only speculating at this point

Records work stoppage and notes how much time was lost

The accident and its aftermath, during which time photographs were taken of the accident site, accounted for a work stoppage of one hour and ten minutes. During that time, all work at the site ceased and did not resume until 10:20 a.m., after police who were called to the scene and EMS personnel had left.

Recommendations

Conclusion follows through on the assessment by describing if the accident or incident was preventable and what has been, can be, or will be done to correct the problem and alter conditions that led to its occurrence

To prevent similar occurrences, our company should consider the following actions in the future:

- Conduct weekly inspections to ensure backup alarms and electronic sensors on all skid-steer loaders are functioning.
- Conduct monthly face-to-face reviews of reversing procedures with all drivers of skid-steer loaders rather than relying on a one-time viewing of a one-hour PowerPoint presentation.
- Erect barriers separating areas where heavy equipment, such as the skid-steer loader, is used from commonly used pathways.
- Institute a policy requiring workers-on-foot to maintain minimum clearance from skid-steer loaders.

Skid-Steer Loader Accident Report, February 7, 2020

FIGURE 11.28 (continued)

Unitas Shoes

To: Jill Brody, President
From: Gustavo Suarez, IT Manager
Subject: Eliminating Loss Resulting from Data Mobility
Date: February 10, 2020

The purpose of this report is to explore the problem of data mobility and the risk it poses to our intellectual property (IP), proprietary personal information and customer data, and ultimately to revenue and profits at Unitas Shoes.

← *Opening defines the problem, notes its cause(s) and resolution, and notes any further steps that should be taken*

Background

← *Establishes the report's purpose and sets out the circumstances in which the problem was discovered and the causes of the problem the report investigates*

As the maker of exclusive, high-end footwear and luxury leather goods, Unitas enjoys a unique position in the Canadian marketplace in competing with foreign brands such as Christian Louboutin and Jimmy Choo and in having secured a niche market of discriminating buyers throughout the country and more recently in select centres such as New York and London. Our unique designs are showcased at Toronto Fashion Week, Montreal Fashion Week, and other headline events in the fashion industry. Our beachhead into Canadian and foreign markets has been enhanced through extensive exposure in publications such as Elle Canada and Fashion and a print-ad campaign in Vogue. All of these factors contribute to Unitas' remarkable 20 per cent growth in sales in 2019; however, that growth cannot be sustained if the distinctness of our brand is not protected.

Instances of corporate theft are on the rise in all industries, and the fashion industry is no exception. Users find it relatively easy to take data away on a USB drive or even by using e-mail for this purpose. The reality of present-day data mobility in an Internet- and network-connected world is that any data that resides on internal storage devices is at risk.

At Unitas, there has been one confirmed breach to date. The centerpiece of our Fall 2019 collection, John Ruddington's design for an aubergine suede stiletto, was leaked via e-mail by an intern who had secured permanent employment with one of our competitors. The design was then copied and mass produced using quick-to-market manufacturing techniques and inferior materials and fabrication. The security breach was discovered by the intern's supervisor two days after the incident, but it was too late to reverse the damage that had been done. The shoe was featured in the window display of every Rock Bottom Shoes outlet weeks before our design made it to market. Although the discrepancy in quality was appreciable, especially to our discriminating customers, the design had lost much of its cachet and sales were sluggish, with projected sales for the product falling flat by slightly over $18,000.

FIGURE 11.29 Sample Problem-Investigation Report

Describes the methods and approach taken and criteria applied in resolving the problem; also reviews findings and discusses their significance

Findings

Companies in a similar position to Unitas's have several options for stemming the flow of data loss through data mobility. The first step is to conduct a loss-prevention audit. A data-protection audit is a systematic and independent examination to determine whether activities involving the processing of personal data are carried out in accordance with an organization's data-protection policies and procedures.

To ensure this process runs smoothly, it will be necessary to encourage and secure the support of all staff. The two loss-prevention auditors I contacted, J & B Associates and Tucker-Bonwit IT Support, estimated that an audit of this kind in a company the size of Unitas would take approximately one week. Our company must also take steps to ensure that we are in full compliance with the Personal Information Protection and Electronic Documents Act (PIPEDA), which establishes laws that regulate the collection, use, and disclosure of personal information by private-sector organizations. For this purpose, we may need to revisit, review, and update our company privacy policy. The audit and any measures that result from it must be in full compliance with data-protection standards. Aims in this process are as follows:

- To assess the level of compliance with all data-protection acts.
- To assess gaps and weaknesses in the data-protection system.
- To provide information for data-protection system review.
- To verify that there is a documented and up-to-date data-protection system in place and that data are protected at rest, in transit, and in use.
- To verify that all staff are aware of the existence of the data-protection system, fully understand it, and know how to use it.

After an audit has been conducted, companies experiencing data loss have several options beyond this, including disabling USB ports. The inconvenience and severity of such measures, however, might create significant work-flow issues and cost us the goodwill and morale of Unitas employees.

Companies such as Ferrari have been able to avert losses by deploying the latest version of security software that offers multi-factor authentication, database encryption, a secure virtual perimeter, and disk and file encryption. In a well-publicized case, Ferrari was able to quickly detect a theft of IP when a former employee lifted designs for special gases to be used in the tires of the company's Formula One racing cars. New security software from Verdasys, as used by Ferrari, and other software leaders including McAfee and DW (Digital Watchdog), provides a

FIGURE 11.29 (continued)

level of protection not offered by our current security software. To implement a DW
6 security system at Unitas would cost in the range of $10,000 to $15,000 a year,
but those costs would be partially offset by a reduction in lost revenue that normally
results from data loss.

Conclusion

Although conducting a data-loss audit can cause temporary disruption to workflow
and raise concerns among employees that they are under suspicion, this routine
activity, along with the upgrading of data-loss prevention software that secures data
across the connected enterprise, significantly reduces the threat of data loss. At this
time, I ask for your authorization to initiate this process by conducting a search for a
data-loss prevention auditor.

Eliminating Loss Resulting from Data Mobility   Page 3

Notes what has been or should be done and by whom. It also briefly outlines any disadvantages of the proposed solution and states how the corrected problem makes for a better outcome.

FIGURE 11.29 (continued)

- **Approach and findings:** describes the methods and approach taken and criteria applied in resolving the problem. It also reviews findings and discusses their
  significance.
- **Conclusion:** notes what has been or should be done and by whom. It also briefly
  outlines any disadvantages of the proposed solution and states how the corrected
  problem makes for a better outcome.
- **Appendix or attachment (optional):** supplies supporting data and evidence
  that cannot be easily included in the preceding sections.

Summary Reports

Before managers and other decision-makers can formulate a solution to a problem,
they must gain a full understanding of the problem from clear, credible, and concise
information that can help them grasp the fundamentals of an issue quickly and easily.
Busy managers rely on well-prepared summaries that put key facts and opinions at their
fingertips.

Writing a summary report involves careful analysis of source documents, such as
journal and newspaper articles, and the ability to distinguish essential information from
amplifying material. To write a summary report that accurately reflects the organization
and emphasis of the original article, follow these steps:

- **Scan, then carefully read, the source material.** Scan the article for its general
  topic and overall organization, then read it carefully and identify its central ideas.
  Underline significant facts. Studying keywords and headings can provide important clues to the information that may be most vital to your summary.
- **Decide what you can do without.** Eliminate amplifying material. Try to condense
  the material to one-third to one-fifth the length of the original or less, if possible.

- **Use underlined points to create a draft of your summary.** Hold to the structure of the original material but use your own words and add transitional expressions to make the sentences in your draft fit together. Do not introduce new material that was not in the original article or document.
- **Add introductory and closing remarks that provide context.** Indicate the title and author of the source material and offer to provide further information as needed.

Analytical Reports

There are several different types of analytical reports—justification/recommendation reports, feasibility reports, and comparison/yardstick reports—each organized to answer a specific type of question. Whereas informational reports emphasize the presentation of facts, analytical reports pass on information with the intent of persuading readers to follow a specific course of action. An indirect writing plan can help readers see the logic of a recommendation. The "analysis" in an analytical report is focused on how to solve a specific organizational problem.

> Which health insurance package should our company choose?
> Should we open an overseas branch?
> Which brand and model of laser printer should our company purchase?

Problem Statements, Problem Questions, and Purpose Statements

An effective business report answers questions and solves one or more real and significant problems. Identifying the problem that the report is meant to solve is the first step in approaching the writing task. It allows you to (1) understand what the real problem is (e.g., *Are a clothing retailer's declining profits because of high overhead, poor customer service or inventory control, or ineffective marketing?*); (2) narrow the problem down so that it is solvable in the available time; and (3) ensure that you have the right data and evidence to document the problem and make recommendations that lead to a solution.

Problem statements are most effective when they are unambiguous and precisely defined:

Problem Statement:	A recent breach of online security has forced Ridgeway Products to move from one-factor authentication to two-factor authentication practices in order to ensure the greatest possible security of company and customer data. Ridgeway must decide on the safest and most convenient type of two-factor authentication.
Problem Question:	What type of two-factor authentication should Ridgeway Products use to ensure the highest degree and most convenient form of online security?
Problem Statement:	The cost of maintaining a fully staffed human resources department at First Rate Financial has soared in the past five years. First Rate must determine if the outsourcing

	of some HR functions, such as payroll, would be a cost-effective solution.
Problem Question:	Could First Rate Financial reduce HR functions by outsourcing functions such as payroll?

The type of problem question that is asked determines the type of analytical report that must be written in order to propose a solution.

- **Recommendation report:** *What should we do to increase efficiency of our printers?*
- **Feasibility report:** *Should we expand our customer base by introducing a line of products that appeals to teens?*
- **Yardstick report:** *Which of three proposed options would enable* APL *Technologies to upgrade its file servers?*

Once the problem has been analyzed and written down, it can be crafted into a concise purpose statement that helps to bring focus and perspective to the project or investigation and serves as a reminder of what the report is meant to accomplish. An effective purpose statement sets out clear action-specific objectives (for example, *to investigate, analyze, compare, evaluate,* or *recommend*) and notes organizational conflicts, challenges, and technical problems the report must address:

Purpose Statement:	To investigate a possible reduction in HR costs through the outsourcing of certain functions, such as payroll, at First Rate Financial.

The more complex a report, the more elaborate a purpose statement can be in describing the scope, limitations, and importance of the investigation the report documents:

- **Scope**—What are the factors or issues to be explored? What is the amount of detail to be presented?
- **Limitations**—Do any special standards or conditions (budgetary, technical, geographical, or logistical difficulties or limits on time or resources) apply to the investigation? How might those conditions affect the findings and how broadly they apply to the situation?
- **Importance**—Why is it important that this problem be solved right now? Can the problem be solved? How severe is the problem?

These additional factors, supported by specific, quantifiable facts (how much? when?), contribute to a more detailed purpose statement:

Detailed Purpose Statement:	The purpose of this report is to investigate the outsourcing of certain HR functions, such as payroll, as a means of reducing costs at First Rate Financial. The report will compare costs for four HR service providers. It will also poll employee reaction to proposed outsourcing of payroll services and determine the effect of HR downsizing on company morale. The study is significant, as contracts

for four of the five current payroll specialists are due to expire at the end of the fiscal year and outsourcing payroll services could reduce costs, which increased by more than 25 per cent since 2016. The study is limited to payroll costs and outsourcing in the Central division.

Justification/Recommendation Reports

Justification and recommendation reports, sometimes known as internal proposals, are persuasive documents, submitted within a company, that make suggestions for new or improved facilities, equipment, processes, capital appropriations, or organizational change. While some organizations have a prescribed form for recommendation reports, in most other cases writers can choose from a direct or indirect strategic writing plan depending on the sensitiveness of the topic and the receptiveness of the audience. A direct writing plan frontloads both the report problem and the recommendation for a solution to that problem. Here are the steps in organizing a direct plan recommendation report:

- Describe the problem and establish that it needs a solution; provide any background information the reader might need for decision-making.
- Offer a solution to the problem or announce the recommendation.
- Explain the benefits of the plan, supported by evidence.
- Discuss potential drawbacks and costs and justify expenditures. Compare possible alternatives.
- Summarize the benefits of the recommended action. Express willingness to provide additional information if it is required.

How far writers can go in making recommendations and expressing opinions depends on what their organizations have authorized them to do in preparing their reports.

An indirect writing plan can help writers win over cautious or reluctant audiences. Its strategic approach moves more gradually towards a well-supported recommendation—the strongest option that has first been shown to be logical and better than all the other alternatives:

- Indicate the problem but avoid referring to your recommendation in the subject line.
- Open with a clear, credible, and compelling description of the problem; persuasively establish that the problem is serious, significant, and in need of a solution; provide an overview of data-collection methods and report organization.
- Discuss alternative solutions strategically, from least to most effective. Weigh the pros and cons of each and provide cost comparisons when needed.
- Present the most viable alternative—the option you intend to recommend—last. Describe its benefits and show how its advantages outweigh its disadvantages. Evidence presented should support your conclusion and recommendation.
- Summarize your findings and announce your recommendation; if appropriate, ask for authorization to proceed.

Figure 11.30 contains a sample direct recommendation report. Because the plan is low cost and easy to implement, the writer expects little resistance and has decided to use a direct writing plan. Figure 11.31 contains a simple indirect recommendation report and presents a less effective alternative first in order to build support for a superior option.

Wellness Drug Mart

DATE: July 8, 2021

TO: Julie Marco, Vice-President

FROM: Havier Perez, Assistant Marketing Manager *HP*

SUBJECT: Converting Store Traffic into Retail Sales

A busy store is usually a sign of healthy sales. Although traffic flow throughout our retail pharmacies continues to be high, in the past year the conversion of browsing into sales has dropped by a rate of 12 per cent. Customers pass through the doors of our stores and wait in line by the dispensary while their prescriptions are filled but do not make purchases additional to their medicine orders.

In-store polls have indicated that customers standing in line are dissatisfied with the amount of time spent waiting. Recent store performance reviews showed, however, that Wellness Drug Mart customers wait no longer than 15 minutes on average for their prescriptions to be filled. This misconception of external wait times is a common one. A recent retail study found that people standing in line perceive that they spend more time waiting than they actually do.

To reduce the perception of extended wait times and to encourage customers to buy as well as browse or wait in line, I recommend that we do the following:

- Purchase ten pagers as part of an on-site paging system.

- Conduct a six-month pilot test on pager use and its effect on sales in our underperforming Woodburn Avenue store.

How On-site Paging Systems Work

Pagers, including a range of models developed by market-leader Beckon Inc, have been used in the restaurant industry for nearly 20 years. These compact, battery-powered, rechargeable devices allow restaurant patrons the freedom to step out of line and go outside or to the lounge area of the restaurant while they wait for their tables. The device vibrates, flashes, or glows to alert patrons that their table is ready. Loss of pagers due to theft or forgetfulness is minimal because an anti-theft, auto-locate tracking mode pages continually until the device is returned.

This technology has recently been adopted by Bargainers Drug Mart Inc. to encourage customers to browse more throughout the store while they wait. Pharmacy customers at Bargainers now have greater control over how they spend their time in the store until their medicine order is ready.

Annotations (right margin):

- Applies memo format for internal report
- Introduces report problem
- Establishes that the problem needs a solution; provides background information the reader might need for decision-making
- Reveals recommendation immediately
- Discusses potential drawbacks

FIGURE 11.30 Recommendation Report: Direct Writing Plan

Vice-President Marco   2   July 8, 2021

An on-site paging system, similar to ones used by restaurants and our competitors, is a relatively low-cost and low-maintenance solution. The number of paging units required can be determined by dividing the average wait time in minutes by 1.5. A ten-pack of pagers is priced at $1050. Beckon specializes in pharmacy paging systems. Consumer guides rate its products as the most durable on the market. The devices operate on a UHF FM frequency (420-470 MHz) within a three-kilometre range. They are powered by low-cost nickel-metal-hydride batteries and battery life is 48 hours on a single charge. Only a limited number of pagers would have to be purchased.

How an On-site Paging System Could Benefit Us

An on-site paging system, requiring ten pagers, would help us improve customer service and encourage sales in three ways:

1. **Minimized wait times.** A paging system would allow customers the freedom to browse without the fear of losing their place in line. The time customers would have spent waiting they can spend the way they want to, with less potential for boredom. Time spent productively should help reduce the perception of long wait times.

2. Increased customer conversion rates. Customers can shop while they wait. In-store traffic should result in higher sales and a better browsing-to-buying conversion rate.

3. Improved customer service. Impatient customers waiting for their prescriptions to be filled frequently interrupt staff pharmacists to ask about the status of the medicine orders. These interruptions result in service errors and slowdowns and can compromise the privacy of other customers. A paging system would boost staff efficiency so that prescriptions could be filled faster and consultations about dosages, drug interactions, and side-effects could be conducted more privately once an order has been filled.

Summary and Action

I recommend that you do the following:

- Authorize the purchase of ten Beckon pagers at $1050, which includes a transmitter and charger.

- Approve a six-month pilot test of the paging system in our downtown Calgary location that provides pharmacy customers with guest pagers and tracks the conversion rate of store traffic to sales.

Enclosure

Marginal annotations:

Discusses costs and justifies expenditures

Summarizes the benefits of the recommended action; lists benefits for readability and emphasis

Gives specific details of the actions to be taken

FIGURE 11.30 (continued)

BASKERVILLE Printing

Inter-office Memo

DATE: October 18, 2021

TO: Austin Wilson, Vice-President

FROM: Mirella Herzig, Production Manager *MH*

SUBJECT: Meeting High-Volume Printing Demands

At your request, I have examined methods of increasing printing output and reducing turnaround time while maintaining current quality standards and colour printing capabilities. To carry out this study, I have consulted industry associations and reviewed professional publications; I also networked with industry contacts about their output systems.

This report presents data documenting the severity and significance of the problem, two alternative solutions, and a recommendation based on my analysis.

Significance of Problem: Lack of Speed and Flexibility Results in Losses

Until recently, our offset lithographic environment has been effective in driving volume; however, since late 2016 our company has not been equipped to meet the increasing demand for short-run work, such as real estate books and stock prospectuses, which now accounts for 65 per cent of our business. Due to slow turnarounds on short-run rush jobs, many of our long-time customers are reluctantly turning to our competitors for quicker delivery and overnight service. Revenues for the first and second quarters of 2021 were down by 15 per cent from the same period in 2020, in part due to the loss of accounts for short-run business.

Another source of customer dissatisfaction is a lack of flexibility in the service we provide. Other print shops have the capability of updating large print runs on demand without having to commit to one version for the entire run. When one of our customers inspects advance copies and decides changes are needed, an entire press run, often in excess of 10,000 copies, has to be discarded. Below are two solutions other print shops have implemented to reduce turnaround times and eliminate waste.

Alternative 1: Purchase a Reconditioned Offset Press

The option that would present the fewest changes to workflow involves the purchase of an offset press, ideally one of a new generation of presses that use computer-plate systems and offer ease of operation, ergonomic design, and quality enhancements. Offset lithography continues to be the most common high-volume commercial printing technology. Offset presses, including the reliable Graumann models we

Subject line highlights benefits without referring to the recommendation

Identifies the report purpose and data collection methods

Previews report organization

Clear, credible, and compelling description of the problem; persuasively establishes that the problem is serious, significant, and in need of a solution; provides an overview of data-collection methods and report organization

Discusses alternative solutions strategically, from least to most effective

FIGURE 11.31 Recommendation Report: Indirect Writing Plan

Vice-President Wilson   2   October 18, 2021

currently use, deliver high image quality, offer unsurpassed flexibility in the choice of printing medium, and are cost effective for high-volume printing jobs. The front-end cost load of offset printing reduces the unit cost as the size of the print run increases. As a result, customers are eligible for substantial volume-based discounts.

Evaluates alternative objectively →

Other key advantages of offset technology include limited downtime and low costs for maintenance. Lithographic equipment rarely breaks down. Service calls are infrequent because veteran operators can usually troubleshoot and fix certain offset problems. A workforce like our own that is already accustomed to offset technology and familiar with the existing offset infrastructure could be quickly and easily trained, at minimal cost, to use a slightly more advanced lithographic press of similar design to ones already in the pressroom.

Although customers appreciate the quality and cost-effectiveness offset offers on high-volume jobs, they are generally dissatisfied with extended delivery time and high unit costs for short runs. The purchase of an offset press might help to drive up overall volume, but it would not address the shortfall in short-run capability we are currently experiencing. Although cheaper models are available, the most reliable offset presses offering the greatest flexibility are expensive. Purchasing a slightly older or reconditioned model would reduce costs. The price range listed below is typical.

Weighs the pros and cons of each alternative and provides cost comparisons when needed →

Cost range: $65,000 to $110,00 for a one-colour to five-colour Graumann Printmeister GTO 52 offset press

Presents the most viable alternative—the option the writer intends to recommend—last; fescribes its benefits and shows how its advantages outweigh its disadvantages; evidence presented supports conclusion and recommendation →

Alternative 2: Purchase a Colour Digital Press

A less expensive, long-term solution is to purchase a colour digital press. A digital press is a computer-controlled device. Unlike an offset press, it is plateless and uses electrostatic toner instead of ink to image virtual printing forms (Henry, 2007, p. 1). In digital printing, many of the mechanical steps required for conventional printing, such as colour proofs and films, are eliminated, and less drying time is required. Digital presses have quick turnaround on short-run jobs, and as a result attract their own volumes.

Digital capability allows commercial users to load a project file received via the Internet, print a proof, run the job, and trim the sheets in under an hour. The benefits for printers include reduced set-up costs for small press runs and easy customization of pieces such as client brochures and letterhead. Electronic updating is possible on demand, even in the middle of a press run. Digital presses also take the guesswork and ambiguity out of achieving colour consistency and now offer an almost unrestricted selection of sheet sizes, including sheets as large as 14 × 20 inches.

FIGURE 11.31 (continued)

Vice-President Wilson   3   October 18, 2021

Although digital presses may be offline more frequently for maintenance, good vendor support can minimize lost production time. The cost of consumable items such as image drums may add to operation and unit costs, but industry specialists advise that digital-press purchasers should negotiate an all-inclusive click rate that reflects the actual cost of maintenance, parts, labour, and supplies. Lithographers who make the transition to digital print production can expect to spend up to six months phasing in the new technology and integrating it with their current workflow (Henry, 2007, p. 4).

Cost: $10,000 for Xylon's GraphX digital press, with 36 ppm colour output
           and 40 ppm black-and-white output

Conclusions and Recommendations

Our print shop built its reputation on a guarantee of speedy delivery and quick turnarounds. The majority of our business, which comes from real estate and brokerage houses, depends on the continued capability of our shop to provide quality, cost-effective services for multi-format, high-volume print jobs and short-run work. If our goal is to genuinely do the most that we can for our customers, we should embrace a combination of technologies and integrate digital output systems into our offset environment. Done well, the work that digital capability would help to recapture could qualify our company for more offset jobs and make our business a one-stop source for the printing services that customers demand the most. Although the integration of digital technology will involve workflow adjustments and start-up training, it will help our business stay competitive and secure the last-minute jobs we might miss without the addition of this technology.

← Links need to recommended solution, summarizes findings and gives reasons for making recommendation

I recommend that we purchase a digital press within the next three months. With your approval, I will investigate possible printer options for our company based on brand name, cost, required features, run length, maintenance, and environmental factors.

← Reveals recommendation based on logic of findings and conclusions

References

Henry, P. (2007, March). Going digital, staying lithographic. *American Printer*, 1–8.

FIGURE 11.31 (continued)

Feasibility Reports

Any new project carries the possibility of failure. Before undertaking a new project, organizations must determine the project's chances for success. Feasibility reports present evidence on the advisability of doing a project or proceeding with a specific course of action. Does it make good business sense? Is it right for the company? Is it practical and workable according to certain criteria? Can the company afford the costs involved? Feasibility reports answer these types of questions based on specific criteria and careful analysis. Managers rely on the evidence and advice that feasibility reports present when deciding whether to commit resources to a new project. Feasibility reports use a direct writing plan to announce the decision first.

- **Opening paragraph**—identifies the plan and reveals your decision/recommendation about it; offers an overview of the report.
- **Introduction/Background**—describes the problem or circumstances that led to the report and discusses the scope, methods, and limitations of the study and the amount of data that could be collected to answer the feasibility question.
- **Discussion**—in logical sequence, presents a detailed analysis of the benefits and risks of the plan along with other positive and negative factors, a calculation of costs, and a schedule for implementation; when appropriate, presents graphical elements to support data and interpret the results.
- **Conclusions**—summarizes data and significant findings.

The report in figure 11.32 assesses the feasibility of converting an unused side-lot and office storage room into an space for employee recreation and lounging.

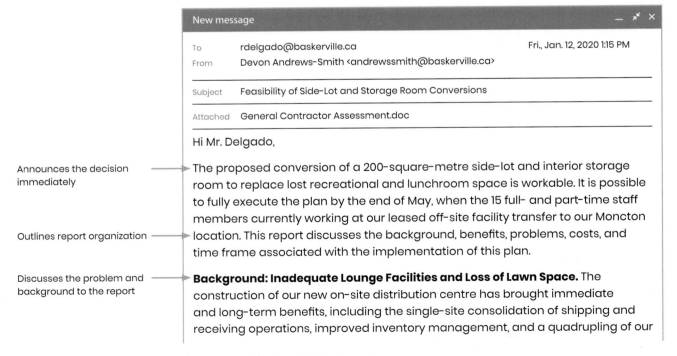

Announces the decision immediately

Outlines report organization

Discusses the problem and background to the report

New message — ⤢ ×

To   rdelgado@baskerville.ca   Fri., Jan. 12, 2020 1:15 PM
From   Devon Andrews-Smith <andrewssmith@baskerville.ca>

Subject   Feasibility of Side-Lot and Storage Room Conversions

Attached   General Contractor Assessment.doc

Hi Mr. Delgado,

The proposed conversion of a 200-square-metre side-lot and interior storage room to replace lost recreational and lunchroom space is workable. It is possible to fully execute the plan by the end of May, when the 15 full- and part-time staff members currently working at our leased off-site facility transfer to our Moncton location. This report discusses the background, benefits, problems, costs, and time frame associated with the implementation of this plan.

Background: Inadequate Lounge Facilities and Loss of Lawn Space. The construction of our new on-site distribution centre has brought immediate and long-term benefits, including the single-site consolidation of shipping and receiving operations, improved inventory management, and a quadrupling of our

FIGURE 11.32 Feasibility Report

storage capacity to 700,000 units. Because this 10,000-square-metre facility now occupies a former green space where employees gathered in good weather for lunch and coffee breaks, staff members are now without a designated outdoor recreational space and have no option but to eat and socialize inside. The result has been an overcrowding of our 30-seat lunchroom. The lunchroom simply cannot accommodate our 70-member staff during the peak noon-to-2:00-p.m. period.

This problem of overcrowding will likely become more severe as the remaining 15 staff members at our leased Saint John facility relocate to our main office and distribution centre over the next three months. These problems were factored into an assessment carried out by outside general contracting consultants, who indicated that the structural soundness of our office building would permit relatively low-cost renovations.

Benefits of the Plan: The proposed plan calls for (1) the creation of a combined green space and patio space through the re-sodding and landscaping of a partially paved, 200-square metre side-lot currently used for overflow parking and (2) the enlargement of the staff lunchroom through the removal of a drywall partition that separates the lunchroom from Storage Room B, followed by the interior redecoration and lighting redesign of the 10- by 14-metre space. The plan proposes practical repurposing of under-utilized space on our premises. One of the objectives in bringing all staff on site, instead of having them in two locations, was to promote collaboration and goodwill in the workplace by alleviating the malaise and isolation experienced by offsite workers. Providing attractive and functional indoor and outdoor spaces in which staff can socialize will help to improve morale and working conditions and contribute to the maintenance of good professional relationships between office and warehouse staff.

Describes the advantages of the proposed plan

Problems of the Plan: Loss of Overflow Parking, Work Disruptions, and Safety Hazards. A foreseeable problem will be compensating for the loss of three overflow parking spaces that are generally unused, but which may be needed as more staff members are brought on site. With the re-appropriation of ten of the current twenty spaces reserved for visitor parking, I expect that the shortage of staff parking could be eliminated with limited inconvenience to our customers, suppliers, and visiting authors.

Describes the disadvantages of the proposed plan

Another problem is ensuring a safe and healthy working environment while the indoor remodelling is carried out. Noise from interior demolition and remodelling may disrupt employees in adjacent areas while they work; fumes from paint, drywall compound, and other chemical agents may present a hazard to office employees and result in downtime. In compliance with the Occupational Health and Safety Act, we expect to conduct periodic environmental assessments to monitor hazard levels and confine most construction activities to weekends and after hours.

FIGURE 11.32 (continued)

Presents costs and schedule ⟶

Costs. Implementing this plan involves direct, one-time costs for landscape design, interior design, construction and landscaping materials, fixtures and furnishings, building permits, and general contracting. Barring any structural weakness in our building, the costs involved are within the $80,000 estimate for the project.

Time Frame. Drafting a request for proposals and initiating the bidding on contracts for remodelling and landscaping projects should take us about one week. With time allowed for project development and the submission of bids, the review process will take another five weeks. Once construction begins, I expect that the remodelling and landscaping work will take at least two months. By July 1 the plan for expanded and upgraded indoor and outdoor recreational space will be fully implemented, with benefits for employee morale and work environment.

| Send | 📎 | + | | 🗑 | + |

FIGURE 11.32 (continued)

Comparison/Yardstick Reports

Yardstick is a term that describes a standard for comparison. A yardstick report compares and evaluates two or more solutions to a single problem and answers the question, Which option is best? The report begins by establishing criteria—standards by which all options can be measured fairly and consistently. Criteria can be dictated by management (for example, cost limits) or emerge from the study research. Some criteria are necessary while others are simply nice to have. The criteria can also be used as bolded headings in the body of the report, where information for each category is weighed and presented. Conclusions are drawn about each option.

To make sure readers understand the reasons for choosing one option over another, writers can organize their information in the following order:

- Identify the problem, need, or opportunity that led to the report.
- Determine the options for solving the problem or alternatives for realizing the opportunity.
- Establish the criteria for the comparison of options; explain how the criteria were selected.
- Discuss each option according to the criteria; draw inferences from the data and make an evaluation of each option.
- Draw conclusions by ranking all the options or classifying options into acceptable/unacceptable categories. Consider if the problem, company resources, or priorities have recently changed in a way that might affect the conclusions.
- Make recommendations based on the findings and conclusions.

Figure 11.33 presents a comparison report for a company that much determine which among several well-respected firms can deliver the service it needs.

DATE: February 6, 2021

TO: Mike Vizcarra, Vice President

FROM: Manon Dupuis, Public Relations Director MD

SUBJECT: Choice of Corporate-Event Planning Services

At your request, I have investigated the possibility of Instanet hiring full-service event planners to strategically develop and produce its corporate functions and new product launches. This report discusses current problems with the standard planning and hosting of corporate events and sets out criteria for the selection of a corporate-event management company that would best enable Instanet to meet its marketing goals and build client and employee relationships. The report assesses three prospective corporate-event companies in Winnipeg and makes a recommendation based on that assessment.

Introduces purpose and provides overview of report organization

Problem: Producing Memorable Corporate Functions and Events

With the goal of increasing its profile and enhancing its relationship with stakeholders and the general public, Instanet initiated a program of unique and innovative corporate functions in 2014 that to date has included golf tournaments, merger events, and gala dinners. With our company's recent merger, the scale of these events will increase and demand a higher level of logistical support and coordination than can be provided by our current team of dedicated staff volunteers. Costs to produce these large events may be significantly higher. As a result, Instanet must ensure that its corporate events meet strategic goals, minimize potential liability, and bring expected returns on investments. Staging our events safely, successfully, and memorably will help us to attract investors and set us apart from the competition.

Identifies problem and discusses background

Solution and Alternatives: Corporate-Event Management Companies

Event management firms provide strategic development and logistics services to corporations, non-profit associations, governments, and social groups in the hosting of events and activities that reward employees, celebrate milestones, facilitate communication with stakeholders, aid in fundraising, and increase an organization's profile. While some corporate-event management firms specialize in one specific type of event, such as conferences, others offer a wide range of services. Instanet requires a full-service management firm with the expertise, artistry, and precise logistical capabilities to produce many different kinds of events.

Combines functional and descriptive headings

Presents a solution and options for its implementation

FIGURE 11.33 Comparison Report

Vice President Vizcarra   2   February 6, 2021

Our priority is to find an event management firm that will perform event strategy assessment specific to our company and tailor events to our company image. As our mission statement upholds a firm commitment to accountability, accessibility, and diversity, our company events and choice of an event management firm should reflect these standards. I have identified three prospective full-service event management companies in the Winnipeg area that can deliver services that meet our marketing and corporate culture needs: Boudreau & Hodges, The Unique Event Group, and Encore Events.

Determining Selection Criteria

The criteria I used to make my selection among the three firms is based on government publications, professional articles, a web search of event management sites, interviews with officials at certification agencies and at companies using event management services, and conversations with the prospective service providers. The following are three categories of criteria I used to evaluate the management firms:

1. <u>Event management services</u>—including catering and décor coordination; training of speakers and volunteers; accommodation, venue, and entertainment booking; VIP hosting; audiovisual production; development of substantive sessions for conferences; and media liaison, promotion, and public relations communications.

2. <u>Reputation</u>—as assessed according to professional association listings, professional certifications, testimonials from past and current clients, and telephone interviews with known clients.

3. <u>Costs</u>—for management and consultancy services.

Discussion: Criteria-Based Evaluation of Event Management Firms

The following table summarizes comparison data on the services and reputation of each of the three firms.

Outlines criteria and explains how criteria were selected

FIGURE 11.33 (continued)

Vice President Vizcarra   3   February 6, 2021

Table 1

A COMPARISON OF SERVICES AND REPUTATION FOR THREE
WINNIPEG CORPORATE-EVENT MANAGEMENT FIRMS

	Boudreau & Hodges	The Unique Event Group	Encore Events
Event strategy assessment	Yes	Yes	Yes
Venue/entertainment selection	Yes	Yes	Yes
Training of volunteers	Yes	No	No
Catering coordination	Yes	No	No
Management of hosting activities	Yes	Yes	Yes
Marketing promotional assistance	Yes	Yes	Yes
Selection of promotional gifts	Yes	No	No
Coordination of A/V production	Yes	Yes	Yes
Media liaison	Yes	Yes	No
Canadian Special Events Society certification	Yes	Yes	No
Certified protocol officer	Yes	No	No
Reputation (by survey of clients)	Excellent	Good	Fair

◄ Summarizes data for conciseness and readability

Event Management Services

Services offered by the first two firms were comparable, while the recently launched Encore Events did not seem to offer adequate service levels. The companies differed in the way they outsourced essential services and employed part-time staff.

The Unique Event Group and Encore Events do not have resident hospitality and catering experts or protocol officers, and they typically outsource all catering functions to third parties. Companies that have used services of this kind report that this catering arrangement can bring inconsistent results, with hit-and-miss menu selections and cost-overruns. Without a protocol officer, whom etiquette experts agree is essential to the success of high-profile VIP functions, any of our company events that include dignitaries or participation from other countries or levels of government would be subject to embarrassing breaches of protocol in

◄ Compares and contrasts alternatives

FIGURE 11.33 (continued)

Vice President Vizcarra   4   February 6, 2021

the areas specified in Heritage Canada's Protocol Checklist: www.pch.gc.ca/progs/ cpsc-ccsp/pe/list_e.cfm. Boudreau & Hodges employs a graduate of the Western School of Protocol and a Cordon Bleu chef who oversees menu theme development.

Encore Events does not currently have the resources to employ full-time event managers. Instanet would need assurances that Encore Events could provide a consistent level of service and support with its part-time staff; otherwise, Encore Events is better suited to producing small-scale conferences and seminars, which it can support with its exceptional technical services including a dedicated audiovisual department, on-site graphics department, and online conference registration.

Reputation

To evaluate the reputation of each event management company, I consulted its membership listing with Live Events Association (ILEA) Canada, an organization that represents the interests of the special events industry in Canada and offers a certification program. Both Boudreau & Hodges and The Unique Event Group are members but Encore Events is not. Boudreau & Hodges and The Unique Event Group are also members of the Winnipeg Chamber of Commerce.

In surveying recent client feedback and summaries of event experience, I found that each firm caters to a specific and decidedly different clientele. Encore Events specializes in providing services to start-up companies defined by an urban, under-40 demographic and chooses unconventional locations such as industrial warehouses as event venues. The Unique Event Group has special expertise in staging exhibits, shows, and awards galas in the arts community and fashion industry. Boudreau & Hodges is a service provider to publicly listed corporations, similar to Instanet, and has produced federal summits and dinners hosted by the prime minister.

In assembling further evidence of each firm's reputation, I conducted telephone surveys to determine the degree of client satisfaction with services received. Client names and numbers were supplied to me on request by the event planning firms. For the sake of consistency, I telephoned three former clients of each firm and asked the same questions in each case. Most of the company officials I spoke with were satisfied with the services they had received.

FIGURE 11.33 (continued)

Vice President Vizcarra   5   February 6, 2021

Costs

The fees schedules for all three firms are summarized in Table 2, which sets out a comparison of costs for planning and consultancy. Other fees, for catering and venue booking, are on a sliding scale based on the type of event, location, and number of guests or registrants.

While all three companies guarantee value-added services and respect for client budgets, Boudreau & Hodges has the highest fees but also offers the most flexible work arrangements, including the outsourcing of staff on a monthly retainer basis. Because Boudreau & Hodges and Encore Events pass on professional discounts to ← *Refers to data from table* their clients, their somewhat higher consulting fees may not necessarily translate to higher overall budgets.

Table 2

A COMPARISON OF COSTS FOR PLANNING SERVICES

	Boudreau & Hodges	The Unique Event Group	Encore Events
Event strategy assessment session (one time)	$1,800/session	$1,400/session	$1,700/
Project manager	$175/hr	$150/hr	$190/hr

Conclusions and Recommendations

Although Encore Events has a dedicated signage and graphics department that ← *Eliminates less effective* enables it to produce event signage at reduced costs, it does not offer flexible pricing *alternatives from* options and is not listed as a member of the Live Events Association Canada. These *consideration* deficiencies make it a less viable option; therefore, the choice is between Boudreau & Hodges and The Unique Event Group. As both companies offer similar services ← *Narrows the choice* and charge comparable management fees, the deciding factors are reputation and markups on third-party disbursements. Boudreau & Hodges has an experienced staff with protocol training and background in planning innovative, large-scale events on local and national levels for FP Top-100 companies. It stands by a commitment to pass on all professional discounts to clients. The Unique Event Group, on the other hand, has a younger, hipper image but a less business-oriented client list, and it may be more expensive because it does not disclose the discounts it receives on outsourced services. Therefore, I recommend that Instanet hire Boudreau & Hodges to plan and produce its corporate events.

FIGURE 11.33 (continued)

Checklist

Chapter Review

Format and Design

❑ Is the format of your report appropriate to the purpose and audience?

❑ Are headings, white space, and graphic highlighting techniques used to enhance content and improve readability? Are headings consistently parallel?

❑ Does the subject line, if one is used, summarize the topic(s) of the report or encourage reader receptivity?

❑ Is information organized for easy comprehension and retention and adapted to meet readers' needs?

Informational Report

❑ Does your report answer a specific question? Is the purpose of your report made clear in the opening paragraph? Does your report begin directly? Does your report supply sufficient background information to bring the reader up to speed?

❑ Is information arranged logically and methodically? Is information divided into subtopics?

❑ Are the tone and style appropriate to the audience?

❑ Does your report include a summary or an offer of further information?

Analytical Report

❑ Is your report organized strategically, according to a direct or an indirect writing plan? If you expect readers to be receptive, are the conclusions and recommendations summarized at the beginning? If you expect readers to be resistant, are the conclusions and recommendations reserved for the end?

❑ Is the purpose of your report clear? Has the problem you are attempting to solve been fully identified?

❑ Are findings presented in a thorough and logical way? Are findings supported with evidence? Do the findings lead logically to conclusions?

❑ Are the conclusions supported by facts and evidence? Do they relate to the problem identified at the beginning of the report?

❑ Are the recommendations, if they are required, action-specific?

Exercises, Workshops, and Discussion Forums

1. **Analyzing Graphics.** Collect a sampling of graphs and charts. Good places to start include online business publications and websites (e.g., *Financial Post*, *Canadian Business*, *The Economist*). Try to find at least one example of each type of graphic discussed in this chapter. Determine if each graphic is well designed and appropriate for the explanation it supports. Critique the appeal of the graphic

(Does it add interest? Does it make data speak?), and trade opinions on any unusual graphics you may have found.

2. **Matching Graphics to Objectives.** In a group or individually, identify the type of graphic you would use to plot the following data. Consider if more than one type of graphic or illustration could be used:

a) figures showing the number of female students enrolled in university engineering programs nationwide over the last five years

b) figures showing an Internet auction company's share price between January 2021 and January 2022

c) igures showing the revenue and earnings for the same company in the years 2020 and 2021 (year ending December 31)

d) a comparison of revenues from three divisions of a company from 2016 to 2022

e) figures showing the income of a national doughnut franchise based on its three leading products

f) figures comparing the sales of those three products over the past ten years

g) data showing cities in Canada with the highest rates of homelessness

Writing Improvement Exercises

1. **Distinguishing between Informational and Analytical Reports.** For each of the following situations, determine if you must write an informational or analytical report:

a) You have just returned from a conference you attended at the expense of your company and must advise your supervisor of the details.

b) As you do every month, you must inform management of the number of customer-service calls you have received, summarize activities and events performed during the report period, and note any irregular events.

c) You have been asked by your employer, Musicmission.com, to recommend three arts-related charities to which the company might consider donating money on an annual basis, to assess the relative merits and needs of each, and to suggest which of the three the company should select.

d) You have been asked by your boss, the chief of product development, to investigate the feasibility of adding a Senomyx flavouring to your company's canned minestrone soup as a means of reducing salt by up to one-third and eliminating the use of MSG. Pending government approval of the flavour compound, you will examine its potential health effects.

2. **Matching Types of Reports to Situation Descriptions.** Identify the type of report you would write in each of the following cases:

a) A report addressed to your boss, identifying a piece of equipment that should be upgraded or replaced.

b) A report requested by your manager, providing an overview of Slack (a subject she knows little about) and how it might be used by product developers.

c) A report requested by the head of your company's donations committee, prospecting four new charities in the fields of education and community service.

3. **Identifying Types of Headings.** From the list of headings below, identify which are descriptive heads and which are functional heads.

a) Costs
b) Personnel
c) Richmond Hill Costs Less
d) Findings
e) The Manufacturing Process
f) Situation 1
g) Survey Shows Support for Software Upgrade
h) Parking Recommendations: Valet Service

4. **Making Subheads Parallel.** Revise the following subheads so that they all use the same grammatical structure. Each subheading falls under the main heading "New Challenges for Human Resources Management."

Creating an Accessible Workplace

We Must Develop an Effective Recruitment Strategy for Indigenous Candidates

Can We Accommodate Employees Involved in Family Care?

Dealing with Intermittent Absences Caused by Chronic Conditions

Some Considerations for a Cultural Leave Policy

5. **Differentiating between Conclusions and Recommendations.** Indicate whether each of the following statements could be labelled as a conclusion or a recommendation.

   a) Sites A and B are not viable because they are located in the suburbs and lack access to major highways.
   b) Choose Site C, which offers direct access to major highways and a growing market in the downtown core.
   c) Archway Company should review the current benefits package.
   d) Develop an online marketing campaign.
   e) A two-factor authentication system can be fully implemented by the end of 2017.

6. **Designing Graphics.** For each of the following explanations, design a graphic or illustration that conveys the data most effectively.

   a) From 2016 to 2021 (year ending December 31), annual home-building-supply revenues (in millions) were as follows: $150 in 2016, $155 in 2017, $187 in 2018, $191 in 2019, $196 in 2020, and $197 in 2021.
   b) In preparing a report, your time in both hours and percentages will be used as follows: gathering information (10 hours/33.33 per cent); analyzing information (4 hours/13.33 per cent); preparing a recommendation report (3 hours/10 per cent); writing a draft (5 hours/16.67 per cent); revising the draft (2 hours/6.67 per cent); and typing and editing the report (6 hours/20 per cent).
   c) Figure 1 shows the percentage of students, faculty, staff, and administrators who participated in the survey: students (63 per cent),

faculty (22 per cent), staff (9 per cent), and administrators (6 per cent).

   d) Figure 5 shows the annual ratio of sales closings to sales calls, by sales representative: Lauren McAllister (80:102); Rosa Santorini (76:105); Jorge Diaz (95:107).

7. **Analyzing Graphics.** For each of the graphics below, write a brief explanation to support it.

   a) **Projected vs. Actual Profits, 2017-2020**

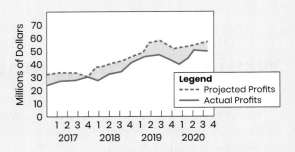

   b) **Cellular Subscribers per Capita, 2020**

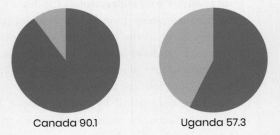

Canada 90.1   Uganda 57.3

   c) **Top Five Companies for Loans to Executives and Directors**

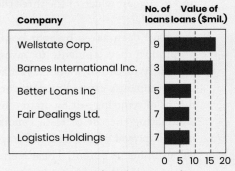

Data source: *Canada's Business Magazine*

8. **Spotting Design Flaws.** Each of the graphics below contains an error. Identify what is wrong in each case.

a) **Undergraduate Enrolment by Faculty**

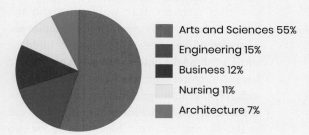

- Arts and Sciences 55%
- Engineering 15%
- Business 12%
- Nursing 11%
- Architecture 7%

b) **Loonie Dives**

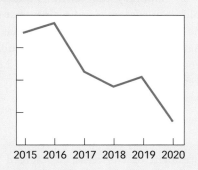

DAILY CLOSE, US CENTS

84¢

82¢   Yesterday's close
           79.03¢ (U.S.)
80¢   down 0.88¢

78¢

     Apr.   May

c) **Transport Truck Accidents**

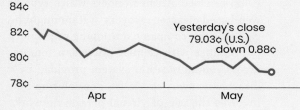

2015 2016 2017 2018 2019 2020

d) **Computer Sales and Leasing by Year**

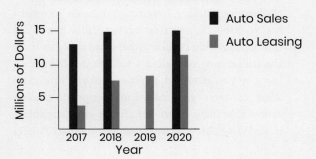

- Auto Sales
- Auto Leasing

Millions of Dollars
15
10
5

2017 2018 2019 2020
Year

9. **Matching Reports to Situations.** For each of the following situations, identify the type of report you would write and discuss how to organize it.

a) Your team project is to provide an expanded database for the Information Management System (IMS). The IMS has been delayed. The original schedule was based on the assumption that the systems analyst responsible for the project would have no problem with the CNG software. An experienced systems analyst is now correcting the problem and is expected to complete the project within the next month.

b) Your team project is to provide an expanded database for the IMS. Before work on the project begins, you must seek authorization to hire two new engineers familiar with the system.

c) Your company's training manager has asked you to seek information about the basic English program that was adopted by Rix Technologies. You have been asked to assess whether some or all of the Rix program elements could be applied to the production of an employee manual at your company.

10. **Analyzing and Revising Problem Questions.** Revise the following problem questions so that they are narrow enough and allow for solutions that can be investigated and implemented within a three-month time frame.

a) What new techniques can Edgeco Industries use to solve the problem of waste disposal?

b) How can Reverb Electronics market its products to teens?

c) What are the best businesses to invest in in developing countries?

d) How can the university improve student services?

e) What initiatives should the municipality undertake to build a greener, more sustainable community before next year's election?

11. **Writing Problem Statements and Purpose Statements.** Write a problem statement, purpose

statement, and, if applicable, a detailed purpose statement for the following report situations:

a) Avatar Fashions manufactures quality shoes and handbags sold online and in retail stores across Canada. Avatar has recently committed to fighting fashion waste in response to consumer concerns and a demand for biodegradable products made in low-waste, energy-conserving facilities, with a target of reducing carbon emissions by 15 per cent. Research is needed to help Avatar determine how these goals might be attainable.

b) Elegance Bridal Studio has been a retail clothing specialist offering a range of bridal gowns, veils, and accessories for over 40 years in a competitive market. Elegance is concerned that its traditional fashion sensibility, modest online retail presence, and conservative store image have contributed to a gradual decline in sales since 2018. It is now September, with the highest volume of sales typically falling between January and June. Elegance Bridal Studio must act quickly if it hopes to win back sales during this important period.

c) Over the past year, operations at Arcan Investment Solutions have been compromised by the forced evacuation or physical lockdown of the building that houses its call centre and administrative offices. At one point, an overnight electrical fire in the building's heating system sent thick, acrid smoke billowing into most parts of the facility. The heavy concentration of smoke made the air unbreathable, leading to serious environmental and occupational health and safety concerns. While the company infrastructure was intact and the server rooms were operational, employees were forbidden from entering the building until a full health and safety assessment had been completed and problems caused by residual smoke damage had been corrected. The workforce, which included more than 200 call centre agents, could not be mobilized for two days. Arcan is worried that it will lose even more business if it does not take steps to put a data protection and disaster-recovery plan (DRP) in place. Arcan wonders which type of web-based disaster-recovery system might be right for the company: a bridging of primary phone lines with cellular phones, a remote-access communication system provided by a disaster-recovery specialist, or a solution that involves the use of virtual private networks or IP phones that could be quickly shipped to a temporary call centre. Because of the volume of customer complaints that followed the fire-related lockdown, Arcan has decided that it needs to act quickly and budget generously for the implementation of a disaster-preparedness plan.

Case Study Exercises

1. **Trip Report.** As the social media manager for your organization, WeAccess, a start-up company with an app that uses crowdsourcing to collect and share accessibility information, you would like to attend Social Media Camp, Canada's largest social media conference. The conference focuses on the latest developments in social media marketing, communications, sales, crowdsourcing, e-learning, content marketing, and e-mail marketing—all of which are relevant to the day-to-day operations and growth of your company. Jibar Mohammed, the president of WeAccess, has agreed to cover the $700 registration fee, with the understanding that you will be responsible for other expenses, including your airfare, lodging, and meals. In return for covering the registration fee, Jibar has asked that you provide regular tweets and updates from the conference, as well as a full trip report detailing why you attended, what events you attended, what contacts you made, and important takeaways that may be of benefit to your organization. Write three to five business-focused tweets

on the conference, and draft a full trip report to be sent in e-mail format. (For purposes of this report, review the events described on the conference's agenda page, http://socialmediacamp.ca/agenda, and imagine that you have attended some of them.)

2. **Investigative Report.** As assistant coordinator of special events for Salk Pharmaceuticals Inc., you have been asked by the coordinator of special events, Tom Byington, to investigate three different models of GMRS (General Mobile Radio Service) two-way radios with which to equip the five team leaders during your annual three-day team-building wilderness retreat. The radios must be able to work within a range of 8 to 13 kilometres, the distance of many treks and canoe trips. Because teams may be outdoors and away from the conference centre for up to four hours at a time, the radios must have a long battery life. You have learned of three reliable brands: the Corsair PR3100-2D (unit price $120), which according to consumer reports has dependable reception and easy operation but does not reach the rated range; the Unicall T6500 (unit price $120), which features good outdoor reception and funky styling but a short battery life and inadequate range; and the Unicall GM885 (unit price $125), an all-round good radio that fares well in different weather conditions and has excellent sound, despite the fact that it does not reach the rated range. The Unicall GM885 has a battery life of 25 hours compared with 12 hours for the Corsair and 14 hours for the Unicall T6500 model. Prepare a report in which you present your findings to your supervisor.

3. **Investigative Report.** For a course or program in which you are currently enrolled, suggest three potential field-trip destinations that tie in with course content: businesses, industries, financial institutions, government agencies, museums, or resource centres. For each excursion, note the size of group the venue accommodates, discuss the allocation of time and resources as well as any special arrangements that may be required, and calculate the expenses involved in undertaking the field trip. Consider the purpose and educational value of each trip.

4. **Periodic Report.** If you are currently enrolled in a work-study program at your college or university, prepare a periodic report for your course instructor or work-placement officer in which you document your work-related activities over the past month. Discuss any irregularities on the job, and highlight solutions to problems you encountered, as well as any special needs.

5. **Investigative Report.** Write a short investigative report that summarizes fact-finding you have done and makes recommendations toward the purchase of a car, a computer and/or office equipment, a camera, or a personal electronics item. Review the criteria you used and options you considered before making your purchase.

6. **Progress Report.** Using the plan outlined in this chapter, write a progress report that summarizes the status of a work, volunteer, or recreational project in which you are involved or a term report you are currently preparing.

7. **Progress Report.** As chief contractor for Grande Construction Company, prepare a progress report for Hilary Murdoch, owner of Best-Temp Employment Services, advising her on the status of renovations to her new downtown office, located in a heritage property. Work is progressing on schedule, perhaps even a little ahead of what you had expected. Although the cost of certain materials is higher than your original bid indicated, you expect to complete the project without exceeding the estimated costs because the speed with which the project is being completed will reduce labour expenses. Materials used to date have cost $90,850 and labour costs have been $217,000 (including some subcontracted electrical work). Your estimate for the remainder of the materials is $85,000; remaining labour costs should not exceed $73,000. As of April 15, you had finished all plumbing work, plus the installation of the circuit-breaker panels, meters, service outlets, and all sub-floor wiring. Replacement of the heating and air-conditioning system is in the preliminary stages. You have scheduled the upgrading of the central office and adjoining storage facilities to take place from April 30 to May 15. You expect the replacement of all drywall, resurfacing of all

wood floors, and installation of lighting systems will take place from May 16 to June 2. You see no difficulty in completing all work by the scheduled date of June 16.

8. **Recommendation Report.** As the circulation manager of *Allegro*, a free monthly music magazine covering the local classical music and jazz scene (circulation 35,000), you would like to gain a higher profile for your publication and increase the advertising revenue on which it depends. One way to achieve these goals is to host and sponsor a free lunchtime salon series of five jazz and classical concerts, held on consecutive Sundays in April and May at a local restaurant. You already know of several outstanding solo artists and ensembles that charge nominal performance fees and would be suitable additions to your program.

The restaurant proprietor has previously let out space for free for similar events. Write a memo addressed to Hal Friedman, publisher and editor of *Allegro*. Although you know Mr. Friedman dislikes change of any kind, you feel the series could succeed based on similar initiatives taken by well-regarded music guilds and organizations in your area. Decide whether a direct or an indirect strategy would be appropriate.

9. **Recommendation Report.** Could one of the services at your university or college—the computer lab, cafeteria, health services, campus bookstore, or parking system—be more efficient? Assess its quality and efficiency based on your own observations and experiences, and suggest appropriate changes in a report to the president of your student council or the dean of students.

Online Activities

1. **Graph Type Exercise.** Complete the three exercises on this web page from Statistics Canada.

   www.statcan.gc.ca/edu/power-pouvoir/ch9/ exer/5214820-eng.htm

2. **Questionnaire Exercise.** Read the comprehensive Statistics Canada web page on important aspects of questionnaire design:

   www.statcan.gc.ca/edu/power-pouvoir/ch2/ questionnaires/5214775-eng.htm

   Then complete the questionnaire exercise on the following Statistics Canada page.

   www.statcan.gc.ca/edu/power-pouvoir/ch2/ exer/5214909-eng.htm#link02

3. **PowerPoint Graphs.** Watch this online tutorial on adding charts to slides in PowerPoint 2016.

   www.youtube.com/watch?v=zrD4FhKt7Qg

(If you are using an older version of PowerPoint, do a quick search to find a similar online video that illustrates how to add charts to the version you are using.) Then return to the writing improvement exercise "Designing Graphics," above, and re-create the visuals outlined in that exercise using PowerPoint.

4. **Incident Reports.** Retrieve the incident report form provided by the University of Winnipeg's Safety Office.

   www.uwinnipeg.ca/safety/incident-reporting/ index.html

Recall an accident/incident that you witnessed on campus or in a workplace, and fill out the report based on what you observed. Was it difficult for you to remember the details of the incident? How much more accurate would the report have been if you had filled it out within 24 hours of having witnessed the incident?

12 Proposals and Formal Reports

Chapter Preview

This chapter explores how to write project proposals and evidence-based formal reports. You'll learn to recognize the distinctions between informal and formal proposals, between informal and formal reports, and between formal reports and proposals. You'll be introduced to methods of data collection along with research strategies, standards for evaluating sources, and methods for acknowledging sources. You'll also be introduced to writing processes, work plans for managing projects, formatting essentials, and strategies for writing reports collaboratively.

Learning Objectives

1. Identify elements of informal and formal proposals.
2. Distinguish between proposals and formal reports.
3. Conduct research by generating primary data and collecting secondary data.
4. Apply standards for evaluating research material from a variety of sources.
5. Apply the writing process to formal reports.
6. Develop a report work plan for a formal report.
7. Write a report as part of a team.
8. Identify elements of formal reports and document sources.
9. Draw conclusions and develop recommendations from report data.

Case Study

ESB Professional/Shutterstock.com

In Ontario, accessibility is a matter of public policy. Under the *Accessibility for Ontarians with Disabilities Act* of 2005 (AODA), provincially regulated companies must file an accessibility compliance report as part of the provincial government's goal to make the province more accessible by 2025.

Good design is an integral part of business communication—a 2010 survey from the Society of Graphic Designers of Canada (GDC) found that two-thirds of respondents noticed a connection between better design and better business performance.[1] Design is particularly important for creating inclusive content that is accessible to people with a range of abilities. With over 6.2 million Canadians living with at least one disability, accessible design is a key aspect of reaching potential employees and customers.[2]

As you compile proposals and formal business reports for a wide audience, there are a few design tips that you can use to make your written reports more accessible. Never use colour alone to convey or signpost information, as the ways that people perceive colour can vary widely. Ensure that you have sufficient tonal contrast for people with different perceptions of colour by printing your report off in greyscale and checking that it is still readable.[3] Choose an easily readable font such as Arial, Calibri, Helvetica, Times New Roman, or Verdana.[4] For printed text, make sure that your font size is at least 12 pt.[5] For digital reports, check that your reader can easily increase the font size, and write descriptive alt text for all visuals.

For more tips on making your business communications more accessible, visit Access Ontario's resource page (https://accessontario.com/resources/).

Proposals

A **proposal** writer's ultimate goal is to persuade readers to approve their solution to a problem—for example, to provide goods or services or to assess, develop, and implement a plan. A proposal may ask for action, business, or funding. It may stay within an organization (**internal proposal**), addressing questions such as the following:

- How can this idea save money? When will the savings occur and how much does the company stand to save?
- How can this new procedure boost productivity or sales?
- How will this plan make the company more competitive?

More often, proposals are sent to potential clients or customers outside the organization (**external proposal**) as a means of generating income. Most external proposals are written in response to a **request for proposals (RFP)** issued by companies and government agencies. Essentially a sales presentation, a proposal formalizes the submission of a bid for a contract. Unsolicited proposals involve a different challenge: convincing readers that a need or problem in fact exists.

Most proposals use a direct approach. Good proposals are persuasive and use words that communicate strength, confidence, and credibility. Unnecessarily tentative, doubtful, or defensive language can undermine the reader's perception of your ability to carry out the tasks you plan and get the job done. Which elements are included, however, depends on the proposal's audience, purpose, and contents.

proposal A business document that suggests a method for solving a problem or that seeks approval for a plan.

internal proposal A persuasive document that attempts to convince management to spend money or to implement plans to improve the organization.

external proposal A proposal issued to governmental or private industry clients outside an organization as a means of generating income.

request for proposals (RFP) A detailed document requesting proposals and bids on specific projects.

THE CANADIAN PRESS/Justin Tang

RFPs are often used in the non-profit industry and for government contracts. In May 2019, the Government of Canada launched an open call for proposals aiming to support the implementation of Canada's goals for the 2030 Agenda for Sustainable Development.

Elements of Informal Proposals

Introduction

The introduction should offer an overview of the proposal and its scope and highlight your qualifications to do the job. For external, sales-driven proposals, mention previous positive associations your company has had with the client.

Background

The background section defines in some detail the problem you aim to solve or the opportunity you wish to address. In addition to identifying the purpose and goals of the project, it conveys your understanding of client needs and how the client stands to benefit from the implementation of the plan you propose.

Proposal, Method, and Schedule

In the proposal section, you should explain:

1. the products or services you are offering
2. how the proposed method for solving the problem is feasible
3. how your company intends to proceed with it and perform the work in the available time
4. what special materials and resources you will use, and
5. when each phase of the project will be completed (create a timeline for this purpose).

If the procedure you propose is complex or involves several steps, use headings to give each section impact and definition. You can also walk the client through the process.

Costs and Budget

The outline of costs and the budget are key. Give a carefully prepared breakdown of costs for the entire project and, if applicable, for each stage of the project process. The budget you submit is a legal contract that does not allow for later alterations, even if your expenses increase, so be realistic about the figures you submit and mention any costs that are impossible to estimate at the time of submission.

Staffing and Qualifications

The staffing section shows that you, your team, and your company are credible and competent. Instill confidence in readers by briefly mentioning the expertise and credentials of project leaders as well as special resources and facilities that equip them to outperform the competition. You can attach resumés and references in an appendix, but take care to safeguard privacy by including only the contact information that you have permission to disclose.

Benefits

The benefits section summarizes the reasons for accepting the proposal so that the client will be motivated to action, helping to resell the proposed plan by highlighting the value of your plan. This approach shows that you are eager to assist the client in maximizing benefits.

Request for Authorization

The closing request—asking for authorization to proceed—can be negotiated after the client has received the proposal. Even without a request for authorization, this section is useful for stipulating the time period in which the proposal is valid and for expressing (1) confidence in the solution, (2) appreciation for the opportunity to submit the proposal, and (3) willingness to provide further information if required.

Integra
Communications Services

710 Conroy Street
Vancouver, BC V2A 1H5
(604) 603-8775
www.integra.ca

November 15, 2021

Ms. Amanda Sullivan, Coordinator
Vanguard Property Development
1400 Oak Tree Way
Vancouver, BC V5S 2T1

Dear Ms. Sullivan:

It was a pleasure to talk with you several days ago and learn about Vanguard Property Development's recent acquisition. Integra Communications Services is pleased to submit the following proposal outlining our plan for a 10-week on-site workshop aimed at improving the quality of document planning and business writing in your workplace.

Our company is prepared, upon receiving your approval, to immediately implement the plan outlined below and to modify it according to our preliminary assessment of writing samples submitted by your staff. We appreciate your ongoing support for our creative training solutions. ← *Courteously expresses appreciation for the opportunity to submit the proposal, for any assistance already provided, or for previous positive associations with the client*

Background and Purposes

We understand that the individualized training modules and self-learning packages currently used by your employees do not provide them with the level of ongoing support for improvement they are seeking. A combination of classroom instruction, regular individual practice, and immediate constructive feedback would more effectively deliver the desired learning outcomes. Your employees build strong basic-language skills and apply them to the written materials they ← *Emphasizes benefits to client* produce on the job. Our goal is to help your employees develop their

---

FIGURE 12.1 Sample Informal Proposal

writing skills through supportive individualized workshops, consultations, and hands-on experience. Our proposed training program is designed to help your employees become more confident and efficient writers able to produce quality documents within allotted time frames.

Proposed Plan and Benefits

On the basis of our experience in conducting on-site workshops and writing training seminars, Integra Communications Services proposes the following plan to maximize benefits to your company:

> **On-Site Workshop.** Participants in a group of not more than 20 will receive 10 hours of instruction through an intensive on-site workshop offered in five weekly two-hour sessions.
>
> Our trainers will provide practical, interactive instruction in an environment that allows participants to share their knowledge and workplace experience. Each workshop will run from 3:30 p.m. to 5:30 p.m., and trainers will remain on hand until 6:30 p.m. to take questions. The 10 hours of classroom time is significantly less than is required for employees to complete a self-directed training module.
>
> **Consultation and Feedback.** Each participant will undergo a preliminary skills assessment, based on work in progress, and receive continuous evaluation that focuses on his or her instructional needs. Through substantial written comments and three 20-minute consultations, each participant will receive immediate and relevant feedback and information on topics ranging from remedial English to strategic document planning. On completing the course, each participant will also receive a one-page status report containing a final assessment and concrete suggestions for further skill development.
>
> **Course Materials.** Each participant will receive a 200-page manual containing learning modules, skill-building exercises, workshop guidelines and topics, printed copies of PowerPoint slides, and assignments specifically adapted to participants' workplace writing tasks.
>
> **Ongoing Support.** Course participants have unlimited access to our comprehensive online writing resources website containing additional writing tips, links to business-writing resources, and self-correcting review exercises that participants can complete at their

FIGURE 12.1 (Continued)

own pace and submit for immediate feedback. For one month after completing the course, participants may also telephone our Writers' Outreach Hotline and arrange a free one-hour consultation with a course trainer.

Course Outline. The following outline corresponds to five primary areas of interest and can be adapted and modified according to the needs of individual participants.

> Week 1: Foundations of Effective Workplace Communication
>> Adapting your message to your audience
>> Organizing routine messages
>> Legal responsibilities for writers
>
> Week 2: Sharpening Your Style
>> Determining tone and word choice
>> Sentence style
>> Editing techniques
>
> Week 3: E-mail Composition and Management
>> Netiquette
>> Handling and processing e-mail
>> Writing better e-mail messages
>
> Week 4: Strategic Document Planning for Routine and Persuasive Messages
>> Applying standard approaches
>> Delivering bad news
>> Writing persuasively
>
> Week 5: Reports and Collaborative Writing
>> Report planning
>> Types of reports
>> Writing proposals

Walks the client through the process with clear headings

Staffing and Qualifications

Integra Communications Services has earned a reputation as a local leader in the communications field by offering quality writing services and ongoing support to businesses and industries in Vancouver. Our trainers, Dr. Gail Simpson; Ezra Nadel, M.A.; and Marie Brossard, M.A., hold graduate degrees in professional communication from the University of Waterloo, the University of Calgary, and Western University, respectively. All are members of the Association of Business Communication and have an understanding of government and corporate

FIGURE 12.1 (Continued)

Proposal to Provide an On-Site   November 15, 2021   Page 4
Business-Writing Workshop

communications environments that comes from years of work with government agencies and businesses such as

- J.G. Hampson & Sons
- Elite Computers Inc.
- Blackwell Investments

Over 90 per cent of our clients report a significant improvement in the quality of their documents and a considerable reduction in the time it takes to process them. For a sampling of client comments and course evaluation surveys, please refer to our website: www.integra.ca.

Cost

The total cost of the course, including a ten-hour workshop for 20 participants, consultations, all learning materials, and ongoing support services, is $3,500. All audiovisual equipment, including PowerPoint projectors and screens, will be supplied by Integra.

Authorization

Our unique approach to professional-writing training will improve the quality of written communication in your workplace. I look forward to discussing the details of this proposal with you and answering any questions you may have. The price in this offer is in effect until April 5, 2022.

Sincerely,

Elizabeth Rocca
Elizabeth Rocca (she/her)
President

EPR:kl

[margin note: Instills confidence by outlining credentials and positive client experiences]

[margin note: Stipulates the period during which the proposal is active]

FIGURE 12.1 (Continued)

Elements of Formal Proposals

Formal proposals differ from informal proposals in format and length. The number of pages can vary from as few as five to as many as several hundred. Formal proposals contain additional elements that sort complex details into easy-to-understand units with customized headings. Elements marked with an asterisk (*) in the following list are optional in an informal proposal.

front matter The parts of a proposal or report that are included before the main body and contain introductory information.

Front Matter
    Copy of the RFP (if applicable)*
    Cover letter/Letter of transmittal*

Abstract or summary*
Title page*
Table of contents*
List of tables/figures/illustrations*
Body of the Proposal
Introduction
Background or problem statement
Detailed proposal and method
Schedule
Budget or cost analysis
Staffing
Authorization
Benefits and conclusion

Back Matter
Appendix
References

> **back matter** The parts of a proposal or report that follow the main body and contain supplemental information.

The next sections provide a closer look at some proposal elements.

Cover Letter or Letter of Transmittal

The cover or transmittal letter, bound inside the proposal as its first page and addressed to the person responsible for making the final decision, explains the proposal's purpose, major features, and tangible benefits. It should either refer to the RFP or mention how you learned about the client needs to which your proposal responds. The letter should mention when the proposal expires and also offer assurances that your company is authorized to make a bid.

Executive Summary or Abstract

The type of summary you write depends on whom the report is intended for. An **executive summary** is intended for decision-makers and gives the proposal's highlights in persuasive, non-technical language. An **abstract** (also one-page maximum) summarizes those highlights in specialized, technical language.

> **executive summary** (or **abstract**) A synopsis of the body of a proposal or report specifying its highlights and recommendations.

Title Page

The **title page** should include (1) the proposal title and subtitle in boldfaced type or upper-case letters, (2) the name of the client organization and/or the decision-maker to whom the proposal is directed, (3) the RFP reference number, (4) the name and title of the proposal writer and company, and (5) the date of submission.

> **title page** A front-matter page of a proposal or formal report that includes the title of the document, the names of the intended recipient(s) and the author(s), and the date of submission.

Table of Contents (TOC)

Best included with longer proposals, the **table of contents (TOC)** should list all first- and second-level headings used throughout the proposal with their corresponding page numbers.

> **table of contents (TOC)** A front-matter list of the first- and second-level headings that appear in a proposal or formal report, all of which constitute an overview of the material to follow.

List of Tables/Figures/Illustrations

If a proposal contains more than six graphic elements, include a **list of tables**, **figures**, or **illustrations** that provides the page number of each item.

> **list of tables/figures/ illustrations** A front-matter list of the titles and page numbers for tables, figures, and other graphics included in a document.

Introduction

If the plan you are about to describe is complex, you can use the introduction not just to offer an overview but also to tell a client how the proposal that follows is organized.

Appendix

An **appendix** allows you to declutter the body of the proposal by archiving specialized materials (e.g., graphics, statistical analyses, tables, generic resumés of project leaders, product photographs, and examples of previous projects) at the end of the document.

appendix A section of the back matter of a proposal or formal report in which specialized supplemental materials are archived.

References

The **references** or **works cited** list uses a formal documentation style to identify the source material for ideas and information you have mentioned in your proposal or consulted in its preparation. This section may be prepared in one of several referencing formats, each with its own distinguishing features and content requirements. Of the two most widely used systems, the documentation style of the **American Psychological Association (APA) style**—which uses a reference list—is favoured by writers in the social and physical sciences and business. The **Modern Language Association (MLA) style**, used in the humanities, features a works cited list. Both styles use short, in-text citations to guide readers to the complete bibliography. (See pp. 452–455 for more on these documentation styles.)

references or **works cited** A section of the back matter of a proposal or formal report that lists, in alphabetical order, the source material cited in the text.

American Psychological Association (APA) style A documentation system used by writers in the social and physical sciences.

Modern Language Association (MLA) style A documentation system used by writers in the humanities.

Checklist

Proposals

- ❑ If the proposal is a response to a request for proposals, does it follow the RFP exactly and meet all specifications and requirements for the job?
- ❑ Does the proposal include a summary of what you propose? Is it clear why the proposal is being made?
- ❑ Does the proposal show that you understand the significance of the problem or challenge the client faces? If the proposal is unsolicited, does it convince the client that the problem or need exists?
- ❑ Are details complete? Are the plan and its implementation fully explained? Does the proposal outline project completion dates, mention staffing needs and resources, include a cost breakdown, and provide evidence to support your ability to do the job?
- ❑ Does the proposal identify the client's competition and develop a customized solution that answers the client's needs? Does the proposal show how the project leader's qualifications, equipment, and resources are superior to those of competitors?
- ❑ Does the proposal outline potential benefits to the reader?
- ❑ Does the conclusion reinforce a positive perception of your company and its ideas? Does it include a date beyond which the bid figures are invalid?
- ❑ Is the proposal positive and forward-looking in its tone? Is its organization reader-friendly?
- ❑ If the proposal asks for authorization, can sign-off be attained easily?
- ❑ Does the proposal follow industry standards in its format and disclosures?

Researching and Collecting Data

Reports are based on evidence. Short, informal reports may require only minimal research since the facts may be already known to you or close at hand. Formal reports, however, often involve extensive research. In either case, your first job is to determine exactly what you are looking for and decide on the best way to find it. There are a variety of types of information available: printed, human, and electronic. Where you search for information and what you use to conduct your search depends on the project and the sources that are available and affordable. Access can depend on the category of information:

- **in-house:** e.g., internal files, memos, reports, or company databases or records
- **publicly available:** e.g., consultants, experts, websites, books, or magazines
- **restricted:** e.g., websites with paywalls, research by other companies and organizations

Researching a report can be as straightforward as consulting a few second-hand sources—a computer printout or a published article—or it can be a matter of setting out and gathering new information first-hand.

- **Primary research** is a strategy that depends on first-hand sources where you generate the data you need, based on your own ideas and observations, by conducting interviews and surveys.
- **Secondary research** involves the retrieval of existing information based on what others have observed and experienced, by conducting a library or an online search.

Because it is easy to be overwhelmed by the task of locating data, you should begin by making a list of keyword-linked topics you need to investigate. Keep in mind the options open to you:

1. **Look for information online.** With the correct search parameters, you can find current articles on virtually any subject. You may also find online databases, company news, mission statements and directories, company profiles, product facts, government information, scientific reports, sound and video files, library resources, online newspapers and magazines, press releases, job banks, and employment information. Some directories, such as GlobalEDGE, are specifically business related.

   The rules of Boolean logic apply to electronic searches. Refine your search using the following commands known as "descriptors" or "Boolean operators":

   - AND—using *and* between your search terms will give you titles of articles containing all of the specified words (e.g., organization AND communication AND systems)
   - OR—linking search terms with *or* will yield documents containing at least one of the specified words (e.g., collaborative OR group OR communication)
   - NOT—using *not* will exclude articles containing the specified term

   When using web sources, evaluate each one carefully to determine its quality, relevance, and value. Look for the name of the site sponsor, note the last time the site was updated, scrutinize author credentials, and make sure the site gives evidence to support its claims.

2. **Do a computer-based search.** Reference libraries and many businesses subscribe to comprehensive databases such as Ovid, Dialog, LexisNexis, and ABI/INFORM.

3. **Find information in print.** *Print* is a bit of a misnomer because so much print material is now available electronically as computerized periodical indexes (such as the *Readers' Guide to Periodical Literature* and *Business Periodicals Index*), book indexes, encyclopedias, directories, almanacs, and online catalogues. Expect sourced material to include academic articles, abstracts, newspaper articles, government documents, and specialty and reference books.

4. **Investigate primary, in-house sources.** It is possible that the information you are looking for is right under your nose, or at least in the internal files and records of your company. There may be previous documents and earlier reports on the same subject waiting to be retrieved, which will save you the trouble of starting your research from scratch. Network within your company to find in-house experts who may have prepared earlier reports.

5. **Conduct interviews.** Chatting by phone or in person with an expert or a seasoned corporate veteran can yield valuable information. See figure 12.2 below.

Locate experts by consulting articles, company directories, membership lists of professional organizations, and faculty expert lists (e.g., the University of Toronto's Blue Book, http://blue-book.utoronto.ca/).

Familiarize yourself with the interviewee's professional background and achievements, so you can converse knowledgeably.

Schedule interviews in advance, estimating how much time your conversation will take. Try not to exceed that limit. Consider providing the interviewee with a list of your questions in advance.

Structure your interview by preparing three or four major questions, but seize the opportunity to ask important questions as they occur to you.

To obtain detailed answers, ask open questions (beginning with *Who? What? Where? When? and How?*). If you simply need to check facts, ask closed, yes-or-no questions.

Establish at the beginning what is on and off the record and what you are permitted to quote.

Record or take detailed notes of your conversation. Write up the results of the interview as soon as possible after it has taken place.

Be patient through temporary lapses and silences—the interviewee may just be formulating a response.

Be friendly and objective, and leave controversial questions for the end. You are participating in a discussion, not a debate.

End by expressing appreciation and asking permission to contact the interviewee for clarification of anything that was said.

FIGURE 12.2 **Good interviews come about through good preparation. Use these tips to conduct a productive, informative interview.**

6. **Quantify observations.** Information that comes from observation can be quite subjective and very open to interpretation. Observations that are reported in terms of measurable results and outcomes may be perceived as more objective and credible.

Formal Reports

Formal reports are business documents generally ten pages long or longer based on extensive research and following a prescribed format or pattern. Formal reports differ from informal reports in more than just length and format: they tackle more complex and difficult problems and have several other important differences. (Table 12.1). These reports present accounts of major projects—the development of new products or services; reorganization at departmental, divisional, or company-wide levels; or analysis of competing products or alternative methods. In order to effectively deliver complex information, formal reports follow a prescribed structure, which includes front matter, the body of the report, and back matter. Many organizations have a preferred "house style," whereby certain elements are treated a particular way according to the guidelines established in a report-writer's manual. If your organization has no prescribed style, follow the writing plan outlined in this chapter.

Preparing to Write Formal Reports

The most effective reports are the result of thoughtful analysis and careful evaluation before the tasks of research and writing begin. As you begin to define the project, you should have a clear idea about the following things:

* **Purpose:** What is the report for?
* **Content:** What is it about?

TABLE 12.1 Informal vs. Formal Reports: Quick-Reference Chart

	INFORMAL	FORMAL
Distribution	usually internal	external or for superiors internally
Style and Tone	some contractions personal tone and language	no contractions impersonal tone and language
Length	usually short	usually long
Structure	less structured several sections	more highly structured multiple sections and subsections
Transmittal	optional	memo (internal) or letter (external)
Title	in subject line	on separate title page
Table of Contents	none	on separate page for any report over five pages
Summary	within report (no heading)	on separate page
Introduction	first section (no heading)	on separate page with heading
Visual Aids	used infrequently	used extensively

- **Audience:** Who is it for?
- **Status:** Will other reports on the same subject follow?
- **Length:** How long should it be?
- **Formality:** How should it look and sound?

One way to start planning is to review the questions in the following "Quick Tips" box.

QUICK TIPS
Report-Planning Review List

Purpose

- What are you being asked to report on and why? What is the subject and situation?
- What is your main purpose? Are you expected to give information, analysis, and/or rec-ommendations? Or is your task to solve a problem or just provide a record for future reference? Does your report have more than one purpose?
- What results do you hope to achieve by writing the report?

Content and Organization

- What details should you include and exclude in order to support your conclu-sions and recommendations?
- What information matters most? How can this information be presented so it is easy to follow?
- How detailed should your analysis be?
- To which plan, direct or indirect, will the reader best respond?
- Could visual material enhance the reader's understanding of the subject?
- Do you have expertise in the subject you are reporting on?
- What research will the preparation of your content require? What sources are most credi-ble? Whom should you consult? What are the most appropriate methods of collecting data? How long will information gathering take?
- If you are working with others, how will responsibilities be shared among you? How can team members best apply their skills?

Audience

- Whom is your report aimed at? Who else will read it?
- What are the reader's skills, concerns, and knowledge of the subject? How much of your knowledge does the reader share? How much background does the reader require?
- What objections might the reader have? How might the reader react?

Status

- Is your report a periodic/interim report (to be superseded by another report in a few weeks or months) or is it a special-projects report (a one-time analysis of a problem or situation written on request)?

Length

- How much are you expected to write?
- How much detail do readers expect?
- How much time do you have to prepare the report? What is the deadline for submission? When must each phase be completed?

Formality

- How formal does your report need to be? What is the setting and audience for your re-port?
- What will happen to the report afterward? Who else will read it?
- Is it for immediate, short-term use (less formal), or will it be presented to senior govern-ing bodies of your organization (more formal)?
- Based on preferences and previous reports, what tone is appropriate?

Writing Style for Formal Reports

Reports often require a detailed and technical style of writing. Be prepared to adjust your style to convey objectivity and build credibility with readers. Here are a few basic dos and don'ts:

- Check organizational style guidelines before you begin to write.
- Use a more impersonal tone than you would for an informal report.
- Write using third-person pronouns, avoiding *I* and *we* as much as possible.
- Use the name of the company or the department to which your report is directed instead of the second-person pronoun *you*.
- Do not use contractions.
- Aim for a mix of sentence lengths, and keep paragraphs to less than seven lines.
- Use verb tenses consistently—use the past tense for completed actions (*respondents were asked*) and for citing references, and use the present tense for current actions (*the purposes of this report are*, *recommendations include*).

Creating a Work Plan

Generating a proper report takes time. The longer or more detailed a report is, the more you need to evaluate and define the project by creating a **work plan**, especially if success depends on working collaboratively. A work plan sketches out the project from beginning to end, making it easier to set priorities, allocate resources, and move forward. A work plan includes the following elements:

- statements of problem and purpose
- a strategy for conducting research
- a preliminary outline
- work schedules for writing and submission

work plan A document that defines the approach, personnel responsibilities, resource needs, and schedule for a major project.

Statement of Problem

As a result of recent expansion, our company has outgrown its current human resources (HR) department. Inaccurately processed claims, increased benefit administration costs, out-of-control operating costs, and the need to reinvest in technology make the outsourcing of some or all of our HR services a viable option for gaining efficiencies.

Statement of Purpose

The purpose of this report is to determine whether consolidation of HR services under one outsourcing provider can control operating costs and facilitate world-class delivery with respect to benefits, HR management, and payroll processing. The report will examine published studies, surveys, and accounts of how other companies achieved their HR objectives.

Sources and Methods of Data Collection

Magazine and newspaper accounts will be examined, as well as "HR Outsourcing: Benefits, Challenges, and Trends," the Conference Board's second study of the benefits of human resources outsourcing (HRO) and changes in the HR marketplace. Our accounting department will undertake cost–benefit analysis to estimate the strategic value of HRO to our business and the cost savings over time. Our HR department will estimate growth in the number of employees in the next five years and the additional number of HR and IT staff required to support that growth using the current systems.

Working Outline

A. What is the scope of programs currently offered by our company?
  1. Who provides them?
  2. Are any programs already outsourced?
  3. Are packaged HR services right for our company?

B. What HR services should we outsource?
  1. Central HR functions?
  2. Technical or administrative functions?

C. What are the benefits and risks of outsourcing?
  1. Risk management
  2. Cost savings
  3. Impact on core functions
  4. Security issues

D. How do we choose a service provider?
  1. What are our selection criteria?
  2. How can we manage our outsourcing relationship?

E. Should we proceed with HR outsourcing?

FIGURE 12.3 Sample Work Plan

Work Schedule

Investigate newspaper and magazine articles	Mar. 10–14
Conduct an internal audit—What do we do best?	Mar. 17–21
Conduct cost–benefit analysis	Mar. 24–28
Investigate system options and service providers	Mar. 31
Interpret and evaluate findings	Apr. 1–4
Compose a draft of the first report	Apr. 7–11
Revise draft	Apr. 14–18
Submit final report	Apr. 21

FIGURE 12.3 (continued)

Time Management

In report writing, time is of the essence. Few reports are assigned without a deadline, so effective time-management skills and up-front planning are essential.

QUICK TIPS

Time Management

- Learn how you work best and design a system that works best for you by figuring out when you waste time and when you work most effectively.
- Set priorities and try your best to ignore distractions. Give the task you are working on the attention it deserves.
- Start early. Don't procrastinate or leave an important task or project until the last minute. Leave room for unexpected occurrences, such as computer trouble or power outages.
- Break tasks into component parts with time for each.
- Ask for additional information and resources if you need them.
- Let people know as soon as possible if you are running seriously behind.

Peer-Reviewing and Team Writing

More than any other type of business document, a report often has multiple authors. **Team writing** a report requires careful collaboration. If you do not establish clear guidelines and processes, different sections of a team-written report can be strikingly unlike each other in tone, sentence and paragraph length, and word choice. Here are some ideas for collaborating successfully with co-workers on a written report:

team writing The practice of multiple writers working together to produce a single document.

- Agree on style points—the degree of formality and use of personal pronouns—before you start the drafting process.
- Tidy up the draft to minimize sharp contrasts in writing styles from section to section.

- Make sure all members of the team are satisfied with the final draft before you begin to edit it.
- Use a program (such as Microsoft Word) that allows each member of the group to make signed changes and comments to the document onscreen.

Elements of Formal Reports

Below are the elements you can expect to find in a formal report. Parts marked with an asterisk (*) do not require headings.

Front Matter
  Cover*
  Title Page*
  Letter of Transmittal*
  Table of Contents
  List of Tables/Figures/Illustrations
  Executive Summary

Body of the Report
  Introduction
  Discussion of Findings
  Conclusions
  Recommendations

Back Matter
  Appendices
  References or Works Cited
  Glossary

Note that for protection and professionalism, formal reports should be presented in a durable cover of vinyl or heavy-stock paper that can be marked with the company name and logo. The title should be visible on the cover, either through a cut-out window or on a label.

Front Matter

The front matter gives report readers a general idea of the document's purpose and offers an overview of the types of information they can expect to find and the specific items that will be covered. Because scope and audience vary every time you write a report, it may not be necessary to include all the front-matter elements described here every single time.

Title Page

The title page includes the following items, centred and spaced evenly on the page: (1) the full title of the report, typed in boldface and/or uppercase letters but not enclosed in quotation marks; (2) the name of the person and group or organization for which the report was prepared, prefaced by *Prepared for*, *Presented to*, or *Submitted to*; (3) the names of the writer(s) or compiler(s), along with their job title(s) and the name of their organization, prefaced by *Prepared by* or *Submitted by*; and (4) the date of submission or the date the report is to be distributed. Items 2 through 4 are typed in a combination of upper- and lowercase letters (known as title case). The title page is unnumbered but is considered page i.

Letter of Transmittal

A letter or memo of transmittal officially introduces the report and provides a permanent record of document delivery. It is written on company stationery and sent in memo form to insiders or in letter form to outsiders. It is usually formatted to allow for a 1¼- or 1½-inch (3.18- or 3.81-centimetre) top margin. A transmittal letter or memo (1) begins with a statement indicating the topic of the report and the fact that the report is being transmitted: *Here is the report on privacy issues you requested on November 3 . . .* , (2) refers to the report's purpose and authorization under which it was written, (3) briefly describes the report and highlights its conclusions and recommendations, (4) expresses appreciation for the assignment and for special help received from others in its preparation, and (5) closes with follow-up action and an offer of assistance in answering questions or with looking forward to discussing the report's details.

Table of Contents

A table of contents (TOC) shows the report's overall structure, listing all the sections or headings of the report in order of appearance and giving an initial page number for each. Prepare your table of contents last, when the report has been completed. List main sections in a column on the left and indent subsections a few spaces, using leaders (spaced dots) to direct the reader to the relevant page number. Use lowercase Roman numerals for front matter page numbers, and do not list *Table of Contents* in your table of contents (keep in mind that the idea is to list every item coming after the TOC). Word-processing programs allow you to generate a table of contents automatically simply by identifying your report headings using built-in heading styles. Leave 1½ to 2 inches (3.81 to 5.08 centimetres) at the top of the page.

List of Tables/Figures/Illustrations

If your report contains only a few tables, figures, and/or illustrations, you can list them in a separate section at the bottom of your TOC. If the report has many graphics and visuals, list them on a separate page immediately following the TOC. "List of Illustrations" is a label that can apply to both figures and tables. Be sure to number tables and figures independently and consecutively with Arabic numbers (meaning that there may be both a Table 1 and a Figure 1).

Executive Summary

Usually written after you have completed the report, an executive summary is roughly 10 per cent the length of the report it summarizes (or less if the report is very long). It can be read independently of the report but accurately reflects the report's most important information without using any technical jargon. Like a well-written précis, an effective executive summary omits examples and instead highlights conclusions and recommendations. Sometimes it is the only part of the report management will read. Place it separately from the report at the end of the front matter or at the very beginning of the body of the report.

Body of the Report

The body of the report begins on page 1. This section, the heart of the report, describes methods and procedures that were used in generating the report, shows how results were obtained, and draws conclusions and recommendations from the results. Not every report will follow the exact formula given below, so use either functional or descriptive headings according to what the project requires.

Introduction

The introduction is both a general guide and a road map that prepares readers for the rest of the report. An effective introduction covers the following topics, any of which may be assigned to a separate section.

- **Purpose or problem:** The purpose statement, usually not more than one or two sentences, identifies the rhetorical purpose of the report (to explain, to recommend) as it applies to the problem the report addresses. Providing a clear statement of goals gives readers a basis for judging the findings and results.
- **Scope:** Sometimes combined with the purpose statement when both are relatively brief, the scope statement sets out the boundaries of your material and defines the limitations of the subject. It tells readers how broad or detailed your coverage is and defines what the report does and does not investigate. Readers may then evaluate the report purely on the terms you establish so it is less likely to be faulted for incompleteness or lack of thoroughness.
- **Background:** Background information puts the report in perspective and may help to fill in the blanks when a report is consulted years later. Avoid giving readers more background than they really need. Instead, give a brief review of events that led to the problem or a description of how other solutions have failed—information that allows readers to understand the design and purpose of the report they are about to read.
- **Organization:** This subsection maps out the structure of the report.
- **Sources and methods:** If you collected primary data by conducting interviews, surveys, or focus groups, outline the procedures you followed and any related details: who your subjects were; how you chose those subjects; what the sample size was; when the collection of data took place; and whether the data you collected is open to dispute. You can also describe your secondary sources.

Besides covering these topics, you may also choose to say a few words about authorization (what the agreed-upon terms under which you are writing the report authorize you to do or suggest) or define key terms that clarify the subject. Almost unavoidably, an introduction will restate information from the executive summary and preview details from the discussion of findings, so use slightly different phrasing to reduce repetition and redundancy.

Discussion of Findings

The discussion of findings is the most substantial section of the report. With careful interpretation and analysis of significant data and research findings, it presents a discussion of the results on which your conclusions and recommendations are based. Choose an appropriate way to arrange your findings (logically, chronologically, in order of importance, by region, or by topic) and then use structural guideposts such as functional or descriptive headings to move readers from one section to the next.

Conclusions

Carefully avoiding bias, use the **conclusions** section to tell readers what they have been waiting to learn—what the findings really mean and what the solution to the problem is. Conclusions repeat, infer from, and pull together points made in the report. In this they differ from recommendations, which are actions the readers are advised to take. Some reports present conclusions and recommendations in separate sections while others combine them, especially if the sections are short. Together or on their own, conclusions and recommendations are no place to introduce new material. In fact, every statement you make in these sections must be justified by a point already discussed, with every result linked to the purpose and methods of the report. Conclusions make the most sense when they are given according to the order in which they are presented in the body and numbered or bulleted for ease of reference.

conclusions The section of a report that restates the main points.

Recommendations

The **recommendations** section makes specific suggestions about what action to take as a result of the information you have presented. Your recommendations should be financially feasible and appropriate to the problem. Presented one at a time as numbered commands beginning with a verb, they should flow logically from findings and conclusions and be supported by the information found there. Number recommendations to make it easier for readers to discuss them, and use the imperative voice to emphasize actions to be taken, adding information as required to tell readers how those actions can be implemented. Some reports include timetables for putting recommendations into effect.

recommendations A section of a report that outlines specific actions to be taken.

Back Matter

The back matter of a report contains supplementary material that accomplishes the following objectives:

- identifies sources that were consulted in researching the report
- provides any additional information that was too detailed or lengthy to include in the body of the report
- defines unfamiliar technical terms used in the report
- makes individual topics discussed in the report easier to find by indexing them

Each part of the back matter starts on a new page and should be given an appropriate label.

Appendix

An optional element located at the end of a formal report, an appendix contains specialized, sometimes lengthy, information that clarifies and supplements the essential information in the body of the report. A report can have more than one appendix (labelled alphabetically as Appendix A, Appendix B, and so forth), but each appendix can contain only one type of information—tables, charts, diagrams, illustrations, raw data, computer printouts, interviews, questionnaires, statistical analyses, or technical support.

Works Cited/References

To avoid charges of plagiarism, support assertions, and help readers access source material easily, cite and document as unobtrusively as possible the sources for any facts or figures you have quoted or referred to in the report. Even if you have summarized or paraphrased an idea, you must identify whose idea it is and where it comes from. The necessity of documenting your source material applies to any words, ideas, or data that isn't your own—anything that is not common knowledge or that does not come from an internal source (internal sources include company sales reports and financial statements). As discussed earlier in this chapter, the APA and MLA styles are two of the most common documentation methods. Each method has two elements: (1) parenthetical citations in the body of the report and (2) a list (of references in APA style and of works cited in MLA style) at the end of the report.

Parenthetical in-text citations identify sources of quotations or ideas that are cited in the body of a report. Whenever you quote, paraphrase, or summarize material from an external source, using either words or ideas that are not your own, you must add a citation to avoid the risk of **plagiarism**. All you have to do to avoid plagiarizing material is to insert the right identifying details in parentheses before you close the sentence in which the borrowed material appears.

plagiarism The passing off of someone else's thoughts or words as one's own.

A references or works cited list includes all print, electronic, and media sources cited in the report. Source material is listed in alphabetical order by author surname. Entries for each work include author (or creator), title, and bibliographical details (including year of publication).

APA Documentation: Parenthetical In-Text Citations

An author–date method is used in creating citations in APA format. Items within the parentheses are separated by commas. Table 12.1 provides guidance on citing the most common types of sources in APA format. For more detailed information, consult the *Publication Manual of the American Psychological Association* (7th ed., 2020).

In-text citations are inserted at the end of the clause or sentence in which the cited information or quotation appears, with closing punctuation placed outside the citation. The following citation identifies the source of a direct quotation:

> Corporate leaders may intentionally obscure their meaning, "but more often they simply twist it out of habit" (Watson, 2005, p.64).

MLA Documentation: Parenthetical In-Text Citations

An author–page method is used in creating citations in MLA format, guidelines for which can be found in the *MLA Handbook* (8th edn, 2016). The author's last name and relevant page reference (with no *p.* or *pp.* abbreviation) appear in parentheses. In-text citations should be placed as close as possible to the content they cite, preferably within the same sentence.

> Corporate leaders may intentionally obscure their meaning, or they may do so out of habit (Watson 64).

If the author's name already appears nearby within the text, then it is possible to include just the page reference in parentheses.

> Don Watson theorizes that "corporate leaders sometimes have good reason to obscure their meaning by twisting their language into knots, but more often they simply twist it out of habit" (64).

Table 12.3 provides guidance on citing the most common types of sources in MLA format.

Table 12.4 provides the general rules that apply to creating a list of references or works cited, showing the differences between the APA and MLA style.

TABLE 12.2 APA In-text Citation and Reference Format

	IN-TEXT CITATION	REFERENCE
Single author	**General citation:** (Author's last name, Date of publication) (Friedman, 2016) **Direct quotation:** (Author's last name, Date, Page) (Friedman, 2016, p. 8)	Author's last name, Initial(s). (Year of publication). *Title of book*. Publisher. Friedman, T. (2016). *Thank you for being late: An optimist's guide to thriving in the age of accelerations*. Farrar, Strauss & Giroux.
Two authors	(Author's last name & Author's last name, Date) (Davidson & Emig, 2015)	Author, Initial(s), & Author, Initial(s). (Year of publication). *Title of book*. Publisher. Davidson, W., & Emig, J. (2015). *Business writing: What works, what won't* (3rd ed). St. Martin's Griffin.
Three or more authors	**First citation:** (first Author's last name et al., Date) (Short et al., 2017)	Author, Initial(s), Author, Initial(s), & Author, Initial(s). (Year of publication). *Title of book*. Publisher. Short, J.C., Randolph-Seng, B., and McKenny, A.F. (2017). *Graphic presentation: An empirical examination of the graphic novel approach to communicate business concepts*. Peter Lang Publishing.
Journal Article	(Author's last name, Date of publication) (Suchan, 2014)	Author's last name, Initial(s). (Year of publication). Title of article. *Title of Journal, Volume number*(Issue), Pages. Suchan, J. (2014). Gauging openness to written communication change: The predictive power of metaphor. *Journal of Business and Technical Communication, 28*(4), 447–476.
Online article	(Author's last name, Date of publication) (Carmichael, 2016)	Author's last name, Initial(s). (Date of publication). Title of article. *Title of Online Periodical*. URL. Carmichael, K. (2016, October 4). How globalization is changing the game for central banks. *Canadian Business*. http://www.canadianbusiness.com/economy/globalization-and-central-banks

TABLE 12.2 (continued)

	IN-TEXT CITATION	REFERENCE
Blog post	(Author's last name *or* Screen name, Date of publication) (Marinigh, 2016)	Author's last name, Initial(s) *or* Screen name. (Date of publication). Title of post. *Website*. URL. Marinigh, L. (2016, October 4). Five steps to building a marketing strategy. *Futurpreneur Canada*. http://www.futurpreneur.ca/en/2016/building-a-marketing-strategy
Organization as author	(Organization, Date) (Statistics Canada, 2018)	Organization. (Date). *Title of document*. URL. Statistics Canada. (2018). *Characteristics related to the age structure of the Canadian labour force in 2017 and 2036*. https://www150.statcan.gc.ca/n1/pub/89-28-0001/2018001/article/00005/age-eng.htm
Web page or Article on a website, no publication date	(Author's last name, n.d.) (Paglarini, n.d.)	Author, Initial(s). (n.d.). *Title*. Website. URL. Paglarini, R. (n.d.) *How to write an elevator speech*. Business know-how. http://www.businessknowhow.com/money/elevator.htm
Web page on a website, no individual author	(Shortened title, Date) (Government of Alberta, 2015)	Website. (Date). *Title*. URL. Government of Alberta. (2018). *Ministry of Community and Social Services*. https://www.alberta.ca/community-and-social-services.aspx.
Personal communication (e.g., an e-mail)	(Communicator's name, personal communication, date of communication) (J. Drake, personal communication, January 7, 2017)	*Personal communications cannot be retrieved by readers, and are therefore not included in the reference list. They are cited in the text only.*

TABLE 12.3 MLA In-text Citation and Works Cited Format

	IN-TEXT CITATION	WORKS CITED
Book by one author	(Author's last name Page) (Watson 64)	Author's last name, First name. *Book Title*. Publisher, Year of Publication. Watson, Joe. *Death Sentences: How Clichés, Weasel Words, and Management-Speak Are Strangling Public Language*. Viking Canada, 2005.
Journal article	(Author's last name Page) (Suchan 452)	Author's last name, First name. "Title of Article." *Journal Title*, Volume number, Issue number, Month and year of publication, pages. Suchan, Jim. "Gauging Openness to Written Communication Change: The Predictive Power of Metaphor." *Journal of Business and Technical Communication*, vol. 28, no. 4, Oct. 2014, pp. 446–76.
Online article	(Author's last name only) (Carmichael)	Author's last name, First name. "Title of Article." *Title of Online Periodical*, Full date of publication, URL. Carmichael, Kevin. "How Globalization Is Changing the Game for Central Banks." *Canadian Business*, 4 Oct. 2016, ww.canadianbusiness.com/economy/globalization-and-central-banks/.

TABLE 12.4 Some general rules for formatting a references page in APA and a Works Cited entries in MLA.

	APA: References	MLA: Works Cited
Arrange entries...	same rules apply for APA and MLA: alphabetically by the first author's last name or by title (if the author is unknown).	
Begin each entry...	same rules apply for APA and MLA: flush left (i.e., at the left margin). Indent each additional line approximately 0.5 inch (1.3 centimetres).	
Type the author's last name...	followed by a comma and his or her initials: *Calter, R. & Mazar, A.*	followed by a comma and his or her first name. For a book by two authors, invert only the first author's name: *Calter, Remy, and Alissa Mazar.*
For works with...	21 or more authors, list the first 19 followed by three ellipsis points and the final name.	three or more authors, invert the first author's name and follow it with "et al.": *Monet, Sigmund, et al.*
For a work with an organization as author...	begin the entry with the organization's name.	begin the entry with the organization's name, omitting any initial *The*.
Capitalize...	(1) the first letter of all proper nouns; (2) the first letter of the title and of the subtitle for works that are not periodicals (e.g., books, articles, web documents, brochures); and (3) the first letter of all major words (i.e., all words except for prepositions, articles, and conjunctions) in the titles of periodicals (journals, newspapers, magazines).	the first letter of all major words (i.e., all words except for prepositions, articles, and conjunctions) in the title of a book, article, web document, newspaper, report, magazine, media production, or video.
Italicize...	titles of books, journals, newspapers, magazines, reports, media productions, and videos.	titles of books, newspapers, magazines, government publications, e-books, online magazines, brochures, and journals.
For articles in scholarly journals, magazines, and periodicals...	italicize the volume number (do not use the abbreviation *Vol.*) of the periodical and include the issue number in parentheses immediately after it. Do not use the abbreviations *p.* or *pp.* for page numbers of articles.	include the volume number, issue number, and date of publication, inserting a comma between each item. Use the abbreviations p. or pp. to specify a page number or page numbers, respectively, in articles. Enclose the titles of articles in quotation marks.
For newspaper articles...	include the full date of publication (Year, month day): 2016, April 7.	include the full date of publication (day month year): 7 Apr. 2016.
For electronic sources...	include a digital object identifier (DOI) at the end of the entry (e.g., doi:10.1177/1050651916651909). If no DOI is available, give the URL for the page from which the material was retrieved (e.g., http://strategis.ic.gc.ca).	include a digital object identifier (DOI) at the end of the entry (e.g., doi:10.1177/1050651916651909). If no DOI is available, give the URL for the page from which the material was retrieved, omitting an opening http:// (e.g. www.canadianbusiness.com). If you retrieved the material from a database, include the name of that database (in italics) immediately before the DOI or URL.

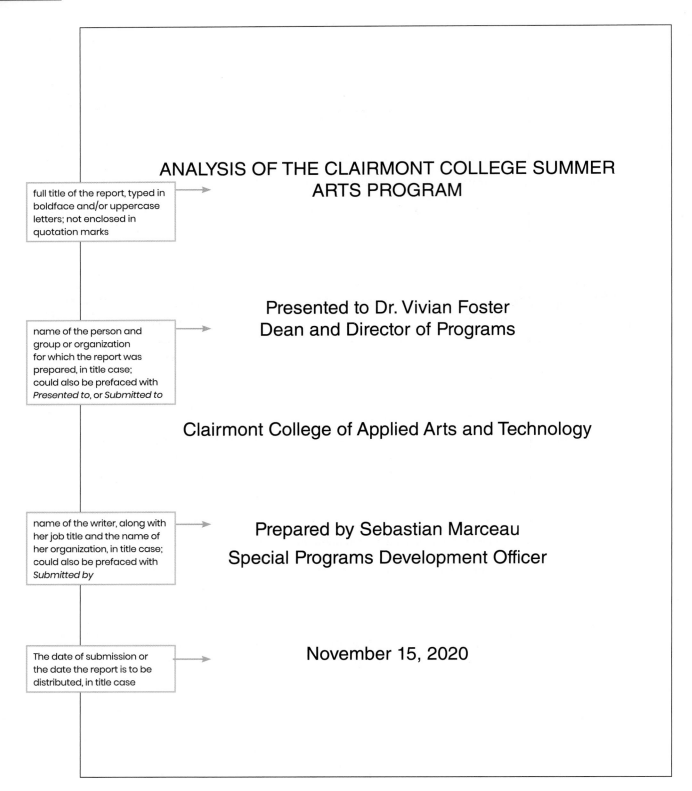

FIGURE 12.5   Sample Formal Report in APA Style

MEMORANDUM

TO: Dr. Vivian Foster, Dean and Director of Programs

FROM: Sebastian Marceau, Special Programs Development Officer

SUBJECT: Assessment of College Summer Arts Program

DATE: November 15, 2020

Here is the report, which you authorized on October 15, about the status of our Summer Arts Program in its first year of operation. The study involved a review of program enrolment figures, revenue variances, staff and classroom expenses, course curriculum design, class size, and student exit evaluations, as well as an assessment of the program mandate and the current and future educational needs of the greater Clairmont community.

Although response to the program has been and continues to be extremely positive, the information gathered shows that, as a result of substantial registration shortfalls in its first year of operation, we should in future expend considerable effort in marketing and refocusing the program to appeal to target audiences. The action plan outlined in this report reflects the results of research within the college and outside arts-in-education research.

I am grateful to summer staff instructors for their input and feedback and to members of the accounting department for their assistance in revenue analysis.

It is my hope that this report will provide you and the college board with the information needed to assess the effectiveness of the first year of the Clairmont College Summer Arts Program, to evaluate its implications, and to plan for the coming year. Please let me know if you have any questions about this report or if you need any further information. I may be reached by phone at (705) 582-2119 and by e-mail at smarceau@clairmontcollege.ca. I look forward to discussing the report recommendations and action plan with you.

Enc.

A letter or memo of transmittal introduces the report and provides a permanent record of document delivery. This report is for company insiders, so it is sent in memo form. It is usually formatted to allow for a 1¼- or 1½-inch (or 3- or 4-centimetre) top margin.

Begins with a statement indicating the topic of the report and the fact that the report is being transmitted.

Refers to the report's purpose and authorization under which it was written

Briefly describes the report and highlights its conclusions and recommendations

Expresses appreciation for the assignment and for special help received in its preparation

Closes with an offer of answering questions or further discussion

FIGURE 12.5 (continued)

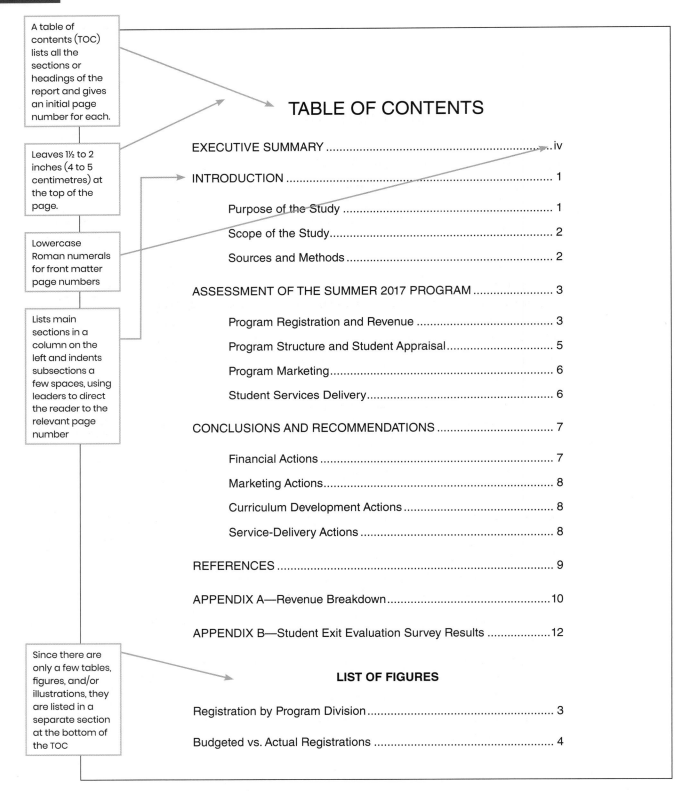

A table of contents (TOC) lists all the sections or headings of the report and gives an initial page number for each.

Leaves 1½ to 2 inches (4 to 5 centimetres) at the top of the page.

Lowercase Roman numerals for front matter page numbers

Lists main sections in a column on the left and indents subsections a few spaces, using leaders to direct the reader to the relevant page number

Since there are only a few tables, figures, and/or illustrations, they are listed in a separate section at the bottom of the TOC

TABLE OF CONTENTS

LIST OF FIGURES

FIGURE 12.5 (continued)

EXECUTIVE SUMMARY

An executive summary is roughly 10 per cent the length of the report it summarizes, and it is sometimes the only part of the report management will read. It should be included on a separate page(s) at the end of the front matter

A substantial shortfall in registration revenues has led to this review of the Summer Arts Program at Clairmont College. The purposes of this report are (1) to assess the continued financial and educational viability of the program based on findings related to its first year of operation and (2) to recommend modifications to curriculum, marketing, and financial structuring that would allow for its sustainability and future success.

The Summer Arts Program, encompassing the Summerworks, Danceworks, and Musicworks divisional programs, was launched in July 2017 after extensive market research indicated that the greater Clairmont community represented a ready market for arts-based educational programming. The program was designed to respond to the needs of adult learners seeking personal development in a supportive learning environment. The program is aimed at enriching the cultural life of the community and at providing a segue to courses at the college.

The results of this assessment show that a general restructuring of finances and curriculum are needed to reduce losses and build a market for the program, if in fact it is to continue.

Outlines the report's most important information without using any technical jargon

As a result of our review and assessment, we recommend the following changes to the Summer Arts Program:

Omits examples and highlighting conclusions and recommendations

1. Reduce course overheads by implementing changes to course delivery and eliminating support-staff positions.

2. Increase class size and reduce the number of hours per course.

3. Apply strategies to encourage students not to withdraw from courses in which they are enrolled.

4. Restructure course curriculum and revise course descriptions to appeal to broader audiences.

5. Implement an aggressive new marketing strategy that would involve print and radio advertising campaigns. Gaining an audience for the program also demands a more proactive approach to community outreach.

6. Upgrade student services and improve campus efficiency during the summer months.

FIGURE 12.5 (continued)

INTRODUCTION

The annotation "The introduction is a general guide that prepares readers for the rest of the report. An introduction will restate information from the executive summary and preview details from the discussion of findings, so use slightly different phrasing to reduce repetition." points to the INTRODUCTION heading.

The Clairmont College Summer Arts Program was established to promote standards of excellence in the fine and applied arts and to provide a community base for personal growth and cultural enrichment in the Greater Clairmont Area. According to its mandate, the Summer Arts Program encompasses three divisional programs: (1) modern and classical dance, including ballet; (2) jazz, orchestral, and choral music; and (3) a cross-section of special interest courses in drama and the visual and media arts.

The annotation "Background information gives a brief review of events, allowing readers to understand the purpose of the report" points to the following paragraph.

As an outgrowth of Clairmont College academic programs, the new arts programming is founded on established notions, voiced by visual artists such as Herbert Read, that "the aim of education ought to be concerned with the preparation of artists" (Eisner, 2004). The Special Programs Committee, which was entrusted with the task of developing programs to promote artists within the broader spectrum of liberal arts education, subscribes to the view that "there are no guarantees or easy solutions to the complex challenges in education, but an arts-rich curriculum can provide a vehicle to self-expression, self-understanding, self-confidence, creative problem-solving and motivation" (Elster, 2002).

Purpose of the Study

The annotation "Identifies the problem that the report will address" points to the following paragraph.

The annotation "Purpose statement is not more than 1–2 sentences, and identifies the rhetorical purpose of the report as it applies to the problem the report addresses" points to the following paragraph.

The Special Programs Committee (SPC) had projected that enrolment in the program would be substantially higher than the actual 2017 registration levels. In allowing for initial registration shortfalls, however, the SPC had also expected that the program would take several years to establish itself in the community and refine its curriculum to meet the needs of target audiences. The purpose of this study is to determine how well the Summer Arts Program fulfilled its mandate and to investigate underlying weaknesses in program funding and curriculum development as a basis for assessing possible changes and the long-term viability of the program. Recommendations for the increasing revenue and enrolment will be made based on the results of this study.

FIGURE 12.5 (continued)

Scope of the Study

This review was intensive and extensive. It paid particular attention to the following concerns:

- Budgetary shortfall
- Underperforming course sectors and curriculum deficiencies
- Service deficiencies
- Customer satisfaction

Sets out the boundaries of the material, telling readers how broad or detailed the coverage is and defines what the report does and does not investigate

Sources and Methods

Our assessment included four elements:

- Budgetary variance reports and revenue statements
- Student exit evaluations surveys
- Meetings with course instructors in all summer program sectors
- Discussions with students previously enrolled in the program

Outlines the procedures used to collect any primary data: who the subjects were and when the collection of data took place

FIGURE 12.5 (continued)

ASSESSMENT OF THE SUMMER 2020 PROGRAM

The findings of this study will be presented in four categories: (1) registration and revenue; (2) program structure and student appraisal; (3) program marketing; and (4) student services delivery.

Program Registration and Revenue

The program had 808 registrants. The budgeted number of registrants was 937 (meaning the program was 129 registrants short of budgeted targets). The diversified Summerworks program accounted for the bulk of registration, at 89.2 per cent, with the smaller Danceworks and Musicworks divisions accounting for only 6.4 per cent and 4.3 per cent of registrations, respectively.

Figure 1 Registration by Program Division, Summer Program 2020

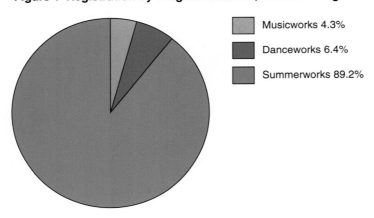

Musicworks 4.3%

Danceworks 6.4%

Summerworks 89.2%

By division, the breakdown of Summer Arts Program registration was as follows:

- Summerworks had 721 registrants, well exceeding its projections of 600. Even with the popular demand for a few such courses as Canadian Gardening and Creativity in the Visual Arts that necessitated the creation of additional sections,

3

FIGURE 12.5 (continued)

many courses ran below their anticipated enrolment average that was budgeted at 12. The average enrolment per course was 10. This unexpected reduction in class size created good classroom circumstances, but weaker-than-anticipated fiscal returns.

- Danceworks had a registration level of 52 (52 at $450 each = $23,400) but still fell far short of the projected 80 students. This contributed to a revenue shortfall of $12,600.

- Musicworks performed below expectations. The budget registration for Musicworks was 251, but the program had in total 35 registrants at $299 per registration, producing only $10,465 of revenue.

The figure below represents budgeted vs. actual registrations by divisional program.

Figure 2 Budgeted vs. Actual Registrations, Summer Program 2020

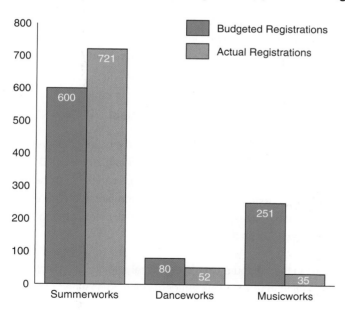

4

A variance analysis was undertaken to explain differences in revenue and expenses:

	Actual $	Budget $	Difference + (−)	
			$	%
Total Revenue	266,635	313,537	−46,902	−15
Total Expense	297,632	278,259	19,373	7
Net Revenue/Loss	−30,997	35,278	−66,275	−188

A full breakdown of revenue and expenses is provided in Appendix A. Total revenues for the Summer Arts Program amounted to $266,635, with a total shortfall for the program of $30,997. The most substantial expenses were incurred through casual and overtime labour—the casual fee paid to the individual who later converted to the Clerk A3 position ($23,011). It is possible to decrease expenses by eliminating this position and by making necessary adjustments to salaries and benefits, particularly by eliminating the $1,000 stipends paid to program guest speakers, for a total saving of $4,500. The cost of Marketing Services —including the production of brochures and a print advertising campaign—also exceeded projections. Instead of placing expensive ads in *Arts Monthly, Clairmont Life*, and *Arts Scene* at a total cost of $1,700, monies could be redirected for a single ad in *The Globe and Mail*, a far more effective venue (at $800 per ad), for a total saving of $900.

Program Structure and Student Appraisal

Student feedback was extremely positive, both in the formal exit evaluation surveys and in informal meetings convened at the college earlier this month. Appendix B provides a tabulation of the results from the evaluation survey issued at the close of the Summer Arts Program. Over 75 per cent of students who completed the survey ranked aspects of the program good or better than expected in all areas. Among former students, there was consensus on the following issues:

1. Course descriptions in the brochure were too general and did not match course outlines, resulting in withdrawals. Students also complained of poor pre-registration counselling. Where customer service is concerned, there is much room for improvement.

2. At 30 contact hours, most courses were too long for students simply studying for personal enrichment. Students agreed that 20 hours per course would be optimal.

5

FIGURE 12.5 (continued)

3. Due to popular demand, the Danceworks program could be modified and expanded to allow for the intake of students aged 10–17. Since September, the Registration Office received over 100 requests for information on the Danceworks program. Most callers were seeking intensive training for younger students in this demographic range.

4. Course start-ups timed to coincide with long weekends discouraged potential registrants.

Under-subscribed courses included Make 'Em Laugh: Stand-Up Comedy Routines, Art II: German Expressionism, and the entire Musicworks program.

Program Marketing

Survey respondents and interviews indicated limited awareness of the program within the community. Few registrants learned about the program through ads appearing in *Arts Monthly, Clairmont Life*, and *Arts Scene*. Current marketing plans allow for (1) the production of a program brochure, (2) a limited direct-marketing campaign aimed at Clairmont College alumni, and (3) a modest print advertising campaign.

Student Services Delivery

Fewer student services are available for the Summer Arts Program in June, July, and August. Food services are available on only a very limited basis. Commuter students complained about the high cost of on-campus parking. Based on an hourly rate, parking fees for students enrolled in day-long intensive courses were prohibitive.

During the week of July 8–12, the physical plant received 12 complaints about the malfunctioning air conditioning and ventilation system, which forced the cancellation of a class in one documented case.

These factors contributed to the lowering of student satisfaction with the overall physical environment and created substantial dissatisfaction among course instructors.

FIGURE 12.5 (continued)

CONCLUSIONS AND RECOMMENDATIONS

The conclusions and recommendations section repeats, infers from, and pulls together points made in the report

During its first year of operation, the Summer Arts Program fulfilled its mandate to provide quality non-credit arts programming to the greater Clairmont area. In exit surveys, students rated the program highly, with more than 85 per cent saying that they would study in the Summer Arts Program again and recommend it to their friends. Based on this feedback and earlier market research, there is sufficient reason to conclude the program is sustainable and worth continuing.

Although the program succeeded in its delivery of quality educational services, it underperformed financially. Registration levels in certain course sectors fell significantly short of projections. The resulting budgetary shortfall may jeopardize the future of the program unless substantial changes are made within the next three months to address these losses. If the program is to be viable in the future, it will be necessary to (1) reduce overheads and (2) refocus and streamline program curriculum.

Conclusions discuss what the findings really mean and what the solution to the problem is

Supported by the findings and conclusions of this study, the following recommendations are offered in the form of an action plan to increase revenue and improve the marketability of the program.

Financial Actions

The recommendations make specific, appropriate, financially-feasible suggestions about what action to take as a result of the information you have presented

1. **Redistribute overhead allocations evenly across all summer program courses.** This would provide a more realistic picture of the profitability–loss status of each program.

2. **Raise the maximum number of students per Summerworks course from 16 to 20**. Although this may present challenges in the delivery of curriculum, with implications for customer satisfaction, it will save the direct expenses associated with opening another section (approximately $1,500).

3. **Consider reducing courses from 30 to 20 hours** (equivalently from 15 meetings to 10 meetings) to lower the price and make the courses more attractive to students. This would reduce revenue, but it would save on the direct expenses.

4. **Avoid scheduling course start-ups on or immediately before long weekends**. Choosing other dates would encourage higher registration.

5. **Eliminate the Clerk A3 position from the Summer Arts Program office**. A downsizing of the Special Programs office would implement a saving of approximately $31,000 across the three program areas and reduce the program overhead load.

6. **Implement loss-prevention by devising ways to minimize the number of student withdrawals from the program**. This will entail several steps:

7

FIGURE 12.5 (continued)

a) Provide more effective customer service.

b) Improve pre-registration counselling through a checklist of questions that can be asked over the telephone to help prospective students make appropriate course selections.

c) Revise course descriptions to reflect the specific content and learning outcomes of each course.

Marketing Actions

1. **Develop a more aggressive marketing campaign.** Reconcentrate monies on *The Globe and Mail*, an effective venue (at $800 per ad), to save $900 over the previous year's advertising costs. Give the summer program prominence on the Clairmont College website or enlist graduating students from the COMM354 Web Design course to develop a related web page.

2. **Become more proactive in terms of community outreach.** Initiatives such as a spring open house could increase awareness of the program during the crucial pre-registration period.

3. **Carry out further market research.** Test newly revised curriculum on focus groups drawn from the community and from among previous registrants.

> Recommendations are numbered to make them easier to discuss, and uses the imperative voice to emphasize actions to be taken

Curriculum Development Actions

1. Eliminate non-productive/non-profitable courses. Replace these courses with more generic courses that could attract larger and more sustainable audiences.

2. Restructure the Danceworks program. Refocus courses to appeal to a younger audience, aged 10–17, through the addition of jazz and hip-hop classes.

5. Offer Saturday intensive courses and dance–drama workshops. This move would attract a new audience, one comprising individuals whose schedules do not ordinarily allow them to take on-campus daytime courses.

Service-Delivery Actions

1. Improve the physical environment of college facilities. Begin by upgrading or repairing air conditioning and ventilation systems so that room temperatures do not exceed a comfortable 23 degrees Celsius.

2. Upgrade student services during the summer months. Issue parking passes to students enrolled in full-day courses and waive the system of hourly rates. Relocate vending machines so that they're adjacent to summer program classrooms and lecture halls for easy access.

8

FIGURE 12.5 (continued)

> Whenever you quote, paraphrase, or summarize material from an external source, using either words or ideas that are not your own, you must add a citation and include a full reference to avoid the risk of plagiarism.

REFERENCES

Eisner, E. W. (2004, Oct. 14). What can education learn from the arts about the practice of education? *International Journal of Education and the Arts, 5*(4). www.ijea.org/v5n4

Elster, A. (2002, Nov. 12). Learning through the arts: Program goals, features, and pilot results. *Journal of International Education and the Arts, 2*(7). www.ijea.org/v2n7

9

FIGURE 12.5 (continued)

APPENDIX A

Revenue Breakdown

A breakdown of the total revenue of $266,635 is set out below:

Summerworks (SW) Registration		
721 @ $337		$242,977
Musicworks (MW) Registration		
35 @ $299		10,465
Danceworks (DW) Registrations		
52 @ $450		23,400
Student withdrawals:		
Registrations		
129 @ $337	($43,473)	
Cancellation fee		
129 @ $32	4,128	
		(39,345)
Administration fee—$12		
Relating to SW — 721 × $12	$ 8,652	
Relating to MW — 35 × $12	420	
Relating to DW — 52 × $12	624	
Relating to other programs		
($23,701 − $8,652 − $420 − $624)	14,005	
		23,701
Other variables such as course-price range differential		
		5,437
		$266,635

A breakdown of the total revenue shortfall of $46,902 is set out below:

Musicworks Program		
(216) @ $299		($ 64,584)
Summerworks Registration Excess		
121 @ $337		40,777

> An appendix is an optional element that provides supplementary information at the end of a formal report. Appendices are usually labelled A, B, C, and so on.

FIGURE 12.5 (continued)

Danceworks Registration Shortfall

    (28) @ $450   (12,600)

$12 Related Registration Fee Amounts

    (−216 + 121 − 28) = (151) × $12   (1,812)

    Unexplained   (9,019)

                          Total   ($ 46,902)

Expenses

Summary of Indirect Expense Variance

Stipend & Benefits—negative variance	$ 5,874
Casual & Overtime—negative variance	23,011
Supplies—negative variance	335
Marketing Services—negative variance	4,802
Staff Expense—negative variance	1,831
Registration Costs—positive variance	(2,460)
Consulting—negative variance	67
Negative variance	$33,460

Summary of Direct Expense Variances

Stipend & Benefits—positive variance	$14,502
Teaching Aids—negative variance	(4,552)
Program Arrangements—positive variance	4,136
Positive variance	$14,086

11

FIGURE 12.5 (continued)

APPENDIX B

Student Exit Evaluation Survey Results

Responses to this survey were provided in confidence to Clairmont College for purposes of program planning and instruction. This survey was administered to students upon course completion. Of a total of 808 students enrolled in the summer program, 760 completed the exit survey.

Criteria	Percentage of Respondents Ranking				
	Excellent	Very Good	Good	Poor	Not Applicable
Performance and enthusiasm of the instructor	34	38	18	10	—
Ability of the instructor to provide a supportive learning environment	25	20	40	5	10
Opportunity for input and feedback	32	48	14	5	1
Physical environment	11	30	36	24	—
Overall satisfaction with the instructor and course	11	30	35	24	—
Innovation and appropriateness of instruction and delivery methods	28	54	12	6	—

Sampling of Comments and Suggestions on How Course/Program Could Be Improved

- Offer weekend or evening instruction to accommodate students' work schedules and child-care responsibilities.
- Upgrade malfunctioning air conditioning system to ensure a comfortable learning environment for all students during the hottest month of the year.
- Assist course instructors through effective and efficient delivery of audiovisual equipment.
- Extend opening hours of food services or relocate vending machines close to classroom locations.
- Improve parking-fee system by issuing passes to students enrolled in full-day courses.
- Raise awareness of program within the community.

FIGURE 12.5 (continued)

Checklist
Reports

The Whole Report

❑ Does the report fulfill your original intentions? Does it present a solution that is practical, financially feasible, and appropriate?

❑ Is the report professional in its presentation? Is the title complete and accurate? Does the transmittal letter tell readers what they need to know about the report? Does the table of contents offer an overview?

❑ Is the report shaped according to the needs of its primary and secondary audiences?

Introduction

❑ Has the problem or report situation been sufficiently analyzed? Does the purpose statement reflect this analysis?

❑ Does the introduction set the stage for the report? Does it supply information that brings readers up to speed and guide them through the report?

Findings

❑ Is the problem subdivided for investigation?

❑ Does each heading cover all the material under it? Are all subheads under a heading in parallel form?

❑ Is your analysis given in sufficient detail?

❑ Are facts and assertions supported by evidence?

❑ Have you used sources that are reliable and appropriate for the type of information you are expected to present?

❑ Do you cite your sources using appropriate documentation style?

❑ Is your language moderate and bias-free?

❑ Do visuals, if they are needed, support and clarify written material, without distortion? Are they straightforward and clearly labelled?

Conclusions and Recommendations

❑ Do facts and findings support conclusions and recommendations? Are recommendations linked to purpose?

❑ Have you achieved what you wanted to achieve in writing your report?

Checklist
Chapter Review

❑ Have you created a feasible plan that will allow you (and, if necessary, your co-writers) sufficient time and resources for completing the proposal or report?

❑ Have you identified the proposal or report's purpose, method, audience, and content?

❏ Does the document include all the required elements?

❏ Is the writing style appropriate? Does it adhere to your company's guidelines and the audience's needs?

❏ Does the document use a reader-centred approach?

❏ Is research needed to support the document's content? If so, is the data reliable and properly cited?

Exercises, Workshops, and Discussion Forums

1. **Evaluating Internet Resources.** Read Georgetown University's guidelines on evaluating Internet resources (www.library.georgetown.edu/tutorials/research-guides/evaluating-internet-content). Based on what you learn, create two lists: one identifying the types of Internet resources that would be good sources of information for a formal business report, and one identifying the types of Internet resources that should be avoided. Compare your notes with those of another member of your class, and discuss any differences between them. Why is it important to be critical of resources you find on the web?

2. **Preparing and Responding to Proposals.** In a small group, establish the application criteria for a provincial government grant that offers assistance to students in operating a summer business. (The maximum grant available is $1,500.) Consider age restrictions, terms of eligibility, restrictions on what the money can be used for, and protocols for reporting expenditures at the end of the summer. Exchange criteria with another group in your class and, on the basis of the other group's requirements, draft a winning proposal.

Writing Improvement Exercises

1. **Analyzing Requests for Proposals.** Search business classifieds, browse trade journals, or visit company websites to find an example of an RFP. Note the specifications and requirements of the job and create an outline of the proposal you would submit. Which headings would be appropriate for the proposal you would have to write?

2. **Creating a Work Plan.** For case study #7 or #8 in the next section, prepare a work plan that lists the problem/purpose of the report, outlines the method of conducting research, establishes a tentative outline, and sets out a work schedule.

3. **Identifying Conclusions and Recommendations.** Identify each of the following as either a conclusion or a recommendation:

    a) Begin an in-house daycare program operating from 8:00 a.m. to 6:00 p.m. five days a week.
    b) Disseminate this report in some form to employees to ensure their awareness of our company's commitment to uphold its ethics and procedures policy.
    c) Over half the respondents use public transit to commute to and from campus at least three days a week.

d) Recruit student leaders to organize, implement, and staff a walk-safe program.

e) The effectiveness of RPG's ethics program during the first year of implementation is most evidenced by the active participation of employees in the program and the 2,498 contacts employees made through the various channels available to them regarding ethics concerns.

f) A safety-monitor program that relies solely on volunteers can be successful because of the availability of volunteer monitors and support for the initiative within the student body.

4. **Formatting Reference Entries in APA Style.** On the basis of the following bibliographic information, create appropriate reference entries in APA style. For additional information on APA style, visit the APA Style homepage (https://apastyle.apa.org).

a) Authors: Jacquie McNish and Sean Silcoff
Title: Losing the Signal: The Untold Story Behind the Extraordinary Rise and Spectacular Fall of BlackBerry
Publisher: New York, Macmillan
Date of publication: 2015

b) Author: Jared Lindzon
Title of Article: "Is the Old-Fashioned Holiday Bonus Dead?"
Title of journal: Globe and Mail
Date of publication: December 28, 2013
Page: B14

c) Author: Deborah Weinswig
Title of Article: "Influencers Are the New Brands"
Title of Journal: Fortune
Date: October 5, 2016
URL: http://www.forbes.com/sites/deborahweinswig/2016/10/05/influencers-are-the-new-brands/#2cfe2ba87fc5

d) Author: The Conference Board of Canada
Title of Article: "Sustainability Practices: 2018 Edition—Trends in Corporate Sustainability Reporting in North America"
Date of publication: April 24, 2018
URL: www.conferenceboard.ca/e-library/abstract.aspx?did=10075&AspxAutoDetectCookieSupport=1

5. **Formatting Works Cited Entries in MLA Style.** Based on the bibliographic information given in the previous exercise, create appropriate works cited entries in MLA style. For additional information on MLA style, visit the MLA Style Center (https://style.mla.org).

6. **Distinguishing Informal and Formal Reports.** Identify the following writing situations as requiring either informal reports or formal reports:

a) You have been asked to investigate the automation of selected HR functions, including technologies, training, resources, maintenance, and IT support. You must report your findings and make recommendations to the director of HR.

b) You have attended the three-day general meeting and conference of certified management accountants held in Edmonton, March 27–29. Your departmental manager has asked you to file a trip report to update him on your activities.

c) Pit Stop, a chain of 1,900 convenience stores, is considering taking the fast-food trend a step further by incorporating several brands into its strategy. You have been asked by the chief of franchise and marketing operations to investigate and make recommendations on three quick-service restaurant franchises with potential to share space with your convenience-store outlets.

Case Study Exercises

1. **Informal Internal Proposal.** Think of a problem or challenge you have observed or experienced at your workplace. Do you have an idea or a solution that would help to reduce costs, improve customer service, improve quality, or increase productivity? Consider the feasibility of what you want to propose so that you may justify expenditures in terms of the bottom line. Write up your idea in a brief informal proposal.

2. **Informal Internal Proposal.** Half your company's workforce travels internationally for business, resulting in a massive carbon footprint and high costs. Make your case for lower carbon travel methods and alternatives to travel.

3. **Informal Internal Proposal.** As a recently-hired innovation specialist for a housewares manufacturer, you are concerned by your company's excessive energy consumption and expensive, non-recyclable packaging. Write a proposal in which you suggest using big data analytics to track energy consumption and changing your packaging to wheat straw that requires 40% less energy to produce.

4. **Informal Internal Proposal.** Roughly one-third of your staff now telecommute, working from home three to five days a week. You require ongoing on-site technical support and repair from a dependable mobile service able to make house calls within one business day. Your telecommuting employees live within a 100-kilometre radius of your office. Investigate the options within your area and make a case to the vice-president of operations in an informal proposal.

5. **Informal External Proposal.** Young At Heart, a local seniors organization, is looking for talented public speakers and entertainers to fill its 30-hour program of events for the year ahead. It is scouting musicians, stand-up comedians, community outreach volunteers, experienced world travellers, and sports enthusiasts to give a series of three hour-long performances, lectures, demonstrations, travelogues, or talks about hobbies. Prepare a short proposal detailing a particular skill, talent, or public service experience and outlining the format and content of each hour-long presentation, with special mention of any audiovisual equipment or materials you will use or require. Explain why the program you propose would be of special interest to seniors.

6. **Formal External Proposal.** Sports Fundamentals, a retail sporting goods chain with 12 stores positioned in major malls and downtown locations, wants a new store image, one that will appeal to a younger, hipper demographic. The company is looking for a creative design concept that will update store exteriors, improve ease of access, maximize retail space (which averages 370 square metres per store), and create an identifiable store brand based on design elements. Write a formal proposal for Omar Khan, president of Sports Fundamentals.

7. **Formal Report.** A chain of clothing retailers has received complaints about the quality of its store maintenance and customer service. You have been asked to inspect one of the chain's stores and note your experiences and observations. Were you greeted when you arrived? Was the store clean and well maintained? Did a sales associate ask about your clothing needs? Did the associate suggest other items in which you might be interested? Was the sales associate polite, courteous, and helpful? Was the fitting room you used clean and well maintained? Did the sales associate return and offer to find other items or garment sizes for you? If you made a purchase, was it processed quickly and efficiently? You make several visits in order to arrive at a fair and proper assessment. Consider if previous complaints about customer service were justified, and make recommendations based on your observations and experiences. Direct your report to Cindy Latimer, vice-president of in-store operations.

8. **Formal Report Outline.** Select one of the following questions on which to base a report, and create an outline that contains functional or descriptive headings.

a) Should online retailers compile customer profiles to help market their products?
b) Are on-site corporate daycare programs worth the cost?
c) Can mobile telework—working from home or car—increase productivity?
d) Do people over 40 have trouble finding jobs in information technology? Is ageism rife in the IT industry?
e) What coaching and development should be provided to managers preparing performance reviews?
f) What are the disadvantages of outsourcing?
g) Can temporary pop-up stores play a role in the marketing of new products?

Online Activities

1. **Writing an Abstract.** Read "Abstracts and Executive Summaries" from the Faculty of Applied Science and Engineering at the University of Toronto, then try the abstract-writing exercise from Mount Royal University.

    www.engineering.utoronto.ca/Directory/students/ ecp/handbook/components/abstracts.htm

    http://uncgsoc301.wordpress.com/exercises/ exercise-6-writing-an-abstract/

2. **Writing a Report.** This exercise, from the Centre for Independent Language Learning (CILL) at the Hong Kong Polytechnic University, presents a business situation involving a training course. Your task is to write a report on the course after first reading background documents and watching a series of interviews.

    http://elc.polyu.edu.hk/cill/reportvideo

3. **Using Formal Language in Reports.** Gain practice in formal writing by completing this CILL writing exercise.

    http://elc.polyu.edu.hk/CILL/eiw/reportformality. aspx

4. **Completing a Report.** Designed to help students improve their writing fluency, this CILL exercise requires you to read a memo report and complete it by choosing the correct option from the drop-down list. You may check your answers at the end of the report, view explanations, and (when finished) read a corrected version.

    http://elc.polyu.edu.hk/CILL/eiw/reportcorrection. aspx

5. **Organizing Your Report.** Complete these exercises from LearnHigher to gain practice in identifying standard report sections and arranging them in logical order. Scroll to the bottom of the page to check your answers.

    http://archive.learnhigher.ac.uk/resources/files/ Report%20Writing/Reports_Organise_Your_ Report_Activity.pdf

6. **Analyzing Annual Reports.** Read Motley Fool's "How to Read Annual Reports" and the Annual Reports Library's "Tips for Reading an Annual Report."

    www.fool.co.uk/investing-basics/ understanding-company-accounts/ annual-reports-and-accounts/

    www.zpub.com/sf/arl/arl-read.html

    Then, in a small group, analyze one of the annual reports from the list below, using the following questions to jump-start your analysis:

    - What are the identifiable sections in the annual report?
    - How do photographs, infographics, and other graphical elements relate to the text of the report?
    - How is statistical and numerical data presented? What types of appeals are evident? In what ways is the report persuasive?
    - How much discussion is there of competition?
    - How does the report's design support the content? How could the design of the report be improved? How does this report differ from others in its industry?

    Bombardier Annual Reports
    http://ir.bombardier.com/en/financial-reports

    Canadian Tire Annual Reports
    http://investors.canadiantire.ca/English/investors/ financial-reporting/annual-disclosures/default.aspx

    IBM Annual Reports
    www.ibm.com/annualreport/

    Canada Post Annual Reports
    www.canadapost.ca/cpc/en/our-company/about-us/ financial-reports/annual-reports/archive-annual- reports.page?

13 Oral Communication

Chapter Preview

Effective oral communication skills are essential to success in the workplace. This chapter focuses on four activities commonly encountered in professional environments: oral presentations, meetings, telephone conversations, and interactions with the media. You'll gain insight into planning and preparing presentations, profiling your audience, and delivering speeches that range from impromptu to formal. You'll also learn useful techniques for developing platform-ready posture and gestures, controlling and projecting your voice, and reducing performance anxiety. Finally, you'll find strategies for designing and using visual aids, making valuable contributions in meetings, and handling questions from audiences and the media.

Learning Objectives

1. Prepare for presentations and briefings by analyzing the occasion and profiling your audience.

2. Gather material, select content, and strategically structure your presentation.

3. Incorporate visual and multimedia aids, including flip charts, handouts, and PowerPoint or Prezi slides.

4. Identify four methods of delivery for a presentation.

5. Master effective public-speaking skills and apply strategies to increase confidence.

6. Handle questions and conduct follow-up.

7. Organize, manage, and participate in meetings effectively.

8. Communicate by telephone productively.

9. Deal with the media and get your message across.

Case Study

iStock.com/RakicN

The elevator pitch—in which a speaker has approximately 60 seconds to "sell" something to a listener—is useful for more than just selling products and services to potential customers. Because it gets the point across succinctly and with emphasis, it is an excellent format for proposing a new idea, promoting a new initiative, or introducing external contacts to your organization's overall purpose or goal.

As small business owners taking part in *The Globe and Mail*'s networking challenge know only too well, the secret to a great pitch is really no secret at all. Attendees had a chance to learn about pitch styles from the challenge's four finalists, but they also got to share their thoughts on what makes a pitch successful. Colin Bell, Chief Commercial Officer at RecycleSmart Solutions, says that the trick is

> to zoom out, pretend that you've never been in your business, and you have to explain it to someone who has no interest. They don't care about your business but you have to get them interested, because the challenge is for entrepreneurs, we're so into our business, we're so inside it, so the really big trick is to come out and pretend that you've never heard of your business but want to become interested in it.[1]

According to Cathy Milne, co-owner of Because You Said So . . . Promotions and Events, "The importance of a pitch is to be clear, concise, to the point—exactly what you want to cover and cover it off quick."[2]

The elevator pitch or speech is a popular approach. The speaker has roughly 60 seconds—the approximate time of an elevator ride—to catch an investor's attention with a concise, strategically planned description that emphasizes how the company works. It identifies the product or service being sold, its market, the revenue model (how money will be made), and the company's leaders, competitive advantage, and competitors.[3]

Oral Presentations

While the prospect of public speaking can be nerve-racking, **oral presentations** represent valuable opportunities to sell your ideas and demonstrate both your competence and your worth to your employers and co-workers. Giving a presentation is in many ways similar to writing a document and draws on the same organizational strategies and audience adaptations. There are also some distinct differences to keep in mind. In public speaking, a presenter has only one chance to make a positive impression. Oral presentations should (1) be simply structured, (2) be arranged around a specific purpose, and (3) clearly identify the dominant idea listeners are meant to retain. The advantage of the spoken word is that it provokes an immediate reaction and allows for instant feedback. Listeners' non-verbal cues—their moment-by-moment reactions—can help you gauge and modify your performance; their comments and questions will tell you if you succeeded in getting your message across.

> **oral presentation** An informative or a persuasive speech delivered using only notes and visual aids to guide the speaker's performance.

Types of Oral Presentations

The term *oral presentation* covers a variety of speaking activities—ranging in length, formality, and style of delivery—which include the following:

- conducting workshops, seminars, and training sessions
- addressing staff at company meetings
- giving talks to clubs, societies, and organizations
- making sales presentations
- making a speech to a conference or gathering
- giving an oral report or briefing

Analyzing the Situation and Audience

An effective presentation starts with knowing what to expect of your surroundings and what the audience expects of you. Understanding the context for your presentation is essential if you hope to connect with the audience and achieve your purpose, whether that purpose is to inform, persuade, or simply convey goodwill. It is essential to keep your audience's needs, expectations, and perspective in mind in order to make appropriate adaptations.

How much assessment you need to do depends on whether you are speaking to colleagues, visitors, or outsiders. Speaking to outsiders presents greater challenges because it is harder to predict if your audience will be receptive and to determine what the audience's needs and expectations might be.

Who is your audience?

- Why will they be there and what will they expect from you?
- What is their attitude toward you and your subject? How can you counter any resistance?
- What is your organizational role, rank, and relationship to your audience?
- Will there be decision-makers in the audience? What are their concerns?
- Are there tensions or conflicts within the audience?
- How knowledgeable will audience members be in the subject area?

- How will this topic appeal to this audience?
- What questions will they want you to answer?

What is the speaking situation?

- What is the purpose of your presentation? What underlying concern has necessitated it?
- What level of formality does your organization expect in oral presentations?
- In what surroundings will you make your presentation? Is the setting formal or informal?
- How large is the room? Will it be equipped with a microphone or PA system? What are the acoustics and seating arrangements like? What are the visual-aid facilities, and how are they placed relative to the audience?
- How much time has been allotted for your presentation? How long will listeners expect you to speak?
- Is your presentation the prime attraction (the only presentation to be given) or will there be presentations from other speakers? How does your presentation tie in with the actions or topics of other participants?
- What will happen before and after your presentation?

An effective presentation is designed around a specific purpose. That means you should have something clear and definite to say and a reason for saying it.

Structuring Presentations

The structure of your presentation is important. Without the integration and coherence that good organization provides, listeners can easily lose the thread of your argument and miss important points. A simple, effective structure that accommodates three to five key ideas is the best way to keep your listeners with you. Three common types are suitable for an oral presentation:

- **Logical structure.** Any presentation worth listening to must be logical in its approach. Listeners should be able to easily understand how each point you make relates to your purpose. You can use signpost words (*my first point*, *my next point*) to guide listeners through your presentation to show how what you have said relates to what comes next.
- **Narrative structure.** The ability to tell an accurate, credible, and compelling story can influence the acceptance of policies, procedures, and ideas. At the management level especially, this skill is valued. Turning your information into a good story can grab attention and make what you have to say memorable. Because statistics alone are abstract and often hard to grasp, narratives provide an important way to ground the information. In order for a storyline structure to work, however, the story itself must be well told, interesting, and relevant to your objectives.
- **Formal structure.** Skilful handling of repetition can aid meaning and retention. This is the idea behind the most common structure for presentations, with its three familiar divisions:

> » introduction (tell them what you are going to tell them)
> » main sections (tell them)
> » conclusion (tell them what you have told them)

Developing a Three-Part Presentation

Introduction

In a world of **sound bites** and instant messaging, audiences have come to expect fast starts and immediate rewards for their attention. You may want to introduce your topic with an attention-getting device, depending on the situation (Figure 13.1). Use your opening remarks to (1) arouse interest, (2) identify yourself and establish your credibility, (3) make your purpose clear, and (4) preview your main points. Part of your introduction can also be reserved for background information or a statement of how you will proceed. An effective introduction prepares your audience to understand your ideas and makes them want to listen to what follows.

sound bite A short, quotable extract from a recorded interview that is edited into a news broadcast.

Body

The body of your presentation should develop your main theme and focus your audience's thinking. Whether your presentation is persuasive or informative, you should balance information with context and analysis so that your talk is more than just a torrent of facts. Give specific examples based on the most recent data available. Depending on your material, you can present your ideas and bring together facts in a variety of ways:

- chronological order (develop a timeline)
- topical/logical order (relate parts to the whole or introduce points in order of importance or reverse order)
- spatial order (map ideas visually)
- journalistic questions (ask *Who? What? Where? When? Why?* and *How?*)
- problem–solution (demonstrate that a problem exists and offer a solution or range of solutions)
- exclusion of alternatives (argue for the remaining option)
- causal order (explain a series of causes and effects)
- comparison/contrast (base assessment on similarities and differences)

State an unexpected statistic or fact or point out an intriguing aspect of your topic.

Ask a question that raises an issue you will address.

Display a key visual aid or perform a demonstration, perhaps one that involves the audience.

Cite a relevant quotation.

Tell a joke or an anecdote, but only if it is fresh, appropriate, and relevant to the situation (and never make a joke at the expense of the audience).

FIGURE 13.1 Attention-getting devices that you can use to introduce a topic.

- pro–con (review the arguments for and against a certain thing)
- process (identify a sequence of steps or stages)

No matter which method you choose, you should clearly announce each point as it comes so that listeners will know when you have completed one point and begun another.

Conclusion

Your conclusion should bring the presentation full circle and leave the audience with a positive impression of you and your ideas. Help your audience understand its significance and remember its main points with a brief summary developed in one of the following ways:

- Restate the main issues you want the audience to remember.
- Restate the point you started with in order to frame your presentation.
- Issue a challenge or call to action (this method is suitable for persuasive presentations).
- Ask a question for the audience to think about.

Your introduction and conclusion are the most crucial in helping your audience understand the value of your ideas.

Oral Presentation Outline

Planning a presentation can be challenging, especially if you have to keep track of a number of points. Use the following template to prepare an outline, or expand it to suit your needs.

Title _____

Purpose _____

I. **INTRODUCTION**

   A. **Use device to gain attention** _____

   B. **Establish credibility** _____

   C. **Involve audience** _____

   D. **State purpose** _____

   E. **Preview main points** _____

   Transition _____

II. **BODY**

   A. **First main point** _____

      Supporting details   1. _____

                                2. _____

                                  3. _____

   Transition _____

    B.   **Second main point** _____

         Supporting details   **1.** _____

                        2. _____

                        3. _____

    Transition _____

    C.   **Third main point** _____

         Supporting details   **1.** _____

                        2. _____

                        3. _____

    Transition _____

III. **CONCLUSION**

    A.   **Summary of main points** _____

    B.   **Closing device** _____

    C.   **Question period** _____

Using Visual Aids

As discussed in Chapter 11, visual aids help you to show what you mean. They also increase the impact of your message, helping to aid retention and involve your audience. Oral presentations enhanced by visual aids are more persuasive, credible, and professional. Visual aids can serve as an aid to your own memory, eliminating the need for additional notes and helping to improve your poise, delivery, and self-confidence. It is therefore important to use effective visual aids to support your presentation.

QUICK TIPS

Visual Aids

- Never allow visual aids to dominate so much that they prevent you from connecting with your audience.

- Use aids sparingly for maximum impact; don't confuse your audience by using too many slides. For a 20-minute presentation, use no more than 12 visuals.

- Make your visuals consistent in size, font, contrast, and spacing. Type should be boldfaced and no smaller than 30-point size.

- Limit the amount of information on each visual. Include no more than two illustrations per visual, no more than five or six numbered or bulleted points, and no more than 35 words on seven lines.

- Prepare each visual carefully and proofread it for accuracy.

- Give each visual aid a title that makes a point.

- Test audiovisual equipment in advance and check the optics of the room to ensure that all participants have unobstructed views.

(Continued)

- Put up your visual aid only when you are ready to talk about it, and give your audience a few moments to digest the information it supplies before you speak.
- Comment on—but do not read from—what you show, and match your delivery to the content of the visual. Remove the visual as soon as you are finished with it.

Types of Presentation Aids

The type of visual aids you use to support your presentation depends on their cost, the formality of the situation, and the flexibility you need to convey your ideas and connect with your audience. Whichever type you use, be careful not to read directly from your aids too often. Limit the number of aids you use and the amount of information you include on each one to curb your reliance on them at the expense of other delivery techniques. In addition, make sure you direct your words to your audience, not to the aids you are using.

Chalkboards, Whiteboards, and Blank Flip Charts

flip chart A large stand-mounted writing pad with bound pages that can be turned over at the top.

Chalkboards, whiteboards, and **flip charts** are flexible and useful aids, suitable for small audiences (under 30 people) and informal presentations. The best approach is to write an essential point and then explain what you have written, standing to the side and turning to the audience. Be sure to write legibly, in letters large and distinct enough to be clear to everyone in the audience.

Prepared Flip Charts and Posters

Prepared flip charts and posters are the most basic of aids. They must be large enough to be seen by the entire audience and clear enough to communicate your points. Visuals must always look professional. Prepared flip charts and posters are suitable for audiences of up to 50 people and can be used to display fairly complicated data of the type that is featured in academic conference and STEM-discipline poster presentations. However, they are awkward to carry around, and their low-tech appearance makes them less appealing to technically savvy audiences.

Videos, Films, Models, and Samples

Films and videos are most effective in the form of short clips, introduced strategically to reinforce key points or concepts. Models and samples can be useful for explaining products, as they can be displayed and manipulated to demonstrate important features and functions.

Handouts

Distributing handouts that summarize your presentation plan or provide a permanent record of graphs can greatly enhance the audience's understanding and retention. Typical handouts include outlines, articles, brochures, summaries, speaker notes, and printed copies of PowerPoint slides. Distribute handouts at the beginning if they will help participants follow your speech; otherwise, give them out at the end to avoid distractions.

Multimedia and Computer Visuals

Computer-based presentations are the medium of choice for business people today. Presentation programs such as PowerPoint, Prezi, and Keynote make it possible to deliver a dynamic, professional-looking presentation to a large audience. Presentation programs make it easy for you to create slides with a variety of formats and features, such as bulleted lists, numeric charts, tables, organizational charts (pie, bar, and line charts), photographs, audio clips, animations, and videos. A major benefit of preparing computer-based visuals is that you can add and adjust their content right up until the time you present. Another benefit is that once you have designed and assembled your slide show, you can take the further step of publishing your presentation on the Internet, through platforms such as Slideshare, or distribute it to the rest of your company online. Many presentation programs also allow you to add voice narration, which can be useful if you are distributing your presentation online.

Using Presentation Software Effectively

With many features, presentation software programs—such as PowerPoint, Keynote, Prezi, LibreOffice Impress, and Canva—are sure to impress, but their slickness can sometimes fail to engage an audience. Don't let the "wow factor" of an electronic presentation overshadow what you have to say. Digital design involves a particular set of considerations. Here are some tips for making the best of what presentation software has to offer:

- **Use templates.** Presentation software programs come with **templates** that combine borders, fonts, and colours for optimal visual effects and offer guidance on a variety of layouts.

  template A stored pattern for a document from which new documents can be made.

- **Choose a colour scheme.** The colours of your slides should relate similar elements, highlight important points, and permit good visibility with available room lighting. Use dark backgrounds with light text only in darkened rooms. Restrict yourself to four or five colours, giving thought to how colour and vibrancy might change when slides are projected. Ensure that your presentation has sufficient contrast to be accessible to a wide audience.
- **Keep slides simple.** Each slide should have a maximum of six lines of text and six words per line (Figure 13.2). Use boldface, sans serif type (e.g., Arial) in consistent point sizes for easy readability. Interspersing or combining text with visual elements can allow viewers to absorb information more readily.
- **Follow the eight-second rule.** Your viewers should be able to comprehend the information on the slide in no more than eight seconds.[4]
- **Make strategic use of images.** An image, especially a well-chosen photograph of at least 150 dpi, can often convey an idea or a concept better than text alone can. Use online photo editors (such as Pixlr or Fotoflexer) to correct images when necessary. If a slide contains text and an image, you can give emphasis to the former by using reverse type within a defined area (e.g., white type inside a black circle) to guide the viewer's eye first to the text and then to the image.[5] Use a photo credits slide at the end of your presentation to acknowledge sources, and remember to check if you require permission before using the photos — many photos, despite being available on the web, are under copyright.
- **Make data graphics clear, concise, and easy to understand.** Seen from a distance, the detail on data graphics and tables may be difficult to make out. To avoid this problem, do the following:
  › Use a clear font for the title and labels.
  › Simplify data and limit the amount of detail.
  › Avoid distracting, busy-looking backgrounds.

> Insert citations at the bottom left of the graphic to clearly identify the data's source.

- **Integrate video and audio clips with care.** Make sure that items add to the content of your presentation and won't distract or frustrate your audience.
- **Put titles on slides for easy reference.** Using titles will help you find slides easily during your presentation.
- **Don't use too many slides.** Consider the amount of information your audience can absorb in the allotted time. Count on spending two or three minutes discussing each slide.
- **Create an agenda slide.** An agenda slide lets the audience know what will be covered in the presentation. For presentation files you plan to share online, you can use hyperlinks to link the topics in the agenda to relevant slides.
- **Include a conclusion and a references slide.** Like a written document, your presentation must contain a conclusion and a references section that lists sources you have cited.
- **Use transitions and animation.** Effects such as dissolve, fade, vortex, or wipeout keep the eyes of your audience focused on the screen between slides. It is usually best to use one transition effect consistently throughout your presentation.
- **If you are using Prezi, use rotation and size to convey meaning.** Rotation can be used to emphasize changes in perspective, thinking, or understanding about a particular topic. The size of objects can be increased for greater emphasis.[6]
- **Proofread the slides before your presentation.** Print a copy of your slides in advance to make sure there are no errors.
- **If you are using PowerPoint, use the "Slide Sorter" and "Outline View" to review your presentation.** These features allow you to see the structure and big picture of your presentation and reorganize slides easily. Slide Sorter can help you gauge the flow of your presentation and its graphical elements; with Outline View you can see charts on the slides in miniature.
- **Produce speaker notes as reminders.** You can set up notes to appear on a second monitor, or you can print them. Consider using your printed notes as handouts.
- **Back up your work.** Copy everything to a USB flash drive, cloud storage, or e-mail it to yourself. Take printouts of your slides to your presentation for ready reference if your equipment fails.
- **Rehearse the slide show.** To ensure your slide show fits the allotted time, do a dry run and record the timing. You can then edit or eliminate slides as needed.
- **Never read from a slide.** Maintain eye contact with the audience and never assume that a slide is self-explanatory.
- **Keep the limitations of presentation software in mind.** Presentation programs can enhance the look of your presentation, but they are not effective for conveying large amounts of complex information. As American statistician Edward R. Tufte has noted, standard PowerPoint templates simplify information to the point that they "usually weaken verbal and spatial reasoning, and almost always corrupt statistical analysis."[7] If you need your audience to think seriously about and analyze complex information, consider using only a few PowerPoint

Suggestions for Successful Networking

- Develop a database of your contacts.
- Become involved in professional activities.
- Call new contacts.
- Make follow-up calls.

FIGURE 13.2 Sample Digital Presentation Slide

slides to show particularly detailed images, supply all audience members with a printed handout that conveys the necessary data, and clearly talk your audience through the handout.[8]

PechaKucha Presentations

Named for the Japanese for "chit-chat," PechaKucha was developed in 2003 for gatherings where designers would showcase their creative work. This format for brief, energetic, and strongly visual presentations limits speakers to 20 automatically progressing image-based slides apiece, each shown for no more than 20 seconds, for a total running time of 6 minutes and 40 seconds. Speakers such as culture critic Lawrence Lessig have adapted techniques from PechaKucha to become more dynamic public speakers and engaging storytellers.

To create effective PechaKucha, decide what you want your audience to remember and select powerful, relevant, and high-resolution images that support this theme and solidify your message. Edit your content carefully.[9]

Methods of Delivery

Whichever method of delivery you choose for your presentation, it should bring out the best in your material and not call attention to itself at the expense of what you have to say. The following methods are the most common ways of delivering a speech to a group:

1. **Script method:** When you have to present extensive or complex data, with no margin for misinterpretation, you may need to prepare a script that you can read from in full. Because it may be difficult to keep an audience with you as you focus on the printed page, make an extra effort to maintain as much visual contact

with the audience as possible, looking up as you begin an important point or sentence. The script itself should be typed in large letters and triple-spaced for easy readability at a glance. Remember that text read aloud can sound boring and expressionless because of flattened inflection, so try to inject some life into your voice by changing your tone appropriately and marking your script to indicate where special expression is required.

2. **Memorization:** While memorizing a speech can enliven the connection with the audience, this method can also backfire if you find yourself struggling to recall what you planned to say. Listeners can easily detect slip-ups and expressions made stale from constant repetition. Consequently, the focus is not on what you have to say but on your inability to remember it. Unless you have a strong talent for memorizing long speeches, you may want to limit yourself to memorizing the general shape of your presentation, its key points, and your opening remarks instead of every word you plan to deliver.

3. **Impromptu speaking:** Certain situations—an informal gathering or a celebration, for example—might call for a short **impromptu speech**, made on the spur of the moment without the aid of prepared notes or the benefit of advance notice. Listeners will not expect new information or specialized knowledge, only the ability to put a new spin on something you already know. A few pleasant, well-chosen remarks, delivered in less than two minutes, are usually all that is required.

4. **Extemporaneous method:** Most oral presentations benefit from a combination of thoughtful preparation and a spontaneous, natural delivery style that engages the audience and holds its interest. Somewhere between ad libbing

> **impromptu speaking**
> A delivery method in which the speaker makes remarks without the aid of prepared notes.

Founded in 1924, Toastmasters International helps people become better communicators and more confident public speakers through its workshop format, in which members make prepared and impromptu presentations. The organization currently has clubs in over 100 countries.

Marmaduke St. John/Alamy Stock Photo

(which leaves too much to chance) and reading aloud word for word (which can lull listeners to sleep) is **extemporaneous speaking**—a form of delivery that sounds fresh and comfortable yet maintains a sense of order from the planning you have done.

Working with memory aids, such as small cue cards, can boost your confidence when speaking in public. They are often just enough to jog your memory, giving you the prompting you need so you can expand on the details. You should be able to fit an outline of your presentation on a single card, along with any quotations or statistics, lettered as large as possible in bold ink and highlighted for quick reference. An additional card can be used for each main section of your presentation, but don't make the mistake of writing out your speech in full. The purpose of cue cards is simply to prompt you to your next main point. If you have had sufficient practice, you may be able to do without the cards altogether. The immediacy your material gains from extemporaneous delivery helps to ensure your message gets across, whether your purpose is to inform or persuade your listeners.

> **extemporaneous speaking** A method of delivery in which the speaker relies on notes rather than script memorization.

Rehearsing a Presentation

Practice sessions can help your delivery go more smoothly by reducing your nervousness, improving your performance, and giving you the opportunity to judge your time and refine your content. Once you have drafted your presentation and prepared your visual aids, you are ready to practise the presentation itself.

- **Practise aloud.** Practise your presentation on-site or set up conditions that closely resemble those in which you will be speaking. Familiarize yourself with using your visual aids, integrating them and noting how long it will take to introduce each item and explain a particular point.
- **Time yourself.** Deliver your speech aloud, staying within the time permitted to you and noting where to pause. Make any adjustments, cutting out or adding material to ensure your presentation is the right length.
- **Master your topic.** Know your material well enough to be able to speak confidently without relying word for word on a script. Overpreparing by writing out your presentation in full and then memorizing it can kill spontaneity. Your delivery will be livelier if you speak from a note card that helps you familiarize yourself with the sequence of the material. Don't count on your ability to wing it or ad lib your way through an entire presentation.
- **Record yourself or ask a friend to listen and give you feedback.** Rehearse in front of a mirror. Video record yourself to detect mannerisms that might be distracting. Aim to develop a well-pitched speaking voice.
- **Get a feel for the room.** Inspect the seating arrangement and, if you plan to use them, make sure the sound system and audiovisual equipment are working properly. Set up or position a screen for optimal viewing.
- **Learn stress-reduction techniques.** Because shallow breathing can make you feel dizzy, breathe deeply several times before you begin. Visualize your success as a speaker. In the days or hours leading up to your presentation, you may find it helpful to try these techniques:

- Practise breathing from your diaphragm (the muscular part of your respiratory system) with a simple exercise. Lie on your back and place your hand on your stomach. With your mouth closed, inhale through your nose and feel your stomach rise; exhale slowly and feel your stomach fall. Try to spend the same length of time exhaling as inhaling, counting to yourself if you have to. Once you are comfortable with the technique, practise while sitting in a chair or standing. You can do this exercise inconspicuously while you are waiting to be called to speak.
- Attune yourself to your body's tension patterns by doing a muscular relaxation exercise. Lying on the floor, clench and unclench each muscle group several times, starting with your right and left fists and progressing to your forearms, shoulders, neck, and so on. Focus on the difference between tension and relaxation.

Delivering a Presentation

When the time comes to deliver your presentation, make every effort to be at your best and project a poised, professional image. If public speaking makes you nervous, put mind over matter and focus on your material and rapport with the audience. Stay in control of the situation rather than allowing it to control you. Being confident and speaking in an animated way, with genuine enthusiasm for your topic, can give your words staying power. Here are a few tips for overcoming nervousness and reaching your audience:

1. **Dress appropriately.** Wear neat, comfortable, professional-looking clothing. Check your clothes for any stains and remove any jewellery that might interfere with a microphone, should you require one.
2. **Arrive early.** Allow time before the presentation to familiarize yourself with your surroundings. Test the acoustics and decide where you can position yourself to be visible to the entire audience.
3. **Maintain good posture and move in a relaxed, controlled, natural way.** If you remain seated during a presentation, sit without slumping in order to improve your voice projection. If you're on your feet, stand up straight and relax your shoulders. You can take a step or two to one side for emphasis at key transitional points; otherwise, stand without swaying from side to side. Avoid unnecessary hand gestures (such as waving, fidgeting, or jamming hands in pockets). The same goes for inappropriate facial expressions (exaggerated grinning or grimacing) or anything that might be distracting.
4. **Pause to collect yourself before beginning.** Adjust your notes, take a breath, maintain your poise, and take control of the situation. Memorize the first minute of your presentation so that you can look at the audience, not at your notes, as you make your opening remarks.
5. **Maintain eye contact and use it to build rapport and gauge audience interest.** The eyes of your audience members will tell you if they are involved and understand you. Listeners staring at the floor and looking around are visual cues that your audience has tuned out. It may take time to get comfortable with your audience, so start by looking for a friendly face and making eye contact for a few seconds before you move on to someone else, occasionally glancing at the whole group.
6. **Avoid long sentences and complicated words.** Use concrete language and short, active-voice sentences that follow natural, conversational speech patterns.

7. **Speak in a clear, audible voice, but don't shout.** Maintain reasonable volume and aim for good, natural voice projection, gauged to the size of the audience and venue. Keep your head up and open your mouth slightly wider than in normal speech to prevent yourself from mumbling. If your voice won't be amplified, ask "Can you hear me at the back of the room?" as you begin.

8. **Pace yourself.** Speak slowly enough to enunciate words clearly and prevent them from running together. Slow down slightly for emphasis and speed up slightly to convey enthusiasm. If you are running out of time, don't speed up; make your content fit into the time you have left by editing your material as you go.

9. **Shape your phrasing, and use inflection to give meaning and add interest.** Your pitch—or tone of voice—should sound natural and match your content. Use a downward inflection at the end of sentences to avoid sounding monotone and to emphasize key points. Never phrase a statement like a question by raising your voice at the end. This habit can make you sound uncertain and nervous. Speak with conviction to project your confidence and credibility.

10. **Never use slang or bad grammar.** Your credibility is on the line—speaking in an unprofessional way is the fastest way to lose it.

11. **Pause briefly to collect your thoughts and create emphasis.** Don't resort to fillers or verbal tics (such as *um*, *like*, and *ah*). Plan your transitions ahead of time so that you can move easily from one topic to the next.

12. **Remember that you are a living, breathing human being, not a statue.** Remain calm and remember to breathe deeply from the diaphragm. Animate your delivery by integrating voice and gestures, leaving one hand free to point to visual aids. Be professional but let your personality shine through.

13. **Bring your presentation to a close.** Thank your audience and make materials available to them. Take questions and make yourself available for follow-up discussion, if necessary.

Handling Questions

Questions from the audience can help you gauge the effect and outcome of your presentation and give you a second chance to get your message across. Audience members may want to obtain additional information, get clarification on a point you made, or express another point of view.

As you begin your presentation, make it clear how you intend to handle questions. When speaking to a large audience, you can usually hold questions to the end and avoid interruptions that can reduce momentum. During informal presentations, you may pause for questions at intervals, allowing you to check that the audience is still following you. Inviting spontaneous questions keeps audience members involved and prevents them from becoming too passive.

In taking questions, stay in control so that the interaction is productive, not just a free-for-all:

1. **Listen carefully to the entire question.** If a question is confusing or hard to hear, ask the questioner to repeat it or paraphrase it yourself for the audience.

2. **Separate strands of complex or two-part questions.** Disentangle parts of a question and deal with them one at a time.

Federal party leaders Jagmeet Singh; Elizabeth May, Maxime Bernier, Justin Trudeau, Andrew Scheer, and Yves-François Blanchet participate in the leaders' English-language debate in advance of the 2019 Canadian national election. In political debates, candidates must practise many of the points discussed in this chapter. They must make prepared statements and more spontaneous rebuttals within allotted time limits, answer questions from the moderator and opponent(s), and impress the audience with their ideas and delivery.

3. **Ensure your answers are long enough but not too long.** Avoid launching into another speech during an end-of-presentation Q&A, but also ensure that your answers are not so short that they sound curt or rude.

4. **Don't feel you have to answer every question.** In some cases, you can say the answer will come later in the presentation or you can throw the question to the audience for feedback and discussion.

5. **Never put down a questioner.** Be courteous, even if a question seems silly. It may be helpful to ask the questioner to explain further.

6. **Be firm with overzealous or long-winded questioners.** Wait for a pause and politely interrupt, asking the questioner to briefly summarize the question.

7. **Stay on topic.** Don't allow yourself to be drawn off topic by an unrelated question or to have words put in your mouth.

8. **Don't start by assuming a question is hostile.** Keep your cool and avoid sarcasm when challenged by an angry questioner. If you overhear nasty asides from the audience, single out the person responsible and ask that person to share his or her comments with the group. If asides turn to heckling, you have several options: finesse your way out of the situation with a humorous reply, give a serious answer, carry on as if you have not heard the remark, appeal for a fair hearing, or ask that the heckler be ejected.

9. **End by thanking the audience for their questions and feedback.** Show that you value the question period as part of the communicative process.

Team-Based Presentations

Working together in a group of two or more can enhance the scope and complexity of a presentation, but when there is a lack of coordination, speakers might end up contradicting or repeating each other or not covering key topics. The presentation can lose its focus and clarity. Such problems can be avoided with proper planning and team effort.

QUICK TIPS

Team-Based Presentations

- Come to an agreement about who will cover which topic areas (conducting research, providing visual materials and handouts, and so on), and decide how the group will be governed (e.g., by majority rule, by consensus, or by shared leadership).

- Establish ground rules for the group, and give priority to presentation development meetings.

- Develop a work plan and set deadlines, working backward from the date of the presentation.

- Know what opinions each person will express to better prepare you to deal with questions and avoid controversy; agree how questions are to be handled.

- Allow time for rehearsals; plan the use of visual aids and how each person can help others use them; coordinate all presentation parts and visuals for consistency; and identify handover cues to indicate when one person will take over from another.

- Appoint a team leader to introduce speakers and help the group maintain its focus.

- Use previews, transitions, and summaries to help the audience understand how parts of the presentation interrelate. Provide a bridge to the next presenter with an introduction such as "Vanessa will now discuss time management."

- Adhere strictly to the allowed time for each speaker, but be flexible enough to accommodate last-minute changes and defer to the expertise of other group members.

Special-Occasion Presentations

From time to time, business people are involved in award ceremonies, commemorations, and other special occasions, and they may be asked to do the following:

- introduce or thank speakers/award recipients
- propose toasts
- give impromptu or after-dinner speeches
- deliver keynote addresses

An effective **special-occasion presentation** is tailored to the specific needs of an event. As a special-occasion speaker, you should be conscious of the impression you

special-occasion presentation A speech made in appreciation, in acceptance of an award, in commemoration of an event, or by way of introduction.

create. In making an introduction, for example, you should show that it is a pleasure and a privilege to perform the introduction. Your remarks should be congenial, gracious, brief, and most of all genuine, based on concrete facts rather than generalities. If public speaking scares you, you can follow a simple script:

> I am pleased to introduce (name of speaker) from (company/organization), who is (position, relevant achievements, and experience).
>
> Please join me in welcoming (name of speaker).

Checklist
Oral Presentations

Strategy

- ❑ Does the opening device spark interest and engage the audience?
- ❑ Does the introduction establish credibility or provide background, as needed?
- ❑ Are ideas and approaches adapted to the audience's needs?
- ❑ Do presentation methods involve the audience?
- ❑ Does the degree of formality suit the situation?
- ❑ Does the conclusion provide a compelling sense of closure?

Content

- ❑ Do facts and information relate to the presentation's purpose?
- ❑ Is the supporting material specific and relevant?
- ❑ Does the presentation fulfill its purpose and provide information the audience finds interesting?
- ❑ Is care taken to clarify ideas that might be misconstrued or prove harmful to the speaker or the speaker's organization?

Organization

- ❑ Is an overview of the main points provided?
- ❑ Do verbal signposts announce transitions to major points? Are these transitions sufficient and logical?

Visuals

- ❑ Are visuals well designed, interesting, and appropriate for the size of the audience and room?
- ❑ Does each visual supply the right amount of information without over-cramming data?
- ❑ Is each visual legible and error-free?
- ❑ Is each visual introduced at an appropriate point in the presentation?
- ❑ Do the visuals add to the presentation and enhance its meaning?

Delivery

- ❑ Is there direct and comfortable eye contact with the audience?
- ❑ Are voice, non-verbal cues, and gestures used effectively? Is the right tone and level of language used in addressing the audience?
- ❑ Are questions fielded effectively?
- ❑ Is the presentation paced according to the audience's level of understanding and interest?
- ❑ Does the speaker communicate interest in, and enthusiasm for, the topic?
- ❑ Does the speaker project confidence and professionalism? Have signs of stage fright been kept under control?

Meetings

Every year, a greater percentage of the average workday is spent in meetings. How you perform in meetings demonstrates your readiness to assume responsibility, solve problems, and work as part of a team. Meetings can be good for your profile, but they can also be good for groups as a whole by bringing leaders to the forefront, providing networking opportunities, and strengthening staff and client relations.

A meeting should be time well spent—a productive exercise that yields results and may even be enjoyable. It must be purposeful and properly managed, and it needs to draw on the strengths and input of its participants. Meetings can have one purpose or several of the following in combination:

- to give, share, or pool information
- to brainstorm, develop, or evaluate ideas and policies
- to find the root causes behind problems, solve problems, and solicit feedback
- to make decisions (through consensus or voting) or help others make them (through consultation)
- to delegate work or authority
- to develop projects or create documents collaboratively
- to motivate members and encourage teamwork

Types of Meetings

Meetings come in all shapes and sizes. They can be conducted face to face or through video- or teleconferencing. They can be **internal**, involving only company personnel, or **external**, including outsiders. Meetings can differ substantially by type (according to purposes such as briefing, planning, project and case management, decision-making, and socializing) in the way they are run. **Formal meetings** operate by strict rules, under the guidance of a leader. Items up for discussion are pre-set by an agenda. Any motion must be introduced formally before it can be debated and voted on. Formal minutes provide a record of each motion, vote, and action taken. **Informal meetings** are run more loosely, making them good forums for problem-solving, brainstorming, and team building. It may not even be necessary to hold a vote if there is general agreement or consensus in an informal meeting.

internal meeting A meeting that involves only personnel from within an organization.

external meeting A meeting that involves outsiders in addition to company personnel.

formal meeting A scheduled meeting that operates according to a pre-set agenda under guided leadership for the purposes of achieving specific goals.

informal meeting A small, sometimes unscheduled meeting that may operate without strict rules.

Preparing for a Meeting

Poor planning and mismanagement can turn meetings into colossal time-wasters. Behind-the-scenes planning helps you to make the best possible use of your time. Consider the following elements before you call a meeting:

1. **Purpose:** Define the purpose of the meeting and distribute an agenda or supporting materials at least two days in advance (see point 6).
2. **Alternatives:** Could your meeting have been an e-mail or phone call? Unnecessary meetings result in lost productivity. Consider if a meeting is truly necessary or if the same work can be accomplished without one.
3. **Participants:** Limit participation to people who are most essential—those who will make the decision, implement it, or provide information crucial to decision-making. If a few key participants are unable to attend, contact them in advance for their views and contributions. Keep in mind that problem-solving is done most effectively in groups of 5 to 15. Large groups of 25 or more are too big for anything more than the presentation of information.
4. **Location:** Meetings are not simply convened; they are staged and strategized. Deciding where to hold a meeting—in your office, in a board room, or off-site—depends on the kind of environment you prefer, how well participants get along, how much space you need, and whether you need to be seen as being in control. Whatever location you settle on, the table and seating arrangement should enhance the flow of information and ideas (see Figure 13.3).
5. **Scheduling:** Establish when the meeting will begin and end by using booking software or a Doodle poll. Ideally, the time should be convenient to key decision-makers or fit in with personal working styles. Unless there is an urgent matter to be dealt

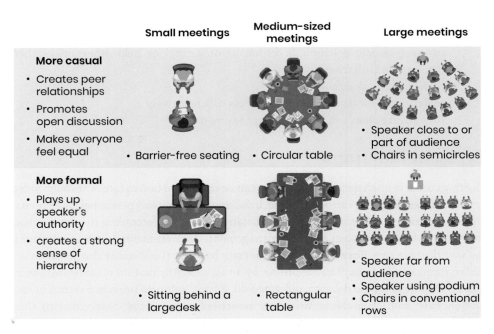

FIGURE 13.3 Seating arrangements can set the tone of the meeting

AGENDA

Jack Pine Resort and Conference Centre

Staff Meeting, February 12, 2021

9:00 a.m. to 10:30 a.m.

Conference Room 4A

		Presenter	Allotted Time
I.	Call to order; attendance		
II.	Approval of agenda		
III.	Approval of minutes from previous meeting		
IV.	Committee reports		
	A. Corporate golf retreat package	Jorge Suarez	15 minutes
	B. Wireless upgrades	Brenda Holz	10 minutes
	C. Parking lot expansion	Mia Bergman	5 minutes
V.	Old Business		
	A. Facility maintenance	Rick Ellers	5 minutes
	B. Safety review	Lu Gan	5 minutes
	C. Overdue accounts	Jamal Smith	5 minutes
VI.	New Business		
	A. Marketing strategy	Ahmed Riyad	15 minutes
	B. New accounts	Jamal Smith	5 minutes
VII.	Announcements		
VIII.	Chair's summary; adjournment		

FIGURE 13.4   Sample Meeting Agenda

with, informal meetings should be set for less busy or less stressful times. Meetings of more than two hours should include a short break (five to ten minutes).

6. **Agenda:** An **agenda** is a tool for focusing the group—a written document distributed in advance that sets the order of business for a meeting, briefly describing items to be covered, identifying who is responsible for them, and allocating a time period for each agenda item (Figure 13.4). An agenda also gives participants the particulars: when the meeting will take place (date, start time, end time), where it will be held, and what preparation they should do beforehand. A copy of the minutes of a previous meeting is sometimes also included when a group meets regularly or when a meeting is a continuation of an earlier one.

> **agenda** A document that establishes the purpose and goals of a meeting and outlines what the meeting will address, thereby helping to focus the group.

Conducting a Meeting

Leading or facilitating a meeting successfully is one of the most important tests a manager faces. While there is no blueprint for the perfect meeting and no guarantee that a few eyes won't glaze over, following certain steps can help you to achieve better meetings that let you build consensus and accomplish what you set out to do and more.

Leading a Meeting

- Distribute a detailed agenda in advance.
- Assign responsibilities: appoint a minute-taker to document the proceedings in a concise yet thorough way, and ask someone else to write on a flip chart or computer to record information that needs to be viewed by everyone.
- Establish ground rules (e.g., turn off your cellphone) and stick to them. Start and adjourn on time. If time runs out for a specific item, decide on it or leave it for a later discussion.
- Focus the group by keeping to the agenda. Identify action items and avoid getting sidetracked by peripheral issues or ramblers—summarize what they have said, politely direct them back to the agenda, and move on.
- Speak up, make eye contact with others around the table, and stay relaxed. Your behaviour sets the tone for the meeting. Analyze non-verbal cues to determine if meeting participants have second thoughts or reservations about the decisions being made.
- Keep hostile participants in check by encouraging a healthy respect for the facts and establishing zero tolerance for name-calling, sulking, and personal attacks. Try to remain neutral in disputes, but make sure that the loudest members of the group don't dominate the discussion.
- Encourage full participation. Ask group members for their input and listen carefully. Allow room for opposing viewpoints and consider different ways of doing things. Acknowledge and respond to what people say.
- Discourage anyone who interrupts.
- Deal with conflict but realize that a degree of conflict is inevitable and even valuable. It can stimulate creative thinking and challenge passive **groupthink**.
- End with a summary in which you paraphrase all decisions and assignments and look ahead to future actions. Raise questions, ask for feedback, and clarify any misunderstandings. Tell participants when they can expect to receive copies of the minutes, and set a time for the next meeting.
- Follow up on action items at the next meeting.

groupthink The practice of thinking or making decisions as a group, whereby conformity is rewarded and dissent punished; the result of groupthink is often poor decision-making.

Participating in a Meeting

- Make eye contact with influential people and sit toward the head of the table if you expect to have something important to say. Link your comments to the remarks of a leader or to something that has just been said.
- Be an active listener, and demonstrate that you have heard and processed what has been said and left unsaid (see Figure 13.5).
- Interact and contribute when you have something to say.
- Don't dominate the discussion or get involved in arguments. Don't be defensive, disruptive, or overly territorial.
- Speak clearly and directly. Do your homework, and be prepared to support your point of view.

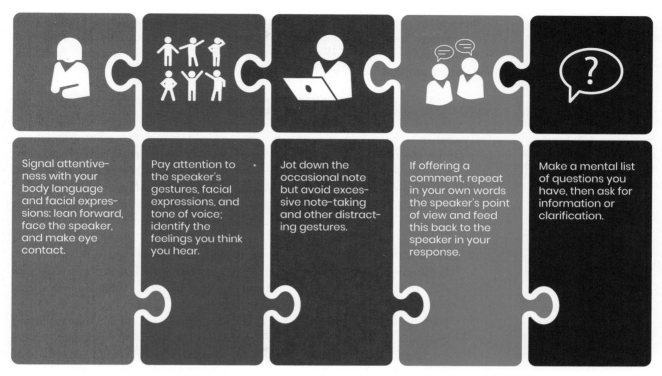

FIGURE 13.5 **Active Listening Skills**

Meeting Minutes

Formal meetings adhere to a system known as Robert's Rules of Order (from a book of the same name). For meetings conducted in this way, a proper process for transcribing **meeting minutes** has to be followed. Formal minutes record the following information:

- name of the group or committee holding the meeting
- date, time, and place of the meeting
- topic/title/kind of meeting (a regular meeting or a special meeting called to discuss a particular problem or subject)
- names/number of people present (for groups of ten or fewer, list names of attendees and absentees)
- statement that the chair was present (include time at which the meeting was called to order)
- statement that the minutes of the previous meeting were approved (if applicable)
- description of old business (if applicable)
- summary of new business and announcements
- record of reports (read and approved), discussions, resolutions (adopted or rejected), motions (made, carried, or defeated), votes (taken or postponed), and key decisions
- list of assignments and due dates
- time the meeting was adjourned
- date, time, and location of the next meeting (if applicable)
- name and signature of the secretary (the person recording the minutes)

> **meeting minutes** A written record of what occurred at a meeting, who attended it, and when and where it was convened.

Templates and software programs are available to assist you in compiling minutes.

In informal meetings, minutes may be taken and later be distributed by e-mail or as hard copy. Informal meeting minutes briefly summarize discussions, report decisions, and outline proposed actions.

Groupware-Supported Meetings

groupware Software designed to facilitate group work by a number of different users.

Collaborative software known as **groupware** can facilitate meetings when group members cannot meet in person. Web-based meetings and online virtual conferences eliminate the inconvenience associated with holding long-distance meetings and can help groups collaborate, exchange information, and reach decisions. Many companies use the following technologies to conduct training programs or team-building seminars or to put colleagues in touch for planning or product and policy development.

virtual meeting A meeting that uses particular software or a website to allow participants in various locations to share ideas and hold discussions in real time.

web-conferencing Synchronous web-supported communication allowing for the real-time transmission of sound and images to various locations.

- **Virtual meetings** allow participants to meet online if they are working at home, in different office branches, or off-site for business travel. As a result, they save time and travel costs. Each participant or group is typically equipped with a computer-based camera, microphone, video screen, and speaker.
- **Web-conferencing** enables images and sounds to be sent in real time to various locations. Although there is some overlap between web-conferencing and virtual meetings, a web conference typically involves one content creator (an individual or a group) sending a video or a computer-generated presentation to audience members in different locations. Some web-conferencing technologies also enable participants to exchange text, audio, and/or video messages in real time. New wireless HD presentation technologies are now making it possible to present, collaborate, and share content directly from mobile devices, with content viewable through room displays and participants' mobile devices.
- **E-mail meetings** allow participants to respond at different times and make the meeting process more democratic by doing away with facilitators. However, e-mail meetings can suffer from the same problems as e-mail in general: there is no guarantee that messages will be read or that they will have enough detail to be useful.

To get the most out of a meeting facilitated by some form of groupware, keep in mind the strategies listed in the following box.

QUICK TIPS

Groupware

- Familiarize yourself with the technology you will be using to participate in the meeting or conference. Download and test any required software or plug-ins.
- Schedule time to participate. Even though you will not have to leave your office or other location, you should set aside a block of time, just as you would for a face-to-face meeting.
- If you plan to take part in a long-distance synchronous (real-time) meeting, be sure to account for any differences in time zones.

Communicating by Telephone

Conducting business via text, telephone, or in-person conversation or performing customer service in responding to customer questions and complaints are interactions that require cooperation—or what Paul Grice called "conversational implicature" or the inferences we draw in conversation. Grice's maxims, or guiding principles for conversations, are those of 1. quantity (being informative), 2. quality (being truthful), 3. relation (being relevant), and 4. manner (being brief and avoiding ambiguity).

Making Calls

Make sure every call you make is necessary and offers the best way to get your message across when compared with other channels.

- **Identify yourself.** When placing a call to someone who does not know you, give your name and identify the organization you represent.
- **Give each call your full attention.** Handle interruptions politely by asking permission to put someone on hold.
- **Plan what you will say.** Notes the topics you intend to cover, information you need to obtain, and objections you may encounter. Anticipate what you will say if you reach someone's voicemail.
- **Be positive, courteous, and accurate.** To get ready for the call, visualize the person to whom you will be speaking. Your voice should sound animated, not flat or canned.
- **Leave clear messages.** When someone is unavailable to take your call, leave your name (including the correct spelling, if necessary), business title, company name, phone number, and a brief message (including the best time to reach you). Include an extension number to spare the caller the inconvenience of consulting your company's phone directory.
- **Mind your telephone manners.** Never eat or chew gum while talking on the phone.
- **Place calls when others are likely to receive them.** Establish a specific call-back time when returning a call. Return calls promptly or redirect them elsewhere as needed.
- **Learn to end a conversation.** As the caller, it is your responsibility to close the conversation. End your call professionally by using a closing phrase (*I'm glad we resolved this concern*) and stating the action you will take.

Receiving Calls

- **Answer promptly.** Make an effort to answer your phone within two or three rings, before the caller is tempted to hang up.
- **Identify yourself clearly.** When answering a call, identify yourself with your full name and department affiliation (*This is Accounts Receivable. Paul Kwon speaking.*). You may also begin your greeting with *good morning* or *good afternoon*—just be sure about what time of day it is.
- **Avoid taking calls during meetings.** Each activity deserves your full attention.

- **Use proper telephone language.** Opt for language that is positive and appropriate.

Don't say	Do say
Hang on a second, okay?	May I put you on hold?
Who are you anyway?	May I ask who is calling, please?
What? WHAT? I am having difficulty hearing you.	Can you please repeat that?

- **Be professional in explaining why you have answered a call intended for a colleague.** Don't give out information that might embarrass a co-worker (e.g., *He's gone to the washroom* or *His mouth is full*). Instead, give a brief, non-specific excuse (e.g., *She's away from her desk at the moment* or *She is unavailable to take your call at the moment*) and indicate when the person will be available to take the call.
- **Excuse yourself when you have to step away from the phone.** If you need leave your desk to obtain information the caller has requested, politely let the caller know what you are doing and that you will soon return. Make sure to put the call on hold—don't simply leave it sitting on your desk.
- **Don't leave callers on hold indefinitely.** Don't leave the caller on hold for more than 30 or 45 seconds. If it is taking longer to find the information you need, give the caller the option of continuing to hold, transfer the person to another party, or offer to call back at a specific time.
- **Apply active listening skills.** Pay close attention to what the caller says and to what the caller's tone of voice reveals.
- **Learn to use your organization's phone system.** Lost or misdirected calls can result in frustration and lost business. Ask for permission when you transfer a call, and give the name, department, and extension number of the person the call is being transferred to in case the call is lost.
- **Take accurate phone messages and deliver them promptly.** A good phone message includes (1) the name of the person for whom the message was left, (2) the caller's name, department, and company, (3) the date and time, (4) the message, and (5) instructions (*please call*, URGENT, or *will call back*).

Using Voicemail Productively

Voicemail is both a convenience and an annoyance. Help callers use this tool effectively to reduce the incidence of telephone tag:

- **Prepare an appropriate greeting as your outgoing message.** Be friendly, informative, and professional (*Hi, this is June Yang of True Blue Marketing. I'm in the office today but away from my desk. Please leave your name, number, and a brief message, and I'll return your call shortly*).
- **Make sure your greeting is up to date.** Re-record your greeting to reflect changing circumstances (e.g., you're on holidays or out of the office for an extended period). If appropriate, leave a colleague's name and number for callers to use in emergencies.
- **Test your message.**

Dealing with the Media

Dealing with the media can be tricky at the best of times. When you speak with reporters or journalists, your image and that of your company are on the line. Many companies hire public-relations officers specifically for the purpose of maintaining a positive public image. It is up to you to guide the reporter to your story and take responsibility for what comes across in an interview. Under your guidance, a media interview can be an opportunity to build goodwill and deliver specific messages to specific audiences through the filter of a journalist. Here are ten rules for getting the best out of an interview:

1. **Prepare by anticipating the questions you might be asked, especially the tough ones.** Be aware of recent events that might affect what you have to say. Decide how candid you will be—which facts are for public consumption and which facts are not.

2. **Know your story, practise telling it, and stick to it.** A good story, crystallized into no more than three key points or a few hard-hitting sentences, does wonders for a message-driven interview. Try to relate the reporter's questions to one or more of your key points.

3. **Remember that tone defines the impression you make.** Stay calm and be positive and helpful, never overreacting to a reporter's attitude. Reporters find negative or defensive language very quotable.

4. **Assess what information will be valuable to the reporter.** Don't release facts or figures that should not be made public. Begin with a brief position statement that sets the tone for the interview. If you don't know the answer to a question, say so and offer to follow up later; if you cannot respond, explain why (*The matter is under consideration* or *It's in litigation*).

5. **Don't get too technical.** Avoid buzzwords and acronyms. Use language that the reporter and the audience will understand.

6. **Speak in sound bites.** Limit your answers to between five and twenty words. Because what you say may be edited, don't flood your answers with too many details. Short answers may help you get your message out more effectively.

7. **Tell the truth.** Remember that nothing is off the record. In cross-examining you, a reporter may be trying to find holes in your argument. Answer or refocus the reporter's question, but don't let him or her put words in your mouth. Correct, as non-threateningly as possible, any misstatements made by the reporter.

8. **Be alert and on guard.** Avoid speculating, making off-hand comments, or saying anything you don't want attributed to you. You have to be able to stand behind what you say.

9. **Make transitions to your key points as you respond.** Keep the interview on track and move back to what is most important, especially if you are interrupted. The following phrases can help you take the initiative:

   While _____ is important, don't forget _____.
   Another thing to remember is _____.
   Let me put that in perspective.
   What I'm really here to talk to you about is _____.

10. **Look your best but be yourself.** Be engaged in the interview and show your enthusiasm, using examples to enrich your story. Let the reporter ask questions; don't try to give all your information immediately.

QUICK TIPS

Television Interviews

- Look at the camera only when instructed to do so. At all other times, look at the interviewer and maintain eye contact to show your interest. Poor eye contact can denote guilt, boredom, or fear.

- Be camera-ready. Dress conservatively yet comfortably, avoiding all black, all white, and small prints (they can create a strobe effect). Remove glittery, over-sized jewellery and empty your pockets. Gesture naturally and avoid fidgeting. Check your appearance before you go on air.

- Speak clearly and distinctly, pausing strategically to avoid fillers such as *ah* and *um*. Remain seated (even after the interview is over) and lean slightly forward in your chair to project energy and interest.

Checklist

Chapter Review

- ❑ Before writing your presentation, have you assessed its context and audience?

- ❑ Does your presentation follow a three-part structure? Have you created an outline to help you organize your ideas?

- ❑ Are your visual aids the best types for your presentation? Do they enhance the presentation's content without dominating your message or distracting your audience?

- ❑ Have you rehearsed your presentation so that you can deliver it confidently and within the allotted time?

- ❑ Do you project a professional, knowledgeable image when making a presentation?

- ❑ Have you given yourself time to familiarize yourself with the environment and to ensure that any required audiovisual equipment is working? Do you have backup copies of your presentation in case there are any technical difficulties?

- ❑ Have you answered audience questions completely while maintaining a calm and controlled manner?

- ❑ Is everyone in your team presentation clear on the ground rules, work plan, related deadlines, and each member's responsibilities?

- ❑ Before calling a meeting, are you sure that one is necessary? If so, have you identified its purpose, required attendees, location, time, and agenda?

- ❑ As a meeting leader, do you circulate an agenda in a timely fashion and stick to it while encouraging full participation and dealing with conflict?

- ❑ Are you an active listener in meetings? Do you contribute your ideas without dominating the discussion or arguing?

- ❑ Do you follow accepted telephone etiquette when making and receiving business calls? Is your voicemail message clear and professional?

- ❑ Have you adequately prepared for a media interview? Have you kept to your message and remained poised and positive?

Exercises, Workshops, and Discussion Forums

1. **Apply Oral Communication Skills in Your Career.** How will you use oral communication skills in your future employment? Interview a professional in your field and share your findings with your classmates. Uphold ethical standards in conducting your interview by asking permission to quote the interviewee.

2. **Analyze Your Audience.** Imagine that you must deliver a briefing to the management and staff of a small company. Reread the criteria in "Analyzing the Situation and Audience" on pages 479–480, then discuss with a partner how you can meet the needs of this diverse group. Assume that your partner has to deliver a similar briefing to the same group.

3. **Face Your Public-Speaking Fears.** In a group of five or six, discuss your fears about speaking in public, then share strategies you have discovered to reduce situational stress.

4. **Overcome Your Public-Speaking Fears.** Prepare a set of cards representing various stages in the presentation sequence (e.g., practising your speech, being introduced, giving your speech). Look at each card and imagine that you are participating in that stage of a presentation. Determine which activity causes the most stress, then try to combat that anxiety and calm yourself with breathing or muscle-relaxation exercises. Repeat the process until you no longer experience stress when you contemplate any aspect of giving a speech.

5. **Change How You Think of Yourself as a Public Speaker.** On the left side of a piece of paper, write down any negative thoughts you have about how you speak. On the right side, write down positive thoughts that counter them. Here is an example:

Negative	Positive
The audience will be able to tell that I don't have public-speaking experience.	Good preparation will compensate for the fact that I don't have public-speaking experience.

Make positive thoughts your public-speaking mantra. If you have any negative thoughts as you prepare, say "stop" to yourself and substitute a positive alternative.

6. **Hold a Team Meeting.** In groups of five or six, hold a meeting to work out the design of a logo that represents the values and strengths of your individual team. Designate a scribe to keep minutes and a chair to lead the discussion as you consider these topics:

- what the team stands for
- how it wishes to be seen
- how the logo can help others see the team in a different way

The design can include a combination of symbols, colours, and shapes, as long as there is a clear reason for incorporating each element. Submit prepared minutes of the meeting to your instructor.

Variation: Propose a slogan or radio advertisement that represents the values of the team.

7. **Hold a Team Meeting.** In a group of three or more, work together to suggest a new law and the reasons for needing it. Appoint a group leader whose job it will be to ensure that each member contributes to the discussion, then write the law in unequivocal language.

8. **Hold a Team Meeting.** In a group of three or more, identify a problem in your community or at your school. By sharing ideas and experience, discuss how this situation could be improved and devise a plan for implementing constructive change.

9. **Hold a Team Meeting.** In a group of five or more, experiment with different types of seating arrangements for meetings. Start by setting up rows of seats, with the audience positioned to face a speaker standing at the front of the room. Use this arrangement for information sharing, problem-solving, and decision-making (a list of possible topics for each session is included below). Next try a U-shaped arrangement, with participants facing each other and the group leader seated at the top (open) end of the U. Repeat the processes of information sharing, problem-solving, and decision-making. Afterward, reorganize the seating for a round-table discussion, and again repeat the processes of information sharing, problem-solving,

and decision-making. What are the advantages and disadvantages of each arrangement?

- Share information about effective listening skills or telephone etiquette.
- Solve a problem that affects campus life or your community.
- Agree on a new parking policy for your campus or a revamping of the menu selection for your school cafeteria.

10. **Evaluate a Meeting.** Alone or with a partner, attend a meeting on your campus, in your community, or at your workplace. Using the following checklist, assess how well the meeting was conducted.

- Is the meeting held in the right place, at the right time, with the right people?

- Does the meeting have and fulfill a specific purpose? Does the agenda reflect this?
- Are ground rules for the meeting properly enforced?
- Are participants encouraged to voice their opinions and ideas? Is the leader fair and does he or she help the group stay focused?
- Do participants know how to prepare for the meeting and how to follow up? Do they know what comes next?
- Is conflict dealt with in a fair and equitable way?
- If the answer to any of these questions is no, write a brief review analyzing how the meeting could have been improved.

11. **Evaluate the Handling of Questions.** Watch a news-related interview or press conference and assess the performance of an interviewee. How effectively does this individual handle tough questions?

Oral Communication and Presentation Improvement Exercises

1. **Introduce Yourself to Your Class.** Give your name and some basic information. If you find this activity intimidating, you may want to follow a simple script:

> Hello, my name is _____ _____.
> I have enrolled in (**name of course**) because
> _____ _____, with the ultimate goal
> of _____ _____.

2. **Introduce a Classmate.** Pair with a partner and conduct a quick interview to learn as much as you can about the other person. Focus on finding out about your partner's classes, school-related activities, work and volunteer experience, hobbies, and notable accomplishments. When you've finished, perform a brief, professional introduction in front of your class.

3. **Give an Impromptu Talk.** Give a brief talk (three to five minutes) on one of the following topics, selected at random or selected for you by your classmates:

   a) The best part of my current/future job/field/industry is . . .
   b) The best way to find a job is . . .

   c) The successful person I most admire is . . .

4. **Prepare a Briefing.** Select a fairly substantial article (750 words or more) from the business or national news section of a daily newspaper. Prepare a brief oral presentation based on the article. If you require additional information, do a keyword Internet search. Following your presentation, submit your outline (including an introduction, main body, and conclusion) to your instructor.

5. **Design a Concise Visual Aid.** Write a series of bullet points (no more than six words per line) suitable for use on a PowerPoint slide that summarizes the following information. Remember to add a suitable title.

> We have four specific corporate goals in the year ahead. The first is to introduce new product lines, including cardio equipment and weight-lifting equipment. Our second goal is to see our company become a worldwide leader. However, if we are to achieve this goal, our company must expand geographically. Plans are now underway to

establish operations in South America and Europe. Finally, we would like to continue 20 per cent and higher sales growth.

6. **Compose a PowerPoint Slide.** Write a short bullet point suitable for use on a PowerPoint slide entitled "What Not to Wear on TV." The point should summarize the important information from the following part of your speech:

   Unless you want to create odd optical effects, you should make an effort to avoid plaid, stripes, herringbone, checkerboard, and white. These patterns and colours tend to photograph poorly.

7. **Prepare a Short PowerPoint Presentation.** Select one of PowerPoint's features or functions, and prepare a short PowerPoint presentation to teach the rest of the class about it. Afterward, submit your PowerPoint notes to your instructor.

8. **Prepare a PechaKucha Presentation.** Develop a PechaKucha presentation on a topic that is relevant and meaningful to you. Follow the guidelines set out in this chapter and in Jason B. Jones's article "Challenging the Presentation Paradigm (in 6 Minutes, 40 Seconds): Pecha Kucha" (www.chronicle.com/blogs/profhacker/challenging-the-presentation-paradigm-in-6-minutes-40-seconds-pecha-kucha/22807).

9. **Prepare a Short, Informative Presentation.** Design a five- or ten-minute informative presentation that incorporates at least one visual aid and explains how to do one of the following:

   - deal with conflict at your school or workplace
   - prepare for an interview
   - devise a budget for your school expenses
   - balance the demands of work and school

10. **Prepare a Persuasive Presentation.** Prepare a five- or ten-minute presentation in which you persuade your audience to buy a consumer product you enjoy using or in which you advocate a particular action your audience can take. Focus on building credibility and capturing attention to help you make your case, and incorporate visual aids that will help you show what you mean.

11. **Analyzing Purpose and Audience for Presentations.** As the president of the student environmental action association at your college, you are scheduled to speak at a series of events. For each of the following, identify your purpose, analyze your audience and relationship to it, your approach and tone, and how you would present content (with or without the benefit of visual aids).

   a) an assembly for incoming Year 1 students introducing them to your student group, among others
   b) a half-day outdoor rally bringing together environmental activists from your community
   c) a national conference on climate change where you are delivering a keynote presentation.

12. **Evaluate Oral Presentations.** As you listen to your classmates deliver one of the presentations outlined above, use the relevant criteria given in the chapter review checklist on page 504 to evaluate their performances.

13. **Polish Your Delivery.** Select a one-page article from a trade journal, business publication, or newspaper and practise reading it aloud, polishing your delivery so it is smooth, well pitched, and free of pauses and fillers. If you like, record your recitation and play it back.

14. **Make a Group Oral Presentation.** Working with three or four classmates, plan and coordinate a group presentation on one of the topics listed below. In advance of your presentation, submit a plan to your instructor that shows how you intend to allocate and share responsibilities.

   - time-management techniques
   - the advantages and drawbacks of teleconferencing
   - the advantages and drawbacks of wireless technology
   - a survey of job sites that offer the best employment opportunities in your field
   - PowerPoint's ability to improve and undermine the quality of presentations
   - foreign ownership of Canadian companies
   - companies' commitment to sustainability or corporate social responsibility

- the role of social media in projecting charitable organizations' credibility

15. **Introduce a Speaker.** Imagine that you have been given the responsibility of introducing a celebrity or business/community leader who has accepted an invitation to speak at your school or organization. Prepare and deliver your remarks. Make sure to introduce yourself, the guest speaker, and the title of the speaker's speech. Include any necessary background information.

16. **Practise Your Special-Presentation Style.** Assume that you have been elected to give a short, impromptu speech at an event honouring a friend or classmate who has reached an important milestone or is receiving an award for service to the community. Explain why you admire the recipient and why the milestone or award is special.

17. **Practise Telephone Communication.** With a partner, take turns placing and receiving telephone calls that correspond to one or more of the following scenarios:

a) **Answering for someone else.** Jenny Chow, owner of Fair Trade Coffees of the World, is calling her accountant, Joseph Li, about a reassessment of her most recent tax return. The call is answered by Amanda Sharp, Mr. Li's receptionist. Mr. Li has gone to the spa for the afternoon and has left instructions that his clients are not to be told of his whereabouts. Ms. Chow is an important client and her call must be handled as tactfully as possible.

b) **Putting a caller on hold.** Brenda Rudnicki, manager and coordinator of Child's Garden Daycare, must place an emergency call to Spectrum Junior, a maker of non-toxic, washable paints, to find out how to safely remove large quantities of hardened paint from a child's hair. She has followed the instructions on the packaging exactly, but much of the paint still remains. The call is answered by customer-relations specialist Marie-Claire Lacasse. Because the colour in question, Dragon Purple, has gone on the market only recently, she must ask Ms. Rudnicki to hold while she confirms the removal procedure.

18. **Record an Outgoing Voicemail Message.** Using the appropriate audio device, record a friendly and professional voicemail greeting that would be appropriate in the field or setting in which you plan to work. Play back the message and re-record it until you are satisfied with its tone and completeness.

Online Activities

1. **Assess Your Presentation Skills.** Take this quiz from MindTools to assess your skill as a presenter.

   www.mindtools.com/pages/article/newCS_96.htm

2. **Analyze an Apple Keynote Presentation.** Watch the following presentation, prepared with Keynote, and discuss how it adheres to the guidelines discussed in this chapter.

   www.youtube.com/watch?v=SUOTJRLkrss

3. **Assess Your Listening Skills.** Take this quiz from MindTools to assess your listening skills.

   www.mindtools.com/pages/article/listening-quiz.htm

4. **Assessing the Natural and Expressive Qualities of Your Speech With AI.** The IBM Virtual Voice Creator using Watson technology was developed to enable users to create unique voice personas and voice-overs for animated video. Using this synthesis technology, users can experiment with the expressive qualities of human speech, including speech rate, voice tract, glottal tension, and tone. Scroll to the middle of the page to "How the IBM Voice Creator Works" and assess the various voice qualities that can be produced, then analyze the own qualities of your voice and which ones you might enhance or alter when making a presentation.

   www.research.ibm.com/haifa/dept/imt/ivvc.shtml

5. **Spot the Fake Smile Quiz from BBC Science.** This 10-minute, 20-question quiz based on research by a University of California psychology professor invites you to spot fake (not Duchenne) smiles. TIP: Are the subject's eyes smiling?

   http://bbc.co.uk/science/humanbody/mind/surveys/smiles/

14 Social Media and Mobile Communications

Chapter Preview

This chapter explores the tools, strategies, and resources for communicating successfully for business through social media channels and through the multimodal channels for wireless communication. Following a brief history of the web and social networking, you'll be introduced to techniques for navigating social spaces, including strategies for effective blogging and micro-blogging. You'll also be introduced to strategies for writing and designing mobile messages in a variety of forms.

Learning Objectives

1. Identify key social media tools, including blogs, micro-blogs, podcasts, social networks, and video- and photo-sharing sites, and consider how to use them effectively.

2. Communicate for business using blogs and social networking platforms, and apply best practices and social media etiquette for business purposes.

3. Identify strategies for user-generated content campaigns.

4. Identify benefits, risks, and challenges associated with social media use in business environments.

5. Identify elements of a social media plan and campaign.

6. Identify privacy issues related to social media use and management.

7. Identify tools for social media measurement.

8. Describe and analyze distinctive features of mobile communications and how mobile information and communications technologies are changing business.

9. Apply best practices for designing and writing messages and optimizing content for mobile devices.

10. Create promotional messages for mobile devices.

Case Study

Pepsi's 2017 "Live for Now" advertisement, featuring Kendall Jenner defusing a protest by handing a police officer a Pepsi, was pulled one day after its distribution. The commercial was severely criticized on social media for "woke-washing," or appropriating imagery of grassroots social movements as a corporate sales tactic.

Every June, consumers have come to expect major corporations to celebrate Pride month by flying rainbow flags from their headquarters, launching new ads featuring LGBTQ+ individuals and families and wishing their customers a happy Pride Month across their corporate social media accounts. This kind of values-based marketing is increasingly popular, particularly for companies with a large social media presence. However, can customers trust that a company's social media presence accurately and authentically reflects their business practices? In June 2019, a joint report by Popular Information and Progressive Shopper found that nine of the most publicly LGBTQ+ supportive corporations in America—including AT&T, UPS, Comcast, Home Depot, and General Electric—had collectively donated almost $15 million to anti-LGBTQ+ politicians.[1]

This practice, where a corporation adopts a progressive stance on social media that is not reflected in their business practices, has been termed "woke-washing," and, when exposed, it seriously degrades faith in a company and its marketing message. You can probably call to mind several examples of corporations that faced heavy criticism on social media for a tone-deaf ad campaign, such as Pepsi's infamous Kendall Jenner advertisement, which appropriated the imagery of the Black Lives Matter movement, or Audi's 2017 Super Bowl ad proclaiming the brand's support for equal pay, which drew attention to the fact that it had only two women on its 14-person executive board.[2] In 2019, Nike was forced to change its maternity leave policy after it released an advertisement addressing the barriers that women face in sport that prompted several former Nike-sponsored runners to call out the company for cutting off sponsorship deals for athletes who became pregnant, forcing some runners to compete while pregnant or resume training almost immediately after giving birth to minimize financial penalties.[3]

How can companies show support for issues that matter to their customers without provoking a social media backlash? As these examples show, social media use by business carries risks as well as opportunities and organizations must be especially mindful of the power of social media as an impression-management tool. Organizations use social media to increase brand awareness and word-of-mouth, boost customer engagement and connect with new audiences, humanize their brand, generate leads and drive traffic to websites, target ads and make sales, engage in social listening to gauge sentiment (what customers think about the brand) and gain intelligence about competitors, handle complaints, respond to crisis, and manage reputation.

Embracing Social Media

A 2017 survey found that Canadians are heavy users of social media.[4] This finding shouldn't be surprising, given that Canada ranks second in Internet penetration among its G8 counterparts.[5] Facebook has continued to have the highest usage among Canadians of any social media platform, with 84 per cent of Canadians having a Facebook profile.[6] In comparison, 46 per cent of Canadians have a profile on LinkedIn, 42 per cent have a profile on Twitter, and 37 per cent have an Instagram account.[7] For Canadian millennials, Facebook, YouTube, Instagram, Snapchat, Reddit, and Twitter rank highest in usage.[8] However, Twitter usage is falling among that age category: only 29 per cent of millennials used Twitter on a weekly basis in 2019, compared to 41 per cent in 2017.[9] In terms of using social media to interact with businesses, Facebook is again the most popular social media site: 59 per cent of Canadians have liked or followed a company on Facebook, while 27 per cent have done so on Instagram, 17 per cent on Twitter, 16 per cent on YouTube, and only 9 per cent on LinkedIn.[10] The social media video app TikTok is currently experiencing a surge in popularity in Canada and elsewhere, with over 1 billion reported downloads worldwide as of February 2019.[11]

Navigating the social media landscape successfully brings a multitude of benefits for businesses and consumers. Social media benefits businesses by

- enabling the broad, rapid spread of marketing materials and product information
- promoting open participation, a sense of community, and dialogue with consumers
- promoting communication with stakeholder groups
- providing a forum for shaping consumer opinions and attitudes
- providing a purchasing venue
- offering a means to evaluate the post-purchase experience through feedback systems[12]

For consumers, social media provides convenient access to

- product information
- product comparisons and reviews
- forums for asking product-related questions
- online shopping
- consumer support

However, embracing social media also presents many risks and challenges. For example, it is next to impossible for individuals or organizations to control conversations about themselves or to manage content in traditional ways. The major risk social media brings is loss of reputation, which can have a negative effect on competitiveness, the loyalty of customers and stakeholders, positioning, media relations, and the legitimacy of operations.[13]

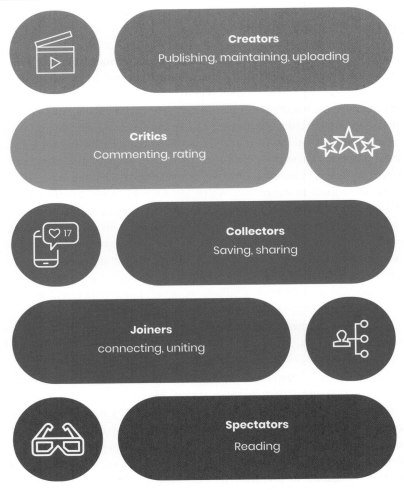

Creators
Publishing, maintaining, uploading

Critics
Commenting, rating

Collectors
Saving, sharing

Joiners
connecting, uniting

Spectators
Reading

FIGURE 14.1 Active social media participants can assume different roles based on their online behaviour, becoming part of social media's participatory culture.[15] Which roles have you taken on while participating in social media?

Participatory Culture and Social Media

The term **participatory culture** is not specific to social media, but it helps in describing an important aspect of the social media experience. Media scholar Henry Jenkins defines participatory culture as a culture with three elements:

- low barriers to creative expression and civic engagement
- support and mentorship among members for each other's creations
- feelings of social connection between members and belief that their contributions matter[14]

Members can participate through affiliation (joining groups such as Facebook or Twitter), expression (producing creative forms such as videos, zines, and mash-ups), collaborative problem-solving (working in formal or informal teams to develop new knowledge or complete tasks, such as through Wikipedia), and circulations (shaping the flow of media through blogging, micro-blogging, or podcasting).[16]

Being part of this new media landscape requires more than just the ability to use a computer. Other social skills, competencies, and "literacies" that are the hallmarks of this culture include the following:

- **judgement**—the ability to evaluate the reliability and credibility of information sources
- **networking**—the ability to search for, disseminate, and synthesize information
- **collective intelligence**—the ability to pool knowledge and compare information for common goals
- **transmedia navigation**—the ability to follow the flow of stories across multiple media platforms
- **appropriation**—the ability to remix and reconcile conflicting pieces of data to form a coherent picture
- **negotiation**—the ability to discern and respect multiple perspectives as shaped by the cultural differences of diverse communities[17]

> **participatory culture**
> A culture in which a person is both a consumer and a producer.

What Is Social Media?

There are many definitions of *social media*. Most commonly, the term applies to the interactive Internet-based and mobile-based tools and applications that are used for these tasks:

- posting and sharing information (such as status updates, responses to blogs, and comments on videos and images)
- conducting conversations
- delivering and exchanging publicly available media content created by end-users, including documents, presentations, photos, and videos

Social media has changed the way individuals stay current, get creative, and stay in touch. Social media users consciously or unconsciously make decisions about how they present themselves online. They disclose information about themselves and create an impression every time they like or dislike something, "friend" or follow another user, post content, or leave a comment.[18] Immediacy and spontaneity underlie the social media experience. Social media allows individuals to see and share events as they happen. A breaking news story or headline can quickly spur responses on Twitter far ahead of the response rate that traditional news outlets allow for. The flow of information through social media can be a strong predictor of trends and a means to listen to and measure public opinion.

Just as profoundly, social media has changed the way businesses collaborate, network, learn, market themselves, recruit employees, share ideas, and communicate with customers, employees, and stakeholders. Businesses can capitalize on social media to achieve different goals:

- generating traffic
- developing a following
- attracting recruits
- creating brand awareness
- facilitating interaction and engagement
- generating revenue
- responding to and mitigating crises[19]

Social media can have several benefits for the external and internal communications of a business. Improved customer care, interaction, and outreach and decreased marketing costs are some of the benefits associated with the adoption of social media for external communications. For example, TELUS rated among the worst Canadian companies for customer service until executives were brought in on conversations that service representatives were having with customers on social media platforms.[20] Companies are also capitalizing on social media to mitigate negative publicity and brand crisis, for example, in issuing product recalls.

Internally, the democratizing effect of social media has helped to alter and soften traditional business hierarchies and improve communications.[21] Best Buy has created its own interactive online learning platform that promotes social learning by enabling employees to share their experiences and ideas. Canada Goose uses Facebook and Twitter to create a positive organizational culture that recognizes employees for their achievements and keeps staff updated with company news.[22]

With social media applications numbering in the hundreds, businesses must be careful to select the best media for the message in order to reach the broadest user-base with the likeliest interest in the product or service. If an organization opts to use more than one social media channel, it must ensure that its messaging is consistent and integrate these channels with more traditional media to reach different content communities.[23]

Types of Social Media

This section provides an overview of five kinds of social media—blogs, micro-blogs, podcasts, social networking sites, and photo- and video-sharing sites—and their relevance in business.

TABLE 14.1 Quick-Reference Descriptions of Select Social Media Sites

SITE	DESCRIPTION
Facebook	A social networking service for connecting and engaging with others via a profile page
Flickr	A photo management and sharing application
Instagram	A video- and photo-posting site that enables users to apply digital filters and share content on other social networking sites such as Twitter and Facebook
LinkedIn	A business and professional networking service
Pinterest	A content-sharing service for organizing and sharing photos and videos, with standard social networking features
Reddit	A social news service featuring user-generated news links
Snapchat	An app for ephemeral content, where photos and videos disappear after a limited time
TikTok	A mobile app for creating, sharing, and collaborating on short lip-sync and comedy videos
Tumblr	A micro-blogging site that encourages the integration of text, photos, and other media
Twitch	A live-streaming video platform, popularly used for video game live streaming, music broadcasts, and "in real life" (IRL) streams
Twitter	A micro-blogging service that enables users to send and read 280-character-maximum tweets
Vimeo	A site for storing and sharing video content that allows users to comment on videos and send private messages to other users
WordPress	A content management system that is most popular as a blog platform
Yammer	A social networking service for collaboration and idea-sharing in the workplace
Yelp	A site for reviewing and discussing local businesses
YouTube	A video-sharing site that allows users to comment publicly on videos and exchange messages privately

Blogs

Blogging is the earliest form of social media.[24] A **blog** is a web page managed by one person or a small team, with date-stamped entries in reverse chronological order. It allows for social interaction, engagement, and feedback through the posting of visitor comments in response to the blog entries. Many large companies maintain blogs to keep employees, customers, and shareholders up to date on important developments while reinforcing and building the company's brand. Corporate blogs represent a shift in the way companies interact with customers and have been shown to build trust, liking, and

blog A web page on which a person posts his or her writings, opinions, and/or other information, usually on a regular basis.

content marketing A type of marketing in which a company provides content of interest to a defined audience in order to boost its profile, attract new customers, and strengthen relationships with existing customers.

involvement.[25] CEOs often maintain blogs on their company websites, in part to improve transparency and reinforce positive perceptions of corporate social responsibility. Corporate blogs are particularly useful for **content marketing**, a popular strategy for gaining attention and trust and converting readers into customers. They can also be useful for promoting particular events and products.

Internal corporate blogs—that is, corporate blogs directed at employees—are often hosted on a company's Intranet. Internal blogs can connect workers with each other, communicate corporate news, and boost morale and employee retention. Employees can use internal blogs to manage projects, exchange opinions on company products and policies, and spotlight work accomplishments. In 2011, TD Bank revamped its internal website into a social media platform supporting blogs, chat forums, and surveys. The site also includes the option for employees to leave comments both on blog pages and at the end of news items.[26]

Bloggers—whether writing to promote themselves or their organization—can make the greatest impact by following a few guidelines:

- **Write consistently and commit for the long term.** Make sure readers know when to expect new content, and never miss a date, even if your blog doesn't receive a lot of traffic at first. A minimum of 50 posts is required for Google to index a blog,[27] and it may take that many posts to build readership.
- **Identify a valuable niche.** Figure out what makes your approach to a topic different or unique.
- **Optimize keywords.** Learn the basic principles of search engine optimization (SEO), and choose keywords that will be most likely to drive traffic to your blog.
- **Determine the right type of post**. Choose the type of post that will get your content across most effectively (see Figure 14.2).
- **Treat your posts as articles.** Use appropriate titles and headings, proper spelling and grammar, and a consistent style. Be clear about authorship, and cite any external sources.
- **Aim for authority and credibility.** Establish authority by sharing industry-related tips readers can apply to their own businesses or lives.
- **Be authentically yourself.** Make yourself relatable by sharing aspects of your everyday life and personality. Always clearly indicate whether a post is sponsored.
- **Incorporate images, videos, and other media.** Long blocks of text can be intimidating.
- **Invite interaction.** No blog is complete without comments, so invite them and use them to understand your followers. Consider inviting guest bloggers or doing interviews.[28]
- **Check out the competition.** Keep up to date with similar blogs and leave comments to build relationships and attract readers to your own blog.

For corporate blogs aimed at external audiences, best practices include the following:

- writing about topics that matter to customers
- educating customers by offering trend and industry news
- writing from a personal perspective rather than a seller's or brand-message perspective
- providing a distinct point of view that complements other brand-based communications[30]

Instructional posts

Easy-to-write "how-to" articles on specific tasks are readily searchable and can be supplemented with diagrams or additional resources.

Cheat sheets

Cheat sheets consist of brief, user-friendly checklists or "top ten" lists, which makes them immensely sharable.

Media posts

Quality images, videos, and infographics increase the shareability factor.

Spotlight posts

Placing the spotlight on a customer or a client humanizes your company.

News posts

News posts keep followers up to date on new products and developments.

Newsjacking posts

Newsjacking posts are useful for showing followers that you are up to date on industry news and presenting your take on current issues.[29]

FIGURE 14.2 A few common types of Twitter posts. Choose a post that will appeal to your target audience.

Micro-Blogs

Micro-blogs allow users to send out short bursts of information to a community of followers in real time. The most popular example of a micro-blog is Twitter, which combines the standard format of a micro-blog with a news-feed function. In its maximum of 280 characters, a tweet has a twofold function: it is both a message and a means of initiating a conversation with followers.

The short, snappy, instantaneous nature of Twitter communication makes it highly suited to sharing the latest, time-sensitive information. The two-way flow of communication on Twitter helps in reputation- and trust-building. Business professionals and their organizations can use Twitter in a number of ways:

- to promote products, services, and brand awareness
- to monitor the competition and their latest projects and initiatives
- to monitor customer satisfaction and public perception of their organizations

micro-blog A blog whose entries are shorter than those of a traditional blog.

- to share and find professionally related knowledge and resources
- to support employee and management communications
- to monitor existing customers and prospect and engage new ones
- to watch industry trends
- to prospect and recruit new hires

Indeed, Twitter has become a major social media platform for brand marketing and promotion, and it is the main platform used by non-profits for social media campaigns aimed at increasing levels of engagement with followers.[31] Businesses and non-profits alike value Twitter as a platform for influencing a target audience's behaviour and fostering awareness.

To realize the full potential of the Twittersphere, consider the following guidelines:

- **Be professional and likeable.** Create a professional-looking profile and username, and strive for a genuine, likeable tone. Consider pursuing diversity and inclusion training in order to avoid reputation-damaging gaffes.
- **Ask questions and respond in real time.** Responding to followers promptly can make them feel valued.
- **Use the right format.** Consider whether tweets, replies, mentions, direct messages, or retweets will best suit your followers' needs.
- **Be selective in what you tweet.** Focus on industry news, professional development opportunities, or a professionally related article or question.
- **Follow only stakeholders and other relevant accounts.** Organize the accounts you follow separate groups and conversation lists (e.g., "Customers," "Competitors," "Professional Associations").
- **Make your content accessible and shareable.** Keep your tweets conversational and free of "marketing-speak." Make them shareable by crafting tweets that are inspiring, intriguing, newsworthy, or appropriately witty.[32]
- **Retweet followers' posts.** However, be sure to confirm that you are not retweeting a statement that might be contrary to your corporate values.
- **Use hashtags.** Hashtags keep your posts searchable and encourage others to join the conversation.
- **Incorporate photos and links.** Add value by incorporating interesting photos and links to articles and videos that provide a fuller context for your tweet. Think of your tweet as an invitation to the reader to learn more.[33]
- **Drive traffic to your blog or website.** Include a link to your blog or website in your Twitter bio, and vice versa.
- **Use Twitter's "Advanced Search" connect with users in your area.** Local customers are often enthusiastic about supporting businesses in their communities.
- **Be strategic in the pace and timing of your tweets.** Keep followers interested, but don't overload their feeds.

Podcasts

Podcasts are audio files that can be downloaded or streamed, usually on a subscription basis, from websites. Many audience members like podcasts because they are highly portable and offer an easy-listening alternative to written content. Most individual podcasts are part of a series, with a new "episode" released on a regular schedule. Listeners can opt to subscribe to the series, in which case an episode is downloaded to their web-enabled device as soon as it becomes available. This arrangement is known as a "push" service, wherein content is "pushed" from a creator to audience members who have asked for or subscribed to it.[34] Podcasts can serve many of the same purposes as blogs. For example, they can be used to educate customers about industry trends and developments, and they can help to position the content creator as an expert. However, they often require more effort to produce than blogs. To offer a meaningful and valuable experience to listeners, podcasts should sound polished and professional. They must be well written and rehearsed, and the final recording must be free of technical glitches and unwanted background noise. A productive approach is to think like a radio producer: be aware that listeners may choose to tune out at any moment, and be careful to provide enough value—whether in the form of entertainment, information, motivation, inspiration, or education—to hold their attention.[35]

Best practices for capturing and recording high-quality audio podcasts that provide listeners with exceptional content include the following:

- **Use a professional-quality recording app.** Record podcasts with an app that replicates studio-recording suite functions, such as Audacity, GarageBand, Audio-Boom, or SoundCloud.
- **Follow a loose script.** While reading word-for-word can result in a monotonous presentation, a brief script that outlines your major points will help to keep you on track.
- **Avoid going solo.** Enter into dialogue or conversation with a co-presenter or guest to create a more dynamic experience for listeners.
- **Seek out and engage with followers.** Promote your content on social media and seek out active users who can share your podcast.
- **Find an appropriate style.** Experiment with podcasting styles to determine how and how much to assert your individual and brand personality.[36]

Social Networking Sites

A **social networking site** is a website that facilitates communication and social interaction through one-to-one or one-to-many conversations between people. Social networking sites such as Facebook enable users to connect by sending messages and by creating personal profiles featuring blogs, photos, and audio and video files that they then invite friends to access. A social media campaign provides access to millions of current and potential customers without the costs associated with more traditional forms of advertising. Companies have been quick to capitalize on and harness the power of social networking, which they use for a variety of purposes:

social networking site
A website that facilitates communication and interaction between two or more people by allowing them to create profiles, send messages, write status updates or posts, and share photos, videos, and other media.

- to create brand communities
- to keep stakeholders and shareholders up to date on products
- to promote products and services, especially to targeted demographic groups
- to publicize events, product launches, and contests
- to carry out marketing research

Non-profits and charities likewise use social media campaigns to publicize their missions and to seek donations and volunteers.

Human resources divisions at companies and organizations across Canada have reported positive results from social media initiatives. Len Posyniak, vice-president of human resources at the Insurance Corporation of British Columbia, sums it up this way: "Immediacy and authenticity are things we can achieve by using social media."[37]

Facebook

Facebook, a giant among social networking sites, offers businesses the benefits of "word-of-mouth" marketing through four basic steps: building a page, connecting with people, engaging an audience, and influencing friends of fans. Consider the following when designing a Facebook page or group:

- **Choose privacy settings with care.**
- **Update your page frequently.**
- **Stay on topic.** Let the focus be your business.
- **Keep your message brief, simple, and relevant to the target audience.**
- **Keep the design clean.** Use links and images where appropriate, but let the brand stand out.
- **Be accurate.** Ensure the correctness and appropriateness of content.
- **Keep the tone spontaneous and informal.**
- **Signpost your company's expertise.**
- **Make the experience interactive and engaging.** Encourage feedback and relationship-building through polls, User Generated Content (UGC), promotions, surveys, and other forms of interaction.
- **Make some content exclusive to Facebook.**

As one of the most popular social media networks worldwide, Facebook can be a powerful tool for building brand communities and promoting products and services. Its "like" feature helps businesses measure user engagement and interest in topics of discussion.

LinkedIn

LinkedIn is another networking site that can help business professionals strategically increase their presence online. Currently the world's largest professional network, LinkedIn had over 630 million users across the globe in 2019.[38] Consider the following best practices (in addition to those discussed in Chapter 10) to optimize your LinkedIn profile:

- **Customize your profile URL.** A URL that includes your name will move your profile to a higher position among search results.
- **Make your profile public.**
- **Complete the summary and experience sections of your profile.** An incomplete profile can result in a lower ranking.
- **Stay active.** Update your status regularly by posting news of activities, information about new products or developments, questions, or links of professional interest. Visit LinkedIn regularly for insights and updates that keep you on top of trends.
- **Connect and network.** Aim for a minimum of 50 connections that include clients, mentors, and business contacts.
- **Solicit recommendations.** Ask satisfied customers and business professionals to recommend you and your company.
- **Stay informed.** Use LinkedIn to stay up-to-date on trending topics and industry news relevant to your business.

Just as LinkedIn can be a resource for job-seekers (see Chapter 10), it can also help recruiters. For example, Nancy Moulday, manager of recruitment at TD Bank Group, reported having trouble finding the right candidates for certain positions when she used the bank's corporate website and online job boards. However, when she started using LinkedIn to advertise job openings, she quickly found that she was able to search for specific qualifications and make more targeted and successful hires.[39] By using InMail, the site's message service, Moulday was able to open a conversation with potential candidates who weren't actively looking on the job board site by establishing some common ground with them and evaluating their level of interest.

Photo- and Video-Sharing Sites

Photo- and video-sharing sites such as YouTube, Vimeo, Pinterest, Instagram, and Flickr allow for the sharing of rich media content with broad, diverse audiences. A similar content-sharing site is SlideShare, where users can post and view slide presentations. Photo- and video-sharing sites carry the risk that copyrighted material will be shared. While most major sites take steps to ban illegally posted content, there have been several cases of major fast-fashion brands selling designs that appear to be copied from independent artists.[40] A 2018 article from Vox found multiple examples of fast fashion brands like H&M, Forever 21, and Zara appearing to copy designs from smaller manufacturers to sell at a much lower cost.[41]

While this practice is technically legal under existing American copyright laws, it can result in lost revenues for smaller designers and artists and provoke a social media backlash against the larger companies.[42] Old Navy was careful to explain that its t-shirt that apparently borrowed its design directly from independent designer Carrie Anne Roberts

photo- and video-sharing site A website with the main function of allowing users to post and share photos, videos, and multimedia.

Canadian comedian and actress Lilly Singh built her career through her YouTube channel, which she started in 2010 under the username IISuperwomanII. Forbes magazine named Singh one of YouTube's highest paid stars with an estimated income of $10.5 million, a *New York Times* bestselling book, and one of the top ten most-followed Twitter accounts out of Canada, a spot that Singh shares with fellow YouTuber Lauren Riihimaki.

was legal since Roberts hadn't trademarked the design. However, it pulled the shirt after receiving a large volume of criticism online.[43] Artists and designers without a significant following or resources for legal action may not have the same success in preventing larger companies from copying and profiting off their designs, and yet they also cannot avoid making their designs vulnerable by posting them on social media without damaging their own business.

Organizations use these sites in a number of ways:

- to share press announcements and keynote speeches with employees and investors
- to upload company photos, public service announcements, and commercials
- to post recruiting videos
- to capture client, customer, and public feedback on company enterprises, products, and services (comments must be monitored)

Encouraging users to post company- or product-related videos on these highly popular sites, often for contests, is another way organizations carry their brand name forward.

User-Generated Content (UGC)

In our age of exploding digital content, online users have been turned into "produsers" (highlighting their hybrid role as producers and users), and their output has been classified as "produsage."[44] Sites inviting user-generated content, such as YouTube, Yelp, and Flickr, provide users with a degree of agency and power, albeit within the arena of a powerful media company.[45]

Recognizing that many consumers are not only willing but eager to develop and share original content online, businesses around the world have devised campaigns to solicit user-generated content in support of their brands and products. UGC campaigns can be effective ways to build interest in a brand and to make customers feel engaged and involved. In 2014, Starbucks launched its "White Cup Contest," which challenged customers to doodle on a cup and upload a photo of their handiwork for a chance to have it selected as the template for a limited edition cup.[46] As of 2019, Instagram users were still regularly posting images under the #whitecupcontest tag, as well as Starbucks's second UGC campaign, the seasonal #redcupcontest. For businesses wanting to achieve similar success through a UGC campaign, best practices include the following:

- **Choose a promotion with your audience in mind.** Analyze your audience to understand interest in your brand. Consider the capabilities and level of technical skills that are typical of the demographic group you are targeting.
- **Look for marketing potential.** Ask for entries that can be repurposed or adapted for use in future marketing campaigns.
- **Offer an enticing reward.** The reward should be at least equal to the value of the efforts expected of participants.
- **Make participation simple and straightforward.** The level of difficulty should not be too high or demanding. Post clear instructions listing specifications for the content and how and where to upload it. The online materials should be easy to navigate.
- **Ensure the legality of what you propose and offer.** Consult with a lawyer to determine who holds rights over submitted content.[47]

The Social Media Advantage

How popular is social media? Globally, Internet users spend an average of 136 minutes a day on social networking sites.[48] Social media use is a powerful trend, and there is little evidence that this trend is temporary. Companies that have embraced the power of social media have realized significant benefits.

As previously discussed, businesses use social media for a variety of purposes and potential benefits:

- internal and external communications
- customer identification and profiling (i.e., developing sales and marketing leads)

- customer care, relationship building, and fan loyalty development
- interaction, collaboration, and engagement
- brand awareness and product promotion
- recruitment
- crowdsourcing
- increased exposure and traffic to websites
- event organization and promotion
- feedback monitoring
- impact measurement

Social media can be an effective platform for promoting and publicizing brands, products, and services, and for building relationships with customers and stakeholders. Moreover, it provides banks of raw data that businesses can harvest and analyze to better understand customers' needs, interests, and priorities. Internally, social media can help to strengthen connections among colleagues and enhance workers' productivity.[49] Workers may use social media to get information to help them solve a work-related problem, ask questions inside and outside their organization, and make professional connections.

Companies such as McDonald's have experienced ups and downs in using social media for marketing and customer relations. While McDonald's US marketers prompted company backlash and bad press in inviting customers to tell their #McDStories, McDonald's Canada took the lead in tweaking this approach and offering to answer any question, no matter how insulting, about its food. The approach worked so well that it was later expanded into television ads and netted the agency that designed the campaign an award at the Cannes Lions International Festival of Creativity.[50]

The Shorty Awards, which honour the best brands, agencies, and professionals on social media, sum up the social media advantage in this way: "Social media gives companies a human touch, bringing customers closer to their favorite brands while allowing marketers to engage directly with their followers in fun and creative ways."[51] Social media has opened up worldwide markets to even the smallest business and made what used to be word of mouth into a global stream that can be heard and seen, instantaneously and spontaneously, by millions.[52]

The Risks and Challenges of Social Media

There is a good deal of euphoria and enthusiasm surrounding the use of social media, but that does not necessarily negate the problems associated with these platforms and applications. The growth of social media has created new risks at a time when organizations are expected to conduct transparent communications and to comply with regulations.[53] There are several key areas of social media that employers struggle with:

1. time theft
2. malicious, negative, or damaging employee comments made about employers
3. leaks of proprietary and/or confidential information[54]
4. damage to brand reputation
5. outdated information
6. use of personal social media by corporate executives

7. corporate identity theft
8. fraud
9. legal, regulatory, and compliance violations[55]

Social networking is a powerful and popular tool, but it can also be a great time-waster, with personal social media use sometimes cutting into work hours. The need to communicate and to stay connected can be overpowering; meanwhile, the fear of missing out by not being online can be detrimental to workflow and productivity. Employees used to sharing details of their personal lives through Facebook or Twitter posts may not understand the potential employment consequences of using social media to express beliefs and views about their work lives, especially when those views have the potential to expose their businesses to harm or risk. Even a casual remark or snippet from an online conversation can be used against a business by its competitors. Corporate takeovers have been fuelled and collective bargaining negotiations have been jeopardized by leaks of this kind.

Learning how to use social media ethically and effectively is something companies continue to grapple with, and the learning curve can be steep. In 2012, for example, Netflix came close to being charged by the US Securities and Exchange Commission (SEC) over information that CEO Reed Hastings had posted to Facebook and that ultimately boosted the company's stock price. The SEC backed down after an investigation, deciding that Facebook was an appropriate way to communicate corporate information.[56] Canadian businesses are becoming increasingly aware of the importance of ensuring their compliance with securities regulations when using social media.

Dominic Dudley/Shutterstock.com

Security breaches of social media accounts are a threat to individuals and businesses, with corporations or hackers seeking to steal private and confidential information to use for their own purposes. In 2018, Canadian data consultant Christopher Wylie, pictured here at an anti-Brexit protest, released documents showing that political consulting firm Cambridge Analytica had used Facebook to illicitly harvest user data for political advertising.

Damage to corporate reputation, threats to employee and customer relations, and fallout from failed or shaky regulatory compliance are likely outcomes when social media is used improperly or ineffectively. It is therefore important for companies to understand their legal obligations and be ethical and transparent in their communications when using social media channels. In this new communications landscape, organizations and their employees must know how to use—and how and when not to use—social media. Faced with the dilemma of social media abuse, employers such as the Government of Ontario have taken the radical step of banning the use of Facebook in its offices.

Facebook and Twitter are not private. Employers may check viewable Facebook profiles or even ask for access to a job applicant's Facebook page before hiring. For this reason, job- and promotion-seekers and others who value their professional reputations should avoid posting potentially embarrassing words and images and be mindful of the online identities and profiles they create. In Canada, labour law protects job-seekers from employers asking for personal information, including social media passwords. Applicants approached for this kind of information have the right to refuse. However, it is equally within an employer's rights to search for employee information that has not been properly protected.[57]

Posts and comments made long ago can have surprising staying power and remain searchable, creating a need for professional "web scrubbers." In 2017, the Federal Public Sector Labour Relations and Employment Board upheld the Correctional Service of Canada's decision to terminate an employee after her Facebook posts showed that she lied about her father's death in order to use her bereavement leave to vacation in Mexico.[58] At least four people were fired and several others faced scrutiny after they were identified as participants in the violent, white supremacist rally in Charlottesville, Virginia, in August 2017 from photos shared on social media.[59] In 2019, Toronto radio host Mike Stafford was fired by Global News Radio after tweeting out racist, anti-Muslim statements. Although Stafford quickly deleted the offensive tweets, they had already been screenshotted and shared by journalist Sean Craig.[60]

Social media also has the disadvantage of making it harder for organizations to control their message and conversations about their product or activities. Social media platforms can function as channels for positive, business-enhancing communication but also carry risks for impression management and reputation, especially when disgruntled customers or employees, through comments, have easy means to voice complaints in a way that can influence public opinion against an organization or its products and services. During a layoff at HMV in the UK in 2013, the social media manager (one of 50 employees let go) live tweeted her outrage and betrayal from the firing session at the expense of the company's reputation and without clear regard for information that must remain private before and after employment.[61] The former employee further embarrassed the company by quoting one marketing director as asking "how do I shut down Twitter?" in the midst of the live-tweeting,[62] portraying the upper management as being out of touch and inept at managing digital business communications. When exposed, this kind of social media illiteracy can seriously damage the reputation of a business that attempts to capitalize on social media without a solid understanding of Internet culture or the platforms with which it is engaging.

A failed social media campaign or one that has caused a backlash is also hard to eradicate, even when controversial, misleading, or offensive product ads have been removed. In 2018, H&M was accused of racism on social media for posting an ad with a black model wearing a sweatshirt that said "Coolest Monkey in the Jungle."[63] The clothing giant had previously been criticized by Indigenous groups in Canada for selling feather headdresses as part of its summer music festival collection.[64] In 2013, just months after the announcement that JPMorgan Chase & Co. was being investigated for its role in the 2007–2008 financial crisis,[65] JPMorgan's official Twitter account launched the #AskJPM hashtag, soliciting questions for senior executives from their followers.[66] After several hours of fielding questions like, "When will you all go to jail?"[67] and "Can I have my house back?"[68] the Q&A was cancelled. More recently, T-Mobile Austria had to act fast to revamp its online security after a spokesperson on their company Twitter feed revealed that the telecommunications giant stores user passwords partially in plain text.[69] The spokesperson for the company responded to customer concerns about cybersecurity by saying that she "really [did] not get why this [was] a problem," and that customers had "not a thing to fear" because T-Mobile's security was "amazingly good."[70] In the wake of several high-profile data leaks, customers were not reassured.

Measuring Social Media Performance

Social media is an important tool for businesses wanting to gauge their effectiveness and improve their performance. The tasks of tracking, capturing, and analyzing important data such as sentiment and content are aimed at determining if that content achieved the desired result. Business marketers who hope to benefit from using the powerful tool referred to as **social media analytics** to track trends and measure sentiment must first decide exactly what to monitor and align those metrics with business goals. Corporate marketers may choose to track data related to trends and activities such as the following:

social media analytics The gathering and analyzing of social media data, which is used to determine usage trends and measure customer interest.

- increases or decreases in the number of followers or friends (consumption or reach metrics)
- the sharing of content among users or the number of one-on-one engagements (sharing and engagement metrics)
- the conversion from social media consumers to paying customers (conversion metrics)[71]

A company can also track what people are saying about competitors and their brands. A few of the best-known social media measurement tools include these three:

- **Google Analytics**—a tool for analyzing visitor traffic and understanding the needs of audience members and customers
- **Hootsuite**—an analytics suite that tracks information about what is valuable to the user through an analysis of links and other factors[72]
- **HowSociable**—a tool that measures social media presence across several different social media sites such Facebook, Tumblr, and Pinterest, assigning a score to each.[73]

Though the practice of social media measurement may raise privacy concerns, the chance for companies to know how they are doing in reaching out to customer communities and thus improve their site content and brands is an opportunity few markets can easily pass up. Michael Wong, director of enterprise business intelligence at RBC, envisions a practical use of analytics: "If there's a conversation that we believe we can perhaps engage in and provide benefit or prospects, we'll step in to provide advice."[74]

Mobile Communication

Mobile devices and wireless communication have made communication from anywhere at any time a reality. According to communications theorist Manuel Castells, it is not only mobility but the concept of connectivity that is important.[75] It is now possible to stay constantly in touch and to be, as linguist and computer-mediated communications scholar Naomi Baron calls it, "always on"—we are, essentially, always on one device or another, whether for business, personal leisure, or gaming.[76] Mobile communications have given the world new phenomena such as mobile youth culture and flash mobs, and they have made it possible for workers to work from anywhere. Indeed, wireless communication has given rise to the mobile network society, transforming the ways we work, find work, play, shop, socialize, volunteer, and form communities.[77]

Communication networks have diffused globally, and the devices that make this diffusion possible are themselves consumer products used by workforces that are dispersed globally. The mobile advantage has been realized in many areas of business, including recruitment, remote workforce management and decision-making, project management, and even training.[78] Sales reps who once had to go solo in the field or be trained on-site at considerable cost now have the support of a team of in-house experts accessible through a device in their pockets. The multimodal nature of mobile communication brings the advantages of text, image, voice, and video to bear on organizational communications and the needs of employees and stakeholders.

Designing and Writing Messages for Mobile Devices

When preparing messages that will likely be read on mobile devices, keep in mind the special challenges these devices present. For example, the portability of smartphones, tablets, and phablets (smartphones with screens of approximately 5.5 inches or greater) means that users are likely to be distracted by background noises and unexpected interruptions from their physical surroundings. In addition, smaller screen sizes and the different user interfaces of mobile devices can affect the readability of messages that have not been properly optimized for mobile devices. Compared to computer monitors, mobile device screens can display far less material at any one time, and most can display only a single window at a time. Usability studies have found that seeing less of a message at any given time and having to zoom and scroll to read it make the content more difficult to remember and divert attention from it, effectively slowing the rate of reader comprehension to 48 per cent of what it is for desktop messages.[79]

To overcome these and related limitations, consider the following guidelines when planning messages that are intended to be—or are likely to be—read on mobile devices:

- Ensure the reader does not have to zoom in to read the content.
- Place the information the reader needs the most at the beginning of the e-mail.
- Use a linear structure, progressing from most important to least important points.
- Keep subject lines and headings under 30 characters in length.
- Position tap targets (e.g., links, check boxes, and form fields) far enough apart to make them easily tappable.
- Ensure links lead to mobile-optimized pages.
- Keep messages as short and specific as possible, and save complex details for a separate message or attachment.

- Ensure that images and design features will be viewable on different screen sizes (e.g., through media queries and responsive design).
- Test-view the message on a mobile device before sending it.
- If the message is meant to be viewed on mobile devices as well as desktop computers, design it for small-screens first.[80]

The above guidelines are particularly important to consider when you are writing e-mails. Checking e-mail is a daily experience for most Canadians, and the mobile optimization stakes are high for e-mails—according to a US Consumer Device Preference Report from Movable Ink, roughly two-thirds of all e-mail is now opened on smartphones or tablets.[81]

Writing Promotional Messages for Mobile Devices

Text message marketing and SMS (short message service) marketing involve connecting with consumers via mobile devices. These forms of marketing are becoming increasingly important in retail advertising and promotion, and they are particularly effective because they allow marketers to reach consumers wherever those consumers happen to be.[82] While many of the techniques for writing persuasive messages previously explored in Chapter 9 apply to mobile marketing messages, promotional messages intended for mobile devices must be especially succinct. Keep the following in mind when preparing these types of messages:

- Confine your message to the offer, its benefits, and details about how to take advantage of it. Additional information is superfluous and will weigh down a message's razor-sharp rhetoric.
- Offer something specific of immediate value.
- Gain attention while avoiding hype, slickly promotional generalizations, and clichés that can make readers mistake your message for spam (e.g., instead of beginning with "Unbelievable prices," catch attention with "50% off winter boots through 12/15/19").
- Create a sense of urgency and timeliness. The channel itself helps in conveying urgency, but also make time-limited offers or state the benefits of acting now.
- Announce the company and brand clearly.
- Communicate exclusivity and make the reader feel special. The promotion should be unique to your message and not widely advertised through a website or other channels. This will help in making the reader feel like an insider.[83]

Optimizing Web Content for Mobile Devices

Mobile-friendly websites are critical for businesses. The dominance of the desktop computer for conducting online searches is diminishing. Google has found that the majority of mobile searches occur in an individual's home or workplace, suggesting that people are choosing to access web content from their mobile devices even when they have access to a desktop computer.[84] Ensuring that websites are optimized for mobile devices is essential to avoid user frustration. A common source of frustration is slow loading on mobile devices; research shows that 57 per cent of users abandon a website if it takes more than three seconds to load.[85] Frustration may also arise when

mobile-friendly websites Websites that display correctly on the small screens of hand-held mobile devices such as smartphones and tablets.

- text is too small to be read without zooming in
- links are too tiny or pushed together too closely to be useful
- content is sized wider than the screen, making it necessary for users to scroll horizontally to see everything[86]

Mobile optimization avoids these sources of frustration by enabling a site to reformat itself to ensure faster loading, easier reading, and a more intuitive, satisfying experience. It recognizes that mobile users have needs and objectives that differ from those of desktop users. A mobile-friendly page accommodates users with

- text that is large enough to be read without zooming
- enabled Pinch-to-Zoom, a useful accessibility tool for users with visual impairments
- dynamic type, which allows users to specify their preferred font size
- content that can be viewed in its entirety without scrolling or zooming
- announcement and validation success or error messages that are enabled for screen readers
- sufficient contrast between the text and background
- links and tappable objects, such as social media icons, positioned sufficiently apart to be easily tapped
- a limited need for users to input text, which may be difficult or imprecise on touch-screen keyboards
- no reliance on software that is not commonly found on mobile devices, which could prevent the page from loading properly[87]
- a structure that favours tight information spaces rather than a long, linear presentation

The most effective and advanced approach to making mobile sites user-friendly involves responsive design. The aim of responsive design is to provide the user with the exact same functionality and content on all devices, regardless of their screen size, memory capacity, or other limiting factors. Responsive design meets this aim by breaking site content into smaller cells and rearranging those cells according to their relative importance and the size of the screen on which they will be viewed.[88] Audience analysis is important to this process, as developing an effective design requires understanding what is important to users and what users' needs will be. The guiding principle of mobile design is simplicity relative to the limitations of the device, the communication channel, and the user: how much screen space is available, how much information can be transmitted and displayed at once, and how much users will be able to pay attention to and remember.[89]

Instant Messaging and Texting for Business

Fast, easy, low cost, and unobtrusive, instant messaging (IM), or the real-time transmission of users' messages with added network-based collaboration tools, is often thought of as personal communication that mimics conversation. The urgency and instantaneousness people associate with IM make this form of communication highly suitable for exchanging short messages on matters of some urgency.

Different organizations set different guidelines on how, when, why, and with whom it is appropriate for employees to use IM. The purposes for which IM will be used influence an organization's choice of which instant messaging system to use; while most IM systems aimed at workplace collaboration provide text-exchange as well as voice, video, and screen-sharing features, each comes with a different range of added features such as offline messaging, group chat, video chat, desktop sharing, bulletin boards, and document management.[90]

Texting/SMS applications can likewise serve different functions based on different organizational needs. SMS applications are commonly used by

- social media platforms (the two-factor authentication that SMS supports helps in protecting account security)
- companies involved in marketing, e-commerce, and online retail (for confirming purchases, notifying customers of shipments, and providing tracking information for packages)
- travel and transportation companies (for communicating alerts and notifications such as arrival and departure updates)
- mobile banking, financial services, and payments divisions (for authentication of online banking transactions, as well as mobile money transfers, mini-statements, and balance updates)
- company customer service divisions (for service change and payment confirmations)[91]

A text message may be short, but it can leave a lasting impression, especially if it is mishandled. Remain professional while using a casual tone for conversational exchanges. The pace of your exchanges won't necessarily allow for conventional planning, but consider your purpose and audience, and think of the outcome you wish to achieve. Although it takes only moments to compose and send a text message, the same principles of planning apply here as for other forms of written communication, though more informally.

- **Consider your purpose.** Are you making a request or providing information? Text messages can lack context, so be as specific as you can about the information you are seeking, and take readers' needs into account. Businesses may use texting to gain a competitive advantage for specific purposes and functions including the following: meeting temporary staffing needs by quickly spreading word of available jobs; building relationships between salespeople and their customers through a few targeted, personal messages; confirming a sale or an order; providing package delivery or shipment progress updates; or providing customer service updates.[92]
- **Consider your audience.** Texting style can vary based on how well you know the recipient and on the recipient's status and seniority relative to your own. Unless organizational style allows for it, avoid being colloquial and using abbreviations and acronyms when writing to bosses and managers.

> NorthMobile svs msg: You can dial *Bill from your NorthMobile wireless phone for quick account balance information
>
> Account: 799321056
>
> Balance: $201.99
>
> Past Due Amt: $0.00
>
> Last Bill: $275.21 due Jul 16, 2020
>
> Last Payment Rec'd: Jun 3, 2020, for $275.21

FIGURE 14.3 Sample SMS text

- **Consider the effect on the reader.** Never send a text to communicate negative outcomes to important decisions or initiatives ("Oops—lost the contract!!!"); in such cases, use a channel where you can better prepare the reader for the bad news. It can also be risky to send a text to solicit new business; instead, focus first on building rapport, and save texting for answering prospective customers' and clients' questions once you have established a stronger relationship.[93]

- **Keep messages short and to the point.** Write in complete but succinct sentences or meaningful phrases that deliver a complete thought, formulating ideas and actions to be taken in as few words as possible. If the message is part of a series of texts, rely on the message thread to provide context.

- **Use a friendly tone.** Avoid using an abrupt tone that sounds harsh and could be off-putting to your reader.

- **Maintain an appropriate degree of privacy.** Consider the degree of privacy your IM system provides. A service hosted over the Internet may carry more risk (potentially resulting in lost data or the compromising of sensitive information) than a system hosted within an organization's private network.

- **Double-check your message before you send it.** Auto-correct and voice-to-text features can distort or alter original messages and recorded speech in unintended ways. Putting trust in your proofreading skills can help ensure your messages are clear.

- **Consider the frequency and timing of messages.** Texting bosses and co-workers outside of work hours may not be appreciated. Likewise, texting clients and customers in the middle of the night could sour business relationships.

- **Consider where you are when you text.** Texting during meetings or while having a one-on-one conversation is generally not condoned. However, recent research shows a growing trend outside North America to multi-communication, or "multi-tasking that involves engaging in multiple conversations at any one time," including conversations conducted via texting.[94]

Checklist

Chapter Review

❑ Be selective about the social media channels you choose to use for both personal and professional purposes.

❑ Keep your social networking profiles and posts current, professional, relevant, and engaging.

❑ Be aware that social media can interfere with productivity and that what you post may be deemed inappropriate and/or unprofessional by employers and customers.

❑ Practise ethical and effective social media use and learn your organization's policies regarding this topic.

❑ Use social media analytics to track the success of your campaigns and to inform your social media plans.

❑ Keep mobile and text messages concise and on topic, and optimize web content for mobile devices.

Exercises, Workshops, and Discussion Forums

1. **Creating a Course Blog or Twitter Page.** Ask your instructor to set up a course-specific blog or Twitter page, with the required privacy settings, to which you and your classmates can contribute your advice on effective social media use. Each member of the class should make a minimum of two postings or tweets.

2. **Analyzing a Facebook or Twitter Campaign.** In small groups, find an example of a Facebook or Twitter campaign for a consumer product or a non-profit fundraising organization. Analyze the elements of this campaign and prepare a five-minute group presentation in which you review its major features and approach and identify a possible target audience. How is the main message, as delivered through social media, different from the message as communicated through the organization's website or other media?

3. **Exploring the Twittersphere.** Log on to your Twitter account, perform a search, and find three hashtags (#) and three users (@) connected to your program, discipline, or future career. Who or what would you consider following? Decide who can help you learn more and connect better. Here are a few steps and considerations that may help you choose:

   a) Browse interests and review Twitter suggestions about which users to follow.
   b) Discover your friends on Twitter; if their professional interests are similar to your own, check who they are following.
   c) Check the user's profile to ensure the bio corresponds to your interests.
   d) See how many tweets and followers your prospects have, review some of their tweets, and check who they are following.

   Present your picks to the class, explaining why you chose them.

4. **Defining Your Social Media Style.** For this activity, work in a small group of three or four. Identify which of the five roles of active social media participants noted on page 512 best describes your daily social media activities. Consider the following questions:

   a) What is your favourite social media site?
   b) What is your frequency of use? How many times a day do you check or post to your social networking sites? Does this frequency change according to the particular site?
   c) How much time per day do you spend on social media?
   d) What are your primary concerns in terms of self-presentation and self-disclosure? Do you edit the photos that you post? Have you ever removed a post to avoid a negative reaction from an employer or to improve job prospects?

5. **Using Social Media for Business.** In a group of three or four, watch the online video "Chris Brogan on Social Media Starter Tips to Grow Your Business" (available online at www.youtube.com/watch?v=pz6PO_Bcr8c) and discuss the strategies he proposes. What other strategies or social media platforms might you use if you were planning to promote a small business online? Make a list, ranking your strategies from most to least important.

6. **Establishing Rules for Business Texting.** Read John Rampton's brief article "The Rules of Business Texting" (available online at www.entrepreneur.com/article/244453). Next, form a group with two or three classmates and discuss what you've read. Do you agree with the rules set out in the article? Can you think of any exceptions to those rules? Can you think of any additional rules that you would add to the list? Make a general list of what to do and what not to do when texting for business.

Writing Improvement Exercises

1. **Writing a Corporate Blog Post.** Create a blog post for a corporate website about a recent work-related achievement or professional-development milestone related to your skills or education.

2. **Writing a Corporate Blog Post.** Find a news story or press release and compose a blog post for a corporate website.

3. **Creating a Personal Profile.** Create a mock-up of your Facebook or LinkedIn profile, then revise and upgrade it to make it more professional and business-ready.

4. **Adapting to Twitter Style.** Write a tweet for each of the following:

a) a rule for using Twitter or social media effectively
b) a principle, concept, or learning outcome from today's class
c) a synopsis or description of your communications course
d) a promotional message for your college or university
e) a summary of last week's class
f) a summary of a news story provided to you by your instructor or searched for by you and your team members

Consider tweeting each one on your class's or your own Twitter page.

Online Activities

1. **Writing a Social Media Message.** Read a selection of consumer reviews (both positive and negative) on TripAdvisor or Yelp, paying attention to elements of social media style. Write a review of a recent trip to a restaurant or hotel, and post it to the site or submit it to your instructor.

   www.tripadvisor.ca/
   www.yelp.ca/

2. **Analyzing Business Blogs.** Review three or more small business blogs highlighted in the Huffington Post article "10 Top Small Business Blogs." Analyze the types of content they offer and how the blogs are designed.

   www.huffingtonpost.com/melinda-emerson/10-top-small-business-blo_b_9417450.html

3. **Tweeting a Media Release.** Read the Twitter tip sheet "What to Tweet." Next, find an online press release related to your industry or area of study, and compose a tweet about it that captures the reader's imagination and attention.

   https://business.twitter.com/en/basics/what-to-tweet.html

4. **Reviewing Shorty Award Winners.** Go to the Shorty Awards website and view a selection of recent award winners. Based on winners' profiles, what traits or qualities seem to define effective social media use? Which ones do you judge to be most effective? How could a company with a less visible social media presence adapt one of the campaigns?

   http://shortyawards.com/#winners

5. **Checking for mobile-friendly design.** Take Google's "Mobile-Friendly Test" to see whether your personal website is mobile friendly. If you don't have a personal website, run the test on a friend's website or a personal website you find online.

   www.google.com/webmfasters/tools/mobile-friendly

Business Usage: A Style and Mechanics Guide

Usage

Commonly Confused Words

There are several categories of commonly confused words: homonyms (words that sound alike but have different meanings), non-standard words (words that fall outside accepted usage), and words whose use depends on whether the nouns they are paired with are count nouns (nouns that name persons, places, or things that can be counted, e.g., *computer, accountant*) or non-count nouns (nouns that name abstractions or entities that can't be counted, e.g., *advice, luggage*). The number sign (#) in entries indicates that the rules of count and non-count usage apply.

a/an   Both *a* and *an* are singular indefinite articles. Use *a* before a consonant sound (*a report*) and *an* before a vowel sound (*an auditor*). **Special cases:** Use *an* before an acronym beginning with a vowel sound but not necessarily with a vowel (*an RSP, an MP*) or before a word beginning with a silent *h* (*an hour, an honest mistake*). If the *h* is pronounced, the word therefore begins with a consonant sound and requires *a* (not *an*): *a hospital, a hostile takeover.*

accept/except/expect   *Accept* is a verb meaning "agree to" or "receive." *Except* is both a preposition and a verb. In its more common use as a preposition, it means "leaving out" or "excluding." As a verb, it means "to exclude." **TIP:** Let the *x* in *except* be a reminder of the *x* in *exclude.* Avoid the common error of typing *expect* ("regard as likely," "suppose") instead of *except.*

> I accept all terms of the contract except the last one.

accompanied by/accompanied with   In these passive forms, *accompanied by* applies to both people and objects, whereas *accompanied with* applies to objects.

> The president was accompanied by the general manager.
> The cheque was accompanied with [*or* by] a letter of apology.

advice/advise   *Advice* is a noun meaning "words recommending a future action." *Advise* is a verb meaning "to give advice." **TIP:** Many verbs end in *-ise* (*advise, apprise, devise*), but only the nouns derived from them end in *-ice* (*advice, device*).

> She advised him to follow her advice.

affect/effect   *Affect* is a verb meaning "influence" and, less commonly, a noun with a specialized meaning used in the field of psychology. *Effect* is a noun meaning "result" and, less commonly, a formal and somewhat pretentious verb meaning "to bring about" or "create." **TIP:** *Affect* is used chiefly as a verb, *effect* as a noun. Think of the *a* in *affect* as standing for its verbal action and the *e* in *effect* as a convenient reminder of the *e* in *result*.

> Restructuring did not affect morale; in the long term it will have a positive effect on productivity.
> The manager effected important changes in workplace safety.

aggravate/irritate   In colloquial usage only, *aggravate* and *irritate* are interchangeable. According to standard usage, however, *aggravate* means "make worse" and *irritate* means "annoy."

> The wildcat strike aggravated the already tenuous labour negotiations.
> Pointless messages on his voicemail irritated him.

agree to/agree with   *Agree to* means "give consent to." *Agree with* means "hold the same opinion" or "be in harmony with."

> The managers agreed to the changes.
> The managers agree with him about the timeliness of the plan.

ain't   *Ain't* is non-standard for grammatically correct equivalents such as *am not*, *is not*, and *are not*. It is unacceptable in all forms of communication for the workplace.

a lot/allot/lots   *A lot* (never *alot*) is an informal way of expressing the idea of "many" or "a great deal"—terms that are in fact preferable in most business documents. *Allot* is a verb meaning "to distribute" or "dole out in portions." *Lots* is unacceptable, non-standard usage in a business context.

alternative/alternate *Alternative* is an adjective that means "available as another choice" or "unconventional" (as in *alternative medicine*). It is also a noun meaning "one of several possibilities" or the freedom to choose between them.

> They optioned several alternative energy sources.
> She had doubts about the plan but disliked the alternatives even more.
> He had no alternative but to terminate the contract.

Alternate is also an adjective meaning "every other," and a stand-alone noun denoting a person or thing that substitutes for another. The verb *alternate* means "change between two things" or describes "two things succeeding each other by turns."

> Seminars were scheduled for alternate Tuesdays.
> Two alternates were named to the team.
> John alternated with Joanne as task-force chair.

a.m./A.M./p.m./P.M.   The abbreviation *a.m.* stands for *ante meridiem* ("before noon"); *p.m.* stands for *post meridiem* ("after noon"). Neither should be used redundantly (as in *8:00 a.m. in the morning* or *3:00 p.m. in the afternoon*) nor with the adverb *o'clock*. Whether the *a.m.* and *p.m.* abbreviations are typed in capital (or small capital) or lowercase letters, the style you choose should be maintained consistently. To indicate the time of day, use figures, not words (*11:00 a.m.*). If the time is on the hour, the colon and zeros may be omitted; otherwise, use a colon to separate the hour from the minutes (*11:30 a.m.*).

among/amongst   These forms are interchangeable in all contexts. *Among* is by far more common, especially in North American usage, whereas *amongst* is more closely identified with British usage and has a somewhat old-fashioned or genteel quality. *Amongst* was once used with verbs conveying movement (*he distributed the memo amongst his co-workers*), but this usage is no longer common.

among/between (#)   Use *among* with three or more people or items, *between* with two.

> There was a dispute among five staff members.
> The dispute between the company and its supplier has been resolved.

Use the objective case of personal pronouns (*me, you, him, her, us, them*) when they follow *between*.

> Between you and me, I think we should reconsider the merger.

amount/number (#)   *Amount* indicates an uncountable quantity. Use it with nouns that name uncountable items (*work, mail, equipment, money*). *Number* indicates a countable quantity. Use it with countable nouns. **TIP:** *Amount* is never used with nouns ending in plural *s*. Uncountable nouns always take singular form.

> He had a number of reports to write—a considerable amount of work for a single day.

ampersand (&)   Use the ampersand sign (&) only in abbreviations (*R&D* for *research and development*, *M&A* for *mergers and acquisitions*) and in the registered names of organizations where it commonly appears (*Royal & Sun Alliance, Procter & Gamble*). The ampersand should not be substituted for *and* in text.

> Their company has long made use of federal government grants to fund R&D.

appraise/apprise   To *appraise* is to "estimate the value of"; to *apprise* is to "inform people of a situation."

as/like   *As* is a subordinating conjunction that introduces a subordinate clause.

> His performance in his new position has been outstanding, as [*not* like] everyone expected it would be.

Like is a preposition and is followed by a noun or noun phrase, not a subordinate clause. It is especially useful for suggesting points of similarity or comparison.

> Norcom, like Telstar, has expanded its foreign market.

If the comparison incorporates a prepositional phrase (beginning with *in*, *on*, or *at*), use *as* instead of *like*.

> In France, as in Germany, the unit of currency is the euro.

assure/ensure/insure   *Assure* means "convince," "promise," or "set someone's mind at rest." *Ensure* means "make certain." *Insure* means "guarantee against financial loss." **TIP:** Think of the noun forms *assurance* and *insurance* to help you differentiate the verb forms more easily.

> She assured him that the team would meet the deadline.
> Her hard work ensured the success of the project.
> Their assets were insured for well over $1 million.

as to   This is an example of bureaucratic jargon. Use more direct substitutes, such as *on* or *about*.

> I reached a decision about [*not* as to] the new recruits.
> His remarks on [*not* as to] the team's performance were helpful.

averse/adverse   *Averse* (usually followed by *to*) means "opposed to." *Adverse* means "harmful" or "unfavourable." **TIP:** Think of the noun forms of these adjectives—*aversion* and *adversary*—to differentiate them more easily.

> She was averse to any plan that would have an adverse effect on efficiency.

backward/backwards   *Backward* and *backwards* are interchangeable adverbs meaning "toward the rear," "in reverse of the usual way," or "into the past."

> He counted backwards [*or* backward] from 10 to 1.

Only *backward* is used as an adjective meaning "reversed" or "slow to develop or progress."

> The CEO's backward policies are partly responsible for the decline in profits.

bad/badly   *Bad* is an adjective describing people, places, and things; also use it after linking verbs such as *feel*, *seem*, *appear*, *be*, *smell*, and *taste*.

> He felt bad [*not* badly] about the cutbacks.

Badly is an adverb used with all other verbs.

The no-refund policy badly damaged customer relations.

beside/besides   *Beside* is a preposition meaning "next to," "near," or "at the side of."

I sat beside him at the annual general meeting.

Besides is likewise a preposition but means "apart from" or "in addition to."

No one besides the team leader liked the proposal.
Besides balancing the departmental budget, the new manager improved employee relations.

Besides is also an adverb meaning "moreover," but this particular usage is more colloquial.

The fund has performed well in the past. Besides, it promises even higher returns in the coming year.

between you and me/between you and I   *See* **among/between**

biennial/biannual/semi-annual   *Biennial* refers to something that occurs or recurs every two years. *Biannual* and *semi-annual* mean "twice a year."

biweekly/semi-weekly   *Biweekly* means "every two weeks"; *semi-weekly* means "twice a week." **Note:** Many people accept "twice a week" as a standard definition of *biweekly*, and many dictionaries list it as an acceptable definition for the word. Therefore, if you use *biweekly*, make sure your meaning is clear. If you are worried about ambiguity, use the phrase "every two weeks" or "every other week" instead.

both/each *Both* means "the two"; it can be used in the following ways: *both consultants, both the consultants, both of the consultants*. *Each* means "every one of two or more persons or things." *Both* is plural; *each* is singular.

She presented a $100 cheque to both of us to cover our expenses. [two people shared $100]
She gave us each a $100 cheque to cover our expenses. [each person received $100]

bring/take Use *bring* when an object is being transported from a distant place to a near place; use *take* when an object is transported from a near place to a distant place.

Please bring the figures for the Anderson report with you to today's meeting.
Please take these files with you when you go.

can/may The once all-important distinction between *can* and *may* survives in formal writing. *Can* denotes ability, whereas *may* is reserved for requesting or granting permission.

Can you finish the research today?
May I help you with your research?

capital/capitol   *Capital* refers to the chief city of a country or province, to accumulated wealth or resources, and to an uppercase letter. In American usage, *capitol* refers to a building where lawmakers meet.

CEO/CFO/CIO/COO/CTO   These abbreviations require capitalization of all three letters and may be used on first reference depending on your audience or readership. Add lowercase *s* to create the plural form (*CEOs*).

CEO = chief executive officer
CFO = chief financial officer
CIO = chief information officer
COO = chief operating officer
CTO = chief technology officer

chair/chairperson/chairman   The gender-neutral *chair* and *chairperson* are preferable to the gender-specific and exclusionary *chairman*.

cite/sight/site   *See* **site/sight/cite**

company names   On first reference, write out the name of the company in full as it appears on company letterhead (where applicable, include *Ltd.* or *Inc.*). Afterward, use the company's shortened name (e.g., *Manulife* in place of *Manulife Financial Corporation*).

compare to/compare with   These forms are generally interchangeable. Use *compare to* to liken one thing to another by emphasizing the similarities of the items being compared. Use *compare with* to imply a greater element of formal analysis encompassing both similarities and differences.

He compared the new security technology to a brick house.
She compared e-business initiatives with more traditional approaches.

complement/compliment   *Complement* is a verb meaning "to go with or complete" and a noun meaning the "thing that completes" or "the full number needed." *Compliment* is a verb meaning "praise" and a noun meaning "a polite expression of praise." **TIP:** The first six letters of *complement* are identical to the first six letters of *complete*.

His fluency in three languages complemented his skills as a communications officer.
Impressed by his credentials, she complimented him on his fluency in three languages.

continually/continuously   *Continually* is an adverb meaning "occurring repeatedly." *Continuously* is an adverb meaning "going on without interruption." **TIP:** The letter *l* "occurs repeatedly" at the end of *continually*, so rely on the double consonant as a re-minder of the word's meaning.

> He lost the goodwill of co-workers by continually interrupting meetings.
> The negotiators reached an agreement after bargaining continuously for five hours.

could of/could have   Helping verbs such as *could*, *would*, and *should* are paired with *have* to convey potential past action. *Could of* is non-standard, and therefore incor-rect, usage.

council/counsel   A *council* (noun) is "an advisory or administrative body"; a *councillor* is a member of such a body. *Counsel* is both a noun meaning "advice" and "lawyer" and a verb meaning "to give advice." **Spell-Checker Advisory:** Only US English rejects the rule of doubling the final consonant before vowel suffixes. American-designed diagnos-tic software, which is often the default software, may flag *counselling* and *councillor* even though their spelling is correct.

> Town council considered amendments to zoning bylaws, but there was no consensus among councillors.
> The company lawyer counselled upper management on the ethics of the pro-posed changes.

courtesy titles   Courtesy titles (e.g., *Mr.*, *Mrs.*, *Ms.*) commonly appear before the ad-dressee's name in the inside address and salutation of a standard business letter. When referring in text to an individual, on first reference use that person's full name without a courtesy title (*Mark Thompson*). Thereafter, refer to the individual by first name (*Mark*), surname (*Thompson*), or by courtesy title plus surname (*Mr. Thompson*).

criterion/criteria   A *criterion* is a standard or principle for judging something. *Criteria* is the plural form that is often mistakenly substituted for the singular, resulting in subject–verb agreement errors.

> There are several new criteria for performance reviews.

data   *Data*—"a series of facts or pieces of information"—is the plural of *datum*, a word that is uncommon and used only in technical writing. *Data* may be treated as a singular noun in all other cases.

> The new data is [or are] consistent with last year's findings.

defer/differ   *Defer* is a verb meaning "postpone" or "yield or make concessions to." *Differ* means "be unlike or at variance."

> According to the contract, they may defer payment for up to six months.

On most challenging technology issues, the team leader deferred to his IT consultants.

The CEO's position on first-quarter spending differed from the CFO's stance.

different from/different than   *Different from* is widely accepted and preferred in formal and professional writing. *Different than* is a colloquialism unsuitable for formal writing but otherwise acceptable when followed by a clause. The British usage *different to* is accepted but uncommon in North America.

Their prices are dramatically different from those of their closest competitors.

Please let me know if your staffing needs are different than they were a year ago.

differ from/differ with   *Differ from* means "be unlike"; *differ with* means "disagree" and usually suggests a disagreement between people.

The manager's recommendations differed from hers.

The task-force members differed with each other over the wording of the agreement.

disinterested/uninterested   *Disinterested* means "impartial, unbiased, objective"; *uninterested* means "not interested." Although some people object to the use of *disinterested* to mean "not interested," this usage is generally accepted.

The matter was referred to a disinterested third party for resolution.

He was uninterested in the new program and decided not to volunteer.

dissent/descent   *Dissent* means "non-conformity" or "difference of opinion." *Descent* refers to family lineage, downward movement, or decline.

There was dissent among committee members over the wording of the agreement.

She packed away her laptop as the airplane made its final descent.

download/upload   *Download* means copy or transfer a document or software from a network to a computer or any other data-storage device. *Upload* means transfer data from a computer or data-storage device to the Internet or a server. *Download* and *upload* are also nouns referring to the transferred files. In Canadian usage, *download* also means to shift costs or responsibilities from one level of government to another.

due to/because of   Use *due to* after forms of the verb *be*. In all other cases, use *because of*, which is generally preferred.

The success of the project was due to the team's effort.

The project succeeded because of the team's effort.

e-/e-business/eBusiness/E-business   The prefix *e-* stands for *electronic* and is common to many relatively recent coinages: *e-learning, e-company, e-commerce, e-mail*. The *e* is capitalized only when the word begins a sentence.

> Our e-business consulting team handles content management and monitors the day-to-day health of the system.
> E-business is the way of the future.

e.g./i.e./ex.   The abbreviation *e.g.* stands for the Latin expression *exempli gratia* ("for example"). It is often used in parentheses to introduce an example or to clarify a preceding statement. The abbreviation *i.e.* stands for the Latin expression *id est* ("that is to say"). Use it to expand a point or restate an idea more clearly. In formal writing, replace *e.g.* with the English equivalent, *for instance* or *for example*. The abbreviation *ex.* is non-standard.

emigrate from/immigrate to   *Emigrate* means "leave one's own country and settle in another." *Immigrate* means "come as a permanent resident to a country other than one's own native land."

eminent/imminent   *Eminent* means "notable, distinguished"; *imminent* means "impending, about to happen."

> The panel of speakers includes an eminent psychologist.
> A change in staffing procedures is imminent.

emoticons   These symbols, which combine punctuation marks to convey strong emotion or tone, are not recommended for most business correspondence. Among the best known are :-) (happy), ;-) (winking sarcasm), and :-o (shocked).

enquiry/inquiry   An *enquiry* is "an act of asking or seeking information"; an *inquiry* is "an investigation." Each is a variant spelling for the other.

etc./et al.   Commonly used at the end of lists, *etc.* is an abbreviation meaning "and the rest" or "and the others." Use it (as sparingly as possible) to refer to things, not people. If a list begins with *e.g.* (meaning "for example") it should not end with *etc.*, as *e.g.* makes *etc.* redundant. The abbreviation *et al.* stands for the Latin expression *et alii* ("and others" or "and other people") and is used in source citations for works with three or more authors (refer to chapter 12 for more detail on the use of et al. in citations).

explicit/implicit   *Explicit* means "expressed clearly, definitely, or in detail." **TIP:** To remember this meaning, think of the verb *explicate*, which shares *explicit*'s word origin. *Implicit*, on the other hand, means "not plainly expressed but implied." Less commonly, it can also suggest a state of containment (often followed by *in*) or an unquestioning attitude.

> He gave explicit instructions that no one should interrupt the meeting.
> There was an implicit trust among co-workers.

farther/further   Use *farther* to suggest greater physical distance; use *further* to suggest greater time or a more abstract quality.

> How much farther is it to the airport?
> Her plan calls for further study.

few/little (#)   Use *few* ("not many") with countable items and *little* ("not much") with uncountable items.

> There were few complaints about the new procedures.
> The new proposal met with little resistance.

fewer/less (#)   These are the comparative forms of *few* and *little*. Use *fewer* ("not as many") with countable items (*fewer investments, fewer reports, fewer losses*). Use *less* ("not as much") with uncountable items and general amounts (*less money, less time, less input*).

> He has less work to do because he has fewer calls to answer.

fiscal/monetary   *Fiscal* pertains to financial or budgetary matters. *Monetary* pertains to money supply.

foreign words and phrases   Foreign words and phrases are used freely in certain disciplines, such as the law, where they are widely understood and integral to the vocabulary of the profession. Used in a more general context, however, foreign words and phrases may confuse readers, and in such cases they should be italicized.

> His lawyer took his case pro bono. [Used in a legal context.]
> The individuals named in the lawsuit were all *sui juris*. [Used in a general context.]

former/latter   When referring to two items, use *former* to indicate the first and *latter* to indicate the second.

formerly/formally   *Formerly* means "in the past." *Formally* means "in a formal, structured manner."

> Jill was formerly an investment counsellor with Mathers–Acheson.
> He knew her to see her, but they had never been formally introduced.

forward/forwards/foreword   Both *forward* and *forwards* are adverbs meaning "to the front," "ahead," or "into prominence." *Forwards* is used to suggest continuous forward motion (*backwards and forwards*). *Forward* is preferred in most other cases.

> They decided to move forward(s) with the project.

Forward is also an adjective meaning "at or near the front," "advanced and with a view to the future," and "bold or presumptuous." In a specific business context, it refers to future production or delivery (*forward contract*).

> Today's forward thinkers are tomorrow's CEOs.

A *foreword* is a preface to a book.

fund/funds   A *fund* is "a reserve of money or investments"; the term *funds* means "money resources."

gone/went   *Gone* is both the past participle of *go* and an adjective meaning "no longer present" or "used up." *Went* is the past tense of *go*. As a verb, *gone* is always preceded by an auxiliary verb; *went* does not require one.

> She went [*not* gone] to the meeting after Steve had gone [*not* had went] home.

good/well   *Good* is an adjective; *well* is both an adjective (meaning "healthy") and an adverb (meaning "effectively").

> Her interpersonal skills are good.
> He is a good judge of character.
> She is well today and will return to work.
> He performed well in the job interview.

got/have/have got   *Got* is a colloquial, non-standard substitute for *have* (*I got timesheets to do*). It should be avoided in formal business messages. *Must* or *have* are more acceptable substitutes for *have got*.

> He must [*not* has got to] submit a new application.
> We have [*not* have got] a week to gather the data for the report.

hanged/hung   *Hanged* means "executed by hanging." *Hung* means "supported or suspended from above" and has many informal usages (*hung out together, hung out to dry*), most of them unsuitable for business correspondence.

> Before capital punishment was abolished in Canada, criminals could be hanged for serious offences.
> They hung their coats in the reception area before the meeting began.

hardly   *Hardly* means "only just" or "only with difficulty." It should not be used with negative constructions.

> I could [*not* couldn't] hardly believe the sudden upturn in the economy.

have/of   Use *have* (not *of*) after the verbs *could, should, would, might,* and *must*.

he/his/him/himself   Decades ago, *he* was used whenever the sex of a person was unspecified (e.g., *if anyone objects he will have to file a grievance* or *each employee has his own office*). Today, this practice (known as "common gender") is widely considered to be gender-biased and should be avoided in business writing. For suggestions on how to avoid using masculine pronouns to refer to people of mixed or unknown gender, see the discussion of gender-neutral pronouns in Chapter 4 (p. 140).

headquarters   *Headquarters* (abbreviated *HQ*)—the administrative centre of an organization—takes both singular and plural verbs.

http:// and **www**   The protocol *http://* (or *https://*) may be omitted if *www* is part of the URL or web address.

I/we   *I* (singular) and *we* (plural) are first-person pronouns that help to establish the moderate informality of a personal business style. While personal pronouns are frowned upon in academic essays, *I*, *you*, and *we* can help business writers express themselves more directly and fluently in their daily tasking-centred messages. In each case, usage is determined by context and readers' needs.

- Use *I* for independent tasking or when you are the sole decision-maker.
- Use *we* (1) for collaborative writing projects, (2) when you write on behalf of a group or speak for a consensus, and (3) when you have the authority to act as spokesperson for the policies and decisions of your organization. *We* should never imply the loftiness of the "royal We" or the condescension of *How are we feeling today?*

imply/infer   *Imply* means "to hint at, suggest, or insinuate without stating plainly." *Infer* means "to draw a conclusion from what is written or said." Generally, the writer or speaker *implies*; the reader or listener *infers*.

> While he didn't say so specifically, George implied that the negotiations were going well.
> The media inferred from George's comments that the strike would be settled by the end of the week.

incidents/incidence   *Incidents* is the plural form of *incident*, an event or occurrence that is either noteworthy or troublesome. *Incidence*, on the other hand, refers not to the event itself but to its rate of occurrence.

> Two recent incidents resulting in complaints against the department require further investigations.
> The increased incidence of absenteeism is cause for concern.

in regard to/with regard to/in regards to/as regards/regards   The expressions *in regard to* and *with regard to* both mean "as concerns," making them interchangeable. *As concerns* is a somewhat stuffier expression meaning "about or concerning." *In regards to*, a misusage resulting from a confusion of these similar phrases, is considered incorrect. *As regards* is an acceptable phrase. *Regards* is an informal complimentary close.

IPO Use this abbreviation for *initial public offering* after the first reference.

irregardless/regardless   Not to be confused with *irrespective* (meaning "regardless" or "not taking into account"), which is acceptable but somewhat stiff, *irregardless* is non-standard and incorrect; instead, use *regardless* (meaning "without consideration for" or "despite what might happen").

it's/its   *It's* is a contraction of *it is*. *Its* is a possessive pronoun. Like other possessive pronouns (*his*, *hers*, *ours*, *yours*, *theirs*), *its* requires no apostrophe to denote possession.

> It's possible to reduce costs.
> The company hasn't released its year-end report.

kind/kinds   *Kind* is singular; the nouns and demonstrative pronouns (*this* and *that*) that agree with it are also singular. *Kinds* is plural; use it to indicate more than one kind. Use it with plural nouns and demonstrative pronouns (*these*, *those*).

> This kind of retroactive agreement is rare.
> These kinds of retroactive agreements are rare.

kindly   *Kindly* means "please" in a polite demand or request (*Kindly refer to the enclosed documents.*). While the courtesy *kindly* conveys is never out of place, some regard it as old-fashioned or overly genteel.

kind of/sort of   These informal expressions mean "somewhat" or "to some extent" and usually imply vagueness or looseness about the term to which they are applied.

later/latter   *Later* means "after a time." *Latter* means "the second-mentioned of two" or "nearer the end."

> Call me later about the arrangements.
> The project manager recently reviewed the Stewart account and the Young account and expressed serious concerns about the latter.
> His responsibilities require him to travel in the latter part of the year.

lay/lie   *Lay* is a verb meaning "to put or place something on a surface." It requires a direct object to express a complete idea. *Lie* means "to be situated in," "to recline," or "to be in a horizontal position." It does not require a direct object to express a complete idea. The present tense of *lay* and the past tense form of *lie* are often confused.

	present	past	past participle	present participle
lay	lay(s)	laid	laid	laying
lie	lie(s)	lay	lain	lying

lay off/layoff   *Lay off* (written as two words) is a verb meaning "remove employees to cut costs or decrease the workforce"; *layoff* (written as a single word) is a noun.

lead/led   *Lead* is both a noun that names a type of metal and the present-tense singular form of a verb (pronounced *leed*) that means "to guide by going in front." *Led* is the past tense and past participle of the verb *lead*.

> Teleway Inc. leads its sector in domestic sales.
> The department manager led a delegation at last year's equity conference.

lend/lent/loan   *Lend* is a verb meaning "to allow the use of money at interest" or "to give someone the use of something on the understanding it will be returned." *Lent* is its past tense and past participle (*I lent, I have lent*). *Loan* is a noun meaning a sum of money lent as well as a verb meaning "to lend," especially "to lend money."

liable/libel/likely   *Liable* means "legally bound" or "subject to penalty or tax." *Liable* is also a synonym for *likely* ("probable") and *apt* ("have a tendency"), but this usage should be avoided in business messages, where it misleadingly implies legal liability or potentially unpleasant results. *Libel* is "a false and defamatory *written* statement." (*Slander*, on the other hand, refers to "a false, malicious, and defamatory *spoken* statement.")

> His negligence left the company liable for damages.
> Given the defamatory nature of the newspaper report, the company sued for libel.

licence/license   As a noun, *licence* means "a permit from authority to use something, own something, or do something." Its variant US spelling, *license*, is usually acceptable in Canadian usage. As a verb, *license* (and also *licence*) means "grant a licence (to a person)."

loose/lose   *Loose* is an adjective meaning "not tight" or "hanging partly free." *Lose* is a verb meaning "cease to have," "become unable to find," or "suffer a loss."

> A loose cable connection caused transmission problems.
> The telecommunications division has been losing money for years.

many/much (#)   Use *many* when referring to more than one item; use *much* with uncountable or single items.

> many: reports, accolades, responsibilities, suitcases, letters
> much: work, praise, responsibility, luggage, mail

may be/maybe   *May be* is a verb phrase expressing possibility. *Maybe* is an adverb meaning "perhaps" or "possibly."

> There may be plans for an additional support network.
> Maybe the company will be restructured next year.

media/medium   *Media* is a plural noun; *medium* is a singular noun. However, there is growing acceptance for the use of *media* as a mass noun with a singular verb.

> Marshall McLuhan claimed, "The medium is the message."
> The media are on our side.
> The media is on our side.

money/monies/moneys   *Money* refers to a form or medium of exchange—coins or banknotes. *Monies*, also spelled *moneys*, refers to sums of money.

myself/I/me   *I* is the subjective pronoun (meaning that it functions as a subject) and *me* is the objective pronoun (meaning that it functions as an object). To determine correct pronoun usage in sentences referring to two or more people, temporarily remove all pronouns and proper nouns except the pronoun in question:

> ✗ The draft proposal was revised by Jen and I.
> ✔ The draft proposal was revised by me.
> ✔ The draft proposal was revised by Jen and me.

Use the objective case if the pronoun follows a preposition:

> Everyone except Paul and me will attend the conference.
> Between you and me, the stock is undervalued.

Myself is the reflexive form of *me*. It refers to or intensifies *I* or *me*. In all other cases, avoid substituting *myself* for *I* and *me* in formal writing.

> I gave myself credit for finishing the report on time.
> The chair and I [*not* myself] offer our heartiest congratulations.

NASDAQ This acronym stands for *National Association of Securities Dealers Automated Quotation system*, the second-largest stock market in the United States. It is also the abbreviation used after an initial reference to the *NASDAQ composite index*.

new economy/old economy   *New economy* refers to the Internet economy; *old economy* refers to the pre-Internet economy.

number   *See* **amount/number**

OK/O.K./okay   These informal forms of *all right* or *satisfactory* are acceptable in most types of e-mail but should be avoided in formal writing.

passed/past   *Passed* is the past tense of the verb *pass*. *Past* means "gone by in time" or "recently completed."

> She passed the test.
> He hasn't travelled in the past month.

per cent/percent/%/percentage/percentile   *Per cent* (also spelled *percent*) refers to "one part in every hundred"; it replaces the % sign (which is used only in statistical reports and on business forms) and usually follows a numeral (*30 per cent of the workforce*). *Percentage* likewise refers to a "rate" or "proportion" out of one hundred but usually follows a descriptive term (e.g., *a small percentage*). *Percentile* is a statistical term used for ranking a score in terms of the percentage of scores below it. It usually refers to a variable resulting from the division of a population into one hundred equal groups.

Shares climbed 15 per cent since the company reported a $200 million profit last week.
There has been a drop in the percentage of investors who support the sell-off.
He was in the top percentile for his age group.

practical/practicable   *Practical* means "useful," "sensible," or "designed for function." *Practicable* means "capable of being put into practice."

His practical approach to debt reduction satisfied investors.
Converting service vehicles to natural gas is not practicable in some regions.

practice/practise   *Practice* (less commonly spelled *practise*) is a noun meaning "a custom or way of doing something," "a repeated exercise that develops skills," or "the professional work of a doctor, lawyer, etc." *Practise* (less commonly spelled *practice*) is a verb meaning "perform habitually" or "be engaged in a profession, religion, etc."

She will open a legal practice when she graduates with her LLB next year.
He will need to practise his French before he transfers to our Montreal office.

precede/proceed   Both verbs, *precede* means "come before" and *proceed* means "go ahead with an activity" or "continue."

A request for tenders precedes the selection process.
Once you receive authorization, you may proceed with the project.

principal/principle   *Principal* is an adjective meaning "first in rank or importance" and a noun meaning "capital sum" or "chief person" (especially the head of a school). *Principle* is a noun meaning "rule" or "axiom." **TIP:** The primary school saying "the prin*cipal* is my *pal*" is a helpful way of remembering the distinction between these homonyms. Both *principle* and *rule* have *le* endings and similar meanings.

The principal was reinvested at a rate of 6.5 per cent.
Her high principles helped her rise above the controversy.

Q1, Q2, Q3, Q4   These abbreviations for the four quarters of the year are appropriate in charts and internal documents, but in more formal documents they should be written out as *first quarter*, *second quarter*, *third quarter*, and *fourth quarter*.

quotation/quote   The noun *quotation* is "a reprinted or re-stated statement made by another person or borrowed from a book or other source, usually enclosed in quotation marks." In business, it often refers to "an estimated cost" or "the current price of a stock or commodity." *Quote* is the informal abbreviated form of the noun as well as a verb. In business, the verb often means "to state the price of a job."

She began her speech with a quotation from *The World Is Flat*.

The quote [*or* quotation] for the project seemed unreasonably high.
At the close of markets today, gold was quoted at $325.

rational/rationale   *Rational* is an adjective that means "sensible" or "based on reason." *Rationale* is a noun that means "the logical basis for something." It is often followed by *for* or *of*.

A corporate sell-off was not the most rational course of action.
By establishing a rationale for the new policy, he ensured the highest degree of compliance.

real/really   *Real* is an adjective; *really* is an adverb. Do not use *real* as an adverb if you want to avoid sounding folksy and colloquial.

Our finest line of desktop organizers is crafted from real Cordovan leather.
He said he was really [*not* real] sorry about the delay.

reason is because/reason is that   *The reason is because* is redundant. Use either *because* or *the reason . . . is that*.

The reason revenues grew was that [*not* is because] the company sold its poor-performing lending business.
Revenues grew because the company sold its poor-performing lending business.

reason that/reason why   The expression *the reason why* is redundant. Use either *the reason that* or simply *why*.

I don't know the reason that [*not* the reason why] he left.
I don't know why he left.

respectfully/respectively   *Respectfully*, a common but relatively formal complimentary close, means "with respect." *Respectively* means "in that order."

I respectfully submit this report for your consideration.
The first- and second-place rankings were awarded to Future Link Corp. and Emergent Technologies Inc., respectively.

shall/will   *Shall* was once commonly used as a helping verb with *I* and *we* to express future action and with second and third persons to express intention or determination. *Will* was used, conversely, to express intention with the first person and the future tense in the second and third persons. Today, there is less confusion about when to use *shall* and *will*. Now less common, *shall* is still used to express a suggestion or pose a very polite question (*Shall we go?*). In legal documents, *shall* expresses obligation or duty (*The author shall revise the work.*), but the formality of the word makes it less suitable for most business messages. *Will* is now used with all persons to form the future tense and to express an assertion or a strong command.

should/would   *Should* expresses duty, obligation (*I should invest more of my disposable income*), advisability (*He should seek legal counsel*), or likelihood (*The markets should improve by the end of the week*). It replaces *shall* in questions that ask what to do or request consent (*Should I revise the report?*). *Would* expresses habitual action (*He would call a meeting every Friday*), a conditional mood (*The company would have met its targets if it had reduced overhead expenses*), or probability (*He would make a good CEO*).

since/because   *Since* usually relates to time. Avoid using *since* as a substitute for *because* if there is any hint of ambiguity, as in the following example: *Since* [meaning both *from that time* and *because*] *he got a promotion, he has spent more on luxuries.*

> He has received five job offers since his graduation last June.

site/sight/cite   *Site* is a noun referring to "a particular place," including a single source for files or services on the Internet. *Sight* is both a noun referring to the faculty of seeing or a thing seen and a verb meaning "observe or notice." *Cite*, also a verb, means "to quote or mention as an authority or example."

> The new site for our company offices will offer easy access to public transit.
> The sight of the month-old sandwich in the cafeteria made him ill.
> Analysts cited increased profit-taking as a reason for caution.

sometime/sometimes/some time   *Sometime* means "at some unspecified time in the future." *Sometimes* means "occasionally." *Some time* means "a span of time."

> The committee will meet sometime in May to make its final decision.
> He is sometimes late for meetings.
> Can you spare some time later this afternoon?

stationary/stationery   *Stationary* means "not moving." *Stationery* refers to writing materials and office supplies. **TIP:** The *e* in the ending of *stationery* should remind you of the *e*'s in *envelope* and *letter*).

suppose to/supposed to   *Suppose to* is non-standard for *supposed to*. The final *d* and the preceding verb *be* are essential to convey the idea of a plan, obligation, or something that is generally accepted. *Suppose*, without *be* and the final *d*, means "assume" or "be inclined to think." *I suppose so* is an expression of hesitant agreement.

> The meeting was supposed to take place last Thursday but was postponed indefinitely.
> I suppose the profit warning will deter investors.

takeover/take over   *Takeover* is a noun that refers to "the assumption of control or ownership of a business," especially the sometimes hostile buying out of one business by another. *Take over* is a verb meaning "to control" or "to succeed to the management or ownership of" something.

than/then   *Than* is a conjunction that indicates comparison. *Then* is an adverb that shows relationships in time.

The XJ copier is faster than the older AP model.
We will do the costing, then submit a bid.

than I/than me   The choice of a pronoun can alter the meaning of a sentence. To check that the pronoun delivers its intended meaning, temporarily add the extra words that are implied.

Hopkins likes golf more than I. [in other words, Hopkins likes golf more than I like golf]
Hopkins likes golf more than me. [in other words, Hopkins likes golf more than he likes me]

that/which/who   These relative pronouns are key sentence builders because they introduce clauses that limit the meaning of the word or words they refer to. Relative pronouns add clarity by defining relationships and, because of this, should be retained in documents intended for translation. On the other hand, too many *that*, *which*, and *who* clauses create a cluttered and awkward syntax. For conciseness, especially in informal documents, revise wordy relative clauses by replacing them with equivalent modifiers.

Awkward: Place copies of claims that have been rejected in the tray that is red.

Revised: Place copies of rejected claims in the red tray.

Awkward: The adjuster who handles small claims is the one that you should speak to.

Revised: You should speak to the small claims adjuster.

It is important to distinguish between *that*, *which*, and *who*. *That* refers mainly to things or animals but can also refer to a group of people (*The committee that revised the proposal*). *That* introduces restrictive clauses adding information essential to the meaning of the sentence. Restrictive clauses beginning with *that* are not set off with commas. *Which* also refers to things or animals but introduces non-restrictive clauses containing information that is helpful but not necessarily essential to the meaning of a sentence. Non-restrictive clauses are set off with commas. Less commonly, *which* can also be used to introduce restrictive clauses. *Who* is a relative pronoun that refers to people; it can be used to introduce either restrictive or non-restrictive clauses.

me yesterday is timely and well prepared. [*that you sent me yesterday* limits *the report* to a particular report]

Your report, which I received yesterday, is timely and well prepared. [*which I received yesterday* just provides more information about the report]

Analysts who recently predicted falling share prices are now optimistic about the stock's performance. [When not set off with commas, the restrictive clause *who recently predicted falling share prices* limits *analysts* to a particular group of analysts.]

Analysts, who recently predicted falling share prices, are now optimistic about the stock's performance. [When followed by a non-restrictive clause set off with commas, the meaning of *analysts* remains general.]

themselves/themself/theirselves   *Themselves* is the only correct form of this plural reflexive pronoun.

there/their/they're   *There* refers to a position or place and is also used to indicate the existence of something at the beginning of an expletive sentence (*There is a new listing on the TSX.*). *Their* is a possessive pronoun. *They're* is the contraction of *they are*.

toward/towards   As prepositions meaning "in the direction of," *toward* and *towards* are equal and interchangeable. It is best to pick one spelling and use it consistently within a document.

unsolvable/insoluble/insolvent   Both *unsolvable* and *insoluble* mean "incapable of being solved." *Insoluble* also means "incapable of being dissolved." *Insolvent* means "unable to pay one's debts."

use to/used to   *Used to* is the only correct usage when referring to something that happened in the past; the *d* ending in *used* is essential.

> He used to work for this company, but now he heads up his own business.

wait for/wait on   *Wait for* means "await"; *wait on* can mean either "serve" or "await."

while   The subordinate conjunction *while* means "during that time" as well as "in spite of the fact that" and "on the contrary." If you are using it to concede a point, *while* must not deliver the unintended meaning of simultaneous action. Unless "during that time" is the intended meaning, replace *while* with *although*, *whereas*, or *despite the fact that*.

Ambiguous:	While there are problems, I think we should proceed with caution. [This implies "proceed with caution only as long as the problems persist."]
Clear:	Although there are problems, I think we should proceed with caution. [This means "proceed with caution in spite of the fact that there are problems."]
Ambiguous:	I thought we should move ahead with the project while they had other ideas.
Clear:	I thought we should move ahead with the project whereas they had other ideas.

who/that/which   *See* **that/which/who**

who/whom   The distinction between *who* (the subjective case of the pronoun) and *whom* (the objective case of the pronoun) is fast disappearing, especially in less formal contexts. *Who* is now the convenient multi-purpose choice for harried writers, but when more formality and absolute correctness are required, use *who* when you need a subject and *whom* when you need an object. If you are having trouble identifying which one you need, refer to the following case chart, then consider the type of sentence *who/whom* appears in: a sentence that asks a question or a sentence that makes a statement.

	case	pronouns of the same case
who	subjective	I, you, he, she, it, we, you, they
whom	objective	me, you, him, her, it, us, you, them

who vs. *whom* in sentences that ask questions

1. Does the interrogative pronoun perform the action (*who*) or receive the action (*whom*) of the sentence?
2. If this is not clear, answer the question the sentence asks, then use the chart above to match up the correct form.

   - Who was responsible for filing the Gustafson report? (*She*, not *her*, was responsible for filing the Gustafson report; therefore *who* is correct.)
   - Whom did CanBiz Magazine hire as its new editor? (*CanBiz Magazine* hired *him*, not *he*, as its new editor; therefore *whom* is correct.)

3. *Whom* commonly follows prepositions such as *to* and *for* (think of the salutation *To Whom It May Concern*).

   - For whom was the memo intended? (The memo was intended for *them*, not *they*.)
   - To whom should the letter be addressed? (The letter should be addressed to *her*, not *she*.)

who vs. *whom* in sentences that make statements

The relative pronouns *who* and *whoever* (subjective case) and *whom* and *whomever* (objective case) are often the first words of subordinate clauses. To test for the correct pronoun, isolate the subordinate clause, then replace *who* or *whom* with the corresponding case of pronoun (see the case chart above). Rearrange the clause to see whether a pronoun subject or pronoun object makes the most sense.

Original sentence:	Employees **who/whom** senior management encouraged reported greater job satisfaction.
Subordinate clause:	who/whom senior management encouraged
Trial substitutions:	✗ senior management encouraged they = who ✔ senior management encouraged them = whom
Correct sentence:	Employees whom senior management encouraged reported greater job satisfaction. [You may drop *whom* from the sentence to lessen the formality: *Employees senior management encouraged reported greater job satisfaction.*]
Original sentence:	The award for business excellence goes to **whoever/whomever** contributes the most to the company in the next fiscal year.

Subordinate clause:	**whoever/whomever** contributes the most
Trial substitutions:	✗ she contributes the most = whoever
	✔ her contributes the most = whomever
Correct sentence:	The award for business excellence goes to whoever contributes the most to the company in the next fiscal year. [In this case, the objective-case-follows-a-preposition rule doesn't apply. The object of the preposition isn't a single word—*whomever*—but the entire clause beginning with the pronoun, making the subject *whoever* the only correct choice.]

who's/whose   *Who's* is the contraction of *who is*. *Whose* is the possessive form of *who*.

> Who's eligible for the new training program?
> Our chief sales representative, whose name is Paul Sharma, will be glad to assist you.
> Whose phone is this?

your/you're   *Your* is a possessive adjective meaning "belonging to you"; *you're* is a contraction of *you are*.

> Please submit your report.
> You're coming to the meeting, aren't you?

Usage Exercise

According to context, select the correct word in each set of parentheses:

1. He (*assured/ensured/insured*) me he would keep the (*amount/number*) of changes to a minimum.
2. The (*affects/effects*) of the (*take over/takeover*) were felt by many personnel. Those most (*affected/effected*) blamed (*backward/backwards*) policies.
3. After (*alot/allot/a lot*) of consultation with printers, the vice-president approved the new design for the company (*stationary/stationery*).
4. With (*fewer/less*) reports to file, there is (*fewer/less*) work to do.
5. She was (*suppose to/supposed to*) settle the dispute (*among/between*) the five committee members.
6. The delegates were accompanied (*by/with*) two members of the support staff.
7. In the (*past/passed*) year, the government has (*past/passed*) new labour legislation.
8. The hiring committee will meet (*sometime/some time/sometimes*) in the next week.
9. The dispute resolution committee agreed (*to/with*) the proposed changes.
10. Because the conference is held (*biennially/biannually/semi-annually*), Sean has two years to prepare his next study of investment trends.
11. (*As regards/In regard to/Regards*) your request to (*precede/proceed*) with the project, I fully support your initiative and ask that you move (*foreword/forwards/forward*) with the plan.

12. (*Between you and me/Between you and I*), I think the need for more (*capital/capitol*) is justified.
13. Lise (*could of/could have*) solved the problem if she had been (*apprised/appraised*) of the situation.
14. Every (*chairman/chairperson/chair*) of the advisory (*council/counsel*) has had (*his own/an*) office.
15. Our team's recommendations differed (*from/with*) (*theirs/there's*).
16. Mai Li plans to apply to (*a/an*) MBA program next year.
17. (*Compared to/Compared with*) his co-workers, Jorge performs (*well/good*) under pressure (*due to/because of*) his superior time-management skills.
18. The cancellation of the flight was (*due to/because of*) mechanical problems.
19. (*While/Although*) the financial officer (*who/whom*) he reports to is supportive, she plans to cut the budget for his department.
20. The committee is looking for applicants (*who/whom*) they feel are best prepared to promote our products in emerging markets.

Abbreviations and Acronyms

Abbreviations

Abbreviations should be used sparingly and only when their meanings are obvious to the reader.

- **Abbreviated titles before and after names:** Use abbreviations ending in periods for titles that precede names (Mr., Ms., Mrs., Prof., Dr., Hon.) or abbreviations for degrees and professional designations that follow names (C.A., Ph.D., M.D., LL.B., Q.C.). Avoid using an abbreviated title both before and after a name.

✔	✔	✗
Ms. Maria DaSilva	Maria DaSilva, C.A.	Ms. Maria DaSilva, C.A.
Dr. Paul Lui	Paul Lui, M.D.	Dr. Paul Lui, M.D.
Prof. Iqbal Khan	Iqbal Khan, Ph.D.	Prof. Iqbal Khan, Ph.D.

- **Abbreviations of months:** The names of all months except May, June, and July can be abbreviated when they are followed by a numeral (*Oct. 5, Jan. 28, June 17*). Use full spelling for the month if it appears on its own or if it is followed by a year (*December*; *March 1998*). Do not abbreviate months in letter datelines.
- **Abbreviations of provinces and addresses:** Use the two-letter postal abbreviations of provinces and territories (AB, BC, MB, NB, NL, NS, NT, NU, ON, PE, QC, SK, YT) in address blocks. Spell out the province's or territory's name in text when it is accompanied by the name of a town or city (*the Markham, Ontario,*

plant will be expanded) and when the province or territory name appears alone (*the Ontario plant will be expanded*). Spell out words such as *street*, *boulevard*, and *avenue* in all inside addresses and in text when no number is part of the address (*please visit our Hastings Street office*).

In general, make abbreviations as clear as possible. If necessary, add periods to abbreviations that might be mistaken for words or typographical errors (e.g., *a.k.a.* or *a.m.*).

Acronyms

An acronym is a shortened form created from the first letters of a series of words. It is pronounced either as a single word (e.g., *NATO*, *CANDU*) or by letter (e.g., *CBC*, *RCMP*). (Acronyms pronounced by letter are usually called "initialisms.") In most cases, acronyms do not require periods. If an acronym is well known, use it without explanation; otherwise, spell it out parenthetically on first reference: *CPA (Certified Public Accountant)*, *AFP (Association of Fundraising Professionals)*. Acronyms are often used for the following:

- **names of corporations and banking institutions**

  BMO   CIBC   IBM   RBC

- **names of organizations and government agencies**

  CAW   CPP   CRTC   CSA   CSIS   NATO   UNESCO

- **abbreviated phrases and compound nouns**

ASAP	(as soon as possible)
CSB	(Canada Savings Bond)
FAQ	(frequently asked question)
GIC	(Guaranteed Investment Certificate)
modem	(modulator/demodulator)
MS	(multiple sclerosis)
radar	(radio detecting and ranging)
RAM	(random access memory)
RFI	(request for information)
RFP	(request for proposal)
RRSP	(Registered Retirement Savings Plan)
RSVP	(répondez s'il vous plaît)
SUV	(sport utility vehicle)
VIP	(very important person)

Numbers

Numbers may be expressed as words or as figures. In general, numbers up to and including ten are expressed as words; numbers above ten are expressed as figures. However, different organizations may follow slightly different rules (e.g., expressing round numbers, such as fifty and one hundred, as words).

Numbers Usage

- **Emphasis:** Numbers under ten may be written as figures in special financial contexts and data references (*The TSX is down 8 points.*).
- **Placement:** Write the number as a word if it begins a sentence (*Fifteen council members attended the meeting.*). Hyphenate words that form a single number (*Seventy-eight applications have been submitted.*). If the number consists of more than two words, revise the sentence so that the number is not at the beginning (*On average, 175 employees apply for this program each year.*).
- **Money:** Use figures to express sums of money greater than one dollar (*The deluxe staplers cost $22.95 each.*). Omit the decimal and zeros when expressing whole dollar amounts (*The starting salary is $50,000.*).
- **Big figures:** Write million or billion as a word instead of a figure with multiple zeros. The number that precedes *million* or *billion* is expressed as a figure (*The company committed $2 million to the project.*). Figures in the millions are generally rounded off to one decimal place, but care should be taken to avoid possible misrepresentation (*Average compensation reached almost $5.5 million this year.*).
- **Related numbers:** Express related numbers (referring to items in the same category) in the form used for the larger number (*Four of the five candidates have graduate degrees.* and *We are prepared to retire 7 vehicles from our current fleet of 32.*). Express the first related number as a word if it falls at the beginning of a sentence (*Seven of the 12 new products released last year exceeded our expectations.*).
- **Consecutive numbers:** Differentiate consecutive numbers that modify the same noun by expressing the first as a word and the second as a figure (*She purchased four 20-year bonds*). If the first number consists of more than two words, express it as a figure (*250 twelve-page inserts*).
- **Decimals and percentages:** Use figures to express decimals (*9.75*). For amounts less than one, put a zero before the decimal (*0.5*) unless the decimal itself begins with a zero (*.08*). In most cases, avoid using more than two numbers after a decimal point. Also use figures to express percentages along with the word *per cent* (*a 10 per cent drop*) or followed by the % symbol in statistical reports (*a 5% increase*). If you are using the % symbol, include it with each individual number (*The share-return price shrank to 45% from 57% the previous year.*). Spell out the percentage at the beginning of a sentence (*Thirty per cent of area residents opposed the development.*).
- **Simple fractions:** Express simple fractions as words in text (*Three quarters of Canadians have Internet access.*) and hyphenate them when they are used as modifiers (*He sold his one-quarter share in the company.*).
- **Time:** To express clock time with *a.m.* or *p.m.*, use figures (*A meeting will be held on February 4 at 2:00 p.m.*). To express periods of time, you can use words or

figures, but figures are best when you need to emphasize important financial or contractual terms (*a 30-day money-back guarantee*).

- **Dates:** Use figures when the number follows the name of the month (*January 15*) and use ordinals (*1st, 2nd, 3rd*) when the number precedes the name of the month (*the 15th of January*). Do not use ordinals in European or military-style datelines (*15 January 2021*).
- **Weights and measurements:** Use figures to express weights and measurements with figures (*each unit weighs 2.2 kg; the office is 5 kilometres from Vancouver International Airport*).
- **Telephone and fax numbers:** For telephone and fax numbers in Canada and the United States, put the area code in parentheses and insert a hyphen after the exchange: *(519) 555-2167*. If extensions are essential, place a comma after the telephone number followed by the abbreviation *Ext.* or *ext.* For internal numbers, include only the extension: *Please call Terry Simpson, ext. 445.* Periods may also be used in place of more conventional punctuation: *519.555.2167*.
- **Addresses:** Write street numbers in figures, except for the number one on its own.
- **Chapters, sections, and pages:** Use figures to designate chapter, section, and page numbers. Capitalize the word before the number when it refers to a chapter or a section (*Chapter 7, Section 3*), but do not capitalize the word *page* or *pages*.

Number Usage Exercise

Correct number usage errors in the following sentences:

1. 45 of the 75 applications for the advertised position were submitted electronically.
2. Project development was documented through a series of 5 10-page reports.
3. Our small electronics division had revenues of $32,900,000.00 in the latest fiscal year, an increase of fifteen per cent over the previous year.
4. When the price of gasoline rose to one dollar and twenty cents a litre, 3 media outlets in the greater Halifax area reported that price gouging was to blame.
5. The association's first conference on biomedical ethics, scheduled for January the tenth, is expected to draw more than three-hundred-and-fifty participants.
6. Our 5 Calgary-area sales centres were among the top 20 dealerships in the country for the 4th consecutive year.
7. Pure Citrus Products was charged with false advertising when it was found that its Premier Juice product line contained only .5 per cent real fruit juice.

Capitalization

Capitalization Guidelines

- **Proper nouns:** Proper nouns, which name specific people, places (geographic locations), and things, should be capitalized. References to language, culture, or ethnicity (*French, Indonesian*) should also be capitalized. Common nouns, naming general categories, are not capitalized unless they fall at the beginning of a sentence.

Proper Noun	Common Noun
First Canadian Place	office tower
Nova Scotia Community College	community college
Air Canada	airline
Hinduism	religion
Lake Athabasca	lake

- **Business and professional titles:** Capitalize business titles only when they precede names or appear in inside addresses, salutations, signature blocks, official documents, and minutes of meetings. Do not capitalize these titles when they follow names or appear alone in running text.

Ms. Shauna Kovick
Director of Human Resources
Technion Enterprises, Inc.
Ottawa, ON K4W 2E9

Sincerely,
David McHenry
Corporate Travel Administrator

Stephanie Di Castro, director of marketing, devised the new campaign.
Vice-President Leung has been assigned to head our Winnipeg operation.
Please consult the district manager before drafting the RFP.

Note that the style guidelines of individual organizations may have different standards.

- **Department and division names:** Capitalize the names of committees, departments, and divisions *within* your organization. It is customary in some organizations, however, to lowercase these names. If in doubt about which style your organization prefers, consult corporate style guidelines. Use lowercase for non-specific names of committees, departments, and divisions *outside* your organization.

The package was forwarded to our Project Management Division.
Antonio was recently transferred to our Accounting Department.
Their sales division was recently downsized.

- **Organization names:** Capitalize all words (excluding non-initial conjunctions and prepositions) in the names of public- and private-sector industries, educational institutions, government bodies, and social agencies, as well as charitable, non-profit, religious, and professional organizations.

Canadian Cancer Society	Environment Canada
HSBC Securities	Ministry of Transportation
Toronto District School Board	Hospital for Sick Children

- **Academic degrees and courses:** Capitalize specific degrees and courses as well as names of academic degrees that follow a person's name. Abbreviations for academic degrees are always capitalized. Degrees and courses referred to more generally are lowercased.

  > Jason Jackson, M.B.A.
  > He earned his Bachelor of Science degree.
  > He earned a bachelor's degree in science.

- **Product names:** Capitalize only trademarked items and manufacturers' names, not general products.

  > Canon copier   IBM computer

- **Compass points:** Lowercase compass points that indicate direction (e.g., *north, south*) and adjectives derived from them (e.g., *northern, southern*). Capitalize them if they name a specific region.

  > Northern Ontario   north of Vancouver

- **Book titles:** Capitalize the initial word and all principal words (not articles, conjunctions, or prepositions) in the titles of books, articles, magazines, periodicals, newspapers, reports, government documents, films, songs, plays, and poems. The titles of major works or publications (such as books, magazines, and newspapers) should be italicized. The titles of all other works should be enclosed within quotation marks.
- **Quotations and bullet points:** Capitalize the first word of quoted material that is a full sentence (*Debashis Chaudry said, "The company is remarkably different than it was a decade ago."*), but do not capitalize the beginning of the second part if the quotation is interrupted mid-sentence. Do not capitalize the first letter of a quotation if the quotation itself is not a complete sentence (*The chair of the advisory board said that it was time to put an end to "fuzzy corporate accounting."*). Capitalize the initial word of a numbered or bulleted item appearing in list form if it is part of a heading or a complete sentence.
- **Nouns preceding letters or numbers:** Capitalize nouns that precede numbers or letters (*Flight 98, Gate 44, Room 3122, Table B*).
- **E-mail and computer functions:** Capitalize all e-mail and computer functions, as in *Click Send*. Copy notations in e-mail (*cc, bcc*) are not capitalized.

Capitalization Exercise

Correct the following sentences by capitalizing words as required:

1. president siddiqui's favourite book is *the world is flat* by thomas l. friedman.
2. winnipeg-based enterprise press plans to launch its first french-language daily newspaper in the competitive montreal market.
3. As stated in article 5 of the senate report, our faculty of business will launch a new program called entrepreneurial studies in the 2016–2017 academic year.
4. the director of public relations will discuss the reintroduction of the gift-card program when she meets with the president next week.
5. tim hortons' famous double-double has helped the chain become the most profitable division of the us fast-food giant wendy's.

Usage-Related Internet Resources

Visit the following websites for more on usage.

1. **APA Style Central (American Psychology Association):** This resource provides information about grammar, usage, and style that is consistent with the guidelines set out in the *Publication Manual of the American Psychological Association*.

    www.apastyle.org/learn/

*   **Common Errors in English Usage (Washington State University):** This page briefly explains commonly confused words and responds to a variety of usage queries.

    http://public.wsu.edu/~brians/errors/errors.html#errors

*   **NetLingo:** This site offers rules for the spelling and hyphenation of Internet terms and explanations of acronyms commonly used online and in texting.

    www.netlingo.com

*   **Usage (Oxford University Press):** Part of the Oxford Living Dictionaries site, this page provides links to clear explanations of common usage problems.

    https://lexico.com/grammar/usage

*   **UToday Style Guide (University of Calgary):** Prepared by the university's communications office, this concise document offers guidance on spelling, capitalization, and other points of usage and style following Canadian Press style.

    www.ucalgary.ca/utoday/styleguide

Salutations and Complimentary Closes: A User's Guide

E-mail

Salutations and complimentary closes are optional in e-mail messages, but they provide a more personalized, reader-centred approach. Greetings and appropriate concluding remarks can soften otherwise abrupt messages, building goodwill and securing compliance. Vary the salutation and complimentary close to fit the tone, subject, and nature of the message and to reflect your relationship to the reader. For example, it is best to refrain from closing with "Cheers" when your message contains bad news. Consider the degree of authority and/or friendliness you wish to project.

Formal Salutation	Less Formal Salutation	Informal Salutation
Dear (recipient's name)	(recipient's first name by itself)	Hello (without using the recipient's name)
Good Morning	Paul Lui, M.D	Dr. Paul Lui, M.D.
Good Afternoon	Hi (without using the recipient's name)	(recipient's name incorporated within first line of message)
	Greetings	

Formal Complimentary Close	Less Formal Complimentary Close
Sincerely	Cheers
Best wishes	Regards
	Best
	Thanks (to show appreciation)

Standard Letters

The most common salutation used in business letters is Dear followed by the addressee's name and a colon. If you are on a first-name basis with the recipient, you may choose to follow Dear with the person's first name only; otherwise, use the person's surname preceded by a courtesy title (e.g., *Ms.*, *Mr.*, *Rev.*, *Prof.*). If you aren't sure of the recipient's gender, use the person's first initial or full first name. Whenever possible, address a letter to a specific person. If you aren't sure of the person's name, make the salutation more generic (e.g., *Dear Colleague*).

Sincerely is universally accepted as the most appropriate complimentary close for standard business letters; however, in certain circumstances, an alternative complimentary close may help you achieve a higher or lower degree of formality. Before making your choice, consider the following factors:

- workplace style guidelines and expected level of formality
- your relationship to the reader and frequency of correspondence
- tone and the nature of the message
- your position within the company hierarchy

Here is a sampling of standard complimentary closes:

Very Formal	Somewhat Formal	Informal
Respectfully	Sincerely	Regards
Very sincerely yours	Sincerely yours	Best regards
Very truly yours	Cordially	Best wishes

Note that in each case, the complimentary close is typically followed by a comma.

Standard Business Phrases and Their Plain-Language Alternatives

As discussed in Chapter 4, plain language is becoming more common in business communication. The following list provides examples of standard business phrases and their plain-language replacements.

Standard Phrases (Wordy/Outdated)	Plain-Language Equivalents
are in receipt of	have received
are of the opinion that	think, believe
as per your request	as you requested, at your request
at your earliest convenience	soon, by (specific date)
enclosed herewith please find	enclosed
forthwith	without delay, at once
in the eventuality that	if
in view of the fact that	because
pursuant to your request	at your request
thanking you in advance	thank you

Grammar and Punctuation Handbook

Subject–Verb Agreement

Nothing detracts from the professionalism of business messages as severely as faulty subject–verb agreement. Verbs—"doing words" that show actions or states of being—must agree with their subjects both in number (singular/plural) and in person (*I*, *he*, *she*, *it*, *we*, *you*, *they*). The primary rule is that singular subjects—those that name just one thing—require singular verbs, and plural subjects—those that name more than one thing—require plural verbs.

S Rule for Third-Person Agreements in the Present Tense

There is a simple way to remember how to make correct subject–verb agreement that applies to singular and plural subject nouns in the third person (subject nouns that can be replaced by *he*, *she*, *it*, *one*, or *they*). For the present tense, agreement with a singular subject noun in the third person is made by adding *s* to the verb:

> The author supports the subsidies.

If the plural subject noun is formed by adding *s* or *es* to the singular noun, no *s* is found at the end of the present-tense verb that agrees with it:

> The authors support the subsidies.

It stands to reason that only one element in the pair—either subject or verb—can end in *s*. If both end in *s* or neither ends in *s*, an error in agreement has been made.

NOTE: The above rule has two common exceptions: the verb *be* (*he/she/it/one is*; *they are*) and the verb *have* (*he/she/it/one has*; *they have*).

Finding the Simple Subject

Part of the challenge in making subjects and verbs agree is finding the simple subject. To do this, ignore intervening phrases that begin with prepositions (words such as *in*, *at*, *of*, and *on*), and make the verb agree with the subject word that comes immediately before the preposition.

> The **author** <u>of the report</u> **supports** subsidies. (singular subject/singular verb)
> The **author** <u>of the reports</u> **supports** subsidies. (singular subject/singular verb)
> The **authors** <u>of the report</u> **support** subsidies. (plural subject/plural verb)

Compound Subjects

Subjects joined by *and* take a plural verb.

> **The company and its subsidiary** manufacture appliances. (compound subject/plural verb)

Only subjects joined by *and* that name a single thing take a singular verb.

> **Red beans and rice** is his favourite dish. (singular subject/singular verb)

Joining Words Not Equivalent to *And*

The following joining words are not equivalent to *and*—they do not alter the number of the subjects that come before them:

accompanied by	except	together with
along with	in addition to	with
as well as	including	

To determine verb agreement, simply ignore the nouns that follow these joining words.

> The **director**, as well as the managers, **is** pleased with the sales figures.

Collective Nouns as Subjects

Collective nouns—common in business correspondence—name groups of things or people: for example, *team, committee, group, family, class, number, audience, jury, couple.* Collective nouns present a challenge to verb agreement because they can be either singular or plural subjects depending on the dynamics of the group. Collective nouns are treated as singular to convey the idea of the group acting together and as plural to convey the idea of members of the group acting individually. Most often, they are treated as singular.

> The **committee is** meeting on Wednesday.
> The **committee are** unhappy with each other's proposals.

To clarify the idea of individual action within the group, add a plural noun such as *members.*

> The **members** of the committee **are** unhappy with each other's proposals.

An exception to the rule: *the number . . .* requires a singular verb; *a number . . .* requires a plural verb.

> The **number** of applicants **is** down this year.
> A **number** of applicants **are** taking M.B.A. degrees.

Singular Subjects in Plural Form

Words such as *economics*, *ergonomics*, *human resources*, *measles*, *mumps*, and *news* are singular. Words such as *physics*, *mathematics*, *athletics*, and *statistics* are singular when they describe disciplines. When these words refer to multiple items, they are treated as plural nouns.

> **Statistics is** a required course for a degree in psychology.
> The new **statistics are** now available.

Amounts and Units of Measurement as Subjects

When the subject names an amount (e.g., of time, money, distance, or weight) thought of as a single unit, the subject takes a singular verb.

> **Thirty dollars** is the closing price for a share of Computex.
> **Two weeks** is too long to wait for the estimates.
> **A 5 per cent increase** in sales **is** expected.

When the subject names an amount thought of in terms of individual things or persons, the subject takes a plural verb.

> **One-third** of the new employees **have** requested parking spaces.
> **Eighty per cent** of the programmers **are** satisfied with the current system.

Titles, Terms, and Organization Names as Subjects

Use a singular verb with the name of an organization, with a work cited by its title, and with words that make up a single term, even if the name, title, or term includes a plural noun.

> **Edgeworth, Flett, & Thompson LLP** has represented us for five years.
> ***The Eight Practices*** is a book that explores the subject of human capital.

Sentences Beginning with *Here* or *There* + the Verb *Be*

When a sentence begins with *here* or *there* followed by a form of the verb *be*, the subject follows the verb:

> There **is a report** on that issue.
> There **are reports** on that issue.
> Here **are** the new sales **figures**.

Subjects and Linking Verbs

Linking verbs—the verb *be* and verbs of perception and sense such as *appear*, *feel*, *seem*, *taste*, or *smell*—join subjects to words that supply more information about them.

The verb always agrees with the subject that comes before it, not the descriptive words that follow it.

> His **concern is** low wages.

If this sentence is reversed, its subject is plural.

> Low **wages are** his concern.

Either . . . Or Sentences

When subjects follow pairs of conjunctions—*not only . . . but also, neither . . . nor, either . . . or*—the verb agrees with the subject closest to it.

> Neither the employees nor the **president wants** to lose customers.
> Neither the president nor the **employees want** to lose customers.

Indefinite Pronouns as Subjects

The following indefinite pronouns are singular and take singular verbs:

another	each	everyone	nothing
anybody	either	everything	somebody
anyone	every	neither	someone
anything	everybody	nobody	something

The following indefinite pronouns are always plural and take plural verbs:

both	few	many	several

The following indefinite pronouns can be singular or plural, depending on the context:

all	more	none
any	most	some

> **Some** competition **is** unavoidable.
> **Some** of our competitors **are** downsizing.

Antecedents of *That, Which,* and *Who* as Subjects

The verb agrees with the word to which *that, which,* or *who* refers.

> The **person** who **finishes** first wins.

Verb Agreement and the Phrases *One of the . . ., One of the . . . Who,* and *the Only One of the . . . Who*

Treat these constructions as follows:

- *one of the* + plural noun + singular verb

  One of the supervisors **is** touring the new facility.

- *one of the* + plural noun + *who* (*that, which*) + plural verb

  John is one of the IT **specialists who work** for our company.

- *the only one of the* + plural noun + *who* (*that, which*) + singular verb

  John is **the only one** of our IT specialists **who works** part-time.

Subject–Verb Agreement Exercise

Underline the correct verb agreement in each of the following sentences:

1. Pressure from investors (*is, are*) partly responsible for the plan to reduce annual costs.
2. Changes in this policy (*is, are*) not expected for at least another year.
3. More than 40 acquisitions in two years (*has, have*) made Briarcorp a market leader.
4. The president, as well as the CEO and CFO, (*anticipate, anticipates*) major changes in the year ahead.
5. Our current strategy of cutting staff in Western Canada and aggressively expanding in the East (*is, are*) controversial.
6. Copies of the manual (*is, are*) now available from accounting services.
7. Eighteen hundred dollars (*is, are*) a fair price for the latest Pentium 4 model.
8. Neither the biggest billboards nor the most eye-catching print campaign (*compensate, compensates*) for a flawed strategy that (*involve, involves*) withdrawing customer service.
9. Neither of the companies (*favour, favours*) a protracted series of layoffs.
10. We have canvassed several firms, but Thornton, Walters, & Estes (*is, are*) our first choice for legal services.
11. Anyone who (*requires, require*) clarification of the new health benefits package should contact human resources.
12. He is the only one of our sales representatives who (*has, have*) not completed the course.
13. Norstar is one of the companies that (*is, are*) cautious about overexpansion.
14. The number of customers satisfied with our services (*is, are*) up significantly this year.
15. Ninety per cent of our customers (*is, are*) satisfied with our services.

Verb Tense Accuracy

Tense refers to the time of a verb's action. Each tense—past, present, and future—has simple, progressive, perfect, and perfect-progressive forms. These convey a range of time relations, from the simple to the complex.

Tense	For Actions	Examples
Present (simple)	happening now, occurring habitually, or true anytime	I walk; she walks
Past (simple)	completed in the past	I walked; she walked
Future (simple)	that will occur	I will walk; she will walk
Present Progressive	already in progress, happening now, or still happening	I am walking; she is walking
Past Progressive	in progress at a specific point in the past or that lasted for a period in the past	I was walking; she was walking
Future Progressive	of duration in the future or occurring over a period at a specific point in the future	I will be walking; she will be walking
Present Perfect	begun in the past and continuing in the present or occurring sometime in the past	I have walked; she has walked
Past Perfect	completed before other actions in the past	I had walked; she had walked
Future Perfect	completed before other actions in the future	I will have walked; she will have walked
Present Perfect Progressive	in progress recently or of duration starting in the past and continuing in the present	I have been walking; she has been walking
Past Perfect Progressive	of duration completed before others in the past	I had been walking; she had been walking
Future Perfect Progressive	underway for a period of time before others in the future	I will have been walking; she will have been walking

Sequencing Past Tenses

When one past action occurred at the same time as another, use the simple past tense in both instances.

When our server **went** down, we **called** for support immediately.

Use the past perfect tense (*had* + past participle) to show that one past action preceded another.

He **had left** the office by the time we **returned** from our meeting.

Shifts in Verb Tense

Shifts in tense are necessary to indicate changes in time; however, inconsistent or unnecessary shifts in tense create confusing and illogical sentences.

✗   When he **applied** for a loan, we **check** his credit history. (past/present)
✔   When he **applied** for a loan, we **checked** his credit history. (past/past)

Other Verb Problems

Speculating about the Future, Making Recommendations, or Expressing Wishes

The subjunctive is one of three "moods" in English. Formed by combining the base form of the verb with the sentence's subject (*work* instead of *works*; *be* instead of *am/are*; *were* instead of *was*), it expresses conditions, requests, wishes, and speculation about future action that is improbable or unlikely. Once common but now mostly restricted in its use to formal English, it survives in certain well-known expressions: *so be it, as it were, far be it from me*. However ungrammatical the subjunctive sounds, use it in formal and mid-level writing in the following instances:

- when you use a clause beginning with *if, as if, as though,* or *unless* to express speculation rather than fact or to describe hypothetical situations that are improbable or unlikely:

  If I **were** you, I would ask for assistance. (situation purely hypothetical—"I" cannot be "you")

  If he **were** to work tonight, he would finish the report on time. (speculation)

- when you use a clause ending in *that* to express recommendations, wishes, or demands:

  It is important that a company representative **be** [*not* is] present to greet the dignitaries.

Speculating about the Past: Appropriate Use of *Could, Would*

In cause-and-effect sentences that speculate about the past, the conditional verbs *could* and *would* belong in the independent clause describing conditions other than they are, not in the dependent *if/unless* clause describing the hypothetical situation that allows for that outcome.

    ✗ If she **would have** telephoned me, **I would have** texted the information.
    ✔ If she **had** telephoned me, **I would have** texted the information.

Emphasizing a Main Verb with *Do*

The helping verb *do* adds positive emphasis to the main verb it precedes. To be effective, this construction should be used sparingly.

> Although there are no plans for expansion, the company **does** intend to modernize its current facilities.

Do can be used to ask questions, and it can be paired with *never* or *not* to express negative meanings.

> **Do** you have experience in risk management?
> John **does not** advocate the expensing of stock options.

Using Passive-Voice Constructions

The "voice" of a verb refers to whether the subject acts (active voice) or is acted upon (passive voice). The passive voice inverts standard **subject + verb + object** word order so that the standard object (the "thing" that receives the action) becomes the subject of the passive verb.

- **active voice:** The financial officer approved the budget.
- **passive voice:** The budget was approved by the financial officer.
- **passive voice:** The budget was approved. (The prepositional phrase containing the original active-voice subject is often omitted.)

The passive voice is formed in this way:

> a form of the verb **be** (am, is, are, was, were, be, being, been) + past participle
> (for regular verbs, the base form of the verb + ed) + (by the agent of the action)

In business writing, the active voice is preferred and should be used whenever possible. There are circumstances, however, in which the passive voice is rhetorically useful.
    Here are some criteria for choosing between the active and passive voice:

- **Conciseness:** The active voice is more vigorous, concise, and direct than the passive voice. It is also less awkward and complicated. The higher word count of the passive construction can, with overuse, make writing sound weak and lacklustre. ACTIVE: *On Tuesday, Jinlu submitted his article to the managing editor.* PASSIVE: *On Tuesday, Jinlu's article was submitted to the managing editor.*
- **Emphasis and disclosure:** The first element in a sentence has the most emphasis. The active voice emphasizes the actor; the passive voice minimizes or conceals the actor and emphasizes the recipient of the action or the fact of the action itself. ACTIVE: *Fiona did not complete the report on time.* PASSIVE: *The report*

was not completed on time. Readers sometimes interpret this use of the passive voice as a sign of evasion or refusal to admit responsibility, so exercise caution in eliminating the final prepositional phrase. The passive voice is appropriate when the question of who performed an action is unimportant or irrelevant: *Bids will be accepted until the end of the week.*

- **Tact and diplomacy:** The active voice is direct, often to the point of bluntness, playing up the personalities that figure in a refusal or denial. The passive voice minimizes the unpleasantness of negative messages by allowing for simple statements of fact, seemingly free of personal malice. ACTIVE: *We cannot activate your account at the present time.* PASSIVE: *Your account cannot be activated at the present time.*
- **Personal/Impersonal style:** The passive voice minimizes or eliminates personal pronouns in instances where overuse conveys the impression of egotism or perceived personal conflict. ACTIVE: *I created this program to reduce cost over-runs.* PASSIVE: *This program was created to reduce cost overruns.* Impersonal passive constructions—beginning with *it is*—may sound antiseptically official and bureaucratic: *It is felt that changes must be made.*

Use the active voice when you need to do the following:

- write concisely
- reveal the doer of an action
- deliver positive or neutral news

Use the passive voice when you need to do the following:

- emphasize an action, not who was responsible for it
- de-emphasize or soften bad news
- take personalities (and their pronouns) out of the picture

Avoiding Logically Mismatched Subjects and Verbs (Faulty Predication)

Subjects and their verbs (predicates) should agree in number and also make sense together.

- ✗ The purpose of the study assesses customer service preferences.
- ✔ The study assesses customer service preferences.
- ✔ The purpose of the study is to assess customer service preferences.

The first sentence is incorrect because a *purpose* cannot *assess*. Two other constructions make for similarly awkward sentences:

- is when, is where

    ✗ A recession is when the economy experiences a temporary downturn.
    ✔ A recession is a temporary economic downturn.

- the reason . . . is because

✗ The reason that we hired her is because she is creative.
✔ The reason we hired her is that she is creative.
✔ We hired her because she is creative.

Use either *the reason* or *because*, but not both, as this amounts to saying the same thing twice.

Using Parallel Phrasing for Items in a Series (Parallelism)

Use parallel grammatical forms to express two or more similar ideas or items in a series. Create balanced sentences by matching single words with single words (nouns with nouns, verbs with verbs), phrases with phrases, and clauses with clauses. Parallel phrasing—like other forms of consistency—improves readability and serves as an aid to memory.

✗ We held a meeting, discussed the matter, and a strategy was devised.
✔ We held a meeting, discussed the matter, and devised a strategy.

Add words necessary for logic and completeness. In the case of the first sentence below, *has . . . pursue* does not correctly form the past tense:

✗ The company has and will continue to pursue aggressive growth targets.
✔ The company has **pursued** and will continue to pursue aggressive growth targets.
✗ Alban has interned and worked for Apex Communications.
✔ Alban has interned **with** and worked for Apex Communications.

Balanced constructions can also be created using correlative conjunctions: *either . . . or, neither . . . nor, both . . . and, not only . . . but also.* Equivalent grammatical elements must be used after each part of the correlative conjunction.

✗ She is not only developing a marketing program but the campaign will also be overseen by her.
✔ She is not only developing a marketing program but also overseeing the campaign.

Parallelism Exercise

Correct faulty parallel structure in the following sentences:

1. Respondents were asked to not only rank the importance of the recycling materials collected but also their preferences in the placement of recycling bins.
2. Neither the chair of the committee wants to seek bankruptcy protection nor its members.
3. Our intention is to develop a work plan, hire suitable people to staff the operation, and working out a schedule.

4. The team was asked to investigate where the raw materials might be available, what the price per unit tonne is, and what the cost to transport raw materials might be.
5. The task force on workforce diversity is committed to promoting an awareness and respect for cultural differences.

Making Comparisons Clear and Logical (Sentences with *Than* or *As*)

Make sure sentences of comparison deliver the meaning you intend. Include all words required to clarify the relationship between the items being compared. Check the correctness of pronouns by mentally filling in implied words and phrases.

> ✗ Recent hires know more about instant messaging than their managers. (This sentence incorrectly compares instant messaging and managers.)
> ✔ Recent hires know more about instant messaging than their managers do. (This sentence compares recent hires' knowledge with managers' knowledge.)
> ✔ Recent hires know more than their managers about instant messaging.

Changing a pronoun can alter the meaning of a comparison sentence:

> Scott likes instant messaging as much as me. (Scott likes instant messaging as much as he likes me.)
> Scott likes instant messaging as much as I. (Scott likes instant messaging as much as I like instant messaging.)

Using Pronouns with Precision

Pronouns should be of the same case—functioning as subjects or objects—and agree in number and gender with the nouns they replace.

- Pronouns that replace subject words: *I, you, he, she, it, one, we, they, who*
- Pronouns that replace object words: *me, you, him, her, us, them, whom*
- Pronouns that indicate possession: *mine, yours, his, hers, ours, theirs, its*
- Pronouns that indicate reflexive action: *myself, yourself, himself, herself, itself, ourselves, yourselves, themselves*
- Demonstrative pronouns: *this, that, these, those*

Avoiding Vague References

Make sure pronouns refer clearly to preceding nouns. Unless a pronoun clearly renames a known antecedent, replace the pronoun with an appropriate noun. Indicate precisely who is responsible for the action of the sentence.

> ✗ On Bay Street, **they** make millions of dollars every week.
> ✔ On Bay Street, **stockbrokers** make millions of dollars every week.

- ✔ **Bay Street brokers** make millions of dollars every week.
- ✗ **They** say the economy is recovering.
- ✔ **Financial analysts** say the economy is recovering.

This, *that*, and *it* must refer clearly to a readily apparent noun or phrase:

- ✔ Management disagreed with workers over benefits, but **it** was never resolved.
- ✔ Management disagreed with workers over benefits, but **the dispute** was never resolved.

Knowing When to Use *I* Versus *Me*

Knowing that it is incorrect to use *me* as part of a subject (e.g., *Tom and me prepared the index*), many writers incorrectly replace *me* with *I* even when the pronoun is the object of the sentence (i.e., when it indicates the receiver of the action). When two or more people are being referred to, determine what pronoun case to use by temporarily removing the other name with which the pronoun is paired:

- ✗ The new clients met with Peter and I.
- ✔ The new clients met with Peter and me.

Me is used after prepositions such as *between*, *after*, and *except*.

> Except for Lydia and me, everyone in the office has accountancy training.
> Just between you and me, the best time to invest is right now.

Pronoun Exercise

Correct errors in pronoun usage in the following sentences:

1. Between you and I, I think the accounts manager has some explaining to do.
2. The change to two-factor authentication was suggested by Giorgio and I.
3. In China, they have a booming economy.
4. Milos and myself were responsible for organizing the team-building retreat.
5. The advantages of launching a clicks-and-mortar operation can outweigh its disadvantages, which requires further consideration.

Correcting Modifier Mishaps

Modifiers—consisting of single words or entire phrases—refine the meaning of other words in a sentence: adjectives modify nouns; adverbs modify verbs, adjectives, and other adverbs. The key to using modifiers effectively is to make sure they relate clearly to the word or words they modify. Sentences with modifier problems are at best ambiguous and at worst unintentionally funny.

Reining in Misplaced Modifiers

The key to using modifiers without confusion is to keep the modifier as close as possible to the word or words it describes. If in doubt about where the modifier belongs, ask yourself, "What goes with what?"

> ✗ She sent a report to the department that was inaccurate. (The modifier seems to belong with *department*, not *report*.)
> ✔ She sent a report **that was inaccurate** to the department.
> ✔ She sent an **inaccurate** report to the department.

Placement of single-word modifiers such as *only*, *even*, and *hardly* can greatly alter the meaning of a sentence. Always position them next to the word(s) they modify.

> **Only** John asked for a 2 per cent salary increase. (no one else asked)
> John asked **only** for a 2 per cent salary increase. (he asked for nothing else)
> John asked for **only** a 2 per cent salary increase. (the salary increase was minimal)

When a modifier—especially a modifying phrase—seems to belong with the phrases that come both before and after it, reposition the modifier so it refers to only one phrase.

> ✗ He told her **on Friday** she would receive PowerPoint training.
> ✔ **On Friday**, he told her she would receive PowerPoint training.
> ✔ He told her she would receive PowerPoint training **on Friday**.

Correcting Dangling Modifiers

Modifiers are said to dangle when they fail to refer to or make sense with another word. Usually dangling modifiers are phrases that contain a present participle (ending in *ing*), a past participle (often ending in *ed*), or an infinitive (*to* + base form of verb) but no subject. The easiest way to correct a dangling modifier is to identify *who* or *what* performs the action of the initial participle or infinitive phrase immediately after the phrase itself. Stating the intended subject clearly saves the reader the trouble of guessing the missing word.

> ✗ Specializing in finance and international business, his credentials are impeccable.
> ✔ Specializing in finance and international business, he has impeccable credentials.

An equally workable means of correction is to change the modifying phrase into a dependent clause by (1) adding a subordinating conjunction, (2) adding a subject, and (3) making the verb complete.

> ✗ Reviewing the agenda, several errors came to her attention.
> ✔ While she was reviewing the agenda, several errors came to her attention.

Dangling modifiers also sometimes result from unnecessary use of the passive voice. To fix such problems, use the active voice in the clause following the modifier.

✗ To qualify for a refund, a sales receipt must be presented.
✔ To qualify for a refund, you must present a sales receipt.
✔ To qualify for a refund, please present a sales receipt.

Modifier Exercise

Correct misplaced and dangling modifiers in the following sentences:

1. To ensure the safe operation of your vehicles, regular inspections by authorized mechanics are recommended.
2. After establishing specifications, the alternatives were weighed by the report committee.
3. To work in quiet and comfortable surroundings, the boardroom is the best place to go.
4. Committed to establishing a career, Anna almost applied for every job that was posted on monster.ca.
5. Our company was fortunate to find new headquarters in the city with two parking lots.
6. Our manager informed us in July no one will go on vacation.
7. We ordered a printer for our office that was unreliable.

Punctuation

Commas

Use a comma

• after a dependent clause that begins a sentence:

Although his business failed, he learned a lot.

• before a dependent clause added to the end of a sentence as an afterthought:

We should meet next Thursday at 1:00 p.m., if you can spare the time.

• between coordinate modifiers that apply equally to the same word:

Ariel submitted a **timely**, **thorough** report.

• before and after parenthetical expressions, non-essential phrases, appositives, and interjections:

The proposal, which took more than three months to develop, was enthusiastically received

- between items in a series of three or more (the final comma before and is optional):

  St. John's, Halifax(,) and Moncton are key markets for our products.

- between two independent clauses joined by and, each with its own subject:

  The **impact** of reduced health-care benefits on employee morale is considerable, and **we** will need to discuss the long-term consequences of this policy change at our next meeting.

Don't use a comma

- between an initial independent clause and a subsequent dependent clause:

  He learned a lot although his business failed.

- between modifiers that don't apply equally to the same noun:

  A **delicious Italian** meal was enjoyed by the conference participants.

- before and after relative clauses beginning with *that* or *who*:

  The report that addressed the failure of the initiative did not assign blame for deficiencies.

- singly between a subject and its verb:

  The lecture will be held tomorrow.

- before and in a compound predicate (i.e., when a single subject belongs to two different verbs in the same sentence):

  Rinaldo took responsibility for the decline in sales and proposed a new marketing strategy.

Semicolons

A semicolon consists of a period sitting atop a comma. Not surprisingly, it performs many of the same functions as the period and the comma. Like a period, a semicolon can be used to join independent clauses, especially when the clauses are closely related or when a conjunctive adverb (a word such as *nevertheless*, *however*, *moreover*, or *furthermore*) links the clauses.

New ethics policies were adopted last year; they have been an unqualified success in helping our company promote values of honesty and transparency.

The shipment of computers arrived today; however, it will be several days before the computer system is operational.

Like a comma, a semicolon can be used to separate items in a series. It is especially useful for separating items in cases where one or more of those items contain internal commas.

Our company plans to establish operations in the following centres: Vancouver, the largest market for our sporting goods line; Calgary, the fastest growing market for our products; and Saskatoon, an emergent and underserved market.

A semicolon shouldn't be used to separate dependent and independent clauses or to introduce a list.

Colons

A colon is a punctuation mark that is primarily used to set off something to follow. Use it after an independent clause (i.e., a clause that can stand alone as a complete sentence) that introduces a list or a long quotation.

Our director of human resources is responsible for overseeing the following areas:
- recruitment and hiring
- employee benefits
- payroll

If an introductory statement does not form a complete sentence, use no punctuation between the incomplete introductory statement and the text that follows.

When proofreading a document
- allow for a "cooling period" before you begin to read,
- allow sufficient time to read slowly and carefully, and
- make several passes over the document.

Colons are also used after salutations (*Dear Mr. Evans:*) and memo guide words (*To:*) and between titles and subtitles (*Technical Writing A–Z: A Common Sense Guide to Engineering Reports and Theses*).

Apostrophes

Apostrophes are used for two principal reasons: (1) to show possession or ownership and (2) to signal omissions (in contractions—*can't, it's, isn't, won't, they'll*). Adding an apostrophe in combination with *s* to the end of most singular nouns communicates possession.

Joanne attended the manager's meeting. (a meeting led or convened by one manager)

The business's customer complaints line was deluged with calls. (*business* is a singular noun)

Marcia is a friend of John's. (in other words, *Marcia is a friend of his*)

Likewise, when a noun is plural and does not end in an *s* or an *s* sound, add *'s* to make it plural.

> The CEO announced the new line of children's toys. (*children* is a plural noun not ending in an *s* or an *s* sound)

When a plural noun ends in an *s* or an *s* sound, add only an apostrophe.

> Joanne attended the managers' meeting. (the meeting of two or more managers)
> Two months' leave of absence seems generous. (*months* is a plural noun)

Add *'s* to each noun of two or more nouns when possession is individual.

> Paul's and Suleman's businesses have grown substantially. (Paul and Suleman each own a business; they do not own the businesses jointly.)

Add *'s* to the last noun when possession is joint or collective.

> Irene and Madeline's business has been nominated for a prestigious award. (Irene and Madeline own a business together.)

Periods

Periods are used at the end of statements, mild commands, polite requests, and indirect questions.

> The restructuring of our central division led to a year of unprecedented gains. (statement)
> Return your completed application form to me by June 1. (mild command)
> Will you please send me a copy of your mission statement. (polite request)
> I asked if they wanted to upgrade their filing systems. (indirect question)

Question Marks

Question marks are used at the end of direct questions or after a question added to the end of a sentence.

> Have you considered telecommuting as a solution to your work-scheduling problems?
> The downturn in the real estate market should help our business, shouldn't it?

Parentheses

Parentheses interrupt the sentence structure, allowing you to add non-essential information or to gently introduce, almost in a whisper, an explanation, definition, reference, or question. Whatever is enclosed within parentheses tends to be de-emphasized, very much the opposite of dashes, which call attention to the set-off text. Two general rules apply: (1) never put a comma before an opening parenthesis and (2) if a complete sentence in parentheses is part of another sentence, do not add a period to the sentence within parentheses. If it is required, you may add a question mark or an exclamation mark at the end of a complete sentence in parentheses that is part of another sentence; however, this practice is rare in business writing.

> The company blamed a high incidence of flaming (the exchange of hostile on-line messages) for the deterioration of employee morale.
>
> His impressive results on the CA exam (he had taken a leave of absence in order to devote himself to his studies) earned him accolades from his departmental manager.

Dashes

Dashes are high-impact punctuation—emphasizing the text they set off—but their impact is at its greatest only when they are used sparingly. Use dashes (1) to set off a list from an introductory statement or (2) to emphasize information that interrupts a sentence. A general rule applies: don't use semicolons, commas, or periods next to dashes.

> His latest sales trip took him to the key markets in the Pacific Rim—Tokyo, Seoul, and Taipei.
>
> The practice of shouting—typing messages in all caps—offends many readers.

Quotation Marks

Quotation marks are used primarily to enclose words copied exactly from a print source or transcribed from overheard speech or conversation. They are also used to enclose the titles of chapters or articles and to give special treatment to words or letters. Single quotation marks ('/') enclose quotations that fall within double quotation marks. When inserting a sentence's punctuation adjacent to quotation marks, place commas and periods inside the closing quotation marks, and place colons and semicolons outside the closing quotation marks. Place question marks and exclamation marks outside the closing quotation marks unless they belong with the words enclosed in quotation marks.

> "The advantage of online retail," the president said, "is the reduction of storefront expenses."
>
> The term "authentication" has an ever-evolving definition given the development of new systems and technologies. (Note that some writers prefer to use italics rather than quotation marks to draw attention to words used as words.)
>
> The article entitled "Building a Team" was among the best offerings in the most recent issue of *Business Monthly*.

Punctuation Exercise

Add correct and appropriate punctuation to the following sentences:

1. Will you please send me a travel expenses claim form
2. The introduction of a fast efficient system of online human resources management is a major advance for our company, isnt it

3. The following individuals have been selected for the conference panel to be held in a months time Preetasha Lai Hector Gonzalez and Vicki Nguyen

4. The departments leading sales reps are all friends of Johns

5. The secret to his success he shared it with us over dinner last night is his commitment to networking

6. Although the project ran over budget it was considered a creative breakthrough for the marketing team

7. Have you heard of the famous Italian design house Prada

8. The way forward the consultant said is to maximize resources without straining them

Internet Resources: Grammar, Style, Punctuation, and ESL

- **GrammarBook.com (The Blue Book of Grammar and Punctuation):** This site provides guidance on grammar, punctuation, capitalization, and the treatment of numbers as well as a number of free quizzes with answers.

  www.grammarbook.com

- **Guide to Grammar and Writing:** This interactive site features grammar lessons with exercises that can be submitted for online correction.

  http://grammar.ccc.commnet.edu/grammar

- **Purdue Online Writing Lab (OWL):** This comprehensive site covers grammar, style, mechanics, punctuation, and ESL-related grammar topics.

  http://owl.english.purdue.edu

- **Grammar Girl:** Grammar Girl Mignon Fogarty provides accessible discussions on a wide variety of topics related to grammar, style, and punctuation. Her podcasts can be downloaded for free on most podcast apps.

  www.quickanddirtytips.com/grammar-girl

Notes

Chapter 1

1. LaRose, B. (2019, June 18). Personal interview.
2. Canham, A., & Olvet, T. (2018, September 16). Why business leaders must cultivate digital change agents. *The Globe and Mail*. https://www.theglobeandmail.com/business/commentary/article-why-business-leaders-must-cultivate-digital-change-agents/
3. Ibid.
4. Conference Board of Canada. (2015, September). *Innovation*. Retrieved from http://www.conferenceboard.ca/hcp/provincial/innovation.aspx
5. Microsoft Canada. (2018, January 18). *Canadian business leaders must enable a culture of creativity and collaboration to survive in the new world of work*. Cision. https://www.newswire.ca/news-releases/canadian-business-leaders-must-enable-a-culture-of-creativity-and-collaboration-to-survive-in-the-new-world-of-work-669900183.html
6. Business Council of Canada. (2018). *Navigating change: 2018 Business Council skills survey*. https://thebusinesscouncil.ca/wp-content/uploads/2018/04/Navigating-Change-2018-Skills-Survey-1.pdf
7. Business Council of Canada. (2016). *Developing Canada's future workforce: A survey of large private-sector employers*. thebusinesscouncil.ca/wp-content/uploads/2016/02/Developing-Canadas-Workforce-March.pdf
8. Deveau, D. (2012, February 13). What companies must do to prepare for the future economy. *Financial Post*. http://business.financialpost.com/2013/02/12/what-companies-must-do-to-prepare-for-the-future-economy/?__lsa=6a50-01aa
9. Wits Language School. (2017, August 17). *Effective communication means business success*. Entrepreneur. https://www.entrepreneur.com/article/330960
10. Towers Watson. (2014). *2013-2014 Change and Communication ROI Report*. https://magneto.net.au/wp/wp-content/uploads/2018/07/2013-2014-change-and-communication-roi-study-towers-watson.pdf
11. The Conference Board of Canada. (n.d.). *Employability skills 2000+*. https://www.conferenceboard.ca/docs/default-source/educ-public/esp2000.pdf?sfvrsn=0
12. Florida, R. (2012, June 27). *Creativity is the new economy*. The Huffington Post. http://www.huffingtonpost.com/richard-florida/creativity-is-the-new-eco_b_1608363.html
13. Martin, R., & Florida, R. (2015, October 7). *Canada's urban competitiveness agenda: Completing the transition from a resource to knowledge economy*. Martin Prosperity Institute. http://martinprosperity.org/content/canadas-urban-competitiveness-agenda/
14. Adekunbi, A. (2019, May 7). *Five ways big data can help your business succeed*. Entrepreneur. https://www.entrepreneur.com/article/333387; Davenport, T., & Bean, R. (2018, February 15). *Big companies are embracing data analytics, but most still don't have a data-driven culture*. Harvard Business Review. https://hbr.org/2018/02/big-companies-are-embracing-analytics-but-most-still-dont-have-a-data-driven-culture
15. IBM Think Big Blog. (2019, June 6). *Toronto Raptors use data-driven command center on path to the NBA finals*. https://www.ibm.com/blogs/think/2019/06/toronto-raptors-use-data-driven-command-center-on-path-to-nba-finals/
16. Dey, L. et al. (2011). *Acquiring competitive intelligence from social media*. Proceedings of the 2011 Joint Workshop on Multilingual OCR and Analytics for Noisy Unstructured Text Data. doi:10.1145/2034617.2034621
17. Beck, U. (1992). *Risk society: Towards a new modernity*. Sage; Giddens, A. (1991). *Modernity and self-identity: Self and society in the late modern age*. Stanford University Press.
18. World Health Organization. (2013). *Risk communication*. http://www.who.int/foodsafety/risk-analysis/riskcommunication/en/
19. Coco, K. (2012, October 25). UN Global Compact: Keynote address to the Association for Business Communication 77th Annual International Convention. Honolulu, HI.
20. Ibid.
21. United Nations Global Compact. (n.d.). *The ten principles of the UN Global Compact*. https://www.unglobalcompact.org/what-is-gc/mission/principles
22. Certified General Accountants Association of Canada. (2011, December). *Regulating sustainability reporting—Is a mandatory approach better than a voluntary one?* http://www.cga-canada.org/en-ca/ResearchReports/ca_rep_2011-12_informed-view.pdf
23. Centre for Sustainability and Excellence. (2017). *Sustainability reporting trends in North America*. https://www.partnersinprojectgreen.com/wp-content/uploads/2017/11/Sustainability-Reporting-Trends-in-North-America-_RS-FINAL-8-22-17Low-res.compressed.pdf
24. Bombardier. (2016). *Planes. Trains. Worldwide*. http://www.bombardier.ca/en/corporate/about-us/worldwide-presence?docID=0901260d8000ede1
25. RBC Financial Group. (2005, October 20). *The diversity advantage: A case for Canada's 21st-century economy*. Presented at the 10th International Metropolis Conference, Toronto, ON. http://www.rbc.com/diversity/pdf/diversityAdvantage.pdf
26. Dimock, M. (2019, January 17). *Defining generations: Where millennials end and Generation Z begins*. Pew Research Center Factank. https://www.pewresearch.org/fact-tank/2019/01/17/where-millennials-end-and-generation-z-begins/
27. Conference Board of Canada. (2013, May). *Helping millennials help you: Managing your young workforce*. https://www.conference-board.org/publications/publicationdetail.cfm?publicationid=2502
28. Conference Board of Canada. (2015). RBC is building workplace-ready skills in millennials. http://www.conferenceboard.ca/e-library/abstract.aspx?did=7021
29. Conference Board of Canada. (2014, September 29). *Canadian organizations need to separate fact from stereotypes to capitalize on future workforce*. http://www.conferenceboard.ca/press/newsrelease/14-09-09/canadian_organizations_need_to_separate_facts_from_stereotypes_to_capitalize_on_future_workforce.aspx; Conference Board of Canada. (2013, May). *Helping millennials help you: Managing your young workforce*. https://www.conference-board.org/publications/publicationdetail.cfm?publicationid=2502; Deloitte. (2019). The Deloitte global millennial survey: Societal discord and technological transformation create a "generation disrupted." https://www2.deloitte.com/content/dam/Deloitte/global/Documents/About-Deloitte/deloitte-2019-millennial-survey.pdf
30. Pew Research Center. (2007, January 9). *A portrait of "Generation Next": How young people view their lives, futures, and politics*. http://www.people-press.org/2007/01/09/a-portrait-of-generation-next/

31. Myers, K., & Sadaghiani, K. (2010). Millennials in the workplace: A communication perspective on millennials' organizational relationships and performance. *Journal of Business and Psychology, 25*(2), 225–238.

32. Deloitte. (2019). *The Deloitte global millennial survey: Societal discord and technological transformation create a "generation disrupted."* https://www2.deloitte.com/content/dam/Deloitte/global/Documents/About-Deloitte/deloitte-2019-millennial-survey.pdf

33. Pew Research Center. (2010, February 24). *Millennials: Confident. Connected. Open to change.* http://www.pewsocialtrend.org/2010/02/24/millennials-confident-connected-open-to-change/

34. Microsoft Canada. (2018, January 18). *Canadian business leaders must enable a culture of creativity and collaboration to survive in the new world of work.* Cision. https://www.newswire.ca/news-releases/canadian-business-leaders-must-enable-a-culture-of-creativity-and-collaboration-to-survive-in-the-new-world-of-work-669900183.html

35. Christensen, C. (2016). *Disruptive innovation.* http://www.claytonchristensen.com/key-concepts/

36. Marr, B. (2018, September 2). What is Industry 4.0? *Forbes.* https://www.forbes.com/sites/bernardmarr/2018/09/02/what-is-industry-4-0-heres-a-super-easy-explanation-for-anyone/#5ab2a5369788

37. Rossow, A. (2018, April 11). Bringing blockchain into Industry 4.0. *Forbes.* https://www.forbes.com/sites/andrewrossow/2018/04/11/bringing-blockchain-into-industry-4-0/#612115a46dc7

38. Baron, N. S. (2008). *Always on: Language in an online and mobile world.* Oxford University Press.

39. Friedman, T. L. (2006). *The world is flat: A brief history of the twenty-first century.* Farrar, Straus, and Giroux, p. 235.

40. Facebook. (2016). Our mission. https://newsroom.fb.com/company-info/

41. Goodwin, B. (2011, July 25). Businesses should prepare for Web 3.0, says Booz&Co. *Computer Weekly.com.* http://www.computerweekly.com/news/2240105143/Businesses-should-prepare-for-Web-30-says-BoozCo

42. Machina Research. (2016, August 3). *Press release: Global Internet of Things market to grow to 27 billion devices, generating USD3 trillion revenue in 2025.* https://machinaresearch.com/news/press-release-global-internet-of-things-market-to-grow-to-27-billion-devices-generating-usd3-trillion-revenue-in-2025/

43. Goodwin, B.

44. CPA. (2019). *Mobile Apps: Risks and Benefits for Business.* https://www.cpacanada.ca/en/business-and-accounting-resources/other-general-business-topics/information-management-and-technology/publications/mobile-apps-for-business

45. Ibid.

46. Carr, N. (2008, July–August). Is Google making us stupid? *The Atlantic.* http://www.theatlantic.com/magazine/archive/2008/07/is-google-making-us-stupid/306868/

47. Stone, L. (n.d.). *Continuous partial attention.* https://lindastone.net/qa/continuous-partial-attention

48. Davenport, T. J., & Beck, J. C. (2001). *The attention economy.* Harvard Business School Press.

49. Chamorro-Premuzic, T. (2014, December 15). The distraction economy: How technology downgraded attention. *The Guardian.* http://www.theguardian.com/media-network/media-network-blog/2014/dec/15/distraction-economy-downgraded-attention-facebook-tinder

50. Hougaard, R., & Carter, J. (2015, November 3). *How to thrive in the attention economy.* http://greatergood.berkeley.edu/article/item/how_to_thrive_in_the_attention_economy

51. Collaborative Consumption. (n.d.). *About.* http://www.collaborativeconsumption.com/about/

52. Ibid.

53. Geron, T. (2013, February 11). Airbnb and the unstoppable rise of the share economy. *Forbes.* http://www.forbes.com/sites/tomiogeron/2013/01/23/airbnb-and-the-unstoppable-rise-of-the-share-economy/#63a7a7356790

54. Heaps, T. (2019). Indigenous business: Canadian economy cannot succeed if the Indigenous economy fails. *Corporate Knights, 18*(2), 29; Vasil, A. (2019). Indigenous powerbroker: Meet the man brokering a path to economic reconciliation. *Corporate Knights, 18*(2), 31.

55. Hilton, C. (2019). Indigenomics in action. *Corporate Knights, 18*(2), 36.

56. Social Sciences and Humanities Research Council. (July 2018). *Toward a successful shared future for Canada.* http://www.sshrc-crsh.gc.ca/society-societe/community-communite/ifca-iac/03-aboriginal_peoples_in_Canada_report-les_peuples_autochtones_en_Canada_rapport-eng.aspx

57. Manitobah Mulkuks. (2019). https://www.manitobah.ca/

58. Bailey, A. (2018, March 8). $1.35 million marina in the works for Toquaht First Nation's secret beach near Ucluelet. *Tofino-Ucluelet Westerly News.* https://www.westerlynews.ca/business/1-35-million-marina-in-the-works-for-toquaht-first-nations-secret-beach-near-ucluelet/

59. Monkman, L. (2019, June 20). *Manitoba's new 'utility scale' solar farm aims to spark First Nations interest in clean energy.* CBC News. https://www.cbc.ca/news/indigenous/fisher-river-cree-nation-solar-power-1.5180646

60. Nk'Mip Cellars. (2019). *About Us.* http://www.nkmipcellars.com/About-Us

61. The Canadian Association of University Teachers. (2019). *Guide to acknowledging First Peoples and Traditional Territory.* https://www.caut.ca/content/guide-acknowledging-first-peoples-traditional-territory

62. Manuel, T. (2019, February 4). *Cultural teachings: Welcome to territory and land acknowledgements.* Reconciliation Canada. https://reconciliationcanada.ca/cultural-teachings-welcome-to-territory-land-acknowledgments/

63. Marche, S. (2017, September 7). Canada's impossible acknowledgement. *The New Yorker.* https://www.newyorker.com/culture/culture-desk/canadas-impossible-acknowledgment; Jones, A. (2019). *Territory Acknowledgment.* Native Land. https://native-land.ca/territory-acknowledgement/

64. Tennant, Z. (2019, January 20). What to learn whose Indigenous land you're on? There's an app for that. *Unreserved*, CBC Radio. https://www.cbc.ca/radio/unreserved/redrawing-the-lines-1.4973363/want-to-learn-whose-indigenous-land-you-re-on-there-s-an-app-for-that-1.4973367

65. Perara, A. I. (September 1, 2017). *Activism skills: Land and territory acknowledgement. Activism Guide.* Amnesty International. https://www.amnesty.ca/blog/activism-skills-land-and-territory-acknowledgement

66. King, H. (2019, January 20). 'I regret it': Hayden King on writing Ryerson University's territorial acknowledgement. *Unreserved*, CBC Radio. https://www.cbc.ca/radio/unreserved/redrawing-the-lines-1.4973363/i-regret-it-hayden-king-on-writing-ryerson-university-s-territorial-acknowledgement-1.4973371

67. City of Ottawa. (2019). *City of Ottawa Reconciliation Action Plan.* https://ottawa.ca/en/city-hall/your-city-government/city-ottawa-reconciliation-action-plan

68. Indigenous Corporate Training Inc. (2015, November 4). *Honouring First Nation reconciliation: An effective example.* https://www.ictinc.ca/blog/honouring-first-nation-reconciliation-an-effective-example

69. Evetts, J. (2012). Professionalism: Value and ideology. *Sociopedia.isa.* Retrieved from http://www.sagepub.net/isa/resources/pdf/Professionalism.pdf

70. Fournier, V. (1999). The appeal to "professionalism" as a disciplinary mechanism. *Social Review, 47*(2), 280–307.

71. Evetts.

72. Delattre, M., & Ocler, R. (2013). Professionalism and organization: Polysemy of concepts and narratives of actors. *Society and Business Review, 8*(1), 18–31.

73. Evetts.

74. Fournier.

75. Chartered Professional Accountants of Canada. (2016). *Building the CPA brand*. https://www.cpacanada.ca/en/the-cpa-profession/building-the-cpa-brand

76. Evetts.

77. Freidson, E. (1994). *Professionalism reborn: Theory, prophecy and policy*. Polity Press.

78. Goffee, R., & Jones, G. (2015, November 12). Authentic workplaces don't try to make everyone the same. *Harvard Business Review*. https://hbr.org/2015/11/authentic-workplaces-dont-try-to-make-everyone-the-same

79. Kahn, W. (1990). Psychological conditions of personal engagement and disengagement at work. *Academy of Management Journal, 33*(4), 692–724.

80. Sorenson, S. (2013, June 20). *How Employee Engagement Drives Growth*. Gallup. https://www.gallup.com/workplace/236927/employee-engagement-drives-growth.aspx

81. HR Reporter. (2018, March 15). *Falling employee engagement 'wake-up call' for employers: Survey*. https://www.hrreporter.com/culture-and-engagement/36248-falling-employee-engagement-wake-up-call-for-employers-survey/

82. Jermyn, D. (Dec. 3, 2018). Canada's top employers continue to raise bar on workplace innovation. *The Globe and Mail*. https://www.theglobeandmail.com/business/careers/top-employers/article-canadas-top-employers-continue-to-raise-the-bar-on-workplace/

83. APTN. (2017). *Communiqué 2017*. https://aptn.ca/pdf/en/APTNCommunique%202017_EN.PDF

84. Pagliaro, J. (2017, September 25). Integrity commissioner censures Rob Ford over knocking down councillor. *The Toronto Star*. https://www.thestar.com/news/city_hall/2015/09/25/rob-ford-broke-council-rules-when-he-knocked-over-counciller-report-says.html

85. Delattre & Ocler.

86. Somech, A., Desivilya, & Lidogoster, H. (2009). Team conflict management and team effectiveness. *Journal of Organizational Behavior, 30*, 359–378.

87. Cohen, S. G., & Bailey, D. E. (1997). What makes teams work: Group effectiveness research from the shop floor to the executive suite. *Journal of Management, 23*(3), 239–290; Tasa, K., Taggar, S., & Seijts, G. H. (2007). The development of collective efficacy in teams: A multilevel and longitudinal perspective. *Journal of Applied Psychology, 92*, 17–27.

88. Jung, D., & Avolio, B. (2000). Opening the black box: An experimental investigation of mediating effects of trust and value congruence on transformational and transactional leadership. *Journal of Organizational Behavior, 21*(8), 949–964.

89. Lorinc, J. (2016, February 29). How Canadian Tire is pioneering tomorrow's retail experience now. *Canadian Business*. http://www.canadianbusiness.com/lists-and-rankings/most-innovative-companies/canadian-tire/

90. Hoegl, M., & Gemuenden, H. G. (2001). Teamwork quality and the success of innovative projects: A theoretical concept and empirical evidence. *Organization Science, 12*(4), 435–440.

91. Chou, H.-W., Lin, Y.-H., & Chuang, W.-W. (2013). Transformational leadership and team performance: The mediating roles of cognitive trust and collective efficacy. *Sage Open, 3*(3). doi: 10.1177/2158244013497027

92. Somech, Desivilya, & Lidogoster.

93. Ibid.

94. Ibid.

95. Tjosvold, D. (1997). Conflict within interdependence: Its value for productivity and individuality. In C. De Dreu, & E. Van De Vliert (Eds.), *Using conflict in organizations* (pp. 23–37). Sage.

96. Somech, Desivilya, & Lidogoster.

97. Lockwood, J. (2015). Virtual team management: What is causing communication breakdown? *Language and Intercultural Communication, 15*(1), 125.

98. N.A. (2017, March 9). 47% of Canadian employees work remotely: Survey. *Benefits Canada*. https://www.benefitscanada.com/human-resources/other/47-of-canadian-employees-work-remotely-survey-94694

99. Newman, S., Ford, R., & Marshall, G. (2018). Virtual team leader communication: Employee perception and organizational reality. https://publications.aston.ac.uk/id/eprint/39015/1/Virtual_Team_Leader_Communication_Employee_Perception_and_Organizational_Reality.pdf

100. Andres, H. P. (2012). Technology mediated collaboration, shared mental models and task performance. *Journal of Organizational and End-User Computing, 24*, 64–81.

101. Marlow, S. et al. (2017). Communicating in virtual teams: A conceptual framework and research agenda. *Human Resource Management, 27*, 575–589.

102. Newman, Ford, & Marshall.

103. Goodman, M. et al. (2017). *CCI Corporate Communication Practices & Trends Study 2017 Final Report*. www.corporatecomm.org/wp-content/uploads/2013/06/Findings-CCI-Practicies-and-Trends-Study-20195-September-2017.pdf

104. Bank of Montreal. (2018, March 14). *BMO named one of the 2018 world's most ethical companies by the Ethisphere Institute*. BMO Corporate Information. https://newsroom.bmo.com/2018-03-14-BMO-Named-One-of-the-2018-Worlds-Most-Ethical-Companies-by-the-Ethisphere-Institute

105. Partly based on Johnson, M. (2003, Winter). The psychology of ethical lapses. *Management ethics*. Canadian Centre for Ethics & Corporate Policy. http://www.ethicscentre.ca/EN/resources/Ethics_Winter_2003.pdf

106. Westin, A. (1967). *Privacy and freedom*. Atheneum.

107. Government of Canada. (2000). *Personal Information Protection and Electronic Documents Act*. http://laws-lois.justice.gc.ca/eng/acts/P-8.6/page-1.html

108. Reuters. (2019, June 20). *Desjardins says personal data of 2.9 million members breached*. Financial Post. https://business.financialpost.com/news/fp-street/desjardins-says-personal-data-of-2-9-million-members-breached

109. Harris, S. (2019, October 16). *Loblaws wanted too much information for $25 gift cards, privacy commissioner finds*. CBC News. https://www.cbc.ca/news/business/privacy-commissioner-loblaws-id-request-25-gift-card-1.5323043

110. The Canadian Press. (2019, April 9). Equifax made breach worse by falling short of privacy obligations to Canadians, commissioner finds. *Financial Post*. https://business.financialpost.com/news/fp-street/equifax-fell-short-of-privacy-obligations-to-canadians-says-privacy-commissioner

111. Gardiner, H. (2012, January 20). Welcome to the new tort of 'intrusion upon seclusion'. *Canadian Lawyer*. https://www.canadianlawyermag.com/practice-areas/privacy-and-data/welcome-to-the-new-tort-of-intrusion-upon-seclusion/271204

112. Office of the Privacy Commissioner of Canada. (2015). *The digital privacy act*. https://laws-lois.justice.gc.ca/eng/annualstatutes/2015_32/page-1.html

113. Office of the Privacy Commissioner of Canada. (2015, November). *The Digital Privacy Act and PIPEDA*. https://www.priv.gc.ca/en/privacy-topics/privacy-laws-in-canada/the-personal-information-protection-and-electronic-documents-act-pipeda/r_o_p/02_05_d_63_s4/

114. Office of the Privacy Commissioner of Canada. (2009). *A guide for individuals: Your guide to* PIPEDA. https://imageadvantage.com/wp-content/uploads/2010/07/Your-Guide-to-PIPEDA.pdf

Chapter 2

1. Van Ruler. B. & De Lange, R. (2003). Barriers to communication management in the executive suite. *Public Relations Review, 2*, 145.

2. CBC News. (2018, March 29). *Walmart ends its involvement in Quebec training program for people with intellectual disabilities.* https://www.cbc.ca/news/canada/montreal/walmart-ends-its-involvement-in-quebec-training-program-for-people-with-intellectual-disabilities-1.4599569

3. CBC News. (2018, March 31). *Walmart 'sincerely apologizes' over confusion around program for people with intellectual disabilities.* https://www.cbc.ca/news/canada/montreal/walmart-apologizes-intellectual-disabilities-1.4601233

4. Rothwell, J. D. (1998). *In mixed company: Small group communication, instructor's manual/test bank.* Harcourt Brace.

5. Bugental, D. E., Kaswan, J. W., Love, L. R., & Fox, M. N. (1970). Child versus adult perception of evaluative messages in verbal, vocal, and visual channels. *Developments in Psychology, 2*, 376.

6. International Communication Association. (n.d.). *Society Information.* Human Communication Research. https://onlinelibrary.wiley.com/page/journal/14682958/homepage/society.html

7. National Communication Association. (n.d.). *Communication defined.* https://www.natcom.org/about-nca/what-communication

8. Dainton, M., & Zelley, E. (2018). *Applying communication theory for professional life: A practical introduction* (4th edition). Sage, pp. 2–3.

9. Weaver, W. (1949). Introductory note on the general setting of the analytical communication studies. In C. Shannon & W. Weaver (Eds.), *The mathematical theory of communication.* University of Illinois Press, p. 3.

10. DeVito, J. A. (2008). *Interpersonal messages: Communication and relationship skills.* Pearson, p. 13.

11. Ibid.

12. Archer, J. (1980). Self-disclosure. In D. Wegner & R. Vallacher (Eds.), *The self in social psychology.* Oxford University Press, p. 183.

13. Kiesler, S., & Sproull, L. (1986). Response effects in the electronic survey. *Public Opinion Quarterly, 50*, 402–413.

14. Thomson, E. (2015, July 22). Great interpersonal skills can be learned. *HuffPost Canada: The Blog.* http://www.huffingtonpost.ca/evan-thompson/learning-interpersonal-skills_b_7847864.html

15. Bradberry, T. (2014, January 9). Emotional intelligence—EQ. *Forbes.* http://www.forbes.com/sites/travisbradberry/2014/01/09/emotional-intelligence/#437796743ecb

16. Bandura, A. (2001). Social cognitive theory of mass communication. *Media Psychology, 3*(3), 265–299.

17. Conference Board of Canada. (n.d.). *Employability skills 2000+.* https://www.conferenceboard.ca/docs/default-source/educpublic/esp2000.pdf?sfvrsn=0

18. DeKay, S. (2012). Interpersonal communication in the workplace: A largely unexplored region. *Business Communication Quarterly, 75*(4), 449–451.

19. Keyton, J. (2011). *Communication and organizational culture* (2nd ed.). Sage, pp. 1–3.

20. Taylor, J. R., & Van Every, E. J. (2000). *The emergent organization: Communication as its site and surface.* Lawrence Erlbaum.

21. Mehrabian, A. (1981). *Silent message* (2nd ed.). Wadsworth Publishing, p. 78.

22. Argyle, M., Salter, V., Nicholson, H., Williams, M., & Burgess, P. (1970). The communication of inferior and superior attitudes by verbal and non-verbal signals. *British Journal of Social and Clinical Psychology, 9*, 222–231.

23. Mast, M. S. (2002). Dominance as expressed and inferred through speaking time: A meta-analysis. *Human Communication Research, 28*, 420–450.

24. Riggio, R. E. (2005). Business applications of nonverbal communication. In R. E. Riggio & R. S. Feldman (Eds.), *Applications of nonverbal communication research.* Lawrence Erlbaum Associates.

25. Hall, E. T. (1959). *The silent language.* Doubleday.

26. Ekman, P., & Friesen, W. (1975). *Unmasking the face: A guide to recognizing emotions in facial expressions.* Prentice-Hall.

27. Di Giusto, S. (2014). *The image of leadership.* Executive Image Consulting.

28. Adam, H., & Galinsky, A. (2012). Enclothed cognition. *Journal of Experimental Social Psychology, 48*(4), 918–925. doi: 10.1016/j.jesp.2012.02.008

29. Canadian Imperial Bank of Commerce. (n.d.). *Frequently asked questions.* https://www.cibc.com/ca/newhrwelcome/faqs.html

30. Hobbs, R., & Martens, H. (2015). How media literacy supports civic engagement in a digital age. *Atlantic Journal of Communication, 23* (2), 120–137; Tardy, C. (2003). A genre system view of the funding of academic research. *Written Communication, 20*(1), 7–36; Canale, M., & Swain, M. (1981). A theoretical framework for communicative competence. In Palmer, A., Groot, P., & Trosper, G. (Eds.), *The construct validation of test of communicative competence,* 31–36.

31. Spitzberg, B. (1983). Communication competence as knowledge, skill and impression. *Communication Education, 39.* https://www.researchgate.net/publication/240519019_Communication_Competence_as_Knowledge_Skill_and_Impression

32. Ibid.

33. Statistics Canada. (2011). *Canada work book.* Ottawa: Minister of Industry, p. 180.

34. Jia, K. (2010, July 28). Building cross-cultural competence. *Financial Post.* http://www.nationalpost.com/building+cross+cultural+competence/3333127/story.html

35. Hofstede, G. (2001). *Culture's consequences: Comparing values, behaviors, institutions, and organizations across nations,* 2nd ed. Sage.

36. Hall, E. T. (1976). *Beyond culture.* Doubleday.

37. Earley, P. C., and Ang, S. (2003). *Cultural intelligence: Individual interactions across cultures.* Stanford University Press.

38. Indigenous Corporate Training Inc. (2012, April 11). *Eye contact and Aboriginal Peoples.* https://www.ictinc.ca/blog/eye-contact-and-aboriginal-peoples

39. Baron, N. S. (2008). *Always on: Language in an online and mobile world.* Oxford University Press.

Chapter 3

1. Folk, S. (2011, May 16). Want to advance your career? Improve your business English. *Financial Post.* http://www.financialpost.com/careers/Want+advance+your+career+Improve+your+business+English/4791013/story.html

2. Boothby, K. (2012, October 12). *Business communication skills have declined in email era.* Postmedia News-Canada.com. http://www.canada.com/Business+communication+skills+have+declined+email/7392043/story.html

3. Lewington, J. (2014, August 26). Recruiters put premium on communication skills. *The Globe and Mail.* http://www.theglobeandmail.com/report-on-business/careers/career-advice/recruiters-put-premium-on-communication-skills/article20206416/

4. Driskill, L. (1989). Understanding the writing context in organizations. In M. Kogen (Ed.), *Writing in the business professions* (pp. 124–145). National Council of Teachers of English.

5. Hansen, C. (1995). Writing the project team: Authority and intertextuality in a corporate setting. *Journal of Business Communication, 33*(2), 105.

6. Colen, K., & Petelin, R. (2004). Challenges in collaborative writing in the contemporary corporation. *Corporate Communications, 9*(2), 137.

7. Ede, L., & Lunsford, A. A. (2001). Collaboration and concepts of authorship. *Publications of the Modern Language Association, 116,* 355.

8. Miller, C. (1984). Genre as social action. *Quarterly Journal of Speech, 70,* 155.

9. Spinuzzi, C. (2003). *Tracing genres through organizations: A sociocultural approach to information design.* MIT Press.

10. Swales, J. (1988). Discourse communities, genres and English as an international language. *World Englishes, 7*(2), 211. http://deepblue.lib.umich.edu/bitstream/handle/2027.42/71887/j.1467-971X.1988.tb00232.x.pdf;jsessionid=648BB97D8AFDE318338F95F0C8937EBC?sequence=1

11. Swales, p. 213.

12. Bitzer, L. (1968). The rhetorical situation. *Philosophy and Rhetoric, 1,* 3.

13. Parker, R. (2014, August 7). *7 ways limitations can boost your content creation productivity.* Content Marketing Institute. http://contentmarketinginstitute.com/2014/08/limitations-boost-content-creation-productivity/

14. Ede, L., & Lunsford, A. A. (1996). Representing audience: Successful discourse and disciplinary critique. *College Composition and Communication, 47*(2), 171.

15. LaBossiere, C. (2013, September 19). Business writing tips to get results. *The Globe and Mail.* http://www.theglobeandmail.com/report-on-business/careers/career-advice/business-writing-tips-to-get-results/article14422915/

16. Ede, L., & Lunsford, A. A. (1984). Audience addressed/audience invoked: The role of the audience in composition theory and pedagogy. *College Communication and Composition, 35*(2), 156.

17. Sutter, B. (2016, April 8). What you need to know about marketing with influencers. *Forbes.* http://www.forbes.com/sites/briansutter/2016/04/08/what-you-need-to-know-about-marketing-with-influencers/#1f0f03b3534c

18. Marsden, R. (2014, October 9). Social media infographic: Identifying your audience. *The Telegraph.* http://www.telegraph.co.uk/sponsored/business/sme-home/11145529/social-media-infographic.html

19. Ibid.

20. Pearson, M. (2015, December 10). Four trends that will shape digital media in 2016. *The Globe and Mail.* http://www.theglobeandmail.com/report-on-business/small-business/sb-marketing/top-trends-of-2015/article27658206/

21. Craciun, E. (2014, October 29). *Benefits of a knowledge management system within an organization.* LinkedIn. https://www.linkedin.com/pulse/20141029121125-2108052-benefits-of-a-knowledge-management-system-within-an-organization

22. Canada Business Network. (2016). *Guide to market research analysis.* http://www.canadabusiness.ca/eng/page/2691/

23. Ibid.

24. Davenport, T. (2014, May 5). 10 kinds of stories to tell with data. *Harvard Business Review.* https://hbr.org/2014/05/10-kinds-of-stories-to-tell-with-data/

25. Bal, M. (2009). *Narratology: Introduction to the theory of narrative* (3rd ed.) University of Toronto Press, p. 5.

26. McLellan, H. (2006). Corporate storytelling perspectives. *The Journal for Quality and Participation, 29*(1), 17–20.

27. Howard, B. (2016, April 4). Storytelling: The new strategic imperative. *Forbes.* http://www.forbes.com/sites/billeehoward/2016/04/04/storytelling-the-new-strategic-imperative-of-business/#5ba906fc69f8

28. McLellan.

29. Howard.

30. Shea, C. (2015, October 15). Jane Goodall on how to get people to hear your message. *Canadian Business.* http://www.canadianbusiness.com/leadership/jane-goodall-on-branding/

31. Lockshin, V. (2016, February 3). *Five ways to improve your storytelling results in 2016.* Charity Village. https://charityvillage.com/Content.aspx?topic=Five_ways_to_improve_your_storytelling_results_in_2016#.V6INJIMrKM8

32. Movember Foundation. (2016). FAQ. https://ca.movember.com/faq

33. Nudd, T. (2012, October 13). 7 basic types of stories: Which one is your brand telling? *AdWeek.* http://www.adweek.com/news/advertising-branding/7-basic-types-stories-which-one-your-brand-telling-144164

34. Pearson, M. (2015, December 10). Four trends that will shape digital media in 2016. *Globe & Mail.* http://www.theglobeandmail.com/report-on-business/small-business/sb-marketing/top-trends-of-2015/article27658206/

35. Lalonde, M. (2015, October 16). *Social impact storytelling: Moving from emotion to action.* The Conference Board of Canada. http://www.conferenceboard.ca/commentaries/oe/15-10-16/social_impact_storytelling_moving_from_emotion_to_action.aspx

36. Ede, L., & Lunsford, A. A. (1990). *Singular texts/plural authors: Perspectives on collaborative writing.* Southern Illinois University Press, p. 20.

37. Harris Interactive. (2013). *The case for better document collaboration.* https://www.perforce.com/sites/all/themes/perforce/images/commons/perforce-document-collaboration-report.pdf

38. Colen & Petelin, p. 139.

39. Putins, P., & Petelin, R. (1996). *Professional communication: Principles and application.* Prentice Hall.

40. Onrubia, J., & Engel, A. (2009). Strategies for collaborative writing and phrases of knowledge construction in CSCL environments. *Computers & Education, 53*(4), 1256–1265.

41. Lowry, P. B., Curtis, A., & Lowry, M. R. (2004). Building a taxonomy and nomenclature of collaborative writing to improve interdisciplinary research and practice. *Journal of Business Communication, 41*(1), 66–99.

42. Onrubia & Engel.

43. join.me. (2014, December). Tooling up for collaboration: Virtual meetings that drive business results. *Forbes.* http://www.forbes.com/forbesinsights/join_me/

44. Morgan, J. (2013, July 30). The 12 habits of highly collaborative organizations. *Forbes.* http://www.forbes.com/sites/jacobmorgan/2013/07/30/the-12-habits-of-highly-collaborative-organizations/2/#71ff04c75729

45. join.me.

46. Word Team. (2015, October 30). Word real-time co-authoring—A closer look. *Microsoft 365 Blogs.* https://www.microsoft.com/en-us/microsoft-365/blog/2015/10/30/word-real-time-co-authoring-a-closer-look/

47. Topping, K. J., et al. (2000). Formative peer assessment of academic writing between post-graduate students. *Assessment and Evaluation in Higher Education, 31*(1), 149–169.

48. Reiber, L. J. (2006). Using peer review to improve student writing in business courses. *Journal of Education for Business, 81*(6), 322–326.

49. *Guidelines for group critique.* (n.d.). http://www.albany.edu/faculty/dgoodwin/shared_resources/critique.html

50. Barrett, T. (2003). *Tentative tips for better crits.* http://www.terrybarrettosu.com/pdfs/Barrett%20%282006%29%20Tips%20for%20crits.pdf

Chapter 4

1. Asprey, M. (2003). *Plain language for lawyers*. Federation Press, p. 62.
2. Canadian Bankers Association. (2000). *Plain language mortgage documents* CBA *commitment*. http://www.scotiabank.com/ca/common/pdf/about_scotia/plain_language_mortgage_documents_cba_committment.pdf
3. Curley, S., Yates, J., & Abrams, R. (1986). Psychological sources of ambiguity avoidance. *Organizational Behavior and Human Decision Processes, 38*(2), 230–256.
4. Stinson, S. (2003, June 17). Software takes the "bull" out of jargon. *National Post*. A12
5. Danesi, M. (2019). Emojis: Langue or Parole? *Chinese Semiotic Studies 15*(3), 243–258.
6. Walther, J. (1992). Interpersonal effects in computer-mediated interaction: A relational perspective. *Communication Research 19*(1), 52–90.
7. Glikson, E., Cheshin, A., & Van Cleef, G. (2017). The dark side of the smiley: The effects of smiling emoticons on virtual first impressions. *Social Psychological and Personality Science 9*(5), 614–625.
8. Ibid.
9. Smith, L., & Rose, R. (2019). Service with a smiley face: Emojional contagion in digitally mediated relationships. *International Journal of Research in Marketing 36*(4).
10. Cuddy, A. J., Fiske, S. T., Glick, P. (2008). Warmth and competence as universal dimensions of social perception: The stereotype content model and the BIAS map. *Advances in Experimental Social Psychology*, 40, 61–149; Judd, C. M., James-Hawkins, L., Yzerbyt, V., Kashima, Y. (2005). Fundamental dimensions of social judgment: Understanding the relations between judgments of competence and warmth. *Journal of Personality and Social Psychology*, 89, 899–913.
11. Qian, D., & Pan, M. (2017). Politeness in business communication: Investigating English modal sequences in Chinese learners' letter writing. *RELC Journal 50*(1), 20–36.
12. Eshghinejad, S., & Moini, M. (2016). Politeness strategies used in text messaging: Pragmatic competence in an asymmetrical power relation of teacher–student. *Sae Open*. https://journals.sagepub.com/doi/pdf/10.1177/2158244016632288
13. Ziv, S. (2019). *A guide to using pronouns and other gender-inclusive language in the office*. The Muse. https://www.themuse.com/advice/using-pronouns-gender-inclusive-language-in-the-office
14. McGregor, J. (2019, July 7) How employers are preparing for a gender non-binary world. *The Washington Post*. https://www.washingtonpost.com/business/2019/07/02/how-employers-are-preparing-gender-non-binary-world/
15. HR Council. (2016). *Diversity at work: Inclusive language guidelines*. http://hrcouncil.ca/hr-toolkit/diversity-language-guidelines.cfm
16. Ober, S., Zhao, J. J., Davis, R., & Alexander, M. W. (1999). Telling it like it is: The use of certainty in public business discourse. *The Journal of Business Communication, 36*(3), 280.
17. Delin, J. (2005). Brand tone of voice: A linguistic analysis of brand positions. *Journal of Applied Linguistics 2*(1), 1-44.
18. This activity is loosely based on an experiment included in a study by Glikson, E., Cheshin, A., & Van Kleef, G. (2017). The dark side of the smiley: The effects of smiling emoticons on virtual first impressions. *Social Psychological and Personality Science 9*(5), 614–625.
19. Friesen, G. and A. Kay (2011). Evidence That Gendered Wording in Job Advertisements Exists and Sustains Gender Inequality. *Journal of Personality and Social Psychology 101*(1), 109–28.

Chapter 5

1. Ovsey, D. (2012, August 7). Spin may be dead, but are business leaders using honest communication effectively? *Financial Post*. http://business.financialpost.com/2012/08/07/spin-may-be-dead-but-are-business-leaders-using-honest-communication-effectively/
2. Stokel-Walker, C. (July 23, 2018). The commas that cost companies millions. BBC Worklife. https://www.bbc.com/worklife/article/20180723-the-commas-that-cost-companies-millions
3. Guffey, M. E. (2001). *Business communication: Process & product* (3rd Canadian ed.). Nelson Thompson Learning, p. 151.

Chapter 6

1. McDougall, M. (2012, August 13). Prioritizing internal communications. *Canadian HR Reporter, 25*(14), 22.
2. Ibid.
3. Houpt, S. (2011, September 13). Workplace e-mail: What's appropriate and what's not. *The Globe and Mail*. http://www.theglobeandmail.com/report-on-business/careers/career-advice/workplace-e-mail-whats-appropriate-and-whats-not/article594205/
4. CBS News. (2015, August 27). *"Reply-all" email catastrophe hits Thomson Reuters*. https://www.cbsnews.com/news/reply-all-email-catastrophe-hits-thomson-reuters/?source=post_page
5. Angus Reid Institute. (2015, February 9). *Canadians at work: Technology enables more flexibility, but longer hours too; checking in is the new normal*. http://angusreid.org/work-tech/
6. Gavett, G. (2015, July 24). The essential guide to crafting a work email. *Harvard Business Review*. https://hbr.org/2015/07/the-essential-guide-to-crafting-a-work-email&cm_sp=Article-_-Links-_-End%20of%20Page%20Recirculation
7. Ibid.
8. Rampton, J. (2015, March 1). *The rules of texting. Entrepreneur*. https://www.entrepreneur.com/article/244453

Chapter 8

1. Maple Leaf Foods (2018, November 26). *Maple Leaf Foods to construct world-class value-added poultry facility in London, Ontario* [Press release]. https://www.mapleleaffoods.com/news/maple-leaf-foods-to-construct-world-class-value-added-poultry-facility-in-london-ontario/
2. Simmons, G. (Nov. 27, 2018). Maple Leaf announces closure of St Mary's/Perth South plant. *Stratford Beacon Herald*. https://www.stratfordbeaconherald.com/news/local-news/maple-leaf-announces-closure-of-st-marys-perth-south-plant
3. Butler, C. (2018, November 28). *Workers at 3 Ontario Maple Leaf Foods plants left wondering about their futures*. CBC News. https://www.cbc.ca/news/canada/london/maple-leaf-foods-plant-london-toronto-brampton-st-marys-1.4922650
4. Ibid.
5. Timmerman, P. D., & Harrison, W. (2005). The discretionary use of electronic media: Four considerations for bad news bearers. *Journal of Business Communication*, 42, 379–389.
6. Jansen, F., & Janssen, D. (2013). Effects of directness in bad news e-mails and voice mails. *Journal of Business Communication, 50*(4), 362–382.
7. Jansen, F., & Janssen, D. (2011). Explanation first: A case for presenting explanations before decisions in Dutch bad news messages. *Journal of Business and Technical Communication, 25*, 36–67.
8. Lazare, A. (2005). *On apology*. Oxford University Press; Kampf, Z. (2009). The age of apology: Evidence from the Israeli public discourse. *Social Semiotics, 19*(3), 257–273.
9. Pfeffer, J. (2015, October 26). Corporate apologies: Beware of the pitfalls of saying sorry. *Fortune*. http://fortune.com/2015/10/26/corporate-apologies-crisis-management/

10. Janssen, D. (2013, October 25). *Apologies in bad news messages.* 78th Annual International Association for Business Communication Convention, New Orleans, LA.

11. McGregor, J. (April 11, 2017). From "tone-deaf" to "textbook': Experts review the United CEO's first—and latest—apology. *Washington Post.* https://www.washingtonpost.com/news/on-leadership/wp/2017/04/11/from-tone-deaf-to-textbook-experts-review-the-united-ceos-first-and-latest-apology/

12. McCann, E. (2017, April 14). United's Apologies: A Timeline. *The New York Times.* https://www.nytimes.com/2017/04/14/business/united-airlines-passenger-doctor.html

13. Pfeffer.

14. LinkedIn Talent Solutions. (2019). *Guide to rejecting candidates.* LinkedIn. https://business.linkedin.com/talent-solutions/recruiting-tips/rejecting-candidates-guide

15. Welch, M. & Jackson, P. (2007). Rethinking internal communication: A stakeholder approach. *Corporate Communications: An International Journal* 12(2): 177–198; Cornelissen, J. (2004). *Corporate Communication: Theory and Practice.* Sage: 68.

16. Mayfield, J., & Mayfield, M. (2012). The relationship between leader-motivating language and self-efficacy: A partial least squares model analysis. *International Journal of Business Communication* 49(4): 357–376; Hendriks, B. and van Mulken, M. (2012). Dear worker: A corpus analysis of internal CEO letters. In G. Jacobs and G. Prescilla, eds. *Researching discourse in business genres: cases and corpora.* Peter Lang, pp. 73–95.

17. Solomon, M. (2015, January 28). 5 social media customer service best practices to handle (or prevent) customer complaints. *Forbes.* http://www.forbes.com/sites/micahsolomon/2015/01/28/5-best-practices-for-social-media-customer-service-to-handle-and-avoid-customer-complaints/#73cd3db56a70; Pollach, I. (2006). Electronic word of mouth: A genre analysis of product reviews on consumer opinion websites. *Proceedings of the 39th Hawaii International Conference on System Sciences:* 1–10.

18. Creelman, V. (2015). Sheer outrage: Negotiating customer dissatisfaction and interaction in the blogosphere. In E. Darics (ed.), *Digital Business Discourse,* Palgrave Macmillan p. 161.

19. Napolitano, A. (2018). Image repair or self-destruction? A genre and corpus-assisted discourse analysis of restaurants' responses to online complaints. *Critical Approaches to Discourse Across the Disciplines* 10 (1): 143.

20. Thumvichit, A., & Gampper, C. (2019). Composing responses to negative hotel reviews: A genre analysis. *Cogent Arts & Humanities* 6(1). https://www.tandfonline.com/doi/full/10.1080/23311983.2019.1629154

21. Solomon.

22. Benoit, D. (1995). *Accounts, excuses, and apologies: A theory of image restoration strategies.* State University of New York Press; Benoit, W. L. (1997). Image repair discourse and crisis communication. *Public Relations Review* 23(2): 177–186; Coombs, T., & Holladay, S. (2007). The negative communication dynamic: Exploring the impact of stakeholder affect on behavioral intentions. *Journal of Communications Management* 11(4): 300-312

23. Blackburn, Mike. (2017, July 14). *Walmart Canada apologizes, says it's pulling infant sleeper that has Twitter all fired up.* APTN National News. https://aptnnews.ca/2017/07/14/walmart-canada-apologiz-es-says-its-pulling-infant-sleeper-that-has-twitter-all-fired-up/

24. CB Insights. (2019, October 16). *323 startup failure post-mortems.* [Research brief]. https://www.cbinsights.com/research/startup-failure-post-mortem/

25. Ibid.

Chapter 9

1. Matz, S. et al. (2017). Psychological targeting as an effective approach to digital mass persuasion. *Proceedings of the National Academy of Sciences of the United States,* 114 (48), 12714-12719. https://www.pnas.org/content/114/48/12714

2. Ibid.

3. Bronskill, J. (2019, June 11). Social media skepticism helping fuel distrust of the Internet, survey fines. *National Post.* https://nationalpost.com/pmn/news-pmn/canada-news-pmn/social-media-skepticism-helping-fuel-distrust-of-the-internet-survey-finds

4. Ibid.

5. Rush, B. (2014, August 28). Science of storytelling: Why and how to use it in your marketing. *The Guardian.* https://www.theguardian.com/media-network/media-network-blog/2014/aug/28/science-storytelling-digital-marketing

6. Mucundorfeanu, M. (2018). The key role of storytelling in the branding process. *Journal of Media Research,* 11(1), 42–54.

7. Dalpiaz, E., & Di Stefano, G. (2018). A universe of stories: Mobilizing narrative practices during transformative change. *Strategic Management Journal,* 39, 664–696.

8. Kelman, H. C. (1974). Further thoughts on the processes of compliance, identification, and internalization. In J.T. Tedeschi (Ed.), *Perspectives on social power* (pp. 125–171). Chicago: Aldine.

9. Panda, M., et al. (2013). Does emotional appeal work in advertising? The rationality behind using emotional appeal to create favorable brand attitude. *The IUP Journal of Brand Management,* 10(2).

10. Darics, E., & Koller, V. (2018). *Language in Business, Language at Work.* Palgrave. p.131; Clampitt, P. et al. (2000). A strategy for communicating about uncertainty. *The Academy of Management Executive,* 14(4), 41–57; Oppenheimer, D. (2005). Consequences of erudite vernacular irrespective of necessity. *Applied Cognitive Psychology,* 20(2), 139–156.

11. Hendriks, B. and van Mulken, M. (2012). Dear worker: A corpus analysis of internal CEO letters. In G. Jacobs and G. Prescilla, eds. *Researching discourse in business genres: cases and corpora.* Peter Lang, pp. 73–95; Cornelissen, J. (2004). *Corporate Communication.* Sage.; Mayfield, J., & Mayfield, M. (2012). The relationship between leader-motivating language and self-efficacy: A partial least squares model analysis. *International Journal of Business Communication,* 49(4), 357–376.

12. Georgetown University Center for Social Impact Communications. (2013). *Digital persuasion: Social media motivates people to contribute beyond clicks* [Press release]. https://www.3blmedia.com/News/Digital-Persuasion-Social-Media-Motivates-People-Contribute-Beyond-Clicks

13. Sexton, J. (2011, February 11). 6 powerful social media persuasion techniques. *Social Media Examiner.* http://www.socialmediaexaminer.com/6-powerful-social-media-persuasion-techniques/. Based on Cialdini, R. (2006). *Influence: The psychology of persuasion* (rev. ed.). Harper Business.

14. Ibid.

15. Dwivedi, Y. et al. (2016). *Social media in the marketing context: A state of the art Analysis and future directions.* Elsevier Science & Technology: 14.

16. Hennig-Thurau, T. et al. (2013). Marketing the pinball way. *Journal of Interactive Marketing,* 27, 237–241.

17. Dwivedi, p.42.

18. Wharton School of Business. (2019). *Digital vs. traditional marketing: What today's c-suite needs to know.* University of Pennsylvania. https://online.wharton.upenn.edu/blog/digital-versus-traditional-marketing/

19. Wiest, B. (2019, March 11). Social media is no longer about products—it's about buying a better version of yourself. *Forbes.* https://www.forbes.com/sites/briannawiest/

2019/03/11/digital-marketing-is-no-longer-about-products-its-about-buying-a-better-version-of-yourself/#7317e5b4734d

20. Wharton School of Business.

21. Bhatia, V. K. (2017). *Analyzing genre: Language use in professional settings.* Routledge. p.45

22. Content Marketing Institute. (2019). *What is content marketing?* https://contentmarketinginstitute.com/what-is-content-marketing/; Holliman, G., & Rowley, J. (2014). Business to business digital content marketing: Marketers' perceptions of best practice. *The Journal of Research in Indian Medicine, 8,* p. 285; Muller, J., & Christandi, F. (2019). Content is king—but who is the king of kings? The effect of content marketing, sponsored content & user-generated content on brand responses. *Computers in Human Behaviour, 96.*

23. Bullock, L. (2019. January 30). 2019 content marketing strategy: Here are 5 content marketing trends that you can't ignore this year. *Forbes.* https://www.forbes.com/sites/lilachbullock/2019/01/30/2019-content-marketing-strategy-here-are-5-content-marketing-trends-that-you-cant-ignore-this-year/#7a7d82715618; Harris, J. (Sept. 2, 2019). *Get a refresh on the what, why, where, and how of content marketing.* The Content Marketing Institute. https://contentmarketinginstitute.com/2019/09/refresh-content-marketing/

24. Yakimova, R. et al. (2017). Brand champion behaviour: Its role in corporate branding. *Journal of Brand Management, 24*(3).

25. Taiminen, K. and Ranaweera, C. (2019). Fostering brand engagement and value-laden trusted B2B relationships through digital content marketing. *European Journal of Marketing, 53*(9), 1759–1781.

26. Castrillon, C. (2019, February 12). What personal branding is more important than ever. *Forbes.* https://www.forbes.com/sites/carolinecastrillon/2019/02/12/why-personal-branding-is-more-important-than-ever/#6e6deb712408.

27. Scolere, L. et al (2018). Constructing the Platform-Specific Self-Brand: The Labor of Social Media Promotion. *Social Media + Society*; Peters, T. (1997). The brand called you. *Fast Company, 10*(10), 83-90.

28. Duffy, B. E., Hund, E. (2015). "Having it all" on social media: Entrepreneurial femininity and self-branding among fashion bloggers. *Social Media+ Society, 1*(2), 1–11; Gershon, I. (2017). Down and out in the new economy: How people find (or don't find) work today. University of Chicago Press; Vallas, S. P., & Christin, A. (2018). Work and identity in an era of precarious employment: How workers respond to "personal branding" discourse. *Work and Occupations, 45,* 3–37; Lowenthal, P. R., Dunlap, J. C., & Stitson, P. (2016). Creating an intentional web presence: Strategies for every educational technology professional. *TechTrends, 60*(4), 320-329

29. Rush, B.

30. Kaur, W. (2018, May 23). *Five Indigenous creatives on the fashion industry in Canada.* Flare. https://www.flare.com/fashion/indigenous-fashion-in-canada/.

Chapter 10

1. B. LaRose, personal communication, June 18, 2019

2. RBC. (2018). *Pursue Your Potential.* https://jobs.rbc.com/ca/en/job/174163/Pursue-your-Potential-PYP-Indigenous-Peoples

3. CBC News. (2018, January 19). *Don't check Facebook before hiring, says privacy commissioner.* https://www.cbc.ca/news/canada/newfoundland-labrador/social-media-hiring-public-bodies-1.4492935

4. Canadian Interprofessional Health Collaborative. (2010). *A national interprofessional competency framework.* http://www.cihc.ca/files/CIHC_IPCompetencies_Feb1210.pdf; Treasury

Board of Canada Secretariat. (2011, December 2). *Competencies.* http://www.tbs-sct.gc.ca/tal/comp-eng.asp

5. University of British Columbia. (n.d.). *Self-assessment and goal setting document for probationary employees.* http://www.hr.ubc.ca/administrators/files/PROBATIONARY-Performance-Review-Plan-Self-Assessment.pdf; Treasury Board of Canada Secretariat. (2004). *Competency profile for supervisors.* http://www.tbs-sct.gc.ca/gui/cmgs-eng.asp#learning_support

6. Citizenship and Immigration Canada. (n.d.). *Employment in Canada. Integration-Net.* http://integration-net.ca/coa-oce/english/pdf/04employment.pdf

7. Bongard, A. (2019, November 18). Automating talent acquisition: Smart recruitment, predictive hiring algorithms, and the data-driven nature of artificial intelligence. *Psychosociological Issues in Human Resource Management, 7*(1): p. 36

8. Experts at KForce. (2019, January 18). *What you need to know about the future of the job search.* Glassdoor. https://www.glassdoor.com/blog/future-of-job-search/

9. Newton, A. (2013). *Can Pinterest help you find a job?* Monster.ca. https://www.monster.ca/career-advice/article/find-a-job-through-pinterest-ca

10. Zhao, M. (2019). *The rise of mobile devices in job search: Challenges and opportunities for employers.* Glassdoor Economic Research. https://www.glassdoor.com/research/app/uploads/sites/2/2019/05/Mobile-Job-Search.pdf

11. Ibid.

12. Sheppard, V. (2019, August 27). *15 growing Canadian tech startups hiring this September.* MaRS. https://www.marsdd.com/news/15-growing-canadian-tech-startups-hiring-this-september/

13. Rai, H., & Kothari, J. (2008). Recruitment advertising and corporate image: Interface between marketing and human resources. *South Asian Journal of Management, 15*(2): p. 48.

14. Whitaker, M. (2019, August 19). How to read a faculty job ad. *Chronicle of Higher Education.* https://www.chronicle.com/article/How-to-Read-a-Faculty-Job-Ad/246921

15. Farooqui, S., & Nagendra, A. (2014). The impact of person-organization fit on job satisfaction and job performance. *Procendi Economics and Finance, 14:* 122.

16. Huang, W., Yuan, C., & Li, M. (2019). Person–job fit and innovation behavior: Roles of job involvement and career commitment. *Frontiers in Psychology, 10:* 1134. https://doi.org/10.3389/fpsyg.2019.01134

17. Kristoff, A. L. (1996). Person-organization fit. *Personnel Psychology, 48:* 1–49; Sekiguchki, T. (2004). Person organization fit and person job fit in employee selection: A review of the literature. *Osaka Keidai Ronshu, 56;* Edwards, J. R. (1991). Person-job fit: A conceptual integration, literature review, and methodological critique. In C. L. Cooper & I. T. Robertson (Eds.), *International review of industrial and organizational psychology. International review of industrial and organizational psychology, 1991, Vol. 6* (p. 283–357). John Wiley & Sons.

18. Wong, C. M., & Tetrick, L. E. (2017). Job crafting: older workers' mechanism for maintaining person-job fit. *Frontiers in Psychology, 8:*1548. doi: 10.3389/fpsyg.2017.01548; Huang, W., et al. (2019)

19. Cappelli, P. (2019, May–June). Your approach to hiring is all wrong. *Harvard Business Review.* https://hbr.org/2019/05/recruiting

20. Ibid.

21. Sheppard, V. (2019, August 27). *15 growing Canadian tech startups hiring this September.* MaRS. https://www.marsdd.com/news/15-growing-canadian-tech-startups-hiring-this-september/

22. Forbes Agency Council. (2017, November 24). Is the business card dead? 16 experts share their thoughts. *Forbes.* https://www.forbes.com/sites/forbesagencycouncil/2017/11/24/

is-the-business-card-dead-16-experts-share-their-thoughts/#64419e679922

23. UBC Student Services. (n.d.). *Informational interviews.* University of British Columbia. https://students.ubc.ca/career-resources/informational-interviews

24. Hinds, J., & Joinson, A. N. (2018). What demographic attributes do our digital footprints reveal? A systematic review. *PLOS ONE, 13*(11), Article e0207112. https://doi.org/10.1371/journal.pone.0207112

25. Girardin, F., Calabrese, F., Fiore, F. D., Ratti, C., & Blat, J. (2008). Digital footprinting: Uncovering tourists with user-generated content. *IEEE Pervasive Computing, 7*(4): 36–43. https://doi.org/10.1109/MPRV.2008.71; Madden, M., Fox, S., Smith, A., & Vitak, J. (2007, December 16). *Digital footprints.* Pew Research Center. https://www.pewresearch.org/internet/2007/12/16/digital-footprints/

26. Sundheim, K. (2013, December 4). Can LinkedIn survive the social media bubble? *Forbes.* http://www.forbes.com/sites/kensundheim/2013/12/04/can-linkedin-survive-the-social-media-bubble/

27. Cheston, A. (2012, May 11). Recruiters say: Avoid LinkedIn at your peril. *Forbes.* http://www.forbes.com/sites/work-in-progress/2012/05/11/recruiters-say-avoid-linkedin-at-your-peril/

28. McKissen, D. (2019, September 25). *Here's an example of the perfect LinkedIn profile summary, according to Harvard career experts.* CNBC. https://www.cnbc.com/2019/09/25/example-template-of-perfect-linkedin-profile-according-to-harvard-career-experts.html

29. Harvard Extension School. (2013, August 2). *Optimizing your LinkedIn profile. Harvard Extension Hub.* http://www.extension.harvard.edu/hub/blog/extension-blog/optimizing-your-linkedin-profile-checklist

30. Ibid.

31. Ibid.

32. Adams, S. (2012, November 30). 4 ways to use Twitter to find a job. *Forbes.* http://www.forbes.com/sites/susanadams/2012/11/30/4-ways-to-use-twitter-to-find-a-job/

33. Kingston, C. (2013, April 10). How to use Twitter for business and marketing. *Social Media Examiner.* http://www.socialmediaexaminer.com/how-to-use-twitter-for-business-and-marketing/

34. Dorsey, A. (2013, September 4). *More than just a resume: Share your volunteer aspirations on your LinkedIn Profile.* LinkedIn. https://blog.linkedin.com/2013/09/04/more-than-just-a-resume-share-your-volunteer-aspirations-on-your-linkedin-profile

35. Writing Tutorial Services, Indiana University. (n.d.). *Personal statements and application letters.* https://wts.indiana.edu/writing-guides/personal-statements-and-application-letters.html

36. Flynn, M. (2010, September). *A guide to writing effective personal statements for jobs.* University of Birmingham. https://intranet.birmingham.ac.uk/as/employability/careers/documents/public/appforms-writing-supporting-statements.pdf

37. Boston College. (2013, October 11). *Resumes, cover letters, & LinkedIn profiles.* Boston College Career Center. http://www.bc.edu/content/bc/careers/jobs/resumes.html

38. Cotterill, S. J. (2007). *What is an ePortfolio?* ePortfolios 2007 Conference. Maastricht, The Netherlands; University of British Columbia. (2010, August 26). *What is it? ePortfolios.* http://elearning.ubc.ca/toolkit/eportfolios/; Learning Technologies for Medical Science. (2011, January 7). *What is an ePortfolio?* ePortfolios. http://www.eportfolios.ac.uk/definition

39. Stockdale, L. (2014, February 27). How to make a great video interview. *The Guardian.* https://www.theguardian.com/careers/careers-blog/how-to-make-video-cv

40. Ibid.

41. National Research Council of Canada. (2012, August 7). *How to prepare for behavioural competency interview questions.* https://nrc.canada.ca/en/corporate/careers/how-prepare-behavioural-competency-interview-questions

42. Alberta Learning Information Service. (n.d.). *Be prepared to answer behaviour-descriptive questions.* https://alis.alberta.ca/look-for-work/interviews-and-offers/be-prepared-to-answer-behaviour-descriptive-questions/

Chapter 11

1. Panchadar, A. (2019, January 29). *Email rival Slack says it has 10 million daily active users.* Reuters. https://www.reuters.com/article/us-slack-users/email-rival-slack-says-it-has-10-million-daily-active-users-idUSKCN1PN2T2

2. Fischer, M. (2017, May 1). What happens when work becomes a nonstop chat room. *New York.* http://nymag.com/intelligencer/2017/05/what-has-slack-done-to-the-office.html

3. Slack team. (2018, April 11). 7 marketing reports you'll never have to pull again [Blog post]. *Slack.* https://slackhq.com/7-marketing-reports-youll-never-have-to-pull-again

4. International Data Corporation. (2017). *The Business Value of Slack* [Report]. Slack. https://a.slack-edge.com/eaf4e/marketing/downloads/resources/IDC_The_Business_Value_of_Slack.pdf

5. Tufte, E. R. (1983). *The visual display of quantitative information.* Graphics Press, p. 51.

6. Harrison, L., Reinecke, K., & Remco, C. (2015). *Infographics aesthetics: Designing for first impressions.* Tufts University. http://www.cs.tufts.edu/~remco/publications/2015/CHI2015-Aesthetics.pdf

7. Ibid.

8. Eckstein, I. (2019, July 15). *The science behind the most popular infographics.* SeigeMedia. http://www.siegemedia.com/creation/infographics

9. Morin, A. (2014, February 4). How to use color psychology to give your business an edge. *Forbes.* http://www.forbes.com/sites/amymorin/2014/02/04/how-to-use-color-psychology-to-give-your-business-an-edge/#1ddbaae52e28

10. Harrison et al.

11. Fisher, N. (2014, June 3). Seeing is believing: Infographics revolutionizing the patient experience. *Forbes.* http://www.forbes.com/sites/nicolefisher/2014/06/03/seeing-is-believing-infographics-revolutionizing-the-patient-experience/#77fc3f1f458c

12. Arcia et al.; Kern, L. (2013, August 30). Infographics: All the rage, but a must-do for your business? *Forbes.* http://www.forbes.com/sites/kernlewis/2013/08/30/infographics-all-the-rage-but-a-must-do-for-your-business/#6bcedd6e936a

13. Insurance Bureau of Canada. (2009). *Incident and accident reporting.* http://www.ibc.ca/en/business_insurance/risk_management/incident_and_accident_reporting.asp

Chapter 12

1. Graphic Designers of Canada. (2010). *Study demonstrates Canadian businesses using design increase success, reduce risk.* https://gdc.design/tools-resources/design-buyers/2010-harrisdecima-survey

2. Statistics Canada. (2018, November 28). *Infographic: New Data on Disability in Canada, 2017.* https://www150.statcan.gc.ca/n1/pub/11-627-m/11-627-m2018035-eng.htm

3. The Association of Registered Graphic Designers. (2019). *Access ability 2: A practical handbook on accessible graphic design.* Revised and supersized second edition. The Association of Registered Graphic Designers, p. 17. https://

www.rgd.ca/database/files/library/RGD___Accessibility_Handbook___2019_07_15.pdf

4. Ibid, p. 21.
5. Ibid, p. 27.

Chapter 13

1. Scarrow, K. (2013, July 23). Want to improve your pitch? Here's how. *The Globe and Mail.* http://www.theglobeandmail. com/report-on-business/small-business/sb-growth/the-challenge/20130716thechallengepitch-1080p5000kbpscopymp4/article13319914/
2. Ibid.
3. Paglarini, R. (n.d.). *How to write an elevator speech.* Business Know-How. http://www.businessknowhow.com/money/elevator.htm
4. Moldinado, P. (2009, June 4). *How to design an effective presentation* [Video]. Youtube. http://www.youtube.com/watch?v=HJgeF3ALlog
5. Ibid.
6. Prezi. (2016). *Five simple steps to a great Prezi.* https://prezi.com/support/article/steps/five-simple-steps-to-a-great-prezi/
7. Tufte, E. R. (2003). *The cognitive style of PowerPoint, 1. The University of Edinburgh.* https://www.inf.ed.ac.uk/teaching/courses/pi/2016_2017/phil/tufte-powerpoint.pdf
8. Ibid., 26.
9. Koka, N. (2018, May 11). Tips for Presenters. *PechaKucha.* https://www.pechakucha.com/cities/mumbai/blogs/tips-for-presenters-2

Chapter 14

1. Ennis, D. (2019, June 24). Don't let that rainbow logo fool you: These 9 corporations donated millions to anti-gay politicians. *Forbes.* https://www.forbes.com/sites/dawnstaceyennis/2019/06/24/dont-let-that-rainbow-logo-fool-you-these-corporations-donated-millions-to-anti-gay-politicians/#7204d27b14a6
2. Jones, O. (2019, May 23). Woke-washing: How brands are cashing in on the culture wars. *The Guardian.* https://www.theguardian.com/media/2019/may/23/woke-washing-brands-cashing-in-on-culture-wars-owen-jones
3. Kennedy, P. (Host). (2019, June 12). Woke washing: The problem with 'branding' social movements [Radio series episode]. In Kelly, G. (Executive producer), *Ideas.* CBC. https://www.cbc.ca/radio/ideas/woke-washing-the-problem-with-branding-social-movements-1.5171349
4. Gruzd, A., Jacobson, J., Mai, P., & Dubois, E. (2018). *The State of Social Media in Canada 2017.* Scholars Portal Dataverse. https://doi.org/10.5683/sp/al8z6r
5. Canadian Internet Registration Authority. (2019). *Canada's Internet Factbook.* https://cira.ca/resources/corporate/factbook/canadas-internet-factbook-2019
6. Gruzd, p. 4.
7. Ibid.
8. Insights West. (2019). *2019 Canadian social media insights,* p. 9. https://insightswest.com/wp-content/uploads/2019/06/Rep_IW_CDNSocialMediaInsights_June2019.pdf
9. Ibid., p. 8.
10. Ibid., p. 15.
11. Deschamps, T. (2019, May 23). Meet the Toronto stars of TikTok, Gen Z's new social media obsession. *The Toronto Star.* https://www.thestar.com/life/2019/05/23/meet-the-toronto-stars-of-tiktok-gen-zs-new-social-media-obsession.html
12. Aula, P. (2010). Social media, reputation risk and ambient publicity management. *Strategy & Leadership, 38*(6), 43–49; Mangold, W., & Faulds, D. (2009). Social media: The new hybrid element in the promotional mix. *Business Horizons, 52*(4), 357–365.

13. Aula, p. 44.
14. Jenkins, H., with Purushotma, R., Weigel, M., Clinton, K., and Robison, A. J. (2006). *Confronting the challenges of participatory culture: Media education for the 21st century.* MacArthur Foundation, p. 8. https://mitpress.mit.edu/books/confronting-challenges-participatory-culture
15. Ibid.
16. Ibid., p. 3.
17. Ibid., p. 4.
18. Kaplan, A. M., & Haenlein, M. (2010). Users of the world, unite! The challenges and opportunities of social media. *Business Horizons, 53,* 62.
19. Hemley, D. (2013, June 25). 26 tips to create a strong social media content strategy. *Social Media Examiner.* http://www.socialmediaexaminer.com/26-tips-to-create-a-strong-social-media-content-strategy/
20. Bhargava, R. (2011, October 28). *9 ways top brands use social media for better customer service.* Mashable. http://mashable.com/2011/10/28/social-customer-service-brands/
21. Ibid.
22. Arrbutina, D. (2012, June 4). Social recognition. *Canadian HR Reporter, 25*(11), 15.
23. Kaplan & Haenlein, p. 66.
24. Ibid., p. 63.
25. Dwyer, P. (2007). *Building trust with corporate blogs.* ICWSM 2007 Conference. http://icwsm.org/papers/2--Dwyer.pdf
26. Johne, M. (2011, October 21). Firing on all cylinders with social media. *The Globe and Mail,* p. B15.
27. Kiisel, T. (2012, November 13). 5 keys to successful small business blogging. *Forbes.* http://www.forbes.com/sites/tykiisel/2012/11/13/5-keys-to-successful-small-business-blogging/#526f668f717b
28. King, C. (2012, October 30). 21 business blogging tips from the pros. *Social Media Examiner.* http://www.socialmediaexaminer.com/blogging-tips-from-the-pros/
29. DeMers, J. (2014, September 23). The 6 main types of blog posts and how to use them. *Forbes.* http://www.forbes.com/sites/jaysondemers/2014/09/23/the-6-main-types-of-blog-posts-and-how-to-use-them/#7608b279216d
30. Lionel Menchaca, quoted by Lee Oden (2011). Big business blogging, the right way, Intel #ISMP. *TopRank Marketing.* http://www.toprankblog.com/2011/07/big-business-blogging-dell
31. Guidry, P., et al. (2014). Moving social marketing beyond personal change to social change: Strategically using Twitter to mobilize supporters into vocal advocates. *Journal of Social Marketing, 4*(3), 240–260; Stelzner, M. A. (2009). *Social media marketing industry report.* http://www.i-marketing-net.com/wp-content/uploads-neu/resourcen/SocialMediaMarketingIndustryReport.pdf
32. The Social Shop (2014, March 30). Tips for Engaging your Twitter Community. *The Social Shop Blog.* https://thesocialshop.co.uk/tips-for-engaging-you-twitter-community/
33. Ibid.
34. Levinson, J. C., & Lautenslager, A. (2014, July 1). Why you should use blogs and podcasts to market your business. *Entrepreneur.* https://www.entrepreneur.com/article/234239
35. Ibid.
36. Ibid.; Price, S. (2015, September 15). 4 reasons to podcast with your mobile device. *Speaker Blog.* http://blog.spreaker.com/2015/09/15/4-reasons-to-podcast-with-your-mobile-device/
37. n.a. (2011, November 21). How is HR using social media? *Canadian HR Reporter, 24*(20), p. 15.
38. Aslam, S. (2019, September 6). Linked in by the numbers: Stats, demographics & fun facts. *OmniCore.* https://www.omnicoreagency.com/linkedin-statistics/

39. Siliker, A. (2011, September 26). Recruiters connect via LinkedIn. *Canadian HR Reporter, 24* (16), p. 2.

40. Lieber, C. (2018, April 27). *Fashion brands steal design ideas all the time. And it's completely legal.* Vox. https://www.vox.com/2018/4/27/17281022/fashion-brands-knockoffs-copyright-stolen-designs-old-navy-zara-h-and-m

41. Ibid.

42. Ibid.

43. Ibid.

44. Bruns, A. (2007). Produsage: Towards a broader framework for user-led content creation. *Creativity and Cognition Conference 6*, ACM, Washington, DC. https://eprints.qut.edu.au/6623/1/6623.pdf

45. Van Dijck, J. (2009). Users like you? Theorizing agency in user-generated content. *Media, Culture, & Society, 31*(1), 41–58.

46. Sui, E. (2015, Mach 12). 10 user-generated campaigns that actually worked. *HubSpot.* http://blog.hubspot.com/marketing/examples-of-user-generated-content#sm.00oozudhc718g5frmt8efieg8ovb3

47. Ibid.

48. Clement, J. (2019, August 14) *Daily time spent on social networking by internet users worldwide from 2012 to 2018 (in minutes).* Statista. https://www.statista.com/statistics/433871/daily-social-media-usage-worldwide/

49. Pew Research Center. (2016, June 22). *Social media and the workplace.* http://www.pewinternet.org/2016/06/22/social-media-and-the-workplace

50. Krashinsky, S. (2013, July 10). 23 award-winning Canadian ads and marketing campaigns. *The Globe and Mail.* http://www.theglobeandmail.com/report-on-business/industry-news/marketing/canadian-winners-at-the-cannes-lions-ad-festival/article13124965/

51. The Shorty Awards. (n.d.). The Shorty Industry Awards: Highlighting the Best Social Media Campaigns. *Shorty Awards Blog.* https://blog.shortyawards.com/post/2699401810/the-shorty-industry-awards-highlighting-the-best

52. Financial Executives Research Foundation. (2013, September). *Social media risks and rewards,* p. 1. Grant Thornton. https://www.grantthornton.in/globalassets/1.-member-firms/india/assets/pdfs/adv-social-media-survey.pdf

53. Ibid., p. 1.

54. Neilsen, C. (2012, March 31). *The double-edged sword of social media.* Panel discussion, Faculty of Business, Ryerson University.

55. Financial Executives Research Foundation, p. 7.

56. Ibid.

57. McQuigge, M. (2012, March 28). Company wants your Facebook password? Just say no. *The Globe and Mail,* p. B19.

58. *Chatfield v. Deputy Head* (Correctional Service Canada), Federal Public Sector Labour Relations and Employment Board. (2017). https://www.fpslreb-crtespf.gc.ca/decisions/fulltext/2017-2_e.asp

59. LaChance, N. (2017, August 17). *More Nazis are getting identified and fired after Charlottesville.* The Huffington Post. https://www.huffpost.com/entry/more-nazis-are-getting-identified-and-fired-after-charlottesville_b_599477dbe4b0eef7ad2c0318

60. Kundacina, A. (2019, July 25). *A Toronto radio host is getting called out for tweeting and deleting racist comments.* Narcity. https://www.narcity.com/news/ca/on/toronto/michael-stafford-is-getting-called-out-for-tweeting-and-deleting-racist-comments

61. Dobson, S. (2013, February 25). We're live tweeting from the HR firing session! *Canadian HR Reporter, 26*(4), 11.

62. Jones, S. (2013, January 31). HMV workers take over official Twitter feed to vent fury over sacking. *The Guardian.* https://www.theguardian.com/business/2013/jan/31/hmv-workers-twitter-feed-sacking

63. West, S. (2018, January 19). H&M faced backlash over its 'monkey' sweatshirt ad. It isn't the company's only controversy. *The Washington Post.* https://www.washingtonpost.com/news/arts-and-entertainment/wp/2018/01/19/hm-faced-backlash-over-its-monkey-sweatshirt-ad-it-isnt-the-companys-only-controversy/

64. The Canadian Press. (2013, August 9). H&M faux feather headdress pulled from shelves after complaints items are offensive to aboriginals. *National Post.* https://nationalpost.com/news/canada/hm-faux-feather-headdress-pulled-from-shelves-after-complaints-items-are-offensive-to-aboriginals

65. Henry, D. and Rudegeair, P. (2013, August 7) JPMorgan faces criminal and civil probes over mortgages. *Reuters.* https://uk.reuters.com/article/uk-jpmorgan-probes/jpmorgan-faces-criminal-and-civil-probes-over-mortgages-idUKBRE9761A420130807

66. Greenhouse, E. (2013, November 16). JPMorgan's Twitter mistake. *The New Yorker.* https://www.newyorker.com/business/currency/jpmorgans-twitter-mistake

67. Ibid.

68. Bloomberg News. (2013, November 14). JPMorgan kills Twitter Q&A amid flood of mocking and insulting tweets. *Financial Post.* https://business.financialpost.com/executive/c-suite/jpmorgan-twitter-qa

69. Kan, M. (2018, April 6). T-Mobile Austria is OK with storing passwords partly in clear text. *PC Magazine.* https://www.pcmag.com/news/360301/t-mobile-austria-admits-to-storing-passwords-partly-in-clear

70. Ibid.

71. Seave, A. (July 22, 2013). How social media moves consumers from "sharing" to "purchase." *Forbes.* http://www.forbes.com/sites/avaseave/2013/07/22/how-social-media-moves-consumers-from-sharing-to-purchase/

72. Deckers, E., & Lacy, K. (2011, September 5). Ten tools to use for social media measurement. *The Globe and Mail.* http://www.theglobeandmail.com/report-on-business/small-business/sb-tools/ten-tools-to-use-for-social-media-measurement/article600410/

73. Brandwatch. (2019, September 27). The Top Social media Monitoring Tools. https://www.brandwatch.com/blog/top-social-media-monitoring-tools/

74. Kite, S. (2011, June 1). Social CRM's a tough, worthy goal. *American Banker.* https://www.americanbanker.com/news/social-crms-a-tough-worthy-goal

75. Castells, M., et al. (2006). *Mobile communication and society: A global perspective.* MIT Press.

76. Baron, N. S. (2008). *Always on: Language in an online and mobile world.* Oxford University Press.

77. Castells et al.

78. Udell, C. (2011, November 8). Dear companies, you should start using mobile devices as training tools for your employees. *Business Insider.* http://www.businessinsider.com/you-should-use-tablets-and-smartphones-to-make-your-business-more-efficient-2011-11

79. Nielsen, J. (2011, November 28). *Mobile content is twice as difficult.* Nielsen Norman Group. https://www.nngroup.com/articles/mobile-content-is-twice-as-difficult/

80. Hacker, W. (2015, April 6). *Delivering better mobile email messages with mobile-first, responsive design.* UX Matters. http://www.uxmatters.com/mt/archives/2015/04/delivering-better-mobile-email-messages-with-mobile-first-responsive-design.php

81. Sterling, G. (2015, January 28). *Majority of emails opened on Apple devices, Android users pay more attention. Marketing Land.* http://marketingland.com/majority-emails-opened-apple-devices-android-users-pay-attention-115945

82. Shankar, V., et al. (2010). Mobile marketing in the retailing environment: Current insights and future research avenues. *Journal of Interactive Marketing, 24*(2), 110–121.

83. Gunelius, S. (2012, March 28). Five tips for better text-message marketing. *Entrepreneur*. https://www.entrepreneur.com/article/223231

84. Google. (2016, April 6). *Mobile friendly websites*. https://developers.google.com/webmasters/mobile-sites/?utm_source=wmc-blog&utm_medium=referral&utm_campaign=mobile-friendly

85. Mills, I. (2014, April 16). 5 reasons you absolutely must optimize your website for mobile. The *Huffington Post*. http://www.huffingtonpost.com/ian-mills/5-reasons-you-absolutely-_b_5122485.html

86. Google. (2014, November 18). Helping users find mobile-friendly pages. *Google Webmaster Central Blog*. https://webmasters.googleblog.com/2014/11/helping-users-find-mobile-friendly-pages.html

87. Ibid.

88. Budiu, R. (2014, April 13). *Scaling user interfaces: An information-processing approach to multi-device design*. Nielsen Norman Group. https://www.nngroup.com/articles/scaling-user-interfaces/

89. Ibid.

90. Bahny, W. (2013, February 13). *Five enterprise instant messaging systems*. TechRepublic. http://www.techrepublic.com/blog/five-apps/five-enterprise-instant-messaging-systems/

91. Tolentino, J. (2015, March 2). *What types of companies are using* SMS? TNW: The Next Web. http://thenextweb.com/future-of-communications/2015/03/02/what-types-of-companies-are-using-sms/#gref

92. Rust, A. (2015, October 20). *5 situations when texting makes for good business*. Business 2 Community. http://www.business2community.com/communications/5-situations-texting-makes-good-business-01355317#xcU39XHy05bMHRPc.97

93. Rampton, J. (2015, March 31). The rules of business texting. *Entrepreneur*. https://www.entrepreneur.com/article/244453

94. Turner, J. W., & Reinsch, N. L., Jr. (2007). The business communicator as presence allocator: Multicommunicating, equivocality, and status at work. *Journal of Business Communication, 44*(1), 38; Cardon, P. W. and Dai, Y. (2014). Mobile phone use in meetings among Chinese professionals: Perspectives on multicommunication and civility. *Global Advances in Business Communication, 3*(1). http://commons.emich.edu/gabc/vol3/iss1/2/

Index

Index

603

Nk'Mip Cellars, 13

noise, 48

non-profits: social networking and, 519

non-verbal communication, 53–9; components of, 55–9; job interview and, 356

noun conversions, 128–9

nouns, 128–9; abstract, 125; collective, 567; concrete, 125; count/non-count, 535; proper, 560–1

number (grammatical), 159

number/amount, 537

numbers: lists and, 187; use of, 559–60

offshoring, 8–9, 25

OK/O.K./okay, 549

Old Navy, 521–2

Olvet, Tony, 3

one of the . . ., 570

online articles: documentation of, 453, 454, 455

openings: bad news and, 257, 263; direct-approach message, 213; memo, 185

optimization: mobile, 529–30; search engine, 516

oral presentations, 479–95; delivery of, 487–9, 490–1; outline for, 482–3; PechaKucha, 487; purpose of, 480; rehearsing, 489–90; special-occasion, 493–4; structure of, 480–1; team-based, 493; three-part, 481–2; types of, 479

organizations: authentic, 16; as author, 454, 455; professionalism and, 16; teams and, 21

organizing: writing and, 84, 99–100

Ottawa: land acknowledgement in, 14

outlines, 84, 99–100; alphanumeric, 376–7; decimal, 376–7; oral presentation, 482–3; preliminary, 95

outsourcing, 8–9

overload: as communication barrier, 48

paragraphs: coherence of, 171–3; development of, 171; e-mail, 193; effective, 169–73; length of, 169

paralanguage, 53, 56–7

parallelism, 160, 575–6; lists and, 186; report headings and, 374

parentheses, 582–3

participants, meeting, 496

participatory culture, 513

participles, 578

parts of speech, 153

Pascal, Blaise, 128

passed/past, 549

PechaKucha presentations, 487

peer-reviewing: reports and, 447–8

Pepsi, 510

per cent/percent/%/percentage/percentile, 549–50

periods, 582

person (grammatical), 159

person-organization fit, 328

Personal Information Protection and Electronic Documents Act (PIPEDA), 30, 31–2

personal statements: job-seeking and, 352

persuasive messages, 289–321; social media and, 312–15; types of, 286–305

Peter, Tom, 315

phablets: messages for, 528–9

photo-sharing sites, 514, 521–2

phrases, 153; assertive, 142; business, 565; embedded, 164; foreign, 544; participial, 156, 578; prepositional, 130–1, 156

Pinterest, 326, 515, 521

piracy, 7

plagiarism: 29, 126, 452; e-mail and, 195

plain language/style, 118–20, 565; international movement for, 119

planning: writing and, 84–6

plasticity, 51

podcasts, 514, 518–19

policy: as buffer, 258

politeness, 127–8

Politeski, James, 212

Popa, Claudiu, 7

portfolios, career/electronic, 354

positive attitude: writing and, 135–6

posters, 484

postscripts, 310

posture: non-verbal communication and, 57; presentations and, 490

Posyniak, Len, 520

Power Point, 372, 484, 485, 486–7

practical/practicable, 550

practice/practise, 550

precede/proceed, 550

predication, faulty, 574–5

prepositions: phrases and, 130–1, 158

presentations: *see* oral presentations

prewriting, 84, 86–99

Prezi, 484, 485, 486

price-fixing, 27, 30

Pride Month, 510

principal/principle, 550

print: research and, 442

privacy: breaches of, 30; employees', 182; job application and, 353; texting and, 531; workplace and, 30–3

Privacy Act, 30, 31, 32

Privacy Commissioner, 7, 30

problem questions, 408–10

problem–solution strategy, 298

problem statements, 408–10

"produsers," 523

professionalism, 15–20; unprofessional behaviour and, 18–20

profile: audience, 88; online, 330, 331; professional, 315

promotion: social media and, 314–15; user-generated content and, 523

pronouns: coherence and, 172; first-person, 165; gender-neutral, 140; indefinite, 569; personal, 120, 134, 136–7, 165; reference and, 158; relative, 155; use of, 576–7

proofreading, 84, 102–5, 173–4, 377

proposals, 393, 431–40; external, 433; formal, 438–40; informal, 434–8; internal, 410, 433; as legal contract, 434; sample of informal, 435–8

proposal section: informal proposals and, 434

provinces: abbreviated, 557–8

proxemics, 55–6

psychological reactance, 253

Publication Manual of the American Psychological Association, 452

public relations, 503

punctuation, 153, 174, 579–84; emphasis and, 160–1; Internet resources on, 584

purpose: meetings and, 495, 496; writing and, 86–7

purpose statements, 408–10; formal reports and, 450

"push service," 519

Q1, Q2, Q3, Q4, 550

quantification: observations and, 443

questions: behavioural interview, 356–7; hypothetical, 157; job interview, 356–7; journalistic, 96; media, 503; open/closed, 157; phrasing of, 157–8; presentations and, 491–2; problem, 408–10; spontaneous, 491